S0-AKT-676

The Vallejos of California

By

MADIE BROWN EMPARAN

Madie Brown Empáran

Richard R. Emparan

PUBLISHED BY
THE GLEESON LIBRARY ASSOCIATES
UNIVERSITY OF SAN FRANCISCO
MCMLXVIII

Library of Congress Catalogue Card No. 68-56147

DESIGNED AND PRINTED BY LAWTON AND ALFRED KENNEDY

DEDICATED

TO

MY DEAR HUSBAND

RICHARD RAOUL EMPARAN

AND

TO MY CHILDREN

ROBERT, COLLEEN AND NATALIE

WITH REMEMBRANCE OF GENERAL VALLEJO'S GRANDCHILDREN
WHOM I KNEW AND WHO APPROVED THE MANUSCRIPT OF

THE VALLEJOS OF CALIFORNIA

Francisca Vallejo McGettigan

Eleanora Benicia Haraszthy Dowdall

Madeleina Frisbie Marron

Adela Vallejo Peters

Alma Cutter McLennan

Harvey Brown Vallejo

Anita Emparan Thomson

Carlos Vallejo Emparan

Richard Raoul Emparan

Table of Contents

Foreword

Naturally, I feel extremely complimented upon being asked by the author, Madie Brown, to write the Foreword of her book, THE VALLEJOS OF CALIFORNIA. No one, I feel sure, could have brought more careful research, more heartfelt enthusiasm to the accomplishment than my dear and versatile friend, Madie Brown.

She knows her General Mariano Guadalupe Vallejo from cradle to grave as completely—no! more completely—than any one of the General's surviving relatives or descendants, and what to them might have proved an onerous task, to her has been a source of never-failing joyous satisfaction, with the consciousness of a loving tribute convincingly paid, a worthwhile deed authentically done.

The short sketches of the General's children are diversified and interesting, sketching a true picture of each and drawing the reader into "the bosom of the family" as it were, and diffusing an atmosphere of romance especially reminiscent of those poetic days of romance and charm.

We thank you, Madie Brown.

FRANCISCA VALLEJO MCGETTIGAN

Preface

I like to think of this book, THE VALLEJOS OF CALIFORNIA, as a tapestry of a distinguished California family. I have been merely the weaver, the colorful threads and designs are the Vallejos'. I have assorted the strands and woven them together; in some instances I have unravelled the tangles and tied some knots. There may be broken threads and rents in the tapestry but I have preferred to leave the imperfections rather than to mend them with suppositions and conjectures.

This book could not have been written without the help of MARY BEAN, of Laguna Beach, a Spanish scholar who has translated several hundred of the Vallejo family letters, as a gift of friendship. Her ardent interest coupled with the excellence of her translations, simplified my work immeasurably. Another dedicated Californian was GLADYS WICKSON of Berkeley, whose excellent editorial supervision prepared the manuscript for publication. Also remembered gratefully is BROTHER HENRY of the Christian Brothers who translated letters and documents. The assistance given by the nine grandchildren of General Vallejo, whom it has been my privilege to know, has not been forgotten, especially the youngest, RICHARD RAOUL EMPARAN, who bears a remarkable likeness to his grandfather.

Throughout the book will be found portions of many letters, in order that the Vallejos, their friends and contemporaries, in and out of official life, may tell the story themselves and thus the vitality of the original telling is not lost in the re-telling. In my narration I have attempted to provide an accurate historical background with continuity of action.

The originals of the letters can be found in the Bancroft Library, that treasure-house of Californiana at the University of California. Others can be read in the State Library in Sacramento and in the Henry E. Huntington Library in San Marino. A lesser number are in the libraries of the Society of California Pioneers, the California Historical Society and the University of San Francisco.

MADIE BROWN EMPARAN

General Mariano G. Vallejo

In the opinion of many historians, the most prominent of the early native Californians was Mariano Guadalupe Vallejo, a son of Don Ignacio Vicente Ferrer Vallejo, the founder of the Vallejo family in California. Don Ignacio Vallejo came to this Spanish province on the shores of the Pacific from Jalisco, Mexico in 1774—five years after Padre Junipero Serra founded at San Diego the first of the Franciscan missions.

The ancestral threads of the Vallejos are woven into the tapestry of America from almost the time of its discovery. In 1500, just eight years after Columbus had discovered the New World, a Vallejo, Admiral Alonzo Vallejo, was sent to Santo Domingo to serve under the new Governor, Don Francisco Bobadilla. The latter had been sent by the Spanish Crown to depose Columbus and his brothers, who were to deliver up to him all fortresses, ships, and other property. In addition and with considerable show of arrogance, Bobadilla took up his residence in Columbus' house, claiming that his orders included sending him back to Spain in chains, which he proceeded to do. Columbus endured the indignities heaped on him, because he felt that when he arrived in Castile, everything would be explained and redressed.

To Admiral Vallejo was assigned the task of guarding Columbus on the ocean journey. Admiral Vallejo, whom Bartholomew Las Casa, Spanish historian and Bishop of Chiapas, called "a Hidalgo of honorable character and my particular friend." Admiral Vallejo was from Burgos, Spain, the cradle of the Castilian monarchy. The Burgos Cathedral there is considered the finest specimen of Gothic architecture. Its carvings have been called the work of angels.

Admiral Vallejo was generous in nature and treated Columbus with deference; he and Andreas Martín, the master of the ship would have taken off Columbus' chains, but, to this suggestion, the discoverer of the New World would not consent. "No," said he proudly, "their Majesties commanded by letter to submit to whatever Bobadilla should order and I will wear them until they shall order them to be taken off and I will preserve them afterwards as relics and memorials of the reward of my services."

During the voyage Columbus penned a letter to Prince Juan's teacher, a lady high in the favor of Queen Isabella. "The slanders of worthless men" wrote Columbus, "have done me more injury than all my services have profited me. I was judged as a governor of a well-regulated city . . . but I ought to be judged as a Captain sent to subdue a numerous and hostile people of manners and religion opposite to ours, living not in regular towns but in forests and mountains . . . Spain heretofore poor has suddenly become rich." This letter was read to the noble-minded Isabella, who, finding how grossly Columbus had been wronged and the royal authority abused, joined her husband in sending Columbus a letter of gratitude and inviting him to court where they assured him that his grievances would be redressed, his property and privileges restored.

As the pattern of the New World began to take bolder outlines on the loom of Time, two of the Vallejos, brothers of Admiral Alonzo Vallejo sailed for the shores of Mexico with Hernando Cortes in 1519. One was Don Pedro Vallejo. The bravery and sagacity of this conquistador added vivid threads to the expanding North American fabric. Don Pedro became one of the governing officials of the province of Panuco on the Gulf of Mexico where he was "lord of great silver mines and master of peons innumerable." The other Vallejo brother settled near the capital in the valley of "Las Anilras," where he remained for many years, subsequently establishing himself with his family near Xalostotitlan (now Jalostotitlan, 100 miles from Guadalajara), where the family had a farm, dedicated to and named after Nuestra Senora de las Canadas. The Vallejos remained in the province of New Galicia (Jalisco) for 200 years. Throughout these years, many of the Vallejo family were educated to be soldiers or priests. Ignacio Vicente Ferrer Vallejo, born at Las Canadas on July 29, 1748 and baptized at nearby Jalostotitlan on August 14th of the same year, was in his boyhood being prepared, at the behest of his Castilian parents, Don Geronimo Vallejo and Dona Antonia Gomez, for Holy Orders; but young Ignacio Vallejo abruptly terminated his ecclesiastical training by enlisting in 1773 at Compostela in the California-bound expedition of Captain Fernando Xavier de Rivera y Moncada and his leather-jacketed soldiers. Ignacio Vallejo was stationed first at the San Diego de Alcala Mission, where he was put in charge of irrigation projects and was cited for bravery during the bloody Indian revolt of November 1775. Altogether he served at seven of the eight missions founded by Father Serra. He was present at the founding of the Presidio of San Francisco in September 1776 and at the rites in connection with the founding of the San Francisco de Asis Mission, the next month. Other ways in which Ignacio Vallejo's abilities were made use of in this remote western region (similar to the one of his forebear's friend Columbus had described, nearly three centuries earlier as inhabited by "a numerous and hostile people") were as carpenter and overseer of crops. Militarily, his highest rank was *sargento distinguido.* It is recorded when the Spanish King, Carlos III, was in need of money in his war with England, he asked for funds from this far-flung outpost of his empire. From the Mission San Carlos in Monterey, the King received $106; Don Ignacio who served at the Mission 1781–1784 contributed $10. In 1799 Don Ignacio Vallejo had been picked from active military duty to take over the duties of Corporal Gabriel Moraga as comisionado of the Villa Branciforte founded by royal Spanish decree.

Ignacio Vallejo's wife was Dona Maria Antonia Isabela Lugo, whom he saw for the first time the day of her birth, September 1, 1776. He was a guest in the San Luis Obispo home of his friend Don Francisco Lugo, who had come from Sinaloa, Mexico, to California in 1769. At the time of Ignacio

Vallejo's visit, Lugo's wife Dona Juana Maria Rita Martinez, was expecting a child, and the medical training Don Ignacio had acquired while studying to be a priest qualified him to act as a physician. His "fee" was the request for the hand of his tiny patient in marriage when she should become of sufficient age. The Lugo infant was baptized on September 2, 1776 in the Mission San Luis Obispo by Padre Pablo de Mugartegui and was christened Maria Antonia Isabela with Don Pablo Antonio Cota as godfather. At this mission was planted the first olive trees in California. Don Ignacio kept up his friendship with the Lugo family and on September 9, 1790, he petitioned Comandante Fages for a license to wed Maria Antonia Lugo. She was then fourteen years old and had lost her mother, but she and her father gave their consent willingly. The wedding occurred in Santa Barbara at the Mission on February 18, 1791 with Padre Antonio Paterno officiating. Jose Raymundo Carrillo from the Presidio of Santa Barbara and Juan Manuel Alarcon, one of the leather-jacketed soldiers, were the witnesses. In spite of the disparity of some twenty-nine years in their ages, the marriage was known to have been a happy one, lasting forty-one years. They were blessed with thirteen children, eight girls and five boys. Their children were:

MARIA ISIDORA	married MARIANO SOBERANES
MARIA JOSEFA	married JUAN FRANCISCO ALVARADO JOSE RAIMUNDO ESTRADA BENIFACIO MADARIAGA
JOSE IGNACIO	soltero
JOSE DE JESUS	married SOLEDAD SANCHEZ
JUANA MARIA GERTRUDIS	soltera
MARIA MAGDALENA	married ANTONIO DEL VALLE
MARIA PRUDENCIANA	married JOSE GALE AMESTI
MARIANO GUADALUPE	married FRANCISCA BENICIA CARRILLO
MARIA GERONIMA ENCARNACION	married JOHN B. R. COOPER
MARIA PAULA ROSALIA	married JACOB PRIMER LEESE
JOSE MANUEL SALVADOR DEL MUNDO,	married MARIA DE LA LUZ CARRILLO
MARIA DE JESUS	married HONORE FORTOUL
JUAN ANTONIO	soltero

Their eighth child Mariano Guadalupe, or "Guadalupe" as the family always called him, was to add not only renown to the name of Vallejo but a certain luster to the whole fabric of California's history. The radiance reflecting unto the 1960s when two Presidents of the United States, John F. Kennedy and Lyndon B. Johnson, both chose the name of Mariano Guadalupe Vallejo for the Polaris submarine (SSBN 658). It was launched on October 23, 1965 at Mare Island with Miss Patricia McGettigan, a great great granddaughter of General Vallejo as sponsor.

2652 MARIANO DE GUADALUPE DE RASON

Baptismal Record of Don Mariano Guadalupe Vallejo

Dia 5 Julio de 1807 en la capilla del R. Pres° de Monterrey bautice solemnemte a un Nino nacido la noche del dia anterior hijo legitimo de Ygnacio Vallejo naral de la haciendo de Na Sra de los Canadas, y Sargento de la Compª de ath° Monterrey y de Maria Antonia de Lugo natural de la Mission de S. Luis Obispo de esta California. Pusele pʳnombre Mariano de Guadalupe. Fue su Madrina Ysabel Cota naral del Pres° de Sta. Barbara en Ath° No California, a quien adverti lo devido. Nota la bredicho haciendo de las Canadas pertece al Obispo de Guadalajara. Para que conste lo firme.

Fr. Baltasar Carnicer

2652 MARIANO DE GUADALUPE DE RASON

Translation

The fifth of July, 1807, in the chapel of the Royal Presidio of Monterey, I solemnly baptized a male infant born the night of the previous day, legitimate son of Ygnacio Vallejo, native of the ranch of Our Lady of the Canadas and Sergeant of the Artillery Company of Monterey, and of Maria Antonia de Lugo, native of the Mission San Luis Obispo of this California. Name given, Mariano de Guadalupe. Godmother Ysabel Cota, native of the Presidio of Santa Barbara in Upper California. To whom these notes concern, they are from country of the Canadas of the diocese of Guadalajara.

Therefore I affirm (sign)
Fr. Baltasar Carnicer

GUADALUPE VALLEJO—CHILD OF MONTEREY

By a strange coincidence this child of old Monterey, who in manhood revered the ideals of George Washington and advocated the annexation of California to the United States, was born on July Fourth of the year 1807. He was baptized in the Chapel of the Royal Presidio of Monterey by Father Baltasar Carnicer on July fifth. The infant's godmother was his first cousin, Ysabel Cota, daughter of Rosa Maria Lugo; her husband Pablo A. Cota. (Subsequently Ysabel became the wife of Jose Dolores Pico.)

Guadalupe Vallejo attended the school of the old soldier Miguel Geronimo Archuleta where he was taught the catechism and Padre Ripaldo's Christian Doctrine and also the schools of Don Manuel Boronda and Salvador Aspiroz. Among Guadalupe's classmates was his nephew Juan Bautista Alvarado, two years younger than himself. Likewise students at that time in Monterey were Jose Castro, Ignacio Martinez, Cayetano Juarez and Antonio Maria Pico.

So well did Jose Maria Estudillo teach young Vallejo penmanship that for three years (starting when he was thirteen) he prepared the writing examples for the schools in San Diego, Los Angeles, Santa Barbara, and Monterey; nor did he ever lose the ability to write a beautiful, legible hand. In Monterey, he served as an altar boy. Recalling those days in later life, Vallejo said: "A thousand times did I help Father Vicente Francisco Sarria say Mass; a thousand times did I receive sweets from him after Mass for my progress in reciting the litany in company with other children my age. He administered First Communion to me with his Heavenly manner . . . Father Sarria wanted to send me to Mexico in the year 1821 with Governor Sola to study to be a priest."

Pablo Vicente Sola, governor of California from August 1815 to November 1822, recognized the ability of young Vallejo and sought to interest him in politics and in world affairs. He gave him Mexican newspapers and allowed him to read official reports. At the cost of many candle-burning hours, he acquired, as he put it, "the precious and enduring treasures of education." "Wisdom," Vallejo said, "is not like the gifts of Fortune, exposed to vicissitudes and losses. It is dependable and durable wealth." He acquired mathematics and bookkeeping, as well as some knowledge of English from working for Monterey merchants, Nathan Spear and David Spence.

At sixteen years of age, Vallejo presented a petition to the then-governor Luis Arguello, to enroll him as a cadet in the Presidial Company of Monterey. He had been acting as secretary to the governor and, as such, drew up the document transferring California's fealty from Spain to Mexico. Vallejo's personal endowments plus his father's military services were sufficient to secure his enrollment as a cadet on January 8, 1824. In 1825 he was promoted to the rank of corporal, keeping the company's books and performing other military tasks; in 1828 he was a sergeant and an ensign (alferez) in 1829. His first important military mission was the quelling of the uprising of the Indian Estanislao in May 1829; later he was sent on a reconnaissance of the country east and north of the bay of San Francisco, with instructions to map the area and name the geographical points.

Vallejo was assigned to the Presidio of San Francisco whose comandante was Ignacio Martinez. At that time, 1830, Vallejo said, "I went to the summit of Mt. Tamalpais with the botanist named Douglas, he burying one of his books on the top." In September of 1831 Ignacio Martinez retired and Alferez Vallejo was named comandánte.

Young Vallejo, possessing as a contemporary account pictured him "a fine form and a handsome face," it was not surprising that he had "*novias*" (sweethearts) in the persons of Ana Avila and Maria Zuniga in Monterey. They were quickly forgotten when another military mission sent him to San Diego where he met on January 24, 1830 Francisca Benicia Carrillo whose face he said was the most beautiful he had ever looked upon. He won her consent and that of her parents, but, being an officer, it was necessary to receive permission to wed from the Mexican officials. He wrote for this in October from Monterey where he had gone for the Territorial elections.

Most Excellent Sir:

Citizen Mariano Guadalupe Vallejo, Ensign of the regular Company of the Port of San Francisco, greets your Excellency most respectfully, stating that he is 23 years of age, as is attested by his baptismal certificate, which he attaches, marked No. 1 and has pledged his troth with Dona Francisca Carrillo, single, fifteen years old, as is attested by her baptismal certificate marked No. 2, the legitimate daughter of Don Joaquin Carrillo and Dona Maria Ignacia Lopez of honorable parentage as is shown by the judicial certificate Marked No. 3 herein.

The supplicant as well as his betrothed having the consent of their respective parents as attested by these documents No. 4 and 5 also enclosed; beg your Excellency to be pleased to grant the necessary permission to contract their matrimony, a favor which they hope to receive from your Excellency.

October 15, 1830 MARIANO G. VALLEJO

It was seventeen months before the lovers received official acquiescence and the wedding took place in San Diego on March 6, 1832. Shortly thereafter Vallejo was ordered back to the Presidio of San Francisco.

VALLEJO'S "COLD WAR" AGAINST THE RUSSIANS

In 1833 Vallejo visited the Russian settlements at Bodega and Fort Ross returning May 5 with the conviction that northern California should be colonized against further encroachment from the Muscovites. He esteemed the Russian; the officers he had met acted like gentlemen. Nevertheless, the Russians were the *first squatters.* He placed no credence in Peter Kostromitinov's statement that his countrymen sought only the opportunity to fish and gather furs—a place from where food could be shipped to their Alaskan settlements.

Vallejo's idea of the colonization of northern California was in agreement with that of Governor Jose Figueroa who had written, "Many of the objects that the Superior Government has in view but the principal one is to arrest as soon as possible the progress of the Russian settlements of Bodega and Ross." Figueroa commissioned Vallejo to lay out a pueblo in the valley of Sonoma and appointed him Administrator of the secularization of the San Francisco Solano Mission, situated near the foothills where Vallejo planned to locate the new pueblo. In the "Historia de California" he tells of this period in his carrer:

General Figueroa ordered me to proceed to found the town of Sonoma and following his orders in June 1834 I embarked 80 cavalrymen in two schooners and set out for the Sonoma landing but because we did not know the Bay Currents very well, the trip took us fourteen days. First, the schooners became grounded in the mud near Novato where we were attacked by several hundred Indians but their attack was ineffective. When the vessels were freed we went on to the landing of Padre Ventura (now known as Lakeville) where I landed my troops and camped.

After two days I made a treaty with the Licatiuet Indians, we re-embarked and after three days we dropped anchor at the place known then as Point Tolar, now

Midshipman's Creek. I reconnoitered the land for a day and night, then embarked the next day, and after three hours arrived at the Sonoma slough and going up it, stopped at Pulpulpa, now called Poppe Landing. There I met Captain Pulpulpa and the great chief Solano who awaited me at the head of 3,000 warriors and they had the horses which I had sent over land for my troops in custody. I camped there and entered into negotiations with the Indians. Two days later my camp was surrounded by about 11,000 Indians who came to greet me.

After breakfast I mounted my troops and took them to a spot near the springs known by the name *Chiucuyen* and now as Lachryma Montis. After eight days of feasting and dancing I finally was freed of so many dancers and proceeded to outline and lay out the new town. First I outlined a plaza, 212 varas square. I left the small building which had been constructed as a church to the east of the plaza. I built a barracks about 100 varas west of the church and after that I outlined the streets and divided the lots as prescribed by law. In this task I was ably assisted by Captain Richardson, the same, who, a year later built the first house in San Francisco.

On December 2, 1834 Vallejo arrived in the Valley of Sonoma with his Cavalry Company from the Presidio of San Francisco. They were to remain at the pueblo of Sonoma. The soldiers were:

Damo Antonio Rodriguez	Cayetano Juarez	Jesus Valencia
Pablo Pacheco	Salvador Altamo	Mariano Sorelo
Felis Berreyesa	Franco Mesa	Franco Garcia
Ygnacio Pacheco	Rafael Galindo	Ygnacio Borjornes
Vicente Miramente	Ramon Mesa	Ygnacio Miramonte
Franco Schocin	Jose Mirando	Prado Mesa
Ignacio Olivas	Jose Condero	Jose Maria Albina
Jascinov	Antonio Bernal	Nasanio Galindo
Manuel Cantna	Ygnacio Hio	Apolinario Mirando
Ygnacio Hiosesaro	Antonio Pena	Antonio Herandes

At the site of the San Francisco Solano Mission at this time were members of the *Compania Cosmopolitana*, the Hijar-Padres group of Mexican colonists, composed of talented artisans whom Vallejo helped; furnishing them with shoes, shirts, hats, trousers and other needed supplies. Among them was Apolinario Sepulveda, who engraved Vallejo's military card with the Mexican eagle, holding the serpent, surrounded by cacti and weapons.

In June of 1835, Vallejo brought to Sonoma (or Solano, as it was then called) his young pregnant wife and baby son Andronico. They found it necessary to occupy rooms in the abandoned San Francisco Solano Mission—a natural procedure, as Vallejo had been appointed Comisionado of Secularization of that mission; but it prompted Padre Jose Lorenzo Quijas, unhappy over the secularization of his mission, to leave for the Mission San Rafael.

One of the first things Vallejo did was to prepare in his own hand and perhaps with the help of his wife, an inventory of all the articles found in the deserted mission; these included church vestments and ornaments, sacred pictures and statues, furniture, books, musical instruments, agricultural implements, carpenters' tools, cots and other plain furniture. Sixty-eight women's skirts were recorded; the padres had hoped to encourage modesty among the Indian women.

Antonio Ortega, a mission guard and a former member of the Hijar-Padres group, was selected to be the major-domo at a salary of $500 per year while Vallejo's brother Don Salvador Vallejo served as administrator. Padre Quijas who departed August 1835 for San Rafael, accused Vallejo and his two appointees of irregularities. He said the first (Vallejo) had acted with moderation; but the second (Ortega) had acted with great brutality and immorality and was, in addition, irreligious while the third (Salvador Vallejo) had acted with impudence, effrontery and insolence. Vallejo complained that although Padre Quijas was still officially the Curate for San Francisco Solano, he ignored that establishment all together except when it was time to collect his pay. Vallejo objected to the payment which he considered excessive as the padre no longer came to the mission.

Remembering the time when he first came to the Valley of Sonoma, Vallejo said "the face of the earth in all those splendid valleys and mountain sides was a mass of clover and the wild oats covered a large section of the country standing more than waist high. All the bays and creeks were literally alive with fish and along the coast and bay shores, there was no end to the delicious clams and shell fish. The elk and deer and antelope and all the smaller animals were literally in immense quantities all over the country and bear, many of the largest Grizzly . . . I came not as a priest among the people, yet a man trusting in the love and guidance of God. I came instructed by my Government to do what I could for the inhabitants of the country and to ward off incursions from Russia on the one hand and from the people over the Rocky Mountains on the other." "It seems to me," said Vallejo, "that there was never a more peaceful or happy people on the face of the earth than the Spanish, Mexican and Indian population of Alta California. We were the pioneers of the Pacific Coast, building pueblos and missions while General Washington was carrying on the war of the Revolution and we often talk together of the days when a few hundred large Spanish ranches and Mission tracts occupied the whole country from the Pacific to the San Joaquin. No class of American citizens is more loyal than the Spanish Californians but we shall always be especially proud of the traditions and memories of the long pastoral age before 1840."

GENERAL VALLEJO'S INDIAN POLICY

Differences with Padre Quijas continued but Vallejo's chief concern was for the Indians. They still resented the intrusion of the white man and there was also warfare among themselves. General Vallejo's Indian policy was regarded as excellent and effective. His wealth, his recognized power and the friendship of Chief Solano contributed to his success. His treatment was just and liberal to the Indians at peace but there was prompt and severe punishment of any manifestation of hostility. There was a time when Vallejo felt that he must discipline his ally Chief Solano. Comandánte Vallejo had a circular printed on the Zamorano Press on October 6, 1838 which stated that Solano had abused the trust and confidence placed in him by conniving for the seizure and sale of Indian children. A rumor had been spread that Vallejo had consented to the kidnapings. This report he denounced as slanderous, explaining that Solano had been arrested and a force of men sent out to rescue the children and restore them to their parents. Vallejo made it clear that Chief Solano had been plied with whiskey by those responsible for the crimes. On being sobered up in the guardhouse Chief Solano became ashamed and asked for forgiveness.

Vallejo in referring to his Indian policy said, "My first object was to make an uninterrupted campaign against the tribes that threatened our borders for the purpose of destroying some and making friends with others."

Vallejo's elder brother, Don Jose Jesus Vallejo, commenting on the Indian campaigns, said, "In the course of those nine years he (Vallejo) went on more than a hundred campaigns against the heathen savages; and, finally, if one takes into consideration the fact that the secularization of the Missions San Rafael and San Francisco Solano might have caused a general uprising of the Cainamero, Suisun, Licatiut and Napajo Indians, and of other tribes directly or indirectly allied with them, who would have liked the property of the towns on the pretext that they were the property of the ex-missions, as many of you who read these lines will see that my brother had reason and to spare in opposing the interference of civil authorities who had little or no knowledge of the situation."

During the Smallpox epidemic which began in 1838, Vallejo did all in his power to encourage vaccination, urging the civil and military officials as well as the Administrators of the Missions to explain its use to the natives. Chief Solano was vaccinated and became immune. Vallejo estimated that in two years 60,000 to 75,000 Indians died from the plague.

To strengthen Chief Solano's power among his Indian subjects, Vallejo did all he could to show him honor. Solano was given a fine horse with silver trappings, a complete uniform, somewhat gaudy with fancy riding boots and a silver watch and a Guard of Honor of 44 Suisun and Napajo Indians. Solano, his Indian name was Sem-Yeto, was over six feet tall and strikingly resembled the portraits of General Andrew Jackson.

With the aid of Vallejo's brother Captain Salvador Vallejo and Chief Solano, friendly relations were finally established among most of the tribes. As for the mission Indians to whom cattle had been given, after the secularization, Vallejo at their request took care of the livestock for them on a share basis. His wise handling of the Christian Indians property helped them and also increased his own fortune. About fifteen Indians remained at the Mission San Francisco Solano and were employed by Vallejo in his home.

THE DEATH OF GOVERNOR JOSE FIGUEROA

On September 29, 1835, Governor Jose Figueroa, who had selected Vallejo to found Sonoma and to colonize northern California, died at San Juan Bautista. His death was a personal and official loss to Vallejo. Vallejo's first land grants enabling him to become a man of affairs and property, had been given him by Figueroa.

When Figueroa arrived in Monterey on January 15, 1833, he was carrying with him a proclamation of Amnesty to all the participants in the irregular proceedings of 1831–32. The Governor was immediately impressed with twenty-five-year-old Vallejo and ordered him to join his company at the Presidio of San Francisco.

In February of the next year, Vallejo from the Presidio wrote to Figueroa, complaining that the Villa de Branciforte refused to report the census lists to him and asked what were the limits of his domain. The Governor in answer advised Vallejo, the Comandante, that his jurisdiction comprised all the territory north of the Las Pulgas rancho and of a line parallel with boundaries of the ranchos of Castro and Peralta, that is, all the northern frontier and down to San Mateo and Alvarado and Niles on the Contra Costa. All the functions of local government—executive, judicial and economical—were to be exercised by the Comandante. Later that year Figueroa informed Vallejo that the Territorial Disputacion had ordered the formation of a civil government which would exercise the political functions—Vallejo remaining with the military command alone. On that same day, Figueroa wrote to Vallejo the letter which follows:

Political Government of Alta California
General Comandancia of Alta California

This government, satisfied of the zeal and activity which characterize you, as well as the patriotism which animate you, sees in your note of the 24th of October ultimo, a new proof of your desire for progress, and of your untiring efforts for the enlightenment of your country and of your fellow citizens.

In consideration of this, it takes pleasure in making known to you that with the consent of the Most Excellent Territorial Disputacion, it has adopted entire the plan you have presented in your note referred to, with respect to the pueblo of San Francisco, declaring its boundary to be the same which you described in said note, that is, commencing from the little cove (caleta) to the east of the fort, following the line drawn by you to the beach, leaving to the north the casamata and fortress; thence following the shore line of said beach to Point Lobos on its southern part; thence following a right line to summit of El Divisadero, continuing said line towards the east to La Punta del Rincon including the Canutales and El Gentil; said line will terminate in the Bay of the Mission of Dolores.

This government, as a proof of the confidence with which your services inspire it, has directed that you should have the honor of installing the first ayuntamiento in that pueblo of San Francisco, for which you have already done so much.

In consequence you will proceed in the time and manner prescribed by law, in the election of the municipal authorities, in order that they may be installed the first day of January of the coming year, 1835, designating for town houses the buildings you deem most fit.

God and Liberty
JOSE FIGUEROA

Monterey, November 4, 1834
Don. Mariano G. Vallejo
Comandante Militar of San Francisco

A true Copy
Zamorano

The Zamorano Press moved to Sonoma about the middle of 1837. Jose de la Rosa did most of the governmental and ecclesiastical printing, although Vallejo sometimes did the press work himself.

Vallejo's friendliness toward foreigners had been noticed as early as 1835 by Richard Henry Dana, who said, "Don Guadalupe Vallejo spoke English well, used to hold many conversations with me."

In 1841, a fleet of six vessels arrived in the Pacific waters, commanded by Lt. Charles Wilkes, head of the U.S. Navy's Exploring Expedition. The Lieutenant addressed a letter to Vallejo, spelling his name in a way which must have amused the latter who after all, at this time was only thirty-four years old.

General Viejo [Old]
Comandant of the Government Forces, Administrator of Justice, etc.
Of the Northern Frontier, Alta California

General:

I have the honor to inform you of the arrival in this harbour of the Squadron under my command and beg leave to ask your friendly exertions in obtaining the quantity of provisions referred to in the list herewith, as soon as possible. Your reply through the officer who will hand you this communication at the earliest most convenient moment will much oblige

Your Excellency's Most Obedient Servant
CHARLES WILKES

U.S. Ship Vincennes
Bay of San Francisco
October 22, 1841

Lieutenant Wilkes anchored the Vincennes at Sausalito and sent Lieutenant J. Ringgold and his assistants to Sonoma. They reported "Upon paper, Zonoma is a large city and laid out according to the most approved plan. In reality however, it consists of only the following buildings: General Vallejo's house built of adobes of two stories which fronts on the public square and is said to be one of the best houses in California. On the right of this is the residence of the General's brother Salvadore and to the left the Barracks." Mention was also made in their account of the dilapidated Mission San Francisco Solano and of three or four more houses and that "there were in the course of construction in 1841 a neat little chapel and a small building for a billard room."

General Vallejo received Lieutenant Wilkes' officers with great politeness and sent word to Wilkes that he could furnish him with the requested supplies, including fresh and dried meat, wheat, corn, lima beans, sweet potatoes and lard.

Military Commander of the Northern Frontier

In 1836 Juan Bautista Alvarado, the son of Vallejo's second sister Maria Josefa, by her first husband, was popular with the Californians and had led a brief rebellion, declaring that Alta California was independent of Mexico under the governorship of Alvarado with Vallejo raised from the rank of Lieutenant to Colonel of Cavalry, comandante-general. The governorship was contested by Jose Antonio Carrillo who claimed it for his brother Carlos Antonio Carrillo of Santa Barbara. Alvarado refused to give up his office. Capturing the leaders of the insurrection he sent them for safe keeping to Vallejo in Sonoma remarking it has been said, as he did so, "If I sent them to the devil they would not get what they deserved, I therefore sent them to Vallejo."

A remark made no doubt when he was under the influence of California wine which he was known to indulge in frequently.

On September 15, 1838 the national schooner *California* arrived with Captain Andres Castillero, the comisionado of the supreme government, carrying Mexican dispatches announcing Alvarado's appointment as governor of California and Vallejo's promotion to Colonel and naming him comandánte-general of the Northern Frontier of Alta California by Senor Moran, Minister of War.

General Vallejo found matters at Santa Barbara in a condition which were not in agreement with his ideas of military discipline. Alvarado and Castro had never been soldiers and cared little to enforce military discipline, allowing the officers to call them "Juanito" and "Jose." In a few days Vallejo had the guardhouse crowded with offending soldiers. He soon found himself involved in such a storm of protests that he was forced to admit that in an army of unpaid relatives, the old Spanish discipline must be modified.

As military head of the Northern Frontier, Vallejo was in control of an area which today comprises the counties of Marin, Sonoma, Mendocino, Humboldt, Del Norte, Solano, Napa, Lake, Yolo, Colusa, Siskiyou, Shasta, Tehama, Plumas, Lassen, Sierra, Placer, Nevada and El Dorado.

Captain John Augustus Sutter

Governor Alvarado gave permission to "Capt" Augustus Sutter, an arrival of 1839 in California (after a roundabout journey from Switzerland) to locate in the Sacramento Valley; however he warned Sutter to stay away from the area commanded by Vallejo, saying that the latter's jurisdiction extended as far as the Sacramento and San Joaquin rivers. The so-called "Autocrat of the North" believed that his command covered Sutter's grant of eleven leagues.

Sutter desired Vallejo's friendship, as he was unhappy over the treatment he had received from the authorities in Monterey. On November 8, 1841 Sutter wrote to Jacob P. Leese (who had received a grant to the Rancho Huichica near Sonoma on October 21, 1841) telling of his, Sutter's potential strength and of the aid he expected from emigrants, hunters, Shawnees and Delawares as well as from the French frigate when it should arrive. In part, in Sutter's spelling, the letter read:

It is too late now to drive me out of the country, one step they do against me is that I will make a Declaration of Independence and proclaim California for a Republic, independent from Mexico. I am strong now . . . I will be a faithful Mexican but when this rascle Castro should come here, a very warm and harty welcome is prepared for him, 10 guns have well mounted for protect the fortress and two field pieces. I have also about 50 faithful which shot their musquet quik . . . I wish you to tell the Commandante General that I wish to be his friend and I am very much obliged to him for his goodness and kindness when my people passed in Sonoma; the beauty in the Valley of the Moon, General Vallejo make so much flowrich. If he will join me in such a case, I should like it very mych. But all is out of question so long they let me alone and trouble me not but I want security from the government.

Leese showed Sutter's letter to Vallejo who made a copy of it and on January 21, 1842, sent it to Mexico City to the *Minister of War and Marine*, with the comment: "Sutter, styling his place the Fort of New Helvitia and himself as governor of that fortress, exercises arbitrary and despotic power . . . receives foreigners, no matter whence or how they come . . . and finally he makes seditious threats as proven by the enclosed letters."

If Vallejo and Castro were displeased with Sutter, Governor Alvarado was not. In January 1842 he reported that Sutter had been obliged to defend himself with only eight men because Vallejo had refused him assistance. Alvarado was pleased to note that Sutter had attracted some 300 Indians, who lived near his establishment, and had started a primary school for them; indeed the Department of Alta California was, according to the governor, indebted to Sutter for much of the tranquility it enjoyed and had no cause to regret its concession to him.

When Lansford W. Hastings arrived at Sutter's Fort on July 11, 1843 with a party of emigrants from Oregon, they were given passports by no other than the formerly bankrupt Swiss citizen, John Augustus Sutter. Vallejo, evidently jealous of his own "Channel of authority" wrote to Sutter on July 26, 1843 the following letter, tinged with sarcasm:

There is in my possession the note dated the 19th of the current month in which you inform me that you have dispatched a messenger to his Excellency, the Comandante General and Governor of the Department, informing him of the arrival of some families coming from Columbia with the intention of settling in the country and that you as legal authority of the new government, granted passports to the emigrants constituting yourself as responsible for their conduct.

I do not doubt that you are legal authority, although I have no more basis upon which to found my assertion than your statement and the annotation on your note; but the latter only says: Justice Court of the District of the Sacramento River and you are not ignorant that *this* is the seat of the principal authorities of the Frontier of the North. I am Chief of the line from Santa Ines to Sonoma, it is understood, all that is comprised in its jurisdiction, and this embraces also your establishment; consequently I cannot help feeling surprised that you should have addressed yourself directly to the Government, I, being the channel through which you should have sent the communication.

The government to which Vallejo referred was that of General Jose Manuel Micheltorena, who had been appointed governor on January 22, 1842, by President Lopez de Santa Ana. Micheltorena took with him to California from Mexico an army consisting of 150 pardoned convicts and one hundred regular soldiers, who, being poorly clothed and often hungry pillaged the land of the Californians. Governor Alvarado had during his administration assigned to Sutter the duties of "*encargado de Justicia y representante del gobierno en las fronteras del Rio del Sacramento*," and Sutter lost no time in exercising the privilege of his office.

In Sutter's autobiography he recorded "Vallejo and others of the Californians, against whom, rather than the Indians I kept my fort and guns in order. They were jealous of my establishment. I gave passports to those entering the country and they did not like it. I was friendly with the emigrants . . . I encouraged emigration while they discouraged it. I sympathized with the Americans while they hated them."

SUTTER'S CORRESPONDENCE

About eighteen months after receiving Vallejo's letter of July 26, 1843 Sutter wrote to Victor Prudon, a Frenchman who had come to California in 1834 with the Hijar-Padres Compania Cosmopolitana. Sutter's letter was dated January 1, 1845 from New Helvetia.

My reasons for not writing is that I lacked an opportunity since your young man was afraid of bad weather . . . I was astonished to hear over there the news that I had sold my establishment to the Government and in fact Senor Estudillo told me that you had gone to see those gentlemen at the Moquelumne River so that it seems that they have not kept the matter secret. What is your opinion about it, Sir? Do you think the Government will buy it? I wish I was certain so that I might take the necessary measures. In case the Government decides about this purchase, do you think it would be possible to obtain a part of the sum on account, enough to pay part of my debts?

I could put them in possession of the establishment at the end of the harvest. It seems to me that the Government ought not to neglect the affair: for next Autumn many emigrants are bound here from the United States and one thing comforts me, that there will be many Germans, French and Swiss among them. I have received letters to the effect from a few friends through the last party of ten men. At all events nothing could be more necessary for the Government than a respectable position in this place. Among the emigrants who intend coming are gentlemen of great means, Capitalists.

A ship is going to bring us printing material and I intend to have a newspaper published, half Spanish and half English. Such progress is made throughout civilization and here we are so much behind. Even in Tahiti, there is lithography and a newspaper is published, L'Oceanic Francaise. We expect a ship from New York in the course of about a month; it will bring us all the necessary implements of agriculture selected on purpose for our valley comprising many ploughs with farmer's garments.

Sutter went on to say that if a ship could enter without paying custom duties or at least pay only a moderate rate, it would benefit the whole country. In April, he said, a ship with a cargo well-suited for the Sacramento Valley would arrive. The owners expected to buy a lot near the Bay or the Sacramento River, erect a warehouse and keep a stock of articles that farmers needed which would be sold on credit and payment made in wheat or any of the products of the country, especially salted salmon. The other merchants who transact business, in this unfortunate country, Sutter said, refused to receive anything but leather and tallow. Sutter wrote further:

Among the people in the Upper Valley are a few bad characters who stole some of my horses and some mares and cows of Mr. Corelua's. I must try to imprison some of the principal ones and I hope I can depend upon Captain Fremont and his men. He will doubtless enable me to make his countrymen prisoners, for to overlook such acts would be the worst influence for the future. I shall try to do it alone and if I have not sufficient power to succeed I shall write to Senor Vallejo for an auxiliary.

In a few weeks the launch will come to Sonoma with some of Mr. Beaulieu's garments and will bring at the same time some tanned leather for Senor Vallejo. How inconvenient it is for us in the North that the Capital should be so distant. It takes at least four or five months before receiving an answer . . . I will make no more reports to the Government except to Senor Castro as he is nearest and he can make his statement to the Government if he judges it necessary.

I have not as yet received an answer from Padre Real about the letter that you were kind enough to write for me about the fruit trees and vines. You know that Senor Castro has given me permission on receiving as much as I need. Advise me, if you please on what I can do. Will it be possible to receive some vines and trees in Sonoma? If you could have them ready in about three weeks, something like 2,000 of them, I would pay you as much as they cost. . . . If this country derived any utility from the Custom House, one would not complain so much, but it is only good to provide for a lot of useless officers who devour the very marrow of the country. If at last a paper could be published that would unseal the blind men's eyes. I trust that you may take a part and interest in that affair of printing.

I am now constructing a mill with two pairs of mill-stones, for a great quantity of flour will be needed next Autumn when the emigrants arrive . . . A much better road some 400 miles shorter has been discovered and the Captain Fremont has also found in the last chain of mountains a much easier passage than the one known so far. Every trip they make some new discovery . . . The crowd of emigrants, arriving in the United States increase the population to such an extent that it will find its way even to the Pacific shores. A year or two and no power will be able to stop the emigration.

An emigrant himself and a naturalized Mexican citizen, Sutter had managed to get along with the several governors who had ruled since he came to California, and he was convinced that it was to his advantage to welcome the emigrants coming from the United States—to make his establishment known as a place of recuperation for the throngs who had fought weather, terrain, food shortage and hostile Indians. And so it was that after their first brief stop at William Johnson's ranch on the Bear River, the emigrants pressed on toward Sutter's New Helvetia, where they had been led to expect not only genial hospitality but a chance to work.

During the summer of 1845, Sutter and Thomas Oliver Larkin, the American consul, carried on a correspondence and exchanged various newspapers; on July 15th, Sutter wrote Larkin:

I send you a newspaper from St. Louis, sent me over the Rocky Mountains with a somewhat exaggerated description of California. The Company which arrived on the 10th inst. from the Oregon consists of 39 men, Widow and three children, of which I send you a list [Sutter's list included not only the names but also occupations]. All of this people have a decent appearance and some very useful Men amongs them . . . A little later will arrive here direct from the U.S. a very large Company, more than 1,000 souls, familys from Kentucky and Ohio and a good many enterprising Gentlemen with some Capital to improve the Country under lead of L. W. Hastings, Esq.

On October 8th of the same year, Sutter again wrote to Larkin:

Yesterday Mr. Sublette from St. Louis arrived here with his party, consisting of fifteen men . . . A good many of this Emigrants have Cash more or less. Some of them have several thousand dollars in Gold. Not one Company has arrived before in this Country which looked so respectable as this. I have a great chance to buy plenty of well broken Amer. oxen and Wagons from the young men which prefer horses that can travell in the Country.

My establishment will gain a great deal by this emigration. I employ a good many necessary mechanics. A first rate Doctor will remain here who is well provided with Medicines and instruments, like wise a clerk. I have now three blacksmiths at work and have so many gunsmiths, I have work for them . . . I think it will be difficult for the Emigrants to obtain lands for them[selves] under the present circumstances, therefore I spoke with some persons who have good titles for land to let the Emigrants have small pieces of their Grants, say a mile or two for a family and nearly all are willing to divide a part of their land with them. I shall give likewise a good Exemple.

DR. JOHN MARSH

Many of the great number of emigrants that came to California in the 1840s had been lured thither by the reports of Lansford W. Hastings, Dr. Marsh and others; Consul Larkin felt that Marsh, an educated man with an accurate knowledge of California, could be of special help in attracting American settlers to California so as to prepare it for annexation to the United States. On July 8, 1845 Larkin wrote Marsh: "Now you as a settler and extensive landholder in California have a great interest in this stake . . . I should like to have you . . . come forth into the field and write for the country you intend to live in. You are a good writer, know all the country, its people and resources, its climate, rivers, bays and soil. Do by all means sit down to the task, write everything you can regarding California and I will have it published in the New York papers. I am so confident of your skill that I assure you, your letters will be copied in every paper." Agreeing to Larkin's plan, Marsh wrote to his old benefactor, United States Senator from Michigan, Honorable Lewis Cass. Portions of his letter follow:

You will probably be somewhat surprised to receive a letter from an individual from whom you have not heard, or even thought of, for nearly twenty years; yet although the lapse of time has wrought many changes both in men and things, the personal identity of us both has probably been left. You will, I think remember a youth whom you met at Green Bay in 1825, who having left his Alma Mater (Harvard) had spent a year or two in the "far, far West" and was then returning to his New England home and whom you induced to turn his face again toward the setting sun; that youth who but for your influence would probably now have been administering pills in some quiet Yankee village, is now a gray-haired man, breeding cattle and cultivating grape-vines on the shores of the Pacific. Your benevolence prompted you to take an interest in the fortunes of that youth; and it is presumed you may not be unwilling to hear from him again.

I left the United States in 1835 and came to New Mexico and thence traversing the states of Chihuahua and Sonora, crossed the Rio Grande at its junction with the Gila . . . and entered this territory at its southern part. Any more direct route was at that time unknown and considered impracticable.

I have now been more than ten years in this country and have traveled over all the inhabited parts of it. I have resided eight years where I now live, near the Bay of San Francisco, at the point where the rivers, Sacramento and San Joaquin unite together to meet the tide-water of the bay, about forty miles from the ocean. I possess at this place a farm about ten miles by twelve in extent, one side which borders on the river which is navigable to this point for sea-going vessels. I have at last found the far West and intend to end my ramblings here.

Dr. Marsh knew of Senator Cass's interest in Indians, he therefore devoted a good portion of his letter giving him a physical description of the California Indian, his dress, food, customs and language—not only of the wild Indians but also of the domesticated ones who worked at the missions and in the homes of the Spanish families.

Dr. Marsh did not neglect to report on California's resources:

I think it (California) cannot long remain in the hands of its present owners. If it does not come into the possession of Americans, the English will have it . . . The agricultural capabilities of California are but very imperfectly developed. The whole of it is remarkably adapted to the culture of the vine . . . Olives, figs and almonds grow well. Apples, pears and peaches are abundant and on the southern part, oranges. Cotton is beginning to be cultivated and succeeds well. It is the finest country I have ever seen; Hemp, flax and tobacco have been cultivated on a small scale . . .

The raising of cattle is the principal pursuit of the inhabitants and the foreign commerce of Upper California employs from ten to fifteen sail vessels, mostly large ships . . . More than half of these are American and belong exclusively to the port of Boston. The others are English, French, Russian, Mexican, Peruvian and Hawaiian. The exports consists of hides and tallow, cow lard, wheat, soap, timber and furs.

California, although nominally belonging to Mexico is about as independent of it as Texas and must ere long share the same fate. Since my residence here, no less than four governors have been driven from the country by force of arms. The last of these, Micheltorena, with about four hundred of his soldiers and one hundred employees were driven away about a year ago.

Upon receiving Marsh's letter, Senator Cass handed it to the press, by which it was given countrywide publicity, and, when called to the attention of President James K. Polk, the letter's contents are claimed to have influenced his decision to wrest California from Mexico.

Vallejo spoke highly of Dr. Marsh, commending his services as a physician and regretting that Marsh's taciturn manners prevented him from becoming a general favorite, but Vallejo was well aware of the problems involved in a great emigrant influx.

EMIGRATION OF AMERICANS

On November 22, 1845, Vallejo wrote to the Mexican officials informing them that, "The emigration of North Americans today forms an unbroken line of wagons from the United States to this Department, and how can they be turned back without force and resources? It is necessary, Sir, it is indispensable that the Supreme Government should send us both. This has been for some years my incessant supplication. Troops and money! Only by uniting both can they save us from the imminent danger that surrounds us. It would be very desirable to close the door of communication between the United States and this country, even at some sacrifice. Castro made propositions to Sutter for the purchase of his establishment; he, Sutter, said he would cede it to the Government for one hundred thousand dollars. I grant this is a very high price to pay for a few pieces of cannon, a not very scientifically constructed bastion, some moats, ten or twelve adobe houses and corrals of the same material but the security of the country is what is being paid for and that is priceless."

William F. Swasey, who worked at Sutter's Fort for awhile, tells of the visit of General Jose Castro, Andreas Castillero, Victor Prudon and Jacob P. Leese in November of 1845 to treat with Sutter for the purchase of his establishment. Sutter declined their proposition.

Because of the threat of California's annexation to the United States, General Almonte, the Mexican minister, ordered Vallejo to forbid American emigrants from entering California or remaining in the country without passports; but no means of accomplishing such an objective had been furnished him. Recalling the situation in northern California at that time,

Vallejo said, "Years before, I had urgently represented to the Government of Mexico the necessity of stationing a sufficient force on the frontier else Sonoma would be lost; which would be equivalent to leaving the rest of the country an easy prey to the invader . . . The instructions sent me in reply to my repeated demands to fortify the country were that I should at once force the emigrants to recross the Sierra and depart from the territory of the Republic. To say nothing of the inhumanity of these orders, their execution was physically impossible; first, because I had no military force; and, second because the immigrants came in the autumn when snow covered the Sierra so quickly as to render it impracticable." In spite of the bitter feeling that existed in Mexico and the orders sent to California, the emigrants were received with kindness by the Californians.

The letters in which Vallejo had "urgently" described the situation to his superiors are in the Military Archives in Mexico City. Through the courtesy of a request from Chief Justice Earl Warren when he was governor of California, the author was given permission to do some historical research in the Mexican archives by the Director of the Military Archives, General Ruben Garcia Velasquez de Leon, the Secretary of the National Defense of Mexico.

I read the letters in which Vallejo had asked that more soldiers be sent him and their salaries paid, in order that he might keep the emigrants from crossing the Sierra; if the aid was not forthcoming, he wished to be relieved of his command. In closing his letter of December 11, 1841, Vallejo had written, "I beg of your Excellency to carry my request to the Supreme Government that they may deign to relieve me of the charge of the General Command with which they have honored me."

Mariano Guadalupe Vallejo's military service had been rewarded with large land grants wherein he pastured his herds, raised grains, farm produce and wine grapes. His energy and ability, combined with the labors of Indian workers produced a fortune unrivaled in California, much of it being acquired on the lush acres of the Rancho Petaluma. When Vallejo petitioned for this land on March 15, 1834, he was required to furnish three witnesses who would testify to his birth, marriage and character, and to the fact that the land he desired did not belong to any particular mission, town or corporation; furthermore, that he had plans for its development. The region of fertile valleys and forested hills of 66,622.17 acres was given to Vallejo in two separate grants; one by Governor Jose Figueroa in June 1834 and the other by Governor Manuel Micheltorena in June 1844. In that year Vallejo had advanced 2,000 pesos in gold coin to Micheltorena at his request.

In awarding the Petaluma grant to Vallejo, Governor Figueroa realized its strategic location—a deterrent to the Russians who had established a foothold at Fort Ross. Soon after receiving the grant in June 1834, Vallejo, knowing it was a natural and easy passage to Sonoma, started building in a small way but with large plans. Large sums of money were spent on the Petaluma Rancho in building houses, a corral, fences and in cultivating the land.

Cattle and horses were under the supervision of skilled vaqueros. Among the buildings was a large tannery in which shoes were manufactured for the soldiers. In the blacksmith shop were turned out the horse-shoes, tools and other needed metal articles; manufactured goods ranging from hand-made nails, blankets, and women's dress materials, to soap as well as the usual tallow and hides, were carried in coast-wide ships as far as San Blas.

Vallejo found a market for his wheat among the Russians who came regularly each year with two and sometimes four vessels to buy for their Alaskan settlement. The large adobe house on the Petaluma Rancho with its barred windows, constructed to act as a fort if necessary, was begun in the middle 1830s but never completely finished. According to the testimony of Salvador Vallejo, a witness when General Vallejo presented his case before the U.S. Land Commission, the large house had cost his brother $80,000 to build. The other witnesses were J. B. R. Cooper, James M. Hudspeth, George Yount and Jose de la Rosa. The petition filed May 21, 1852. The case submitted on briefs December 19, 1854. The case went to Court of appeals, then to Supreme Court which supported Vallejo's right to the land.

In March 1857, after confirmation of the grant Rancho Petaluma, Vallejo sold the large Petaluma Adobe and some adjoining land to William Whiteside and his wife for $25,000. The Whitesides kept the Petaluma Adobe for two years and sold it to William D. Bliss for $30,000.

The largest land area given to Vallejo was the Suscol Rancho of 80,000 or slightly more acres. It had been formerly a Nacional Rancho or stock farm operated for the benefit of the Mexican soldiers. It was deeded to Vallejo as part-payment of the debt that the Central Mexican Government had owed Vallejo for some years.

On June 19, 1844, the Abstract of title stated

Whereas the citizen Mariano Guadalupe Vallejo, Colonel of Cavalry, and Military Commandant of the Frontier of Sonoma, has solicited from this Government the purchase of the land known by the name of "Suscol" in the jurisdiction of said frontiers, bound on the north by the lands called "Tulocay" and "Suisun," and on the east and south by the Straits of Carquines Mare Island, and Napa Creek; the necessary measures and investigations by the Supreme Government of the Mexican Nation sold him the said land of "Suscol for the sum of five thousand dollars, which the Government has received to its satisfaction, declaring to him the ownership thereof by these present letters in virtue whereof he may occupy and possess it, freely and exclusively destining it to the use and cultivation which may best suit him without any restriction.

Therefore I command that these Presents serve him for a title to be recorded in the corresponding book and acknowledged by all the authorities of the Department of the Republic, and be delivered to the party interested as private property bought from the Government of the Department in due and legal form.

Given in Monterey, on the 19th of June, 1844

MANUEL MICHELTORENA
Francisco Arce, Secretary ad interim

Two years before, in June 1842, Vallejo had acquired the four-league Rancho Suisun, granted originally to Chief Solano who had petitioned for the grant in 1837 saying the land belonged to him by inheritance from his ancestors and that he was actually in possession of it but he wished to conform to the new order of colonization. General Vallejo paid $1,000 for the Suisun Ranch to Chief Solano. The small-pox epidemic had so decimated the Indian Chief's tribes that he preferred the money to the land. Money was better than beads!

On July 4th, 1845 Fremont was in Sonoma where he organized a battalion of 224 men. In his *Memoirs* he said, "I sent out parties for horses to mount the battalion and to bring in cattle for their support. The horses were taken principally from the estate of General Vallejo and the cattle from the government stock-farm at Suscol." As was mentioned above, the Suscol Rancho became the property of Vallejo in 1844, therefore at the time Fremont outfitted the men for horses and cattle, he was taking the cattle as well as the horses from Vallejo.

Among other purchases which Vallejo made were Rancho Yulupa from Miguel Alvarado, the major-domo of the Petaluma ranch; the Agua Caliente grant from Lazaro Peña, a grant so large that Vallejo could afford to give a tract of two leagues by one quarter for music lessons for his family to Andrew Hoeppner. Other Vallejo land was the "Pozo de los Marineros," 371 acres near the Presidio of San Francisco, given to Vallejo by Governor Jose Figueroa who had also given the first Petaluma grant. Vallejo also owned land in the Potrero which he had acquired from the De Haro estate, having belonged to Francisco De Haro, the first Alcalde of San Francisco. In Mendocino County, Vallejo owned eight square leagues of land known as the Yocaya Rancho which was conveyed to him on August 16, 1852 by Don Cayetano Juarez. And there was the Rancho Temelec (where General Persifor F. Smith once lived); the "Entre Napa" and other acreages so it is safe to surmise that Vallejo's holdings at one time amounted to over 175,000 acres.

For a number of years Vallejo had been cognizant of the political ambitions of the European governments, his personal wealth having put him in a position to serve as the attentive but unofficial host of California. This position was considerably strengthened by the warmth of his hospitality and his peculiar grace of manner, which joined with his well-informed mind gave him a reputation that extended beyond California; even to Europe. In fact, among the visitors who sailed into the port of San Francisco and sought his acquaintance, were the official representatives of the four great powers. Socially the visitors may have made an impression but politically—No! Vallejo said of them:

> I remember when there came to my home in Sonoma, Sir George Simpson, Governor of India; Governor Douglas and Mr. McLaughlin with all their retinue in 1838 and in 1841 and they asked me if I would work for the protection of England . . . I

told them this; that I'd be hanged if I would accept any European power to keep this country. Afterwards the French Consul Hascet, a Frenchman who was in Monterey and another who was in Los Angeles came to ask me to seek the protection of France and I gave them the same answer and a little harder because they understood Spanish . . . We belong to the American continent and are opposed to European heads.

Thus Vallejo was the first person on the Pacific Coast to endorse the principles of the Monroe Doctrine (enunciated December 2, 1823) which stated henceforth no European power could be permitted to extend its system over any government in the Western Hemisphere whose independence had been acknowledged by the United States.

As mentioned before, Lieutenant J. Ringgold of the Wilkes Exploring Expedition was one of the first American officers entertained by Vallejo, and incidentally the Lieutenant did not think much of the village of Sonoma. Another visiting officer was Commodore Thomas Ap Catesby Jones who had entered the Bay of Monterey with two Naval vessels and under whose orders the American flag had been raised on October 19, 1842, only to be replaced two days later with the Mexican flag which he had taken down. The Commodore's apologies were accepted and he was entertained by the forgiving Californians. Consul Larkin wrote of that time to the New York Herald's Bennett saying, "During the time the vessels lay at anchor here the officers spent their time ashore hunting wild deer or dancing with the tame dears, both being plentiful in and around Monterey."

At the time of Commodore Jones' visit David Spence wrote to Vallejo that Monterey had been captured by United States Naval forces. Vallejo ordered all military commanders to assemble their forces to San Francisco and issued a proclamation calling upon the people to take up arms for their country. However, before Vallejo himself could leave, a message was received from Captain Mariano Silva, saying that Commodore Jones had replaced the Mexican flag with apologies and salutes.

Commodore Jones wrote that he desired to visit Vallejo in Sonoma. The General sent directions but the Commodore chose another route; he and his men in "strange uniforms" were arrested by Lieutenant Ramon Carrillo and taken to the Indian camp at Huichica. Chief Solano brought them to Sonoma Barracks where Vallejo met the Commodore who asked the General, "Is this the kind of reception you prepare for your guests? It was now Vallejo's turn to offer apologies. The guests were saluted with a 13-gun salute, and entertained for several days.

General Vallejo repaid the call aboard the *Cyane* anchored at Sausalito. He was received with a 13-gun salute. On his departure Vallejo was presented with two globes made in Boston in 1832; one a celestial globe and the other a terrestrial globe. They now grace the historic Vallejo home in Sonoma.

In May, 1846 after Vallejo had returned to Sonoma from Monterey, he received a letter from Pablo de la Guerra who was an advocate of independence for California. He asked Vallejo which he would support, Castro's idea of a French protectorate, Pico's party in favor of England or absolute independence. On the margin of this letter, Vallejo wrote that he had replied that it was preferable for the Californians to be annexed to the United States, rather than to be ruled by lords fifteen thousand miles away.

California's Year of Decision

Mexico's neglect of her province of California and Vallejo's realization that his native land was not strong enough to be independent caused him to advocate the linking of California's destiny with the great Republic to the East. He felt that California's interests would be better served under American rule.

In the spring of 1846 (Vallejo gives the date as March 27th) at a meeting in the home of the American Consul, Thomas O. Larkin, the California Junta debated the future of the province. General Jose Castro ended a long speech by saying: "I pronounce for annexation to France or England, but I hear some one say 'No Monarchy' but is not Monarchy better than Anarchy? Then Vallejo's secretary Colonel Victor Prudon arose and said: "Up to today, I was in favor of total independence . . . but after listening to the arguments of General Castro who presented the defenseless condition of California and its inability to resist attacks of foreign powers, I am of the opinion that we should annex California to the United States of America. I am as you know a native of beautiful France. I love France with the love of a son but I love California with the fervent idolatory of a lover and when the time comes to vote, I shall cast mine for union with the United States of America." General Vallejo followed Colonel Prudon with an impassioned speech, saying in part:

> I cannot coincide in opinion, the cession of our country to France or England. It is most true to rely any longer upon Mexico to govern and defend us would be idle and absurd . . . My opinion is made up that we must persevere in throwing off the galling yoke of Mexico . . . We have indeed taken the first step by electing our own governor. In contemplating this consummation of our destiny I feel nothing but pleasure but I ask you to share it. When we join our fortunes to hers, we shall not become subjects but fellow-citizens, possessing all the rights of the people of the United States and choosing our own Federal and local rulers. We shall have a stable government and just laws.
>
> California will grow strong and flourish and her people will be prosperous happy and free . . . Look not therefore with jealousy upon the hardy pioneers who scale our mountains and cultivate our plains but rather welcome them as brothers who come to share a common destiny.

The foregoing words were first printed in Lt. Joseph Warren Revere's book *Tour of Duty in California*. Revere, a Spanish scholar, had been in charge of the garrison in Sonoma for a time and before the publication of his book, he called upon Vallejo. Together they went over Revere's notes of Vallejo's speech in Spanish and the English translation; Vallejo approving.

General John Charles Fremont in his *Memoirs* referred thus to the Spring 1846 meeting of the Junta in Monterey: "From Mr. Samuel Hensley, a leading American settler, I learned that he had met General Guadalupe Vallejo, who had command of the Northern District of the Department and one of the most influential men of Upper California. The General, Mr. Hensley said, had informed him that he had attended a convention composed of Castro, five other delegates and himself from the different districts of California at which the proposition of separating from Mexico and establishing an independent government under the protection of a foreign power had been debated; however the majority in the convention was not in favor of placing the country under the protection of the United States.

The Governor at that time, Pio Pico, was not friendly to the Americans. "We find ourselves threatened by hords of Yankee emigrants, who have already begun to flock into our country, and whose progress we cannot arrest. Already have the wagons of that perfidious people scaled the almost inaccessible summits of the Sierra Nevada, crossed the entire continent and penetrated the fruitful valley of the Sacramento. What that astonishing people will next undertake, I cannot say!"

Thomas O. Larkin, a half-brother of Captain Juan B. Cooper (husband of Vallejo's sister Encarnacion) must have been glad to have had the meeting of the Junta held in his home at this critical time. Since April 2, 1844, the day he was appointed American Consul, he had been working to win over the Californians to the idea of annexation to the United States. Larkin kept a secret file in which he noted his opinion of the native Californians and early settlers in California. These brief biographical sketches were written by the consular secretary, William F. Swasey, under the dictation of Larkin; one copy of these sketches was sent to Mr. Buchanan, Secretary of State, one was given to Commodore Stockton and one copy was recorded in Mr. Larkin's consular book. "These sketches," said Swasey, "were written from Mr. Larkin's own volition without direction, knowledge or suggestion of any one else and he was so anxious that they be kept secret that he directed the record of them should be sealed up and not to be opened until after his death."

From Consul Larkin's Dossier:

MARIANO GUADALUPE VALLEJO:

Born in Monterey, aged 36 years, named as a cadet when 15 or 16 years of age. Holds the commission of Lieut. Colonel which he received from Bustamente; his father a Spanish Sergeant, equal in power to a Captain of the present day; a man of large property; married; very studious for a Californian; of much knowledge and general information; anxious to improve himself and country. In 1837 assisted Castro and Alvarado in expelling Mexicans.

From that time has gradually retired from active military life although he has always had some command at his place of residence: Has been formal stiff, pompous and exacting towards his countrymen and foreigners of the lower and middle class. Within a year has become pleasant and condescending, anxious for popularity and good will of others. In Sonoma he has immense tracts of land, herds of cattle and horses and extensive houses; is hospitable to those who are highly respected or recommended to him. Ostentatious and for a Californian a close observer of every passing event. As a private person has but little regard for Mexico, as an officer more; is confident that Mexico will not assist or protect California and that his own countrymen have not the capacity. Has given much work and employment to the laboring American emigrant. Always speaking in their favor.

He has no wish for Government pay (it owes him twenty or thirty thousand dollars) Speaks English indifferently. Would always prefer rank, perhaps office after affairs are well settled. Has much influence all over the country. Had his part of California the most free from robbery or insubordination with more safety of life and property than any other town in California.

BEAR FLAG INCIDENT

Early on Sunday morning, June 14, 1846, General Vallejo, his brother Salvador, his secretary Victor Prudon and Rosalia Vallejo's husband Jacob P. Leese, all men in their thirties, were made political prisoners by a group of American settlers. The latter have been called the Bear Flaggers, because their hastily-made flag showed a crudely drawn bear looking up at a star drawn in with blackberry juice and the words "California Republic." At the bottom of the flag of unbleached cotton was a band of red flannel. The flag, three by five feet, was hoisted in place of the Mexican ensign on the flag-pole in front of the barracks of the Sonoma plaza. Three days later Jose Castro reported the incident in a proclamation:

> The contemptible policy of the agents of the United States of North America in this Department has induced a number of adventurers who, regardless of the rights of men have designedly commenced an invasion, possessing themselves of the town of Sonoma, taking by surprise all the place, the military Commander of that border, Colonel Mariano Guadalupe Vallejo, Lt. Col. Victor Prudon, Captain Salvador Vallejo and Senor Jacob P. Leese . . . There is still time to rise in mass.

Castro was naturally incensed because seven months before he had conducted a hearing of emigrants in Sonoma telling them that he would permit them to remain provisionally in California under the vigilance of Colonel Vallejo, obeying the laws, applying within three months for a regular license, promising to depart if this was not granted.

Castro wrote Larkin that the course pursued at Sonoma was the most atrocious and infamous that could be imagined. The settlers, he said, had "attacked the rights of the people, breaking the established social compacts, profaning the sacred soil of another nation . . . Senor Thomas O. Larkin, will permit the undersigned to say to him frankly, that he has witnessed with extraordinary coolness the invasion of the Department . . . the undersigned believes that the Consul of the United States, will agree with him that the acts committed by this party of foreigners, Americanos, has the appearance of actual and downright robbery."

It is interesting to read how General Vallejo, himself, years later remembered the unexpected event:

> A little before dawn on June 14, 1846, a party of hunters and trappers with some foreign settlers, under command of Captain Merritt, Doctor Semple and William B. Ide surrounded my residence at Sonoma and without firing a shot, made a prisoner of myself, then Commander of the Northern Frontier and of Lieutenant Colonel Victor Prudon, Captain Salvador Vallejo and Jacob P. Leese. I should state here that down to October 1845, I had maintained at my own expense a respectful garrison at Sonoma which often in union with the settlers did good service in campaigns against the Indians; but at last tired of spending money which the Mexican government never refunded, I disbanded the force and most of the soldiers who had constituted it, left Sonoma. Thus in June 1846 the Plaza was unprotected although there were ten pieces of artillery with other arms and munitions of war.
>
> The parties who unfurled the Bear Flag were well aware that Sonoma was without defense and lost no time in taking advantage of this fact and carrying out their plans. If the men who ran up the Bear Flag had flown the flag that Washington consecrated, there would have been no war on the frontier of Sonoma, for all minds were ready to give the embrace of brothers to the sons of the great Republic that had our admiration.

On another occasion Vallejo added a personal detail to the Bear Flag incident. He had delivered in Santa Rosa the baccalaureate address before the graduating class of the Pacific Methodist College and was the guest of its president Dr. Finley for dinner. Vallejo's arrest was mentioned and Vallejo exclaimed to Dr. Finley, "And they tied me to a chair! Me! Vallejo!"

Most historians list 33 names as members of the Bear Flag Party. Vallejo listed 19 of the "Bandera del Osos" with his own terse comments; Dr. Robert Semple was "Buen Oso" and Ezekiel Merritt and Granville Swift were listed as "Oso Malo."

Some months before, being pressed by the Mexican authorities, the California officials had ordered the American settlers to leave California and had forbidden them to take any of their property with them, threatening them with extermination should they presume to remain in the country. These orders were made known to Captain Fremont, who was in California on his Third Topographical Expedition, undertaken in the interest of science and commerce.

In January of *1846* (which has been called the "Year of Decision") Fremont, accompanied by Consul Larkin, had made his official call on Don Jose Castro, the commanding general of the Department of California, and was cordially received. But on March third Lieutenant Chavez brought a communication from Castro to Fremont, then encamped at W. E. P. Hartnell's ranch in the Salinas Valley, ordering him and his men out of California. Surprised at Castro's breach of faith, Fremont refused to comply. Instead, he made camp on a hill, Gavilan Peak, four miles from San Juan Bautista. There he raised the flag of the United States. Later, when the staff was blown down by the wind, Fremont interpreted it as an omen that he should leave, realizing, too, that he had no official orders to raise the flag. While his campfire was still smoldering he made his way toward Oregon. His journey was interrupted by Lieutenant Archibald H. Gillespie of the Marine Corps, who had left Washington, D.C. with orders from the President and the Secretary of the Navy to see Larkin and to find Fremont.

Before leaving the Sacramento Valley, Lieutenant Gillespie told some of the American settlers that, if matters worsened, he would recall Fremont; his camp would then provide temporary protection. Gillespie overtook Fremont near the shores of Klamath Lake where his party of fifty men were encamped. The Lieutenant gave certain information to the *Pathfinder* which Fremont believed absolved him from his duty as an explorer but thrust upon him the duties of an officer of the United States Army, an officer who now had authoritative knowledge that his government intended to take California. He believed that "affairs had assumed a critical aspect and that the time had come when it was unsafe to leave events to mature under unfriendly or mistaken direction." As stated in Fremont's *Memoirs* he decided "to govern events, than to be governed by them."

Going south, Fremont camped at Marysville Buttes and sent word to the settlers to come to his camp; the message was delivered by an Indian agent on the 8th of June. William Brown Ide who was to be one of the leaders of the settlers, arriving two days later at Fremont's camp, has recorded in a letter to Senator Wambaugh how Fremont outlined to the settlers his "plan of conquest"—First: Select a dozen men who have nothing to lose but everything to gain. Second: Encourage them to commit depredations against General Castro and thus supply the camp with horses, necessary for a trip to the United States. Third: Make prisoners of some of the principal men and thus provoke Castro *to strike the first blow*, in a war with the United States. This constituted Captain Fremont's plan of *neutral conquest* of California. He emphasized the indignities he and the settlers had received from Castro—indignities that justified them in any measure they might adopt for their safety; but if they waited to receive the first blow, all hope of resistance would be in vain. Talking with the group, Fremont said he was not at liberty to offer aid. He spoke privately to Ezekial Merritt, however, and gave him orders. In the *Memoirs* Fremont wrote:

> Among the settlers was a man named Ezekial Merritt. He was tall and spare, what I understand by raw-boned, a rugged man, fearless and simple; taking delight in

incurring risks but tractable and not given to asking questions when there was something he was required to do: Merritt was my Field-Lieutenant among the settlers. Looking over the field I saw that prompt precautionary measures were necessary in order to avail myself of such advantages as my position afforded. Acting upon this necessity, I sent Merritt into Sonoma instructed to surprise the garrison at that place.

"Stuttering Merritt," as he was known by his companions, could neither read nor write. John Bidwell said Merritt was "an old mountaineer and trapper, lived with an Indian Squaw and went clad in buckskin fringed after the style of the Rocky Mts. Indians. He chewed the tobacco to a disgusting excess and stammered badly. He had a reputation for bravery because of his continual boasting of his prowess in killing Indians. The handle of the tomahawk he carried had nearly a hundred notches to record the number of his Indian scalps. He drank deeply whenever he could get liquor." This was the kind of man that Fremont chose to lead the surprise attack on Sonoma Barracks.

To fully understand the armed group on that early Sunday morning's visit, Vallejo asked to have his brother-in-law Jacob P. Leese sent for, to act as interpreter. Leese, an American from Ohio, had married Vallejo's sister Rosalia and they lived on the west side of the plaza. Upon being told of the situation by Don Jose de la Rosa, Leese hurried over to the Casa Grande. He reported, "On my arrival I must say that I was really astonished to see such a rough looking set of men. I supposed to find them the regular troops ordered by the United States government (but on the contrary). I found the General and two other officers arrested (leaving out any remarks relative to the family and children looking on, which is too tender for me to relate.)"

Leese approached a man who was about "six feet, six inches high and about fifteen inches in diameter, dressed in gray buckskin with a fox-skin cap." Leese asked Doctor Semple (for that was the name of the tall man) for what reason General Vallejo and the officers were being arrested and who was the commander. Semple replied that there was no particular commander. He explained that their objective was to make California a free and independent government; that General Vallejo had a great deal of influence and property as well as arms. This conversation was translated to Vallejo who requested Leese to say that he had a large quantity of arms under his charge which belonged to the Mexican government; however he would not oppose their undertaking if they would not molest private persons or property.

It has been said that at that time Vallejo signified his readiness to collect and take command of a force of his countrymen, saying that his devotion to the cause of annexation to the United States was well known and his opinion has been too often expressed to leave room for doubt as to his integrity and sincerity, while his position in the community was sufficient guaranty of his ability to perform all he had promised. But the majority of the men whom

Vallejo had addressed were ignorant of the Spanish language and were prejudiced against the Mexicans. Not knowing of the sterling qualities and the expressed political opinions of the prisoner, they were naturally suspicious of his good faith.

Leese suggested that a guarantee be given both parties. This was approved, so agreements were drawn and signed; the Californians promising not to take arms against the insurgents and they, in turn, were not to disturb private property nor harm the prisoners nor the members of their families. With this assurance given, General Vallejo at once placed at the insurgents' disposal fifty horses and gave them the keys to his storehouse with permission to take all the provisions they might require. The insurgents' leader, Ide, said, "We were to be provisioned by the generosity of our captured General." Ide promised Vallejo that the horses would be well cared for and an exact account kept of all stores consumed by necessity, that no waste would be permitted and that they would, to their utmost ability, pay full value for everything required.

The prisoner's interpreter was well acquainted with some of the men; he said he knew that they were intemperate and suggested that the *aguardiente* be destroyed for fear they might get intoxicated and create a disturbance. This was approved. Some of the men complained of being "hongry." A bullock was immediately killed, and sugar and tea were also given them for breakfast. According to Leese, this was the extent of the refreshments served by Vallejo.

One of the men wanted to strike Captain Salvador Vallejo, now that he was a prisoner. Leese told the filibusters not to think of old grudges as it would violate their recently signed treaty and would place a stain on the American character.

When Leese thought that things had quieted down, he went home for breakfast. In the course of half an hour, he returned to General Vallejo's home and was surprised to have two of the men tell him that he must inform the General that it was necessary to take him and the other prisoners to Captain Fremont's camp.

Leese asked Ide if Fremont had anything to do with the movement and was told that Captain Fremont had planned the undertaking. Leese immediately informed Vallejo who felt great satisfaction, knowing that Captain Fremont was an American officer who had been brought back into California by Lieutenant Gillespie and would no doubt straighten things out.

Leese and Vallejo thought that the signed agreements were sufficient guarantee to allow Vallejo to remain in the Casa Grande and the other prisoners in their homes but the "long Captain in leather," Semple, argued that as so many of the men were intoxicated it was better to take the prisoners to Fremont's camp for safe-keeping.

While the members of the party were busy searching the premises for arms and ammunition, finding nine pieces of artillery and two hundred stand of small arms, Vallejo managed to send for his friend Don Jose de la Rosa, a former printer on the press brought from Mexico by Don Agustin Zamorano. The General directed "Don Pepe" (as he was intimately called by the Vallejo family) to proceed with a message for Captain John B. Montgomery, whose ship, the *Portsmouth*, was anchored near Sausalito. Vallejo's request for help was not for himself, "he did not ask Captain Montgomery to take part in the matter or even to intercede for his own release," but he asked the Captain to send an officer to Sonoma or in some way use his influence with the insurgent garrison to prevent any injury to the defenseless inhabitants of Sonoma.

At the time of his arrest, Vallejo made no mention of his own emotions but he must have been deeply stirred; a brave young man—he was not yet 39—forced to surrender without a chance of removing his loved ones from the threat of marauders. Vallejo had settled an untrodden wilderness; he had known the treachery of Indians and foiled their uprising and plottings against his life. As a skilled horseman, he was able to catch with his lariat and toss the bull, and he could securely lasso the grizzly bear. Never had he known fear; but as he left his weeping wife and children, there was fear in his heart.

CAPTAIN FREMONT'S ORDERS

About eleven o'clock, June 14, 1846 the three prisoners and Jacob P. Leese, the interpreter, rode away under the armed escort of ten of the Bear Flaggers commanded by Captain John Grigsby, Robert Semple and Ezekial Merritt, all on horses from the herds of General Vallejo.

At the time of Vallejo's arrest Cayetano Juarez, born in Monterey (1810) three years after Vallejo's birth there, managed to escape from Sonoma where he was a guard, to Napa where he notified Dona Maria de la Luz, the wife of Captain Salvador of the arrest of her husband and his brother. Juarez disguised himself as a squaw and led a group of men to where the Bear Flaggers camped the first night with the prisoners at Vaca's Rancho. In the dark of the night when the Bear Flaggers were all asleep, Juarez approached Vallejo and told him a rescue party was close at hand awaiting his command. Vallejo confident of his release by Fremont, urged the men to return to their homes.

The second night was spent by the prisoners and their guards at Harvey's ranch on the Sacramento; the third day the party arrived at Fremont's camp on the American River. General Vallejo, according to Leese, stepped forward and said to Captain Fremont, "I am your prisoner." "No," replied the Captain. "You all are the prisoners of these people," pointing to the guards. Leese in his dictated narration said that Fremont went on with a long "rigmarole" of how he had received nothing but complaints from the Sacramento people, about General Castro, and that he would keep the prisoners in Captain Sutter's Fort until grievances were settled. The prisoners themselves had grievances: they told how their property had been taken (some 100 horses besides the ammunition). Fremont said it would be made right. The sun was going down, and Fremont, in order to terminate the interview, called six of the Indian horsemen and ordered them to deliver the prisoners to Sutter's Fort. This was the 16th of June. The entry of that day in the diary of Captain Sutter read:

> Merritt and Kit Carson arrived with news of Sonoma being occupied by the Americans and the same evening as prissoners, Genl. Vallejo, Don Salvador Vallejo, Lt. Col. Prudon and Mr. Leese and given under my charge. I have treated them with kindness and so good as I could, which was reported to Fremont and he then told me that prissoners ought not to be treated so: then I told him, if it is not right how I treat them, to give them in charge of somebody else.

And that was exactly what Fremont did for the following reason: "Captain Sutter was an officer under the Mexican government and I thought it best to place in charge of the Fort, Mr. Edward Kern who is already known as the topographer of my exploring expedition."

Captain Sutter discussed the situation at the Fort with William Leidesdorff, the American vice-consul at Yerba Buena: "I was appointed second in command. I accepted this in the hope that when Mr. Kern has to join Captain Fremont again, I will be his successor. I can assure you it is not very pleasant to have another commander in one's own house."

John Bidwell was another to whom Captain Fremont had assigned duties at Sutter's Fort. In recalling that time Bidwell said:

> Fremont gave me special directions about the prisoners and I understood him to put them under my special charge. For want of a suitable prison, the prisoners were placed in Sutter's parlor which had but one door and this was now guarded by a sentinel . . . that their meals were regularly and properly brought and sometimes I would sit by while they were eating. One day E. M. Kern, artist to Fremont's exploring Expedition called me out and said it was Fremont's orders, that no one was to go in or speak to the prisoners. I told him that they were in my charge and he had nothing to say about them. He asserted that they were in his charge and finally convinced me that he had been made an equal if not the principal custodian. I then told him that as both were not needed, I would go over and join Fremont at Sonoma.

IDE'S PROCLAMATION

The members of the Bear Flag Party left in Sonoma were busy collecting ammunition and food supplies. William Brown Ide, who had assumed the leadership, spent the hours between one and four o'clock of the morning of July 15th writing a proclamation. In it he requested all persons to remain at peace, pursuing their rightful occupations without fear of molestation. He called attention to the fact that he and his brave companions had been denied the privilege of buying or renting land and that they had been ordered to leave the country by Proclamation. The object of his group, he said, was to overthrow a government which had robbed and destroyed the Missions, a government that had exacted heavy tariffs to provide for its favorites. In its place his party wished to set up a government which would give civil, religious and personal liberty to all.

Besides the Proclamation, Mr. Ide wrote a letter to Commodore Robert Field Stockton relating at length the hostilities between the American emigrants and the Californians. He wrote of the capture of General Vallejo's fortress at Sonoma on the morning of June 14th, where the Bear Flag was hoisted. "This day," wrote Ide, "We proclaimed California a Republic . . . With this, as we learn from various parts of the country, the Spaniards are not only satisfied but pleased . . . It is our object and earnest desire to embrace the first opportunity to unite our adopted and rescued country to the country of our early *home*."

The letter for Captain Montgomery was given to William L. Todd (nephew of Mary Todd Lincoln) who had volunteered to carry it. It was Todd who had made the Bear Flag which was flying over Sonoma. He arrived at Sausalito, where the *Portsmouth* was anchored, the same day as Vallejo's courier Jose de la Rosa. Upon coming aboard, De la Rosa was received by Captain Montgomery; Lieutenant Washington A. Bartlett, a fine Spanish scholar, was called to act as interpreter.

Senor de la Rosa reported what had occurred in Sonoma, saying that General Vallejo had asked him to ask the Captain to exert his influence to prevent any acts of violence; that he hoped an officer could be sent to Sonoma or a letter that would have the effect of saving the helpless inhabitants from violence. Captain Montgomery replied as follows: "Sir: You will say to General Vallejo on my part, that I at once and entirely disavow this movement as having proceeded under any authority of the United States, or myself as the agent of my Government in this country or on this coast. It is a movement entirely local and with which I have nothing to do, nor can I in any way be induced to take part in the controversy which belongs to the internal politics of California. If they are Americans, as they avow themselves, they are beyond the jurisdiction of the laws and officers of the United States, and must now take the responsibilities of the position in which they have placed themselves, being answerable to the laws of Mexico and California . . . If my individual efforts can be at any time exercised to allay violence or prevent injury to innocent persons, it shall be exercised; but as an officer of the Government of the United States, I cannot have anything to do with either party . . . You will assure General Don Guadalupe Vallejo of my sympathy in his difficulties but I cannot positively interfere in the local politics." This was translated to Senor de la Rosa, who said he understood and would convey Captain Montgomery's remarks to Don Guadalupe Vallejo at the earliest moment.

William Alexander Leidesdorff, who had been appointed vice-consul in 1845 by Consul Larkin, sent the Consul a copy of Ide's "Proclamation" on June 19, 1846 with a letter; a portion which follows:

Sonoma was surprised on Sunday morning last, by 34 men. Their present force it is impossible to give as no one pretends to know how many they now have at their camp on the Sacramento and in the surrounding country. They took prisoners Don Guadalupe and Salvador Vallejo, Col. Prudon and Mr. Leese, these they escorted to their camp on the Sacramento. They also arrested the Alcalde but he accepted a commission under the new Commander of Sonoma and now continues his duties under that commission.

The prisoners were assured that no injury to their persons should be permitted, when General Vallejo at once placed at their disposition fifty horses and all the provisions they might require in the Garrison. The Commander-in-Chief assured him that the horses would be well cared for, and an exact account kept of all stores consumed by necessity and no waste permitted. And that to their utmost ability they would pay full value for everything required.

Before Don Guadalupe left under his escort he directed Don de la Rosa to proceed to Captain Montgomery (if he could leave the place) and request him to send an officer or otherwise use his influence with the Garrison to prevent any injury to the defenseless inhabitants, but he did not ask Captain Montgomery to take any part in the matter or even to intercede for his own release.

Closing his letter, the vice-consul at San Francisco wrote:

I think the "Proclamation" will call many to their "Banner" which is a white "field" with a red border, a large "star" and a "Grisley Bear," such is the flag of young California.

Mrs. Vallejo was permitted to send her brother with an open letter to Genl. Vallejo (on the 17th) and also an account of the interview of de la Rosa with Capt. Montgomery . . . The proclamation seems to please many who have read it. I have no idea what the California officers intend to do in the premises.

Soon after the interviews with Don Jose de la Rosa and William L. Todd, Captain Montgomery prepared an order for Lieutenant John S. Missroon to proceed in one of the ship's boats to Sonoma and there to call upon the commanding officer of the party having possession of the town. In his official order Captain Montgomery wrote, "I deem it my duty to use my friendly endeavors with the dominant party to secure for the defenseless people of Sonoma that security of life, property and privilege to which all are entitled . . . I wish you to endeavor as far as propriety will permit to obtain a promise of kind and humane treatment toward General Vallejo and his companions."

LT. MISSROON'S VISIT TO SONOMA

Lieutenant Missroon took with him the two messengers and Montgomery's young son. They reached Sonoma about sunset on June 16th. The Lieutenant called upon the commanding officer, William B. Ide, and received from him both verbal and written assurance of his intention to maintain order and to respect the persons and property of all persons residing within the limits of his command. Ide also gave Missroon a copy of the Proclamation which was to be delivered to Captain Montgomery. After the interview with Ide and a visit to the Sonoma Alcalde, Jose de los Berreyesa, Lieutenant Missroon said,

"I then called upon the family of General Vallejo and moderated their distress, by the assurance of safety for the General, which I had received, and informing them that the prisoners were held as hostages." To show her appreciation Senora Vallejo provided rooms in the Casa Grande for Lieutenant Missroon and the young Montgomery lad. They, on their part, offered to deliver some food and mail to her husband.

Dona Maria Antonia Lugo de Vallejo, the mother of General Vallejo, was also greatly troubled. She wrote to Consul Larkin, asking him to send some trustworthy person to Sutter's Fort to make certain that her son was alright. Larkin hired John Murphy for the purpose, at the rate of 100 pesos, he succeeded in bringing back to Monterey a letter from Vallejo to his mother. At this time permission was given to Senora Benicia Vallejo's brother, Don Julio Carrillo, to carry letters and gifts of food to the prisoners at the Fort. Upon arriving there, he, too, became a prisoner upon *Fremont's orders.*

General Jose Castro wrote asking Captain Montgomery for an explanation of the conduct of Fremont in taking possession of Sonoma and making prisoners of the two Vallejos, Prudon and Leese. The Commander of the U.S.S. Portsmouth, irked by Castro's complaints, replied that he "begs leave to assure General Castro of his entire conviction that Captain J. C. Fremont of the United States Topographical Engineers, whose visit to California has reference only to scientific researches, is in no manner whatever, either by authority of the United States Government or otherwise connected with the Political Movement of residents of the country of Sonoma." Montgomery went on to say that upon the request of General Vallejo, delivered by his messenger Don Jose de la Rosa, he had sent an officer to Sonoma who found not the anarchy and disorder apprehended by General Vallejo but that perfect order and quietude prevailed throughout the place.

In spite of Captain Montgomery's opinion of Fremont's activities, the man most responsible for the arrest of General Vallejo and his companions was, of course, Captain Fremont. He gave orders and they were followed. When Captain Fremont arrived in Sonoma on June 25th with his force of 72 men, without any salutations, he approached Ide and asked, "Who wrote that Proclamation for you?" Fremont, perceiving that Ide was not taking the least notice of his insolence, continued, "H—ah! your name was on it." He turned and left Ide abruptly but returned in a few moments, accosting Ide in a civil manner and remarking that he was happy to see and understand that the Proclamation was all it should have been, that every word was as he would have it. He complimented Ide on his style of diction, told him that it compared favorably with the best writers in the States but he regretted that no mention had been made of the insults that he, Fremont, had endured at Castro's hands.

Two days before Captain Fremont visited Sonoma, he had received a long letter from Captain Montgomery. In it the naval officer said: "The last few days have teemed with important events. Although aware that the public mind in California was prepared for a change of government, I little expected the movement to take place at this time or in the manner it has. The capture of the horses and the surprise of Sonoma were master-strokes . . . Castro must feel sensibly the loss of the two Vallejos and Prudon as well as the arms and munitions taken at Sonoma. I have exchanged communications with the commanders on both sides and others, preserving a strict neutrality and avowing my purpose of scrupulousing adhering to this principle; while I confess my sympathies are wholly with the gallant little band in arms for mutual defense."

Reference to the capture of the horses and to the surprise of Sonoma as masterstrokes must have fed the ego of Captain Fremont who had planned both. After his visit in Sonoma, he went to San Rafael where the shooting of the twin de Haro brothers and Jose de los Berreyesa (the father of the Alcalde at Sonoma) occurred upon Fremont's order. This savage act caused Captain Montgomery to confess in his journal: "This course of Captain Fremont renders my position as a neutral, peculiarly delicate and difficult. Having avowed, not only my own but Captain Fremont's entire neutrality and non-interference in the exicting difficulties of the country . . . it can scarcely be supposed, under the circumstances, that I shall be regarded as having spoken in good faith and sincerity."

At Sutter's Fort

Over at Sutter's Fort, the prisoners were being gradually deprived of all privileges. Lack of exercises and proper food, to say nothing of their exposure to a great number of malaria-carrying mosquitos and fleas, took toll of their health. Captain Montgomery, hearing of General Vallejo's illness, allowed Doctor Alexander Henderson, the assistant surgeon of the *Portsmouth*, to accompany Lieutenant Revere to Sutter's Fort. Of that visit there, the latter part of June, 1846, Revere wrote:

> We were met and welcomed by Captain Sutter and the officer in command of the garrison. All about were thick bearded fierce looking trappers and hunters armed with rifles, bowie knives and pistols; ornamented hunting shirts, gartered leggins, long hair turbaned with colored handkerchiefs. I found during the visit that General Vallejo and his companions were rigorously guarded by the 'patriots.' But I saw him and had some conversation with him which it was easy to see, excited a very ridiculous amount of suspicion on the part of his vigilant jailors whose position as revolutionists who lacked United States approval was a little ticklish. It engendered in them that distrust which is inseparable from low and ignorant minds in dangerous days . . . Indeed they carried their doubt so far as to threaten Sutter for the capital crime of being polite to the captives.

Jacob Leese, in speaking of their treatment, mentioned that "old Captain Sutter called in frequently through the day and seemed to console us by saying we would be liberated in a few days. When the next morning I was informed by surprise that word was sent to Captain S. that if he would visit our room again that Captain F. would hang him on the branch of the old oak tree that is in the corner of the Fort."

A letter written by Leese was carried by John Bidwell to Captain Fremont, requesting Fremont to give him his liberty. He had been placed at Sutter's Fort unjustly, Leese said, because he was an American by birth and he wished no such stain on his character as that of opposing his own country; that if Fremont wished his services, he was at Fremont's disposition. Captain Fremont never answered Leese's letter.

On July 6th, just one day before the United States flag was raised in Monterey, Vallejo wrote to his brother Don Jose de Jesus Vallejo:

> I am sending this letter to you with the object of relieving your mind about the fact that we have not been killed, at least up to this time. Salvador is here and although we are all prisoners it is under the force of circumstances. We believe that our detention is no more than political, indispensable for the progress of the new order of things. We believe fundamentally that this is the beginning of a complete turnover in the country; but not without a change founded on justice and on the law that will be a relief from the present miserable state of things. Don Luis, Don Victor Prudon and Julio, my brother-in-law are also detained here and all together we owe much to Senor Sutter in whose house we are staying, we owe him for a thousand favors to us and we shall be eternally grateful to him.
>
> Our own persons, our families and our property has been solemnly guaranteed to be returned to us in due respect to us so we ought to rest assured of it under the safeguard of law as well as under the good faith of men so I hope it will turn out and your loving brother begs you to publish this letter. M. G. VALLEJO
>
> Here also are Vicente Peralta, Jose Noriega and Robert Ridley.
> It would be well to notify their families.

The injustice of the treatment given Vallejo and his companions was recognized by a young Virginian, Charles E. Pickett, who had come to California by way of Oregon. He was pressed into services at Sutter's Fort as one of the guards of the Sonoma captives. By his kindly treatment and understanding, he won the life-long friendship of Vallejo. Some time after Vallejo's return to Sonoma, Pickett tried a bit of farming on a piece of Vallejo's land, at the same time reporting for the *California Star*, Sam Brannan's newspaper. Pickett dubbed himself "Philosopher Pickett." In his writing he advocated reforms which annoyed the politicians who called him insane. However, many of Pickett's suggested reforms were later placed on the statute books.

UNITED STATES FLAG RAISED IN CALIFORNIA

After several days of indecision (haunted by memories of Commodore Thos. A. Catesby Jones' premature raising of the United States flag in California in October 1842), Commodore John Drake Sloat, who had recently arrived from Lower California, wrote to Captain Montgomery on July 6, 1846 from his flagship *Savannah* in Monterey Bay:

Since I wrote you last evening, I have determined to hoist the flag of the United States at this place, as I would prefer being sacrified for doing too much than too little . . . If you consider that you have sufficient force, or if Fremont will join you, you will hoist the flag of the United States at Yerba Buena or at any other place and take possession in the name of the United States.

It was on board the Savannah that Captain Fremont visited Commodore Sloat who seemed excited over the gravity of the situation. The Commodore asked Fremont under what instructions he had acted in taking up arms against the Mexican authorities. Fremont said, "I informed him I had acted on my own responsibility and without any expressed authority from the Government to justify hostilities. He appeared much disturbed by this information and gave me distinctly to understand that in raising the flag at Monterey he had acted upon the faith of our operation in the north. Commodore Sloat was so discouraged that the interview terminated abruptly . . . He did not ask for another interview."

However Captain Montgomery proceeded to carry out Commodore Sloat's orders and, in turn gave orders to Lieutenant Joseph Warren Revere. Revere left the *Portsmouth* early on July 9th, for Sonoma. Of his historic visit to Sonoma, Lieutenant Revere said, "Having caused the troops of the garrison and the inhabitants of the place to be summoned to the public square, I then read the proclamation of Commodore Sloat to them and then hoisted the United States flag upon the staff in front of the Barracks under a salute from the artillery of the garrison. I also caused the proclamation to be translated into Spanish and posted in the Plaza."

According to James McChristian, a by-stander, Revere handed the Bear Flag which he had taken down to Captain Montgomery's young son, sixteen-year-old John Elliot, who placed the folded flag in the left-hand pocket of his Navy pea jacket. On July 25th, young Montgomery wrote to his mother in Charleston, Massachusetts, that he had the original and only flag of the California Republic in his possession and esteemed it as a prize. He drew a picture of the flag and added the comment, "The cubby came down growling."

Unfortunately, young Montgomery and his brother lost their lives in California. Their father turned over the flag to the Boston Navy Yard in May, 1848. In February of 1855, California's United States Senators, William M. Gwin and John B. Weller, wrote to the Secretary of the Navy, J. C. Dobbins asking that the original Bear Flag be given them for delivery to the Society of California Pioneers which had been organized in 1850.

The Secretary wrote that the flag had been recently deposited with the Navy Department and it not being connected particularly with the United States Naval Service he could see no objection to having it placed in the State of California with those whose early history it was associated.

The original Bear Flag was given to the Society of California Pioneers in September 1855 in time for it to head the Admission Day parade of that year. The flag was cherished until it was destroyed in the Pioneer's Building at

Fourth and Market Streets during the San Francisco Earthquake and Fire of 1906.

On that early morning of July 9th, 1846, Lieutenant Revere had left the Portsmouth with three American flags. Besides the one he hoisted in the Sonoma Plaza, he forwarded one to Bodega where Captain Stephen Smith lived. Stephen Smith had come to California in 1841 at the personal advice of Daniel Webster, who had informed him that sooner or later the United States would be in possession of California and that in consequence it would become a great country; the third flag was carried to Sutter's Fort by William Scott of Sonoma. Years later (1879) in Lititz, Pennsylvania, Captain Sutter described in a letter the raising of the American flag at his fort in Sacramento on July 11, 1846:

> For me it was a very important and happy event. Before, under the Bear Flag, my life was in danger and it is a wonder that I had not been shot by some of Fremont's ruffians. I had received the American flag which Lieutenant Revere sent from Sonoma in the night by the courier. I was walking about because I gave up my last room and bed to Major Reading and another gentleman.
>
> I told the Courier to tell nobody that he brought the flag, that I would have her up by sunrise or before. I went to a few of my employed men to assist me to fire a salute when we got up the flag, which was so heavy from two mounted six pounders in the yard that all the window panes where the prisoners were and those where Major Reading was, broke all to pieces and then everybody came to see what was the matter and I tell you the the Bear Flag men made very long faces. And I went up to congratulate the prisoners and I told them we could now speak free as the great protecting flag of the United States flies and need no more be afraid of Fremont's spies.

When the imprisoned Californians heard of the Stars and Stripes flying in California, it raised hopes in their minds that now they would be returned to their homes. They asked to see Captain Fremont. The Captain sent word that he would grant Vallejo an interview. While the prisoners waited, Vallejo wrote Fremont: "Yesterday I had the pleasure of receiving a note from you by one of your officers, that today we would have an interview with you which I have been waiting anxiously all day long but since this is very advanced I fear that you will no longer have time. As much as to calm uneasiness of the gentlemen who share my prison as well as for my own satisfaction I wish you would let me know whether our imprisonment is now ended which as you know has been made more severe by an absolute solitary confinement since the 16th of June. I do not have to tell you anything regarding the way in which we have been deprived of our liberty since you are not ignorant of it; but the national flag of North America which today flies over this fortress leads me to suppose that the change has already taken place and to expect an advantageous future for this country whose fate cannot be a matter of indifference to me."

Captain Fremont gave no answer to Vallejo's letter. He left Lieutenant

Kern in charge with instructions not to release the prisoners except on direct orders. About this time Vallejo wrote to his wife:

Sacramento, July 22, 1846

My Good Francisca:

From a vaquero that came from Napa on several errands for Salvador and Julio I have learned that all the family is well and from the same source I have also heard that Salazar would be coming soon and from whom I am anxiously awaiting to hear about home. We are all well. Even though Salazar has left here, I would request you to send me by some Indians of Soscol that know the road (Petronio knows it well) two hands of paper, that is to say, ten packs because there is none here and if we delay we will not have anything to write on, also send the chess game, that is in one of the little drawers of the desk the very small ivory one, also some purgative salts.

Please tell Alvarado (mayo-domo at Petaluma Rancho) to write and tell me about the work and the harvest and tell him not to kill at Petaluma more than 100 fat herd for lard and to Senor Elenterio, 150 at Soscol and that the hides from Soscol be brought to Sonoma. We are waiting daily for mail from Monterey and then perhaps we will be free to return to our homes . . . Julio is well and sends greetings to all. I do the same. Take care of the children and give them an embrace affectionately in my name. Do not forget greetings for Rosalia and her children. Wishing you happiness.

Your affectionate
M. G. VALLEJO

Not being able to secure an interview with Captain Fremont, Vallejo decided to answer a letter he had received from the American Consul and present their case to him. This he did on July 23rd. The letter in Spanish was sent by courier to Monterey:

Fort New Helvetia on the
Sacramento River. July 23, 1846

Mr. Thomas O. Larkin
Sir:

I, last night, through the hands of Mr. John Murphy received your most appreciated communication which I answer. I perceive the interest you take in our misfortune and for your good offices I shall forever recognize the obligation and do now, most sincerely thank you . . . The deprivation of our liberty from our domestic hearth by order of Captain Fremont on the 14th of last month . . . I have at last seen the standard of North America hoisted and our situation is still the same; we have heard tell of some proclamation by the Commodore in all parts of the country (excepting this place, perhaps maliciously) and our situation does not change; neither have we been allowed to see any of them. Although we hear people talk of security and guarantees.

At the same time we were made prisoners at our house, a written document was exacted from us in which we promised on our word of honor, on our lives and interests not to take up arms against the cause of the persons who took us and another was written by them in which they promised security and respect to our lives, our families and our property; ourselves remaining in our houses but before the signatures were dry; this treaty was broken and they conducted us to this place; I have both of these documents in my possession to justify myself at any time and prove to all the world that we aught not to have been treated in this manner I have related to you.

The National flag of N. America flys in this part of the country. It protects the inhabitants and their property, it distributes equal justice and I hope we shall share a part of that equal justice by receiving our liberty. This is what I believed the moment I saw the American flag flying that we should be set at liberty but nothing of this has happened, on the contrary, we remain just as we were, without ever having given the least motive for suspicion of any kind. I swear it to you by the faith of a man of honor.

Our families have been absolutely abandoned since the date above mentioned in Sonoma. At the time we were surprised in our homes, there were no men in them but ourselves. Consider yourself our situation and affliction. Since our imprisonment, quantities of cattle and horses belonging to myself and others have been drove off in groups of such magnitude that there is not a single horse left on the ranches to saddle. I thereby do most heartily beg of you in the name of friendship to use all your kindly influence with the Commodore for our liberty and our return to our houses . . .

I remain as always with all consideration, Yours most affectionately.

M. G. VALLEJO

Larkin received Vallejo's letter on the morning of July 29th. That evening he carried the letter out some miles at sea to Commodore Sloat where he read it to him. The Commodore, before leaving on the *Levant*, ordered Commodore Robert F. Stockton, whom he was leaving in charge of California, to release General Vallejo.

Regarding Vallejo's letter, Larkin wrote to his friend Jacob P. Leese on the night of July 29th:

This morning I rec'd letters from Don. M. G. Vallejo and Senor Prudon to Como. Sloat, which in a boat I carried out to sea some miles; the Como. having left the Port in the *Levant* for home. On reading the letter to him I returned with it to Commodore Stockton and did not have the translation before sunset . . . You may believe I commiserated your situation. I engaged Mr. Murphy on Don Guadalupe's expense, to go direct to your place of confinement to know your state. I supposed on raising our flag you would all enjoy its protection.

The letter of Senor Vallejo was well wrote, mild, firm and respectfully and fully to the purpose. The Como rec'd the English copy on board at sunset and by 9 this night sent his secretary to me with the letters I now send. And he was to sail to-morrow and myself to be gone 25 or 30 days. I asked him to answer Don Guadalupe's letter before we left. You will see his anxiety by his dispatch.

It is not for me to question the motives of those who made you prisoners. I know nothing about them nor did I say more to Messrs. Fremont and Gellespi than I could not understand your imprisonment and thought you would be put at large any time You will show this letter to Don Guadalupe and those interested in the safety of your person.

The vast increase of your property hereafter to you, I hope will in a manner compensate for the actual property you may have lost by your absence; your personal sufferings are another thing. The when, why and wherefore of it all, I suppose the authors will in proper time give their reasons and motives. That you may safely return and find your families well is the wish of THOMAS O. LARKIN

As you have not seen the Proclamation, I now send it.

Consul Larkin felt that Captain Fremont's conduct in the North was a serious hindrance in the way of a true conquest of California. He thought it delayed the raising of the United States flag a full week as the greatest obstacle to Commodore Sloat's work lay in the results already produced by the "gallant" marauders at Sonoma—the folly of the Bear Flag Party.

RELEASE OF GENERAL VALLEJO

Upon receiving orders from Commodore Sloat to release General Vallejo, Commodore Stockton wrote immediately from the United States Frigate *Congress* to Vallejo, saying:

I have the honor to acknowledge the receipt of your letter of the 23rd addressed to my predecessor, Commodore Sloat. I hasten to inform you that one of the first acts of my administration was to order your immediate release from confinement and I hope before this reaches you, that you will be at liberty. I was not aware of the name and rank of others confined with you; I now send by courier (notwithstanding I have already sent one today) to Captain Montgomery for the release of your friends as well as yourself.

Commodore Stockton signed his letter "R. F. Stockton—Commander-in-Chief."

It was on the first of August, 1846 that orders came to Sacramento for the release of General Vallejo and his brother-in-law. The brother-in-law was supposed to be Jacob P. Leese but, by some misunderstanding, it was another brother-in-law, Julio Carrillo, who was discharged with Vallejo on August 2nd. A parole was signed for M. G. Vallejo and Julio Carrillo by Lieutenant John S. Missroon with John A. Sutter as witness. The document stated that in consideration of being set at liberty, they pledged not to take up arms against the United States; they were not to furnish supplies, carry communications or in any way assist any person or persons who might be opposed to the United States. They were not to leave the home district without permission from the Commander at Yerba Buena. If the pledge was not faithfully kept, their lives were to be forfeited. A rather humiliating document for a man of honor to sign. That Captain Montgomery, who had been appointed the Commander of the Northern District of California, thought so too, is evident from his letter to Vallejo: "I have now, Sir, the additional satisfaction today, that reposing full confidence in your honor and sincerity, I have directed Lt. Revere to mitigate the terms of your parole by obtaining from you simply a promise of friendship to the United States of strict neutrality in all differences pending between them, the existing and former governments of this Department which will leave you pretty (much) at large to attend to your business concerns without hinderance and restraint."

Back home in Sonoma, Vallejo did not forget his prison-mates; on August

4th he wrote to his brother Don Salvador and to Colonel Prudon, telling them that they would soon be at liberty. On August 7th, Salvador replied complaining that three days had passed and they had received no word. "We go on, always in our little room, telling a thousand stories and scrutinizing one by one, the words of our letters, especially the order of Senor Commodore. We are all well as of today. We are only troubled by the uncertainty of our position."

Colonel Prudon wrote that they didn't have any hope of being free until the return of Captain Fremont. Mr. Kern had told him that he couldn't set them free unless Captain Fremont desired it. In closing his letter Prudon said, "We all believe very strongly that it would be very propitious for you to write Captain Montgomery in your own hand . . . It would be good to get Captain Montgomery to send a very decisive, speedy order to Kern."

Don Salvador Vallejo, Colonel Victor Prudon and Jacob P. Leese were released on parole the next day, August 8th, by Lieutenant J. L. Missroon of the U.S. Navy.

Leese on returning to Sonoma, wrote to Consul Larkin, the man to whom he was most grateful for his release. It was August 12th that he wrote:

I have the pleasure once more to pass you a few lines to inform you that I am in the Bosom of my family after having been separated from them, for which reason, I am not able to inform you as yet. I received your kind letter to me of the 29th of last month and through which I am perfectly satisfied that you have been my liberator in this cause and for which all I can say in a declaration to you that Proven Friends is never to be forgotten. I should be happy to say moor [sic] to you but hope to see you shortly.

Dear Larkin you know you have a friend here and moor so now than ever at your command, also the same with my family which will never be forgotten. I do then close to say excuse and receive the best respects from my wife and family.

From your friend and well wisher, I am

Yours and Truly.

JACOB PRIMER LEESE

Vallejo acknowledged Captain Montgomery's letter, mitigating the parole terms which had been brought to him by Lieutenant Revere. Vallejo thanked the Captain for being able to return to his family. He wrote, "The flag of the U.S. unfurled, we were saved by a miracle; it saved the country and will conduct it without a doubt (as no other government could) to that height of prosperity to which nature destined her." Vallejo further stated in the letter that he has welcomed Lieutenant Revere to his house and will help him in preserving order; and by Revere sends his promise of friendship for the United States and neutrality in the war.

General Vallejo stated that he weighed only 96 pounds on his return from Sutter's Fort. The first days at home he spent in convalescing from the effects of his imprisonment. Once again, Captain Montgomery sent Dr. Henderson from his staff to attend the General. With Vallejo when he returned to Sonoma was the courier John M. Murphy, who later married Virginia Reed of the Donner Party. Murphy said in telling of the journey, "He took me with him. When we got there (Sonoma) he brought out all his fine clothes, his uniforms, made a pile of them and then burned them." However, Vallejo kept his epaulets, sent him in 1841 by President Bustamente—"the first instance," Vallejo said, "of a present from a Chief of the Republic of Mexico to a native Californian."

Vallejo had been home a little over a month when he wrote to Larkin on September 15th:

> I left the Sacramento half dead and arrived here almost without life but am now much better . . . The political change has cost a great deal to my person and mind and likewise to my property. I have lost more than one thousand live horned cattle, six hundred tame horses and many other things of value which were taken from my house here and at Petaluma. My wheat crops are entirely lost for the cattle ate them up in the field and I assure you that two hundred fanegas (about 25,000 bushels) for sowing in good condition as mine was, is a considerable loss. All is lost and the only hope for making it up is to work again.

Vallejo's fellow-Californians might think that Mexico would regain the province but he, himself, had no such idea. He was convinced that the United States meant to add California to its territory. In December 1842, when Commodore Thomas Ap. Catesby Jones was visiting Vallejo, he assured Vallejo that it was a foregone conclusion that the United States would have California soon at all hazards and that his (Jones') action in October of that year in hastily raising the Stars and Stripes upon California soil, under the impression that war was raging between Mexico and the United States, was in accordance with secret orders to checkmate any such movement that might be made on the part of the British Naval Commander. By a strange coincidence, the day the United States flag was raised the second time in Monterey (July 7, 1846), Consul Larkin received a letter from Commodore Jones who told how a Board of Inquiry at Washington, D.C., had just turned in a delayed report exonerating him from all blame in connection with the flag raising in Monterey in October 1842.

Through his contacts with American officials, with Yankee merchants and American emigrants, as well as through his extensive reading, Vallejo was well acquainted with American institutions and republican ideals. Why should Californians shrink from incorporating themselves with the happiest and most free nation in the world, destined to be the most wealthy and powerful? For him the separation from Mexico would entail no heartache. He had experienced many disappointments in the years he had worn the Mexican uniform. The act of burning his Mexican uniform was no mere bit of sentiment. His actions were to speak louder than words. While still under parole, he offered his services against the threatened invasion of the Walla-Walla Indians. This offer was accepted by Captain Montgomery who wrote,

"The conditions of the country, menaced as it is by a large body of armed Indians in the neighborhood of Fort Sacramento, caused me to accept with gratitude the offer of your services."

VALLEJO—INDIAN SUB-AGENT

The Walla-Walla Indian invasion did not materialize; the California volunteers with Vallejo and his brother Don Salvador in the temporary service of the United States were dismissed. Captain Montgomery in command of the northern district again wrote Vallejo:

> Permit me . . . my dear Sir, to express to you individually and in behalf of my Government, my hearty thanks for the services you have rendered and for the prompt and sincere manner in which you are pleased to tender your assistance to the Government of the U. States in the present emergency and thus feebly expressing my obligation to you. I desire also to convey them to your recent associates in arms, who were acting under your orders whose ready obedience to your call on behalf of our existing authorities has done much toward allaying national prejudices and unfriendly suspicion among the various classes composing the Society of California and of hastening arrangements for the establishment of peace, order and good government, the blessing of which I trust through the mercy of a kind Providence will soon reward their faithfulness.

Although the Walla-Walla war scare was over, General Kearny felt that the Indians on the north side of the Bay needed watching. He offered Vallejo the appointment of sub-agent for the Indians on the north side of the Bay of San Francisco including those on Cache Creek and on the lakes. He offered the same position to Captain Sutter for Sutter's area. Both consented to serve. At that time, April 14, 1847, Kearny wrote to Vallejo:

> In offering this appointment to you, it may be proper for me to remind you that the Indians have lately assumed a threatened attitude, and given some alarm to the inhabitants not only near Sonoma, but to those north and east of it. I am in hopes that by good advice and prudent counsel and the well-known influence which you possess over these Indians, they may be induced by you to remain quiet and refrain from committing any further acts of depredation or hostility upon the people or their property . . . Will you explain to the Indians and to their chiefs the change which has taken place in the government of this country, that they must look upon the Californians and Americans as one people and any offenses they may commit upon the one will be punished in the same manner as if committed upon the other . . . I will endevour to obtain and furnish you with a quantity of Indian goods, to be given as presents to such chiefs and bands as may conduct themselves peaceably and quietly. You will please report to me, from time to time any occurrences which you deem worthy of notice and offer such suggestions relative to the Indians and Indian affairs as may be expedient to you. Your salary will be $750 per year.

The *well-known* influence that Vallejo possessed over the Indians was based on his understanding of Indian or human nature. Once when he was asked if he had much trouble with the Indians in the early days, he replied, "Oh, no,

I had no trouble; I let them go to Hades their own way. It was only when the missionaries tried to show them a new road that there was trouble." It was fortunate that Vallejo had no need of money at this time of his appointment as Indian sub-agent, otherwise he could not, on such a small salary have contributed so generously to the money being collected for the rescue of the Donner Party in the Sierra. Serving with him on the fund-raising committee was William Leidesdorff, Samuel Brannan and William D. M. Howard. The meeting was held at the Portsmouth House in San Francisco.

A year later Vallejo was still serving as Indian sub-agent but Colonel Richard B. Mason was the military commander and civil governor of California. On May 25, 1848 he wrote Vallejo that he had received his letter of the 22nd on the subject of threatened Indian hostilities and protesting the removal of Captain Brackett's company from Sonoma. Colonel Mason replied that Brackett's company was needed in Lower California and that he apprehended no real danger from the Indians as long as the inhabitants felt so assured that they could leave their homes and go to the mines. Colonel Mason concluded his letter, "I am much pleased to hear that you will visit those Indians and use your efforts to pacify them . . . I am sure your well-known prudence, judgment and knowledge of Indian character will render those efforts eminently successful. I received on the 20th of last month a letter from you without a date, offering the resignation of your commission as Indian sub-agent . . . I should have acknowledged the receipt of that at an earlier day but for the difficulties of finding some one to fill your place."

On the same day that Colonel Mason wrote to Vallejo he wrote to Major James A. Hardie, Commanding West Military District at the San Francisco Presidio, ordering him to visit Sonoma and get the facts as reported by General Vallejo and Alcalde L. W. Boggs. Mason told Hardie that he must be guarded in crediting the reports and rumors about this Indian disturbance and that he "must bear in mind that the people north of the bay are exceedingly anxious to keep Brackett's company there and would in all probability kick up a disturbance with the Indians if in no other way their object could be effected."

HOSPITALITY TO THE BOGGS FAMILY

During the winter of 1846–47, General Vallejo provided shelter for Missouri Ex-Governor Lilburn W. Boggs. The travel-stained Boggs family arrived in Sonoma on a cold day and spent the first night at the home of Jacob P. Leese. The next morning Vallejo offered Boggs the use of the large adobe building on his Petaluma Rancho. Preceding the Boggs' arrival, Vallejo had ridden over on horseback and had made arrangements for their reception, even to the stringing a line of home-made lanterns on the upper balcony as a beacon for the tired wayfarers. Of that memorable night, Lilburn Boggs' son William (born 1826 in Missouri) wrote:

My father's family and myself and wife were kindly tendered the use of the building by General Vallejo when we reached Sonoma. It was the first shelter we obtained and it was not completed. It is a large square constructed with the usual court (Spanish style) with verandas twelve feet wide on the upper story. The front of the building, looking toward Petaluma also had the wide veranda. The walls on the south and east were covered with a tule thatch to protect them from rain. It was Vallejo's summer rancho residence and had been occupied by the family before the General tendered it to us to winter in. The lower rooms were used for storing grain, hides and other ranch products.

The Vallejo family furniture used during the summer sojourn was still in the rooms above. On our arrival in the night at the ranch, General Vallejo who had gone ahead of our worn-out teams, had aroused his Indian servants to prepare supper for us. The tables were spread with linen table cloths; sperm candles were in the chandeliers and we had a regular Spanish cooked meal, wholesome and plenty of it. With Spanish hospitality the General waited on the table, helping all the large family. After supper he handed Mrs. Boggs a bunch of keys to the various rooms and assigned one well furnished apartment to her and me.

Vallejo told the Boggs family, "Kill all the cattle you want, take all you can use. We do not care how many cattle you kill, but there is one thing we do ask, that is, whenever you kill a steer, hang the hide on a tree or on a fence somewhere so the coyotes cannot destroy it. That is where we make our money; from the hides."

A few weeks after the Boggs family arrived at the old adobe, William Boggs' wife gave birth, on January 4, 1847 to a son while the prospective father (an enlisted soldier in the war against Mexico) was in Yerba Buena. Vallejo called at the adobe and found that the "Baby Gringo" was still without a name. The family requested the General to supply one, which he did, naming the baby after himself, Guadalupe Vallejo Boggs.

That baby, when grown and living in Salem, Oregon said in a letter (1892) to a Sonoma friend, "If ever a chord of the heart was touched with kindness, Senor Vallejo could do it. It was under his hospitable roof I was born. In 1847 he gave my father and mother possession of the Petaluma Adobe. I was raised with his children and well do I remember them and their many acts of kindness. The General never met me on the street or in any place but that he had to pat me on the head and tell when I was an infant, he and his wife saved my life by having a sheep killed and wrapped me in the warm pelt to keep vitality in me. The Vallejos have a warm place in my heart."

Guadalupe Vallejo Boggs' father was always a close friend of General Vallejo and enjoyed his companionship in spite of the differences in their ages. In later years he wrote to Edwin A. Sherman of Oakland, telling him of a visit Commodore Ap Catesby Jones made to Vallejo in Sonoma. He said that the tall gaunt Welchman arrived wet and muddy, and dressed in gum boots and an oil cloth hat, with a shotgun and game bag. He enquired of Boggs for General Vallejo. Boggs then pointed out the General, who was standing on his front verandah looking eagerly for the Commodore and his suite. Jones remarked, "I am Commodore Jones, General, how do you do?" In amazement Vallejo replied, "You, Commodore Jones? And all over with mud and splash." Whereupon he escorted the Commodore into the Casa Grande where he was made to feel at home. A few days later William Boggs was asked to join the General and the Commodore on a horse-back trip to the Carquinez Straits to look for a Navy Yard site. The three were invited to dine on the sloop-of-war *Preble* lying at anchor in the Straits near Benicia and commanded by Captain West. Boggs said that Commodore Jones did not seem to have any more authority on the ship-of-war than either General Vallejo or himself; but he seemed to enjoy telling stories of his farm life and of his two sons who were midshipmen in the Navy.

The January of 1847 which the Lilburn Boggs family spent in the Petaluma Adobe was memorable because, on the 13th of that month Captain Fremont signed a peace treaty at Cahuenga Pass with General Andres Pico, who had put up a gallant fight against the Americans and had won their respect. Vallejo's youngest brother Juan Antonio made mention of the event in the following letter written on January 21, 1847 from Monterey:

Guadalupe:

Don't be surprised that I have not answered your letter for some time for circumstances have brought about the delay, as you are well aware. First, the events of war or peace regarding the country in the pueblo of Los Angeles area seem to have been taken care of by some treaties made by Senor Fremont with the Angelenos from below. A greater part of the Northern people came on the scene when surrender was being made to the American Authorities. Now the country is forever to be American for I believe Mexico has totally given it up.

The Government of the United States is taking over in a very solid manner, the land as well as on the sea. The Commodore (Stockton) who has recently anchored and headed here has arrived here with his frigate and has aboard they say 500 men; a few days later there arrived here another transport with 150 soldiers. In a line there are tents for their quarters at the Fort (Presidio of Monterey). Some of them have brought their families. I don't know what is going to happen in the future.

My mother and the whole family greet you affectionately. All of us feel sorry about the turn of events, the up-setting of your property and the rest.

JUAN ANTONIO VALLEJO

The "up-setting" of Vallejo's property and the uncertainty of the future during the early days of the American occupation caused the usual optimistic Vallejo to lapse into a depression. With some exaggeration, he wrote on July 5, 1847 to the Commissioner from Mexico, Andres Castillero, "Well things happened in which I have been very unfortunate so much so that I was a prisoner in a dungeon. I have lost all my possessions and I am destitute along with my family. Mr. Limantour has been good enough to lend me some amounts and I have offered to pay him if the Mexican Government will take pity on me and pay for my personal losses and perhaps it will, if you can exert your influence in a decisive manner because on it depends the future subsistence of myself and family.

VALLEJO'S FRIENDSHIP WITH AMERICAN OFFICERS

American officers were anxious to cultivate the friendship of General Vallejo, and lost no opportunity to express their displeasure and regret over his imprisonment. Washington A. Bartlett, one of the young officers on the Portsmouth (who later became the Alcalde of Yerba Buena and changed the village's name to San Francisco), wrote to Vallejo on August 6, 1846.

Your note of the 30th ulto. I have had the pleasure to receive and embrace the first opportunity to reply, regretting exceedingly the circumstances that caused your long detention at the Sacramento and still more that it caused your present illness from which I trust a kind Providence and our medical faculty will soon relieve you . . . Captain Montgomery has constantly regretted you were not liberated on the day the American flag first waved over New Helvetia which certainly would have been the case had his command extended to that post.

He has directed me to assure you, Sir, that among his first communications to Commodore Sloat, he stated the names of all persons who had been arrested by the party which had been in arms against the California authorities and requested instructions as to the course he should pursue with regards to them: at the same time making particular mention of your case and requesting that his friend General Vallejo be at once set at liberty and permitted to rejoin his family and the reason as yet unexplained, no reply was received to this dispatch until a few days ago, since then Captain Montgomery received an order appointing him Military and Naval Commander of San Francisco, Sonoma, New Helvetia and the pueblo of San Jose, with the adjacent country, when he at once gave the order for your release . . . Now that he has been able to place an officer of the United States (Lt. Revere) in command at Sonoma with a competent force to maintain order and protection under it which you so reasonably expected when the flag was first unfurled in California.

The *Portsmouth* officers were frequent guests at General Vallejo's home, but the responsibilities of its commander, Captain Montgomery, kept him from accepting the General's repeated invitations. When the Commander was ordered south, he wrote Vallejo that he had hoped to visit Sonoma but Dr. Henderson under whose professional care he had been for some time, felt that his present state of health would not admit of the journey. Eight months later Montgomery, returning to the Bay region, wrote Vallejo on August 6, 1847: "After a much longer absence than I had anticipated, the *Portsmouth* again entered the Bay of San Francisco and agreeably to my promise I am very desirous of making you a visit at Sonoma before leaving here again, perhaps for the last time . . . I should exceedingly regret, my dear General, the necessity of departing without seeing you and your respected family . . . Should I not reach Sonoma in less than a week from today, you may naturally infer my disappointment and conclude that the only prospect left me of having the pleasure of personally greeting my esteemed friend, is dependent on his kindness in making a visit to the *Portsmouth* where sincere and cordial welcome ever awaits you from your numerous friends on board. Can you not, my dear General, return with Lt. Revere in the event of my not arriving at your hospitable residence previous to that time."

While social contacts were a pleasure to Vallejo, he was not remiss in looking after his own and the Californians' property interests. With these interests in mind, he sent to General Stephen W. Kearny and to the press copies of the orders he had received from the former Mexican Governor Figueroa, directing him to build a pueblo and to colonize northern California. To the California Star published by Sam Brannan, Vallejo wrote:

March 10, 1847

Sir:

Being necessary to make public my instructions I have received privately, from the civil government of Upper California to start the colonization of the frontiers of Sonoma, should they be deemed worthy by you of insertion in your estimable columns—said instructions—the originals I have the honor to hand you herewith—by their contents and for other causes I shall make public in due time, you will be persuaded as also the public at large, that I could not until now, that the circumstances urge it, to make public these documents and if I do so now, it is because of the situation in which some persons, residents in that part of the territory are placed

In an editorial the *California Star* published the following:

The documents which we publish today in relation to the authority of General Vallejo to colonize the country in the vicinity of Sonoma will be read with interest by every citizen of this part of California; and particularly by those interested in the lands placed at his disposition.

The causes which induced the Mexican authorities to enjoin secrecy upon General Vallejo are believed no longer to exist therefore the publication of the papers placing under his control a large district of country is not only proper at the present time but become necessary in order to remove all doubts from the minds of those who have derived their titles to all the land from him. These papers form the principle link in the titles to all the land placed at his disposal and the publication of them will enable one interested to have a copy of them in his own possession.

General Kearny in reply to Vallejo's communication wrote him on April 6, 1847:

I have to acknowledge the receipt of yours yesterday enclosing a copy of two communications to you from the former Governor Don Jose Figueroa, each of June 24, 1835, on the N. side of the Bay of San Francisco and Sacramento River by granting lands to such Persons as may wish to settle there, said Grants to be confirmed by the Territorial Government upon proper application.

In relation to the subject above referred to, I have only to remark that the instructions to you from Don Jose Figueroa may no longer be exercised, yet there is no doubt that whatever has been done under his instructions and which he was authorized to give, will be fully recognized and confirmed by the government of the United States.

The Communications from Governor Figueroa, dated June 24, 1835, follow:

Monterey, California
June 24, 1835

Don M. G. Vallejo
Military Commandant & Director of Colonization of the Northern Frontier:

"In conformity with the orders and instructions issued by the Supreme Government of the Confederation respecting the location of a village in the Valley of Sonoma, this Commandancy urges upon you, that, according to the topographical plan of the place, it be divided into quarters or squares, seeing that the streets and plazas be regulated so as to make a beginning. The inhabitants are to be governed entirely by said plan. This government and commandancy approves entirely of the lines designated by you for outlets—recognizing as the property of the village the public lands and privileges, the boundaries of Petaluma, Agua Caliente, Rancho de Huichica, Lena de Sur, Salvador, Vallejo and La Vernica, on the north of the City of Sonoma, as the limits of its property, rights and privileges, requesting that it commence immediately around the hill, where the fortifications is to be erected, to protect the inhabitants from incursions of savages and all others. In order that the building lots granted by you, as the person charged with colonization, may be fairly portioned, you will divide each square (manzana) into four parts, as well for the location of each as to interest persons in the planting of kitchen gardens, so that every one shall have a hundred yards, more or less, which the government deems sufficient; and further, lots of land may be granted, of from one hundred and fifty to two hundred yards, in opening for outlets, for other descriptions of tillage, subject to the Laws and Regulations of the subject, in such manner that at all times the Municipality shall possess the legal title.

"This Government and Commandancy-General offers you thanks for your efforts in erecting this new city, which shall secure the Frontier of the Republic, and is confident that you will make new efforts for the National Entirety.

"God and Liberty.

"Jose Figueroa"

[copied verbatim, without attempt at correction] SEALS

MILITARY GOVERNMENT OF UPPER CALIFORNIA
CIVIL GOVERNMENT OF UPPER CALIFORNIA

Monterey *June 24, 1835*

In a separate note of this date, you will receive the instructions which determine the extent of your power respecting the building of a town in the valley of Sonoma in place of that which had been marked out and begun in the valley of Santa Rosa.

Many are the objects that the Superior Government has in view; but the principal one is to arrest, as soon as possible the progress of the Russian settlements of Bodega and Ross, in order to make ineffective all the ulterior designs of that government to ours, which would cause great difficulties to the nation.

To verify the scheme spoken of and in accordance with the supreme resolutions relative thereto, you are empowered to solicit families in all the Territory and other states of the Mexican Republic, in order to colonize the Northern Frontiers, granting lands to all the individuals who may wish to establish themselves there and these grants shall be confirmed to them by the Territorial Government and when the grantees apply for the same. The title that they may receive from you will serve them as sufficient guarantee, as you are the only one empowered by the Supreme Government to grant land in the Frontier under your command.

The Supreme Government is satisfactorily convinced that you are the only officer to whom so great an enterprise can be trusted and in order to accomplish it in the right manner, it is willing to defray all the necessary expenses towards it and recommends you to use a just and prudent economy in this particular keeping an exact amount of all and advising the government of the same. Should it happen that the Territorial Government may not be able at any time to aid the colony with the articles which they may need, it requires of you to supply them for the time being.

VERY PRIVATE

The topographical situation of the Frontier on the northern side of the Bay of San Francisco and Sacramento River may be somewhat difficult to colonize but this Government trusts that for the honor of the National Government and your own proper interests in the social order that you will not let escape an opportunity to deserve the premium to which all men aspire—POSTHUMOUS FAME—ultimately this Territorial Government knows and is persuaded of all that you have informed it, respecting the danger to which this Frontier is exposed on account of your neighbors of the North and it recommends that the Mexican population be always greater than that of the foreign, who in virtue of the colonization should solicit lands in that precious portion of the Territory trusted to you by the Government, for which it again charges you only to give titles to those who may prove they merit them, bearing in mind the importance of the part of Bodega and Cape Mendocino, which points are too necessary for the preservation of the National Welfare.

The Government omits recommending the secrecy that this note requires which you will not make known only in the last extremity and it confides in that you will labour with assiduity in an object so sacred in which are concerned the general good and the peculiar welfare of the Territory in which you were born. It is warranted by the prudence, patriotism and good faith of which you have given so many proofs, offering again to make them known to Government, God and Liberty.

JOSE FIGUEROA

To the Military Commander and Director of the Northern Frontier

GIFT TO LORENZO WAUGH

Vallejo's apprehension as to his finances in no way curtailed his hospitality. The young officers in the different American services were the recipients of courtesies characteristic of the General's Castilian forebears, and his thoughtfulness was not reserved for officials alone. Many of the emigrants were beneficiaries. He supplied them with cattle and with land. He once remarked, "Land is plenty. God made it for us and I have plenty." This remark was made to the Methodist minister, Lorenzo Waugh, who had come to California in the fall of 1852, after a month's journey across the plains. Waugh decided to settle on a tract of land about five miles north of the area which is now Petaluma and there he wintered in a redwood camp. The spring of

1853, he built a redwood house. Waugh had been told that he had built on government land but others thought it was part of General Vallejo's Petaluma Rancho.

Waugh decided to ride to Sonoma and try to get a good title from Vallejo. In his autobiography Waugh says, "So I rode over and found him [Vallejo] at home; I described to him the place where I was located and told my purpose was to secure a home to stay on, so if the place was on his grant, to try to make arrangements to secure the title; that I was an old wornout Methodist preacher and with a young family which I wished to raise and provide for. Said the General, 'We welcome you to California, with your family. You are the kind of man we want; families come to stay, to make their homes and to cultivate our beautiful lands. God made this beautiful country for people to live in. I know the place where you have stopped and I do not know whether it is my grant or not. When the land is surveyed, then we shall know. I appreciate your efforts in trying to instruct and benefit mankind and especially your efforts among the Indian tribes; now you go right on where you are and if that place suits you; make your improvements, make them good and feel yourself at home. If that place proves to be mine when surveyed you shall have a home and it will not matter about your money whether it is much or little."

Soon after the interview Waugh received a letter written in Spanish from Vallejo confirming what he had said; Waugh therefore went ahead and planted fruit trees and grapevines and fenced a portion of the 160 acres.

The Petaluma grant was surveyed and confirmed by the Land Commission whereupon in March 1857 Vallejo sold the Petaluma Adobe and some surrounding land. In June of the same year, Vallejo was called to Monterey by the death of his youngest brother Juan Antonio. He left his landholdings in charge of his lawyer who had power of attorney. The lawyer sold Waugh's holdings. The itinerant preacher was astonished and engaged D. O. Shattuck as his lawyer. In the meantime Vallejo returned and sent for Waugh to come to his San Francisco office. The General received Waugh in a pleasant manner and said, "Well Mr. O had bought your place over your head, I am told, without notice either to me or you. But, this is about the way things are going now, all for self. My lawyer knew very well I did not wish your place sold in any such a way . . . Now you may think I am just like the rest, ready to sacrifice my word and honor for a little money or land, *all for self;* but I will convince you this is not the case; Mariano Guadalupe Vallejo is not that kind of man and does not intend to be. I remember all I told you, and now I want you to say just what will make you safe and whole in this matter. You just say where you wish a home. There is a tract of 320 acres near you, a fine place, nicely watered, a place I had intended for one of my boys. If that place will suit you and make you safe, you go to your attorney and have him make out a deed for that land and bring it to me."

Waugh's lawyer filled out the deed and Vallejo affixed his signature and paid all fees giving to the Temperance-lecturing Methodist minister a munificent homestead. When the story of the gift of 320 acres of land was published in Lorenzo Waugh's book, Vallejo wrote to the author saying, "Permit me to send you by means of this letter, my most cordial congratulations upon the success of your book entitled, "Autobiography of Lorenzo Waugh." Vallejo sent a copy of the book to his son Platon, who in acknowledging it wrote on April 2, 1884 to his father:

> The little work of Lorenzo Waugh is quite interesting and well written relating to his home in California. I think the gentleman is grateful and takes a very pretty way of acknowledging such spontaneous and remarkable generosity . . . And we who may be supposed to be one of the boys mentioned in the story do not begrudge the stranger his little home, 300 or 400 acres and endorsing our dear father's generous gift like a chip of the old block wish the gentleman all the comfort and happiness here below.

LAND GRANTS

A *landed proprietor* is what Lt. Revere called his friend, General Vallejo. Revere wrote in his book *Tour of Duty in California*: "There are some wealthy men in California—they are few and far between—and their wealth is in their lands and products of their lands. General Vallejo formerly general and commander-in-chief, has a large amount of land, acquired by his own daring and adventurous settlement of the north side of the Bay. For these lands he holds titles in due form directly from the Mexican government, and of course his titles cannot possibly be disturbed without resorting to the most shameless and barefaced robbery, which the people of the United States will never tolerate . . . He has, it is true, a large amount of land and if our government owns it, they could sell it perhaps in the course of ten years for two hundred thousand dollars. But unless they would be willing to rob a man of so much money out of his pocket, they should not think of stealing it in the shape of land. I will venture to say that this vast enterprise of General Vallejo is of a hundred times greater service to California than the parceling out of his lands into small lots could be. I believe he actually supports more human beings on his estates than the same land would support if sold in small tracts. Under his superintendence, for he is a man of a cultivated mind and superior judgment, as well as a man of capital—there is little doubt that in a few years these estates will show immense results."

General Vallejo's estate showed "immense results" but he was not to benefit from the development because there were those who resorted to "shameless and barefaced robbery" which the people of the United States *did* tolerate.

As early as March 1849 Rev. Walter Colton, U.S.N., serving as Alcalde in Monterey, expressed his opinion: "The land titles in California ought to receive the most indulgent construction . . . To disturb these grants would be alike impolitic and unjust; it would be to convert the lands which they cover to the public domain, and ultimately turn them over to speculators and foreign capitalists. Better let them remain as they are; they are now in good hands . . . No Californian grinds the face of the poor, or refuses an emigrant a participation in his lands . . . If he has a farm, and I have none, he will divide with me, but who ever heard of a Yankee splitting up his farm to accomodate emigrants?"

The United States delayed action on the Mexican Land Grants through 1848, 1849, and 1850. In 1851 the Land Commission heard claims on Land Grants in California. The U.S. Government declared every grant of land legally void and lost unless the owners would sue the United States in Court and gain there. If the Land Commission confirmed a claim, an appeal was granted and it was taken to the United States District Court. If confirmed there, an appeal was often granted and the claimant was compelled to take the case to the United States Supreme Court at Washington. All this involving the claimant to expenses for witnesses, interpreters, high fees for lawyers, costs for transcripts amounting to several hundred dollars.

Squatters took his lands, occupied it while the owner was forced to pay the taxes on the land. In consequence he was often finally forced to sell a portion of his land to pay for the litigation.

VALLEJO RECEIVES OFFICIAL APPOINTMENT

It was in the middle of January, 1847, that Vallejo received an official dispatch which read:

TO ALL WHOM IT MAY CONCERN—GREETINGS

Having by authority of the President and Congress of the United States of North America, and by right of conquest, taken possession of that portion of Territory heretofore known as Upper and Lower California and having declared the same to be a Territory of the United States, under the name of the Territory of California and having established laws for the government of the said Territory; I, Robert F. Stockton, Governor and Commander-in-Chief of the same, do, in virtue of the authority in me vested and in obedience to the aforementioned laws appoint MARIANO G. VALLEJO—a member of the Legislative Council of the Territory of California for the term of two years.

Given under my hand and seal on this 16th day of January, Anno Domini, One thousand, eight hundred and fort-seven at the Cuidad de los Angeles.

R. F. STOCKTON
Governor, etc

A week later, Colonel Fremont wrote to the perplexed Vallejo:

I have the honor to transmit to you the Commission of a member of a Council of State, intended to exercise the functions of a legislative body in the Territorial Government of California.

Your great influence in the country, with the high respect and regard entertained for your person by the Californians will render your service of great value in tranquilizing the people and effecting the restoration of order and civil government.

I shall feel great pleasure in being associated with you in the accomplishment of these objects and trust that it will not be incompatible with your private engagements to accept the post offered you.

[Fremont never one to be unduly modest, signed the letter:]

J. C. FREMONT
Governor, Commander-in-Chief of California.

ADVICE OF FRIENDS

When it was learned that General Vallejo had been asked to serve on the Legislative Council, his close American friends proceeded to offer advice. From Los Angeles, Thomas O. Larkin who had also been appointed to the Council, came the following letter to Vallejo, dated January 22, 1847:

You have a letter from Colonel Fremont and a Commission to you as a member of the new Council. I hope you will not allow any business to prevent you from accepting and attending in March. Your non-attendance will sorely disappoint our Commodore, Fremont and myself. The Commodore thinks you told him you would accept if the rights of the Californians were respected. If you accept, many Californians will by degrees accept.

From Monterey, Larkin's business partner Talbot Green wrote:

I learned you are appointed one of the Council of Legislation which I hope for the good and interest of California you will accept as their [sic] is many questions that must come before the country which in my opinion there is no one who understands the interests of the country better than you; a great many land titles that are not exactly in form and the rights of the individuals claiming the missions; all of these questions will have to be settled before your assembly. You will please write direct to Mr. Larkin in my care whether you accept the appointment or not. I am well aware the pay is no object to you. The salary will be $2,000 per annum and mileage.

Robert Semple, erstwhile member of the Bear Flag Party and publisher of California's first newspaper, *The Californian*, expressed his opinion thus:

From a conversation with you, I was afraid you would not accept the office . . . I am fully aware of your delicacy of feeling as to the acceptance of office but my dear General, you must remember that it is a duty you owe yourself and your children as well as your country to accept a position where your talents and suavity of manner will have a powerful tendency to tranquilize the country and give confidence to the people of the good intentions of the American people, to place the old inhabitants of California on the same footing as themselves.

And Robert Semple's partner in the publishing business, the Reverend Walter Colton, wrote from Monterey, January 31, 1847 to Vallejo in this vein:

The Californian, Dr. Semple has often spoken of you to me and we have often expressed the desire to each other that you might consent to be a member of the first legislature. It is all important to take wise steps to make a good impression at first. There is no man in California who better understands her true interests than yourself. Your information, talents, the weight of your character are greatly to be desired in the first legislation. We fear too, should you decline a seat in the Council, it might be ascribed by the Californians to a want of confidence in the Government or a disaffection to it. This we Americans all know would not be true. We are all therefore deeply desirous that you should accept the appointment . . . Excuse my freedom in urging your acceptance of the appointment as a duty to California in the present crisis. It is understood that Governor Alvarado has accepted.

Reverend Colton, who had been the first American Alcalde of Monterey, admired General Vallejo greatly. After Colton left California, he wrote a book *Three Years in California* which he dedicated to "his friend" in the following gracious manner:

GEN. MARIANO GUADALUPE VALLEJO
One of California's Distinguished Sons
in whom
The interests of Freedom, Humanity and Education
Have found an able advocate and munificent benefactor

Four of the letters received by Vallejo were in agreement that he should accept membership on the Legislative Council, however two expressed a contrary viewpoint. William Leidesdorff, former American vice-consul who operated the City Hotel on Portsmouth Plaza (first hotel in Yerba Buena) advised Vallejo not to accept membership. The other negative letter was from Lieutenant Joseph Warren Revere who wrote to the General on January 29, 1847 from the *Portsmouth* birthed at San Diego:

My dear General:

You will receive this letter by the *Cyane* which will leave tomorrow for San Francisco. Undoubtedly you will hear a better account of the events that have taken place in this part of the country since our arrival than I could give you . . . The predominant opinion still is that events of the 8th and 9th of this month have not been conducive to bringing a permanent calm to the country, a circumstance for which we can thank the rash conduct of Fremont, after the Californians had decided to sue for peace; and a universal disgust is publicly expressed toward the course pursued by this officer—both as regards his rash acts and subsequently.

General Kearny came to the country with orders from the President to conquer it and organize a government . . . Now he sees himself pushed aside by Commodore Stockton, just at a time when he is carrying on his legitimate functions and sees himself obligated to remain inactive in the Territory until he receives confirmatory news from Washington D.C. where he has sent one of his engineering officers to bring back the decision of the government.

The arbitrary conduct of Commodore Stockton had its origin in his own selfish interest when Fremont said to him in the pueblo of Los Angeles that if he wasn't made Governor of California, he (Fremont) would go over to the side of Kearny. Stockton fearing that Kearny would get credit for the pacification of the country "bought off" Fremont with the title.

Under the circumstances in which we find ourselves, I should be very sorry to see you accept the position of Councilor which I know will be offered to you and many of your friends among the officers would be sorry too. You now occupy a neutral position, full of dignity and I am sure General Kearny will have the support of the President of the United States and that Fremont and his transitory cabinet will not have much time to exist . . . With sincerest good wished to all the family from all the *Portsmouth*, Your faithful friend,

J. W. REVERE

There was a close feeling between Vallejo and Lieutenant Revere, who had been sent to raise the flag of the United States in Sonoma on July 9, 1846 and had remained in command of the northern frontier until early September. He was the one American officer who always wrote to Vallejo in Spanish. The General still remembered that it was Fremont who organized the American settlers, instructing them to "surprise the garrison at Sonoma," giving orders for his imprisonment at Fort Sutter, and it was Fremont who was responsible for the harsh treatment of himself and his companions. Vallejo's first inclination must have been to refuse. But there were more than personal feelings involved; his American friends thought he could be of service to his native land, and he remembered that he had written thanking Larkin for his interest and help and had said, "I shall forever recognize the obligation." After much soul-searching, Vallejo decided to recognize his obligation to his native land and to Consul Larkin, his friend.

On February 15th, 1847 he wrote to "*Governor*" Fremont, accepting the office of Councilor, conferred, Vallejo said, by Commodore Stockton. Vallejo said that he recognized his lack of ability but that he would do his best for California, for whose welfare he had always felt the deepest interest. He hinted that he was still a *prisoner of war*, but, he would be ready to start for Los Angeles as soon as Larkin would come for him.

SERVICE RIVALRY

It was not long before Vallejo was in the midst of American politics—politics between the Services. John Charles Fremont who was now Colonel Fremont was the center of the Army vs Navy skirmish with General Stephen Watt Kearny his chief adversary.

In June of 1846, the then Colonel Kearny was stationed at Fort Leavenworth, Missouri and received there a confidential letter from W. L. Marcy, the Secretary of War, which said in part: "It has been decided to take the earliest possession of Upper California. An expedition with that view is hereby ordered and you are designated to command . . . It is expected that the naval forces of the United States which are now or will soon be in the Pacific will be in possession of all towns on the seacoast and will cooperate with you in the conquest of California."

Kearny at the head of 1600 men crossed the deserts and captured Santa

Fe. Continuing his march to California, he met Commodore Stockton's courier Kit Carson who gave him information of the conquest of California. Kearny turned back the greater number of his troops only to find how badly he needed them when he was intercepted and defeated December 6, 1846 by the Californians at San Pasqual near San Diego. Kearny had to accept help from Commodore Stockton, however his humiliation was somewhat assuaged when he learned later that Commodore Shubrick had arrived succeeding Commodore Stockton in command.

General Kearny reached Monterey in February and on the first of March issued a Proclamation telling the Californians that the President of the United States had instructed him to take charge of the civil government and to guarantee them freedom in religious worship and protection of person and property. At about the same time he wrote a lengthy report to Washington, D.C. to General Roger Jones, adjutant General U.S.A., telling him that Commodore Shubrick "acknowledged me as the head and commander of the troops in California which Commodore Stockton and Lieutenant Colonel Fremont had hitherto refused. We agreed upon our separate duties . . . Upon Commodore Biddle's arrival I had a full understanding with him relating to our duties and I take pleasure here to acknowledge the great courtesy I have received from both of these gentlemen."

FREMONT VS KEARNY

In Los Angeles, Lieutenant-Colonel Fremont was exercising his newly-bestowed executive authority by contracting debts for the California Battalion and conferring appointments in San Diego and Los Angeles. General Kearny on April 11, 1847 expressed his resentment toward Fremont to Commodore James Biddle, who was then commanding the United States Pacific Squadron:

> I claim for myself, as governor of California by virtue of instructions from the President of the United States, no such power as is attempted to be exercised by Lieutenant Colonel Fremont, the President having assigned "to the commander-in-chief of the naval forces the regulation of the import trade and the conditions on which vessels of all nations, our own as well as foreign, may be admitted into the ports of the Territory."
>
> Lieutenant Colonel Fremont has no authority for considering himself governor of California, and attempting to perform the duties of that office except what he may have derived from Commodore Stockton of the Navy; and he well knows that the President of the United States has assigned that duty to myself, having been officially informed of that fact by a circular of March 1st, signed by Commodore Shubrick and myself . . .

General Kearny had some time before sent Colonel Mason to Los Angeles with a letter for Fremont, telling him that Colonel Mason was clothed with full military authority and "that any instructions he may give, you will consider as coming from me." Upon arriving in the South, Colonel Mason asked Fremont to give him a list of the appointments he had made and furnish him with records or papers touching upon the civil affairs of the Territory during the time he claimed to be governor of California. Fremont gave a written reply, saying that "such brief record of my official acts as Governor of the Territory that was preserved by me has been forwarded to the United States. My position here having been denounced as usurpation by General Kearny, I could not anticipate from him any call for these papers."

The failure to obtain any records from Fremont was reported to Kearny. With Colonel Mason's report was enclosed an original order issued by Fremont to Captain Richard Owens, directing him not to obey the order of any officer, that did not emanate from him [Fremont] nor to turn over the public arms to any corps without his special order. Such insubordination could not be tolerated by General Kearny. He went to Los Angeles and summoned Fremont to appear before him. During a stormy interview Fremont handed General Kearny a written statement in which he said that he and his California battalion had been mustered into the Navy under Commodore Stockton and that he felt that he owed his allegiance to Stockton. In this fateful letter, dictated to Kit Carson but signed by Fremont, the Pathfinder had said:

> I feel myself, therefore, with great deference to your professional and personal character, constrained to say that until you and Commodore Stockton adjust between yourselves the question of rank, where I respectfully think the difficulty belongs, I shall have to report and receive orders as heretofore from the Commodore.

General Kearny, upon reading the letter and perhaps remembering his friendship with the Benton family, advised Fremont to destroy it and put himself under his orders or he would end his career in the army. Fremont refused. He remained in southern California with Stockton.

From the Headquarters of the Tenth Military Department—Ciudad de los Angeles on May 13, 1847 General Kearny reported to General Roger Jones, Adjutant General, U.S.A. "I leave here tomorrow for Monterey and will close my public business there as soon as possible and then proceed to St. Louis . . . I, this morning started Lieutenant Colonel Fremont to close his public business there before he leaves for Washington. His conduct in California has been such that I shall be compelled, on arriving in Missouri, to arrest him, and send him under charges to report to you."

As early as January 30th, Kearny had requested from W. L. Marcy, Secretary of War permission to return to Missouri "provided the Peace of the country is firmly established and placed beyond the fear of interruption."

Stephen Watts Kearny left California on May 31, 1847 leaving Colonel Richard B. Mason of the First Dragoons as Governor of California.

MILITARY RULE

California as a conquered province was subject to military rule. The different military governors all followed the local customs and appointed alcaldes for the pueblos; an alcalde combining in himself the duties of both mayor and judge. In Sonoma 1847, John H. Nash, a good-natured illiterate man, was given the office of alcalde of Sonoma by local residents. General Kearny refused to recognize his appointment and named Lilburn W. Boggs instead. But Nash would not relinquish the alcaldeship; consequently, Lieutenant William T. Sherman, upon Colonel Mason's orders (he having succeeded Kearny) went to Sonoma and Nash was arrested in the Green residence where he was boarding. He was taken to Monterey and released upon his promise to give up all the records.

In February 1847, Lilburn W. Boggs, who was living at General Vallejo's Petaluma Adobe, sent the General a book containing a copy of the *Constitution of the United States* with Rules and Regulations for the government of both Houses of Congress. Boggs told the General that in the back of the book was Jefferson's *Manual of Parliamentary Practice* which he said was the text of common law for all legislative bodies in the United States. It was Jefferson's Manual which two years later was selected to be the law for the Convention forming the first Constitution for California.

With Boggs presiding and Vallejo a member of the Committee, a meeting was held in Sonoma on February 26, 1847 for the purpose of making plans for the citizens north of the Bay to organize civil government. An Assembly was created in Sonoma and Yerba Buena. General Kearny sent a letter to John N. Nash at that time Alcalde of Sonoma, saying that he had received a copy of the proceedings of a meeting presided over by L. W. Boggs which related to the legislative council: Kearny tartly concluded his letter, "I will thank you to inform all concerned that I have not called for any such council, nor at present do I contemplate doing so." When it was known that the military officers in Monterey looked with disfavor upon the plan, it was dissolved.

MILITARY TRANSFERS

The spring and summer of 1847 was a time of transfer for many of the Military and Naval officers in California. Captain William Mervine and Lieutenant Joseph Warren Revere, the two young officers who had been frequent guests of the Vallejos were leaving California with regrets. They were somewhat cheered with the knowledge that they had bought California land and had plans to make the Golden State their home.

Captain Mervine of the United States ship *Savannah*, wished to purchase a parcel of ground a mile square on Sonoma Creek, opposite Jacob P.Leese's embarcadero, and to buy a lot next to the one on which Leese lived, facing the Sonoma Plaza.

REVERE'S SAN GERONIMO RANCHO

Lieutenant Revere, while in command of the military post in Sonoma in October 1846, purchased the Rancho Geronimo consisting of two square leagues (dos sitios de ganada mayor) about five miles from the old mission of San Rafael in what is now Marin County. Revere had first seen this valley shut in by lofty hills covered with redwood forests and pines, and with a free-flowing stream, when he was hunting elk. He was determined to possess it. When he was about to leave, he wrote Vallejo on June 7, 1847 from the *Portsmouth:*

There is a possibility I will return soon to the eastern part of our country and I regret that the happy event will deprive me of the pleasure of seeing you. I am sorry that up to now, you have not found a manager for San Geronimo. I had in this instance hoped I could relieve you of the bother. My friend and correspondent Don O'Farrell received so many instructions to do me favors, it must have given you a lot of bother. Now that my plans are not completed I am dependent on my friends. He will be responsible for such expenditures you may consider for live stock and other things.

Expect soon to return and make the ranch my home. I am very glad I decided before leaving San Francisco not to sell any part of the land. That is still my desire for the reason I have received word, confidentially from the United States that California lands are going to be very valuable. Also I am not like you, a "grand Senor"; also selling part of the ranch would damage the value of the remainder.

San Geronimo was stocked with horned cattle and mares. When Revere returned to California in February 1849, as a government timber agent, he found that in his absence the cattle had increased to about 500 head of all kinds, roaming at will; the mayor-domo or manager engaged to take charge of the San Geronimo Ranch was also roaming, off to the bonanza placers. Revere formed a party of his neighbors, Indian servants and vaqueros and went to the gold territory on Feather River where they camped and prospected.

The Revere party's trading netted more gold than their digging. The cattle the group took with them sold at a great profit; a boat laden with dry goods, groceries, crockery and hardware, sold at even greater profit; butcher knives bringing twenty dollars, common iron spoons five dollars, and ordinary wash-bowls fifteen dollars. Flour which had come from Chile, Revere sold for $100 a sack. Calico shirts worn by members of the Revere party were sold unwashed for $20.

After the trip to the mines, Revere returned to his ranch. From a friend in command of a brig from Honolulu he secured a few barrels of potatoes, poor and small, about the size of a walnut: These he planted on his ranch and left them in charge of his Indian servants while he attended to his duties as a timber inspector.

Revere's crops turned out beyond his most sanguine expectations, and he had the satisfaction of reaping a splendid harvest which was disposed of at high prices. He built a new house and planned other improvements.

Near the end of 1849, Revere resigned his commission as lieutenant in the United States Navy, hopeless of promotion in spite of twenty years of service. He was reluctant to abandon his profession, but he enjoyed being a California rancher. To quote him: "My health was never better, my physical powers never greater than when I was a ranchero in that glorious country."

Upon Lieutenant Revere's departure from Sonoma in 1847 the barracks had been turned over to Company C under Captain J. E. Brackett of Stevenson's New York Volunteer Regiment. Later Company H commanded by Captain John B. Frisbie, occupied the premises. The Sonoma barracks or Quartel was an adobe structure, built during the years 1839, 1840 and 1841 by mission and neophyte Indians and two white men under the supervision of General Vallejo.

Just as General Vallejo had made friends quickly with the first American officers, so did he with the new contingent. A month after Colonel Stevenson's arrival, the Colonel was writing to Vallejo in a semi-formal jovial manner: "General Vallejo having proffered me some young horses, I will accept them with thanks for his kindness. He may select colours, black, bay, grey, and the favorite California colours named by Mr. Bartlett, the day we called at Mr. Coopers."

General Vallejo was not the only one at the Casa Grande who interested the young officers. There were several beautiful daughters. It was said it was not unusual to see half a dozen horses tied in front of the house. Although fond of company, himself, the General thought it wise to discourage such wholesale hospitality. One Sunday morning Colonel Joe Hooker was announced with two military friends. Vallejo met them at the door and took no pains to hide his displeasure. To the first officer he thundered, "What brings you here today at this hour? The embarrassed visitor muttered something about wanting to buy some beef cattle; the second man, upon being questioned, said he had come about buying some horses. When it came to Joe Hooker's turn, he frankly replied that he had called for no other purpose than to see the young ladies. Vallejo turned to the first two officers and said that he was not in the habit of doing business on Sunday but would be glad to see them on any other day. To Colonel Hooker he said, "Please step into the parlor, my daughters will soon be here."

Colonel Hooker had come to Sonoma in 1849 with General Persifor F. Smith. Hooker had won his third brevet in Mexico for his actions at the storming of Chapultepec. After the fall of Mexico City, the months were pleasant ones for Colonel Hooker whose affable ways and commanding appearance had made him a favorite with the Spanish ladies. They called him "el Capitan hermoso."

Hooker acquired 550 acres near what is now Agua Caliente and erected a small cottage which he later sold to George E. Wattriss.

FOUNDING OF BENICIA

General Vallejo had long foreseen that a metropolis would some day be situated on the great bay of San Francisco and he and Dr. Robert Semple believed that such a city could be developed on Vallejo's land at the Carquinez Straits. A site was chosen and named "Francisca" after one of the baptismal names of Senora Vallejo. A contract was entered into by the two men Vallejo and Semple on December 23, 1846. On January 19, 1847 the document was taken to Yerba Buena and presented for filling to Washington A. Bartlett, appointed by Captain Montgomery as the alcalde of the San Francisco district, with headquarters in the village of Yerba Buena. Upon receiving Semple's document Bartlett believed that if a name sounding like San Francisco were given to another town on the bay it might retard the development of the pueblo over which he presided so he issued the following order on January 30, 1847:

> Whereas the local name of Yerba Buena as applied to the settlement or town of San Francisco is unknown beyond the immediate district and has been applied from the local name of the Cove on which the town is built. Therefore to prevent confusion and mistakes in public documents and that the town may have the advantage of the name given on the published maps, It is hereby ordered that the name of San Francisco shall hereafter be used in all official communications and public documents or orders appertaining to the town.
>
> Washington A. Bartlett
> Chief Magistrate

The ordinance was published in *The California Star*, Sam Brannan's newspaper. Thus the village's name would correspond to the port, presidio and mission of San Francisco.

Dr. Semple decided to remove his residence from Monterey and in May he wrote Vallejo, "When I saw you at Santa Clara, you spoke of Mr. Larkin's desire to become interested in the City of *Francisca* . . . I am aware that the building of a city will greatly increase the value of your land and should you be desirous to avoid the labor of making a city, you could not probably trust it to the hands of a more energetic man than Mr. Larkin . . . I am now selling my business here."

In explaining in later years (January 25, 1874) his actions in connection with the founding of Benicia, Vallejo wrote his son Platon. A portion of that revealing letter follows:

> In the course of time Don Thomas O. Larkin, an American gentleman who in addition of being very influential, rich, a great friend of all my family and principally because he had done some very important services for me at the time of my imprisonment when the Bear Flag was raised on the 14th of June, 1846, asking me very diplomatically to allow him to enter as a partner in the founding and in the speculation of the City of Benicia. Not being able to refuse, we met together, Dr. Semple, Larkin and I to discuss the matter. As a result of the conference, instead of the one mile which I had given before to Semple, two more were added, to which I agreed willingly, extending the project. I made a title in favor of the two men mentioned, it being well understood among us that although they would be and were already the actual managers, or better said, the directors of all the business since I didn't understand English well nor the forms or formulas of the titles in that language.

On May 19th, 1847, Vallejo and his wife Francisca Benicia granted to Thomas O. Larkin and Robert Semple a tract of land embracing an area of five square miles which was a portion of their estate known as Soscol. Vallejo stipulated that a ferry should be operated by Semple, which was carried out —the first public utility in California.

Larkin recognized the handicap the new town would be under if it had a name so like San Francisco, the new name of Yerba Buena. It was thereby decided to give their town another Christian name of General Vallejo's wife, namely "Benicia" whereupon Dr. Semple published the following notice in *The Californian.*

NAME CHANGED:

The name of the City of *FRANCISCA* recently laid out at the Straits of Carquinez on the Bay of San Francisco has been changed to *BENICIA CITY.* At the request of my partner and several other persons, I have consented to the change. The reason for the change is that this town of Yerba Buena is by the order of the Alcalde called San Francisco and it was thought that the names being so much alike might create confusion . . . No one dreamed of changing the name 'Yerba Buena' until I handed in my deeds to be recorded for the present site of the City of Benicia with the name of the City of Francisca. The Alcalde next day issued an order that the town of Yerba Buena be hereafter called San Francisco.

The first house in Benicia was commenced in August 1847. There were upwards of 200 lots sold and some were donated for schools. General Vallejo was unable to visit Benicia often, but its development was of such concern to him that he appreciated the following report of its progress from Dr. Semple:

I received your letter a few days ago, intimating a desire to know something of the progress of Benicia. There are none more willing to do so than myself for I think the place promises to be one of the largest and handsomest cities this side of the mountain and its progress is now as rapid as I have expected.

There are not so many persons here as there have been but the fact that a number of the citizens have gone to the Redwoods to get timber to build their houses. I do not want to place the lots on the market now; they would not sell for much and would injure the place but in a month or two, when business opens, I shall sell some lots for I am resolved to be out of debt by May.

In recalling the story of the founding of Benicia, Vallejo said: "After Semple, Larkin, Phelps and others assumed the management and direction of the city, they denied the debt to me; they took over everything as if something had possession of them."

THE GOLDEN YEAR OF DESTINY

Gold had been found in California in various places long before 1848. Vallejo himself had bought it from the Indians and had sent the gold dust to Mexico hidden in the sealed quills of a vulture; but it took the Americans living in California to tell the world of James W. Marshall's discovery of the precious metal in Captain Sutter's mill-race on January 24, 1848.

Ten days afterwards, a treasure greater than California's gold was given to the United States when the treaty of peace was signed with Mexico. This treasure had long been desired by the United States. By the opening of President Polk's Administration, the acquisition of California was favored by both parties, the Whigs and Democrats. Daniel Webster had said that the port of San Francisco was twenty times as valuable as all Texas. Polk sent John Slidell to Mexico to obtain a cession of California to the United States, knowing that England had designs on California. It was said that the Mexican Republic's financial obligations to certain English capitalists aggregated to more than fifty million dollars. There was thought of proposing to Mexico that the debt be canceled for the transfer of California to Great Britain.

Slidell's mission was a failure and it was not long before there was a formal declaration of war. Nicholas P. Trist, the chief clerk of the State Department, was sent to Mexico to conclude a treaty of peace. Trist had been a Secretary to President Jackson. He had been educated at the United States Military Academy and had studied law under Thomas Jefferson and was named one of Jefferson's executors (he later married Thomas Jefferson's granddaughter). He had also been the United States Consul at Havana, so he was well fitted for the important task confided to him.

Owing to disagreements with General Winfield Scott in command in Mexico, and the envoy's readiness to consider counter-proposals from the Mexicans, Trist was recalled.

After the United States victory at Contreras (the battle at which General Bennet Riley had distinguished himself and was given the yellow sash which he later wore at the Constitutional Convention Ball in Monterey)—and the subsequent occupation of Mexico City, the Mexicans were ready to negotiate.

Trist's recall had left the United States without an accredited representative. The flag of the United States was floating over the Mexican capital, but General Scott declined to take any responsibility in the matter. In this crisis, Trist rose to the occasion and "assumed the risk of punishment for what might be construed as an act of monstrous insubordination." Actuated by unselfish and wise patriotism and diplomacy, he resolved "for good or evil" to send home a treaty of peace.

On February 2, 1848 Trist wrote the State Department that the treaty was "signed an hour before at the City of Guadalupe, a spot which agreeably to the creed of this country is the most sacred on earth, as being the scene of the miraculous appearance of the Virgin for the purpose of declaring that Mexico was taken under her special protection."

The document, perhaps the only treaty negotiated and signed by a private citizen without authority from his Government, was given to James L. Treanor, the correspondent of the New Orleans "Delta" who carried it to New Orleans and forwarded it to Washington, where on March 10, 1848 it was ratified by the United States Senate by a vote of 38 to 15. The ratification by the Mexican Government was brought to the United States. President James A. Polk appointed Ambrose H. Sevier and Nathan Clifford to go to Mexico as commissioners to exchange ratifications of the treaty as amended by the United States Senate.

The ratifications were exchanged on the 30th of May, 1848 at Queretaro, Mexico. However, the news of ratification did not reach California until August. On the seventh of that month Colonel Richard B. Mason, military commander and civil governor of California issued a proclamation to the people of California announcing the ratification of a treaty of peace and friendship between the United States of America and the Mexican Republic by which Upper California is ceded to the United States." He told the people of California that by the conditions of the treaty that those who wished to become citizens of the United States were absolved from all allegiance to the Mexican Republic. Those who wished to remain Mexicans would be at liberty to do so and retain their property but they would have to make known their election within a year from 30th of May past.

Colonel Mason closed the proclamation by saying: "Americans and Californians will now be one and the same people, subject to the same laws, and enjoying the same rights and privileges; they should therefore become a band of brothers, emulating each other in their exertions to develop the wealth and resources, and to secure the peace, happiness and permanent prosperity of their common country."

Vallejo must have rejoiced as two years before in Monterey he had expressed much the same sentiments when he told the Californians to welcome the Americans as brothers and said, "If California would join her fortune to the United States, they would have a stable government and just laws. California would grow strong and flourish and her people would be prosperous, happy and free."

Nicholas P. Trist, who had made the signing of the peace treaty possible, was ordered home by President Polk, who refused to pay his salary. However, in 1871 Congress appropriated $14,559.90 of Trist's salary which had been withheld. In 1870 Trist was appointed the Postmaster of Alexander, Virginia, by Gen. Grant.

The gold discovery changed the character of California. Its people who, before, had been engaged in cultivating their ranches and guarding their herds of cattle, were at the mines. Laborers of every trade left their workbenches and tradesmen their shops; sailors deserted their ships and soldiers their garrisons. Sonoma had lost two-thirds of its population. Most of the houses were empty and there was not a single carpenter nor blacksmith in the village. Those who went early to the mines came back too rich to resume their trades. Even those who borrowed money did not hesitate to pay high interest. Vallejo and Frisbie were present when Ben Kelsey lent a Mr. Griffith $25,000 at 25 per cent interest; the principal and interest were paid.

In Benicia, Robert Semple was having his labor troubles; he wrote Vallejo,

"Since the gold fever broke out, I find it impossible to keep my men." Semple's partner, Larkin, spent very little time in Benicia; he was either in San Francisco or in Monterey. This was a disappointment to Semple who wrote him, "If the place is not worth coming to see, it is not worth knowing about; your interest reminds me of a man who was so eager for the dime, he could not see he was surrounded by dollars."

Upon the completion of the conquest of California, Larkin's official position as the United States Consul had expired. He offered his services to Secretary of State Buchanan. In reply the Secretary wrote: "I thank you for this offer of your services. I have determined that under the circumstances of the case, you should continue at least for the present as Confidential Agent in the Californias. From the fact that the Californias are yet considered foreign territory so far as to enable me to continue your agency. You are not to infer that the President contemplated any contingency in which they shall ever be surrendered to Mexico."

Larkin received from the President the Commission of Naval Agent for the North West Coast of America. He was required to furnish a bond of $30,000 which prompted him to write to Jacob P. Leese on October 18, 1847: "I therefore call on you as one of my oldest friends in this country, to do me the favor to sign the bond with Don M. G. Vallejo and Don Salvador and Don Francisco Pacheco." Leese consented to be Larkin's guarantor as did W. A. Leidesdorff.

Several months after the gold discovery by Marshall, Larkin sent by the flagship *Ohio* to Secretary Buchanan an account dated June 1, 1848 of the gold discovery. Another letter with greater detail followed after Larkin himself had made a trip to the mines.

As early as February 10th, Vallejo had learned of the gold discovery from Captain Sutter, himself. The General's comment at the time had been, "As the water flows through Sutter's mill-race, may the gold flow into Sutter's purse."

When the first gold dust was brought to the pueblo of Sonoma there was much doubt as to its genuineness. Alcalde Boggs and the military officers pronounced it genuine and in a short time, miners began to arrive with large quantities of the dust; it could be bought for four to five dollars an ounce. Change smaller than one dollar was scarce; a blacksmith was employed in cutting Mexican dollars into halves and quarters. For a time the pueblo of Sonoma was a sort of distribution point whence supplies were drawn for gold seekers. Vallejo opened a mercantile store there, also one in Napa and one in Benicia. His partner in these enterprises was Captain John B. Frisbie who had disbanded Company H of Stevenson's Regiment at Sonoma in August of 1848.

General Vallejo and Alcalde Boggs paid a visit to the placers; they saw Sutter's mill and tail-race, picked up a few glittering small nuggets and were content to return to Sonoma. However, from a prepared, unsigned, undated document in the Bancroft Library, it appears that Vallejo had considered going into partnership with Alexander Rotscheff in placer mining. According to several statements in the contract, the machines to be used were to be in imitation of those used in Siberia and would be capable of washing 10,000 to 20,000 buckets a day; they would save labor and not lose the least bit of gold. Rotscheff stated that he had already solicited Washington for the privilege of using said machines. The *sixth* statement on the contract suggests to the reader that Rotscheff wanted free transportation to Europe:

"Don M.G.V. will supply the necessary money or bond for the transportation of Don A.R. and Don V.P. [evidently Victor Prudon] to Paris and Don A.R. will leave him a note for said amount which will be honored in Paris. Seventh: Don A.R. guarantees his return to San Francisco, barring accidents, within six months, counted from the day of his departure from California."

The General's brother-in-law, Jacob P. Leese, joined a party for the mines, which included Jasper O'Farrell. It was the first group to prospect on the Yuba River and the first to discover gold in an area which was to become the great placer-mining center.

With the influx of men from every country and clime, with all degrees of conduct and morals, there was an insistent demand from the law-abiding residents that California be made a State in order to receive the benefit of American laws. U.S. Senator Stephen Douglas introduced a bill to give statehood to California but Congress adjourned without providing a new government for it.

VALLEJO REBUKES A NATIVE CALIFORNIAN

In June of 1849, Vallejo had interested himself in the case of Don Theodore Robles who had been banished by Don Antonio Maria Pico, alcalde of San Jose. On the 30th of June Vallejo wrote Pico:

Doubtless you are going to wonder at my addressing you, asserting my little or no influence in behalf of Don Teodore Robles, which individual has been banished from his place in a way, hardly decent . . . You ought to believe and know that neither you nor the jury have now enough authority to sentence to banishment a man who has not had proved against him legally any crime . . . The time is past when each Alcalde or Justice of the Peace does what he pleases for no other reason than because it suits him. No, Sir! The Law is the only thing to which man is subject and authority derives from that Law. Our new compatriots see our lack of culture and crudeness and are right in giving us so little consideration. It is possible that you in discharging one of the duties of the Magistrate of a town which elected you to protect its rights and especially those of the sons of the country are turning into an oppressor?

It is very easy for me to see that you as the authority, have shown yourself very hard and unjust to a son of the country and moreover in front of the new peoples that are watching us and can believe, although it may be without justice that the Mexican Laws are absurd, as the conduct of the very ones, which are used to transact some business, show them to be . . . Where are we heading, if our own countrymen turn against us? What can we hope for, then? What? Is it not enough, the situation in which we find ourselves—without knowing the language, nor the customs, nor the Laws, nor anything of the North Americans? I again ask you to see to it that Don Teodore Robles may remain in the place where he lives without being molested . . . I have no other purpose than that of undoing a wrong and of helping a Californian when he is persecuted without just cause.

Years before Don Antonio Maria Pico had been a schoolmate of Vallejo in Monterey. If the letter in behalf of Vallejo's friend bore fruit, the General was able to thank Senor Pico in person as the San Jose Alcalde was a delegate to the Constitutional Convention in Monterey.

CONSTITUTIONAL CONVENTION

General Bennett Riley, California's military governor in 1849 in an effort to help the situation and with the advice of former governor Colonel Robert B. Mason, issued a Proclamation calling for an election of delegates to frame a State Constitution. The delegates chosen from Sonoma District were Joel Walker, Robert Semple, M. G. Vallejo, and Lilburn Boggs. For some reason Boggs did not attend the Convention.

September first, 1849, was the opening day of the Constitutional Convention in Monterey but there was no quorum present. Vallejo was in Yerba Buena; as he wrote his wife: "This afternoon I am leaving for Monterey in the steamship after waiting these five days with a very bad temperature, accompanied by a heavy and continuous cold which takes from me all desire to go out into the street."

Monday, September 3rd, the Convention was called to order in the two-story light yellow sandstone edifice built by the Reverend Walter Colton, with convict labor. Chairman Kimball H. Dimmick announced the names of the elected delegates. When the apportionment for the districts was announced, Senor Jose Antonio Carrillo, the delegate from Los Angeles (said to be the right hand of Pio Pico), arose and told the delegates that he was surprised that Los Angeles was put upon the same level with Monterey by being given five delegates. He said it was known that Los Angeles had doubled the number of its inhabitants and that the resolution should be amended to give Los Angeles seven delegates.

On Tuesday afternoon, September 4th, the delegates elected Dr. Robert Semple, president of the Constitutional Convention. Two of California's most distinguished sons, 47-year-old John A. Sutter, an adopted son from Switzerland, and 42-year-old Don Mariano Guadalupe Vallejo, a native son of Monterey, California, escorted Semple to his seat. Present as an observer for General Persifor F. Smith was Lieutenant William T. Sherman.

The flags of the United States were draped above the head of the president and behind him on the wall was a chromo of George Washington. As Semple rose to address the gathering of law-makers on the western coast, the tall

42-year-old Semple may have been thinking of his brother James Semple, who had been United States Senator from Illinois (1844 to 1847).

Dr. Semple began his address: "Fellow Citizens: While with an open heart, I feel grateful for the honor conferred upon me, yet I must say that I feel a regret that it has not fallen into abler hands. I shall expect a due feeling of forbearance on your part . . . We are now, fellow citizens, occupying a position to which all eyes are turned. The eyes not only of our sister and parent States are upon us but the eyes of all Europe are now directed toward California. This is the preliminary movement of the organization of a civil government . . . I am satisfied that we can prove to the world that California has not been settled entirely by unintelligent and unlettered men. So far from this, population consisting of persons who had nothing to do at home, it has drained from the States, many of the best families and most intelligent men in the country. The knowledge, enterprise and genius of the old world will reappear in the new, to guide it to its destined position among the nations of the earth."

The sessions—often morning, afternoon, and evening—kept Vallejo busy, as he had been appointed on several committees. However, he did find time to visit his mother and other Monterey relatives, and for writing short letters home. On September 28th, he wrote to his wife:

Francisca:

We are finishing up the labors for which we came here and I believe we shall be able to leave here by the 7th of October. Take care of everything. My mother and all my relatives greet you affectionately. The Capital from now on will be the village of San Jose. Tell Fannie that I hope when I reach Sonoma, she will already know English so she can teach me.

Your husband,

GUADALUPE

In later years, Vallejo, recalling the Convention, said: "While I was in the convention of which Semple was the president and Larkin a member also, the conduct of my partners in Benicia City was such that the idea came to me, as an inspiration to raise up another city in competition to Benicia, which city is now Vallejo."

The Convention which had enjoyed beautiful Autumn weather, was in session for almost another week after October 7th. There had been some impatience over the delay caused by much speech making. One of the delegates, C. T. Botts of Monterey who was often on his feet, said he knew there were those who expected the Convention to manifest railroad speed, but he recalled, "We passed twenty-eight of the most important sections in our Constitution in less than two hours."

Vallejo presented the following resolution to the Convention:

That three Commissioners be elected by ballot to draft a code of laws for the government of California, to be submitted to the Legislature for their approval at the first session thereof.

Mr. Tefft from San Luis Obispo felt that the people had not sent delegates to the Convention to form a Code of Laws but to form a Constitution; he felt it was presumptuous to contend that all the legal talent and ability was centered in the Convention. If the Commissioners were appointed by the Convention, the Legislature would indignantly reject any code of laws they might present to them.

L. W. Hastings of Sacramento said the Legislature would be very grateful to the members for making laws for them, thus leaving them nothing to do but sit in their seats and draw their sixteen dollars a day. Francis J. Lippitt of San Francisco opposed the adoption of Vallejo's resolution. He said it was impossible for three men or 30 men to draw up a code of laws in less than two years.

Vallejo rose in defense of his resolution: he said that he had no other motive than to provide for the rapid passage of laws by the Legislature. It was a matter of economy to pay the three Commissioners rather than an entire Legislature. The sessions of that body would not be so protracted if their business was in advance prepared. If the Convention objected to paying the $3,000 or $4,000 for the Commissioners, Vallejo said, he would pay it himself, willingly. He regretted that his limited knowledge of the English language prevented him from replying to all the arguments adduced by those gentlemen who did not speak his tongue.

When Vallejo's resolution was put to a vote, there were 18 yeas; De la Guerra and Sutter voting with him. However, there were 36 nays; among the negative voters were Carrillo, Halleck and Larkin.

On Wednesday, October 10th, there was discussion of the proposed boundary of California. William C. Shannon, delegate from Coloma, wanted information from Mr. Hartnell or Mr. Halleck regarding an ancient Spanish document. Mr. Hartnell suggested that "Perhaps Mr. Vallejo may be able to give the desired information." In reply Vallejo said, "I have myself seen in the archives of the California government, a document issued in the time of the Spanish Government, dated 1781, in which the boundary from the 32d deg. 30 min. to the 42d deg. 30 min. of north latitude divides the Great Desert, leaving one half to the jurisdiction of New Mexico, and the other half to Upper California: I do not say that this line was ever formally laid down by official survey, but that such a line did exist dividing the Great Desert in two is, I think, sufficiently established by the document to which I refer."

Mr. Halleck next spoke and said that he and Mr. Hartnell had about a year before overhauled the old archives and found among them in the old custom house the first map that was ever drawn of California. From this map Halleck said all the maps of California have been made. Jose Antonio Carrillo said, "I recollect perfectly well having seen a document among the archives of the government at Los Angeles when I was alcalde of that place and I examined it with great care, and I have no doubt myself that an order was sent from the Spanish government in 1781, making this line from 32 or 32½ degrees north latitude to 42, cutting the Great Desert in two."

In spite of a few long-winded speakers, the six weeks of debate were carried on in a spirit of amity, and resulted in a State Constitution for California; the constitutions of Iowa and New York most often serving as examples. Notable was the prohibition of slavery by unanimous vote.

On Friday, October 12th, a copy of the complete constitution was given to General Bennett Riley, with the request that he forward the same to the President of the United States. A resolution was passed thanking Dr. Semple for the faithful and impartial manner in which he had discharged the arduous and responsible duties of the chair.

THE CONVENTION BALL

The delegates to the Convention by assessing themselves $25 each raised $1,000 to provide a ball for the entertainment of the citizens of Monterey, a village of 1,500 people. The Convention hall was cleared of the rostrum and the delegates' desks, and was decorated with pine boughs from the nearby forests and with red, white, and blue bunting.

At eight o'clock the guests began to arrive; among them in full uniform was General Riley, wearing the yellow sash he had won in Mexico at Contreras. He was accompanied by other officers stationed in Monterey.

Handsome Don Pablo de la Guerra from Santa Barbara was floor manager and, as "El Tecolero," gallantly welcomed some sixty members of the gentler sex—dark-eyed senoritas and fair-skinned "Norte Americanos." Among the latter was Jessie Benton Fremont, dressed in a red brocade and dark skirt (in contrast to her Washington City ball-gowns of tarlatan and satin). Her husband who had resigned from the Army after his court-martial, was away prospecting for gold on his Mariposa land of 40,000 acres which had been bought for him by Consul Larkin for $3,000.

Mrs. Fremont, the daughter of U.S. Senator Benton of Missouri, was always ambitious for her husband, and no doubt thought it wise to attend the ball, making personal contacts as Fremont's name had been mentioned as a candidate for the United States Senate from California. Fremont's sponsors argued that he was the logical candidate, since Fremont's explorations had made him a popular hero, and his maps were guiding the long lines of covered wagons westward. Besides, his services they thought had helped to secure California for the United States.

Bayard Taylor, the reporter for Horace Greeley's *New York Tribune*, attended the ball in borrowed evening clothes. Among the distinguished guests he particularly noticed was General Vallejo's tall erect figure. His quiet dignity impressed Taylor, as did also the good-humored Swiss Captain Sutter who was short and stout. Music was provided by two violins and two guitars playing three pieces alternately—the waltz, the quadrille and the graceful contra-danza which was like a minuet, the steps being taken slowly to waltz time. At twelve o'clock a supper of baked turkey, roast pig, beef and tongue was served; with wines and liquors in the courtyard on the lower floor. Most of the guests left about two o'clock a.m.; however, some remained until dawn.

Padre Antonio Ramirez who had opened a number of the Constitutional Convention sessions with prayer, was at the ball in his clerical cassock and remained until a late hour.

LAST DAY OF CONVENTION

The morning session of the last day of the Convention, October 13th, was presided over by Captain Sutter; the delegates taking their seats around the hall which still retained the decorations of the ball. In the afternoon Dr. Semple, weak from a siege of typhoid fever, managed to resume the chair. Several resolutions were passed, one tendering thanks to the Trustees of Colton Hall for the use of the building.

The engrossed copy of the State Constitution, which had been prepared on parchment by Lieutenant Hamilton for the sum of $500, was circulated among the delegates for their signatures. At that moment, the American colors were run up on the flag staffs in front of the Government buildings and the guns fired a salute. Captain Sutter, with deep emotion, sprang from his seat and exclaimed, "Gentlemen, this is the happiest day of my life. It makes me glad to hear those cannon. They remind me of the time when I was a soldier. Yes, I am glad to hear them, this is a great day for California." The members gave three cheers, whereupon, on motion of Mr. Gwin, Captain Sutter was asked to address General Riley on behalf of the Convention after its adjournment. Then, on motion of Mr. McCarver, the Convention adjourned *sine die*. The members went in a body to General Riley's house, where Captain Sutter addressed the General as follows:

> I have been appointed by the delegates elected by the people of California to form a Constitution, to address you in their names and in behalf of the whole people of California and express the thanks of the Convention for the aid and cooperation they have received from you in the discharge of the responsible duty of creating a State Government. And, Sir, the great and important service you have rendered our common country and especially to the people of California and entertains the confident belief that you will receive from the whole people of the United States when you retire from your official duties here that verdict, so grateful to the heart of a patriot, "Well done, thou good and faithful servant."

General Riley was deeply touched with the words of appreciation and replied: "Gentlemen—I never made a speech in my life, I am a soldier, but I can *feel*. And I do feel deeply the honor you have this day conferred upon me. Gentlemen, this is a prouder day to me than that on which my soldiers cheered me on the field of Contreras. I thank you all, from my heart. I am satisfied now the people have done right in selecting delegates to form a Constitution. They have chosen a body of men upon whom our country may look with pride; you have formed a Constitution worthy of California. And I have no fear for California, Gentlemen, I congratulate you upon the successful conclusion of your arduous labors; and I wish you all happiness and prosperity."

In order that the State Constitution might be ratified by the people and the public officials chosen, General Riley called for an election to be held November 13th. As a result of the election Peter H. Burnett was given the honor of being California's first governor. In the Sonoma District, there was a contest between M. G. Vallejo and Jonas Spect, a Methodist clergyman. It was thought first that Spect had been elected State Senator but when the final authentic returns came in from Larkin's ranch, they proved that Vallejo had been elected State Senator.

CALIFORNIA'S FIRST STATE LEGISLATURE

The members of the first State Legislature assembled in the pueblo of San Jose on December 15, 1849. A quorum not being present, the body adjourned until Monday, the 17th. The citizens at the November election had chosen all the public officials except the United States Senators. This was left to their Representatives in the State Legislature. Seven names were presented: John C. Fremont, William M. Gwin, Henry W. Halleck, John W. Geary, Robert Semple, Thomas Butler King, and Thomas J. Henley. Not a native Californian was mentioned!

Colonel Fremont, in the interest of his candidacy, sought out Vallejo for an interview, with the result that Senator Elect Vallejo of Sonoma District not only promised to vote for him but also wrote to his nephew, Senator Pablo de la Guerra of Santa Barbara, advising him to do likewise. Vallejo wrote:

> It is essential that you and the other Californians give your vote to Captain Fremont; this I advise for the following reasons: First, because I admire and value every independent man, persevering in his endeavors and endowed with valor in every test. These three I consider to a great extent are combined in the person of Fremont; Second, that since the United States has been in control, swarms of corrupt politicians have come, some with pretence that they are representing California . . . These people do not know us and consequently don't like us, although they talk otherwise; what interests them is to exploit us.
>
> You and others who live in Santa Barbara will have little of this but I and my neighbors who live in the very nest of the hawk would soon be victims, if we don't guard with a vigilant eye the people who break the laws and especially those who represent us in Washington where with one blow of the pen, they can make us happy or miserable . . . Fremont has a good heart; not even his enemies have dared to accuse him of being corrupt and not a few times have I heard him say that he had a great appreciation for the Californians and for that reason I consider him worthy of our vote. I have promised to vote for him and I hope you too will vote for that

gentleman who promises much good. What I have listed are the reasons, which in my role as a public figure makes me prefer Fremont to Mr. Butler King, for whom I have a real appreciation.

Fremont made me a visit and gave me complete satisfaction for the rough and violent treatment that the "bears" rained upon me and the troops that accompanied him when I was a prisoner of war. Among other things he told me that though he very much wanted to better my condition, he could not do it because his companions watched all his actions. I send these lines to let you know that in working for the election of Fremont I have no other motive than the interests of California and seeing it being represented with dignity in Washington.

Vallejo's credulity in this instance can only be explained by his fervent desire to have a man of "dignity" and education, instead of a professional politician represent California in Congress.

On December 20th the two Houses of the California Legislature proceeded to elect two United States Senators. The names were called and the voting was *viva voce*. General Vallejo was not present to cast his vote for Fremont because of the error, already mentioned, in reporting the returns from the Sonoma District. Jonas Spect cast the vote for Fremont. Vallejo's thirty-year-old nephew Pablo de la Guerra heeded his uncle's advice and voted for Fremont for United States Senator.

John Charles Fremont was declared to have received a majority of all the votes cast on the first ballot and was "duly elected to the office of United States Senator." After two more ballots, William M. Gwin was elected as the other United States Senator from California.

That evening the newly-elected Senator Fremont rode 70 miles through the winter's wind and rain to Monterey to greet Mrs. Fremont. At the door of their home, he called to his wife, "I couldn't wait; I've ridden from San Jose to be the first to greet Jessie Fremont, Senator's Lady from the State of California."

State Senator Vallejo

With the correction of the election returns from Sonoma County, Vallejo took his seat as State Senator on December 27th; he was introduced by State Senator Pablo de la Guerra, the nephew who was to serve four years.

Lieutenant-Governor John McDougal, presiding officer of the State Senate, was aware of Vallejo's ability. He appointed him on the Committee of Claims, Engrossed Bills, Militia, Privileges and Elections, Roads and Fences, Corporations and the Committee of Counties and County boundaries. On motion of Vallejo, a special committee was appointed to report to the Senate on the "Derivation and Definition of the Names of Several Counties." Vallejo became the chairman and presented his written report on April 16th. It was so well received, being filled with authoritative historic information, that 2,000 copies in English and 1,000 copies in Spanish were ordered and printed for the use of the members of the Legislature.

It is interesting to note how Senator Vallejo voted on some of the bills. One was introduced "to strike out the word *eighteen* as an age at which females might marry without consent of parents and insert the word *sixteen*." He voted no. Then the word *thirteen* was suggested for insertion; Vallejo voted no again. The age *seventeen* was suggested and Vallejo still voted no. As a father who then had four daughters, he was particularly interested in this bit of legislation. A resolution was introduced for postponement of a bill to prevent the immigration of Free Negroes and Persons of Color into California. Vallejo voted for postponement. The vote of Senator Vallejo helped to pass "An Act for the government and protection of the Indians."

On January 3, 1850 Vallejo wrote to his wife, Francisca:

> There hasn't been one single good day . . . I think as soon as the weather moderates I'll take a run up to the house and see all the family. I am not happy away from home; I miss all when I don't see them and it is a great emptiness that I suffer both physically and mentally. Take good care of all the family and see that they don't fail to study every day, Give counsel to Jose and Andronico since they are young men, about the things they need, as well as the girls who are already in their adolescence and need good example and advice. Kiss and embrace all the little ones especially [5 yrs] Uladislao. Tell him to be happy. When you receive this letter give all the children something with which to buy sweets, also give some to the Indians. Greet Don Pepe (Jose de la Rosa) and have the room where he lives well fixed up.
>
> (Signed) I am, as always,
>
> GUADALUPE

As early as January 28th, Senator Vallejo had learned that many of the members of the Legislature were dissatisfied with San Jose as the site of the seat of Government. He wrote his wife: "Tomorrow I'll be very busy working to get the Capital to Sonoma or to the Soscol, near the mouth of the Soscol Estuary where I have offered a piece of land." Vallejo's offer of this land and $370,000 for the public buildings, Vallejo incorporated into a formal Memorial. Senator David C. Broderick, who was the chairman of the Committee on Public Buildings and Grounds, presented, "An Act to take the sense of the people of California upon the subject of the Permanent Location of the Seat of Government." At the same time Senator Broderick presented his report in writing. The Committee on Public Buildings, he said, had under consideration various propositions for the permanent location of the seat of government, all of which were of liberal character but the Committee would not hesitate to recommend the acceptance of General Vallejo's offer. In his remarks Broderick continued:

> Your Committee cannot dwell with too much warmth upon the magnificent propositions contained in the Memorial of General Vallejo. They breathe throughout the spirit of an enlarged mind and sincere public benefactor, for which he deserves the thanks of his countrymen and the admiration of the world. Such a proposition looks more like the legacy of a mighty Emperor to his people than the free donation of a private planter to a great State, yet poor in finances but soon to be among the first on earth.

Your Committee in view of the magnitude on the subject, and near the close of this first session of the Legislature and believing that the people of the State should be consulted upon so great a question recommend the passage of the bill.

Both Houses passed the bill and it was signed by Governor Burnett on Monday April 22nd, the last day of the first session of the Legislature. In the absence of Lieutenant-Governor McDougal, the president pro-tempore of the Senate, E.Kirby Chamberlin, in accordance with a joint resolution of the two Houses, adjourned *sine die*, the *First* Legislature, the Legislature which had laid the foundation of Laws for California.

Referring to Vallejo's offer, "The Annals of San Francisco" [1854] said, "His princely proposition to the State to make a point on his estate the seat of government is well known; and some idea of the people's universal estimation of his integrity may be gathered from the fact, that in all the angry discussions to which it gave rise, his high and honorable motives were never questioned."

CALIFORNIA ADMITTED TO THE UNION

The Californians had elected their two Representatives, George W. Wright and Edward Gilbert and their first Legislature had chosen William M. Gwin and John C. Fremont as their United States Senators.

There was some delay in admitting California to the Union. While waiting, the California Delegation prepared a Memorial addressed to both Houses of Congress stressing the fact that its Constitution resulted from a spontaneous movement by the American settlers. The Memorial closed with these words:

"This people request admission into the American Union as a State. They understand and estimate the advantages which will accrue to them from such a connection while they trust they do not too highly compute those which will be conferred upon their brethren, They do not present themselves as supplicants, nor do they bear themselves with arrogance or presumption. They come as free American citizens, citizens by treaty, by adoption and by birth, and ask that they may be permitted to reap the common benefits, share the common ills, and promote the common welfare as one of the United States of America.

WILLIAM M. GWIN
JOHN C. FREMONT
GEORGE W. WRIGHT
EDWARD GILBERT

Henry Clay introduced his famous *Omnibus Bill* which included the admission of California. Speeches from the "Big Four" of the Senate followed. Senator John C. Calhoun's opposition speech was read by Senator Mason of Virginia while the ill leader of South Carolina listened. Daniel Webster gave one full of oratory and logic and Senator Seward of New York declared in his maiden speech that "California is already a State. She can never be less."

The Senate by a vote of 38 to 14 decided on August 13th, 1850 to admit California. The bill encountered strenuous resistance in the House but finally it was ratified on the 7th of September by a vote of 150 to 56. On September 9th, 1850 the new President Millard Fillmore (President Zachary Taylor having died July 9th) placed his signature on the bill making California the thirty-first state of the American Union.

The Land Commission

In 1851 a Land Commission of three members was sent to California to hear the claims of the land owners. Vallejo early filed his claims for his land. Confirmation was received from the Land Commission in regard to the Soscol and the Petaluma Ranchos. In both cases appeals were granted and the cases taken before the U.S. District Court. While waiting for the decision in the case of the Petaluma Rancho, an attachment was placed upon it by the principal law firm handling land cases, its members being Henry W. Halleck, A. C. Peachy and Fred Billings. This firm in order to collect from Vallejo the sum of $15,252 evidently legal fees, attached not only the Petaluma Rancho but also the Casa Grande (then being used as a girls' school, *St. Mary's Hall*) and the barracks, both of these buildings facing on the Sonoma plaza, and in addition Vallejo's new residence at Lachryma Montis.

Henry W. Halleck, the senior member of the firm, had come to California in January 1847, after a sea voyage around the Horn. Among his fellow passengers on board the *Lexington* was young William T. Sherman who, like himself, was to become one of the famous Civil War generals. On the voyage to California, Halleck spent his time reading Wilke's Exploring Expedition, Dana's *Two Years Before the Mast* and Forbes' account of the California Missions, in order to acquaint himself with the California scene.

In the law firm, Halleck's partners were A. C. Peachy, a city attorney of San Francisco, and Frederick Billings who had been the attorney-general of California. When the firm sent out their professional announcements, they included as references the names of 28 leading native Californians and pioneer citizens, among them General Vallejo.

Vallejo—A Democrat

While in San Jose attending the Legislature, Vallejo was asked to serve on the Democratic Party Committee. To the invitation he replied:

> Your polite communication has informed me that I have been placed upon the Democratic Committee . . . With many thanks for the compliment, more flattering because wholly unsolicitated but I must beg to decline the honor conferred upon me until I become more truly acquainted with the principles of our two great parties that are trying to get control of the politics of California.
>
> Such being my firm determination, you will I hope not press me for the present for I do not consider it consistent with the interests of the State to take a hasty resolution or embrace blindly principles which I have not yet had time to study carefully.
>
> When the platforms and principles of each party are placed clearly before me, I shall be happy to act with one or the other but in the meantime I must beg the privilege of voting for the man whom I believe will most, especially without regard to party sustain the interests of California.

Later Vallejo became a member of the Democratic Party and remained a Democrat the balance of his life. His future son-in-law, young Captain John B. Frisbie, was a Democrat. The latter had won the admiration and confidence of General Vallejo to such an extent that on July 3, 1850, Vallejo executed a document appointing "John B. Frisbie of the City of Benicia" his true and lawful attorney with control over most of Vallejo's property, especially that of the Soscol Rancho. Frisbie immediately began to promote the development of the area as the proposed site of the Capital of California. To advertise, he wrote for publication:

This place, the proposed seat of Government, for the State of California is bound on the East by the City of Benicia, on the South by the Straits of Carquinez and on the West by the Bay of Napa . . . As a location for a large city its topography is unsurpassed in California . . . I am authorized to dispose of a limited number of lots upon liberal terms and I invite the attention of Capitalists and the public generally to the new City.

Frisbie was not the only person helping to develop the city of Vallejo. George W. Wright, one of California's first two Representatives in Congress, was also interested. On the stationery of the House of Representatives, he wrote on January 25, 1851 to Vallejo:

You will please accept my heartfelt thanks for your unbounded kindness in making me one of the original proprietors in the City of Vallejo . . . Our Bill for a Sectional Dry Dock with basin and railway has passed both Houses and the Secretary of the Navy has a contract with Messrs Lecoy & Co. for the construction of the dock at one million, four hundred and forty thousand dollars . . . I consider the location of the Government Docks at this point as being of the utmost importance to Vallejo; it will necessarily bring all the shipping to that port for repair. I have used every exertion to locate the mint at Vallejo but the committee has reported against it.

On February 19th, General Vallejo appeared before Robert R. Pierpont and signed the statement in reference to his bond for $500,000 in connection with the Capital site development.

"MARIANO G. VALLEJO of the City and County of Sonoma being duly sworn, doth depose and say he is the person named and described in the foregoing bond: and deponent further saith that he is worth in property, real and personal, one million dollars over and above all liabilities or demands against him. And deponent further saith, that his entire estate is unencumbered and further deponent saith not."

At the same time John B. Frisbie swore he was worth $75,000 and Salvador Vallejo, $250,000.

SECOND SESSION OF THE LEGISLATURE

General Vallejo, having drawn the short term as a State Senator, was replaced at the second session by Martin E. Cooke who represented the 11th Senatorial District, which then comprised the Counties of Sonoma, Solano, Napa, Marin, Colusa, Yolo and Trinity. At this second session, held again in San Jose, Senator Cooke gave the Majority Report of the Committee for the Permanent Site for the Seat of Government. He reported that "it appeared that the people had in their sovereign capacity as electors have instructed this Legislature to fix the permanent location of the Capital at Vallejo." That site had received 8,949 votes of the people, while San Jose, the nearest competitor among 19 other suggested places, received 1,371 votes.

Opposition had developed against the Vallejo site, and this opposition was expressed in the Minority Report presented by Senator George B. Tingley, who said that the proposition was deception; it looked handsome when arrayed in tall figures but it was a speculative project. He said that no deed had been made to the State, and it was not known if Vallejo could make a good title.

The last charge was answered by Vallejo, who wrote to the Senate and Assembly that he had executed title to the State and had placed the same in the hands of the Governor. Vallejo also said that he had named General Persifor F. Smith and John B. Frisbie as Commissioners to serve with three others, who would be selected by the members of the Legislature. The Commissioners were to select the sites for the various public buildings at the new site for the Capital. On the 19th of February, Vallejo gave bond for $500,000 and as recorded before, he swore he was worth in property, real and personal, one million dollars.

Soon after the Legislature convened, Governor Burnett sent in his resignation and Lieutenant-Governor McDougal was inaugurated as the second Chief Executive of California.

As Senator Fremont's short term as United States Senator from California would expire March 4th, the two Houses met in joint session to fill the vacancy. Among the candidates besides Fremont, were T. Butler King, a former Congressman from Georgia, and John W. Geary, San Francisco's first postmaster and also first Mayor. One hundred and forty-two ballots were cast. None of the candidates having received a majority of votes, this session of the Legislature adjourned without naming the new Senator. The Legislature was to meet again in January 1852.

THIRD SESSION OF THE LEGISLATURE

The delegates to the third session of the Legislature met in the "City" of Vallejo, on January 5, 1852 in spite of Governor McDougal's protests. Senator George B. Tingley who had led the opposition against the transfer of the Capital from San Jose to Vallejo in the first place, presented a protest against *remaining* at Vallejo. Tingley said that General Vallejo had not provided a suitable building for legislative purposes, nor offices to protect the archives and property of the State. He said that he believed that the General would not redeem his bond nor his obligation of $370,000 to the State. Aside from this opposition there had been unfavorable publicity; the San Francisco Evening Picayune editorialized as follows on July 16, 1851:

VALLEJO—WHERE IS THE CAPITAL?

When the last Legislature acceded to the proposals of General Vallejo and determined to remove the seat of Government from San Jose to the imaginery City where it is now located, many and indeed nearly all the intelligent men who were not interested personally in the matter, prophesied that the whole movement would speedily explode and show the folly of the originators of the scheme and produce serious loss and inconvenience to the State. The prophecy will be verified. In the first place it was obviously impossible for General Vallejo or any other individual with resources less than infinite to fulfill the stupendous promises that he made to the State.

General Vallejo had tried to provide a satisfactory building for the sessions of the Legislature. A three-story frame building had been started on Capitol Hill, but due to the scarcity of labor, it had been left unfinished. Vallejo drew up a contract with J. Bacheldor and A. P. Petit for its completion. They were told to eliminate the contemplated dome. The finishing work was to be done for $16,000. The basement of the State House was leased to James M. Estell, no doubt for the purpose of providing liquid refreshment. The money to pay Bacheldor and Petit was perhaps secured from James King of William, as, shortly before (September 24, 1851) Vallejo borrowed $18,000 from the San Francisco banker giving a mortgage on a portion of the Petaluma Rancho.

The Legislature only remained four days in Vallejo. The members found the State House unfurnished and the rostrum not built. Chairs were scarce; boards were placed on stools and nail kegs. Rooms were hard to find; one hundred persons were forced to seek quarters on the steamer *Empire* on which they had come to Vallejo. Food was limited and there were no laundry facilities. The legislators began to complain. On January 9th, they voted removal of the Capital to Sacramento where they had been promised the good things of life. They left on the same day aboard the *Empire* for Sacramento, where they were welcomed with a ball.

John B. Frisbie had been in Sacramento lobbying for his father-in-law's project. He wrote to A. C. Peachy who was a member of the Legislature, saying that General Vallejo had instructed him to submit the proposition that his bond be canceled and that the town of Vallejo be retained as the seat of Government; in consideration the General would deed to the State the public buildings already erected and also one undivided fourth of the town of Vallejo. Should this proposition fail, Vallejo proposed that the contract removing the seat of Government be canceled and General Vallejo reimbursed for actual expenditures. Having written the foregoing to Peachy, Frisbie wrote the same day to Vallejo:

> There is now a fair prospect of bringing the Vallejo business to a conclusion; the present indications are that the capital will go back and you released from your bond. A concurrent resolution passed the Assembly this morning directing the Archives back to Vallejo after the close of the present session; tomorrow we shall

try the resolution cancelling the bond and I have no doubt that it will pass. Whatever is done, I think will be without delay.

Sacramento River floods rather than Vallejo's proposition drove the legislators back to the town of Vallejo for the 1853 session. In January of that year Vallejo sent a communication to the lawmakers saying, that due to unforeseen embarrassments resulting in a large measure from the repeated removals of the State Archives, he must ask to have his bond canceled. The only answer from the Legislature was the passage of the Concurrent Resolution, imposing on the governor the duty of demanding from Vallejo the sum of "$500,000 mentioned in his bond."

On January 27th, 1853 Vallejo wrote to His Excellency John Bigler, Governor:

> My attention has this moment been called to a concurrent resolution of the Legislature imposing upon your Excellency the duty of demanding from me certain sums of money recited in a bond executed by me on or about the 4th day of February A.D. 1851 to the State of California . . . I have already advised the Legislature in a communication addressed to them at its last session that in consequence of unforeseen embarrassments resulting in a very great degree from the repeated removal of the State archives from Vallejo to other points since the passage of the Law establishing the seat of Government at Vallejo, the resources upon which I mainly relied to discharge the bond referred to had been entirely destroyed and the enterprise brought into discredit.
>
> I was compelled to ask that myself and that the securities might be discharged from any further liability upon the said bond and that the same should be cancelled and annuled and I beg through your Excellency to renew this request . . . I hope that this proposition may meet the approbation of your Excellency and the Legislature.

The Concurrent Resolution was approved by the Governor, but, before the action could be carried out, the Legislature passed an Act on February 4th to remove the seat of Government from the City of Vallejo to the City of Benicia, thus accepting the invitation of Mayor David M. Fraser of Benicia. This act of the Legislature moving the seat of Government to Benicia, caused Vallejo to feel that it relieved him legally from the performance of his bond; if a Release could be approved by the Attorney-General, S. Clinton Hastings; the Attorney-General upon being requested, approved the Release on February 14th and a copy was transmitted February 17th to the State Senate and Assembly at Benicia by Governor John Bigler.

Being apprehensive of the outcome of the Capital business, Vallejo some time before, was glad to shed the financial burdens connected with the complex politics of State Government and return to the security of his home and the comparative simplicity of Sonoma's local government. He accepted membership on the Sonoma City Council on May 4, 1851 and was appointed on a Committee to grade and improve the Plaza, repair the bridge at its southeast corner, and make plans for building a school house. Vallejo was asked to give legal names to the Sonoma city streets. He changed the name Calle Principale, the wide street entering Sonoma, to *Broadway*. Other streets were named Spain, England, France, Germany, Russia, Brazil, Chile and many other countries of the world. Truly, the first birth of the Nations in California.

1851—LARKIN BUYS BOOKS FOR VALLEJO

It was in January of 1851 that Governor McDougal placed Mariano G. Vallejo and James Estell in charge of the State Convicts, the prison grounds and buildings for ten years. By the contract Vallejo and his partner undertook the guarding, safekeeping and maintenance of all convicts in consideration of their labor, without cost, trouble or expense to the state. No doubt Vallejo was only too glad later to sublease the contract to John S. Hays, sheriff of San Francisco and to John Caperton.

When Vallejo, at home in Sonoma, learned that Thomas O. Larkin was planning to take a trip east to look after his real estate holdings in New York City, Vallejo gave him $1,000 to buy some books and school materials. In June the General received a letter from Roe Lockwood and Son, Book Sellers, Publishers and Importers of Foreign Books in New York City:

> About two weeks since, Thomas O. Larkin showed us a Commission from you to purchase some Spanish, French and English books together with some music and drawing materials to the amount of one thousand dollars. Unfortunately we did not have on hand at that time the Spanish books you ordered. Some we had sold but a short time before and some we had never imported. We offered to order them but Mr. Larkin said that would take too much time for us to do so. After looking over our stock, he ordered a set of the Spanish classics in 47 volumes for your own library. He then authorized us to add a good collection of smaller Spanish books and the other articles you mentioned . . . We are aware of the high position you hold and you can by your influence give us considerable amount of business which we hope you will do so.

The books were shipped. While many of them were destroyed in the Casa Grande fire of April 13, 1867, the 47 volumes of Spanish classics rest in their scarlet covers on an upper shelf of General Vallejo's bookcase in his historic home. Besides his own books, Vallejo found room to store those belonging to Philosopher Pickett. Regarding them, on October 21, 1851 Pickett wrote to Vallejo from Sacramento:

> The frequent fires in San Francisco have destroyed nearly all the newspapers of olden times in this country which causes me to feel more solicitous of those left along with my books in your care. Please take the best of care of my effects and you will greatly oblige me by collecting and preserving all such papers as you may have stored away. I observed one of the boxes was open when we looked at them a few weeks since; this, you had better have it nailed securely.
>
> I shall write you to send them to me when I get established in San Francisco. I am trying another plan to raise money to start my paper. All my Californian friends must take it and give it as wide circulation as possible as I intend opening their eyes

to the great mass of villainy going on in this once happy and contented but now infamous blood stained polluted land. I wish to show the rancheros of California who are being swindled and robbed out of all their property; that it is not the Sydney rogues nor Squatters who are doing it but the big talking and swelling bugs, Legislators, Judges, lawyers, bankers, merchants and speculators in whom they have trusted and hithertofore placed great confidence; those are the real rogues and the men to be dreaded. Be kind enough to speak to Mr. Boggs, Don Salvador and others you may think has them, to preserve all the old newspapers spoken of.

LACHRYMA MONTIS

On March 28th, 1850, on a motion introduced by Senator Vallejo at the first session of the State Legislature, the town of Sonoma was incorporated as a city. Jasper O'Farrell was sent to survey it. O'Farrell was the pioneer civil engineer who had enlarged and corrected the first survey of Yerba Buena, made by Captain Juan Vioget, and had also, with the aid of James M. Hudspeth, surveyed the site for the town of Benicia in the spring of 1847. The original survey of the pueblo of Sonoma had been made in 1840 by Vallejo, assisted by Captain William Richardson and Augustin Davilla. As a result of O'Farrell's survey in 1850 and E. T. Peabody's map, Sonoma town lots of 109 square varas were put on sale at the price of $9.25. The alert Yankees were the early birds and bought up the more desirable lots. Many of these men had come to California to mine for gold but soon found it was easier to acquire precious metal by dealing in real estate.

The activity around the plaza in Sonoma was such that General Vallejo decided to move from the Casa Grande to quieter surroundings. He selected an area northwest of the town on the shelter of an oak-covered hill. He chose the spot because of the artesian spring, whose abundant water had attracted the Indians there long before Vallejo saw it. The Indians called it *Chiucuyem*, which Vallejo translated into the Latin equivalent *Lachryma Montis* (Mountain Tear). It was on this spot that Vallejo camped with his soldiers for eight days before proceeding to the area near the San Francisco Solano Mission to found the pueblo of Sonoma under orders of Governor Figueroa.

Vallejo, once the owner of leagues of land, found that in 1850 he had to go to the American settlers to buy the acreage he needed for his homeplace near the spring. One of the 109 square vara lots (No. 344) which a John McCracken had bought in June, 1849 for $50, was sold to Vallejo eleven months later for $1,000. This was the lot on which Vallejo built his *almacen* or brick store-house, which provided temporary storage for his fruit, wine and general supplies for the ranch and home. In the loft he stored grain. The building was erected from timbers cut and numbered in Europe. The panels were filled with bricks which had been used as ballast in sailing vessels. Its large timbers were joined with lock-joints and the smaller ones with wooden pegs. The lot on which the Vallejo residence at Lachryma Montis was built was bought, together with eight other lots from the Canadian Oliver Bolieu for $6,000 on November 20, 1849. The lots numbered on the early map as Nos. 341, 342, 343, 345, 346, 352, 353, 354, 356.

At the time that Lachryma Montis was in the process of construction, bricks often cost $1.00 each and lumber $500 per 1,000 feet. The residence was built of redwood cut from Vallejo's forests and prepared at his lumber mill. It was quite unlike his earlier adobe home; however, he put adobe bricks between the walls for insulation. It was and is a two-story frame dwelling of the Victorian period, so-called modern gothic; a duplicate of such a house was built for Joseph Bonaparte, the exile King of Naples in Bordentown, New Jersey.

At the time Joseph Bonaparte was in the United States, young Joseph Warren Revere was in Rome, Italy. With a small group of American officers he called on Napoleon's mother, Mme. Letitia, who received them cordially and asked after her son Joseph. One of the young officers had recently seen him which pleased her.

When it was learned that Vallejo had bought the property with the spring, the City Council of Sonoma passed an ordinance declaring the spring was public property. Whereupon Vallejo protested to the Council:

> Your petitioner having learned with astonishment that an ordinance passed your Honorable Body lately, declaring certain Spring public property. Your petitioner believed when he purchased the land, he purchased also the waters, no exception having been made; he has no objection to allowing the City any privilege within the power of your petitioner when not conflicting with his private interests but consider it as done without due consideration and would solicit the repeal of such ordinance.

The ordinance was repealed and the General had the spring of tepid water as his own. Its genial influence stimulated vegetation and the growth of his orchards. Tropical fruits did especially well. Vallejo had 200 flourishing orange trees. As many as 600 oranges were taken from one tree. He had fifty pomegranates and an equal number of fig trees. Other fruits on the place were olives, pears, cherries, nectarines, peaches, apples, lemons; the pomelo (Oriental grapefruit revered as good luck by the Chinese) and several varieties of berries: also the tuna of the cacti and one banana plant.

Vallejo's deep interest in horticulture had continued from the time of his planting fruit and vines in the rear of the Casa Grande. A Mr. Warren asked Vallejo to exhibit at the Agricultural and Horticultural Fair which he was promoting in San Francisco. Captain Sutter sent one of Warren's circulars to Major Bidwell in August, 1852, saying, "I wish you could make it convenient to be present at this Fair; if you have to exhibit anything, it would be good to communicate with Mr. Warren on account of the room. I hope to get a silver cup for the grapes."

On September 5th of the following year Mr. Warren wrote Vallejo: "We have many times learned of your devotion to agriculture and the great success which has attended your efforts and we most earnestly desire your co-operation for the coming exhibits. We do assure you that it would add a great value to the Fair to see fruits and other specimens from Gen. Vallejo's grounds. You must be aware, dear Sir, that in a new country like this, the people look upon the early pioneers with a veneration and a respect most worthy. We would esteem it a special kindness if you would favor us with a call when in this city that we may lay before you the full plans of the coming Fair and receive your aid and counsel in matter of how we may best advance this noble work." Vallejo was agreeable to Warren's suggestion. He exhibited at the Fair (1853) and was awarded a silver medal for his fine fruits.

MAYOR M. G. VALLEJO

On May 3, 1852, Vallejo was elected Mayor of Sonoma; he received 60 votes, his opponent C. Bruner received two votes! In Vallejo's first message as Mayor, he thanked the citizens of Sonoma for the distinguished honor they had conferred on him by selecting him to preside over the councils of the city; he said he felt a diffidence in his own ability, but their confidence was a source of pride and an incentive to faithful and efficient discharge of the trust. He also added that he was pleased with the gentlemen selected to work with him on the Council. In closing he said, "You will not regard it as affectation, Gentlemen, when I tell you that as a citizen, I have watched the growth and prosperity of Sonoma with paternal interest. It is peculiarly the land of my predilection. At an early period of my life while the entire country, north of the Bay of San Francisco was peopled exclusively by the savages I had occasion to visit professionally the Valley of Sonoma; impressed by the beauty of the scenery and the benignity of its climate, its pure mountain streams and its rich and fertile soil, I, at once, notwithstanding the danger by which a settlement in the midst of hostile savages was encompassed, determined to establish here my home. Marked, have been the changes since that time. A spiritual and enterprising people have followed the indolent Indian and this noble valley, then but a magnificent hunting ground, teeming it was true with the most luxurient vegetation but as wild as the race who tracked it, has since become what we now behold it, one of the richest agricultural districts known to civilization."

Mayor Vallejo told the Councilmen that he felt that the education of the children should be given the first consideration, and that among the matters of secondary importance was the improvement of the plaza. He said its present condition was a source of severe criticism from every stranger who visited Sonoma, and that it was not a very gratifying testimonial of the taste and enterprise of Sonoma's citizens. Mayor Vallejo offered to give a lot facing the plaza for the public school, but it was not accepted as it was thought the site would be too public.

On January 26, 1853, Vallejo as Mayor signed an ordinance whereby "all merchants, groceries and hotels facing the plaza were to pay licenses at the rate of three dollars per month, the money collected to be used for the improvement of the Sonoma plaza, such as grading and leveling the public square.

Mayor Vallejo maintained and enforced strict obedience to the City of Sonoma's ordinances but in so kind a manner that none took offense. When vaqueros and rancheros, his own countrymen, would come racing and whooping into town and be arrested for fast driving in the streets, he would enforce the penalty of the law with the fine of $5 in each case, and if they did not have the money, he would pay the fines for them, himself.

The first years at Lachryma Montis were busy and fruitful. Aside from his interest in the politics of Sonoma, Vallejo was busy with the development of his estate and the education of his children. His fortune at this time was ample. How near Lachryma Montis came to being an answer to Vallejo's quest for comfort and material happiness is answered by the following dissertation written by Vallejo.

TO LIVE HAPPILY ONE NEEDS

To have a good home, good furniture, good carpeting, good bedrooms, good fireplaces for fire in cold weather; water in abundance for everything and in addition good and excellent baths; a good kitchen with its accompanying utensils; a great deal of wood to poke, a good dining room, many and abundant vegetables of all kinds all the year round; in season a great deal of fruit of all kinds, always fresh and preserved, chickens, eggs, milk that is always fresh, ducks and geese; a cook and laundress, etc.

To have a hundred acres of irrigable land planted with fruit trees, grape vines and garden stuff, both to sell and for the use of the family; a permanent water spring, a house located near the spring, good storage houses for keeping the horticultural implements, a buggy for driving gentle horses both saddle and for harnessing. To have another hundred acres (in all 200 acres) of good high land for pasturage which is well forested for different uses which has many cords of wood and in addition stables for horses.

Daily, Vallejo was called upon to meet visitors whom he said he alone could entertain and answer all their questions as if he were a public information officer. Often he was called away from home to give information. A case in point was when on June 6, 1855 he was called before the United States Land Commissioner M. A. Thompson to give a Deposition in regard to the "Nicasio" grant. He was asked what office he held under the Mexican government and what was the nature of his functions in regard to the San Rafael Mission. "I was charged with Colonization, as Director; San Rafael was entrusted to my general superintendence." Vallejo was then asked, "Had you the power as Director to grant mission lands? If yes, where is the decree granting said power and how came Figueroa to make this grant through you?" Vallejo replied: "I had the power to grant Mission lands and other lands;

the power was embodied in my instructions from said governor [Figueroa] to grant lands. These instructions were a matter of public notice and I suppose they are in the archives of the government, taken by the Bear Flag Party in 1846, and I have not seen them since." In closing the questions, Vallejo was told to state how long the Indians had been in possession of the land they cultivated, known as "Nicasio." "Said Indians," replied Vallejo, "were born on said lands and were on them before the secularization and are still in possession. I can not say accurately how much of the land they cultivated."

Vallejo's correspondence was heavy and some letters interesting as the one received from Henry La Reintrie marked "*Confidential.*" La Reintrie, formerly secretary to Commodore Thos. Ap C. Jones, wrote Vallejo in June 1856 that he was "determined to fathom the claim of Jose Y Limantour to the land to which I believe he has set up a fraudulent title." In his letter La Reintre asked Vallejo eleven questions. Among them—"Do you remember the visit which Commo. and suite paid you at Sonoma in December 1842?" Were you on board the *U.S. Cyane* when she lay at Saucelito in December, 1842? Did you receive from Commo. Jones at that time, two globes, one a celestial, the other a terrestial globe?" To these questions Vallejo had in pencil written on the reverse side of the letter: "Que aqui en Sonoma tengo los globos." And to La Reintre's query: "What was the name of the vessel you sold to Jose Y Limantour?" Vallejo had written—"Joven Fanita."

As has been mentioned, these globes, made in Boston in 1834, are in the library of the state-owned Vallejo Home.

In 1853 Jose Y Limantour presented his extraordinary claim to some six hundred thousand acres of land in California, the islands of the Farallones, Alcatraz and Yerba Buena, the peninsula of Tiburon and to four square leagues of land in San Francisco. These grants were signed by Governor Micheltorena and dated 1843. The Land Commission rejected the six hundred acre grants but confirmed those to the San Francisco leagues and to the islands.

The U.S. District Court pronounced the alleged grants forgeries. The fraudulent character of the documents was largely due to Professor George Davidson of the U.S. Coast Survey who had been called as an expert witness for the government. Limantour was arrested and released on a thirty thousand dollar bond. He deposited the money with his bondsmen and fled the country.

EDUCATION FOR THE CHILDREN

Vallejo wished to see that his own children as well as those of others be given a good education, the lasting wealth which could not be affected by the vicissitudes of life. Knowing this, Captain Sutter sent to General Vallejo a young man, "who wished to take the place of preceptor to instruct children of a respectable family." In the letter of introduction, the Swiss Captain wrote, "knowing that you intended always to do a great deal in the education of your children, therefore I take the liberty of recommending the gentleman

. . . You will excuse me not writing to you in Spanish but knowing that you understand English well, I took this liberty. I had wished very much that I could have had the pleasure of seeing you here at Hock Farm but I think it is about with you like me, plenty to do at home."

During the Mexican regime the Vallejo children had tutors, but now that the United States had acquired California, General Vallejo preferred sending them to the better American schools. Andronico, the eldest boy, was sent to Maryland with Platon, who was twelve years old. Uladislao, eight years old, the restless one, was sent to Dr. Blake's school in Benicia. The girls were quite young, so their father thought it best to keep them at home. Vallejo encouraged the Episcopal minister, Dr. John L. Ver Mehr, to open a seminary for young ladies in Sonoma by offering him the Casa Grande for the school.

Dr. Ver Mehr, who had taught school in the girls' school, St. Mary's Hall in the East, was a linguistic scholar of Austrian and Spanish lineage. He emigrated to the United States in 1843. During the Gold Rush, Rodman Price asked Dr. Ver Mehr to establish a mission in California. Arriving in San Francisco in September 1849, he found that his missionary field had been occupied several months by the Rev. Flavel Mines. The disappointed minister decided to found a new parish; its chapel he named *Grace*. There he remained preaching until the year 1853, when he decided to leave the foggy and windy atmosphere of San Francisco for the benign climate of Sonoma. When he arrived in August, 1853 he found that he was unable to move into General Vallejo's house, so he rented school quarters in the home of Senora Josefa Fitch at a rental of $300 a month, until the summer of 1854 when Vallejo redeemed his promise by allowing Dr. Ver Mehr to occupy the spacious Casa Grande at the nominal rent of $145 a month. Adela, Natalia, and Jovita were all pupils at "St. Mary's Hall."

The Vallejo children were growing rapidly, and so were Vallejo's orchards and vineyards. Between educating his children, developing Lachryma Montis, paying legal fees and taxes (the native Californians had never paid taxes on land), General Vallejo was hard pressed financially. Frisbie wrote him during the business depression of 1854, "I have never known a more difficult time to raise money than the present. It is like draining blood from a stone." Needing money, Vallejo in 1956 started proceedings against the United States Government to recover rent for the occupancy of the Barracks. In reference to this coming suit, Frisbie wrote Vallejo on July 16, 1856:

Colonel Stevenson has an order from the Court of Claims at Washington to take testimony in your case for rent of Quarters. I think the Government took possession of the Barracks in July 1846. This will have to be proved by some one residing in Sonoma at the time. Cooper perhaps, or any old resident that your judgment may suggest, also the continued occupation by Brackett in 1847, followed by myself in 1848 and by General Smith from 1849 to 1853. The witnesses that have occured to me are Cooper, Griffith, Cox, Cornwell, Brockman of Napa and Sonoma. I will see Cornwell and Cox myself. Those residing in Sonoma, please see yourself as soon as possible and inform me when you can procure their attendance in San Francisco, the sooner we have the proof in, the sooner you will get your money.

It was a fact that some branch of the United States Services had occupied the Barracks after the raising of the United States flag in California until 1853. General Persifor F. Smith, Commander of the Pacific Division of the Army wrote to General Jones in Washington that "a small company of dragoons is posted at Sonoma . . . I am about to move my headquarters to Sonoma." This he did the latter part of June, 1849 with his staff of Lt. Colonel Joe Hooker, Major Phil Kearney and Lt. George Stoneman, the latter became governor of California.

During the legal proceedings in the U.S. Court of Claims, one of the witnesses for the United States Government was Don Jose S. Berreyesa, son of the elderly Berreyesa who had been shot, together with the De Haro twins, on order of Capt. Fremont in June 1846. When the case opened Jose S. Berreyesa was questioned at length, he testified that he had come to Sonoma as a soldier from Santa Clara in 1837; that he had been employed as a writer for General Vallejo; he had received an appointment as a corporal, and was given a grant of land. During the examination he was asked, "Are you friendly or unfriendly to the General?" He replied, "I have never liked him as a friend." Another question put to Corporal Berreyesa was, "Are you his enemy?" The Corporal answered, "I have said he was not my friend." In pursuit of the same line: "Are you his enemy in any degree?" Berreyesa's answer: "We are enemies in sentiment, in the way of thinking . . . I am an enemy of his interests and property which in my conscience I consider not his property."

Vallejo was able to prove that he had erected the barracks with his own resources. Vallejo did not get the full amount asked but he did receive compensation from the United States government.

With the passing of time, this same Berreyesa realized how wrong his enmity against Vallejo had been. One evening he came to Vallejo's home to offer apologies for the things he had said. The General graciously welcomed him and accepted Berreyesa's apology, saying, "That is quite all right. I never believed a word you said about me. Come in to dinner, the family is just sitting down."

A WAYWARD SON

Among the traditions of the Vallejo family is a story about a little orphan boy, Jose Altamira, whose knowledge of Indian dialects enabled him to warn General Vallejo of a threatened uprising against him. Jose's reward was the gift of being accepted as the General's foster son along with the name of Vallejo. For schooling, he was sent to Valparaiso, Chile, under the guardianship of Faxon Dean Atherton. There he was enrolled in the College of the Sacred Hearts of Jesus and Maria, established by the French Fathers.

On August 10, 1843, Atherton wrote Vallejo that Captain John Wilson had left with him 500 pesos to pay for the expenses of young Jose Vallejo. He reported that he felt that Jose was a youth with many natural gifts and with a desire to study. "As for the school," Atherton said, "in my opinion it is the best that can be had for him. They [the Fathers] take good care of youths of his age for whom there is nothing like horseback rides and carrousels . . . but all such is taken away from him and by the time he returns to his own country he will remember little about being a good horseman."

Two years later, on September 8, 1845, Atherton wrote to Thomas Oliver Larkin, "I wish much that some one would come soon and return to C. [California] again as I desire to send young Vallejo back, he having become tired and desirous to return and has learnt all that will be of any great use to him. Besides his funds have given out, some time since and my own are not in such a state as will admit of too much outlay on the accounts of others. The young fellow is a very decent fellow and has made good progress, writes a good hand, understands arithmetic well and has made a good advance in other studies, especially music of which he appears very "aficionado."

On March 18, 1846 we again find Atherton writing to Larkin, discussing the situation in California, asking many questions: "Are there many Americans coming over the mountains? . . . What is the feeling of the natives towards them? How would they like annexation?, for instance Vallejo, Pio Pico, Alvarado, Bandini, etc."—And a few words relative to Jose Mariano Vallejo. "I endeavored to procure a passage on board the *Congress* for young Vallejo but they are so full of passengers it is impossible. If his father should be in Monterey, have the goodness to tell him that he must send some funds to pay his debts. Already I have advanced three hundred dollars and the poor devil himself has no means of paying."

On December 5, 1846, Vallejo wrote Jose:

Beloved Son:

It was under unfortunate circumstances that I received your last letter because I was a prisoner in the fort of Sacramento at the beginning of the change-over in this country, now in the possessions of the Americans as you probably know. You can imagine how worried and disturbed I was, and especially so to receive news from you that neither my letters nor my remittances of money for your course of studies have arrived at their destination. I am now remitting in care of Mr. Atherton a draft in triplicate for 500 pesos and I am recommending to another gentleman that he open for my account a sight draft to cover the costs of your education and necessary expenses.

I wish like you, that Andronico were there acquiring the precious and enduring treasure of education, but as yet this has not been possible. In spite of attempts because of his physical makeup, although apparently strong, he cannot stand a sea voyage. He gets so very seasick that I don't dare to send him off on a ship. It is possible *now*, it will not be necessary for parents to send their children away in order to give them an education. I hope soon we will have in California, where up to now, ignorance and stupidity have been enthroned, establishments in care of capable professors who will dissipate the dense darkness in which we have lain dorment until now. A fortunate era for youth! I only wish, dear son, that your father had had an opportunity such as you have to acquire an education. Make the most of it, Jose.

You have of course learned something of Mythology and know that Saturn (the god Mercury) has wings. Yes, my son, and Time has wings and flies very rapidly. I would give all my possessions to return to your age and find myself in the circumstances in which you find yourself now. But you well know the scarcity that has existed up to now of all means of education and that little which I was able to acquire was at the cost of sleepness nights, hard study and steady persistence. But I lacked some one to direct and guide me and you have them, willing and capable. Show appreciation therefore by application to your work and by fulfilling my hopes ... I don't think it is necessary but it behooves me to admonish respect and deference toward your teachers.

Andronico, Fanita, Adela and Natalia received the stamps which you sent them. They send you affectionate embraces. They await anxiously your return to the bosom of your family and they miss you more and more. Greetings from Guadalupita, Jovita and Uladislao. And finally your parents send you their blessing and wish you everything that is good.

M. G. VALLEJO

Jose wrote to his father from Valparaiso complaining that he had not received any letters, and that "there was no greater torment than when not getting any news." He said that he had heard about the "ruckus" that D. Jose Castro had made and about the taking of Sonoma by those of the English tongue. Jose said he knew that his father, Uncle Salvador and Don Luis were prisoners, and it distressed him so much that it hindered his studies. He added in his letter, "I wish I knew when you were going to send for me. I am a big boy now and could be of use to you in something. In regard to the sciences, I am getting along fine and you will not have to reproach me. This year I came out on top with awards in the second division in mathematics, arithmetic, algebra, double duty accounting with geometry." And as to impress his father with his maturity he gave his opinion on the Mexican-United States situation, saying, "As to the taking over of Mexico by the United States, my idea is, they are not going to take anything, because the most powerful countries are opposed to the business; France, England and Spain who has already sent a fleet to Vera Cruz to stop them but as to California, it doesn't know whether they [U.S.] will keep her."

Atherton, the faithful guardian, reported to Vallejo on February 6, 1847: "After much labors, finally I have been able to arrange with the officials of the American warship 'Preble' that they take your son, Jose, to his native land which he has desired to see again so much. I think you will find him very advanced in his studies especially in the French language and Arithmetic; for this latter, his teachers tell me he has much talent. In the examinations of this past December he produced very excellent reports in several branches of studies. He is taking to you the report card passed by his teachers where they show his advancements. I hope you'll be pleased as he is truly a youth of very good qualities, good hearted, very correct and very moral in his conduct and

I hope very much that you'll place him in some Commercial house for which it seems to me he has a great aptitude and I believe he won't take long in establishing himself in Monterey or San Francisco. I am enclosing to you his account to date the amount due me, 539 pesos."

Four months later Jose, a tall, handsome youth, was on his way to California, however, not on the *Preble.* On June 3, 1847, Consul Larkin from Monterey wrote to Vallejo: "I have the pleasure of informing you of the arrival of your son, Jose from Valparaiso in the Chile barque *Confederation,* Captain Jones. He is now with his Aunt Cooper. With this you have two letters. The supercargo has given me Mr. Atherton's draft on you for $100, which I will pay if I can. It is for passage money." A week after receiving Larkin's letter with the enclosures, Vallejo with controlled anger, wrote to Jose:

Senor Larkin whom I esteem, wrote to me saying that you had arrived at Monterey on the Chilean corvette the *Confederacion* which pleases me. At the same time, I received from the Captain of the boat, a letter in which he told me what he thought about your conduct at his table, insulting him and the American flag, besides your saying that 'all Norte Americanos in California should have their throats cut quickly.'

Inpudent young man! What right have you to speak like that? Are these the principles of courtesy you have learned at college? Is that what your teachers taught you? Have you forgotten that you have received benefits from the Americans? Do you ignore the fact that only the depraved and ingrates abuse hospitality? Without doubt such conduct is very bad. I disapprove and feel a great disappointment. In writing this letter I order you that you immediately give satisfaction to the Captain of the boat and I forbid you to ever express yourself again in such a manner to the Americans for you have neither right nor reason to do so.

There is no known letter of apology from Jose for his conduct. On June 19, 1847, he wrote from Monterey saying that his visit to Sonoma was delayed "because of my clothes and also on account of the wedding of Cousin Carmen (Prudenciana Amesti's daughter to James McKinely). They begged me to stay because the wedding is real soon so dear father, excuse me for a few days . . . I am charged to send you the deepest affection of your beloved mother and your devoted brothers and sisters and acquaintances, all anxious to see you . . . Please plan something for me to work at when I return. I am not earning a cent here." Work was provided for Jose by his father at the Petaluma Rancho. He was engaged in selling Vallejo's horses.

In September 1850, part of the Petaluma Rancho was leased to some French colonists, the Deslander and Lebret Company which had been promised a cow a week for food. They wrote Vallejo that they were without supplies as the cattle constituted their food, and they had been told by Don Jose Vallejo that, since there were no vaqueros on the ranch, it was impossible to catch a single wild cow. The writer for the French colonists added, "You will understand how it is difficult for us to make those laborers work when they don't eat."

Two years later, in September, 1852, the General's brother Don Salvador asked Jose for 228 mares which were in addition to the 162 horses Salvador had already received. These were to be paid for, from the money Don Salvador expected to receive from his claims upon the United States Government. The General wrote Salvador regarding this matter and enclosed a bill for $12,120 which he itemized for rent, oxen, plows, mares and colts; included was 1800 feet of rope, costing $130. Vallejo added the following sharp words: "In regard to this business, I never would have said a word about it, if it were not for the deal you tried to make with Jose, in which I would have come out skinned."

While Jose was working on the Petaluma Rancho, something unpleasant occurred and once again Jose was a disappointment to his father. Some unknown mediator sent Jose an unsigned letter which read:

Jose:

Your father will perhaps be able to forgive you after death; but before it would be very difficult. Never forget that you have offended him with the greatest of insolence and contempt. His honor (upon which your own depends) you have deliberately violated in a thousand ways, sometimes by your actions and at other times by abuse and derogatory language against him and all the family . . . Where did you ever develop such tendencies and conduct? Running away from home and the atrocious sarcasm, ridicule and scoffing directed against your own father were the first signs and indictations of your waywardness.

You have just about exhausted your father's good will toward you. He made it a point of honor to always be at your side, helping and guiding you in the social life of which you were to be a part but unfortunately you made a mockery of his hopes for you . . . The sacrifices that your father has made for you children merit a better recompense; he is certain he complied with the duty which nature willed he should fulfill and now his recompense is black ingratitude. Ingratitude has no legal punishment, in fact there is no chastisement great enough for the ingrate, especially when ingratitude is directed against the man who has filled the place of father and benefactor and against one who trying to better an inferior social position has compromised his own credit in attempting to benefit the ingrate.

My position as mediator between you and your father is too delicate. If you can understand such things; never did a mediator come out with a whole skin in a situation like this . . . when you understand your position better and have corrected with proper decency your faults and bad behavior, both past and present, you will gain some realization of your misdeeds.

A note, found on the back of the mediator's original letter and in the handwriting of Jose Mariano Vallejo, bore this message: "Senor Papa, if I am not to be forgiven, I hereby return this letter so that it will not be a painful reminder."

Vallejo may have forgiven Jose but he did not forget. The association was never close again. Jose's correspondence, hereafter, was with Senora Vallejo. Jose was living in San Pablo when he fell in love. He wrote to Sonoma:

My esteemed mother:

I have not been able to marry because I do not have Papa's permission, although I am told to marry if I want to. But I am appealing to you through Anita who is one of the finest little girls hereabouts and who is in a position to visit with you and my brothers and sisters, the only objects of my veneration in this world. Mother, I am in the deepest despondency; few are my friends. Do what you can for me and you will have your reward in Heaven.

Your unworthy son who kissed your feet.
JOSE VALLEJO

On April 12, 1861, Senora Vallejo wrote to the unhappy one saying: "In accordance with your wish, I spoke to your father about your desire to marry and I do not think he is in any way opposed. If he is offended and angry with you, it is because of your recent mismanagement of money matters and it is very probable that getting you out of this fix, will sadly jeopardize his financial and social standing. As far as your marriage is concerned, your father says to go ahead at any time it may suit your convenience—that he wants you to be happily married. His only comment being that he would advise you to think well before you marry."

Jose Mariano Vallejo married but on February 6th, his wife Loreta died leaving a baby girl.

In 1870 Jose married Susana Higuera, a granddaughter of Don Ignacio Martinez. Martinez had been Jose's father's commanding officer when Vallejo, as the young Alferez, marched against the Indian Estanislao. Martinez was granted the Pinole Rancho where the town of Martinez, named for him, is located. There Jose Vallejo served for a number of years as an interpreter at the Contra Costa Court House. He reared a large family; his descendants have been people of education and refinement.

THE MOTHER OF GENERAL VALLEJO

There was much concern among the members of the Vallejo family in the spring of 1855 because Grandmother Vallejo, Dona Maria Antonia Lugo de Vallejo, then 78 years old, was ill. The older children of the General, Andronico, Fannie, Adela, Natalia and Platon had been good about writing and sending chocolates to *Querida Abuela.*

Dona Maria Antonia had never learned to write; in her young days, that was a privilege reserved for boys. She would hardly have had time to attend school as she had begun housekeeping at the urge of Don Ignacio Vallejo when she was only fourteen years old and became in time the mother of thirteen children. In spite of her lack of scholastic training she expressed herself well in letters which others wrote for her.

She was a deeply religious woman. In June of 1844, she felt impelled to write to four of her children—three sons, Jose de Jesus, Guadalupe and Salvador, and one daughter, Rosalia—a joint letter, telling them to receive the illustrious Bishop with all outer show of honor and respect due to his holy character as a Prince of the Church. They were admonished to ask for his blessing and to listen to his instruction. She said, "I hope to God that His Divine Majesty will give to all of you the Grace to make a good confession of all your past sins . . . I love you so deeply and desire your eternal happiness. It causes me great pain to think of the possibility of your being damned. Many times I would have preferred not to give you birth than to have such anxiety. God bless you, children of my soul. May He give you and me the Grace we need so much."

Grandmother Vallejo, like all grandmothers, then and now, enjoyed the letters from her grandchildren, although in her case they had to be read to her. Her son Guadalupe's eldest daughter Fannie had in August 1850 just passed her fifteenth birthday and wrote to Nana Antonia, of course in Spanish. Here, translated, in part is her letter:

My very dear Grandmother:

Many greetings from all the family. We are all well. I have the greatest pleasure in writing you these lines and it would give me the greatest pleasure to see you and all the family. It has been a long time since you were here in Sonoma; we can hardly remember it now.

My papa says he is going to take us to Monterey but I don't know when, but he says very soon . . . The other day we went to Benicia but we had the misfortune of having the calash turn over. Fortunately none of the family were in it. We had just taken little Benicia out of it . . . My mother was as pale as a corpse from such a fright . . . Some time ago we took a trip to the ranch, that was my Aunt Rosalia's. We are sending you a box of apples so you can try the apples of Sonoma. They aren't good except for eating. My godfather (Captain Cooper) told me that he was going to bring Rogerio for me to see but he went to China. Then I learned on his return, the Captain went to the United States with Rogerio.

Fannie ended her letter by telling her grandmother that she was enclosing a coin for Nana Antonia to buy chocolates.

Fannie's mother also wrote to her mother-in-law. She took a sheet of her finest stationery, which looked like a Valentine with its edging of paper lace, and wrote:

My very dear mother:

I don't want to miss adding my letter to the ones of my children to you, to send you a very close embrace. I, myself would like to go and give it to you personally which I hope will be soon. It would have been done if Guadalupe's many occupations had not prevented it.

Give my greetings to my young sister and all the others. Tell them I will come to see them soon. Receive my sincere affection. F. BENICIA VALLEJO

Here, I send you this $20 bill to help you buy the crackers to go with the chocolate.

Rogerio, a favorite grandson of Senora Vallejo, was the son of her daughter Encarnacion and Captain John B. Cooper. The Captain had taken Rogerio to enter a school in New England. From there Rogerio wrote:

Dear Grandmother:

I thought I would write you a few lines. I am very glad you sent me the hair rope. I received the letter from Father with much pleasure. I learned from the letter that my father wrote that he was coming to Boston in about two years if he lived and I hope he will come here so he may see what is going on and that I may be able to see him again.

I live in a boarding house and go to school and sleep in the same house and we live very near the water and we have a little new boat and we go rowing in her. I wish when Father writes me another letter he would tell me when you sent the rope and how you sent it. I do not believe I shall get it as I have not heard where it is. I wish you would ask my brother John to write me a letter and tell me how he gets along on the farm and tell me how many bulls he has eaten since I came away. So I will close my letter. WILLIAM ROGERS COOPER

Please direct in care of La Fayette Burr
Newport, R.I.

General Vallejo wrote as often to his mother as his busy life allowed. Few of his letters to her remain but those few indicate his deep affection for her. This one, written in 1851, relates to the business of establishing the permanent site of California's State Capital:

I am flattered to know that within some time I can satisfy my best desires and my families' to visit you and to spend some days in your goodly company and among the family. It is now some time as you know that we have been trying to make the trip but you know also the important and difficult business that has lately taken up all my time and energy. Thanks to God the most trying part is over although there is still much to arrange. I think our departure will not be long delayed and we are preparing little by little for the trip.

Some days ago a boil developed on my cheek. It got worse and it was finally necessary to open it and now I feel more relieved but it kept me from writing and it bothered me a lot. Thousands of greetings to the whole family and receive dear mother, the affection of your son who soon will have the pleasure of embracing you.

VALLEJO'S UNCLE, DON ANTONIO MARIA LUGO

Six years before, Vallejo's mother was sitting on the porch of her home, overlooking the Bay of Monterey; sitting near her was a granddaughter, when several horsemen came into view. Dona Maria Antonio Vallejo exclaimed, "There comes my brother." The young girl, Magdalena del Valle, who was living with her grandmother, cried, "Oh, Grandmother, yonder comes three horsemen but no one can tell who they are at this distance." The older woman quickly replied, "But, girl, my eyes are sharper than yours. The tall man in the middle is my brother whom I have not seen for twenty years. I know by the way he sits in the saddle."

This brother, Don Antonio Lugo, a noted horseman, was two years the senior of Dona Maria Antonia and was the owner of vast lands. He could ride for days and nights without his horses touching foot on land that was not his own. Don Antonio was six feet high in his stockings, handsome in features and physique, and said to be a pure type of an aristocrat Spaniard. The girl, Magdalena, mentioned above, was the granddaughter who had been put in the care of Grandmother Vallejo when the infant's mother Senora Magdalena Vallejo del Valle died in July 1825. The father, Antonio del Valle, went to Santa Barbara.

It is known that Vallejo's mother, after bringing up her own thirteen children, undertook the care of several of her grandchildren. When Senorita Magdalena del Valle was a young woman of twenty-seven, Dona Maria Antonia dictated a letter on July 23, 1852, to her youngest son Juan Antonio, who was ranching in the Pajaro Valley and was a close friend of Lieutenant William T. Sherman. She said:

My dear Son, Juan Antonio Vallejo:

In the first place I am well, without any news at home. The dentist (Henry G. Blankman) has asked me for Magdalena to make her his wife. I answered him that she can do anything according to her wish. And she tells me that she wants to marry him. Then he said that because of that, he came and wants to marry at once. He went and talked with Father Ramirez and the Father told him that he has to wait until he has a license and the Vicar of San Francisco which will be here on Friday of this week. Then as soon as the license comes they are going to take their vows. My son, I should like for you to be present if it is possible. I have nothing more to say other than, may God keep you well and with every happiness, for those are the desires of your mother.

MARIA ANTONIA LUGO DE VALLEJO

During February 1853, General Vallejo was in San Francisco and on the 12th he wrote to his mother a note carrying sad news:

My dear Mother:

The opportunity of the departure of Juan Antonio allows me the sweet pleasure to send this, so as to give my blessing. This letter you will probably receive within ten hours and with all my soul I wish I could be the carrier of it, but I can't be at the moment. I believe that soon I'll be back with all my family and yearn for the moment.

On the 31st of January, I lost a four year old little girl (Benicia) Notwithstanding her innocence, I ask for your prayers. Cares of the family multiply upon me each day, so that they are making me old. I am sending you my portrait, made just before Juan Antonio left. Andronico writes me every fortnight and sends greetings. He begs you not to forget him; he is in a Catholic College and attended the council of 54 Bishops.

Your Son who loves you dearly,
M. G. VALLEJO

LAST ILLNESS OF VALLEJO'S MOTHER

It was on May 3rd that Juan Antonio Vallejo wrote from Monterey to his brother Guadalupe in Sonoma, telling of the serious illness of their mother:

Yesterday, your mother and mine was very disturbed in the evening and therefore spent a thoroughly restless night and the same for all of us. As this night approaches the situation of her condition remains the same for she has been moaning in her delirium. When the door squeaks, she asks if the visitor is one of her sons; she would say 'some one is knocking; Senor Jose de Jesus Vallejo [eldest son] is coming.' That is the song that goes on continually in her long illness.

I warn you that this is the last letter I am going to write you even if she is still sick. I wrote you twice but perhaps you haven't received the letters. I beg you to show this letter to Salvador, send it on to him; you can do it more safely. In the future do not say I did not give you both warning of the illness that our dear mother is suffering. If God doesn't cure her soon, we will be orphans, motherless ones.

Four days later, on May 7th, 1855, the Vallejo boys and their sisters were "motherless" ones. Juan Antonio wrote informing them of their sad loss. Captain John B. Cooper, with whom Senora Vallejo was living at the time of her death, wrote this short note to Sonoma:

Don Guadalupe Vallejo, Esteemed Brother:

Today at noon your mother died, apparently without pain and with all her faculties, blessing all her children. The poor dear felt very badly because she couldn't look upon Rogerio [grandson] before dying. Considering the grief, all the family is more resigned than I thought possible. Maria and Antonio cry but the little one is quieter; but I know all grieve.

Dr. James L. Ord attended Senora Vallejo in her last illness. His statement for professional services was $500; $150 had been paid; the balance was to come from her estate. Dr. Ord came to California on the same ship with Lieutenant William T. Sherman and was his roommate in Monterey before marrying Augustia de la Guerra Jimeno in 1856. Dona Augustias had been left a widow in 1853 with eleven children. One of her daughters, Carolina (Senora Moise Kahn) was greatly beloved by her uncle "Tio Guadalupe."

The San Francisco Alta printed on May 13, 1855 this death notice:

Died at Monterey on the 7th inst. Dona Maria A. Lugo de Vallejo, aged 78 years, wife of the late Ignacio Vallejo. She was born at San Luis Obispo married her godfather when 13 years old and had 156 children, grandchildren and great grandchildren. She retained her memory and faculities until a few weeks of her death.

The mother of Vallejo survived her husband, Don Ignacio Vallejo, twenty-three years. It was in the spring of 1831 that Don Ignacio, finding himself in bed with a sickness which Divine Providence had considered it well to inflict upon him and "with his senses perfect" he had drawn his will.

First, Don Ignacio said, he wished to be interred in the habit of the Franciscan order in the Sacristy of the Church of the Presidio of Monterey. He asked in his will that intercessory prayers be said for him, the number depending upon the proceeds from the sale of twenty head of cattle from his ranch (Bolsa de San Cayetano) which contained at least one thousand head. He wished his debts to be paid, down to the last real. He stipulated that six head of cattle were to be sold as alms for the widows of the Presidio; the balance to be divided in two parts: one part to his wife Maria Antonia, and the other to be divided equally between his sons and daughters. His drove of mares was to go to his sons, Guadalupe, Jose de Jesus, Salvador, and Juan Antonio.

Don Ignacio further stated that, "I have on my ranch a mill that it is my desire that it will be for my wife, Jose de Jesus and Rosalia; to Jose de Jesus, because of the work he has put into it and to Maria Antonia and Rosalia because of the great care they have taken of me during my illness." He added, "Anything coming from my military pay, I leave to my wife, Maria Antonia, as the only heir."

In closing, Don Ignacio stated that he owed Don William Edward Hartnell 406 pesos, one real. He named his sons Jose de Jesus and Guadalupe as executors. Witnessing the signing of the will by Ignacio Vallejo, were two members of his Cavalry Company of the Presidio of Monterey, Sergeant Juan Hernandez and Corporal Francisco Sota. Fourteen months after making his will, Don Ignacio Vicente Ferrer Vallejo had passed away on May 10, 1832, aged 84 years. He was buried in the Cemetery of the San Carlos Mission by Fr. Ramon Abella.

THE WILL OF DONA MARIA ANTONIA LUGO DE VALLEJO

Wills often reflect the character of the testator; such was the case with the will of Vallejo's mother. She had written one in 1853 and another, her last one, dated January 25, 1854. This was signed with an "X," and it was witnessed by Manual Dias, Gabriel Avila and William Roach. Portions of her will follow in translation:

In the Name of God, the All-Powerful, Amen:

I, Maria Antonia Lugo de Vallejo, native of the State of California, being by the mercy of God, sane and in complete control of my faculties, do order this my last will in the following terms—

I commend my soul to my Maker and my body to the earth from whence it was made, charging my beloved son, Juan Antonio, that at my death, he is to take charge of my burial in the way that seems best to him, provided that everything should conform to the rites of our Holy Roman Apostolic Church in which Faith I have lived and expect to die.

I attest to having been married to Don Ignacio Vallejo, now deceased, from which marriage we had the following children, to wit: Isidora, Maria Josefa, Ignacio, Jose de Jesus, Magdalena, Juana, Prudenciana, Mariano Guadalupe, Encarnacion, Rosalia, Salvador, Maria de Jesus and Juan Antonio . . . All my wealth of whatever kind there may be, be it fixed or moveable . . . should pass intact to my children Juan Antonia and Maria de Jesus.

Upon designating these two children as my only heirs, I hope and trust that my other children in no way interpret this preference as motivated by a greater predilection since my mother love extends equally to all of them; rather have I been prompted to it by the knowledge that all the others are more than usually endowed with good fortune and also to show in this special way my particular acknowledgment of gratitude to my son, Juan Antonio, for having been the one who in my advanced age took care of my interest, doubtless to the detriment of his own and very especially of my person.

To fulfill this my last will, I name as my only executor, the aforementioned, my son Juan Antonio who being worthy of my complete confidence I relieve him of all surety or bond whatsoever that the Law may require and I can relieve him of it since it is my expressed and considered wish that from the moment of my death, he may enter into the discharging of his duties as executor and may enjoy his inheritance without bond of any kind.

The will was filed August 13, 1855. The probate clerk, James H. Gleason of Monterey, called the witnesses; the first one questioned being Gabriel de Avila:

Q. State your name, age and place of residence.

A. My name is Gabriel de Avila, Age is 37 years, reside in Monterey, Monterey County.

Q. Was your acquaintance with Maria Antonia Lugo de Vallejo and if so, state whether or not she is still living and if not when and where she died.

A. I was acquainted with her and I knew that she died in the city of Monterey, County of Monterey, about four or five months ago.

Q. Look on document marked A, now shown to you, purporting to be the last Will and Testament of deceased and say whether or not you have seen it before and if so when and where and under what circumstances.

A. I saw the same on the 25th day of January last year in the house of J. B. R. Cooper in the city of Monterey, Monterey County at which place the deceased was living. The Will of deceased was there signed by her making a cross in my presence and in the presence of the witnesses whose names appear thereto. The witnesses, William Roach, Manual Dias and myself signed our names to the Will as witnesses at the request of the deceased and in her presence and the presence of each other.

Q. State whether or not the deceased at the time she signed the Will was of sound mind at the time and not under any bodily restraint.

A. The deceased was of sound mind at the time and not under any bodily restraint and she declared to me that she had executed the same voluntarily and the same was read over to her by E. L. Williams and explained by him to her.

(Signed) GABRIEL V. O. AVILA

Sworn and subscribed
Before me, the 13th day of
August A.D. 1855

The same being read over to the witnesses in Spanish by J. H. Gleason who was duly sworn interpreter before signing.

The next witness called was Manual Dias, a former Alcalde of Monterey, aged 43 years, who answered the same questions and stated that he believed Senora Maria Antonia Lugo de Vallejo to have been over seventy years. Judge H. Rumsey, Judge of the Probate Court of Monterey County, received the Will of Senora Vallejo naming her son Juan Antonio Vallejo as executor.

In June 1855, Aaron Lyons, Sheriff of Monterey County, had had his under-sheriff Thomas K. Munk deliver a true copy of the Will to Rosalia Vallejo and her husband, Jacob P. Leese; to Encarnacion Vallejo de Cooper and to her husband John B. R. Cooper; to Prudenciana Vallejo de Amesti, and to Maria Jesus de Vallejo. Munk stated he had not been able to locate Jose Amesti nor Juan Antonio Vallejo. The last named was served with a true copy of the Will ten days later.

Senora Maria Antonia Lugo de Vallejo left an estate appraised at $23,535 besides her Bolsa de San Cayetano Rancho, valued at $6,000, and the improvements thereon (viz. six houses in good condition and four or five houses of little value, and fences appraised at $5,000 by Jacinto Rodriguez and Rafael Pinto. She left certain parcels of real estate in Monterey. On a 50 by 50 lot on the west side of Pierce Street, south of Soberanes, she owned an adobe dwelling. A frame house was also on Pierce Street north of Pinto, and another on the east side of Alvarado.

The counsel for Prudenciana Amesti objected to the Will being in probate, so the executor, Juan Antonio Vallejo, had to employ D. S. Gregory as an attorney; but before anything could be done in settling Senora Vallejo's estate, Don Juan Antonio Vallejo was killed on May 26, 1857, by a fall from his horse while he was lassoing a bull on the San Cayetano Rancho in the Pajaro Valley. Don Juan Antonio's neck was broken and death was instantaneous. He left no will, so his brother, Don Mariano Guadalupe Vallejo, was appointed administrator. This necessitated Vallejo staying in Monterey a good deal of the time, and, while there, he was often the guest of his sister Rosalia Leese in her home which had belonged to Thomas O. Larkin. (It had been deeded to Jacob P. Leese on January 8, 1850 for a piece of Leese's property in San Francisco.)

On June 26, 1857, Vallejo inserted this advertisement in the public press and gave a bond for $40,000.

ADMINISTRATOR'S NOTICE

Letters of Administration having been granted to the undersigned upon the estate of Juan Antonio Vallejo, deceased. Notice is hereby given to all persons, holding claims against the estate of the said Juan Antonio Vallejo, deceased, late of Monterey County, California to present same with the necessary vouchers to the undersigned at his residence in Sonoma, California within ten months from the date hereof or they will be forever barred.

M. G. VALLEJO

Don Juan Antonio Vallejo's debts amounted to $5,032.27. Among his debtors was his brother Don Salvador, who was allowed the payment of $1,100 for twenty-two horses sold to Juan Antonio in 1851. Don Juan Antonio's personal property was valued at $13,692; in it was included a carriage valued at $200, two sofas at $15 each, a silver watch, valued at $22, and a trunk at $6. A supplemental inventory listed a brass bedstead, bureau, washstand, round table, a dozen chairs, old clock, four large mirrors, Chinese box, nine dozen tumblers (the last named evidently from the Tavern which he kept with an adjoining billiard parlor). His personal jewelry consisted not only of the silver watch but he also had a gold watch, a gold pencil case, and 41 gold coins. The inventory of the ranch, which included the equipment and animals amounted to $2,760.

With the entire Vallejo clan as heirs, it was not easy for Vallejo to serve as Administrator and attempt to please so many relatives. Don Victor Fortoul, the husband of his youngest sister Maria de Jesus, was especially difficult. He tried to raise the question that the estate of Don Ignacio Vallejo, with Don Jose de Jesus Vallejo and Don Guadalupe Vallejo as administrators, had not been settled. Even Vallejo's oldest brother, Don Jose de Jesus, petitioned for the removal of Guadalupe Vallejo as administrator of the Juan Antonio Vallejo estate.

CALIFORNIA'S BUSINESS DEPRESSION

The last half of the decade of the 1850s was filled for Vallejo with anxiety and vicissitudes of both a family and business nature. Because of the Gold Rush, San Francisco's growth and progress had been rapid. Then followed a business depression. The financial storm which had commenced in 1854 had increased in violence and extent until it caused the failure of many of the largest financial institutions. Naturally it affected Vallejo's vast holdings. Added to this stringency was the difficulty occasioned by the swarms of locust-devouring "squatters" who *squatted* on any unoccupied land which appealed to them, and roamed about picking up unbranded calves.

Because of the necessity of appearing before the Land Commission whose rooms were in San Francisco, Vallejo maintained his own office in San Francisco. During a visit there in July 1855, the General was presented with an invitation which, if he accepted it, must have provided social diversion and some brief relief from business. The invitation was signed by W. F. Sherwood and H. P. Ord and read:

> There are now in town some ten or twelve members of the Constitutional Convention held in Monterey in 1849. Three or four of us met this morning, individually and unanimously resolved to have a little pleasant talk and dinner together tonight at 9 o'clock at the Bella Union Restaurant upstairs. Pablo de la Guerra, Gwin, Erwin, Norton, Corrarrubas, Larkin and all the members we can find in town will be there. We expect you without fail.

The latter half of the 1850s was scattered with vital statistics for the Vallejos: the immediate Vallejo family was increased by the births in 1856 and 1857 of two daughters, Luisa and Maria. In 1857, Vallejo's youngest brother, Juan Antonio, as was mentioned, died from the fall from his horse. In 1858 Vallejo's second daughter, Adela, married Doctor Levi Cornell Frisbie. In 1859, on January 13th, the Vallejos lost a beautiful six-year-old daughter, the lovely child with long black curls, Benicia Isabel. Her body was buried in the family cemetery on the nearby hill where were buried two little sons, each named Plutarco, and two little daughters, Guadalupe and the first little Benicia. The bereaved father made note of this second Benicia:

At Lachryma Montis, Valley of Sonoma, the 13th day of the present, Benicia Vallejo, daughter of General Vallejo, of the age of six years.

A loving flower has been touched by the Angel of Death in the beautiful garden of Lachryma Montis and transplanted to the Land of the Sun to live in Eternal Light.

Benicia was one of the little ones of California and the dearly beloved of my throbbing heart, mourning is now in the father's house for the one who in life gave so much joy and happiness. Such is certain—"The Kingdom of Heaven."

It was necessary for Vallejo, after the death of his younger brother, whose holdings had been in Monterey County, to spend some time there to liquidate the estate as he had been appointed the executor. On August 24, 1858, he wrote his wife:

On the 18th at nine in the morning I left San Francisco and after a voyage of eight hours with delightful weather and extremely calm I arrived at this place (Monterey) . . . Just at the beginning I was pleased with the novelty of again seeing the place of my birth and the persons with whom I was brought up from my infancy to adolescence . . . I am sorry to tell you that there is nothing more monotonous than Monterey . . . I find nothing that I desire which is to associate myself with those of my taste. I meet with little congeniality.

Yesterday I went to the River Carmelo with the sole object of bringing back some demi-johns of drinking water, for right here there is not even that and what was my surprise upon arriving at the river to see it absolutely dry, so dry that I returned without any water whatever, a surprising thing that one would not expect to see.

I walked three miles up stream through the canyon of the river and not even one pool remained nor any liquid whatsoever that would fill one demi-john with water. After I returned from the Carmel the only thing I could do was to join a small caravan that was going out to the Canada Verde a favorite place for picnics and with the family of Rosalia (Leese) and Carmelita Soberanes; we went out to eat some dry meat (jerky) to drink some bottles of wine and to bound around in the sand like boys that do not know how to spend their time. On returning I got so covered with dust that I can no longer bear myself. Then I remembered Lachryma Montis and I wanted to fly in order to enjoy the advantages of water. What a difference from one place to another . . . Now the coachman of the stage is coming and he is urging me to finish soon.

RICHARD HENRY DANA JR. RETURNS TO CALIFORNIA

In 1859 California was paid a return visit by the author of *Two Years Before the Mast*. Dana arrived on August 13th on the superb steamship *Golden Gate*. Twenty-four years before (January 14, 1835) as a common sailor, he had arrived on the Brig *Pilgrim*, after a voyage of 150 days from Boston. When he saw San Francisco transformed into a city of 100,000, and reflected on what he once was and on what he had seen in Yerba Buena—and on what *now* surrounded him—he said, "I could scarcely keep my hold on reality."

During this visit Dana called at the United States Navy Yard, where he met an acquaintance of the early days, Don Mariano Guadalupe Vallejo, with whom he had held many conversations in English. As Dana recorded it, "He received me with true earnestness and would not hear of my passing his estate without visiting him. He reminded me of a remark I made to him once when pulling him ashore in the boat when he was Commandante of the Presidio. I accepted the old gentleman's invitation so far as to stop at Vallejo for breakfast."

On the 9th anniversary of California's admission to the Union (1859), San Francisco put on quite a celebration. Vallejo brought down from Sonoma his carriage (which had come from Paris) and rode in it with General Fremont.

VALLEJO, MAYOR AND VINTNER

The growing of grapes for wine had held great interest for Vallejo since the days when he had transplanted the withering vines from the abandoned missions of San Rafael and San Francisco Solano, to his own land. In 1860, his vineyards were under the supervision of P. A. Giovanari and his wine cellars under Dr. Victor J. Faure. That year Vallejo planted 4,000 bearing grapevines and 10,000 cuttings and had made 8,000 gallons of wine. He was a regular exhibitor at the Fairs in Petaluma, Marysville, San Francisco and Sacramento, winning first and second premiums for his white wine, red wine and champagne. The awards of silver goblets, berry spoons and pitchers of silver must have delighted Senora Vallejo.

The Vallejo wine cellars were in the old Sonoma barracks; the thick walls had been plastered inside so as to be clean, yet dark and cool. Visitors spoke of the "perfect sweetness of the atmosphere," and had commented on the cleanliness of the wine press, distilling apparatus, wine vaults, in contrast to some places in other sections of the state where the implements were left in bad order. Of interest to visitors were the pictures in the wide hall and over the door of the wine vaults; Maidens with baskets of fruit, fruit-pieces, and several convival pieces—all emblems of the vine, from the grape to the wine made from it.

The old vineyard of Lachryma Montis, according to General Vallejo, was on lots numbered 354, 355, 356, 369, 370 and 371.

In May 1860, Vallejo was elected Mayor of Sonoma for the second time. His first term had been eight years before. Of his 1860 election Vallejo said, "Although there is no salary, it was an honor to be elected without opposition." A salary, however small, would have been welcomed by Sonoma's first magistrate; only the month before Thomas P. Madden, an attorney who had loaned him money, had written, "Please send me your check for $200 by return mail, being the amount of interest due on your note. I am hard up for money."

After the summer months were over, the financial picture was a little brighter, and Vallejo offered to lend some money to the husband of his wife's kin, Colonel Henry S. Burton, who was preparing to leave with his wife Ampara for the East. On the 2nd of October Colonel Burton wrote Vallejo, "Will you do me the favor to send $500 of the amount you so kindly offered to me to Mr. James Walsh & Company . . . Your unwavering kindness to my wife and myself has won our esteem and friendship and I think that whenever we have the pleasure of meeting you in the Atlantic States we shall have the power, as we now have the wish of showering you with our gratitude."

SUPER-ABUNDANCE OF LITIGATION

It has been said that the possession of much property can be ruinous, and Vallejo was learning this. The United States had confirmed Vallejo's title to the 66,622.16 acre Petaluma Rancho on March 16, 1857. Three weeks later, he sold the old Petaluma Adobe and some adjoining land for $25,000 to William Whiteside, who kept it for two years and then sold it for $30,000 to William D. Bliss. At the time that the Court confirmed Vallejo's title to the Rancho Petaluma, it refused the appeal of the Squatters. However, the Court allowed the appeal in the case of the Soscol Rancho. This ranch of some 80,000 acres had been deeded to Vallejo by Governor Micheltorena on March 15, 1843, as part payment on the debt owed Vallejo by the Mexican government. The case was taken to the United States Supreme Court. This meant heavy expenses for Vallejo in Washington, D.C. Thomas P. Madden, John B. Frisbie's friend, was in the Federal City in November 1861 and telegraphed back to California that the Soscol case would have to be argued. More legal fees! Vallejo was satiated with lawyers who took so much of his wealth. He remembered some of the pettifogging ones of the Gold Rush days. Of these he said, "But all the evils became negligible in comparison with the swollen torrent of shysters who came from Missouri and other states of the Union. No sooner had they arrived than they assumed the title of attorney and began to seek means of depriving the Californians of their farms and other properties. The escaped bandits from Australia stole our cattle and our horses but these legal thieves clothed in the law took from us our land and our houses." No wonder that Vallejo had the temerity to say to the wife of one of his attorneys (Wm. W. Chipman) that he hoped there would be no lawyers in heaven.

The Justices of the Supreme Court were not adverse to taking Vallejo's property. But what a blow it was to him when the United States Supreme Court on March 24, 1862 reversed the lower courts confirmation of the Soscol Rancho on the technicality that the grant had never received the sanction of the Supreme Government of Mexico. Justice Robert Cooper Grier and Justice James Moore Wayne dissented from the opinion of the other members of the Supreme Court. Justice Grier reasoned:

If this treaty is to be executed in good faith by this government why should we forfeit a property for which a large price has been paid to the Mexican government on the assumption that the Mexican government would not have confirmed it but would have repudiated it for want of formal authority? Vallejo was an officer of the army, high in the confidence of the government. His salary as an officer had been in arrears. In time of difficulty he furnished provisions and money to the government of the territory. How do we know that Mexico would have repudiated its sale of 80,000 acres as robbery of its territory when two decent colonists having a few horses and cows could have 100,000 for nothing. I believe the Mexican Government would have honestly and honorably dealt with their valued servant and the same obligation rests upon us by force of the treaty.

When the decision of the United States Supreme Court was announced, reversing the lower courts' confirmation of the Soscol Rancho, Vallejo wondered why he had not heard from his son-in-law; Frisbie got around to writing to Vallejo on April 20, 1862:

Mr. Brooks informs me that you have not heard from me since the receipt of the news of the disaster to Soscol. I wrote you and handed the letter to Madden and supposed he had sent it. My dispatch from Washington was received at mid-night of the 3rd inst. On the following day I quietly secured Land Warrants enough to cover all the land I had in my possession, some three thousand acres. . . . I have also covered by consent of parties, lands upon which I hold mortgages to the amount of $30,000. My friends in San Francisco came promptly and generously to my aid furnishing me the means to accomplish the objects named. I had to, in a few hours to raise $15,000 and frankly stated my necessity and the cause of it; the generous response to my appeal has left an impression of gratitude upon my heart deeper and stronger if possible than the indignation I feel at the infamous outrage perpetrated by the Government in its criminal violation of its treaty.

General Vallejo must have been disappointed that Frisbie so concerned with his own affairs that he gave no thought of his father-in-law who had shared his wealth with him. Vallejo wrote to Frisbie in June:

It was not my intention nor is it now that you should be bothered in any way in helping me get out of the sad, critical and agonizing state in which are found the few properties which remain to me. My letter is reduced to asking you to tell me if it remains in my possession or if I have some rights to the Sobrante, the Zabacca and the Potrero, in order for me to dispose of it. My huge debts to Madden and Borel are paid; I said paid as they have good mortgages, ample enough to be paid in money to which is added, that they will be bound to take them . . . What wears me down and bothers me most are the accounts of the servants and workers; the rest is nothing. The Wheel of Fortune is very fickle and it isn't strange for me to see it turn, distributing the results of chance—taking from some, giving to others. It hit me among the first and—patience. I insist that you don't trouble yourself. Anything you do for me now is late. I only want to know if I have some rights in the properties.

In answer Frisbie wrote the General:

> I am truly grieved at your great pecuniary embarrassments, can the more readily sympathize with you as I am suffering from the same and even more difficulties; Credit and Squatters at the same time either of which evils is quite sufficient to drive the most even-tempered man to desperation. The interests held by you and myself in the Sobrante, I regard as our joint property, share and share alike subject to the debts with which it is charged. I think about one thousand dollars. The Potrero property is held in the same manner. The Zabacco is practically the property of Mr. Atherton who loaned me the entire amount of the purchase money and now holds the mortgage upon it about $42,000 quite as much as it would sell for.

This distressing report from his son-in-law forced Vallejo to make the supreme sacrifice, that of placing a mortgage on Lachryma Montis and the nearby vineyard Quiquiriqui. It was made out to Thomas P. Madden, the lawyer friend of Frisbie, for $17,500 on July 21, 1862.

On December 26, 1862, Frisbie wrote the General, "I leave for the East on Thursday . . . this step had become imperative and yet I feel great apprehension of serious disturbance upon the Soscol . . . I am extremely anxious to see you prior to my departure; the new United States Registrar who has it in his power to accept or reject the school warrants location, has expressed a wish to see you in regard to a piece of cavalry ordinance he has invented and which he is anxious to bring to the attention of the Mexican Government. He requested me to ask you to come down and see him. He has politely placed in my hands $50 to pay your expenses to the City; this gun is his hobby and weakness and through it I believe we can establish such friendly relations with him as will enable us to secure favorable mention by him on Soscol matters. Your cooperation and aid however is indispensible. I therefore beg that you will come down immediately. I will then detail fully my plan of action."

Frisbie went to Washington, D.C. and there he lobbied for a bill which would protect the *bona fide* purchasers of the Soscol property. Frisbie's expenses were defrayed by these purchasers. The bill which passed February 17, 1863, allowed them to acquire title to their land by paying the Federal Government $1.25 an acre.

During the days of "super-abundance of litigation," one of the attorneys who did legal work for Vallejo was a young lawyer, Henry Alexander Gaston, who had come to California in 1854. After graduating from Oberlin College and Yale University, Gaston married Josephine Battin, a brown-eyed beauty with a halo of chestnut brown hair, who was a cousin to Julia Gardener, the wife of President Tyler. Mrs. Gaston and her children joined her husband in California in 1856.

In the early 1860s the Gastons were living in Napa. One day, Henry Gaston and his wife drove to San Francisco where many of Gaston's clients lived. Leaving his wife seated in their carriage he went into the Occidental Hotel to transact some business. Meanwhile a distinguished looking gentleman approached the carriage, doffed his hat with a sweeping bow and started speaking to her in Spanish. Mrs. Gaston replied, "Senor, I am sorry, I know no Spanish." Just then Mr. Gaston emerged from the hotel and cordially shook hands with the gentleman, then said to his wife, "My dear Josephine, allow me to present General Vallejo." The General was embarrassed for a moment; then said, "Ah Senor Gaston, a thousand pardons, but with such an exquisitely beautiful wife, you will understand the great temptation of any gentleman to become acquainted with her. So there may be no misunderstanding, Senor Gaston, I merely asked the gracious lady in Spanish if I had not had the honor and pleasure of meeting her previously."

SAN CAYETANO RANCHO

"Que es nessario!!!! Dinero!!!" so said Vallejo. Yes. "What is necessary? Money!!! The disaster to Soscol forced Vallejo to seek other sources of revenue. As one of the heirs to the Vallejo family ranch, *San Cayetano Rancho* near Watsonville, Vallejo went again to the Pajaro Valley, where he spent a great deal of time in the spring of 1864 trying to bring the Vallejo heirs into agreement. Vallejo's father, Don Ignacio, had received the title to the Rancho Bolsa de San Cayetano. After his death in 1832, the eldest son Jose de Jesus, one of the executors of the estate, made application to the Mexican Government, and the grant of some 9,000 acres was confirmed to the Vallejo family. Subsequently a Patent was received by the family to the San Cayetano Rancho from the United States. From this ranch Vallejo wrote home:

I am alone in my mother's home in a house on an elevation from which you can see the sea, the village of Watsonville; all the people who pass in their wagons or other vehicles; a river in front. Also you can see the town of Santa Cruz, the pine forest of Monterey and you can always hear the heavy roar of the waves of the big sea as they break on the beach.

However much I have done to finish up the business which brought me, I haven't been able to end it on account of the brother (husband of Vallejo's sister Maria de Jesus). He (Fortoul) has brought a suit to force the partition of the land and I don't know yet when it will end. I have worked hard to sell my part but they have offered me so little for it that I haven't wanted to do it. They have offered me 10,000 pesos for what is worth 30,000 and it seems hard to sacrifice my last hope after so much expense like those unpaid bills in Sonoma. I don't know what to do but I am hoping the stormy clouds will clear up a bit.

The financial horizon did not clear. "So much money invested in Law—for nothing," so wrote Vallejo, who was forced to put a mortgage on his home-place, Lachryma Montis, and the adjoining vineyard Quiquiriqui. The mortgage was held by Thomas P. Madden. Vallejo somewhat depressed wrote his wife:

To remain poor because the most powerful government in the world has squatted on my most valuable pieces of property is not my fault. The fact is that I have not been able to defend them successfully because of the lack of material means to oppose the Government.

I have had hopes for three years of getting out of my troubles with the accursed Soscol business which has embarrassed me on top of everything else making me in debt to those who have been serving me and beginning the mortgage on the property. I came here to clear myself of the debt on this property with the hope of realizing at least some $15,000 but I haven't been able to accomplish it because of circumstance which I couldn't help and which, if I had been able to foresee I absolutely would not have come.

I have suffered much physically and mentally, making unheard efforts to sell and to get money to take home but the *Devil Money* has disappeared from the country. Everyone barks, cries and whines for it.

Some days past I was in Monterey . . . There are many families in such misery that were it not for fishing, they would die of hunger. Thank God, I said, that at my home are geese, ducks, chickens and all kinds of vegetables to eat. I made a point of comparison and was somewhat consoled and I even wished inwardly to share with them the abundance which my family had compared to them.

There was a rift in the clouds of despondency when news reached General Vallejo at San Cayetano that his son Platon had received his M.D. degree from the Medical College of the University of Columbia. The General was filled with parental pride and happiness, as he wrote to Platon's mother on May 6, 1864:

You must know that Platon received his Doctor's degree and did very brilliantly in the examinations, leading more than 70 youths who graduated at the same time. I am very happy over that and all the papers speak very well and some with admiration. How I wish we could see him soon. Poor Platon, he went away a child and will soon return a man with a distinguished and respected profession. I wonder what he will say when he learns Jovita whom he left in school is married and has a baby.

Vallejo's financial worries continued. There was "Squatter" trouble near Sonoma. Don Jose de la Rosa, "Don Pepe," family friend of many years, warned the General:

The Squatters of the Agua-Caliente are very agitated against you, they mean to spy on you . . . Just today the Sheriff of Santa Rosa has put up a public notice for the payment of the taxes. I don't know if the time limit is for two days or weeks. They will put up for public auction in Santa Rosa the grain, barley, the vines of "that cock of the walk of Lacrima Montis." Ula will give you the detailed news of what has happened better than I. Speaking of news of the Squatters, this same Nathanson heard it in Pauli's store all that had been said. Nathanson wanted to warn you secretly and put you wise to it all.

The months of June and July of 1864 found Vallejo in San Francisco, trying to get some money to pay the Madden Mortgage and other unpaid bills. Benjamin S. Brooks, a trusted attorney of Vallejo's, was well acquainted with Vallejo's financial affairs, offered a bit of advice:

It is better for you in solitude to examine the state of affairs and to determine the best thing to do, not only for today but also for the future years for yourself and all your family. It is necessary right now to practice economy and before any settlement it is necessary for your wife to have the idea in its full meaning. It is certain that there are debts that are not paid, even in their interest . . . All the receipts are consumed in expenses. It is possible to live on other smaller holdings in order to pay the debts. But to do this, it is necessary to abandon the house for some years.

If you won't rent your house it would be better to close its doors, for you well know that the cost of living there is prohibitive. To effect this, it is necessary first of all that your wife feel the necessity of this kind of economy. She would not have to worry about the pruning of the vines and care of the gardens growing so fast and in full production.

The Vallejos couldn't think of giving up their beloved Lachryma Montis. Surely, they thought, there must be another way. Discouraged, the General wrote his wife from San Francisco, July 20, 1864:

The more I work and the more I make myself hunt for the means to get money to pay the Madden mortgage and other unpaid bills of which you know, the less hope I see of succeeding. Seeing then, that it is necessary to take a prompt and resolute decision, in order to save the house and lands of Lachryma Montis before Mr. Madden's mortgage absorbs it all with the interest which is accruing all the time I believe it is opportune and absolutely necessary to sell Quiquiriqui with vineyards and houses.

I regret it but it is necessary to pay the debts soon before things get into a worse state. I see that a frightful crisis is coming close and one must prepare oneself to see it in time. If I could wait longer and see a better aspect to business I would wait a little longer, but nothing is clear; on the contrary all the future is dark threatening a monetary storm. I want, nevertheless to put you and the family in safety, in order to be serene, fulfilling thus the duty of a man and a father. There is not one peso here, nor is one to be had. This letter is for you alone.

The Vallejos' son-in-law, John B. Frisbie, had often received financial aid from the General but all Frisbie could do during this financial crisis was to offer sympathy:

I know your pressing need of money and believe me when I assure you that were it in my power to offer relief you would promptly receive it . . . You speak of abandoning your homestead to Mr. Madden. I sincerely trust you will think better of this as I believe it can be saved to you. It is my purpose if possible to pay the interest upon it so that you can enjoy the entire proceeds for the maintenance of your family and in addition to this I fully intend if it is ever in my power to do so, to pay off the mortgage and thus secure to you and Mrs. Vallejo a fair competence. I am young and can therefore better endure reverses than one advanced in life as yourself. Certainly nothing can more afflict me than to see you suffer and most sincerely do I hope and sincerely believe brighter days are in store for you. I pray you to bear patiently as possible your present misfortune and look happily in the future.

Vallejo was unable to clear with Frisbie's well-meaning words the Madden mortgage. Before the year was over, Madden wrote the General as follows:

"Please advise me as to the success of your negotiation for the sale of the Pajaro. I am waiting with much anxiety to hear from you." Shortly after the harassed Vallejo confided to his son Platon: "In order to save it (the home) all my inherited property in the Pajaro, I turned over to Mr. Madden for $15,000 (fifteen thousand pesos). Even yet it is in danger but I believe it will be saved."

GENERAL VALLEJO'S FIRST TRIP EAST

With Vallejo's finances somewhat improved, he decided to accompany his son-in-law John B. Frisbie on his trip East. They sailed from San Francisco on January 4, 1865 on the Pacific Mail Steamship *Constitution*, which in addition to 315 passengers carried the United States mail and over one million dollars in treasure. Two weeks later, off the coast of Guatemala, Vallejo wrote to Platon:

> After my departure from San Francisco, nothing has occurred of more importance than that great danger we had at the exit from the port, in avoiding some boats. It was the most stupendous and greatest thing that all the men, from the porter to the best man on board, had seen; the devil was about to carry us off in the hugh waves. Now that I have escaped from that, I hope nothing more like it will happen to me; calmness is my element . . . Every one says the view of the sea is sublime. I don't doubt it but it is very boring. If I could, I would dry it up and would find myself a better mode of travel . . . Tomorrow we reach Panama.

After twenty-three days of navigation, over 5,000 miles of two oceans, Vallejo and his son-in-law reached New York City on January 27th. The General reported home, "The cold of the country is unbearable. One can reconcile oneself to it only by the pleasure of seeing an immense multitude of both sexes skate in Central Park . . . This frozen park is the enchantment of every one . . . New York is an immense and admirable city . . . Frisbie has taken me everywhere and with solicitude has tried to impress me with the wonders of his native land. It is surely marvelous and I confess that everything here is big and ought to be more so after the passage of a few years."

The two California travelers left for Washington, D.C. on the last day of January, 1865. According to Vallejo the train on which they rode, traveled fifty miles an hour, and when their train passed another train, a foot away, it went like a breath. On February first, Vallejo visited the Capital; on the second he wrote:

> I was in all the departments and I can do no less than admire its grandeur. I have sat in the same seats where Washington sat and all the great men of the United States. I have seen it all and touched everything. Today, it is quite certain that soon there will be peace; that today or tomorrow the deputies from Richmond are coming to parley with the government. Day before yesterday Congress passed the law abolishing slavery and it has produced a universal sensation.

Vallejo was referring to the passage of the 13th amendment by the House of Representatives on January 31, 1865, abolishing slavery throughout the

United States. The resolution had been approved earlier by the Senate. The "Deputies from Richmond," mentioned in his letter, were the Confederate Commissioners. They met with President Lincoln and Secretary of State Seward on February 3rd on board the *River Queen*, which was anchored off Fortress Monroe in Hampton Roads. Alexander H. Stephens, who headed the Southern Commissioners, was Vice-president of the Confederacy; with him was John A. Campbell of Alabama, a former Justice of the Supreme Court; the third member was R. M. T. Hunter, assistant secretary of War in the Richmond government and president *pro tem* of the Confederate Senate.

From Washington City, Vallejo went to Philadelphia and Baltimore, two cities he considered beautiful. While in Baltimore he thought of his two sons, who ten years before had attended school in nearby Emmettsburg. Returning to New York City, Vallejo found the weather still cold. In a letter to his wife he said, "I am still alive but I don't know how I have been able to endure the cold of this country . . . This city of New York is a town in which every one walks, goes and comes in the streets without recognizing or talking to one another and hub-hub and confusion is such and the noise so great that one talks in shouts to be heard . . . The most beautiful thing is New York Harbor at night. The harbor is surrounded by more than two million inhabitants—it is small and all the cities are lighted with gas and the lights are reflected in the water. Also thousands and thousands of boats move about, also lighted up. Just imagine that you are looking at a starry sky on a dark night, with the stars below in the water. This is indeed very beautiful. Every one is money mad; it seems to me that the people are crazy. Friendship is for the sake of self interest alone and I have not regarded it so up to now and it makes me unhappy, just to think about it. The madness they have is desperate madness."

Vallejo's business in New York was delayed, so he planned to use the waiting time in seeing more of the Eastern portion of the United States. The latter part of March he went to Niagara Falls. While there he bought a souvenir booklet, "Table Rock Album," filled with poems and quips taken from the public register. Vallejo, who had a sense of humor, must have been amused by such comments as, "finest shower bath in the world," "Why are the Falls like a woman? Because they both are always making a lot of noise." To express his own reaction, he wrote on a fly-leaf of the little book, "Niagara is Nature's stupendous prodigy, the best description is silence and the prostrating of oneself and see in it, the Hand of the Eternal."

VALLEJO VISITS BOSTON

The first part of April found Vallejo in Boston where he visited over seventy points of interest, among them Bunker Hill Monument, Old South Church, Franklin's Birthplace, Harvard University and Faneuil Hall. Because of his interest in fruit culture, he made a point of visiting Horticultural Hall.

On the Boston Common, Vallejo saw the Great Elm, then over two hundred years old, near the Old Elm was the Frog Pond which, in Vallejo's guidebook (the gift of a friend by the name of S. I. Morris), was said to be called "Cochituate Lake" by the super-genteel people. On Washington Street, near the westerly corner of the Common, stood the Washington Elm, under whose shade George Washington first drew his sword as Commander-in-Chief of the Continental Army, July 3, 1775—just one year after Vallejo's father arrived in California from Mexico.

On April 7th, 1865 Vallejo visited the Boston Museum whose buildings had cost nearly a quarter of a million dollars. The main building was said, officially, to be spacious, a superb building: its front adorned by elegant balconies decorated by rows of round glass globes, like enormous pearls which at night were luminous with gas. At the summit of the grand staircase was the Grand Hall of Cabinets; in the hall were pieces of statuary and works of Art, and, arranged in glass cases were curiosities from all parts of the known world, not an inch is thrown away. Among the one thousand costly paintings in the Art Gallery was Sully's "Washington Crossing the Delaware," and colonial portraits by Copley, West, Stuart and others.

Days in New York City

The traveling General Vallejo returned once again to New York City and was there when the assassin's bullet ended the life of President Lincoln. He saw the martyred President's body pass through the city's streets on its way to Springfield for burial. From Vallejo's window in the Fifth Avenue Hotel, he watched the funeral procession for six hours, a procession composed of numerous organizations, floats depicting a nation's grief and bands of music playing funeral dirges. Vallejo wrote his impressions to his daughter Natalia who had been born on the late President's birthday and had danced at his first Inaugural Ball in March of 1861.

The end of May came and Vallejo was still in New York. He wrote his wife:

> It's already a month since we should have left for California but so many things have happened which have upset everything, paralyzing the affairs which at the beginning of our arrival had all prospects of having a quick conclusion and a successful one but the war and the assassination of President Lincoln have caused the delay of everything and moreover have kept us here longer than I wished to be. Never-the-less, perhaps I shall be able to leave here by the first of June.

Vallejo was delayed again and the middle of June found him still in New York. He was living at the Barcelona Hotel. He took time out to go to C. D. Frederick's Photographic Studio and had some excellent photographs taken.

Help Given Agent of Benito Juarez

By late summer Vallejo was back in California, busy winding up the contract with General Placido Vega, the agent for Benito Juarez. General Vega came to California to solicit funds for military supplies and munitions for the Juarez campaign against Maximilian, Archduke of Austria, who had been made Emperor of Mexico. Victor Castro, Augustin Alviso and M. G. Vallejo furnished $8,000 in gold coins. Senora Vallejo approved the aid given by her husband; she wrote, "Help General Vega as much as you can; since in helping Vega you help all good Mexicans."

Vega was able to secure help from others beside the native Californians. Samuel Brannan not only fitted out, at his own expense, a regiment of frontiersmen from California and placed them at the disposal of Juarez, but he also purchased over one million dollars of Mexican bonds.

The greatest amount of financial help given to General Vega must have come from Vallejo's two compatriots, Alviso and Castro, as Vallejo found it necessary to deed to Thomas P. Madden some 59½ acres known as Lachryma Montis and the vineyard Quiquiriqui; also 90½ acres of land comprising 96 Sonoma town lots. This was on February 24, 1866. On the same day, the Vallejos filed abandonment of Homestead on the Lachryma Montis property. Early in 1866, Vallejo decided he was unable to take up the mortgage held by Thomas P. Madden, attorney and financier, which with unpaid interest had reached the figure of $27,364.19, so on January 25th Vallejo and his wife deeded to Madden the lands and premises known as Lachryma Montis and Quiquiriqui.

Mortimer Ryan, who had been the overseer of Lachryma Montis, had a lien on the property by a decision of the 7th District Court of Sonoma in a judgment against Vallejo, August 25, 1865. On February 17, 1866 Ryan made a quit claim deed to Madden. On March first Madden agreed:

> In consideration of a deed to me executed by General Mariano G. Vallejo conveying to me in fee simple absolute the property in Sonoma, mortgaged to me by the said M. G. Vallejo, I do hereby covenant and agree to and with the said Vallejo that he may occupy, possess and enjoy the said premises with their appurtenances for the term of five years from the day hereof, paying rent therefore at the rate of one hundred and fifty dollars per month in gold coins of the United States.

Madden also stated in the document that at any time during the said term of five years, he would, upon the payment of twenty-one thousand dollars in gold coin of the United States convey the said premises by deed to the said Mariano G. Vallejo.

Fifteen months later Vallejo, unhappy over the situation Madden had placed him in and remembering what he had done for Frisbie, wrote his wife, "There are men to whom are entrusted interests so freely and for such a long time that they get so attached to the property to believe it is theirs." Naturally Vallejo had in mind his son-in-law, to whom he had entrusted property for John B. Frisbie to manage. On June 26, 1867, Vallejo wrote to Frisbie: "I find myself unable to buy of Mr. Madden the property heretofore sold and conveyed him by me. It is my wish that he would sell the same to you and that you make the purchase and take the contract and management thereof—all for your account." On the reverse side of Vallejo's copy of his note to Frisbie he had written: "A copy of a letter that I wrote to Frisbie in order that he would accept and receive from Thomas Madden the title to Lachryma Montis with the idea that he would redeem it with a part of my interests Frisbie has in his name—Madden is very hard to do business with. He is heartless."

Nothing was done by Frisbie about redeeming Lachryma Montis until the five years mentioned by Madden had almost terminated. On December 9, 1871 General Frisbie paid Madden $21,000 for the mortgaged property. A week later Vallejo wrote his wife: "I now have the title of Lachryma Montis and this has lifted a great weight from me. I have a half of million pesos in stocks which very soon will be at par; Now to pay off some schemes in Sonoma. But I charge you to tell no one anything for it will be better not to for now. If you say anything to the children, warn them to guard the secret well. The girls will go to school sure. As soon as I come home to lay the roof, you can if you wish spend Christmas in San Francisco."

In spite of Frisbie's action in paying Madden for the property, Frisbie did not deed Lachryma Montis and the other property to Vallejo until April 12, 1872; then the deed to Lachryma Montis was made out to Francisca Benicia Vallejo.

After Vallejo's son Uladislao had gone to Mexico with General Placido Vega, Vallejo considered going. He discussed the possibility in a letter dated March 17th, 1869, to his son Platon:

> I owe you two answers to two letters; the first relative to my fall from a ladder and the last one in which you beg me in the name of my children and the children of my children, not to go to Mexico . . . with Vega. Believe me, my son, I am not going to Mexico for pleasure. I am going through necessity. I need the wherewithall to live and seek means of meeting my obligations . . . You have heard it said that your Papa was always rich, that he had been robbed and although he hopes, he should not lose time in earning something for his children.
>
> The blind man who has never seen
> So he does not know what it is to see
> Does not live so joyless
> As the one who afterwards is blind.
>
> So it is, my son, the people who have never been rich can not sense how those suffer who have become poor. Believe me, Platon, I will do whatever I can, not to have to leave for Mexico but I don't promise it to you. I thank you for the advice and I receive it as from your good heart. But I have a wife, your mother whom I love a great deal, three minor children and seven others who make me happy when I see them and I want to make the last effort to help them.

The General did not go to Mexico; so he sold the certificates, issued by the Mexican Government and which he had bought from General Vega, to Charles J. Jansen of San Francisco.

After two years in Mexico, Vallejo's son Uladislao was anxious to come home. From San Francisco, Vallejo wrote the voluntary exile's mother: "I have been hunting for some money to send Uladislao who asks me for it to come here. At last I have arranged it so that it is possible for him to receive in time $150 so that he can come by way of Guadalajara where a gentleman will take him as far as San Blas. There, General Vega will take care of the rest . . . I have managed to sell the wine of Quiquiriqui but they won't pay for it until after three months . . . I have to collect $500 which Mr. Brooks is to give me and that really has kept me here. If he gives it to me soon, it will put Lulu and Maria in the college of Santa Clara. The wine that Dr. Faure makes, no one wants to buy. I don't know what the devil is the matter with it."

TRANSCONTINENTAL RAILROAD JOURNEY

The transcontinental railroad had been completed in May 1869. John B. Frisbie decided to visit Washington, D.C. with the idea of bringing to the attention of the members of Congress the matter of making the City of Vallejo a port of entry and Mare Island a first-class Navy Yard. Vallejo left with the Frisbie party to help look after the junior members. While on the trip, he made these notes dated October 2nd, 1869:

I left Vallejo, California on the 27th of September accompanying Frisbie. I tried to help Fanny, my daughter, Frisbie's wife with all their family which is very large and too young yet to care for themselves alone. We travel swiftly day and night of course, but very comfortable.

The work which has been done in three years to cross the Continent is stupendous; to see it, is one thing; to hear about it, is another matter . . . I recall now that the Suez Canal was started once in Solomon's time. Confucius, the great Chinese law-maker spoke in his time of that work, the grandiose dike. Thirty leagues. What times those were; What times these! At last the Suez Canal is finished after L. Napoleon set to work on it twenty years ago.

What a difference. The railroad that crosses the American Continent was made in three years; a thousand miles a year and at the end of the last year, a Yankee invented a machine to construct twelve miles of track in one day. I am writing this on the iron road.

I would need to write more than the Bible and its Concordance if I wanted to describe the country, its mountains, deserts, its climate, etc. but I will just say that the City (Chicago) is large, beautiful, the streets well planned, beautiful edifices, large establishments of Art.

HOUSEKEEPING VALLEJO

During the latter part of 1869 and the early part of 1870, Senora Vallejo was living in Fannie's home in Vallejo while her daughter was in Albany, New York, putting the Frisbie children in eastern schools. Senora Vallejo was glad to visit in Vallejo where she could be near her children. Adela and Platon, both married, lived there and the two young daughters, Luisa and Maria, were attending St. Catharine's Convent in nearby Benicia. General Vallejo was in Sonoma, El Soltero, busily engaged in improving the grounds of Lachryma Montis and keeping house with his brother Don Salvador. On November 6, 1869 he wrote his wife:

Today, Saturday I received your letter dated the 3rd of this month to which I answer saying: I found the house very clean and so it should have been since you had been here and so it won't suffer harm, every day I ventilate it, opening the windows without touching anything, leaving it as you left it, since you well know that I don't like ever to disarrange or mix up in anything that another does.

As soon as afternoon comes I close the windows of your room and I go down to mine without anything else to do than read and write or make verses as always . . . My expenses are greatly reduced, they won't amount to more than 4 reals a day . . . Here I endure and suffer but it is here I belong and my lot; in another time I spent the money in order to make a decent place because I knew ahead of time the financial castastrophe that was coming down on us. When the property was threatened by auction, I sold, in order to save it; all my property inherited in the Pajaro and turned it over to Mr. Madden for fifteen thousand pesos ($15,000) . . . There are two cords of wood in the storehouse. Around these parts there is a handful of Indians, Simona, Caridad, Guidora, Jerera, etc.

Another letter to Francisca of more than family interest was dated January 3, 1870:

I am so alone, alone in this lovely place. Although alone, I am not fond of absolute solitude; by nature I like company, educated and refined company. I don't like to be the one who always does all the talking . . . I suffer as the result, although here I have books but my eyes are very tired from so much reading . . . Now on to something else. The Italians work very well. I think they are men of good conduct . . . After they planted some vegetables today they finished the ditch, from the white door by the side of the Castile roses up to the place where the water leaves the tank, but what a ditch! Wide, deep and well made, so at last the property is getting better each day and it begins to look now as it did when I had lots of money.

If you were to make me a visit one of these beautiful days, you would find everything in good order. The house is well swept and ventilated . . . La Isadora (Chief Solano's widow) is washing my clothes; tomorrow I shall iron everything except the shirts!

La Isadora, then nearing ninety years of age, had been given a little shack on the Lachryma Montis estate by Chief Solano's faithful friend, General Vallejo. When Henry Cerruti, Bancroft's literary agent, interviewed her several years later (1874), she told him: "The Indians who knew me at the time I was the wife of Captain Solano and who then called me the Princess, still treat me like a princess and also some of the white people such as Remino, Berreyesa, Gonzalo, Captain Salvador Vallejo, and many others who from time to time come to Lachryma Montis to visit me, still call me Princess . . . After marriage with the great Solano, Prince of the Suisines, Topatos, Yoloites, Churactes, he was made Prince of the Topates after having conquered them and who during his lifetime made every one tremble."

While Vallejo wrote that he was *alone*, he was not lacking in masculine companionship. A frequent visitor was Jacobino, a little Italian boy, son of a neighboring vineyard worker. The child adored Vallejo and was amused by the pictures Vallejo drew of the nearby train, engine, cars and caboose, and by the verses the General composed to accompany the drawings, moreover the General's pockets were usually supplied with chocolates and maple sugar cubes for his little friend. Jacobino said he didn't like the way the Patrona [Senora Vallejo] left the Patrono alone.

Not being able to afford all the help needed to keep up Lachryma Montis, Vallejo did a lot of the heavy work himself. He complained that his heart pounded hard, but he felt it was from "old age"—the only thing, he said, that doctors could not cure. But the General knew how to relax, judging from a letter of January 29th, 1870 to Platon:

Today, dawned more beautiful and bright than ordinarily; calm reigned in the air; the sun came out illuminating with its rays all the valley whose hills form the great declivities everywhere, sown with trees of dark green on a background of light green, giving forth the ethereal air which gives life to the living creatures. The whole day has been blessedly calm; it seems that the descriptions of the climate of beautiful Italy is similar to the climate today in this valley.

The afternoon and dusk have been particularly beautiful and indescribably lovely in my poor opinion. And it is the month of January. The sun has sunk in the west and here begins the business of this letter. We are sitting at the table, your Uncle Salvador, Ygnacio Soberanes and Juan Angula. We dined on goose, very well stuffed with red chili, good bread, a bottle of wine and for desert, a frying pan full of excellent beans a la Mexicana, tea and water.

As soon as we had risen from the table, a fire was lit in front of the staircase that leads to the pool; two benches were placed near the fire; I drew near in a white armchair and Salvador in another; the guitar was brought and the song and dance began. Jef seated on the end of a bench seemed with his shadow to be inscribed on the walls of the storehouse. In the big green door, a group of Italians applauding the singing. The night calm but very dark; the driveway, the fountain playing, truly it seemed the place of a pastoral scene, a natural one to which was added enough of the artificial that Lachryma Montis possesses.

The singing and music continue; your Uncle regales us, the spectators, with a thousand stories; salty little lies to lighten the fiesta. Ignacio doesn't stay behind. I enjoy everything, half silent; Juan laughs without a care and Jef does too. Now at nine o'clock at night they are going to dance the jarabe.

Several weeks later (March 30, 1870), Vallejo writes to his wife:

I am cleaning up all the side of the little fence in front on the inside because the Italians are staking up and planting tomatoes. Tomorrow perhaps I shall begin to clean up the road, and the paths of the fountain of the orange trees which are badly rutted from so much rain—so the side of the house is going to appear very clean. The weeping willow with the green foliage is very, very, very pretty; it gives a nice shade . . . The poplars are beginning to show some green; the orange trees are commencing to throw out new shoots and then the lemon, blossoms.

Salvador is well; as always send greetings to all; he is so loth to write that it hurts me to tell him to write although he receives letters from the girls as you know. Tell me if I should send the sewing machine because if you are not going to do anything with it, it would be useless to send it to Vallejo . . . Salvador made a stew yesterday, very tasty and we thought of you . . . The little Chinese makes my tea and toast twice a day and that's enough for me . . . It is 6 in the evening; the sun sets among clouds of fire, the sky was magnificent at the same time the moon came up white as silver among the magnificent cloud effects. I enjoy those phenomenons of Nature.

Senora Vallejo's absence from Lachryma Montis was prolonged by her visit to New York to be with her eldest daughter Fannie Frisbie. The General was pleased that his wife was to have the trip across the continent, seeing many of the interesting places he had seen six months before.

SONOMA WATER COMPANY

In the early days, the waters of the spring of Lachryma Montis had drawn the Indians to the hillside where General Vallejo later developed his estate. These waters had nurtured his vineyards and orchards, and now, in 1873, the crystaline water would be the means of increasing his income. The spring produced 6,000 gallons an hour—enough water to supply not only his ranch but also the citizens of Sonoma who had no wells.

An agreement was made between Vallejo, his wife, Benicia, and William Carlisle and James Forsyth to bring water from the Lachryma Montis spring to the town of Sonoma in 3-inch redwood pipes. The parties of the second part, Carlisle and Forsyth, were to enlarge and deepen the east and north side of the pool. The total length of the main pipe, 8,000 feet, was to be placed at such a depth as not to interfere with public travel. The Vallejos were to allow no ducks, geese or pigs to have access to the pond, nor any animal having a tendency to injure the purity of the water, they were to pay half of the costs of keeping the system in order, and were to have the privilege, after five years, of taking over the water system by refunding the original cost. In reporting progress to Platon, Vallejo wrote on January 29, 1874:

I am busy with a little program of "Sonoma Water Works" which will soon start. It will give me a certain rent of 100 pesos at least a month; increasing always. Everything is done and ready to start. The pipes will be here soon as they can be bought and this will give a push to this little village which is already beginning to grow. The pipes will run along all the driveway to the entrance, from there all along the street to encircle the plaza and the other streets and the plaza will be improved with trees.

Most of Vallejo's time was given to the development of the water system and to the selling of basalt blocks from his quarry for paving the streets of San Francisco. However, he found time to be sociable with Henry Cerruti, one of Hubert H. Bancroft's "literary gentlemen" who was in Sonoma for the expressed purpose of gathering historical material. One evening Vallejo entertained Cerruti and Professor Henry L. Oak, Bancroft's assistant, at dinner.

After the meal, Vallejo began to narrate a few episodes of days gone by, when Cerruti explained, "A gentleman whom I did not know entered the courtyard of the General's villa and notified him that the water pipes had been landed in the vicinity of Sonoma; this piece of intelligence highly pleased him. He forthwith rang the bell and ordered a bottle of wine and four glasses. He then introduced the recently arrived person as Mr. Carlisle. "The redwood pipes came from A. M. Jewell and Company, San Francisco, manufacturers of redwood pumps and irrigation patent pipes. The pipes had been charred inside to keep the water sweet; they were in pieces of six to fourteen feet connected with tenon and sockets, and were priced at fourteen cents a foot. In September of 1875, Vallejo sent out signed notices:

> You are hereby respectfully requested to make an economical and judicious use of the water of the Sonoma Water Works for your domestic purposes, so that all subscribers may be equally benefited thereby. Any extravagance and wastefulness or gross carelessness in leaving the faucets open all night will be charged accordingly.

The Sonoma City Water rates were for a family of not over five persons, $1.50 a month, each additional person 10 cents; for watering one horse or cow, per month 25 cents. Where bathtub is used, 50 cents. Hotels, for each bedroom 25 cents, Saloons $1.50 a month. For washing vehicles, such as carriages, buggies and spring wagons per month, each 75 cents. No street sprinkling allowed with hydrants.

CALIFORNIA HISTORICAL RESEARCH WORK

Henry Cerruti, one of the guests that evening, was an Italian in his late thirties who liked to be called *General Cerruti*. He had been a soldier of fortune in Spanish America and for five years, so he said, was Consul-General for Italy in Columbia; hence the title "*General*." After arriving in San Francisco he was given employment by Hubert Howe Bancroft. Cerruti without mentioning Bancroft's name, had written General Vallejo on March 22, 1874, telling him that he was gathering historical data: "I am very desirous, citizen Vallejo, that you should find it convenient to supply me all possible data concerning your family." Cerruti asked if he should go to Sonoma to copy information from the archives of the Vallejo family, or whether it could be sent by mail. Two days later Vallejo sent his reply to Cerruti:

> I very much appreciate the comments you make mentioning in the History of California which you are about to include the humble name of the Vallejo Family, a name with which the undersigned feels honored to be identified. However humble and insignificant, this name is related and connected in such a close manner with the history of Upper California since its founding.
>
> Senor Consul, that its ommission in such a history would be like the ommission of periods, commas and accent marks in a beautifully written discourse. I should like with all my heart to be able to send you written records of all the points you ask for completing the history but it is best that I should follow your idea of having

you come to Sonoma to make your own notes, It would be too heavy a task and on top of this, my rhetorical style would not be appropriate for your purpose. It is therefore my desire to be the narrator of the historical and biographical episodes that you request rather than trust their composition to my poor talent in such matters. You can consider yourself at home here in Sonoma and I shall be at your orders.

A Mr. William Dixan published a book in England in 1876 and quotes Vallejo as saying, "You asked about the history of California. My biography is the history of California." Cerruti was to find that was true. It was well that Cerruti came to Sonoma at this time; his companionship was a diversion for the General as, shortly before, he had been most despondent. At the time of his greatest depression he had written to Platon:

> There are very exceptional situations in life which are not in the reach of all . . . Mine for instance—an accumulation of bitterness and vexation in every sense, weary of struggling against Fate for a long time now, despairing sometimes of life itself, in a sea of difficulties which embitter it at every instant; exasperated always; the soul uneasy and the heart hardened, disgusted at many men (almost against humanity). With unavoidable debts which Honor, Duty and Society demand, I have been held in anxiety, hellish, frightful and therefore unusual. Nevertheless, I have been able to endure and resist with a certain studied calm all the tempest of censures with outward sang-froid with an austere philosophy, if you will, but in reality, burning in an abyssal inferno of griefs that have poisoned my blood.

There was sufficient reason for such despondent moods; General Vallejo, like many of the Hispano-Californians, had been mistreated, swindled and robbed, often by the very people he had befriended.

Cerruti, with his fluent knowledge of Spanish and his urbane manners (to say nothing for his flair for bestowing delicate flattery), soon won Vallejo's confidence and cooperation. At first, Vallejo only gave a small amount of historical material for Cerruti to read, and he required that it be copied at the Vallejo residence. As Vallejo's confidence in the young Italian grew, Cerruti was permitted to take a bundle of the documents to the Union Hotel, where he was staying, to copy: still later, intriguing with the aid of Vallejo's convivial brother, Don Salvador, bundles of documents were sent to Bancroft's Library in San Francisco where they were copied by the staff.

It was not long before Vallejo realized that his new friend was Bancroft's agent, but that mattered little, now that his interest was aroused. During one of Cerruti's visits to Lachryma Montis, the General told him: "I believe that Mr. Bancroft is in earnest and means to give to the world a true history of California. I was born in this country and once I undertook to write its history. But when I had written about nine hundred pages a great fire burned my dwelling and my poor manuscript which had cost me many long hours of hard work was burned together with the rest. By mere chance my servants succeeded in saving several bundles of documents, referring to the early days of California . . . I will, however, write to San Jose and order my trunk to be sent to Sonoma . . . In it you will find many official papers that are of inestimable value to any person engaged in writing the history of this country. I will place implicit confidence in you; the documents of public interest you will be allowed to copy and letters of a private nature, you will return to me. You must admit that I go to a great deal of trouble for the purpose of contributing my grain of sand toward the completion of the great work undertaken by your friend yet I will be more than repaid if Mr. Bancroft's history be worthy of my country."

To Cerruti's request that the General permit him to take the papers to Bancroft's Library where men could be employed to copy the documents, Vallejo had replied: "Well, be it so while you are about it: there are two other chests of documents which I have never disturbed since the fire. Take them also." Embolden by his success, the eager "literary agent" suggested that Vallejo *give* Bancroft the documents, thus saving the heavy expense of copying them. "No Sir," the General exclaimed, "at all events not now. And I charge you to make no further allusions to such a possibility, if you value my favor. Think you, that I regard these papers so lightly as to be wheedled out of them in a little more than two short months by one almost a stranger. You have asked for my recollections; those I am now prepared to give you." "Good," said Cerruti, taking up his notebook. "All ready, General, you may begin your narrative."

Cerruti's presumtuousness was too much for Vallejo. "My friend," he said, "you are in a hurry, you are more Yankee than Italian. It seems to me that you intend to write history on horseback. I do not approve of this manner of writing books. You seem to forget that history is the light of truth, the witness of past events. I am willing and ready to dictate every thing I can remember but I wish it clearly understood that I must be allowed my own way. I will not be hurried or dictated to. It is my history not yours. If those terms suit you I am ready to commence." Vallejo's rebuke was well received. Upon being told of Vallejo's reactions, Bancroft said that the work was lifted from the category of personal narrative to the higher concept of exact history.

Mr. Bancroft, with his daughter and a niece, visited General Vallejo at Lachryma Montis. Cerruti left the two men together. After this visit, Bancroft considered moving his library to Sonoma where Vallejo, in his enthusiasm, had offered land and buildings. Cerruti noted that Bancroft had made a good impression on Vallejo, so he ventured to ask permission to send a box of documents to the Bancroft Library and was happy to receive a favorable answer. After three days spent in searching among the trunks, Cerruti filled three boxes with historical documents and shipped them by Wells-Fargo Express to San Francisco. A few days later, Vallejo and Cerruti took the stage to Lakeville, then the cars to Donahue where they boarded the steamer *Antelope*.

On board the Antelope Vallejo had a shave. When it was finished, he gave the barber half-a-dollar and was handed some change which the General refused, saying that cigars and liquors were sold at double price on board the steamer, and he could not see why the barber should not receive double pay. Cerruti after his shave refused the change, saying, "Allow me, dear sir, to follow the example of my illustrious friend, General Vallejo."

Immediately upon arriving at the pier in San Francisco, the General and Cerruti went to the Bancroft Library where the General saw eight Mexicans copying his documents. The workers arose and bowed as the General passed. Two hours were spent by the distinguished visitor examining the library. Vallejo saw documents bearing the signatures of Columbus, Queen Isabel the Catholic, Philip the Second, and various other notables who figured during the 15th Century. It was evident that Vallejo was impressed and pleased. Cerruti saw his opportunity and suggested once again that General Vallejo give his documents and papers to Bancroft, thus saving a year's labor of copying. The General gave a quick answer, "He deserves them. Tell him they are his."

Hubert Howe Bancroft was literally speechless with astonishment and joy. He knew that the Vallejo documents would cause his library to be unequalled in original California material and that Vallejo would accept no compensation for them. However, Vallejo did accept Bancroft's hospitality at his princely residence in San Francisco. With his youngest son Napoleon, and his two youngest daughters Luisa and Maria, the General spent three weeks at the mansion, where Bancroft gave a series of festivities including a ball for his guests.

COLLECTING DOCUMENTS

The enthusiasm of Vallejo for Bancroft's quest was such that he was not content to give merely his own documents; he wished to acquire others from his relatives and friends. Accordingly the General and Cerruti went to San Jose and Santa Clara but being dissatisfied with the prospects in these two towns, they decided to go to Monterey.

In Monterey Vallejo was happy. "I love to go to Monterey," he said, "for there I may yet find a little of the dear and almost obliterated past. There is yet the ocean that smiles to me as I approach and the venerable bearded oaks to which I raise my hat as I pass under them. There are streets still familiar and houses not yet torn down and streams and landscapes I may yet recognize as part of my former belongings."

At this time Philip Roach became a candidate for governor and wanted Vallejo to run on the ticket with him as lieutenant-governor. Cerruti was disappointed that Vallejo refused. He wrote to Dr. Platon Vallejo, "I am sorry that General Vallejo should refuse to accept the position as Lieutenant-governor offered to him by a large circle of his friends who had promised to bear the expenses of the election."

CHRISTMAS AT MONTEREY

The Christmas holidays of the year 1874 found Vallejo in Monterey where, on Christmas eve, he attended a dinner and a Cascaron Ball at the home of Don Jose Abrego, the husband of his niece Josefa Estrada. Vallejo said that a thousand cascarones (egg-shells) were broken, some on himself. These cascarones emptied of their original fillings and then packed with perfumed tinsel and bits of confetti were sealed and when broken their glittering contents were scattered on the dark tresses of the senoritas as they whirled past in the dance.

Although Vallejo was fond of dancing, he was not in Monterey for pleasure but for the painstaking business of dictating the history of Alta California and the collecting of ancient documents. He wrote his son Platon that he must continue his writing, that if he stopped there would be no one to contradict the mercenary liars who had defamed the Californians:

I owe you three answers to your long letters but in spite of my desire and always the good intention of doing it, I haven't been able because of always being almost all the time busy with people who visit my office, dictating or talking; opening and reading many old documents of others and even more, making notes so as not to forget what may be erased from memory from one moment to the next.

My historical works continue "their majestic march." There have been written already 900 pages subject to correction, rectification, amending and augmenting and I have reached only the year 1836.

I shall not stop moistening my pen in the blood of our unfounded detractors without losing sight of certain accursed writers!!! who have insulted us, such as Mofras, Shea, Robinson, Gleason and others. You know I am not vindicative but I am and I was born Spanish. To contradict those who slander "tis not vengeance, it is regaining a loss." I want to believe because I feel it is so, that "good ought to be rewarded and evil punished." But it pleases me to believe that there should be a hell with lakes of fire, hot lead and regions of demons with red-hot pinchers to pull out the tongues of slanderers. I am human and weak. I regret to tell you I can't pardon some things, although I know that sentence that "God does not pardon the one who does not pardon."

Some months before Vallejo had expressed himself to Bancroft his feeling about fraudulent writers such as De Mofras.

Today I received your always welcome letter of yesterday, the fifth and I answer it first, to greet you on your fortuitous arrival in California from the States in the East, and second to thank you for the kindness you have given me through the Press in honoring my humble name, without any cause whatsoever. My whole object in cooperating somewhat in the literary endeavors into which you have hurled yourself has been to help you and nothing more.

Accustomed since my youth to work for the advance and material progress of my fellow citizens, I have not been able to remain indifferent to the call of our mutual friend General Cerruti made on me in the name of Science and History; but when I came to recognize the fine talent that form your hallmark, I resolved even with danger to my health, to write for the second time as much as I remember of the story of my country since I am certain and sure I am not mistaken in thinking that you will do justice to all and in your work you will separate the *chaff from the grain* [written in English]. You have a very vast and extensive field in which to work; in it you can refute fraudulent writers such as De Mofras, audacious ones like Shea and another bunch of stupid ones that without knowing California and its government and without having traveled through it scarcely and studied the country have gone to Europe to write not what they should but a series of lies of the most absurd and untrue kind.

Duflot de Mofras mentioned by the General, visited Sonoma in 1842. Vallejo remembered that the French traveler had written in his account of his visit to California that "the Comandánte [Vallejo] at Sonoma had pillaged the Mission of San Francisco Solano to the point of demolishing the church in order to build his own house out of the materials." This was untrue. The large church was in ruins; it had never been completely built—only the walls and floor tile were started. Vallejo, himself, rebuilt the chapel for his soldiers as mentioned before. With his own hands, he prepared an inventory of the furniture and articles he found in the Mission San Francisco when he was sent to secularize the mission. The original inventory of this mission in Vallejo's handwriting is today in the Archives of the Santa Barbara Mission.

Vallejo was anxious to present the true story of the "Osos" or "Bears." In writing to Bancroft he said: "I have caused Captain Cayetano Juarez to come to Lachryma Montis, in order that he may aid me to write all which appertains to the evil things of the 'Bears' in 1846–47. Captain Juarez, who was a witness present at the time and a truthful and upright man, and myself are engaged in recalling all those deeds, just as they occurred. What I relate is very distinct from what has been hitherto published by writers who have desired to represent as heroes these men who robbed me and my countrymen of our property. American authors desire to excuse those robbers with the pretext that in some cases the 'Bears' captains gave receipts for the articles of which they took forcibly possession but as those receipts were worthless, the Californians have the right to say that the Bears or a majority of them were robbers."

Juarez, knowing that Vallejo was continuing to dictate to Cerruti, Bancroft's literary agent, wrote skeptically to Vallejo: "Notwithstanding I have heard that the books you are writing and have written impartially, I have my doubts as to your ability to meet with an American publisher bold enough to write the truth with reference to the revolutions of which we were made the victims, the inhabitants of the frontier town, the Bear Flag Party did not respect our houses. If you succeed in having published one quarter part of the evil that the Yankees inflicted upon us, you will effect a miracle. They stole large numbers of horses and cattle, that were driven to Oregon and other places."

VALLEJO VISITS W. E. P. HARTNELL'S WIDOW

With his two youngest daughters, Luisa and Maria, Vallejo went to Salinas City to call on William Hartnell's widow, Dona Teresa de la Guerra y Carrillo, the eldest daughter of Captain Jose de la Guerra y Noriega. The Captain, formerly from Spain, was for many years Santa Barbara's most noted public servant, the "Pericles" of the Community. Senora Hartnell was the sister of Don Pablo de la Guerra who had recently died, aged 54 years, after a distinguished career of service to his native country and to the land of his adoption. His casket, covered with the flag of the United States, was entombed in the family vault beneath the church of the Santa Barbara Mission in February 1874.

During Vallejo's visit to Senora Hartnell, mention was made of the visit of Monsieur Duflot de Mofras to the Hartnell Rancho El Alisal, early in 1842. At that time Hartnell was away in San Diego attending to official business. A stranger came to the Hartnell door and announced himself as Duflot de Mofras, the French King's agent. He said he had obtained permission from Mr. Hartnell to visit El Alisal. Dona Teresa, knowing that her husband was proverbially hospitable, ordered a room prepared for Monsieur de Mofras and extended him an invitation to dinner. While at his hostess's table, he found fault with every one of the dishes but did full justice to the wine.

Senora Hartnell had stored in her guest room a barrel of the choicest wine sent to her from Santa Barbara by her father for use by the priests when saying Mass in the Hartnell's private chapel. Next morning upon the Hartnell's guest not making his appearance at breakfast nor answering calls, his room was entered and the servants found him stretched out on the floor drunk. When this rude and crude guest left, it was found he had rifled a trunk and taken a new suit of Mr. Hartnell's clothes. Upon Mr. Hartnell's return home, he assured his wife that he had never seen the Frenchman, much less given him authority to stop at his home.

Dona Teresa Hartnell cooperated with General Vallejo in every way, giving him many valuable documents. After his visit, Vallejo wrote Platon: "I was out of Monterey, collecting old documents which I got from the widow of Mr. Hartnell . . . As for De Mofras I will hunt him down as I would a bear and I shall tie him with skill. I'll put a rope around his neck and he'll land and I won't lose my temper when he falls, so shall others fall who have based their writings on the calumnies of the accursed Frenchman . . . I am finishing the year 1836. I have only ten years left which historically are very complicated since thousands of political episodes happened; changes of governors, military movements, battles, missions and missionaries, etc., etc. Also at the end the Americans came, in whose chapter or chapters, ought to be painted as they are . . . I have gotten together many documents from people which they had hidden. When they have seen the equipment in the office I occupy and have heard read some snatches of history they have been convinced that it is a big and serious thing. General Cerruti takes greater pains every day and makes good use of good material with his abundance of words and eloquent style of his rhetoric."

Cerruti remained with Vallejo in Monterey, Vallejo paying most of the expenses. The warmest friendship existed between the two men. However, they were not without their little differences. Vallejo would say, "Cerruti wishes to hurry me and I will not be hurried." Cerruti used to say that Mr. Bancroft would not be satisfied unless a certain number of pages were written every week. Vallejo would ask, "Who is writing this history, myself or Mr. Bancroft?" On the other hand, Cerruti would tell Mr. Bancroft that he would be very pleased when the work was completed; that if he remained another month he would be an old man as he only saw old people, conversing of days gone by. "At my meals I eat history, my bed is made of old documents and I dream of the past."

VALLEJO VISITS HIS OLDER BROTHER

One of the side trips made by Vallejo and Cerruti was to Mission San Jose to see Vallejo's older brother Don Jose de Jesus, who was seriously ill. Cerruti remarked that the chief difficulty seemed to be to keep the General from killing his brother with historical questions lest he die without telling the younger man all he knew.

General Vallejo was not as unconcerned over his brother's illness as Cerruti thought. From Mission San Jose, Vallejo wrote his wife:

> I arrived at this place in which I found my brother close to death; he recognized me when I embraced him in the bed; we cried together, his wife cried too and all his daughters were crying . . . I took his hand, caressed it, patted it and so we remained almost all afternoon and a good part of the night. The next day he seemed a little more alive, I, always at his side.

Vallejo went on to say that telegrams had been sent to Plutarco, the son of his brother and to Dr. Platon Vallejo. The two arrived and Platon gave much hope which comforted the family. Vallejo ended his letter, "If he continues to improve in the two days that follow, perhaps they will let me leave . . . It seems I must give him life, for that reason, his wife and daughters implore me not to leave . . . The girls wish you to pray to San Antonio that he make their Papa well."

Vallejo once again wrote to his wife on April 18th from the Mission San Jose:

> It's two days since my brother seemed a little better, speaking distinctly; his vision is better and chest good to a point. He can move his hand and foot from one side to another even where the stroke of paralysis stiffened him. Everything seems improved although he can't walk. To change his bed every day I have to open his room and Plutarco gives the bath, then puts him in another bed and so when the bedclothes are changed he can get back into bed. The Doctor has many hopes for his

recovery. When Luisa's letter was read to him, he wept easily and he wanted thanks to be given to everyone because they prayed to St. Anthony for him and why he believes he will get well. He receives the Sacraments regularly. I think I will leave this week and if he is relieved I shall return home and I will bring the girls to remain here some days. He wants to know them better and seeing them will relieve him because what happens when my family visits him. He gets better when I come and more so when Platon comes. But he weeps when Platon goes away . . . My brother sends thousands and thousands of greetings, Soledad, the same of love . . . On going through San Francisco I found that Napoleon is engaged to a little American girl from California named Miss Brown and that it is very formal.

Sister Mary Teresa, who was a teacher at the Convent of the Sacred Heart in San Jose, couldn't be with her father, so she wrote on April 10, 1875 saying to Vallejo: "Uncle, what is the matter with Papa? Tell me frankly, have we any hope for his recovery of his health . . . I want to ask 1,000 questions. A thousand thanks for leaving all your business to come to console our afflicted family." Don Jose never fully recovered but lived seven years more.

Another trip taken by the history seekers was to Santa Cruz. They boarded the steamer *Senator* and as the vessel approached the town, Vallejo who had been on the deck for the entire voyage, recognized on the wharf Francisco Rodriguez waving a red handkerchief to him. Upon leaving the steamer, Vallejo went directly to the old soldier (who had served under Captain Salvador Vallejo) and embraced him. Rodriguez enquired about his former commander, saying he had never seen a brave man who could come up to the standard of him. The General invited Rodriguez to Lachryma Montis as he said that his brother Salvador, owing to his old wounds and age, could not travel.

Another soldier, Perez by name, came up and seized General Vallejo's hand, saying, "Praise be to God, my General, for I am rejoiced to see you as young as ever." In parting, General Vallejo laid one of his hands on Rodriguez' shoulder and the other on the head of the faithful Perez and, with dim eyes, blessed them.

VALLEJO'S LAST EVENING IN MONTEREY

The latter part of August, 1875, Vallejo wrote to Platon from Monterey:

I think I'll have to give the last stroke of the brush to the history of California in Vallejo where I shall repair as soon as possible. I expect to leave here next week for home via Vallejo to be there for the wedding of Fanita [Fannie Frisbie's daughter] to which I am invited. In Vallejo we will have time to revise and correct the history which has extended to the fourth volume of 425 pages each. The fifth is started but we have reached the time of 1844 in which the events are very complicated, deeds are multiplied of which many persons who still live were witnesses and they are anxiously awaiting the publication of my work, some purely for curiosity and some to criticise it with all their force and others await it with envy . . . Be that as it may, the history will come out and it will be as you've heard me say many times, the truth impartially written so it can serve posterity as a guide.

On the eve of Vallejo's departure from Monterey on a summer evening in 1875, he was visited by his friends and relatives who wished to bid goodbye to a countryman who had given so much of his time preserving for posterity the records of the founders of Alta California.

Vallejo addressed the group thus (as recorded from an undated clipping from a Monterey paper):

It is indeed a great pleasure to be convinced of the deep interest you manifest in the success of the history of California which I have written and I assure you that your approval of my literary labors is the only reward I had in view when I undertook my historical journey and I thought it highly flattering to my pride to be made the recipient of such high marks of esteem as you bestow upon me. I must state that I perceive with regret that you fail to give others a share of the glory to be derived from my work. Allow me, therefore, dear friends and former companions in arms to assure you that if I have been enabled to bring to a successful completion the History of California from 1769 to 1845, I owe it in a great measure to many of you who have freely come forward and kindly loaned me your family papers and granted to one unpretending historian the benefit of your recollections.

I am indeed sorry tonight I have not time to refer to every one of you who have rendered me valuable assistance. I will however mention the names of those who have placed themselves to greater inconveniences for the purpose of fostering the progress of my historical work. Foremost among my helpers I must cite Jose Abrego, Senora Teresa Hartnell, Juan B. Alvarado, Maurice Gonzales, Jacinto Rodriguez, Benito Diaz, David Spence, Jose de Jesus Vallejo, Rev. Father Casanova, Monterey, Father Cassidy of San Jose, Father Adam of Santa Cruz, Florencio Serrano and Senora Rosalia V. de Leese.

To these I have named and many others I am most grateful for their assistance and information. With regard to the use which I intend to make of the manuscript I will allay all fears you may entertain on the subject by informing you that I intend giving it to Hubert H. Bancroft, author of the Native Races of the Pacific States, who has kindly consented to compile my writings in the great Encyclopedia which he is preparing for the public. You can therefore rest contented and confident that the History of California whose four volumes I have just completed will be given to the world under favorable auspices and under the name of the most conscientious writer of this enlightened century.

VALLEJO-BANCROFT CORRESPONDENCE

When Vallejo had completed the arduous task of recording California's history he wrote on November 16, 1875 a letter to Hubert Howe Bancroft, a portion which follows:

Years ago, at the urgent request of many Californians who desired to see the deeds of their ancestors correctly transmitted to posterity, I undertook the pleasant, though arduous task of recording my native country's history from the date of its settlement by Europeans to the year 1850, when our California became a State in the American Union.

Fortune, however, did not smile upon my undertaking since my manuscript, the result of long and careful labor, was destroyed by the flames that on the 13th day of April, 1867, consumed my residence at Sonoma.

Two years ago, impelled by the same motive, with undiminished enthusiasm for the work, and with a higher idea than ever of its importance, I decided to recommence my task. . . . Though I held, during many years, a prominent position in California, I deemed it proper to mention my acts only when I could not possible avoid it. Personal disputes and petty differences among my countrymen in the early time and with Anglo-Americans in later years I have touched upon lightly as is consistent with historical accuracy. I have no wish to contribute to the revival of any national, religious or personal prejudice, and it is no part of my plan to flatter friends or abuse enemies.

I had at first, my friend, intended to give my labors to the world in my own name, but having noticed with much satisfaction the ability and exactness displayed in your work "*The Native Races of the Pacific States*," I concluded to place my *five* volumes of manuscripts at your disposal, to use as you may think best, being confident that you will present to us a complete and impartial history of California.

Hubert H. Bancroft replied ten days later, November 26, 1875 saying in part:

I have carefully examined the *five* large manuscript volumes upon which you have been occupied for the past two years and which you so generously placed at my disposal. In the name of the people of California, those now living and those who shall come after us, permit me to thank you for your noble contribution to the history of this western land. . . For a period of 30 years from 1815 to 1845, your work stands without a rival among your predecessors in its completeness and interest, and I confidently expect to find it as accurate as it is fascinating. . . . We have in a lighter vein charming recollections of school boy days; popular diversions of young and old; indoor music, dancing and feasting and the outdoor picnic, race and bull fight; ceremonial displays under Church auspices and official receptions of high dignitaries.

I have to thank you not only for this most valuable and timely gift but for some fifty large folio volumes or original papers . . . as well as for your generous interest in the task I have undertaken and your interest among your countrymen in my behalf.

To none of the many who have aided or may aid in my work shall I be placed under greater obligations, General and to none shall I ever more cheerfully acknowledge my indebtedness than to yourself.

Very Sincerely
HUBERT H. BANCROFT

Christmas of 1875 was made interesting for Vallejo by a gift from Hubert H. Bancroft. Vallejo wrote of this gift to Platon: "The 24th past I received a gift from Senor Bancroft as a Christmas present, some five volumes bound as for the library of a Prince. The books are titled *Native Races of the Pacific Coast*." In appreciation of the gift Vallejo wrote a sonnet (which he thought the most difficult form of poetry), extolling Bancroft's work.

Some months earlier, in June 1874, Vallejo wrote Bancroft in part:

I have read with much attention and special care the first volume of your very stupendous literary work which General Cerruti has had the kindness to present to me in your name and allow me to assure you that I was impressed favorably with the accuracy with which you described the peculiarities of the indigenous races of the states in the north Pacific . . . I took the greatest interest to all that pertains to the territory of Upper California especially the part in which you describe the Indians that dwelt from San Diego to the southern frontier of Oregon . . . At various times and under different circumstances I have had to be in contact with the indigenes, and therefore I can assure you that from 1824 to 1847 I have spent my life surrounded by thousands of them; I have used them in various occupations and have had infinite opportunities to study their character, their manner of living, their religious belief, their method of educating their young, their method of entering into a campaign, their style of building their homes and rafts as well as the rites that preceded their burials, in view of which I can in all conscience declare that all you have written on the subject is in perfect accord with the truth.

With the historical work completed, Vallejo returned to his home in Sonoma. The November rains were cold and the roads filled with mud. Senora Vallejo was visiting her sister Josefa Carrillo de Fitch in Healdsburg. Vallejo alone with his ailing brother, Don Salvador, and in a depressed mood wrote his wife:

Since the next day after you left, it has been raining all the time; the cold weather is beginning to be felt and therefore the fireplace gives to bodies of the old and sick the warmth they lack. Some three days ago we had a heavy storm and the wind was so strong that I thought all the trees were going to be cut into pieces but they have resisted and the only complaint I have is that all the honey locust pods and fig tree leaves have been lost and I will have a lot of work in sweeping up the leaves but then if you want nice things done, you have to work for them.

Salvador has been very ill and the girls begged him to come to the room occupied by Napoleon so he can take baths and also so they can cure his pains with mustard plasters but all of this is to no avail and he is getting somewhat better, only using as medicine a few "good drinks" . . . I am feeling like hell—cannot read which for me is something terrible. I am able to write with great trouble and not being able to read or write makes me feel like a fool. I am starting to feel the rheumatic pains and they come in a bad time as very soon we will have the cold weather of January and February. Here in Sonoma, it is getting to be a place for old people; some die too fat, others too thin, others from drinking and most of them from being loafers and good-for-nothing bums, Holy Virgin! Please make a miracle.

DEATH OF DON SALVADOR VALLEJO

With the coming of the year 1876, Vallejo's elder brother, Don Jose de Jesus, continued to improve in health, but his younger brother Don Salvador, born in Monterey on January 1, 1813, grew increasingly worse and passed away at Lachryma Montis on a Thursday morning, February 17th. Don Salvador had married Maria de la Luz Carrillo, the lovely sister of Senora Vallejo, on September 8, 1840 in the San Francisco Solano Mission. Don Salvador took his bride to the adobe home (now Swiss Hotel), which he had built west of his brother's Casa Grande. At the time of Don Salvador's death, the newspapers spoke of him "as a man of strong prejudices who had never become reconciled to the American occupation of the country." This viewpoint was refuted by Salvador's friend Felipe Fierro, editor of *La Voz Del Nuevo Mundo*, who wrote:

> A few facts will suffice to set his (Salvador's) memory right before the American people and the world . . . It is true that he was severe on Fremont and Sutter but to a host of American officers and civilians who upheld with honor, dignity and integrity the proud flag of the Union, have received at his hands their meed of praise.
>
> That Major Vallejo loved the flag rendered sacred by the services of Washington and his compeers . . . is proved by the fact that when the misguided Southerners hoisted the flag of the rebellion, he raised a force of native Californians and marched at their head to take his share of the sufferings of the battlefield in defense of the Union and her free institutions. He held his commission of Major from Governor Stanford.

The flags in Sonoma flew at half-mast in honor of the intrepid fighter who had helped to make the pueblo of Sonoma a safe place in which to live, both in the middle 1830s and in September 1846, when hostile Indians of the Walla-Walla tribe threatened.

Nicholas Carriger, a pioneer from Tennessee, recalled the generosity of Don Salvador. He believed that Major Vallejo deserved a pension because as Carriger said, "When a large number of emigrants' wagons were camped in the vicinity of Sonoma, filled with sick women and children, the Major used to come around every morning at five o'clock and offer the sick people sugar, chocolate, flour, beef . . . his acts of kindness were many and he never begrudged the services he rendered us. When the news of the Donner family reached Sonoma, he was amongst the first to start to their assistance."

For twelve years Don Salvador spent much time at Lachryma Montis in the home of his brother where he was a great favorite with the General's children. This did not please Senora Vallejo too well. She felt that he should not have left his wife, her sister, at Las Trancas in Napa County, to care for their children alone.

Don Salvador at the time of his death was no longer a wealthy man, but the General felt that his brother's estate could well reimburse him for certain expenses. He presented the following bill:

CHARGES AGAINST THE ESTATE OF DON SALVADOR VALLEJO

For five thousand dollars loaned for the rebuilding of his home	$5,000
For twelve years of maintenance, that is, room and board, washing & ironing at $20 (20 pesos a month $240)	2,880
For payment to Dr. Wells, in his last illness	40
For payment to Dr. Van Geldern, in his last illness	20
For the coffin for his burial	20
For digging the grave	5
For Funeral carriages from Vallejo	20
For clothing for twelve years	500
March 17, 1876	$8,485.00

In answer to a letter of sympathy received from an intimate family friend, Mrs. W. W. Chipman at the time of Don Salvador's death, Vallejo wrote on March 4, 1876:

Receive my sincere thanks for the words of sympathy you sent in your letter dated the 23rd of last February regarding the death of my brother, Don Salvador. Death is a mystery and I would give all I possess in this world and all I hope ever to possess to know what my dead brother knows. Perhaps there is a new light on the other side. Who knows? We come into the world in a miraculous manner, knowing nothing until reason penetrates the modus operandi. Also we suffer at death and where do we go?

On the 24th of the same month, Vallejo wrote to Mrs. Chipman again:

After the death of my brother, another misfortune followed. In San Jose, Tonita Vallejo daughter of my brother Jose de Jesus died and last week a niece of my wife, the daughter of Felicidad (Senora Victor Castro) died. Her name was Jovita Castro, so we have been in sorrow all the time. Without doubt, all in this world, as well as ourselves, will come to know what is on the other side of Eternity. I hope there will be no lawsuits, nor lawyers or taxes or earthquakes; no mud in the streets, nor dust nor wind or other manifestations of nature. If not, it will be a real paradise, as it is pictured by wise men.

According to the family, another manifestation of nature which Vallejo disliked was an electric storm.

The letter-writer of the Vallejo family was the General, so he was the one who informed his relatives of the death of Salvador. In reply to his letter, Prudenciana Vallejo de Amesti wrote from her home in Monterey on April 11, 1876:

Dear Brother Guadalupe:

Yours that you wrote me on the 28th of last month is in my possession and I am well aware of what you tell me. I see you don't like to write sad things and in truth they are sad, the memories you call to mind of the death of our dear brother and the others.

In answer brother, let me say to you that we ought to resign ourselves to everything, that is in sadness or happiness. You were not so ignorant that you did not know that there is no tranquillity and joy of spirit outside our religion. Brother, we are now of an age to think seriously of the things necessary to the salvation of our soul; not to wait to take care of such matters when one scarcely can. You'll probably say, I have turned priest in order to preach to you and give you advice. No, sir, this is from your poor sister who loves you and appreciates you . . . Write to me for I always receive your letters with pleasure.

Vallejo needed no preachment from his devout sister nor from his equally devout son, Platon, nor from his priest nor anyone. Vallejo was a man of faith, a faith developed through years of living through fast-moving scenes and vitalized during quiet hours of meditation and reflection. On one occasion he wrote Platon expressing his belief: "All is changing in the world; agitated and renewed under the excelling supervision of the Intelligence of the Supreme Maker. In everything can be seen the finger of God directing the Universe, without missing accounts of a single atom of all the materials flying invisible through space. He who directs us and protects us with Infinite Mercy, shield us with hope, giving us commandments to obey and thus reach Divine Truth."

VALLEJO SPEECHES

There had been so much publicity in regard to the historic research work which General Vallejo had done for Bancroft that his daily mail was filled with requests from writers and newspaper scribblers and with invitations to make speeches. An impromptu talk which no doubt he himself enjoyed, as it required no preparation, was given by the General on a Saturday evening in Dashaway Hall, San Francisco. When General Vallejo was observed at their meeting by members of the Democratic Club of the 10th Senatorial District, he was loudly cheered and called upon for a speech.

Vallejo told the audience that in 1850, when the Whigs and the Democrats started solicitating members for their parties, he and other Californians knew nothing of the distinctive principles of either party. He and his nephew, Pablo de la Guerra, decided before taking sides that they would listen to representative men from each group explain the differences. They listened to what T. Butler King and others had to say on the Whig side; viz, that the Whigs were the rich folks, the gentleman's party and the laws should be made to favor them. Then, Vallejo said, they heard what General Halleck and others had to say about the Democrats that they advocated laws to operate upon the poor and rich alike and they had always best conducted public affairs.

The General then told his appreciative audience that he had advised his nephew that the Democratic Party was the one to join and that he had acted with it until the South seceded when he supported the war measures of the Government. Because of this, he said, some Monterey and Sonoma Democrats had called him a *Black Republican* and caused his defeat as an elector. In spite of this, he told the gathering that he would support the Democratic nominee.

When Vallejo felt that the rabble-rousing sand-lot orator, Denis Kearney, a Democrat, was "a disgrace to this civilization" he voted for the Republican George Perkins for governor.

CENTENNIAL ORATION

There was one request for a speech which Vallejo felt he could not refuse. It was the invitation from Reverend Joseph Sadoc Alemany, Archbishop of California, to deliver the oration on the occasion of the centennial anniversary of the founding of the Mission San Francisco de Asis. As usual when undertaking anything of a scholarly nature, the General discussed it with Platon. He wrote him:

I had to come from Sonoma last Sunday to this city (San Francisco) to arrange for the talk for the 8th, to finish it and study it a bit. As it is not a romance, the speaker must be bound to dates and names of people and as there are many, it isn't easy to keep them all in mind. Therefore I will have to read most of it. It is work of somewhat of a difficult task for me alone. What I am going to write is not fiction. It is the real and true history of the San Francisco Mission, the Presidio of San Francisco and the history of the city of San Francisco with its flaws and dirt. The Archbishop gives me only thirty minutes.

The Archbishop and others have suffered equivocation and errors in history. I shall correct them. The Monitor, the Chronicle and others claim that the founding was the 8th or 9th. Both are foolish. The fourth of October is the day. I have the basis for proving it. Friend Savage (Bancroft's researcher) writes Spanish well and helps me a great deal.

On October 8th (1876), the ceremonies began at ten o'clock in the morning at the San Francisco de Asis Church (Mission Dolores), with a Pontifical Mass and sermon. At their conclusion, exercises were held at the old Mechanical Pavilion where about 10,000 people heard the speeches of Governor Irwin, John W. Dwinelle and General M. G. Vallejo. The General gave his speech in Spanish. How beautiful must have sounded the names of the early navigators and of the Franciscan Padres when Vallejo spoke them in his native tongue.

The ceremony of the foundation of the San Francisco de Asis, according to Vallejo, took place on the fourth of October. Don Jose Joaquin Moraga and his soldiers, Don Fernando Quiros, his two pilots and the major part of the crew of the packet were present, also the four padres, Palou, Thomas de la Pena, Cambon and Nocedal. The priests participated in the Mass which was sung with the ringing of bells and the firing of salutes.

Vallejo gave a condensed synopsis of the events by which the Port of San Francisco came into possession of Spain. He spoke of the navigator Cabrillo and of the English buccaneer Sir Francis Drake, who had anchored and perhaps remained a month in the small bay which Vallejo said the Californians called the Port of Tomales. Vallejo added, "It is an absurdity to suppose there can be any connection between Sir Francis Drake and the Port of San Francisco except in the imagination of some visionary geographer."

General Vallejo told his attentive audience, "It is not only the diary of Father Palou that serves me as authority to fix upon the exactness the day of possession and foundation respecting the garrison and Mission. This data I had obtained, a long time before I had even seen or read the diary, from the lips of military men and settlers who were eye-witnesses to the ceremonies; that is to say from Lieutenant Moraga and from my father Don Ygnacio Vallejo." Vallejo mentioned twelve others by name and said there were still others but he did not wish to be too lengthy.

In his speech Vallejo recalled that when he was adjutant of the garrison of the San Francisco Presidio he was present with the soldiers under his command at the October 4th, 1830 Foundation celebration of the Mission.

Among the priests there were Padre Buenaventura Fortuni of the San Francisco Solano Mission and Padre Juan Amoros from San Rafael. Vallejo further recalled that when he was a child that Padre Amoros was chaplain at the Royal Presidio Chapel and there on January 3, 1813 Padre Amoros baptized Vallejo's younger brother Salvador. Vallejo told that when Father Amoros came to celebrate Mass in the chapel of the soldiers on Sunday he always brought a few sweet figs, dates and raisins in the sleeves of his habit which he distributed after Mass to the boys of the Sunday School after he had given instructions in Christian Doctrine. Vallejo continued speaking of Father Amoros: "I speak with much feeling of kindness toward Father Amoros because I am cognizant of his great virtues, his pure heart and sincere devotion. Moreover, it was with him I made my first confession and from his holy hands I received for the first time the consecrated bread of the Eucharist."

Vallejo mentioned the names of many of the early-day Padres, saying he had met Padre Jose Altimira who had established the San Francisco Solano Mission in Sonoma. Vallejo having given much time to praising the Missionaries "To whom," he said, "is due the civilization of so many thousands of souls" he thought it appropriate "to make a few remarks in defense of the good name of the individuals who governed this country during the Mexican administration whose reputations have been sometimes wantonly attacked."

Vallejo referred to the Missions' wealth saying "That the Missions were rich we all knew but that the Mexican governors robbed the Missions is an absurdity." Vallejo mentioned that the four Mexican governors Arguello, Echeandia, Victoria and Figueroa either left California poor or died poor there. The wealth of the primitive days of the Missions was sent according to Vallejo to Spain, Mexico and Italy. "Neither the Governors nor the Californians ever partook of that wealth."

In closing his speech, General Vallejo asked his audience, "What shall be the destiny which the Supreme Benefactor has prepared for this portion of our beautiful native land for the next coming hundred years? I entertain the full conviction that the Hand of the Great Creator by which is guided the progress and happiness of mankind, will carry us to the highest degree of excellence in all the branches of knowledge. Then it is to be hoped that those who will celebrate that day taking retrospective view of the present epoch will remember with gratitude what this generation by Divine aid has established for them to carry on until they reach moral, intellectual and physical perfection. And let us from this moment send cordial salutation to our fortunate descendants who will see the brilliant dawn of the *second* Centennial of the Foundation of the Mission of San Francisco de Asis.

DEATH OF CERRUTI

While the General was still in San Francisco, he received a telegram from his wife telling him the news of Henry Cerruti's suicide on October 9th 1876 in Sonoma. Cerruti who had lost heavily in mining stocks (about $30,000) went up to Sonoma to the Union Hotel where he had formerly stayed and carried out his threat, made to his co-workers at Bancroft's library, to take his own life. He took morphine, chloroform and strychnine. Senora Vallejo was sent for and personally administered an antidote but it failed to revive him. Mr. Bancroft was in New York at the time. He wrote Vallejo, "I am very sorry about Cerruti. He was a good man and very honest; but he fell into the hands of men without honor or conscience. They rushed him, he was ruined and he ruined others and had no alternative than to commit suicide when he saw he had been deceived. Poor man."

Vallejo in commenting on Cerruti's death, wrote to his friend Caroline Chipman:

> When I went to the Centenary (Mission San Francisco de Asis) I spent days and nights (8 days) composing and writing the speech in Spanish. After the celebration, I intended visiting you in the evening, when I received a telegram from Sonoma in which I was informed of the suicide of General Cerruti. I had to leave the city at 7 in the morning in order to assist at his funeral. Poor Cerruti!
>
> This followed the failure of Frisbie and not only did he (Frisbie) fail but he involved me to my ruination. I lost $156,000 and this has caused me not only sorrow but more, a deep embarrassment, almost to the point of losing my faith and committing a transgression . . . others can ruin one and leave one in an accursed situation. All these difficulties and tribulations have made me sick physically and emotionally. I was hoping to arrange my affairs with F. (Frisbie) in Vallejo but he, F. arranged them differently. That's the way the world is. "When one thinks there are hams in the pantry, there aren't even sticks" says a Spanish proverb.

Vallejo told Mrs. Chipman that "You are most kind to tell me that my letters are poetic and that you like my Spanish style. A thousand thanks for the compliment. Perhaps there is or rather there must exist between us a certain intellectual understanding. Your letters charm me and your conversation transports me to the region of thought which flies increasingly on to the mansion of memories. You know that memories are a precious gift of Heaven which carry us to the imaginery spaces, where we relive our past life. When I make you a visit, and talk, talk and talk in Spanish not English which language I cannot speak and it annoys me not to be able to express my ideas."

FAILURE OF FRISBIE

The death of William C. Ralston, president of the Bank of California, the year before had caused the so-called *Bonanza stocks* to go down rapidly. The decline in values had not only caught Cerruti but John B. Frisbie as well. Frisbie was president of the Vallejo Savings and Commercial Bank whose depositors had been gradually withdrawing their money, with the result that the bank closed its doors.

The emotions of Vallejo during these difficult days are revealed in a letter to his son, Platon, dated October 26, 1876:

As I am so beset with so many evils that have befallen me since the failure of Frisbie, I haven't written you or answered your letter of the 18th. Perhaps you will have seen the last letter I wrote to Frisbie; he answered me then and I think he did his best for eloquence. Perhaps, from now on he will conduct himself better when he rises again. God grant it. But one has said, "And when I acknowledge my fault, what do I eat." Frisbie ought not to have jeopardized or risked what was not his, neither in his speculations nor in the stocks.

I am hunting for and gathering together what old paper I have in which I may be able to get something to support my family. Up to now I have been very foolish; from today on, I shall try not to be and I shall try to twist whatever necks come to my hand. To be an honest man among so many scoundrels is practically impossible. The world is bedevilled. One can't live in it without being a rogue, through and through.

I received from Father Luis a letter very worthy of his fine mind which gives me more pleasure and pride than the Archbishop's and why? Because in a little poem I wrote, he suggested to me the idea of using in English the words "One Hundred Years Ago," when giving the talk on the 8th of this month. I am very grateful to him because I know he is sincere. His letter is a treasure for my private archives.

Believe me in spite of my physical and mental forces, I am truly bored, tired of living in this place which is so solitary. Perhaps the forced philosophy that I have carried on my shoulders for so many years finds me now desperate and with the last blow to my fortune I shall become older than a Centenarian. Every illusion that is lost makes more grey hairs come. I not only have entered into maturity but I have passed the zenith of my life; my mind has reached its completeness and withdraws silently meditating the mysteries of existence, elaborating on ideas to start the voyage to Truth. Each day that passes draws me near the tomb. And in spite of the memories of past joys, these fly like a shadow, there being nothing left but the trail of false deceptions of youth. What to do? Conform oneself to the inexorable law of Fate.

But it is very hard after 68 years to have to go searching for the means to live and to seek our daily bread with a thousand anxieties. I can't forget about Frisbie since he scarcely told me in what or how he has lost every thing. Of course you probably read the letter of Frisbie and you see that he says that in his losses he involved me too. What a crime!

Some of the people in the town of Vallejo were affected by Frisbie's financial losses, having been depositors in his bank. Vallejo felt extremely sorry for them. On January 11, 1877, he wrote to Platon:

At last I am going to answer your two letters, one dated the 28th of December just past, and the other the 4th of this month in which you tell me the sad state of many people in Vallejo suffering and lacking even the most necessary things for life which causes me great pain perhaps because of my sympathy. Poor people are always to be pitied especially those who have little children to support and have no more resources than their work which if it is lacking leaves them the alternative of robbing or begging, or committing suicide.

What a difference between the present time and those that preceded the usurpation by the Americans. If the Californians could all gather together to breathe a lament, it would reach Heaven as a moving sigh which would cause fear and consternation to the Universe. What misery! And it is much more intense than when everyone without exception lived in abundance. This country was the true Eden, the land of promise where hunger was never known, nor charity—if you can just utter such an expression since no one had to exercise it.

VALLEJO WRITES TO THE POPE

Archbishop Alemany had told Vallejo he could have thirty minutes for his address at the Centennial of the Mission San Francisco de Asis. Having so recently gathered historical information for H. H. Bancroft, it was not too difficult a task to write his speech with the help of Spanish speaking Thomas Savage, a literary agent of Bancroft. Vallejo decided to send a copy of his address to the Pope. On November 8, 1876, he wrote to Pius IX:

To His Holiness Pius IX:

On the 8th day of October just passed there was celebrated in San Francisco the Centenary of the founding of the Mission of the same name under the auspices and direction of the Illustrious Archbishop Fray Jose Alemany, His Illustriousness had the kindness to name me the orator of the day to narrate the story of said founding, which I did on said day before an immense crowd that gathered from all parts of the State of California and other parts of the Republic. The speech to which I refer I have the honor, Most Holy Father to enclose in this letter asking you to accept it is a gift which a Catholic Californian makes to you; a Californian, son of one of the founders of this privileged land who has seen in it since his infancy, Christianity unfold, being a living witness of the apostolic work of the missionaries who planted here the seed of the Gospel.

M. G. VALLEJO

A copy of his letter to the Pope, Vallejo sent to his son Dr. Vallejo. On November 27, 1876 not having heard from him he sent the following letter:

I don't know what to think of your silence in respect to my plan to write a letter to the Pope including for him a copy of my speech of the 8th of last October; I'm inclined to think that the Fathers that I wanted to consult have not approved. As to this I ask myself: "Why should it be improper for a Catholic regardless who he is, to address the Vicar of Jesus Christ? Isn't the Pope, the father of the Church to whom the faithful have the right to and address in all the circumstances of life? As you have said nothing to me on that, I have believed that you don't approve of my sending the speech and even less that I should write directly to His Holiness.

JOURNEY TO MEXICO

The natural resilience of John B. Frisbie, supported by the financial help of a brother-in-law, Patrick Lynch of New York, enabled Frisbie to plan a trip to Mexico, taking General Vallejo with him. Vallejo had long wished to visit Mexico, the native land of his father. He had heard much of the Republic south of the border from his son Uladislao who had visited there several times. Vallejo had read even more information in his Spanish Encyclopedia with 55 pages devoted to Mexico—its Agriculture, Industry, Commerce, History, Literature, Science and Arts.

Vallejo left California in May, 1877 which was six weeks after his protracted visit with his daughter Jovita Haraszthy, trying to smooth out her marital difficulties. Vallejo met Frisbie in Chicago and together they continued to New Orleans, where they arrived on May 19th and registered at the St. Charles Hotel. Vallejo said that everything looked dilapidated. Modern conveniences were lacking, and he thought the inhabitants seemed listless owing to the extremely hot climate and the ravages of the late war. In the 500 miles of travel, Vallejo had not been sick a day which he thought said a lot for a man who was almost seventy years of age.

The crossing of the Gulf of Mexico took seven days. Arriving at Vera Cruz, the port where Hernando Cortes burnt his ships, Vallejo found the weather sultry. From there he and Frisbie traveled by train "through the most picturesque mountains in the world" to Mexico City. Vallejo, like many another tourist, was indisposed for the first few days in the Capital City. When he recovered, he started sight-seeing as described in a letter home:

> The Cathedral and its sanctuary are stupendous works. The Church of Our Lady of Guadalupe, some two miles from the Cathedral is the most beautiful perhaps in the world as far as its architecture and ornamentation. There is the Portrait of the Virgin of Guadalupe. I climbed the Sanctuary, knelt and kissed the feet of the Lady and touched her with my hands. The thick frame and the rays of light are of solid gold. The immense passage-way from the altar to the seats of the Bishops and Canons are of pure silver. I sat down on purpose in the Arch-bishop's seat and the Father who was guiding me said that the Archbishop Alemany had sat there too. In the center of the pavement is the vault of the illustrious Viceroy Bucareli who contributed so much to the founding of California.

General Vallejo was interviewed by a reporter of a Mexican newspaper, *The Monitor Republican*. Quite aware he was talking for a Mexican publication, he commented, "I am an American because the treaty of Guadalupe placed me on the other side of the line, dividing the two nations but I was born a Mexican [sic]; my ancestors were Mexican and I have always maintained with my sword the honor of Mexico. I have both Mexican and American children and I desire for my native land all the prosperity and progress enjoyed by the country of some of my children and mine by adoption. The day that Mexico has a railroad which devouring distance unites it with California, commerce and industry will flourish." The reporter added his comment, "We hope the Government will see the advantage of General Vallejo's project and give him a concession." Vallejo as well as Frisbie made contact with Don Matias Romero, the Mexican Secretary of the Treasury. Vallejo wrote from the Hotel Iturbide on June 7th:

> Sr. Ministro Dn. Matias Romero
>
> My respected Sir:
>
> General Frisbie and I are travelling together. And as we are stopping at the Capital of the Mexican Republic, we desire to visit the people we know who reside in it. We had the pleasure of knowing you in Washington D.C. some years ago and

it would be very pleasing to us to greet you personally for which interview I ask you to indicate to me the day and hour in which it can be effected.

Three days later Vallejo received this reply:

Replying to your appreciated letter of this date in which you were pleased to tell of your arrival at the Capital manifesting to me your desire to see me. I have the pleasure to say that I shall do so with the greatest will, if you will take the trouble to come to the Secretariate of the Treasury tomorrow at six P.M.

The California travelers had met Senor Romero in Washington, D.C. in 1865. Don Matias Romero was a small, thin man with a large bald head and large black eyes. It was this same Don Matias Romero who, as a friend of General Ulysses S. Grant acted as his escort when Grant made two unsuccessful trips through Mexico, hoping to promote railroad and mining interests between the United States and the country which Grant had come to love, when he was a young officer during the Mexican War. When General Grant was an ex-president of the United States and was swindled by his Wall Street partner (Ward) and left practically penniless, Don Matias Romero, the Mexican Minister, called at Grant's New York residence and offered funds. Grant, at that time said, as he left the room that he would have to consult his wife, Julia. When he returned to his parlor, he found that Romero had gone, leaving a check for a thousand dollars on the table.

In Mexico City, Vallejo stayed at the Hotel de Iturbide, a beautiful stone building with balconies surrounding the inner patio. It had been the residence of the ill-fated Emperor Iturbide. While living in this historic palace, an aide-de-camp from the National Palace brought Vallejo a photograph of the President of Mexico, inscribed thus—"Mexico June 19, 1877, To General Vallejo—Your servant and friend—Porfirio Diaz."

While in Mexico, Vallejo managed to find time to write to the different members of his family; sometimes utilizing the services of the professional letter-writers of Mexico City. The following are portions from some of his letters:

Unhappy country, so rich, so beautiful! Now I shall tell you something about this city, so famous in the annals of our history. The early Spaniards, our true ancestors founded it about 356 years ago and they continued the subsequent years up to 1821 to build it up with monumental edifices, secular in nature, worthy of the grandeur and munificence of their creators. Since the last date (1821) nothing has been improved nor built except for some houses of adobe such as the mission ranch house with tile roofs and other roofs of shingles (without nails) held down so that the wind wouldn't carry them away with stones or rather rocks, a thing which amazes and shames one. How backward is this country.

The City of Mexico contains three hundred thousand inhabitants and of that number there are two hundred and sixty thousand Indians who infest the streets half naked; some in skins and others in tatters without shoes; laden with charcoal, mats, ollas, etc; the Indian women selling tortillas and other kinds of edibles with one child held by the hand and another nursing . . . There are in this city, many good things for the time when another class of people will come to revive it. An

immigration of at least five million white families is necessary for this country.
It has many elements of prosperity and riches but they can't be exploited today. Agriculture is in its infancy and the Mexicans haven't the means to export the products to the rest of the countries of the world, in spite of having very rich lands. The mines are very rich, a thousand times richer than those of California but the uncertainty resulting from the continuous revolutions halt their exploitations although they work some of them. I haven't seen one single broom with a handle with which to sweep and they give the reason that the Indian woman would be deprived of their earnings from selling their brushes of straw and cane.

Vallejo and Frisbie remained in Mexico six months, Frisbie studying the social, political and financial economy of the country. He believed that there was a great opportunity for legitimate and commercial enterprises, what with the natives providing the cheap labor and skilled labor providing the management. Capitalists would then be encouraged to invest. Frisbie could foresee prosperity for Mexico and wealth for its developers. He was anxious to return to the United States, to make the proper contacts with the moneyed men of the East. Vallejo was in no hurry to embark from Vera Cruz which was suffering from an epidemic of yellow fever. He thought for awhile that he would return home by a steamer leaving from Acapulco. He wrote, "I shall become acquainted with this interesting part of the country (Lower California), where I shall be able to survey probably a country side that very soon will be worth to me some thousands of pesos. From there I shall continue to San Francisco. To make this trip, I think some $600 is enough, almost equal to what I need to make the trip returning by the Eastern States. With this idea in mind, Vallejo went as far as Cuernavaca. There he made a change in his plans which he dictated through a professional letter-writer on October 6, 1877 for his wife:

I left Mexico City day before yesterday, heading for Acapulco to take the ship which passes from Panama to San Francisco; but I reached this place (20 leages from Mexico City) and found that in order to reach Acapulco, there are three hundred miles yet with a sun each day of 104 degrees; very bad beasts of burden, mules, and saddles very old and weak. The prospect seemed very unfavorable to me and I abandoned the trip. I am returning to Mexico City and shall take the train to Vera Cruz and from there go to New Orleans . . . Fifteen or twenty days have passed in which there has been no Yellow Fever and I am trusting God that I shall arrive . . . I believe that Frisbie left today for New York. He invited me to go along but the fever is a terrible sickness. It is infernally hot. I believe I have never felt it so much. I am carrying in my trunk thousands of Mexican things for all.

Vallejo's last letter from Mexico was to his wife and was written on October 17th on stationery of the Consulate General of the United States of America:

On the first ship that reaches Vera Cruz, I shall leave for California via Syracuse. Now, there is no fever, Frisbie went on ahead 'risking his skin' but he went through well, thank God. He was under pressure and had a great need to be in Washington during these days, for that reason he went . . . When I left Vallejo I weighed 231 pounds; four days ago I weighed myself in Cuernavaca and I weighed 191 pounds. I am dried up from not eating or rather eating badly. I can't walk. I'm so thin but I'll be patient because it is foolish to let myself die among these people.

Vallejo left the Capital City of Mexico November 14th, 1877 and sailed from Vera Cruz on the fifteenth on the "City of Merida" which (according to Vallejo, a magnificent ship) bound for New Orleans from which he took a train to New York. He arrived in Syracuse on November 23rd. There he found his daughter Adela who was visiting Adelita, the granddaughter who had just married a "young man named McCarthy." Vallejo expected to leave for California just as soon as Frisbie returned from Washington, D.C.

Vallejo wrote on December 8th to his wife:

Lynch [Frisbie's brother-in-law] told me last night that Frisbie would come to-morrow, Sunday, so that we shall not leave until next week if there is not some obstacle that prevents our trip. It is as cold as a glacier; everything is covered with snow. The house in which I am as a guest belongs to Adela's son-in-law, Adelita's husband. He as well as the others take care of me with careful attention and affection . . . The house from the lowest (floor) is kept at a good temperature by the heaters which are used in winter.

I have so much to say about the things in Mexico that my head doesn't contain all the ideas; it seems to me my brains are bursting or that my cranium will break from thinking so much of that unfortunate country. What vanished illusions. And to think that things can't be remedied by the Mexicans themselves, is a deep grief to me.

VALLEJO RETURNS HOME

Soon after his return home, Vallejo, after writing to H. H. Bancroft received from him the following letter, dated December 28th, 1877 from his residence at 556 11th Street, Oakland:

My dear General:

I am just in receipt of your kind letter, announcing your safe return for which we all cannot be too thankful. I am impatient to see you and hear from your own lips all about your adventures in Mexico. You and General Frisbie have made yourselves famous since you have gone.

Of course I will send the Native Races. I am sorry to have made you so much trouble. Shall I send the books by mail or to the Consul here. I hardly know how Cerruti sent things to Mexico. Poor Cerruti. I have just been writing up my LITERARY INDUSTRIES in which you and he figure to the extent of several chapters. In the history of California, likewise your name appears oftener than any other man.

I hope all my work will be done to your satisfaction. It is good to know that you are back again. Tell me the day when you will be in San Francisco so that I may meet you there. I would be delighted to see you at my little house in Oakland which I have rented for the winter only. My kindest regards to Mrs. Vallejo and the young ladies. Mrs. B. and Kate desire to be kindly remembered.

Very Sincerely
H. H. BANCROFT

Financial problems were waiting for Vallejo, to be met in the new year of 1878. A new contract had to be executed with the Italians, Antonio and Angela Caminata and Giusepe and Francisco Fosati, as the vineyards they had been caring for on a share basis, had been destroyed by the phylloxera and had to be uprooted. Vallejo had found the Italians very satisfactory in working his vineyards.

With the idea of making a bit of needed money, Vallejo tried to conclude a scheme with two New Yorkers whereby they would pay $8,000 in gold if he accompanied them to Mexico, where his prestige would facilitate their getting a permit from the government for construction of a railroad from Acapulco to Mexico City. In explaining the proposition to Senora Vallejo, Vallejo wrote her: "With $8,000 I can do something; for example I would leave $2,000 to you for all expenses; $1,000 for Maria (Maria was engaged). $1,000 for life insurance of $40,000; $1,000 for the trip going and returning, and to spend in Mexico for food and clothing $3,000 more. So if I should drown or if I get killed you would have $40,000 and if nothing happens, nothing will be lost. Nevertheless, I don't like the trip but necessity knows no law."

Nothing came of the Mexican Railroad scheme. It was necessary however for Vallejo to spend a great deal of time in San Francisco seeking out witnesses and locating and translating documents in connection with his claim to a portion of the old San Francisco Presidio, the Pozo de la Marineros (the Sailors' Well). The son of Juan B. Alvarado from San Pablo was helping him and both were staying at the Palace Hotel. "We are here just gabbing together," Vallejo said, "Every day we take breakfast together, same for lunch and we are enjoying ourselves greatly, walking about the immense corridors, and pillowed on beds of comfort for just one dollar a day. Nevertheless it is a lot of money for those who have it not."

Vallejo, indeed, "had it not." He had reached that low financial point where he had to ask for small personal loans. He wrote his wife that he had directed Lulu to ask her brother Platon to lend him $100 to pay the Hotel and the witnesses and notaries in connection with his litigation. He asked his daughter Adela "to go to the Doctor (her husband). She has enough money, she tells me so. I dared to ask her for a loan of $1,000 and when returning it, paying her $50 a month. The Doctor refused and this caused me some embarrassment. It is the first time I have bothered them in my life."

Being refused by Doctor Frisbie, Vallejo wrote to his sister Encarnacion (Mrs. John B. Cooper). As he explained to his wife, "I wrote to my sister about a loan but there was no reply . . . I have searched among my old friends (for whom I have done thousands of favors when I had the money) for a little silver with which to transact well my business and not one of them wanted to loan me a single dollar. They are a bunch of ingrates and more over they are ungrateful, among them Mr. Brooks and Mr. Madden who are, according to what every one says, quite rich so that I am chagrined. I asked a loan from Mr. Brooks of some $200 but he answered, 'I haven't got anything for my expenses.' Who knows what I will do? From our own people one can't expect anything; they are all poor, very poor. Friend Pickett yesterday loaned me one dollar. I thanked him for the good will with which he did it although I didn't need it since I had in my purse five dollars. I invited him to eat and spent on the meal 4 reals."

Pickett was a friend who truly wished to help Vallejo. He knew of James G. Fair's debt owed Vallejo and thinking he might help in this matter, had written Vallejo as early as November 23, 1876.

> I wrote you a letter a few days ago. I write now to suggest that you send me an answer to that and this one couched in a certain style and for a certain purpose which I will explain. I propose to show such a letter to Mr. Fair and try to have him comply with what I unsuccessfully essayed last winter. Write the letter in English and mention in as strong language as the truthful condition of your affairs will justify, just what the condition is. You can state that the failure of Frisbie has cut off your only source of revenue for the support of your family and you are in the deepest distress and straits of poverty.
>
> Write me this letter very soon if disposed to let me use such an appliance to try and secure a few thousand dollars. Do not stand upon false pride in the matter. Of course this prompting is mine and our whole plan will be kept secret. Enclose me a separate note saying whether you or Frisbie have made any effort to have Fair refund the old obligation or whether you have had any intimation of his doing so.

Vallejo replied to Pickett on November 25th saying:

> I received your two letters on time but I have not answered them (in English) because of a certain mastership is necessary to touch the point which you refer to in your last letter which I received just today, dated the 23rd. If you have a day or two to spare, you could come to my house, we could talk about the matter and of others of interest to both of us.
>
> I'm alone, that is to say without the family and besides I must relieve my soul somewhat, conversing with a person of confidence and a friend such as you. So I beg of you that as soon as you receive this letter you embark on the steamer and come to my house where you are always welcome and I'll be waiting for you.
>
> Postscript in English — Sonoma Steamer leaves every morning San Francisco and gets here about noon. The *Donahue* leaves San Francisco at four.

James G. Fair was ungrateful, and one might go as far as to say dishonest in not repaying Vallejo. Fair had been financed in the early 1850s in his first mining operations by Vallejo who had given him a clear deed to 320 acres near Petaluma. Fair was to repay later. He made a payment of $600 but neglected to make any further remittances, although he was rated as being worth between 15 and 20 million dollars.

Vallejo did not write the letter for Pickett; instead, he took the case to the Superior Court, only to find the debt had been outlawed. In despair and in need of money, Vallejo turned to some one who might have been Mammy Pleasant. To quote his words to his wife at this time: "I asked a loan from the Negress, a little money," and "The Negress is still not here and says nothing about the promise."

Vallejo told his son Platon that, in order to aid themselves a little, some families were coming to Lachryma Montis to live. "We shall give them room and board." He also thought of turning Lachryma Montis into a resort: "The place can be made not only a resort to compare with the world-famous Del Monte but something to surpass it, the climate, location, trees, mountains, view, water, road facilities and distance from San Francisco."

The gloom of insufficient money was somewhat lifted by the promise of his son-in-law John B. Frisbie made him before leaving California to live in Mexico. As Vallejo informed his wife: "I think I'll have according to his (Frisbie's arrangement) $100 each month and this will help in my present circumstances which joined with the small rent from the Italians and the water are $150 per month. The account books Vallejo kept through his later years show in fact, that it was the income from the Sonoma Water Works, together with the rental from his pastoral land for truck gardens, which provided the most of his meager income. There were checks from Frisbie from Mexico, usually for $50 but they hardly ever came more than every other month.

In spite of his harassing financial worries, Vallejo thought of other people in trouble or sorrow. Tramps (pobre mozos) were given small hand-outs.

In the spring of 1878 Vallejo's young friend, Raquel Sears, lost her husband Jacob Rink Snyder on April 29th. To her he wrote on May 2nd a letter of condolence which is one of the few letters the author has seen that General Vallejo wrote in English:

Dear Friend:

I know no words can make amends for the great loss you have sustained. I deeply realize from having passed through a similar bereavement, that expressions of condolence wholly fail to restore the loved and lost one, yet I cannot but hope that the heartfelt sympathy of a sincere friend will not be deemed intrusion on your grief. It has been well said that "we weep for the loved and lost because we know that our tears are in vain."

I would ease your sorrow yet I know not how. We can only acknowledge that the affliction is God's will. Over in the beautiful land to which I trust your life companion has gone, we may not doubt he is free from pains that he so long endured here and when we gather at the river, is it not a sweet connotation to think that among the loved and lost he may meet you on the other side.

Commending you to Him who doeth all things well, I remain in the tenderest of friendship.

Your sincere friend,

M. G. VALLEJO

In accordance with one of Mr. Snyder's last requests, the Society of California Pioneers, with Samuel Brannan attending, had taken care of the details of the funeral of Jacob R. Snyder who had come to California in 1845. After the funeral on May 2nd, 1878, a few of the members of the Society paid an impromptu visit to General Vallejo's home. In welcoming the unexpected guests, the General was assisted by his daughters Adela Frisbie and Luisa Vallejo, Luisa being one of the reigning belles of the Sonoma Valley. Major W. F. Swasey, who headed the party, made a few felicitous remarks in which he recalled some of the numerous services rendered by their host to the Americans in the days prior and subsequent to the Conquest. Vallejo in turn, in order to relieve the tension of their sad pilgrimage to Sonoma, narrated incidents serio-comic in character, and upon his invitation sampled some of the choicest wines of Sonoma Valley.

General Vallejo welcomed these contacts with his American friends of the early days. For the moment they seemed to relieve his mind from the depressed feelings which were almost constant. There was one person with whom he could discuss his moods, namely his favorite son Platon:

> I haven't written to you nor answered your letter just past because I have been sick, sad and consequently have been peevish and bored to a superlative degree . . . As the halo of riches and abundance does not surround me, to those that it does, I seem "a zero on the left." Nevertheless I suffer everything without laments and complaints, hoping that at least some day they may recognize my sacrifices. This way of speaking may seem an enigma but one may not always put on paper real bitterness which does damage to people of reason and those do not know who are infatuated with the business, "I don't merit those things."
>
> If I had the wherewithall I would come to visit you all. I say "all" because there are in Vallejo several of my children and their families but the "dispossessed" do not have any business making trips. Here I vegetate and nothing more; my mind in imagination flies back among its memories which are a gift of Heaven because they make our past life, present, before us, and our memories, that force of the soul, goes back into space . . . I have a great desire to see your little girls. Kiss Felipa and also Francisca and a thousand affectionate regards for Adelita, without forgetting Lyli [Platon's wife].

Vallejo's *ennui* in the spring of 1878 and the tearful departure of his oldest daughter Fannie Frisbie and her family for their new home in Mexico were as nothing compared to the shock received when he opened Arpad Haraszthy's telegram announcing the death of Arpad's wife, Jovita, on May 5th, of apoplexy. Delays in the permission for Jovita's funeral from the Cathedral added additional grief to Vallejo's sorrow.

The Vallejos had lost seven children, six as infants or very young; but now it was a grown daughter—one whom he had persuaded the year before to remain with her husband instead of getting a divorce. Her death left a cruel void in his own heart, to say nothing of the despondent husband and two motherless children.

Maria Vallejo, the youngest daughter, who had been in the midst of plans for a large wedding to James Harry Cutter, was permitted to have a quiet one at Lachryma Montis on May 12th.

THE ARTIST, ORIANA DAY

It was fortunate that soon after these financial and tragic personal troubles, Vallejo was given a new interest. With his natural enthusiasm, it was easy for him to become absorbed in a project. His son, Platon, had some close friends, Mr. and Mrs. John A. Day, living in Vallejo. Mr. Day worked as a $1,200 clerk on Mare Island; his wife Oriana Day was an artist who formerly lived in Boston. Perhaps at the suggestion of Dr. Vallejo, she decided to paint a series of pictures of the old Presidios and Missions of California as they once appeared, and General Vallejo consented to help her.

Accordingly Mrs. Day was invited to visit the Vallejos at Lachryma Montis so that she could execute a painting of the north side of the Sonoma Plaza as it was when General Vallejo was the Comandante-General of the Northern Frontier of California. Of Mrs. Day's visit, the General wrote Platon on June 21st, 1879:

Mrs. Day and her daughter arrived at Lachryma Montis yesterday on the stage and have spent the night at our home. Today, the Senora went to see the ruins of the founding church and the remains of the house of the mission and at the same time the surroundings of the plaza. We went down Broadway where she got a view of the mountains, at her pleasure, so as to correct, if it were necessary . . . a view of the northern part of the houses on the plaza, which you suggested to her. I think she noted how much was necessary and Mrs. Day will finish her picture very satisfactorily.

I truly like the painting (and the artist too). One can see she is dexterous in the handling of the paint brush and she likes her profession. I told her to paint the tree boxes with the trees in front of the houses, also the cannons, the bell of the barracks and enough Indians (quite a few Indians) who were always about, showing interest in the gatherings; also to paint the battery on the hill to the north of the plaza, etc, etc., I told her to reduce the number of doors to the houses.

Mrs. Day is a lovely lady and her daughter, a fine girl; both of them very kind and agreeable persons . . . Mrs. Day is so beautiful that she can't do less than paint very beautiful things, since she is so, herself.

Another letter relative to Mrs. Day's work soon followed:

Much, very much I think of the beautiful artist and the work she has undertaken. Would to God, I could be at her side to cooperate in some way in her tasks and to admire both things, first, herself and her pictures afterwards . . . I should like the artist not to commit an error.

Nothing new in these parts except that we have an iron railroad. Steamer every day going and coming from "*Frisco*"; excursions every Sunday; a weekly periodical; some new factories and the old Barracks redone in a beautiful and unrecognizable manner compared to what it was. It is something to wonder at.

Two months later, Vallejo still interested in Mrs. Day's work, wrote Platon:

I received a letter from Mrs. Day in which she tells me that she has finished the picture in a satisfactory manner; that you were in her studio and were "highly delighted with it." God grant it is so, in addition to the artistic execution, the painting is the *only one of its kind* . . . I have wanted very much to leave here to make a visit to Mrs. Day and her family but I haven't been able to. It is possible that next week I shall do it and then I shall take with me the pictures of the missions that she wants to copy. What a bonanza for an artist. If I could be with her in the studio I would help her in many things, explaining thousands of things pertaining to the case since they were and are familiar to me.

As time went on, Vallejo once again expressed his views concerning Mrs. Day's work to Platon:

I hope that Mrs. Day doesn't lose heart to continue to its conclusion her great artistic work, "The Illustration of California Early Life." Greet her for me and tell her that on the least expected day I am going to surprise her in her studio with her palette in her hand and her brush on the picture, in order to greet her and to ponder at her work and *more* to see *her*. On New Year's Day I made her a present of a very interesting book with illustrations and very pretty passages; a new book on the voyages to the North Pole.

About this time, Vallejo was also assisting the writers who were preparing a History of Sonoma County to be published by the Alley Bowen Company. When the book was printed, the Company sent Vallejo a copy saying that it was "a means of expressing our gratitude to you for the very kind assistance that your eminent capability and very great knowledge of the subject, placed you in a position to give us . . . May it be deemed worthy of a place in your library."

The year the book was published, 1880, nature was not in a mood of co-operation with the usual benign climate. During January the valley had been covered with snow. Vallejo said he had never experienced a colder winter. In twenty years the orange trees had not suffered so much, in spite of their being stronger and better able to resist the temperature. One night, Vallejo said, one of the last of the freeze, the dawn showed that the ground of the orange grove was covered with more than 4,000 almost-ripe oranges and almost half of the leaves—all this on account of the cold. The locust trees in front had so many seed pods and leaves on the ground that, according to Vallejo, "It's going to take a lot of work with the broom."

When spring came, Vallejo went over to the Petaluma Adobe. Of this visit, he wrote Platon:

I ordered a picture taken of what was my old house which I had not visited for some thirty years and although almost in ruins, it nevertheless doesn't fail to show what it was in those days . . . It is a sad memory but one bows to that which says that 'all is perishable in this world.' I compare that old relic with myself and the comparison is an exact one; ruins and dilapidation. What a difference between then and now. Then Youth, strength and riches; now Age; weakness and poverty.

Platon answered his father's letter promptly, saying:

Your letter of May 11th came duly at hand and brought with it the photograph of the old Adobe house of Petaluma. That old house with its balcony all around but particularly that front corner in the picture nearest the west and looking over the valley from a beautiful eminence or summit of a hill has always been the object of my dreams. Indeed, often in my life when in the midst of the most interesting surroundings in the middle of this nineteenth century, my mind would fly to that porch and I would see myself a little child standing near the banister looking down and away into the beautiful valley covered with flowers and filled with beautiful cattle and horses rolling in fat and happily sunning themselves in the sun's golden light like a blessed people enjoying existence in a happy land. Petaluma has a charm for me and there is an enchantment about that place even yet. Petaluma, Sonoma and Soscol are three chambers in my mind where the scenes of my childhood are pictured in the most enchanting light and most beautiful colors. And now that I have grown up and find myself weaned from this natural home of my own, I find in it plenty food for reflection.

VALLEJO'S SEVENTY-THIRD BIRTHDAY

On Vallejo's seventy-third birthday, Senora Vallejo was away visiting one of her married daughters. On the afternoon of July 7th (the day celebrated by the family instead of his natal day, July 4th), Natalia who lived nearby, came with her husband Attila Haraszthy bringing their gifts. The General said they gave him a bottle of ink, three reams of paper, 400 envelopes, a box of pens, 1000 postal cards, 50 postage stamps and a pen knife. Fine gifts for one who wrote so many letters. Vallejo said he had been told not to write such lengthy letters and not to trouble to compose them so carefully as his eyes tired easily although he saw well. In discussing his correspondence Vallejo wrote to Platon:

> Between Luisa and your Papa, we spend for postage stamps each month from $2.50 to $3.00. Just imagine how many letters leave from Lachryma Montis. Among the members of my family, (greater than the tribe of Abraham) and among the great many friends that I have and that Lulu has, we have a regular post office.
>
> As for me, that keeps me occupied since I have to write each in a different way according to his character, instruction and intelligence. Also there comes to me from time to time, letters from literary people, whom one must indulge according to the string they play.
>
> Very often some youths who wish to enrich their albums with my autograph. An American lady from Oakland whom I don't know and have never seen, asked me to send to her "with some greetings" my autograph. In Castilian, I sent to her "guard in the deepest recesses of your breast the charm with which you ward off the storms of life, your innocence." As some person has to translate it into English, the thought will have a double effect.

VALLEJO'S DIFFERENCES WITH THE CLERGY

Dr. Platon Vallejo was a man deeply dedicated to the faith of the Roman Catholic Church and often wrote pious letters to his father who termed them "sermons." The General, himself, was dedicated to that faith of his Castilian fathers, and to the tenets of the same church. He once wrote Platon on March 11, 1872:

Your sermon-letter dated the first of this month I received on time . . . Do you think I am afraid or ashamed that someone will "point the finger at me" for the way I fulfill my duties as a Catholic? Well, you deceive yourself, if I haven't done it since Father Luis was here it is because I haven't in all conscience been able to do it—not because someone "points" at me. It is a duty I owe myself as a Catholic and the younger members of my family as an example.

In Sonoma it has been impossible for me to go to church—the weather very very rainy all the time, other times there wasn't any Mass, other times sick, etc. This is not an apology or an excuse—I know as well or better what I owe to myself and to my family. At my age, (64!!!) "experience, science and conscience" reach a culminating point; the last-mentioned above all is what guides the actions of man. Conscience is the omnipotent judge which holds us up, attracting us always, always toward working good. I want, I desire, I need to do what you charge me.

Frequently during his life Vallejo found himself in disagreement with the clergy. However, he held great reverence for the old padres, Serra, Saria, Amoras, Payeras, Victorio and Magin, grey-frocked missionaries who had built the missions. A present-day friend was Reverend Angelo B. Casanova of Monterey who located the grave of Padre Junipero Serra at the Carmelo Mission.

When Vallejo first came to Sonoma, the Mission San Francisco Solano had been abandoned under the threat of Secularization, and there was some misunderstanding with Padre Lorenzo Quijas who had gone to the San Rafael Mission. Later, the relationship between the two men must have improved, if one is to judge from Padre Quijas' correspondence with Vallejo; the first stilted, formal salutations gave way to friendly, cordial greetings.

Padre Santillan, the Indian priest stationed at Sonoma, was not admired by Vallejo. Charles E. Pickett (Philosopher Pickett) told how in January 1848, he and the General had enjoyed a game of billiards and afterwards as they passed the old Mission church, they had looked in. There they saw Padre Santillan, preaching away to one solitary listener, old Berreyesa. Santillan was so drunk he had to lean against the wall for support. Pickett suggested they go in, but Vallejo said he preferred to run that little Indian rascal out of town.

The differences between Vallejo and the Catholic clergy in the earlier years were concerned with administrative policies, but in 1878 Vallejo's feelings against the clergy became poignant and personal, when his daughter Jovita was refused funeral honors from the Cathedral in San Francisco. Vallejo's resentment increased when Archbishop Alemany sold to Solomon Schocken the Mission San Francisco Solano Church, where according to Vallejo many of his 16 children were baptized. At the time of the sale, some nearby land was claimed by the Archbishop which Vallejo said was his own—a situation which prompted Platon to write his father one of his "*cartas sermonas*":

It behooves you to show them great and good intention to preserve the Holy Church, our Mother, like a true and gallant son and brave descendent of a long line of heroes; the property which was Hers and which today, you, without asking one single penny restore safely into the hands of the Archbishop, in order that the work which your father with the renowned Serra began, may go on and flourish here in the beautiful Valley of Sonoma . . . Give it to Her. Do not think to keep it. Say "This is yours, it is yours. It is yours now."

Replying on October 9, 1881, Vallejo explained how he felt on the subject:

Your letter of the second of July, I answered the same day. In it is mixed the question of some pieces of property that never were the property of the mission or of the church and this I say and swear with my hand on my breast. If they had been or if they were, do you, who know me, think I would not have ceded them to the Church without going to court with the Archbishop? When it has been just for me and I have been able to, I have helped the Church and the Fathers individually, now I cannot. I am poor and have a family to support.

It is not just for me under any circumstances as the father without any resources of any kind (many times without the wherewithall of spending for the day, that is to say without means to buy the necessities of life) to have to make a gift to the Archbishop of a piece of property that has cost me considerable money which I need at the present time. I have tried to put an end to the matter peacefully; but the *men of peace* make war upon me.

Your above mentioned letter is no more than an introduction or a prologue to that which followed, dated the eighth of August of the present year which intentionally and by design I did not wish to answer. It is so long, full of errors that it would tire me to answer it, point by point.

The people who have advised Senor Alemany are those of a "wide conscience" or in other words, with much science and little conscience; one of them Mr. Caserly, the one famous in guileful tricks in Washington.

About a month ago I was on the steamer *Donahue* with Father Harrington and he offered to talk about the places in Sonoma; we talked for a long time and he was convinced of the error of the Archbishop, so convinced was he that he asked me for the original titles upon which I based my claim; I sent them to him with an explanatory letter but I have not received either the papers or an answer to my letter. I am of the opinion that to fight with the clergy is worse than fighting bulls . . . Fortunately, I can make an honorable exception to the clergy—one single individual—that is Father Luis, the only one in whom I have faith because he has proved it by precept and example.

Reverend J. F. Harrington was secretary to Archbishop Alemany. It was Father Harrington who invited Vallejo in the name of the Archbishop to serve as vice-president of a group interested in helping several hundred Sisters of Charity exiled by the Mexican government in 1875. The General in accepting said that "The Sisters of Charity are walking angels whose heavenly mission is to alleviate suffering, inspire hope to the forsaken and lead back to the path of virtue those of either sex who have gone astray."

A year later, the disagreement over the property was not settled. Vallejo was trying once again to explain the situation to Platon to whom he wrote on August 2, 1882:

I am writing this to tell you that the property in question between the Archbishop and me has never been what His Illustrious Highness calls "church property," neither was it adjudged so at the time of the secularization of the Mission San Francisco Solano in the year 1835 by the Commission . . . The allegation of the lawyers is a falsehood. The Mexican Government in performing its rights before the American invasion lawfully conceded that property to a Mexican citizen with full rights to it in conformance with the laws and rules of those times. And so it exists in the public records of the country. The Archbishop wants to hold on to it at all costs since it has the Patent of the President of the United States.

The Archbishop doesn't need the lands in question for anything. He will sell them the same way he has sold the house of the Mission with its land and in addition for decorating, the church which I *built for my soldiers* and which ultimately cost me nearly $4,000 to build; he sold it I say for $3,000 to Schocken . . . the church in which are buried the bodies of some Catholics such as the mother of your Mama, an uncle (Juan Carrillo) of yours and several others.

Schocken has been begged by two daughters of your grandmother that they can exhume her, they being given three months of grace. What a shame! But it is the Archbiship, a Catholic who has consummated the deal in spite of the just displeasure and feeling of this parish, which has finally said "Amen," For that property I paid $500 and believe me, and you know it would be a great loss to me and my family. You also know that too many times I lack even the most necessary things for life . . . I ought to insist on recovering that property because my claim on it is just.

With the sale of the old mission building, Senora Vallejo wrote her husband saying that she wanted the body of her mother moved to where their dead children were buried. She also wrote to her sister Josefa Fitch, living in Healdsburg, asking her to assist financially in this desire. It is not known whether the two daughters of Senora Maria Ignacia Lopez de Carrillo were able to have the body of their mother moved to the Vallejo family burial grounds in Sonoma.

WELCOME VISITORS TO LACHRYMA MONTIS

The members of the Chipman family were frequent visitors to Lachryma Montis. Luisa was devoted to the Chipman girls, Alice, Fannie and Lizzie, all near her own age. The girls that her father said "the three are as lovely as Roses of Castile." Mrs. Vallejo and the General enjoyed having them as guests. The last named wrote their mother, then Caroline Dwinelle; her first husband William Worthington Chipman had died on November 16, 1873 and she had remarried. Mr. Chipman had been the founder of the City of Alameda. Vallejo's letter was dated October 26, 1880:

Alice arrived with Lulu last night. Do not worry about her as we will care for her as though she was our own daughter. Why did not Fannie come also? Alice is so pretty and as lovely as her mother. I never tire of looking at her. May Heaven keep you always happy is the wish of your old friend.

A month later after a visit to his friends, the General writes to Caroline Dwinelle on November 17, 1880:

The other day when I was at your home and was most certainly check-mated three times at chess. I left my room very early in order to take the half after 7 boat so as to arrive at Vallejo at 11 A.M. I ask a thousand pardons of you, your husband and all your lovely daughters (the three Graces) for having deserted such good and amiable company. "Business before pleasure" so say the Americans. Besides your husband was ill and it would have been wrong to disturb him. I am sending a box of fruit for all of you. Greetings to Mr. Dwinelle and Liza.

Another letter to Caroline Dwinelle upon Vallejo hearing of the unexpected death of her second husband John W. Dwinelle, the noted jurist; it was sent by Vallejo on February 3, 1881: "Troubles even though sad and hard to bear are sent to us to test, in this world of misery, the bravery of the big souls, such as yours, dear Lady. Have courage and philosophy and patience in your present affliction and God who is capable of doing all things well will help you in every way."

COLONEL PETER DONAHUE'S LOAN

The Sonoma Valley Railroad Company (narrow gauge) was formed in 1878. Funds ran out and the stock was sold to Colonel Peter Donahue. It was in 1881 that the third engine of the line, the largest, the "General Vallejo" pulled the train with Sam Lewis at the throttle, down Spain Street where it was welcomed by members of the Vallejo family who decorated it with garlands of flowers. Miss Luisa Vallejo, then in her early twenties, climbed on the pilot of the locomotive and sang The Star Spangled Banner.

It was this same year, 1881, that Vallejo's acute need for money caused him to write to Colonel Donahue for a loan:

I am in need of $1,500. If you would be kind enough to furnish me this amount at the rate of ten per cent per annum, you would confer a great favor. I will give you as security all the small lots, west of the White Gate, up to Attila Haraszthy's property, twelve in all, as you may have seen as laid down on my little map which was left at your depot here. Please answer me at your earliest convenience.

It was in that year of 1881 that Colonel Donahue wished to extend the Sonoma Valley Railroad from the Sonoma Plaza to Glen Ellen. He met with opposition from the property owners along Spain Street, which made the Colonel more anxious than ever to acquire a right of way; the railroad would cross Vallejo's property diagonally, making three curves, and, at the same time, making Vallejo's lots unsaleable. Donahue's loan gave Vallejo immediate relief, but it was to be the cause of grief and worry in the years ahead.

Vallejo tried to interest Mr. Donahue in developing Lachryma Montis as a resort. He said at the time, "I am certain that under the management of Mr. Donahue and Mr. Burton this place can be made not only a resort to compare with the world-wide famous "Del Monte" but something to surpass it. The climate, location, trees, mountains, view, water, railroad facilities and distance from San Francisco go to make a whole which with the addition of capital can be made the most beautiful Summer Resort on the Pacific Coast."

ORIANA DAY'S ART WORK

Mrs. Oriana Day continued her art work. Father S. Vilarrasa of Benicia visited her studio and expressed his approval of her paintings of the missions. In appreciation Mrs. Day sent him a painting of the San Carlos Mission which the padre from Benicia called "a precious gift." General Vallejo continued his interest in her painting and wrote regarding it: "Mrs. Day has finished her work and is ready to show it in San Francisco. Those who have seen and passed judgement on the above mentioned collection of oil pictures say they must be worth fifty to a hundred thousand pesos . . . It is probable that one of the millionaires like Stanford or Crocker will like to enrich their saloons with artistic and unusual pictures, and she, Mrs. Day, will get her price, for in addition to being a true '*Yankee*' she is a beautiful and charming woman."

Vallejo had often spoken of the beauty of Oriana Day; judging from her photograph, one is inclined to agree. His letter to Platon continues: "Dr. Edwardo Vischer undertook with me the gathering up of the collection of the missions over a period of 22 years; four sets were made. One was sent as a gift to the Emperor William of Germany, another to Pope Pius IX; from both we received autographed letters; another set was given to his son Herbert Vischer and the other to me. The day he finished the work, he arranged his papers; I was with him in the afternoon and at four o'clock in the morning of the next day, he was found dead in his bed. What a misfortune. He was a fine person, very scholarly and admired by all who knew him."

Some time later, February 1, 1883, the husband of Oriana Day asked Doctor Vallejo if he had a set of Vischer's drawings of the Missions. "I hope," Mr. Day said, "that they will remain in your possession and that Bancroft will not get hold of them. He evidently wants to get all that your father has." When Oriana Day had first started her work, General Vallejo had written Platon:

> I would have sent you today by Express the interesting collection, compiled by the late Mr. Vischer, had I not feared that the last pictures mounted under glass would break and be lost. Truly the collection, you should have and save, since you are the only one of my children who would know how to appreciate its merit and future importance. When I no longer exist and you would arrive at my age or before, you will know even better its merit. Therefore if you want to pay your respects to and compliment the artist, why don't you take the cars in the morning in Vallejo, take the stage in Napa and reach Sonoma at noon? If you bring a grip you can carry the collection in it and can very well return to Vallejo the same day.

Oriana Day opened a studio in San Francisco in the Phelan Building and invited a reporter from the *Bulletin* to view the paintings. The reporter wrote in his column that there were two scenes in which General Vallejo appeared: one was a review of the Mexican troops at the Presidio in Sonoma, showing General Vallejo on horseback, accompanied by Chief Solano and Chief Marin; the other was a life-size portrait. As Vallejo explained to his son Platon:

Mrs. Day is very anxious for the history of each mission to be put in a big book with illustrations, that is to say, the history of each mission with its accompanying pictures. I see it already in my imagination, such a book, richly printed and I believe it can be sold for a great many pesos. Each public and private library ought to own such a book not only in California but in the United States and in all the civilized world. You should be my secretary, no one can write on the subject in English better than you.

The question arose as to the propitious time for Vallejo and his son to commence writing the text for the book of the Missions. Platon's idea was: "Let us begin, money or no money. Let us do it for the love of the thing." Vallejo answered that while he had a great deal of material with which to start the work, it was necessary to see the archives of each mission and to travel. Money was needed. Vallejo thought that the speech he had prepared for the Centenary of the Mission San Francisco de Asis would help. He told Platon that he would send to him twenty-five blank books, one for each mission and one for each Presidio, so that when he was writing, each thing would be in its proper place without mix-up. Not having heard from Platon, the General wrote him: "Some months past, by the Express I sent various books relating to the history of the Missions of California, also 21 blank books, labelled each one of them with the name of each mission in order to facilitate the work without confusion . . . Now how have you progressed in the history of the missions which we have at hand? Mrs. Day asked me some days ago something about the business and I answered her, 'that everything was going well'—a little lie which can hurt no one."

The twenty-one blank books remained *blank*. Not one inaccurate statement in them! The illness and death of Platon's beloved wife, Lily, mother of his four little daughters, took from him all desire and energy to write. Vallejo understood this. The project of the illustrated history of the California Missions never materialized.

Death intervened in another direction. Oriana Day passed away on May 26th, 1886. Her legacy to her friend Dr. Vallejo was her oil painting, "General Vallejo Reviewing His Troops Before the Casa Grande," which was presented to the Doctor by Mrs. Day's daughter Florence Rice Gamage. Seventy-four years later this painting was willed to the historic Vallejo home by Dr. Vallejo's daughter Adela Vallejo Peters. Today, the painting restored by the noted painter Al Sondag, hangs above the mantel in General Vallejo's library.

1882—THE YEAR OF THE VALLEJO'S GOLDEN WEDDING

The first week of the year 1882 was saddened by the death of Vallejo's oldest brother Don Jose de Jesus, who died on January 6th at Salinas City, "passing" as Vallejo said, "from the finite life to the Infinite . . . of my relatives there remains three, Prudenciana (Mrs. Jose Amesti), Encarnacion (Mrs. John B. Cooper), Rosalia (Mrs. Jacob P. Leese) and I remain their only brother." Vallejo thought that Don Jose de Jesus was eighty-five years old at the time of his death. His widow Soledad Sanchez survived him ten years.

Mariano Guadalupe and Francisca Benicia Vallejo had been looking forward to the year 1882 which would mark the occasion of their Golden Wedding. The General went shopping in San Francisco for two roasted turkeys and a "*weding kek*" *para comer el dia que cumpli 50 anos de casado que sera 6 de presente*, as recorded in his account book. The dinner, the evening of March 6th, was for members of the family only. However, when the citizens of Sonoma remembered the anniversary of their most loved couple, the American flag was at once raised on the plaza and by those citizens who had flag staffs. A collection was taken up to purchase a gold-mounted cane with an appropriate inscription, also, the Sonoma Quadrille Band was engaged to serenade General Vallejo and his wife. About half past nine the group appeared in the orange grove of Lachryma Montis and commenced serenading the distinguished couple. The members were all invited into the parlor where the Vallejo's talented daughter, Miss Luisa, joined the chorus in song. Later dancing was enjoyed.

The most unforgettable features of the evening were the toasts and speeches around the long dining room table, amply loaded with Sonoma wines and cakes. When one of the guests made an allusion to the ungrateful treatment of the General by some of the Americans in the past, Vallejo replied that he felt no resentment; he was glad, he said, to have thwarted the schemes and prevented the acquisition of California by England or France. If Mexico was compelled to lose it, it was his desire that the Americans should have it. The distribution of land and cattle, and other assistance given to emigrants to help build up the country, were things he did not regret. He treasured, instead, what his old and well-tried friend Charles E. Pickett had said, namely that if he, Vallejo, had no wealth or money or lands to bequeath to his descendants, he would leave them an untainted reputation and a record of worthy deeds of which doubtless honorable mention will be made in history. In remembering the days when he was a cattle king, Vallejo pointed out that "formerly our cattle roamed by thousands, yet not one was stolen, for the unwritten law of the land granted to the weary traveler the privilege of killing cattle whenever he wanted beef so long as he placed the hide where the owner could easily find it. Since the transfer of California to the United States many native Californians have been hanged for stealing cattle and I firmly believe that some of the victims did not know that under the new Government it was a crime to possess a steer for which they had not a bill of sale."

Short speeches were made by Messrs. Peters, Mullen, Charles E. Pickett, A. F. Haraszthy, General Murray Whallon and Doctor Ball. The last named presented the gold-headed cane saying: "General, feeling under deep obligation to you for the many kind acts shown the American people in so warmly welcoming and protecting the early emigrants hither who came as poor strangers to a strange land and having full knowledge of your many good qualities and important services rendered the Government under whose flag you were willingly transferred a citizen, we, your immediate friends and neighbors come to congratulate you and your noble wife that God has spared you to attain in health so goodly a patriarchal age and to celebrate so important an epoch in your lives. As a small token of our respect and esteem, we present to you a cane, hoping that you may live to that period when from age alone, you will require its support."

On this festive occasion, General Vallejo wore his richly embroidered satin vest which he had worn the day of his wedding in San Diego fifty years before. The bride's raiment no doubt had long ago been given to her daughters of whom she had reared six.

In departing, Mr. Peters, the superintendent of the Sonoma Valley Railroad said he was sorry he had not had time to generate enough steam in the locomotive *The General Vallejo* to take the entire party for a moon-light ride on the train.

THE YEAR OF 1882

In the spring of 1882 Reverend Lorenzo Waugh took his friend Charles J. Hittell to the old Petaluma Adobe where Hittell made a fine sketch of the historic structure; then they went to Sonoma where Hittell sketched the old spliced pole which had held the noted "Bear Flag" 36 years before. While in Sonoma they went out to Lachryma Montis to call on General Vallejo and found "the noble old pioneer in good health and spirits," owing mainly of course, said Reverend Waugh, to his life of temperance and strict sobriety.

The General gave his visitors a stirring description of the wonderful country when it was inhabited by vast numbers of naked Indians, full, fat and saucy, feeding on the abundant luxuries of the country.

The interview, said Waugh, closed "with a beautiful treat on the part of the General, not of wine or brandy, but a full server of sweet, luscious oranges picked by the General's own hand from the charming orange grove, in the sweet and fragrant atmosphere where we sat in the open air."

DEATH OF GOVERNOR JUAN B. ALVARADO

Immediately after the Golden Wedding celebration, the Vallejo household became busy with plans for the marriage of Luisa to Don Ricardo de Emparan. Vallejo's account-book listed $69.25 as "spent for different things for Luisa's wedding." This favorite daughter's story of her wedding is told elsewhere in "The Vallejos of California."

On the last day of March, 1882 Governor George C. Perkins paid a visit to Vallejo, so the account-book recorded. Governor Perkins had remembered that Vallejo had voted for him, in spite of the fact that Perkins carried the Republican banner and Vallejo was a staunch Democrat.

On the afternoon of July 13th, 1882, a telegram was delivered to Vallejo which read, "Father died this afternoon." It was signed by H. V. Alvarado, son of Juan Bautista Alvarado.

Alvarado was only two years younger than his uncle Vallejo; they had been schoolmates in Monterey and as young men, began their civic careers together. In 1836 young Alvarado had raised the standard of Independence and proclaimed the Free and Sovereign State of Alta California. Forthwith he appointed his uncle Guadalupe "Military Commander of the Frontier of the North." In 1838, the Mexican Government recognized Alvarado as Acting-governor and in 1839 appointed him Governor, an office he occupied until 1843.

When the Americans raised the Stars and Stripes, Alvarado was far-seeing enough to understand that it was futile to resist, but, as the following letter to Vallejo shows, he was never reconciled to the occupancy of his native land by the Yankees.

When a Californian in Monterey asked Larkin why would the United States wish to take California. His answer was because Mexico can not attend to it. A gringo answered Vicente Peralta along the same line when found killing a head of cattle on his ranch. "why have you killed my cattle? asked the Californian. The thief answered, "Because you have too much and cannot eat it all." It shouldn't be strange that a common thief should speak that way but it is indeed strange that the Consul of the United States should have given that answer when we consider that General Micheltorena granted Larkin's small son, still a nursing child, eleven leagues of land in the Sacramento . . . The Americans have become rich with our gold.

The mention of Larkin's child brings to mind that in May 1847 the Larkin children's ranch of which John S. Williams was supervisor, was stocked with 580 head of cattle and about 200 horses, mares and colts from General Vallejo's ranch near Petaluma.

Don Juan Bautista Alvarado died at his adobe residence in the village of San Pablo, Contra Costa County, at the age of 73. His wife Dona Martina Castro passed away several years before when it was said Alvarado had to borrow money for her funeral. He was survived by three sons and two daughters.

Before the year 1882 was over, General Vallejo lost a faithful friend, Charles E. Pickett, whom Vallejo called "a good friend and a good man." Philosopher Pickett had gone to Yosemite Valley where he saw "the tumbling of the lofty Yosemite Falls." He became ill and, in spite of the devoted care of a Mrs. Jane Gallison, owner of the Mariposa Hotel, to which he was taken in his distress; he passed away on November 16, 1882.

THE YEAR 1883

In the spring of 1883, Governor Stoneman appointed Vallejo as a member of the newly created State Board of Horticulture, with the well-known fruit grower Ellwood Cooper of Santa Barbara, as president. Vallejo consented to serve as Treasurer. In September of the same year, Vallejo was a guest at the Palace Hotel in San Francisco and wrote thus to his wife:

Yesterday I received your simple but judicious note. I appreciate the good wishes which in it you send me which I shall not forget. Besides the experiences that I've acquired in my long life in business of every kind, I have the conviction that it is time that I look after NUMBER ONE. Number one is you and myself. We have completed our mission in society, we have a large and scattered family; we brought it up, educated it and gave them position, not contrary to their will, according to our religion and society. We shall have some satisfaction to think how we have survived to see the obligation which was contracted in our marriage over fifty years ago, now fulfilled. Thanks be to God who gave us long life to see our children's children and to die in peace, blessing them.

I desire to work and own some little capital, enough so as to be happy, remodel our house, the Spring of Lachryma Montis and the pipes . . . something to allow us some rest without cares and tribulations . . . You must realize that I am not here just for the pleasure of being here. Here, business is done, here resides persons spending time, taking advantage of every occasion, the rich, the big fish, always want to swallow the little ones.

I have an appointment in the morning, another for two in the afternoon, afterwards two or three. There will be more for another day . . . One can't depend on any one. It is an uninterrupted chain of talk and when it seems a business comes to its final terms, everything is resolved in nothing and all the treadmill begins anew. I am tired and bored. I've tried since I have been here three times to go to the theatre and have always left hurridly, sick in my eyes. You know, I dislike theatrical foolishness. There is enough in those who go through life and in every role we play.

After finishing the above letter, Vallejo wrote an encouraging one to son-in-law Ricardo de Emparan, the husband of Luisa, with whom he was promoting some business in Mazatlan. In the letter, Vallejo quoted one of his favorite proverbs—"When God gives, fill your hands." One little verse he was fond of quoting to the family. Translated from the Spanish; it reads:

Let no one here murmur of the absent one
Of defects not one's own; be silent
And he who to this prescription does not agree
Readily from the table can he rise.

THE YEAR 1884

The year 1884 found Vallejo still in need of money. One of the probable sources appeared to be the contracts he entered into with L. W. H. Green of San Francisco to obtain from the Mexican Government the exclusive right to sell or plant Eucalyptus trees or seeds throughout the Republic of Mexico.

Mayor Adolph Sutro of San Francisco bought the Eucalyptus trees that were planted on Mount Davidson, and in the area west of Twin Peaks from Mr. Green.

Vallejo usually stayed at the Palace Hotel when he was in San Francisco, his room costing him only $1.00 a day. While there in May, 1884, he borrowed $1,000 from its owner, William Sharon, who at that time was in the midst of defending himself against the charges brought by the "Rose of Sharon," Sarah Althea Hill, the sister of Morgan Hill, who founded the town of the same name.

Vallejo left the Palace Hotel to visit his married daughter, Maria Cutter, who was living in the City. While on his way to her home, he fell to the pavement with such violence that, he remarked, he almost killed himself. "Fortunately by making a supreme effort," Vallejo wrote, "I managed to prevent the *domi* (street car) from catching me between the wheels, breaking an arm, a leg or my head. Thank God, I can tell the tale. Nevertheless the fall hurt me enough. My ribs and spinal column were injured so much so that ever since I have been confined to my room on orders of the doctor . . . The doctor says that old people do not recover except after a long time from such shake-ups."

It was on July the Fourth that Vallejo delivered an address at the time of laying the corner stone of the new Court House in Santa Rosa and it was on this day he reached his 77th birthday. He enjoyed the following recognition of his natal day in the Daily Evening Post:

All the friends of the genial old gentleman and their name is legion will join heartily with his children in wishing him 'many happy returns of the day.' General Vallejo is one of the best known and highly respected of the Californians and he likes to be called a Californian . . . No one looking at the old typical Spanish gentleman, walking with a firm step and erect figure, would think he was an old man; nor is he, for, although he has seen many a summer pass and a cold winter take its place. Old Time seems to have had the same kind friendship for him and touched him lightly with his defacing finger.

Vallejo had a number of correspondents to whom he enjoyed writing; one was Carolina Jimeno Kahn, whose grandfather had been the distinguished Don Jose de la Guerra y Noriega of Santa Barbara who had died 26 years before. Carolina's mother was Senora Augustinias de la Guerra Jimeno Ord. In a reminiscencing mood on October 23rd he wrote to Carolina telling her that their friend Mr. Poull Newman had been named the Minister to the Capital of Mexico by Calamacira, the king of the Hawaiian Islands, and that Luisa had returned from Mexico. He went on to say:

Lulu, I believe is going to live in San Francisco. Napoleon, also will soon go to Oakland with his family. Then your Aunt and I will be left alone, like before having a family with the difference that then I was 24 years and she was 16. Now she is 68 and I am 77 but we have accomplished our mission in this surely laborious life—but we have fulfilled it. What experiences after fifty-three years of married life! Sixteen children, to raise them, educate them and get them established, not contrary to their wishes. How many cares in childhood! How many worries in youth! And how much trouble in manhood! Always thinking, always the same anxiety for each one of them, always the same cares, maybe more. However thinking philosophically, it is very gratifying to see one's self reproduced to be father, mother, grandparents, great grandparents, and assuming the title of PATRIARCH!!!!

THE YEAR 1885

In June of 1885 occurred the death of Lily, Platon's young wife. The General looked upon Lily as another daughter, and knowing that she had been deprived of her own father in childhood, he lavishly bestowed his affection upon her. He deeply felt her passing. Only in reading was there any alleviation of his sorrow.

Vallejo was a subscriber and a great reader of newspapers as well as of books. Much of the newsprint was destroyed after reading it, but he saw to it that the September 9th, 1885 Admission Day Edition of the *Sonoma Democrat* (Santa Rosa) was saved. In it was a full account of the celebration of the 35th anniversary of the admission of California into the Union. Santa Rosa was elaborately decorated with evergreen arches and with numerous mottoes, flags and tri-colored bunting. One thousand Native Sons of the Golden West marched in line interspersed with nine brass bands. General George Stoneman, governor of California, was the speaker of the day. He recalled the days when "Women were rare as Angel's visits and as highly prized. One might travel from street to street without seeing a bonnet or ribbon or hear the musical rustle of the chaste crinoline."

In the Admission Day edition were pictures of Governor Stoneman, the Grand Officers of the N.S.G.W., General Sutter, and General A. M. Gwinn, the organizer of the Native Sons of the Golden West who, in 1865, married the widow of James King of William. There was also a picture of General Vallejo. Under his likeness was printed a biography which began: "To General Mariano Guadalupe Vallejo belongs the distinction of being the most influential, the ablest, the most patriotic, the best friend of Freedom among all the native Californians who took part in the events which preceded the acquisition of the country by the United States."

Two full columns of Vallejo's history followed, closing with the paragraphs: "Gen. Vallejo on his release (from Sutter's Fort) at once made his great influence as a friend of the United States felt throughout the country. He took active interest in public affairs always on the side of order and good government. He was elected a member of the Constitutional Convention which met in Monterey and was a Senator from the Sonoma District in the first Legislature of California. And from that period down to the present, he has been an enterprising, useful and honored citizen of Sonoma. In priority of settlement he is the first of all the inhabitants now living in this county." The article continued, "In person General Vallejo even at his advanced age is a strikingly handsome man. He is tall and erect in carriage with the military air of one disciplined in arms in his early youth. He is a brilliant conversationalist, an eloquent speaker, even in English which he acquired late in life. To these accomplishments, may be added the grace of gesture and manner which he inherits with his blood from an ancestry of Spanish cavaliers."

GRANDFATHER VALLEJO

By the autumn of 1885, the healing force of Time permitted the General to turn his thoughts and rejoice in the birth of another grandson on October 30, 1885, Raoul Ricardo Rolando, the third child of Luisa Vallejo Emparan who was living in the paternal home. General Vallejo and his wife became the godparents of the infant, their thirty-sixth grandchild, on November 5, 1886 at the St. Francis Solano Church on Napa Street.

Luisa's three little children, Anita, Carlos and Raoul brought happiness to Grandfather Vallejo and his household. The old gentleman frequently could be seen sitting on the porch or under the Honey Locust trees, usually with a book in his hands; resting his eyes, he would watch the little boys play, interrupting them when the train passed, so that each child could salute Sam Lewis, the engineer.

THE YEAR OF 1886

January 1886 arrived for Vallejo with continuing need for money. He wrote to his son-in-law Frisbie in Mexico for a loan but to no avail, as Frisbie's answer contained only regrets: "I am pained to say in reply that it is utterly impossible for me to send the money you desire. I would be only too happy to avail myself of it to come to your relief. Herewith you will find a draft for $50 payable to your order."

In February, an anxious reminder of a debt of some standing came from James Mervyn Donahue who wrote Vallejo: "I am directed by the executors of the estate of my late father, the attorneys thereof to remind you of the note secured by mortgage for $1,500 which expires April 7, 1886. As the inventory of the estate must according to law be filed within a few weeks, I trust you will see the necessity of making necessary arrangements for its due payment at your earliest convenience." Vallejo replied immediately:

> In answer to your request to pay the amount of the mortgage referred to in your letter. I am sorry to state that I am not able at such short notice to fulfill my obligation . . . At the time of making the mortgage to Peter Donahue on lots in Sonoma, numbers 30, 387, and 388, he was to release the mortgaged property whenever it could be sold for building lots. He set the price at $8.00 per front foot and I have been unable to sell any at that price. In consideration of my giving the right-of-way through my place, Colonel Donahue would cancel the mortgage, I now make the same proposition to you, implicitly relying that your respect and piety for your deceased parent will induce you to treat me in the same manner as your father would have done if he were personally present and alive. When the railroad was extended through my place, I was advised by Mr. Peters to make no objection or demands and that in consideration of my giving the right-of-way through my place, Colonel Donahue would cancel the mortgage. I have always believed this and I

believe now that Colonel Donahue would have fulfilled his promise if permitted by Providence to do so.

To add to these financial worries, Vallejo was notified about this time that he should replace the wooden water pipes with iron ones. Vallejo wrote Platon to see if Father Luis, as he hinted, would loan a sum of money with which he could replace the water works in Sonoma exchanging the wooden conduits with iron pipes.

MAJOR SHERMAN'S INVITATION IN 1886

On a May morning in the year 1886, an old carriage stopped at the "White Gate" entrance to Vallejo's estate on Spain Street. Inside the carriage sat the General with the mail he had just called for at the village post office. "*Kee*," the Chinese houseboy, sat in the rear on a small raised footman's seat. Before he could alight and unfasten the gate, one of the little Italian neighborhood boys, perhaps little Jacobino, arrived and did the chore; smiling, the General tossed him a coin.

The General did not care for walking. Cerruti once said that Vallejo would never walk if he could ride—a rule which prompted him, when in town, to give a lift to any package burdened friend he might see. The private road to Lachryma Montis had been laid out as West Third Street, running from Spain Street to Alp Street at the base of the hill, and Vallejo had petitioned the Sonoma Council to buy it. He owned the lots on both sides, he said, and had planted trees at great expense. His request was granted and the land sold to him for $5 an acre, or for $20 for the entire roadway.

Before explaining why this morning in May 1886 was memorable for the General, it might be of interest to describe the scene as he drove home. Cottonwoods cast their alluring shade over the roadway which, in turn, was bordered by the fragrant Roses of Castile, planted under the supervision of Senora Vallejo. The carriage made its second stop at the Red Gate, just beyond the railroad which Vallejo had permitted to cross his property, as mentioned earlier. Near the end of the roadway and high among the branches of the last two trees, was a treehouse which had been the joy of his children and was now the center of interest for his grandchildren when they visited Lachryma Montis.

The pair of horses, all that remained of his vast herds, turned to the left and came to a halt in the courtyard. Vallejo alighted and went into his study with his mail. The residence as well as the "*Almacen*," the nearby brick storehouse, were in need of repairs. Forty-five years younger than their owner, the buildings were not in as good condition. General Vallejo would be seventy-nine on the fourth of July, but there was about him a certain illusion of youth; attributed in part to his well-developed physique, the result of outdoor living and temperate habits. Vallejo's young friend Otto Van Geldern once said, "I can see the old General as the host of his table, drinking a toast to the ladies in the ruby colored wine of the Valley as a cavallero and chivalous knight, but it is utterly impossible for me to imagine him leaning against a bar with his foot on a brass rail."

Vallejo's military training had left him with an erect carriage, which, coupled with his courtly manners made him a man one rarely forgot. One could well believe that within himself was *El Paraiso Escondido,* the Hidden Paradise, the name he sometimes gave to his home. It was a kind of inner retreat, which the vicissitudes of life, loss of fortune and harassing cares could not long disturb.

Once in poetry, Vallejo spoke of his spirit as an eternal fire. And when one thinks of him in this way, one realizes that, early in his life, the fires of youth had generated in him the power to conquer a wilderness and lay the foundation of a new Western Empire. During his middle years, when the aggressive Yankee expansion was taking place in California, this fire smoldered. Now in his sunset years, the fire of youth was a glowing ember imbedded in a philosophy which caused him to say to Carolina de la Guerra Jimeno Kahn, a favorite relative, "I enjoy memories, I forget the bad ones."

Vallejo was no man to live in the past; and as he assorted his mail on that particular day in May, not only the individual letters but the fragrance of the jasmine, which climbed the trellis under the open window of his study, made the present vivid and compelling. One might think he conducted a Bureau of Information from the number of enquiring letters he received. One letter was from a State official who was investigating the effect of rainfall on vegetation and wished the General to send him the dates of the very dry and very wet seasons prior to 1849. General Nelson Miles from the San Francisco Presidio wanted to know the history of the old Spanish cannon at the San Francisco Presidio. A. F. Rogers of the United States Coast and Geodetic Survey asked the correct spelling of the name "Carquinez," saying "I have the honor to apply to you as the best authority, I know upon the subject, the orthography of Spanish and Indian names."

Professor Hilgard of the University of California wrote a letter of thanks for a plant which Vallejo called "Cruz de Malta" but which Hilgard identified as an ornamental foliage plant known as "Euphorbia Lathyris."

But the letter in this particular morning's mail which held a special interest for the General was an envelope addressed in the small, neat handwriting of his friend Major Edwin A. Sherman. It bore the date of May 28, 1886. Under the golden seal of the *Associated Veterans of the Mexican War* was the following:

You are cordially invited as an American citizen and as one of the members of the first Constitutional Convention which met in Monterey, September 1, 1849, to frame a Constitution for the State of California, to be present at the celebration of American Independence and also of the 40th anniversary of the raising of the American flag at Monterey by Commodore Sloat of the United States Navy, July

7th, 1846; the joint celebration of which will take place on Monday July 5th, 1886. We also desire that you shall raise the flag of Spain which will be honored by a National salute, then lowered by your own hands; then you shall raise the flag of Mexico which shall also be honored by a National salute and the National hymn of Mexico played by the band, then you will lower the Mexican flag, after which the American flag will be raised by another person, a Government officer . . . Trusting to receive your letter of acceptance at the earliest date.

EDWIN A. SHERMAN, *Chairman.*

General Vallejo's first impulse may have been to send a gracious letter of regret, as he was 79 years old and found traveling somewhat difficult. But upon reflection he decided to favor his old friend and do his part toward making the celebration a success. Major Sherman had served in the Mexican War from 1846 to 1848, and his knowledge of the Spanish language had been valuable to the United States Government. In 1852, Sherman located in Sonoma where he was named city clerk at the time Vallejo was mayor, the latter having succeeded John Cameron, Sonoma's first mayor.

When the General decided to accept Sherman's invitation he dictated to Luisa who had for some time been acting as his amanuensis, his answer:

Edwin A. Sherman et al Sonoma, May 31, 1886
Dear Sirs:

Your letter of the 28th of the present month in which you invite me to attend and act as one of the vice-presidents in the celebration of the American Independence and also of the 40th anniversary of the raising of the American flag at Monterey was duly received and in reply I will state that I most cordially accept your kind invitation with which you honor me.

I will be at Monterey on the third or fourth of July as according to your letter the celebration will be held on the Fifth of the same month. Hoping that this will meet with your approbation, I remain

Your Most Obedient Servant,
M. G. VALLEJO

Realizing that he would be expected to say a few words, Vallejo went to his bookcase and took out two volumes from his Spanish Encyclopedia: No. 17 for the history of *Espana* and No. 27 for that of *Mexico.* His anticipation was heightened when he received a short note from Major Sherman saying, "We have concluded that it is best that you should raise the Spanish and Mexican flags and *not* lower them but leave them flying until evening when they can be lowered at the proper time by some one else."

The Vallejo household at Lachryma Montis was astir early that July morning, making ready for the General's trip to Monterey. His wife packed his black leather valise and slipped in a list of things which she wanted him to purchase in San Francisco. He was good about shopping, even to the bringing home of *pan Francais.* One could be sure too that he would add *dulces para la casa* to the list; and if his money held out, he would purchase a ticket to the Louisiana Lottery. The General bought the lottery tickets quite regularly—a *boleta* only cost $2.50. While he had never won anything, one never could tell! At any rate, he must have received his money's worth in dreaming what he would do with his winnings.

FORTIETH ANNIVERSARY OF RAISING OF AMERICAN FLAG IN CALIFORNIA—1886

On Monday, July fifth, 1886 in Monterey, the Associated Veterans of the Mexican War, the Pioneer Societies, the Native Sons of the Golden West, and other patriotic organizations formed in line under the direction of Dr. Westfall, the Grand Marshal. They marched to the water's edge where stood the old Custom House, in front of which a large platform had been erected, with two flagpoles, one at the northeast and one at the southwest corner.

Governor Stoneman, like many governors before and since, sent a substitute; Representative William L. Duncan, who acted as Master of Ceremonies. Chaplain James O. Rayner offered a prayer. The Chaplain had been present at Sitka, Alaska, when the Russian flag was lowered and the American flag raised by the officers of the United States Cutter *Lincoln* in 1867.

After the invocation by the Chaplain, the Master of Ceremonies introduced "The most distinguished general, statesman and patriot which California has produced, born in Monterey, subject of Spain, faithful military officer under Mexico, our honored guest and fellow-citizen, General Mariano Guadalupe Vallejo."

General Vallejo in his frock coat rose, leaving his derby hat on his chair, stepped forward and began reading the speech which he had prepared in Spanish. First he offered his sincere gratitude for "the unmerited honor which you have bestowed on me in selecting me to raise on this memorable day . . . the flags of Spain and Mexico, that in no remote time in the past, waved in this historical city with equal glory with the *Banner of the Stars*."

Vallejo spoke of the Catholic monarchs Ferdinand and Isabella, of the immortal Columbus, and of the voyage of *La Santa Maria*, *La Pinta* and *La Nina*, "those vessels ploughing the seas that were destined to work a great revolution in the history of the world." He recalled to the audience the incident of Don Hernando Cortes burning his ships at Vera Cruz in 1519 that there might be no retreat. Vallejo then spoke of how Mexico, inspired by the example of the United States, had struggled for its independence from Spain and had become a Republic. The General concluded his speech by referring to the war between Mexico and the United States which resulted in the cession of a part of the Mexican territory, saying, "I am commissioned by you today to raise those two flags (Spain and Mexico) in sign of respect to your predecessors, I accept with pleasure this duty, for I was born on this piece of land and reared under the ensigns of Spain and Mexico, the two, which I salute at this hour with all the fervor of my soul." Vallejo then spoke a few words extemporaneously in English and reverently raised the Spanish and Mexican flags, which were saluted by guns from the ships in the harbor. A great-grandson of Commodore Sloat, Master J. B. Whittemore Jr., a lad of ten years of age, brought forward the American flag and presented it to Captain Charles F. Williams of the United States Marine Corps, who then raised it to the top of the original flagstaff where, forty years before, the flag of the United States had been hoisted by order of Commodore Sloat.

In the evening after the festivities, General Vallejo and Major Sherman were walking among the ancient live-oak trees in the gardens of the palatial Del Monte Hotel, built six years before by the "Big Four"—CharlesCrocker, Leland Stanford, Mark Hopkins, and Collis P. Huntington. The two friends were talking of old times; suddenly the General turned and, embracing Sherman as a father would a son, said, "Major Sherman, you are the only living man for whom I would have done what I did today, in hoisting the Spanish and Mexican flags on the old Custom House, but I appreciated your motive in thus representing the history of California from its state of solitude and Indian barbarism, when Spain first took possession until its occupation by the United States and its cession by treaty with Mexico. Here in Monterey I was born and educated under the monarchial flag of Spain and saw it give way to that of the Republic of Mexico under which, from my young manhood until the American occupation, I began and finished my military career; and then to become a citizen of the United States and not an English or French subject or of any European monarchy . . . My heart thrills with tender memories of the past, while I feel unspeakable pride in having here, on the very spot where I was born, aided in laying the foundations in framing the Constitution for the State of California and the land of my birth."

Major Sherman in answer said: "Well, General, you have lived and have been under more flags and have become a citizen of the United States without having to take out naturalization papers in California than any man I ever knew or heard of." At this, Vallejo laughed and said, "Well, I never looked at it in this way but it is a strange truth."

After a pleasant evening together, the two friends parted. It was their last goodbye as they never saw each other again.

The rest of the mild summer evening, Vallejo sat on the veranda of the Del Monte Hotel smoking and watching the display of fireworks on the grounds. It had been a joy to see such old friends as Philip Roach, Monterey's last Alcalde and first Mayor; John Porter, Elisha O. Crosby, and several other members of the State Constitutional Convention. But Vallejo had left these friends that morning to clasp in his arms John W. Murphy, who had come from San Jose to attend the celebration.

It was Murphy who had made in 1846 the long ride from Monterey to Yerba Buena, a distance of 125 miles between sunrise and sunset, changing horses three times, in order to carry Commodore Stockton's message to Captain Montgomery, ordering the release of Vallejo from Sutter's Fort. And it was Murphy who bore the dispatch to Sacramento which liberated Vallejo from Sutter's Fort, and who then escorted the ill Vallejo to Sonoma. In gratitude, at that time, Murphy was offered 500 young heifers from Vallejo's herds.

On Major Sherman's return to his home in Oakland, he saw to it that General Vallejo was elected an Honorary member of the California Pioneer Society of Alameda and Contra Costa Counties. Vallejo accepted the honor in a letter dated August 6, 1886:

I assure you that I consider myself highly honored to belong to the California Pioneers of that section of our country and I hope that in the future I may be able to be of some service in the progress of our State, as we the Pioneers should not rest until California heads the list and is far ahead of all the other states that compose this glorious Union. I would like to be able to do in the future much more than what little I have done in the past. I received your translation of the few remarks which I made in Monterey on the fifth of last month and I assure you that it could not have been done better by the ablest scholar, it is a perfect translation and you have conveyed my ideas exactly into the English language. I have also received the badge which you kindly sent me and will wear it with pride on all occasions when I am required.

When Bancroft's *History of California* was published in the middle 1880s, Vallejo's so-called annexation speech became a debated historical incident. Hubert H. Bancroft wrote in Volume V of his *History of California:*

A desire to be strictly accurate, the leading motive of all historical researchers, compels me to state that I believe all that has been said of this meeting, including the eloquent speeches so literally quoted, to be purely imaginery. No such meeting was ever held and no such speeches were ever made . . . I am very sure that General Vallejo's memory has been greatly aided by his imagination.

Professor Josiah Royce shared Bancroft's views. In his *California from the Conquest* he said, ". . . no official or other contemporary MS record of such a meeting is known to Mr. Bancroft's library, nor is such a record discoverable in the archives; and as for Mr. Larkin, he, who could not possibly have been ignorant of such a junta, knows absolutely nothing about it as appears from his letters to the State Department."

It is quite possible that Consul Larkin sent his official account of the Junta to the State Department and the Department kept the information in a restricted file. That Larkin was not ignorant of the Junta is evident from a portion of his letter, dated April 10, 1846 to the American Vice-consul, William A. Leidesdorff at San Francisco: "We have Senors Castro, Castro, the Prefecto, Carrillo, Vallejo, Alvarado and Prudon here, acting as a council of war. They may hold sessions for a month to see what good can be done for the country."

General Vallejo resented Bancroft's denial; to think that Bancroft who had been so eager to get Vallejo to write the history of California should doubt the act which had caused Vallejo such tremendous sacrifice, was more than

Vallejo could take in silence. It had been no easy thing to lay aside his official allegiance to Mexico and be willing to provoke displeasure among his relatives in order that his beloved native land might come under the benevolent rule of the United States which Vallejo had called "The wonder of the World."

Vallejo and Bancroft! Castilian and Puritan! Native Californian and Adopted Californian! Both for love of California undertook the task of recording its history. They had begun their work together in 1874. Heretofore Vallejo had contented himself with noting Bancroft's errors in Bancroft's *History of California* by writing comments on bookmarks inserted in his personal volumes of the History by such remarks as *Que absurdo!* (what nonsense) written on the margins. But a letter received the summer of 1886 from Vallejo's old friend, Major W. F. Swasey, relative to Bancroft's denial, gave Vallejo the opportunity to express openly his feeling in writing.

Major W. F. Swasey, Sonoma, August 31, 1886
Dear Major Swasey:

I received your letter of the 24th of this month in which you allude to Mr. Bancroft's denial in regard to a certain speech I made at Larkin's house in 1846 in consequence of a Junta held at Larkin's residence at Monterey, Mr. Bancroft calls it a "myth" and a creation of my own imagination and I am sorry that all those persons that were present at the time are dead and gone except yourself. And I assure you that I thank you most heartily for recalling this subject to my memory, as you are the only person surviving that was present, at that time acting Consular secretary to Mr. Larkin.

Mr. Bancroft is certainly very ungrateful and has no reason to doubt what I have told him or written for him in regard to the historical facts of this coast and I wish if what I have written for him, is considered in his estimation all fabricated by me, to return to me what I have written and then Mr. Bancroft will be at liberty to select such a person as he may consider more trustworthy and whose assertions may not be considered as "myths" or lies. When I went to Monterey the following persons accompanied me. Col. Prudon, Captain Salvador Vallejo, Francisco Sanchez, J. B. Cooper, Governor Alvarado and Prado Mesa and our object was to prevent the Junta at Santa Barbara which we accomplished.

You must remember that at that time there arrived in Monterey, the war vessel Chyanne [Cyane] and Captain Du Pont was in command and Mr. Gillespie came on that vessel. On the same night of their arrival Governor Alvarado gave a grand ball at his residence at Monterey and we all suspected Gillespie of being a commissioner or spy and he was immediately sent to overtake Fremont after his retreat from Gavilan Mountain.

When I see you in San Francisco on my next trip, I will tell you of several meetings I had with General Castro and several others, which I do not want to reveal until the time comes.

I am very thankful to you for writing me this last letter so I might be able to put these points which are in doubt in their right light. Hoping to hear from you soon, I remain

Your Most Obedient Servant
M. G. VALLEJO

Major Swasey had come to California in 1845. After spending a short time at Sutter's Fort, he went to Yerba Buena, and, in the spring of 1846 he proceeded to Monterey, where he was appointed secretary to Consul Larkin. Swasey referred thus to Vallejo's letter in his book *The Early Days of Men of California:*

In the latter part of March or early in April, 1846, a Junta composed of the leading Californians and citizens of alien birth met at the house of Mr. Larkin. The meeting took place in a room, adjoining one occupied by the author, who being anxious to know what was going on, listened attentively to their proceedings from which he gathered distinctively that the main object of their discussion was the suggestion of the proposition of throwing off the trammels of the Mexican government and seeking protection of some foreign flag.

Several speeches were made, mostly in favor of England but the meeting finally wound up with a speech made by General Vallejo; the purpose of which was that when the time arrived when it became necessary for the well-being of the Californians to change their allegiance from their mother country, he would be most earnestly and emphatically in favor of appealing to the United States or as he frequently termed it in his speech, "La Gran Republica del Norte"; upon which the meeting broke up or adjourned without taking action.

Mr. Bancroft denies that such a meeting was ever held or that such speeches were ever made and pronounced the meeting a *myth* and General Vallejo's speech, the creation of his own imagination. The author is in receipt of a letter from General Vallejo in which he denounces Mr. Bancroft's language and assertions in most vigorous and justly indignant terms and alludes to the author as the only survivor of those present.

CALIFORNIA'S FIRST ARBOR DAY

It was in the year 1886 that the ceremonies for California's first Arbor Day, promoted by Joaquin Miller, were held on Saturday, November 27th on Yerba Buena Island. Thousands of school children, numerous organizations and dignitaries which included ex-Governor Perkins, General Vallejo and General Howard of the San Francisco Presidio, assembled for the tree planting on the then Goat Island. The exercises began by the reading of a poem by Joaquin Miller. General Vallejo was to have delivered the address but he was unable to climb the hill. The belated arrival of the horse he was to have ridden caused his speech to be read by Fred M. Campbell of Oakland.

In his written address, Vallejo had reviewed the early history of Yerba Buena Island which he said was the headquarters for the tribe of Tuchayne Indians who possessed a fishing station there and "also a large Turkish bath named by them, *Temescal,* considered both a luxury and a sovereign remedy for all ailments." Vallejo said that some years later a pioneer merchant, Nathan Spear of the village of Yerba Buena, brought some goats from the Sandwich Islands. They became so destructive to the flowers and garden truck that the goats were taken to the island where "they increased rapidly; hence the name *Goat Island* which it now bears."

The first tree was planted by Adolph Sutro. The second by Mrs. Chonita

Fuller de Ramirez whose father in 1847 had claimed ownership of the island with Nathan Spear, who had bought it from Don Juan Jose Castro. Castro had received it from his daughter Martina's father-in-law, Governor Juan B. Alvarado. Another tree was planted by General Vallejo.

On June 3, 1931, the old Spanish name Yerba Buena (good herb) was restored by the United States Geographic Board to this island in the San Francisco Bay, known as Goat Island. The secretary of the Board, John J. Cameron, announced, "We were reluctant to change the name because there must be stability, and the name Goat Island was officially adopted in 1895. We are convinced, however, that the people have now made up their minds to use the old Spanish name. The decision was unanimous."

ORANGE CULTURE

The sixth Annual Fruit Growers Convention convened at Sacramento on Monday, November 15, 1886 and was called to order by Ellwood Cooper, president of the State Board of Horticulture. During the sessions, General Vallejo reported that a Mr. Robert Howe of Sonoma had planted some four thousand quince trees about seven years ago, and in October of the present year he had sent to New York, Chicago, and St. Louis, three carloads of the fruit.

A paper on Orange Culture, the king of fruits, was read; discussion followed as to whether it was necessary to irrigate orange trees. It was thought that to plow deeply and cultivate thoroughly would do away with the necessity of irrigation. General Vallejo, the oldest grower of oranges present, added his bit to the discussion. "Nearly fifty years ago," he said, "I planted in the Sonoma Valley the first trees that were raised in this State (Northern part) from seeds that were brought from Acapulco, and succeeded in getting from fifteen or twenty trees. I planted them at my residence near the old Plaza. For four years they were small; I then transplanted them. At nine years old, the trunk was about three inches thick and they commenced to bear nicely and very sweet fruit; I do not say better than from any other localities but very fine oranges, for which I have had premiums awarded at Marysville, San Jose, Sonoma Valley and San Francisco. For nine years the trees grew slowly, the main root grew deep and several branches quite thick, like wood; but after nine years, they began to create a kind of blanket of roots which was very thick." Vallejo continued: "Before that you do not need irrigation. After they begin to get so very thick, it is necessary to dig and clean away and cut out the mass of small roots, and then you begin to put some water there. I have had the experience for years; I have some two or three hundred trees that I planted for experiment so as to get an idea of what we can grow in this section of the country. In our localities here in the north, our climate is good enough in general but not so even as in San Diego and the more tropical regions where they make a business of oranges. I have been in California seventy-nine years and have been in every locality from San Diego to

Shasta. I have studied every ravine, every river, every lake and I am familiar with the climate. I have had experience in my place over fifty years and I tell you if you get good soil, not exposed too much to the north wind, only sheltered a bit, they (oranges) grow everywhere. Perhaps on the flats, they will not do very well where winds strikes them but I have lemons on my place equal to those that grow anywhere and oranges as sweet as any."

Vallejo told the delegates that he had picked as many as 600 oranges from one tree at Lachryma Montis where Cerruti said that when the neighborhood boys came begging for oranges for their sick relatives, "General Vallejo sent every one of the little beggars to the garden with strict injunction to gather the fruit without spoiling the trees."

As early as 1875, Vallejo had 200 flourishing orange trees, 100 of them in full bearing. He had the largest number of pomegranates in any one place in the State, 50 bearing trees. He also had 50 fig trees laden down with fruit. He had lemon, lime and an orchard of 50 fruit-bearing trees. There was one banana plant and 70 acres of grapes in bearing.

SAN FRANCISCO PRESIDIO LAND LITIGATION

In the month of November, 1886 Vallejo brought action against General O. O. Howard to recover a portion of the San Francisco Presidio Reservation, a tract of land of about 371 acres called the Sailor's Well. Vallejo's attorney was Joseph W. McKinley.

In his legal statement, Vallejo said he had owned the land under a grant and a patent from the Mexican Government. He stated that in 1846, when he was being held as a prisoner by U.S. military officers, there was no legal process under any Act of Congress whereby title or rights for the use of said tract could be acquired except by military force. He felt that the military officers had treated him with the greatest disrespect; no leniency had been extended to him, nor was it their desire to deal justly with him; he thought the methods adopted by the U.S. law agents were calculated not to further justice but to defeat it by dilatory and expensive litigation. Vallejo also stated that the transfer from the Federal Courts would cause him great hardship and expense. In spite of Vallejo's plea, the case was transferred to the Circuit Court, December 22, 1886 and was dismissed October 22, 1890. Some months after Vallejo's death. Vallejo's son, Napoleon Primo Vallejo, tried to reopen it only to be defrauded by an Oakland attorney, who took not only his money but it is thought also his father's gold-headed cane, which had been presented to the General as previously recorded on the Vallejos' golden-wedding anniversary.

RIVERSIDE MEETING OF THE FRUIT GROWERS

As an expense-account of $150 had been provided for him, General Vallejo was able to attend the meeting of the Fruit Growers held in Riverside, California, in April 1887. As usual, the members were glad to have the General speak to them. He told them that when he first came to the Riverside area he was about twenty years of age. He was with Father Boscano, and the party was on its way to meet the Indian Chief "San Jacinto." Apologizing for his broken English, Vallejo went on to say that he had never seen anything like the Riverside orange—one might think that they had grafted pumpkins on the orange! He mentioned the fact that this time he had come by fast train but he thought that some day, one might be traveling by telegraph or telephone, so he asked his hearers to pray that *age* might be turned into *youth*. Vallejo moved that the next Convention be held at Santa Rosa, the county seat of Sonoma County. In closing Vallejo said, "Mr. President, if the next convention shall meet in Sonoma, I promise to receive you all and all the Board."

At one of the meetings of the State Board of Horticulture, Vallejo tried to resign from his duties and responsibilities as Treasurer. Antonio Coronel of Los Angeles and William M. Boggs of Napa, two of the Commissioners, spoke feelingly of General Vallejo's great usefulness to the Board as treasurer, and of his being the first and most valued horticulturist in the State. The General was finally prevailed upon to withdraw his resignation.

GENERAL VALLEJO'S EIGHTIETH BIRTHDAY

General Vallejo's eightieth birthday was a festive occasion, and was highlighted by the presentation of a specially-bound volume of birthday greetings, letters handwritten by his descendants in Mexico City—his children and his children's children. The first letter in the book was a letter from Adela who was visiting her sister Fannie at the time; she wrote, "I suppose Fannie ought to have written first, but she is out doing her purchases at the Plaza. I will take her place, in first writing and to wish you dear Papa, many Happy Returns of the Day." On Fannie's return, she wrote in Spanish, telling her father that she had returned from the Plaza and was so tired that she must rest to be able to transport herself in thought to where he was. She concluded her message with these fond words, "I would like to say to you for you to live to be a thousand years old but as that is not probable, may my Papa live many years."

There were short notes, some in English and others in Spanish from the grandchildren; Fannie de Sequeira and her two children Juanita and Agosto; Bennie (Benicia), Josephine, Minnie, Platon, Madeleine, Bernardo and Leo. Fannie's husband, John B. Frisbie, added his greeting: "I pray that notwithstanding your advanced age, there still remains to you many years of happy life."

Mariano Guadalupe Vallejo an octogenarian! He attributed that fact and his youthful appearance to his abstincence in eating and drinking and to his moderation in everything except in the number of children he had had. "I do not deny," he said, "that Nature has been very kind to my physical being . . . I am strong, very old in age . . . Last night I was invited to a ball in Glen Ellen; I came back this morning and felt very lame. Eighty years is too much for dancing with . . . young girls."

Vallejo's spirit of youth was evident to his friends. One of them, George N. Rogers who lived in Mazatlan, wrote him:

Time that waits for no man alive is an exception in your case. Now and then I see your hearty smile in your own printed words and I tell Lola that some men do not seem to have been born to die but live forever. How beautiful it is; nothing among all the magnificent phenomena of life gives a man more pleasure than to see the full force of manhood emanating from a celestial aura, the very soul fibre of an old man. He who attains to that, must have analyzed what life means. Like yourself, like Gladstone of England, and like many obscure persons known to a few, there is a select class of men who live in the world as men with whom every act and every word is Eureka. (Material acquisitions or conquests mean nothing to them unless there is personal growth).

Now my dear General. I have not an axe to grind in writing to you at this time. I wish simply to salute you and to remind you that the old Mexican was Vallejo, who gave away all his land to the Pike immigrants, is remembered by a true friend, as one of the wisest and best of men.

VALLEJO ATTENDS CONVENTIONS

Acting on Vallejo's suggestion, the Eighth Fruit Growers Convention met in Santa Rosa in November, 1887. On the evening of November 8th, Colonel Mark McDonald told the audience that the man who had laid out the country under instructions from the Mexican Government, was present; whereupon the president, Ellwood Cooper, introduced General Vallejo, who said in part:

I would be glad if I could speak the English language correctly but I will try and do my best to speak a few words to you in my broken English. I desire in this connection to thank Mr. McDonald for having mentioned my name as a pioneer of this country; I had over a half of a century ago a presentiment of the future of this (Sonoma County) or Sonoma District as we called it in Mexican times. Then it was composed of the present Sonoma County, Marin, Mendocino, Napa and Lake.

I was then a young man. That is fifty-two years ago. I am eighty at the present day but deducting the fifty years makes quite a transformation. I was then young and very active and the Government had a good deal of confidence in me and sent me all over the country, from San Diego to Oregon to see what would be the best part of the country to open a settlement in. . . . General Figueroa gave me orders to select a point near the Bay to have communications with the South . . . I selected Sonoma Valley and kept two schooners in Sonoma Creek to have connection with the settlement . . . I laid out myself that old plaza of Sonoma into blocks like San Francisco . . . One day the fourteenth of June 1846, I was alone in my house when about thirty or forty armed men with rifles and coyote caps, regular mountaineers, surrounded me.

A celebrated man among them was very tall, his name was Dr. Semple . . . They took me prisoner. When you have eight or ten rifles pointed at your head, you can't make any noise, so by compulsion I made a trip with those people, by orders of General Fremont . . . Soon after, there were half a dozen governors, Commodore Biddle, General Kearny, General Fremont, Governor Stockton; it seemed everybody was governor. I was soon after nominated to be one of the Council of Fremont. Well, I was ready to go to make laws or something, then General Kearny came and said, "Don't you go." He and Commodore Stockton came to my house and I made him a present of half a dozen horses and he went by land and Kearny took Fremont back. I know the history in Spanish but I can't explain it in English, only to give you the points. At last General Kearny was succeeded as Governor. And then there was an election and I went to Monterey as a delegate to the Convention to form a Constitution . . . I was elected Senator from the Sonoma District and when it came to divide the country into counties, I was president of the Commission.

When Vallejo was about to conclude his speech, he said, "I see among you my friend William Boggs. I knew him when he was a young boy, and his son, by the way, is the first California boy of American parentage born in this State. He was born in my house in Petaluma." Mr. Boggs arose, proud to acknowledge his friendship with General Vallejo.

At the Santa Rosa Convention, Vallejo voted for the passage of a Resolution, offered by a Mr. Tompkins, in the interest of Conservation. It read:

WHEREAS, the rapid destruction of the Redwood forests of the State will entail permanent loss to the beauty of our coast counties and already threatens the water supply and consequently the fruitfulness and healthfulness of those counties and

WHEREAS the perpetuation of a large tract of coast Redwoods will be of continuous economic value and of continued and increasing interest to science

BE IT RESOLVED: That the Eighth Convention of the California Fruit Growers hereby endorses the effort of the State Board of Forestry in seeking to secure the reservation of such a tract of Redwood forests and recommends their protection to the earnest consideration of our Representatives in Congress.

The Resolution of Mr. Tompkins was thereupon adopted.

On the fourth day of the Santa Rosa Convention, the secretary read a letter inviting the Fruit Growers to hold their next convention in April, 1888 in Santa Barbara. When Vallejo heard the name *Santa Barbara* he could not stay off his feet.

I must say a few words about Santa Barbara County. I have known since 1822 all the coast from Gaviota, as we called it, to Buena Ventura. In times gone by, we had in Monterey a big lawsuit and a brother of mine was in charge of it, and he took me down to Santa Barbara. When we reached Santa Inez which seemed to us at that time a very long distance from Monterey, traveling as we did in those days from one mission to another on horseback, carrying home-made biscuits on our horses. We went to Soledad, San Antonio, San Luis Obispo, then Santa Inez. We rested there at a big mountain—it was a big mountain then. Now it is no use to talk about big mountains for holes are made and they go through them. That is nothing now; but then we rode up on a mule and it took half a day to reach the top of the mountain, going down the same way. In 1822 we stayed at the house of Dolores Ortega. There were oranges at Santa Barbara in the yard of Comandánte Don Jose de Noriega. He had several trees at the military post.

Well, Santa Barbara now is a very important county—not so large but rich—good climate, plenty of oranges, plenty of olives, good pears, potatoes and everything else and besides that a good gracious people. I would be glad if I were a miraculous man to inspire everybody in this convention to vote with me to go to Santa Barbara with us next April.

Vallejo continued talking, telling how, during his last visit to Santa Barbara, he had stayed at the magnificent Arlington Hotel. When he went to pay his bill, the clerk said, "All paid, Sir, a letter has been received from Los Angeles to the owner of the hotel, to keep you any length of time."

The speech of the reminiscencing General went on and on. He had once again asked the members to vote in favor of Santa Barbara when a delegate, seemingly bored, arose and commented that according to the printed program the selection of the next meeting-place should be made just before adjournment.

A trifle sensitive, perhaps, because of the interruption of his speech, Vallejo said he had not intended to interfere with the regular order of business and he hoped the gentleman would excuse him. Then the venerable Californian proceeded to let the delegates know that he had been a good friend of the United States officials, favoring them in preference to the representatives of European governments; and again the story of his arrest in 1846 by members of the Bear Flag Party. One of the former members of the party was present, a Mr. Gregson who informed the delegates that in those days he was a private soldier whose duty had been to guard a General. The two men shook hands, Vallejo saying, "That Bear business was like medicine from a good doctor." At the conclusion of Vallejo's speech there was much applause and the vote was carried to hold the next convention of the California Fruit Growers in Santa Barbara.

HEARTBREAK

In the dreary grey days of early December 1887, a great sorrow enveloped the ageing General; "the restless and rash" son, Uladislao had taken funds while serving as Sonoma's tax collector, and left for Mexico and later Guatemala. The distraught father took upon himself the obligation to redeem the theft. Informing Platon he wrote:

As you know perfectly about the business of Ula, I do not feel that it is necessary to enter into great explanations. It is enough to tell you that in order to prevent your brother from returning to California with handcuffs on his hands and from going to San Quentin with a ball and chain on his foot, I had, at my age, to go to Santa Rosa on a morning when it was raining buckets in order to persuade one of his bondsmen, Mr. Clewe, not to take any step for his apprehension. . . . On writing you about this, don't think that I believe that you are prosperous and in a position to help me, but I do know you have good friends and among them Father Luis, who is mine too, who might be able to lend me the money for a year with proper interest. I believe that as Ula's bondsmen consider me good for the money on the note, you will be able to find some one who will do as much since I have several deals under way. And furthermore you know I am a good payer.

Just consider that if I put such obligation on myself, it was to cover the honor of my name and of my family and consequently all of you are duty bound to help me get out from under it . . . When Frisbie was here I talked to him although without mentioning this disagreeable affair, of the straits I was in, but he indicated to me that he couldn't help now due to being involved in Mexico. I have then to touch other resources and I trust that you will do your share as it is your duty.

More sorrow for the Vallejo family was to follow; on the second day of February 1888, Natalia's husband, Attila Haraszthy, vice-president of the Sonoma Valley Bank and once mayor of Sonoma, died.

Meanwhile grief over Uladislao's malfeasance had begun to take its toll on Vallejo's strong constitution causing him to remain at home more and more. In April 1888, he was invited by the Argonaut Parlor of the Native Sons of the Golden West of Oroville to attend an anniversary celebration. After explaining to the organization's president that the condition of his health did not permit his acceptance of the invitation, Vallejo wrote: "I take pleasure in deputizing your good self to shake hands on my behalf with all your associates, conveying to them my hearty wishes for a pleasing holiday and successful celebration. Referring to your happy hint in regard to the comely daughters of your Parlor, I cannot, under any circumstances, confer the VALLEJO DEGREE by proxy, for this interesting rite must be performed in *propria personae*, and your assurance that there are many candidates will be an extra inducement for an early visit to your town." The VALLEJO DEGREE to which Vallejo referred was, he thought, his patriarchal privilege of bestowing a kiss on a fair Native Daughter. The rite had started at a meeting of the Native Sons and Daughters of the Golden West at an Admission Day celebration held in Santa Cruz, which Vallejo attended with his son Napoleon.

In November 1888, Vallejo visited the Chico Parlor of the Native Sons of the Golden West. Writing to his wife from the Union Hotel in Chico, he said:

I reached this place today at four in the morning after traveling, sitting up all night on the train. I am a little tired or better said, lacking in sleep but not ill. The day is very dark, raining and the streets muddy. I'll try not to get my feet wet as you warned me. You see I am writing to you so that you don't worry, neither you nor Lulu, nor the rest of the family.

God grant that from here on, for the little time that remains to us of this life, we can walk in peace and harmony. As old people we ought to be able to maintain domestic peace at least among our families and relatives on both sides. If some member among them makes a mistake, we ought to correct and counsel with dignity and prudence, avoiding all scandal. Let him without faults cast the stone, said the Lord, when they were judging the woman. We are not better than the Lord.

His journey to Chico was one of the few trips Vallejo made away from home, but there was very little curtailment in his correspondence. Now that a stain had been cast on the Vallejo escutcheon, he was deeply appreciative of an article which appeared under his photograph in the *Press and Horticulturist:*

The above is an excellent likeness of the oldest member of the State Board of Horticulture and Treasurer of the Board since its organization. Although an Octogenarian he is still hale and hearty, and his straight figure, military bearing and firm step give him a much younger look than one would expect from his age.

Then followed a brief biography, ending with this paragraph:

During the early days of California immigration, Gen. Vallejo was indefatigable in his efforts to promote the settlement of the state, and immigrants had in him a firm friend and counselor; and during his whole public life, extending over a half of century, there is none among the Californians whose public record, in respect to honorable conduct, patriotic zeal, executive ability and freedom from petty prejudices of race, religion or sectional politics, is more favorable than his. As a private citizen he was always generous, kindhearted, maintaining his self respect as a gentleman and commanding self respect of others.

If doing good for the benefit of others meant giving his time and lending his influence the General could still afford to do both. During 1888, he had interested himself in the plight of one of the prisoners at San Quentin whom he believed to be innocent, and Vallejo hoped that his own friendship with the young daughter of the Governor of California might be the means toward helping the man. Little Abbey Louise Waterman had written to General Vallejo on December first, 1888.

My dear Friend:

The beautiful little books you so kindly sent me came a few days ago and how can I thank you for your gracious gift. I shall always prize them above anything I possess because you sent them to me. I wish I understood Spanish that I might thank you in your own beautiful language. I shall begin to study at once so I may read my dear little books.

Father and Mother wish me to present their very kind regards to you and say that they hope to have the great pleasure of seeing you at our home in Sacramento. With best wishes for you and yours, I am with sincere love,

Your Friend,

ABBEY LOUISE WATERMAN

General Vallejo was away at the time Abbey Louise's note came, but on his return, he wrote her as follows:

Thank your dear parents for their kind invitation which I shall accept on my next visit to your charming city. I am delighted to know you so much liked the books I sent you and when you have studied the Spanish language sufficiently to appreciate its literary merits you will see how truly you resemble "El Angel del Hogar" (The Angel of the Home).

As you will soon commence your studies in Spanish I take pleasure in sending you several books which I hope will be useful to you. I shall anxiously look forward to the day when my "Spanish letter" will reach me and pray your progress in your new language may be rapid.

I had the pleasure of seeing your Papa at the Occidental Hotel the other day and we had a pleasant little chat. Since then I have written a private letter requesting him to pay attention to a petition sent by the leading citizens of Sonoma Valley to pardon a man now at San Quentin who is suffering an unjust imprisonment, and who better than "Miss Abbey Louise" can be the soliciting angel for this poor man.

After the holidays of 1888 were over, Vallejo wrote to the Chico Parlor of the Native Sons of the Golden West with reference to his visit there in November:

As a slight memento of my recent visit to your beautiful city, I take pleasure in presenting you herewith with a likeness of myself, in token, that in spirit I am, and always will be with you . . . I shall never forget the spontaneous hearty and hospitable and kindly reception accorded me.

I am proud to say that I am one of you, proud of my native land, our beautiful California, and I am proud of such noble sons. Being as I am, the oldest of your order, I feel toward you as though you were my own, as a father to his children. I feel that the future well-being of the state is safe in your fostering and protecting hands.

While yet California's mountains and plains and meadows were untrodden save by the grizzly, the elk, the antelope and the primitive race, and its streams and rivers flowed clear as crystal, I foresaw the rising tide of progress, the great and wonderful future of this Golden West and I gladly embraced the anticipated opportunity of cooperating with the American ideas, theory and practice of vigorous growth and improvement of California.

During those days your estimable fellow-townsman General Bidwell saw and knew me at the fort of General Sutter where I was obliged to make a brief sojourn and for whom he was then secretary. Chico founded and growing under his intelligent and enterprising care has a bright and prosperous future that will make it with its natural resources second to no other city of the northern valley. I beg to convey through you my thanks to General Bidwell who though absent at the time of my visit to your city presented me with princely hospitality, the freedom of his home.

Upon receipt of the General's letter and portrait, William G. O'Connor, president of the Chico Parlor of the N.S.G.W., wrote him on February 18, 1889:

The Chico Parlor of the Native Sons send you fraternal greetings. We were proud to have you as our guest and happy in showing you honor . . . We trust you will feel assured that Chico Parlor has received at your hands, a gift she values above riches. A memento that has in our eyes no commercial equivalent, something we may hand down to our children's children to remind them of the Grand Old Chieftain of our beloved order.

Draped in the Golden Sash of a Past President, your magnificent portrait hangs in an honored position on our walls, watching with unceasing vigilance the work of the order. Honored Sir and beloved brother, we accept with pride your magnificent gift and trusting we may never prove unworthy of your high regard.

Such affectionate regard stirred deep emotions in the "Grand Old Chieftain," especially when he read the letter by a Mr. John R. McCauley of Alameda, published in the *Sonoma Index.* The letter extolled the products of the Sonoma Valley, especially its grapes, which required no chemicals to be added to the wine made from them. McCauley went on to say:

We might ask the question who is the greatest Californian, living or dead? A great many people would look to some of the railroad magnates or some of the bankers or philanthropists but Sonoma Valley has the honor of taking the palm for the greatest Californian who ever breathed lives in Sonoma, a well known citizen, General M. G. Vallejo. No unsavory record will ever taint the memory of this great man . . . At one time the richest Californian . . . but he gave and gave, till he had nothing to give.

He gave it in Heaven's own way. True there is one large town in Solano County which bears his name and one township in Sonoma County but the greatest monuments that bear his name are in Heaven for his treasures are there with pure childlike faith. He cannot realize the good he has done and if we could but look inside the veil and take a glance at the invisible when the great Vallejo throws off the mortal and puts on Immortality, he will be astonished to see among the souls of the just men, made perfect, some of the very people he befriended in their early days in California.

It was not only his friends who thought well of General Vallejo, but he was also admired and loved by his *parientes.* Early in 1889, he had received a letter dated January 9th, from his niece, Guadalupe, the daughter of his late brother Don Jose de Jesus who had died seven years before.

Well said is the proverb 'works are love' and for a good reason it is. For the newspaper that comes almost daily from you is for me an eloquent sign of your regard for me, thoughts of a grand soul who consoles me by remembrance, assuring me I am not alone in the world, who sympathizes with me in my present situation, considers me and perhaps has pity on me.

I've had the opportunity, dear uncle, from some one who wished to marry me and have me leave the care of my old mother to my brothers, but I've no other choice than this light sacrifice; only a few days more on earth, then to her will be opened the door to Heaven, to her another life.

A few days later, Vallejo replied to Guadalupe: "Truly dear niece, your precious letter of the 9th, caused me to 'bring the colors out of the house.' Your expression, style, amiability and intelligence expressed therein is a proof of your culture . . . You make me blush when you say you are proud of your uncle. Well, hear me, dear child, I am proud to have a niece like you, so loveable, so dear, so intelligent and, to conclude, so beautiful."

The "light sacrifice" was removed from Guadalupe Vallejo on June 2, 1892 when her mother Dona Soledad Sanchez Ortega de Vallejo died in Oakland at the age of eighty-one. Guadalupe survived her mother twelve years. She was sixty years old when her death occurred; until shortly before, she had been busy translating "Ben Hur" into Spanish. Her translations of "America" and "The Star Spangled Banner" were used in the textbooks of the schools of Cuba and the Philippine Islands.

Though older members of the Vallejo family held the General in great respect, one of the younger members, a grandson of Don Salvador Vallejo, was not impressed. During a trip Vallejo made to Las Trancas in Napa, to visit Dona Maria de la Luz Carrillo de Vallejo, the widow of Don Salvador, he accosted a little boy: "Do you know who I am?" "No," answered the boy. Whereupon Vallejo said, "I am General Vallejo." Then the lad, looking up at the General, said, "Well, I am Owen Frisby." This family anecdote was recounted by Owen's brother Uriah Frisby, an octogenarian and grandson of Salvador Vallejo living in Napa in 1963.

SEEKING A PENSION

Friends who remembered the pensions given to Sutter and Marshall by the State of California felt that one should be given to Vallejo. In February 1889, Vallejo received a letter from a Mr. Litzuis who wrote that he had spoken in Sacramento to Assemblyman Howe about a pension for the General, but under the new Constitution nothing could be done. The Sutter and Marshall Requisitions had been put into effect under the old Constitution. Litzuis felt that if Vallejo could come up to Sacramento and circulate among his friends, something might be done. Litzuis added, "If a person is bashful, he will never get anything."

The financial need must have been great, as Vallejo wrote to Lieutenant-Governor Stephen W. White. In reply White told Vallejo, "It would afford me the greatest pleasure to be able to effect the desired result and am now engaged in investigating, in order to ascertain whether it is practicable so to do. Your claims are certainly very great and there should be no failure to recognize them."

In spite of his financial embarrassment, Vallejo's hospitality did not diminish. One who was always welcome was "the deaf one," Theophilus H. d'Estrella, who occupied the guest cottage El Delirio. Estrella, in speaking of Vallejo, said, "On my first meeting, General Vallejo charmed me as he did everybody with his striking and splendid physique and his courtly and dignified hospitality; no one could fail to feel honored in such a distinguished presence." When coming for the day, the teacher for the Deaf and Dumb in Berkeley, would bring his pupils. Vallejo would talk to them in the sign language. He kept an illustrated card with the alphabet for the deaf in his wallet.

The lingering grief over Ula's actions and the worry over his own financial straits were seriously undermining Vallejo's once strong constitution. He was refusing invitations. In April 1889, he sent the following telegram of refusal to the 12th annual session of the Grand Parlor N.S.G.W. "I wish you all a successful and joyful gathering. Sickness prevents me from shaking hands with you, but I am with you in spirit and proud to be the oldest member of the Native Sons of California, which promises to be the most prosperous state of the Union." At this time he wrote to his daughter Maria Cutter:

For two weeks I have been very sick in bed without it allowing it to be known, as far as has been possible for me, neither the gravity of my illness nor the intensity of my pain, in order to avoid grieving your poor mother and Lulu, both of them being also in rather poor health; but anyway, I am improving little by little, so slowly that Lulu has been chiding me because I don't take good enough care of myself.

Maria's husband, Harry Cutter, wrote to his father-in-law that he had heard that he had been quite sick, but now that the pleasant weather had arrived he was hoping that he was all right again: "You have so much of the ambition and spirit of youth that I fear you often task your strength, forgetting you are no longer a 'young buck.' "

On May 13th, 1889 General Vallejo received a letter from Miss N. L. Denman of Petaluma:

I hope you will excuse my troubling you, for knowing your interest in everything pertaining to the early history of our country, I have ventured to ask you for some information. I should like to learn from you any facts about the old "Adobe" three or four miles East of Petaluma, that you can give. When it was built, how large it was originally, how many people lived in it. Was it ever attacked by Indians, when did it pass out of your possession and any other facts of interest. I belong to a Literary Society here and they have appointed me to find out all I can on the subject and I cannot get any book about it.

Three days later, May 16, 1889 Vallejo asked his daughter Luisa to take down a letter to Miss Denman:

Dear Miss Denman:

Your letter of the 13th inst. reached me in safety, and at your request I will narrate some of the interesting facts concerning the old adobe, three or four miles east of Petaluma.

I built the house in 1834 to 1844 and it was of immense proportions, owing to the different departments for factories and warehouses. I made blankets enough to supply over 2,000 Indians; also carpets and a course material used by them for their wearing apparel. A large tannery also, where we manufactured shoes for the troops and vaqueros. Also a blacksmith shop for making saddles, bridles, spurs, and many other things required by the horsemen. I have a blanket still in my possession made there, and although in constant use, is in perfect condition.

My harvest productions were so large that my storehouses were literally overfilled every year. In 1843 my wheat and barley crop amounted to 72,000 Spanish bushels (a "fanega" or Spanish bushel is equal to one and one-half of our bushels) and my ploughmen were about 200 men. Corn about 5,000 bushels, besides a superabundance of all grains for daily use, such as beans, peas, lentils, and vegetables of all kinds. All these products were stored in different departments of this large house, besides giving freely to the Indians who lived in the surrounding country in peace with me. A large number of hides were preserved every year, also tallow, lard and dried meat to sell to the "Yankees."

In one wing of my house, up stairs, I lived with my family when in Petaluma. The south front was 250 feet long, and the building formed a large square, the house having an immense courtyard inside, where every morning the laborers met and called the roll before dispersing for their various occupations.

The house was two stories high and very solid, made of adobe and timber, brought by oxen from the redwoods, and prepared for use by the old fashioned saw, by four kanakas (my servants) brought from the Sandwich Islands by Captain Cooper, my brother-in-law. It had wide corridors inside and outside, some of which were carpeted by our own make of carpets.

Mr. Fowler, father of Mr. Henry Fowler of Napa, was the last carpenter who worked in my old house. I sold it to Mr. White (sic. Whiteside) about twenty years ago for $25,000. It was never attacked by the Indians.

When I was taken prisoner by the Bear Flag party, this house was filled with what I have already mentioned and they disposed of everything.

The meaning of the word "Petaluma" signifies in the Indian language "a beautiful panorama seen in the great declivity from all points." Hoping this reaches you in time, and will give you a full detail of the old adobe is the sincere wish of Yours very truly, M. G. VALLEJO

Anita Emparan, the little granddaughter who lived at Lachryma Montis, celebrated her sixth birthday on June 7, 1889. "Gran-Papa" Vallejo wrote her a short poem in his beautiful script. On June 26th he wrote a more serious document, namely a holographic will.

VALLEJO'S 82ND BIRTHDAY

General Vallejo's own birthday anniversary, his 82nd, came on July fourth but as usual he celebrated it on the 7th, which for some reason he thought was his natal day. The Sonoma Parlor of the Native Sons of the Golden West gave him "an elegant present for which," he told them, "my heart is overflowing with gratitude and words fail me to properly thank you all." It was what he needed most—money. From his dear friend Father Luis came this note: "Allow me to offer my congratulations on the return of your birthday. May your last one be yet far distant and the crowning one of all when it comes. I have succeeded in securing a friend with money willing to invest in developing your waterworks provided we can satisfy him that the investment will prove a safe one."

From Cell No. 601—San Quentin came this letter on July 14, 1889. Addressed to Honorable General Vallejo, it read:

Dear Sir:

Please read this appeal of mine to you. Will you see if you can obtain a pardon for me? General, I've been here in this prison 7 years now and I think I've been punished enough. I have forgiven all who have done me wrong . . . I am thoroughly a reformed man and ready to do what is right and I have made up my mind to never indulge in drinking no kind of intoxicating liquors. General, remember I have no relatives to sympathize with me. I have 16 months more to serve and if you would succeed in obtaining a pardon for me I would cheerfully perform any labor for you. Sir, I hope you will excuse me for taking the privilege of writing to you. I am well treated here by the officers, they are kind to those who tries to do what is right.

The Leeses

A telegram was received the last of July, 1889 telling Vallejo that his sister Rosalia Leese had passed away. She had been ill for some time and in straitened circumstances. Rosalia, several years younger than General Vallejo, had married the merchant Jacob P. Leese who came to California via Los Angeles from Ohio and built the first frame building of any size in Yerba Buena. On July fourth, 1836, Leese gave a party whose guests included the officers and men from the two American vessels in port and a Mexican brig and about sixty Californians from northern California.

Mexican and American flags and bunting decorated the new building and the extra tents. A six-piece orchestra was furnished by Captain Hinkley of the "Don Quixote" barque. Among the guests was General Vallejo who offered a toast which began, "To the Glorious Memory of General George Washington, the hero of this famous day and the Founder of the Independence of the United States of America . . . this great Republic, the Wonder of the World . . . I offer this Toast." Also present was Vallejo's sister Rosalia Vallejo, whom Leese met for the first time. Leese observed in his diary that "our fourth ended on the evening of the fifth."

Almost a year later Leese wrote to his friend Abel Stearns in Los Angeles a letter, dated May 8, 1837 in which he informed him (spelling unchanged):

> I was married to a young lady of Monterey on the 12th of last month in the Mission of Saint Solano; it was something on the sly after the fation of us Yankeys in the western part of the U. States. Cince my marriage it has caused a great deal of talk among the people of the country which was in consequence of its being so sly and not a coustom of the country.

The Leeses lived a few years in Yerba Buena, then sold their property there to the Hudson's Bay Company and moved to Sonoma where Leese was Alcalde for a time. He was given a grant of five square leagues of land "Huichica" and in the town of Sonoma, he was given a lot on the west side of the Plaza. Here the Leeses built an attractive adobe home with a balcony, in which they resided until they moved to Monterey and purchased the Larkin House, from the former American Consul.

Rosalia Leese, who was noted for a proneness to sarcasm, as well as her good looks, harbored a dislike toward all Americans after the Bear Flag incident in Sonoma, where she was living at the time. She had been forced to give up the key to her husband's warehouse.

Mrs. Leese insisted that her children who spoke English as a usual thing, converse with her in the Spanish tongue. The very sound of the English language made her shudder; realizing the sweet Castilian words were being given over to the unpronounceable English jargon.

The unfortunate handling of her dowry by her American husband led to marital difficulties. They finally separated; Leese, writing to his children from New York City in 1871, attempted to explain the situation, in somewhat improved spelling from his early-day letters.

Dear and Ever Remembered Sons and Daughters:

You say that you are very sorry to hear that I was married again. It is true but not with the idea of abandoning my Family. Necessity compelled me to do so as it was impossible for me to get along without a companion and one that I was not ashamed of. There has been no deception in the case. I informed the parties of my having a family in California. In the first place you know well, how unfortunate I have been these past years in all my undertakings as well as the unhappy life I have lived with your mother. You know I transferred to you all the Monterey property as you desired. Never entertain the opinion of my ever abandoning you as I love and remember you all. As soon as possible, I will send you some money. You say that you was informed that I gave my companion $2,000 and a large interest in Lower California stock, all of which is false. She has no need of any interest from me as she has plenty of her own.

After a number of years, Leese returned to California and was reconciled with his children before he died in San Francisco on February 2, 1892 at the age of 83. His funeral was conducted by the Society of California Pioneers. The nieces and nephews of Tia Rosalia had been saddened by her death. At that time Maria Encarnacion Vallejo de Kern, the daughter of Don Jose de Jesus Vallejo, wrote to her Tio Guadalupe (Gen. Vallejo) saying: "Another leaf from the beautiful family tree has fallen into the earth, my dear Tia Rosalia. She has taken flight to Heaven to join our family already there, to be happy in the eternal mansions while we are submerged in shrouds of sadness for the departure of my dear Papa." (Died January 1882.) From Sister Teresa of the San Jose Sacred Heart Convent, another daughter of Don Jose de Jesus Vallejo came these words, "I hope if by some fault she (Tia Rosalia) has been detained in the place of separation the Almighty will pardon her and give her the reward that a good life and virtue find her deserving of."

THE DONAHUE LOAN

In August 1889, Joseph Maguire, attorney for James Mervyn Donahue, son of Colonel Peter Donahue, wrote to Vallejo about the $1,500 loaned him by the late Colonel. This time, Vallejo, who had endeavored to explain the entire transaction to the younger Donahue, turned over the matter to his attorney, Henry N. Clement of San Francisco. Clement sent a letter explaining in detail the transaction to Maguire. In conclusion, Clement wrote: "As you know, General Vallejo is not and never has been a business man. He will sign anything his friends or those he regards as his friends ask him to. The strong and potent facts of the case are (1) that General Vallejo never received one cent for the right-of-way through his place, (2) that the effect of the building of the railroad through his place was to destroy its value as a security for the debt, (3) that he received assurance from both Colonel Donahue and his confidential agents that the mortgage would be cancelled."

Correspondence went on throughout the summer and fall, until the winter when the case was terminated.

VALLEJO'S LAST VISIT TO THE CITY OF VALLEJO

By the fall of 1889, General Vallejo had improved enough in health to visit the city named in his honor. It was his last visit.

While there he stayed at the home of his daughter Adela (Mrs. Levi C. Frisbie). One evening, many of the resident Sons and Daughters of the Golden West called upon him to pay their respects, and as was customary, the young ladies claimed the privilege of saluting the veteran with a kiss. When Adela's husband, Dr. Frisbie, came into the parlor, he could see how intent they were all in receiving the *Vallejo Degree*. Whereupon the Doctor jokingly remarked: "General, I see you are having a flirtation. How do you enjoy it?" The General replied, "No. Not a flirtation, Doctor, that belongs to you young chaps, to do furtively perhaps, but *I* do not need any tactics anyway with these young people whom I love really as my own children. I do not believe in the flirting business; this is the real thing; genuine, original fatherly love and affection for a generation of young men and women whom I am proud to call my own because in them I realize (and they appreciate the fact) that I was instrumental in producing their present State and watched the finger of God in pointing westward and bringing their fathers to reside and develop the productive soil of this our native land. I hope the Almighty will bless them all and that they will develop a great and magnificent people and not allow anything to interfere with the harmony and union which always help to strengthen a people and contribute so much to consolidate into a great nation. The idea of the Native Sons and Daughters is an old one with me, and we had ever since my youth a kind of society, including all the sons and daughters of this beautiful soil and was called 'Hijos e Hijas del Pais'."

Vallejo continued: "But now that they have become so much more numerous, I meet them everywhere I go and they salute me as you see, joyfully like my own children and I realize that my life has not gone for nothing in the effort made long ago to bring to these golden shores and still more blessed hills and valleys, a stock of people at once energetic and able to cultivate the soil and make productive the millions of acres of virgin soil, the most productive on the face of the globe . . . When I look back and reflect that where I once crossed on rafts of logs, now any one can cross from the opposite shore and come by steamboat and railroads to where we sit tonight. I seemed to have lived a thousand years and I begin to think that Adam and Methuselah were not so very old after all. I do not exaggerate when I say I have seen California come from the savage and wild condition into the highest and foremost civilized state in the period of less than one hundred years."

On Vallejo's return from his name city, he did a bit of shopping. He bought hats for Raoul and Carlos, costing $1 each and for their little sister Anita, a "sombresito" which cost fifty cents. Raoul was four, Carlos five and Anita six years old. Soon the rains started—rather unusual for October. Regarding the wet weather, Vallejo wrote his daughter Adela Frisbie:

Here we don't lack much for turning into frogs. It has rained so much these last days that the creeks have risen a great deal. Still the storm doesn't abate and the sky continues to threaten rain. It appears Neptune is irked and has decreed that this year, rain should come two months earlier than usual. Who knows perhaps the seasons of the year have changed around. I am truly very surprised at this deluge of water in this month, since in the 82 years that I have lived, there has not been a similar deluge in October.

How has it been with you in October? I imagine the same, as I have from here seen the clouds covering all that region as far as Mt. Diablo.

The inclement weather continued through the winter. Its severity, together with the ruthless efforts of the widow and son of Colonel Peter Donahue to collect the debt of $1,500, aggravated Vallejo's illness. In spite of his weakened condition, Vallejo painstakingly wrote almost a brief to his attorney, Henry N. Clement, explaining the whole transaction and of the promise of the late Peter Donahue to cancel the debt in exchange for the right-of-way over Vallejo's property. Vallejo concluded his letter: "I hope you will do your best to urge their lawyer to convince Mrs. Donahue that for the memory and for the honor of her deceased husband, she abide by his promise made to me."

The correspondence between Vallejo and his attorney on the subject still continued. Finally, the burden of worry was lifted from Vallejo's mind by the following letter from Mr. Clement:

The original note and mortgage was made and executed by you and your wife in 1881. I have labored under the impression up to this time that you renewed the note and mortgage by giving a new note and a new mortgage . . . I find that you did not renew the note and mortgage in a legal sense. All that you did was simply to sign a paper acknowledging that the old note and mortgage were not paid and hence the old note and mortgage are *outlawed* against you and I am of the opinion that they are of no value and they could not be collected against you to foreclose the mortgage long ago was because they knew it was outlawed . . . The claim is dead in law and I am very glad of it.

THE CONTINUED FRIENDSHIP OF THE BOGGS FAMILY

Another letter which eased somewhat the tedious days of suffering, was one from his old friend, William M. Boggs of Napa. Mr. Boggs was a son of Lilburn W. Boggs whose family spent the winter of 1846–47 as guests of General Vallejo in the old Adobe near Petaluma. After the first winter, the former Missouri governor located in Sonoma where he was appointed Alcalde and later opened a merchandise store. At that time the General was a lavish buyer and a great entertainer; his account ran into large figures. Governor Boggs never sent a bill. When the General disposed of cattle or sold a piece of land, he would settle his account, paying whatever the books showed. Later when money became somewhat scarce with Vallejo, he decided to settle his account with a note, an arrangement which was satisfactory to Boggs.

Some time after the death of Boggs, his son William found the note and, because it bore Vallejo's signature with an elaborate rubric, he decided to keep it as a memento. He put it in his wallet and had almost forgotten he had it. He never considered presenting it for payment. Years later, Vallejo and William Boggs were called as witnesses in San Francisco in a land case. The two friends were sauntering up and down the corridor, waiting to be called. Vallejo, who so often rolled his own cigarettes, asked Boggs for a cigarette paper. Boggs thought of the note and, taking it from his wallet, he handed it to the General in a casual manner. Recognizing the document, Vallejo flushed, stopped and said, "It is my obligation, Sir, I acknowledge it true enough but I regret I cannot pay it. Perhaps at some future time." He handed the note to Boggs who refused to take it, saying as he patted the General on the shoulder, "Why don't you make your cigarette, General? If my father were here he would be only too pleased to know that in this small way we are able to repay you, if only in part for all you did for us and our families in the early days."

This gracious action was quite in keeping with the character of the man who had never forgotten Vallejo's kindness in the early days. His first child, Guadalupe Vallejo Boggs, the little *Gringo*, had been born at Vallejo's hacienda near Petaluma. Now in the winter of 1889 William Boggs heard of Vallejo's serious illness and decided to do something concrete for his afflicted friend. In a spirit of gratitude, he wrote General Vallejo on December 21, 1889:

> It is with much sorrow that I have heard of your illness and suffering and you will excuse me, my dear General, if I inform you that I have taken the liberty to address a strong letter to the Hon. Joseph McKenna, our representative in Congress asking him to act with the Hon. U.S. Senators Stanford and Hearst in obtaining an appropriation for your benefit on account of the past services and many noble acts of generosity you have performed for the American people in former years, and the aid you rendered our United States officers in furthering their plans of operations and your hospitality in entertaining them during the pending of hostilities with your own Country; your kindness to the American emigrants—a thousand other noble acts, when you were in affluence and above all, your noble conduct in advising your Countrymen not to resist the power of a government, that your good foresight and judgment convinced you was a useless waste of life and means to resist.
>
> I have forwarded the communication to Governor Waterman at Sacramento to obtain his endorsement and approval, hoping it may be the means of affording you some relief in your declining years.
>
> Yours ever in gratitude, I remain
>
> WILLIAM BOGGS

At this time a Napa newspaper published the following:

AID INVOKED

General Vallejo is in his 83rd year. He lives in a little house near old Sonoma, the scene of his princely hospitality before California was a State. He is no longer strong physically nor independent financially. He is a broken old man, infirm and almost entirely helpless. Once immensely rich, he is now extremely poor. From a position of affluence, he has come to one of hard poverty. To render him the aid he so well deserves, Mr. William M. Boggs of this city (Napa) has written to Congressman McKenna with the hope of getting relief from the Government. The letter thus written, Governor Waterman will be asked to endorse. Mr. Boggs bases this claim for relief upon the noble services rendered the American people by General Vallejo in the early days—the aid he freely gave the U.S. officers when they came to take possession of the country—his kindness to immigrants and his noble conduct in advising his countrymen not to resist the power of government he had the foresight to see must rule the Pacific Coast Territory.

When in affluent circumstances his ample roof sheltered the weary and from his bounty the hungry were without questionings freely fed. Now that the day of adversity has overtaken him he would carry his burden alone but his friends will refuse to see him suffer without an earnest appeal to the Government he so fearlessly honored and so nobly helped.

William Boggs sent another letter to Vallejo, written Christmas day, 1889, saying: "I have just received a letter from Governor Waterman, in reply to my request of him to endorse my letter to Congressman McKenna, requesting him to do something in the way of obtaining relief for you from the Government. The Governor not only wrote a strong endorsement to my letter but he enlisted others in the case. Among whom is the Honorable Frank Pixley of the *Argonaut*. Mr. Pixley goes to Washington in a short time and he promised the Governor to do all in his power to get you a pension or some other relief financially. The Governor also suggested that the Native Sons make a move in the same direction, hoping now that the ball is in motion we will keep it going until success follows."

It has been said by members of the Vallejo family that when the General read the letters, he shook his head and said, "Es muy tarde" (It is too late). While General Vallejo may have read William Boggs' letters with tears in his eyes, in his heart there must have been a glow of satisfaction in knowing that, in spite of the ingratitude of many Americans he had befriended, there was at least *one* who remembered and was grateful.

LATENESS OF LIFE'S HOUR

The lateness of Life's Hour was realized by General Vallejo. He had in June prepared a holographic will in his beautiful script, and was prepared for the last journey. As the year was drawing to a close, he took Holy Communion from Father John J. Sullivan, the pastor of the St. Francis Solano Church. The rite was observed in the library which had been converted into the General's bedroom. This was to save him the climb upstairs. Luisa prepared a table near the invalid's bed and on it placed candles, flowers, Holy Water, and a picture of the Resurrection. Vallejo was given a white napkin which he held as he was given his Communion. Kneeling about the bed were his wife and children, whom he fondly kissed after he received the Blessed Sacrament. Platon was not present; so Luisa wrote to her brother, telling him, "Raise your heart to God and thank Him as our own dear Papa has taken Communion."

Soon after this, Platon received a note from Dr. H. H. Davis, who was attending General Vallejo: "If convenient I wish you would come over and take a look at your father. I will meet you there if you will send me word of your arrival. He does not progress as I would like to see him doing. I would be satisfied to have you see him again. I have said nothing to the family of having written you in regard to him."

Upon receiving the note from Dr. Davis, Platon turned over his patients in the city of Vallejo to another physician, in order to be with his father. Platon found his father patient in his sufferings, his manner sweet and most affectionate towards his family. The once energetic, intellectual, passionate, and gracious person was prostrate, humble and resigned.

Luisa, who was a sort of head-nurse, felt that her father's days were filled with delirium, because his mind seemed to dwell upon those loved ones who had passed away from this life, recalling them vividly, as if they were present. To Napoleon, her youngest brother who was traveling for Arpad Haraszthy's wine concern, Luisa wrote:

> Adela, Platon, Natalia, Lolita, Tala and I are listening to his wandering mind tell such beautiful things. Poor Papa is out of his mind, most of the time. I am so afraid that he will not know Fannie when she comes. It will be a great disappointment to her not to be recognized by her dear father . . . Mama just came in from the parlor and kissed Papa. He hasn't much to say but he knew her. She came leaning on Andronico's arm. "Hambrear" [hungry] he said, when she came near him.

Fannie Frisbie, who had been telegraphed to come, arrived from Mexico City in San Francisco on January 14th. With her was her son Platon and her daughter Josephine. They went immediately to Sonoma.

Platon assigned to himself the night hours to care for his father. Every evening this forty-nine-year-old son would kneel beside his father's bed and together they would repeat the Rosary. If the General awakened in the night, he would call for Platon to read him the Seven Penitential Psalms and other pious prayers, which Platon was happy to do even though the fire had burned low in the grate and the winter chill was in the air.

With death approaching, Vallejo seemed to become aware of a different level of conciousness, seemingly possessing a sort of sixth sense. He was evidently conscious in some way of Luisa's thought that his mind was wandering and wished to convinced his loved ones he was normal. The General called Platon to his bed and, pointing toward the marble fireplace, said, "That is

North." Platon answered, "Yes, Father." Reaching toward the head of his walnut bed, Vallejo said, "This is South." Again Platon agreed. The General then pointed to the window, "That is East." Again from Platon, "Yes." Vallejo, pointing once again, this time to the door leading into the back hallway, saying, "And that is West." Again an affirmative nod from Platon. "Well then," General Vallejo said, "I am not out of my mind." "Oh no," said his son. "Am I not in my own bed, in my own room, in my own house, at my own Lachryma Montis. And I believe I am not out of my mind but I have heard my mother's voice. My mother died many years ago [1855] but I have on more than one occasion lately heard her voice distinctly." It is comforting to believe that Vallejo's dear mother may have been the first loved one to welcome him into the new life.

The youngest son, Napoleon Primo, also acted as a nurse for the General. He gave what time he could from his work, selling in Oregon his brother-in-law's champagne, "*Eclipse*," to care for his father. It was Napoleon's special duty and pleasure to give him his daily rubbing with sweet oil and see to it that the glass bottle was filled with hot water to warm his feet.

In spite of the attentive care of the physician and the Vallejo family, the General's condition became critical. On Friday, January 17th, his last conscious day, a young lady, little Susie Willis, came to see him. As she was dearly loved by the General, in fact by the whole Vallejo family, she was allowed to see her sick friend. Finding him asleep, she quietly approached his bed, and, after regarding the General a few moments, she bent down and impressed a kiss on his brow. The patient opened his eyes. Taking her hand, he said, "I thought an angel had kissed me, why it is you Susie."

At one-thirty in the dark hours of January 18th, 1890 General Mariano Guadalupe Vallejo, murmuring "Into Thy Hands Father, I commend my spirit," passed away quietly, surrounded by his family. The news of General Vallejo's death was received with sorrow throughout the State. The metropolitan papers carried long accounts of his career; flags floated at half-mast and schools and business houses were closed in Sonoma.

The day of the funeral, Tuesday January 21st, was gloomy and overcast. The historic town, which owed its very existence and name to the honored dead, presented a general appearance of mourning. It was said that the people grieved as though each family circle had been deprived of one of its members.

The General's body lay in state in front of the white marble mantel in the parlor of his home which was filled with floral offerings. On the casket was an immense floral pillow with the legend in purple flowers, "Grandpa from Mariano Guadalupe Vallejo"; this was the tribute from Napoleon Vallejo's oldest son, a lad of fourteen years, who had been named for the General.

After friends had paid their last respects at the Vallejo home, General Vallejo's body was taken through the crape-draped portals of the east porch, then carried along the tree-lined avenue of Lachryma Montis to the strains of Chopin's Funeral March, played by the Military Band of the San Francisco Presidio. It had been sent to Sonoma as a special courtesy to the fallen General by another military man, General Nelson Miles.

The body was taken to the St. Francis Solano Church on West Napa Street for the solemn Requiem Mass. With the exception of a close family friend, Henry Weyl, the pall-bearers were members of the family; the three sons, Andronico, Platon and Napoleon; the sons-in-laws, J. H. Cutter, Ricardo Emparan and Arpad Haraszthy and the honorary ones, Mariano and Agoston Haraszthy (Natalia's two boys) Leo and Platon Frisbie (Fannie's sons), Mariano and Harvey (Napoleon's sons) and a nephew, Ignacio Vallejo (Salvador Vallejo's son).

After the funeral service, which took almost two hours and at which Father Sullivan officiated, the long procession of patriotic societies and delegations circled the Sonoma Plaza, stopping a few moments with bared heads at the site of the Casa Grande, the first home of the pueblo's founder, then marched along West First Street, along to Mountain Cemetery, Vallejo's gift to the city.

The distinguished dead was brought to the burial site between rows of soldiers, standing with arms presented, while a brief burial service was read. There on the hillside in a stone crypt, the illustrious patriot, soldier, statesman and founder of Sonoma was laid to rest. A silken flag, the "Banner of the Stars" surmounted by a golden eagle, the gift of the California State Legislature, was unfurled and was placed among the banks of flowers as a *Guard of Honor* for MARIANO GUADALUPE VALLEJO, the great and good friend of the United States.

Dona Francisca Benicia Carrillo de Vallejo

Dona Francisca Benicia Carrillo de Vallejo

The wife of General Mariano Guadalupe Vallejo was born on August 23, 1815 in San Diego. On the 24th of August, she was baptized and given the name of Francisca Maria Felipa Benicia by Padre Fernando Martín in the chapel of the Presidio of San Diego. The infant's godparents were Don Francisco Maria Ruiz, Teniente Comandante of the Presidio of San Diego, and Dona Josefa Sal, the widow of Sergeant Mariano Mercado.

The child was known as "the baby of the Presidio, daughter of the soldier Carrillo and his wife Maria Ignatius Lopez." The father, Joaquin Carrillo, was born in Baja, California; his wife was the daughter of Jose Francisco Lopez and Maria Feliciano Arballo de Gutierrez. The latter, a twenty-year-old widow of Jose Gutierrez, a Royal soldier who was killed by savage Indians in Mexico, joined Captain Juan Bautista Anza's expedition in 1775 at Tubac, Mexico. With her were her two young daughters, Maria Tomasa, six years, and Maria Estaquia, four years. Soon after the expedition reached the San Gabriel Mission, Dona Maria Feliciana was married to Jose Francisco Lopez March 6, 1776 by Padre Francisco Garces. Thirteen years later her daughter Maria Estaquia Gutierrez married Don Jose Maria Pico whom little Estaquia had first known as a boy of eleven years on the Anza expedition. Estaquia became the mother of a number of children, among them Pio Pico and Andres Pico.

The children of Senora Jose Francisco Lopez born in California were Ignacio and Jose Lopez, Josefa (Senora Vejar) Juana (Senora Juan Osuna) Maria Antonia (Senora Jose Maria Aguilar), and Maria Ygnacia (Senora Joaquin Carrillo), the last named the mother of twelve children, one being Francisca Maria Felipa Benicia.

The Carrillos of European Noble descent were among the first families to come into California. The Joaquin Carrillos of San Diego were blessed with seven daughters and five sons, nearly all of whom figured more or less prominently in the history of California. Joaquin served as a soldier for 22 years. He was highly respected in his own right, but, as he was just a regular soldier, he had no land of his own. Consequently his family were glad to occupy the only house outside the grounds of the San Diego Presidio when it was offered to them. It had been built of adobe by Don Francisco Ruiz, and was surrounded by a beautiful orchard of pears, pomegranates, and olive trees. There, in the huerta or orchard during January 1830, Alferez Vallejo saw for the first time the young Carrillo girl who was destined to share his life. At the time, her lovely face was hidden; she was washing her long dark hair.

In referring to the youthful Francisca in after years, Vallejo said, "I knew her when she was a regular goat amidst those hills . . . in the land of the cholla, the prickley pear and rocks." Francisca was indeed an outdoor girl in that benign climate and was a skilled markswoman. With her large dark, lustrous eyes and regular, classic features, she was considered a beautiful young woman.

It was not long before the mutual attraction between the two young people turned into love. Although Alferez Vallejo stayed only a few weeks in San Diego, he won the consent of his sweetheart and that of her parents. Being an officer, it was necessary for Vallejo to receive permission to wed from the Mexican officials. He wrote for this on October 15, 1830 from Monterey, where he had gone for the Territorial Legislative election. While waiting for the official sanction to arrive, Vallejo occupied much of his time reading the banned books which had cost him four hundred hides and ten kegs of tallow; also excommunication from his church because of the suspicions of the priests, who, Vallejo said, "kept guard over all the ports and bays of California like St. Peter at the gates of Heaven to prevent the entrance of books of a liberal tendency." When Father Duran was convinced that the books would not be placed in the hands of irresponsible or non-intelligent people, Vallejo was able to write his fiancée, "It is now permitted me to improve my education without incurring the danger of being stigmatized as an excommunicated heretic."

Seventeen months passed, before the lovers received official permission to marry. It reached Vallejo at San Juan Capistrano on March 2, 1832, and he lost no time in hastening to San Diego, "to be led captive to the altar." Don Guadalupe and Dona Francisca were married on March 6th, 1832, in the Chapel of the Presidio of San Diego, where 23 years before, Francisca's mother had been married. As it was Lent, a special dispensation was obtained enabling Padre Fernando Martín, who had baptized the infant Francisca, to perform the ceremony. The wedding guests stood in a circle, there being no pews in the churches in those days. Padre Martín blessed the rings and the arras; then he put one ring on Alferez Vallejo's hand and Vallejo put the other ring on his bride's hand; then he gave her the arras (thirteen ounces of glittering California gold), saying, "This ring and these arras I give thee in token of matrimony." Francisca, declining the gift of the arras, placed the gold on the church platter, thereby earning the promised blessing of many future children. The wedding sponsors were Don Juan Bandini, his wife Dona Dolores Estudillo, and Senor Joaquin Ortega.

Acting Governor Jose Maria Echeandia, one of the guests, went with the wedding party to the home of Juan Bandini where the reception was held; there the Governor toasted the young couple, "I drink to the happiness of this young couple whom I appreciate and esteem. I made young Vallejo, the Ensign of Cavalry for his merits and activity in service. I have known his young wife since she was eight years old and I have had frequent occasion to admire her fine manners. May Heaven keep happiness for them and may their children be many and worthy of them, an ornament to our dear California and the cultural society of San Diego." A sumptuous feast and dancing followed. The music was furnished by the San Diego Band and by an Indian orchestra from the San Luis Rey Mission named for Louis the Ninth, Crusader King of France. This mission, within a day's ride from San Diego, supplied the San Diego garrison with corn, wheat, beans, manteca, soap and shoes.

The young bridegroom, although busy with military and legislative affairs, was able to remain in San Diego with his bride most of the spring of 1832, making occasional trips to Los Angeles where the latter part of December he attended the final session of the Legislature. The members had assembled to discuss matters to be presented to the new governor, Don Jose Figueroa. Figueroa arrived in Monterey January 15, 1833, and Vallejo, with his nephew Juan B. Alvarado and their friend Antonio Osio, traveled to the capital to offer their services to the new chief. The Governor was impressed with young Vallejo and ordered him to join his company at the Presidio of San Francisco.

Senora Mariano Guadalupe Vallejo had been left in San Diego, but not for long, as Vallejo sent his twenty-year-old brother Don Salvador to bring his bride to the Presidio of San Francisco which was to be their first home. In spite of the protection of twenty troopers and the care of Don Salvador, it was a rugged journey along the Camino Real for a seventeen-year-old girl who was expecting her first baby.

Francisca found the San Francisco Presidio a dilapidated military post, but, with the enthusiasm of a wife deeply in love, she began "housekeeping" for her husband, in a crude adobe house at this outpost of civilization. Francisca's baby—a boy was born on March 14, 1833. It was the custom in those days for the parents to take the infant for its baptism to the community where the godparents were living. The Vallejo's son was baptized on April 11, 1833, in "la yglesia de este Pueblo de Nuestra Senora de los Angeles" by Padre Antonio de Anzar. The infant was given the name Andonico Antonio with Don Jose Antonio Carrillo and his wife Estefana Pico as godparents. At that time Don Jose Antonio Carrillo was the alcalde or mayor of Los Angeles.

There is a tradition in the Vallejo family that the Mexican authorities, in appreciation of the Vallejo's first-born, gave the young officer a parcel of land in the Presidio known as "*Pozo de los Marineros*" (Sailor's well). As a sign of budding life, Vallejo proceeded to plant an orchard and vegetable garden on it.

The baby died on January 21, 1834 when it was ten months old and was buried at the Mission Dolores. However, the Vallejos were comforted when a second son was born on April 28th, 1834 and was given the name of the little son they had lost. The second Andronico was baptized at the Mission Dolores on May 2, 1834. His care kept Francisca busy, making less lonely the hours when her husband was busy north of the Bay of San Francisco with the secularization of the Mission San Francisco Solano and in making plans for the Hijar-Padres colony from Mexico which was to settle in the Valley of Sonoma.

THE VALLEJOS COME TO THE VALLEY OF SONOMA

In June 1835 Vallejo took his twenty-year-old wife and his year-old son to the Valley of Sonoma, where he had been directed by Governor Jose Figueroa to lay out a pueblo. Some members of the Hijar-Padres colony were already there. Among the members who remained in San Diego for a time and were hospitably received by Dona Francisca Vallejo's mother, were Don Agustin Janssens and six youths. Of her hospitality, Don Agustin said: "Dona Maria Ignacia, wife of Senor Carrillo, treated us in such a kind manner that we could almost look on her as a mother. With her at the time was the widow of Captain Romualdo Pacheco who died in Los Angeles defending the interests of the National Government . . . Mother and daughter did everything possible for our comfort, giving us milk, green vegetables, fruit and whatever else we wished or which they saw we needed without accepting a single centavo. They continued to do for others what they did for us during the whole time they were in San Diego. It is impossible to find words of gratitude to describe the generous conduct of these ladies of Senor Carrillo. To have offered them money would have seemed an offense to them."

After Senor Janssens reached Yerba Buena, he records that he met Vallejo who invited him to go to Sonoma with him in his launch, operated by the Indian Celso. It proved to be a foggy, stormy trip, with most of the time spent in bailing out the boat. Upon arrival at the Mission San Francisco Solano, Janssens found that in matters spiritual it was in charge of Padre Lorenzo Quijas, but, as the mission had been secularized, the area had been converted into a military post with Mariano G. Vallejo in command. He said there were many Indians, perhaps three thousand. This was before the terrible small-pox epidemic.

"After a three months stay in Sonoma," said Senor Janssens, "without hope of progress as the colonists were continually accused of plotting revolution (plots which I believe existed only in the fevered brains of the accusers), I resolved with others to leave." Departing, Janssens reached San Rafael and was told that while the colonists in Sonoma were at Mass, the soldiers of Vallejo had gone to their homes and had taken their arms. "The weapons," said Vallejo in after years, "served later to arm a company of Suisun Indians who did duty as a body guard of my faithful ally, Prince Solano, head of the powerful tribe of Suisunes. This guard of honor was put under the command of Sergeant Fernandez." The action of Vallejo in seizing the colonist's arms pleased Governor Figueroa, who had given the order. "Owing to the skill and military prudence with which Alferez Don Mariano G. Vallejo performed his duty," Figueroa said, "it resulted in no one being wounded or even bruised."

Most of the members of the Cosmopolitan Company, as the Hijar-Padres was called had been comfortably housed, but Dona Francisca Vallejo and her baby son had to find shelter at the abandoned Mission San Francisco Solano.

In one of its adobe-walled rooms was born the Vallejos' third child, their first daughter, on August 4th, 1835. She was named Epifania Guadalupe.

With evidence of an increasing family, Francisca's husband wanted a home of their own. On January 5, 1835 he had petitioned the Mexican Government for a lot on which to build a house, with the result that he was given a parcel of land (later numbered lot 25) on the north side of the plaza, directly west of the Mission.

By the end of 1836, the Vallejo home, the *Casa Grande*, was finished. The adobe bricks for the large, two-story building, with its three-story lookout tower (torreon), were made by the *gentile* Indians, brought in from the mountains by Captain Salvador Vallejo. The bricks were laid by the Indians from the local mission, and the timber was cut and the carpentry work done by a Spaniard and several Anglo-Saxons, with Vallejo, himself, helping at times. The rooms were large and numerous, as if Vallejo knew that they were going to be needed for his family. And they were, for in the Casa Grande were born eleven children: Adelayda, Natalia, Plutarco the first, who was to survive two years; next, Platon; followed by the daughter Guadalupe, who lived to be four years old. Then came Jovita Francisca, bearing one of her mother's names; next, Uladislao, then another boy, Plutarco the second, who lived less than three months. The first Benicia born a year before Napoleon Primo (the youngest son) lived to be four years old, while Benicia the second, born three years after Napoleon, a beautiful child with dark long curls, lived to be almost seven. She was the last child of the Vallejos born in the Casa Grande.

According to Edwin Bryant who served as the second United States Appointed Alcalde of San Francisco from February to May 1847, the Vallejo residence in Sonoma presented a different appearance from any house occupied by native Californians which he had entered. All the rooms, even the main entrance hall and corridors, were scrupulously clean and presented an air of comfort. As he said in his *What I saw in California*, "The parlor was furnished with handsome chairs, sofas, mirrors and tables of mahogany framework and a fine piano, the first I have seen in the country. Several paintings and some superior engravings ornamented the walls." Bryant felt that the owner of the well-furnished home was friendly to the United States. "General Vallejo is I believe strongly desirous that the United States shall retain and annex California. He is thoroughly disgusted with the Mexican ways which is fast sending the country backwards instead of forewards in the scale of civilization and for years has been desirous of the change which is now taking place."

Bryant's description of the Vallejos' home is in agreement with that of the U.S. Naval Lieutenant Wise, who told how he had arrived there at night in 1847 and had been ushered through a spacious porte-cochere into a large sala, where he was graciously received by the lady of the mansion. The apartment assigned to him had its walls papered and there were book cases, prints, and mirrors in profusion.

The Lieutenant was somewhat surprised; he had not believed that such refinement existed in the Territory. After a hearty meal he was entertained by the singing of a number of Russians and Germans, and by piano pieces played by the Vallejo girls. He said that "the little daughters had been properly instructed and performed remarkably well"; he thought, "They were pretty, becomingly attired and what is still more commendable, exceedingly well bred,"—all of which testified to the ability of Andreas Hoeppner, the Vallejos' music teacher and to the training the children had received from their parents.

Although over three centuries had passed since *The Laws of Burgos*, relative to the care of the Indians of the New World, had been promulgated by "Dona Juana," nominally queen of Spain after the death of her mother, Queen Isabella in 1504, Senora Vallejo, during the absence of her husband carried out the rule "if there is no priest present (to baptize infants), the person in charge of said estate shall be obliged to baptize them." She not only baptized the infants but in many cases had delivered them.

Senora Vallejo herself, each year had either a baby next to her heart or on her lap. Besides the personal care she gave her children, she was kept busy supervising her large staff of Indian servants, making each Indian responsible for just one task. As a rule, he or she was not inclined to learn more than one. The Indian who was taught cooking would not wash clothes, and a good laundress would consider herself insulted if asked to spin or sew. Each of the Vallejo children had a particular servant, while Senora Vallejo had two personal maids.

As the wife of General Vallejo said, in recalling those days when the Casa Grande was their home, "Our house was always filled with relatives, particularly as General Vallejo had been able to persuade our *parientes* to settle in the Sonoma District to help in the colonization of Alta California. My mother settled at Santa Rosa; my older sister, Josefa (Mrs. Henry Fitch), at Healdsburg. My brother-in-law (Salvador) with my sister Maria de la Luz, located in Napa Valley and, together with the younger brother Juan Antonio, had a large grant of land near Clear Lake. That was where they kept their cattle."

At the Vallejo ranch at Clear Lake, fine horses were stocked. The General's private caballada, for his own and his family's use, contained one hundred and fifty well-broken horses. Thirty-five were his own private saddle-horses (caballos de silla)—the finest in the country. He told Lieutenant Revere that he had some of his horses twenty-five years. General Vallejo, a graceful rider, usually took a morning and evening ride.

It was said that General Vallejo and his brother Salvador took pains to breed their horses properly; the stallion of each manada was not permitted to roam with its progeny. Many of the selected animals were presented to his visitors, along with silver-ornamented saddles. During the "Bear" revolution, Vallejo lost his entire caballada of about one thousand horses.

From the frequency with which Vallejo's lavish hospitality is mentioned in the writings of those who partook of it, one would think that every person of importance, who visited the Port of San Francisco, came up to Sonoma to be a guest of the Vallejos. To entertain them, many servants were needed. Senora Vallejo found that three grinders of corn for the tortillas were not enough; five were required. Six or seven Indians served in the kitchen, which was located in the long low building at the rear of the tower, next to the residence. The journey to the dining-room often caused the food to become cold before it reached the table. Five or six Indians were busy washing clothes, and a dozen with spinning and sewing.

Numerous Indians who had been trained by the mission padres were employed at the Petaluma Hacienda, producing crops of the different grains and fresh garden vegetables. Various articles were manufactured and sold as far south as San Blas, Mexico.

The General was fond of superintending the work of the Indians, and they performed it willingly. As his wife said: "In consequence of secularization, each head of an Indian family or adult single Indian was to receive a certain quota of livestock, farming implements and a few acres of land if he wanted it. In order to save their livestock, most of them asked my husband for them on a share basis. Most of the local Indians held a deep affection for the General. They were happy in building our new home in Sonoma, the Casa Grande and to work at the Petaluma Rancho." Any harsh Indian policy that Senora Vallejo's husband might have entertained in his youth had been supplanted by one of humane consideration. It was known that he would never tolerate injustice or brutality toward the natives. In 1844, at a time when there was division of authority in the Sonoma District between the civil and military authorities, Vallejo reported to Governor Micheltorena on August 12th:

> The political authority of this place has given passports to several commanders for the detention of the heathen tribes to bring them in by force. I have protested to the said authority, in strong terms; a few days ago a commander passed by with a string of heathens tied with ropes en route to a ranch to work for the Alcalde. The result cannot be other than an uprising as has happened. The tribes of this region are opposed to this sultanic tyranny contrary to the rights of nature.

GUESTS OF THE VALLEJOS

Among the guests entertained by the Vallejos was William Heath Davis, who had come from the Hawaiian Islands to California in 1831 and, in 1847 had married Dona Maria, the daughter of Don Joaquin Estudillo. Davis said that Vallejo enjoyed the companionship of the cultured and educated foreigners, but that he had little in common with the rougher class—miners, trappers, and adventurers, whom he named "*White Indians*." Davis tells of the time when he and Thomas Shaw (super-cargo of the ship Monsson of Boston) were guests at the Casa Grande. They were cordially received, handsomely entertained at dinner, and invited to pass the night. On retiring, they were shown to their apartments. Davis found in his room an elegant bed covered with beautifully trimmed and embroidered sheets, coverlet and pillows, but, on getting into it, Davis discovered there were no blankets; an oversight of the Indian servant. The whole household had retired, so he shivered and shook all night, wishing there had been a little less of elegance and a little more of comfort.

Another guest at the Casa Grande was Sir George Simpson, Governor-in-Chief of the Hudson Bay Company's Territories in North America. At the time of Simpson's visit the General was ill in bed; so his brother Don Salvador and Jacob P. Leese entertained the visiting Britisher and his agents, Mr. Rae and Mr. Forbes. At the morning meal they were joined with Senora Vallejo, her sister-in-law Encarnacion, wife of Captain Cooper and Mrs. Leese. At dinner the General made his appearance wrapped in a cloak and the visitors had the pleasure of being introduced to the "dowager Senora" an, agreeable dame of about sixty." [sic. 66 years] Vallejo's mother from Monterey. Sir George was not a good judge of ages as he wrote in his Journal, "General Vallejo is a good looking man of about 45 years." Vallejo was thirty-five years old at that time.

Sir George thought that the beef stew, plus fowls, rice and frijoles, was ample but he complained that the food was cold due to its long journey from the outside kitchen to the dining room. Moreover he said, "Every mouthful was poisoned with the everlasting compound of pepper and garlic." After dinner, dancing was the order of the day. Don Salvador and one of the troopers played the guitar while "toeing and heeling it at the Fandango, the Cotillion and the waltz." Sir George said that the evening past most amicably and agreeably, winding up after several songs with "Auld Lang Syne" in which the Californians joined. Sir George said the next day (January 5) was Old Christmas and that he should have fancied he was welcoming Auld Yule in the north of Scotland.

Sir George Simpson expressed his appreciation of his visit to the Vallejos in a note to General Vallejo:

> I sincerely hope your health is now perfectly reestablished and should the love of travel induce you to visit England at some future period, I trust you will afford me an opportunity of returning the great kindness and civilities I have experienced under your roof.

BEAR FLAG EPISODE

At the time of the Bear Flag episode, Senora Vallejo had eight living children; the oldest, Andronico, was twelve years old, and the youngest, Uladislao, seven months. Their need of her gave her the courage during those fear-filled days, when her husband was a political prisoner and when her nearest neighbors were the rough-looking Bear Flag men, the "Osos." Senora Vallejo's opinion of them was best expressed through Henry Cerruti, a dinner guest of the Vallejos on a spring evening in 1874, in his *Ramblings in California*: "Madam Vallejo . . . whenever a favorable opportunity presented itself, would fire a full broadside to the Bear Flag crowd to whom justly or unjustly she attributed the loss of a great part of her husband's estate. She described the greater number of the party as rough and uncouth, dressed like Spanish banditti, wearing caps made with coyote and wolf skins, the great part wearing buck-skin pants that reached only to the knees." Her sister-in-law Rosalia Leese described them as "a large group of rough looking men, wearing on their heads, caps made with the skins of coyotes or wolves, some wearing slouch hats full of holes, some wearing straw hats as black as charcoal . . . several had no shirts, shoes were only to be seen on the feet of 15 or 20 of the whole lot."

One of the members of the Bear Flag Party, Robert Semple, agreed with the two California ladies: "Almost the whole party was dressed in leather hunting shirts, many of them were greasy. Taking the whole party, they were about as rough a looking set of men, one could well imagine. It is not to be wondered at, that one would feel some dread falling into their hands."

Most of the Bear Flag followers who remained in Sonoma, after Vallejo's departure, were quartered in the Barracks, next door to the Vallejo residence; however, some of the men with families were housed in the near-by adobe buildings. The John Grigsby family occupied the large house of Captain Salvador Vallejo, on the west side of the plaza, which had been built in 1842.

Before leaving Sonoma with his captors, General Vallejo had commissioned Jose de la Rosa to report to Commander John Berrien Montgomery of the *Portsmouth*, that a group of Americans had taken possession of Sonoma and made captives of himself and several Mexican officers; he asked for Montgomery's assistance to prevent violence upon the defenseless Sonoma families; Montgomery replied to Vallejo's courier that as an officer of the United States he could not interfere, but he would use his friendly endeavors to prevent violence. Captain Montgomery sent Lieutenant Missroon, the executive officer of the *Portsmouth*, to Sonoma. Departing with Missroon were the Vallejo courier, de la Rosa and the Bear Flag Party's messenger, William Levi Todd, and also Montgomery's 16-year-old son John Elliot.

The boy, on July 25, 1846 wrote to his mother who was living in Massachusetts, a long letter in which he said:

I accompanied him (Missroon) to Sonoma. On arriving (June 16th) found a party of 24 men mostly dressed in Buckskin and we were met half way across the Square by a plain man about fifty years old in his shirt sleeves with a pair of pantaloons which certainly had seen better days. His shoes looked as if they had not seen blacking bottles for 6 months and his hat was some what more holy than righteous. . . . This was Captain Ide, he welcomed us to Sonoma . . . Their flag consisted of a

Star Union with a grizzly bear in the center looking up at the Star and under the words "Republic of California." on the lower border was a red stripe of flannel the whole was composed of a piece of white cotton and blackberry juice, there being no paint in the country . . . Mr. M. (Missroon) and myself called on Mrs. Vallejo, he assured her of her husband's safety and she offered us beds in her house which we accepted. She is a very pleasant woman indeed.

Senora Vallejo was given permission to write to her husband and send some food.

Guadalupe:

I and the children are well. Don't worry about the family because the men are taking good care of us. We are sad because we don't know when you will come. My Mama sends you many greetings. She says for you to take good care of yourself. Julio can't do much on the ranches because the Indians are running away. Alvarado (Miguel Alvarado, major-domo of the Petaluma Rancho) is fishing at Petaluma and Senor Venterio is doing the slaughtering at Soscol. Your papers are well cared for. I am sending you a little money, a bit of cereal and bread. When you write to me, make the letters well, otherwise I don't understand them.

FRANCISCA CARRILLO DE VALLEJO

Senora Vallejo's brother Julio Carrillo had been given permission to carry the letter and food to Sutter's Fort in Sacramento, but there he was made a prisoner. The latter part of July, Senora Vallejo sent the following word to her husband: "Senor Langriano entered the granary and stole some things and went about stirring up trouble among the Indians and I notified the Captain and they took him a prisoner. I am very afraid of him. A man arrived here and showed me two letters and told me they were for the purpose of setting you free. He also told me it was necessary for you to bring some men because there were bad people on the road who wanted to kill you. Ask some good men to come with you. I and all at home are well." On July 22nd Vallejo had written his wife, asking her to send him ten packs of paper. In her letter she says she has done so.

Harpers Magazine wrote a story of an American officer calling on Senora Vallejo while her husband was in prison. He offered her an English and an American flag and asked her in Spanish, "Senora, which do you prefer?" She looked at him a moment, then clasped the American flag, kissing its folds, saying, "This is the flag my husband has taught me to love. It is the one he wished to see wave over his beloved California." A short time later Senora Vallejo watched Lieutenant Joseph Warren Revere take down the emblem of the Bear Flag Party and put up the flag of the United States. To her husband in prison she wrote, "For two nights the servants have not slept in my room; the danger is past, for a Captain from Sauzalito, sent by Captain Montgomery, who in a letter recommended him highly to me, put the American flag on the staff where before was the Bear, and since then there are no robberies that I know of; it was like great fiestas, all of us shouting and waving handkerchiefs but the Osos (Bear Flag men) were very sad. I and sister Rosa (Rosalia Leese) are not afraid any more for your life and that of Salvador and Don Luis" (J. P. Leese).

Nathan Spear, a merchant of Yerba Buena, wrote Consul Larkin of the Sonoma ladies, "The women were brim full of wrath and cabbage when they heard the Bear Flag was flying at Sonoma, but when they saw the American flag was hoisted they appeared to be much pleased."

Writing in his *Reminiscences*, Joseph T. Downey, a seaman from the *Portsmouth*, recalled that when the flag of the United States was raised in Sonoma on July 9th, 1846, "The Senora Vallejo was so enthusiastically delighted that she threw open her house to all, friends and foes, and through the live long night she visited the door every half hour to be sure no daring hand would attempt to remove that flag, on which she said hung all her hopes."

When the American flag was raised by Commander Samuel F. Dupont on July 29th, 1846 in San Diego, Senora Vallejo's birthplace, her sister, Dona Josefa Fitch with Dona Isidora Bandini and Dona Arcadia Stearns, furnished white muslin sheets and material from their own gowns, to make the flag of the United States.

SENORA VALLEJO'S BROTHERS

Two of Senora Vallejo's brothers figured in the Bear Flag Episode: Julio Carrillo as mentioned above and another brother, Jose Ramon Carrillo (husband of Dona Vicente Sepulveda, widow of Tomas Yorba). According to William Heath Davis, Jose Ramon Carrillo was an expert horseman and bear hunter with "a personality as gentle as a lamb." Don Ramon figured in stories connecting him with the Juan Padilla group. From *Sierra Petaluma*, he wrote to his sister Francisca Vallejo on June 22, 1846:

> Last night I received your appreciated note in which you tell me that the Captain of the Party told you that he has people to receive me and he told you also, if I do them harm, he will do harm to the family, and in answer I tell you, in order that you may not worry, that these people I have assembled do not have the idea of doing harm to that gentleman nor to his people.
>
> It is true we have many armed Indians and white intelligent people and if we had the intention of doing harm we would have already done it. In order that you may better believe what I tell you, if you wish you can say on behalf of my group of people to the Captain of the Party, that never have we thought of doing the least harm, because the only reason we have banded together was to look after our interests and demands by legal means, and secure the peace that was promised to come to pass as the result of the Articles of the Proclamation that they gave to the Public, promising security of person and property, and finally to tell the Captain that if he finds himself in an agreeable mood to have peace with us in order to avoid other disturbances, all that is necessary for him is to have the goodness to ask me in writing to appear.

The capture and savage slaying of two Americans, Cowie and Fowler, by the Juan Padilla group, cast suspicion on Ramon Carrillo. When he met death at the hands of the Vigilantes near San Diego on May 21, 1864, he became the subject of newspaper comment which grew so bitter that Julio Carrillo came to the defense of his dead brother in a public letter in the Sonoma Democrat dated June 4, 1864: "I wish more particularly to call attention to an old charge which I presume owes its revival to the same source, to wit: That my brother Ramon Carrillo was connected with the murder of two Americans who had been taken prisoners by a company commanded by Juan Padilla in 1846, I presume this charge first originated from the fact that my brother had been active in raising the company which was commanded by Padilla and from the further fact that the murder occurred near the Santa Rosa farm, then occupied by my mother's family. Notwithstanding these appearances, I have proof which is uncontestable that my brother was not connected with this affair and was not even aware that these men had been taken prisoners until after they had been killed. The act was disapproved of, by all the native Californians at the time, excepting those implicated in the killing and caused a difference which was never healed. There are, as I believe, many Americans now living in this vicinity (Santa Rosa) who were here at the time and know the facts I have mentioned. I am ready to furnish proof of what I have said to any one who may desire it."

Senora Vallejo shared her husband's belief that if the flag of the United States had been raised *first* instead of the Bear Flag, the transition period would have occurred without bloodshed. Most of the American officers, stationed in California after the raising of the flag of the United States, were young Army and Navy graduates—which was well—considering the difficult task they had of reconciling a proud people to a new yoke.

A description of General Vallejo's wife at this time has been given by Edwin Bryant: "Senora Vallejo is a lady of charming personal appearances and possesses in the highest degree the natural grace, ease and warmth of manners which render the Spanish ladies so attractive and fascinating to the stranger. The children some five or six in number were all beautiful and interesting." Marius Duvall, Navy surgeon from the *Portsmouth*, visited Sonoma about the same time. "Madam Vallejo is 'muy gorda' very fat" he said, "but still has the evidence of much beauty. She seems to be femininely passive and voluptuous, contented and happy."

This happiness was interrupted by the serious illness of the little four-year-old daughter, Guadalupe Vallejo in January, 1847. Mr. and Mrs. Andrew Hoeppner, Mr. Scott, and Mrs. Grayson were the Vallejo guests at the time and Senora Vallejo had to care for the sick child, leaving the General to act as host.

Senora Vallejo sent her Indian maid, Maleana, to fetch her supper. The thirty-nine-year-old Indian cook Canulo (or Canito) arranged her dinner on a tray which was taken to the Senora's room by Maleana. Shortly afterwards

Senora Vallejo sent her husband some particles of a glass bottle which she had found in her soup. They were so large that she had felt them in her mouth. Notwithstanding she and her six-year-old son Platon had swallowed a portion of the soup. The General excused himself immediately from his guests and went to his wife's room where he examined the plate and found it was covered with glass particles. On questioning the servants, he was told by two of them, Plimayon and Tolma, that they had seen Canulo, the mayordomo of the Vallejo household, pounding glass some days before in one of the rooms of the outhouse.

General Vallejo sought out Canulo and confined him in his room. Upon being questioned, Canulo confessed. He said it was true that he wanted to kill the lady because he was afraid she would punish him for losing his shirt. Canulo said that Ventua, who had recently run away from the Casa Grande, had taught him this manner of poisoning.

On January 10, 1847, Vallejo appeared before John H. Nash, Justice of the Peace (or, as Nash liked to call himself, "*Chief Justice of Sonoma District*") to give a sworn statement of the case. On February first, Canulo, by his sworn confession and the testimony of witnesses, was judged guilty of the crime of attempted murder which, under the Mexican laws, had been punishable by death. As there was no jail in Sonoma at that time, Canulo was sent to Yerba Buena while waiting trial.

A day after Vallejo's appearance in Nash's Court, his baby daughter 'Guadalupita' died and was buried in the Vallejo cemetery near the Lachryma Montis spring.

Two years later, on January 21, 1849, Senora Vallejo gave birth to a daughter who was given her name of *Benicia*. When she was nine months old she became ill and Senora Vallejo wrote her sister, Josefa Carrillo de Fitch, on November 24, 1849:

> I don't want to pass up the chance of writing you some lines and I'll tell you at once my dear Josefa that I am very happy because of the good news you give of your family. As for me, I regret having to say that my little daughter Benicia is quite ill and has been for some days. She has an attack of dysentry which, in spite of the fact that we have treated her with much medication and the doctor visits her once or twice a day, doesn't cease so that the sick child is very weak. So I spend every night awake since ever so often Benicia stirs and cries and her tears as well as the anxiety she causes me, doesn't permit me to sleep.

Little Benicia recovered only to pass away when she was four years old on January 31, 1853.

SONOMA GARRISON

During the American occupation, the Barracks next door to Senora Vallejo's home was filled with soldiers. After the *Bears* left, the quarters were occupied by a garrison under the command of Lieutenant Revere as mentioned before. Explaining how he had been transferred from keel to saddle, the lieutenant wrote: "There being no officers of the Army in the country except Colonel Fremont, the officers of the Navy and Marine Corps were obliged for the present to perform their duties on shore, both as officers of the newly raised California Battalion and as civil magistrates. It fell to my lot to exchange the quarter-deck for the saddle, having been ordered to take command of the district on the north side of the Bay, garrisoned by Company B. California Battalion Mounted Riflemen . . . On taking charge of the military post of Sonoma, I mustered my troop and found the whole force to consist of fifty men. Although my men were not uniformed they were well equipped, each having his private arms . . . Our barracks were roomy and commodious and we had an abundant supply of horses." Revere found that 87 of the horses of the caballada bore General Vallejo's iron brand of two intertwined inverted spades.

Lieutenant Revere said that many of the men were dressed in buckskins. A typical list of supplies issued each man (in this case, to Private Nathan Coombs) on August 7, 1846 was as follows:

I acknowledge to have received from Lt. J. W. Revere the following articles:

1 Blue Shirt $2.31	Blanket $1.93	$4.24
1 Cloth Jacket		7.43
1 Red T Shirt		.88
1 Duck Frock		.93
2 Doz. Buttons		.50
1 Pr. Socks		.27
1 Pea Jacket		9.63
1 Blk s. Hanks		.99
1 Blue T Shirt		2.31
1 lb Tobacco		.25
1 lb Tobacco		.25

Signed NATHAN COOMBS

Contracts were written by Lt. Revere for Jacob P. Leese to furnish the garrison at Sonoma with beef and flour to be delivered daily to the amount of 25c per person.

When Revere was sent to San Diego in 1847, Captain J. E. Brackett, a West Point graduate, occupied the barracks with his Company C of Stevenson's New York Volunteers. Upon Brackett's departure in August 1848, Captain John B. Frisbie arrived with Company H, but in a short time he received orders from Colonel Folsom to disband. Then came General Persifor F. Smith and made Sonoma his headquarters.

Rooms on the lower floor of the Casa Grande were rented to various people, namely to Dr. Frederick Reeger, erstwhile tutor of the Vallejo children; to Lieutenant Griffith, and to Lieutenant Stoneman. In 1852 Vallejo rented one of the rooms as a meeting place for the Sonoma Council, of which he was a member. The monthly rent was $27.50.

THE NEW HOME—LACHRYMA MONTIS

It was little wonder that Senora Vallejo wanted her husband to build another home away from the plaza, which, since the coming of the Americans during the Gold Rush had been filled with dust, noise, profanity and confusion. Agreeing with her suggestion, the General chose a site about half a mile from town, at the foot of a wooded hill from which flowed a tepid crystal clear artesian spring. The approach along Third Street, West, from Spain Street had been planted on each side with cottonwood trees by General Vallejo, and he wished to have it as a private roadway. He wrote the Mayor and Common Council that he was anxious to preserve the avenue of trees—"If protected until it grows with years, it will greatly add to the beauty of the city." On April 4th, 1852 Senora Vallejo received the following deed which stated in part:

Know all men by these presents, that I, John Cameron, Mayor of the City of Sonoma by virtue of the powers in me vested, in consideration of the sum of twenty dollars paid by Benicia F. de Vallejo to the City Treasurer, do hereby Grant, Convey and Confirm unto the said Benicia F. de Vallejo all the piece of land lying in the City of Sonoma known as West Third Street between Spain Street and Alp Street, according to the City Map of the City of Sonoma containing four acres more or less.

The Vallejos built a frame two-story Victorian, gothic-style house, the latest fashion among the Yankees. In it were born the last two Vallejo children—the so-called "little Yankees," Luisa and Maria, a year apart.

Here at Lachryma Montis in 1856, Senora Vallejo posed for her portrait by Stephen William Shaw, early-day painter whose portraits of California's pioneers hang in the Crocker Art Gallery in Sacramento. Shaw's full-length painting of General Persifor F. Smith, a native son of Louisiana, adorns one of the walls of the *Mayor's Parlor* in the old City Hall in New Orleans.

The Christmas of 1856 General Vallejo gave his wife $500 and to Adela, Natalia and Jovita he gave $100 each. The financial atmosphere of 1854 and 1855 had somewhat cleared. On October 7, 1858 he wrote Senora Vallejo from San Francisco:

I believe that tomorrow I shall finish what I have to do right now and be in Sonoma to rest. With much effort I have gotten five thousand dollars and have paid all your little bills and some of mine. No longer do I have to hide myself as far as debts are concerned, I am bringing you a very small present but I want you to tell me that it is pretty when you see it . . . Write me tomorrow if you need something in order that I may bring it. Give a kiss to all the little ones. I want you to be happy when I arrive.

Senora Vallejo had been interested in buying new furniture for the new home; the game table which would hold the General's chess set had cost $70 and was being placed in the library. She planted the grounds with shrubs and flowers. Between the cottonwood trees along the entrance roadway she planted the fragrant Rose of Castile, the favorite of her husband. She was proud of her new home and only too glad to share it with her friends and relatives. One of her cousins whom she wished to entertain was Ampara Ruiz, the wife of Colonel Henry Burton. General Vallejo located her in San Francisco and wrote his wife December 22, 1858:

After repeated searchings for Dona Ampara, I found her in a house. Pleasant and very amiable as she is, I did not kiss her (but I had a great temptation to do so) as I found her very beautiful. After the usual greetings we had a conversation, holding hands for two and one half hours. To be sure I was charmed with her. I do not know whether she or I talked the most. I had a very pleasant time with the lady whom I liked very much, a lady with a good disposition, frank, gay and engagingly provocative, I believe like you. I also believe she understands and appreciates my character and intentions.

I have invited her and her husband to pay us a visit. They promise to be in Sonoma Monday afternoon. Will spend a day in Sonoma. I will try to be in Sonoma that day. If not, try to entertain them. My business in Petaluma I have not been able to settle. Yesterday and today I am very bored. San Francisco is very tiring when you are not busy earning money especially when on the average day some one asks for a loan or alms or another subscription and a thousand other commitments (obligations brought about by circumstances and my position.) Greetings to the children.

CASA GRANDE BURNS

The home from which Senora Vallejo had moved—the home where eleven of her sixteen children had been born—was also dear to her. When it burned on April 13th, 1867, she expressed her emotion to Adela [Mrs. Levi C. Frisbie], the first of the Vallejo children to have been born in the Casa Grande:

On Monday at 3:30 in the afternoon, the Casa Grande in Sonoma burned and I cried as if it were some child of mine that had died. The house in which we had lived for so many years, the house which your father helped to build with his own hands; the house which your Papa built so that I and all of us could live in it, you and all your brothers and sisters.

The little marks you made with your tiny fingers and the first letters that you wrote in the back rooms, which you will remember. While it was burning, I tearfully went to see it and watched it some four hours. How I thought of all the family. Napoleon [then 17 years old] and I were the only ones who were watching it burn. Your Papa didn't want to go, nor your Uncle Salvador.

The people from all the Valley were in the Plaza. It seemed like a fiesta day. It was worse when they brought out a barrel of brandy as the people were almost dead of thirst. Many became intoxicated; they got so close to the fire; it was frightening to see them. They worked hard and saved the store and the Barracks miraculously, carrying the water in pails and a pump; one of those pumps that send the water afar.

At the time of the fire, the two youngest girls, Luisa, eleven years; and Maria, ten, were home, and with their father they watched the mingled smoke and flame from the east porch of Lachryma Montis. It was a scene they remembered all their lives.

Dona Francisca Benicia was her husband's confidante, but she was not always patient with his intense interest in business and politics. When the General as State Senator from the Sonoma District was attending the first session of the State Legislature in San Jose, she wrote him: "I suppose you are busy. I know you are so entertained with your government and with your investments. Yes, I do believe you can forget your family more than the government. . . . Is it that you don't have enough with what we have, neither I nor your family want more." On February 19, 1850, Vallejo replied to her letter saying in part:

You do have reason to believe that you are left alone with the whole burden of caring for the family and that I am leaving you alone with yourself in great concern; but it seems to me that, in spite of my absence, you should not think that I am not working for the family and for its security now and in the future. Without any question, I have very sacred obligations toward my family; but I also have them toward society in general; and the way to reconcile the one with the other is to cooperate (even under the difficult enough circumstances) in the organization of a government by fair means. When this is reached, I shall have the satisfaction of having been one of those who were of help. Don't you think the same way?

I shall bring you something which will, after reading this explanation, make you forgive my absence. Do you think I can be happy away from you and our children? My only pleasure in being away is to receive letters from you and from the whole family and to have the pleasure of reading them.

While in San Jose the General told his wife to "take good care of all the family and see that they don't fail to study every day. Give counsel to Jose and Andronico since they are young men about the things they need as well as the girls who are already in their adolescence." He wrote that she knew how to write well enough but still she did not write to him in her own hand. He then named Fannie, Adelita, Natalia and Andronico, scolding them because they had not written, "Is it that they all forget me?"

The General's wife had a discerning mind, although her formal education had been limited. She once remarked, "In the early days, there weren't schools to teach us as now, and if they taught even a primer so that they could read all the *Faithful Christian* and the Creed and the Litany of the Virgin; this was a great deal. There are those who knew more and those that didn't know, such as I. It wasn't the fault of our parents. It was the custom of former times."

In spite of being thus circumscribed by Spanish traditions, Senora Vallejo held modern ideas. Platon spoke of this characteristic of his mother when describing her to the Oregon author Eva Emery Dye at the time that she was planning to write about the Vallejos. Platon summarized his mother's views as follows:

She was indeed a faithful wife, a devoted mother and true friend. She believed in Women's rights. She believed that *some* women were the equal of *some* men. She believed that all women should be held sacred and that all men should respect them. She didn't covet riches for herself, whilst the poor were struggling. She believed that some women should at least be allowed to vote, to have a choice in the government, of the people and the commonwealth. She felt that some women had the natural ability for ruling justly and thus aid in solving the problems how to live peaceable, economically and happily. She was what we would call a level-headed woman.

Always in the shadow of the limelight of her distinguished husband, Dona Francisca Benicia took pardonable pride in having the city on the Carquinez Strait named *Benicia* in her honor. Thereafter she signed all documents and letters Benicia F. de Vallejo, although General Vallejo continued to call his wife *Francisca.*

CORRESPONDENCE FROM SAN CAYETANO RANCHO IN 1864

When General Vallejo's youngest brother, Don Juan Antonio Vallejo, died in 1857 without having made a will, the members of the Vallejo family automatically became the heirs of his estate. Vallejo as administrator, found it difficult to please so many relatives and the resulting delays prevented his return home. Frustrated, he managed to entertain himself by writing lengthy letters to his wife. A typical one follows:

In the public papers I have seen that Ida Haraszthy has arrived in San Francisco and it is very possible that in New York she may have had occasion to see Platon and I am anxious to know if he is alive or dead. It's been eight months since I received a letter from him and that silence worries me. In the last letter which I wrote to him from Sonoma I remember that I scolded him for not writing to me—it can be that he didn't like such a scolding and for that reason hasn't written to me again. Nevertheless he ought not to be so sensitive nor so touchy unless it could be that he thinks in the American fashion—that is to say, pretending to be independent—which wouldn't surprise me in spite of the fact that he has always been very obedient. Nevertheless, if you can make enquiries of Ida, ask her about him and give her my greetings, felicitating her on her happy arrival home. Also greet Mrs. Haraszthy.

However much I have done to finish up the business here which brought me, I haven't been able to end it on account of the brother Fortoul (husband of Vallejo's sister Maria de Jesus)—he has brought suit, to force the partition of the land and I don't know yet when it will end. I have worked hard to sell my part, but they have offered me so little for it that I haven't wanted to do it. They have offered me 10,000 pesos for what is worth 30,000, and it seems to me very hard to sacrifice my last hope here after so much expense and delays. It seems very hard to me, too, to return home without a single *real* for expenses like those unpaid debts I have in Sonoma.

I don't know what to do, but I am hoping that the stormy clouds will dissipate somewhat and the financial horizon will clear up a bit. I have been hoping that Frisbie who is in Washington will have finished the Soscol business which was again introduced in Congress. The Squatters have made another powerful attempt to overthrow the title and Frisbie went to see what he could do. You already know that this was half-way settled last year, but the devil seems to get mixed up in everything. When I was in Vallejo, Frisbie told me that in spite of the set-backs and expenses I would still get seventy-five or eighty thousand pesos for my share and he would get an equal amount, but it seems to him a good thing to wait a little to sell better.

Now I'm tiring of it all and furthermore I am aging fast. I am already balder than Don Juan Cooper but I'm glad for it's stylish to be bald—in order to go to church and sit up front. Also, about ten of my teeth and four molars have fallen out so that is also stylish. When you see me you're not going to know me—such an interesting figure! Sometimes I get the desire to die or to flee. It's mighty fine to be stylish but to be bald, old and toothless is intolerable. The children aren't going to know me and neither are you. There's only left to me to be blind in one eye and lame to seem to be a grandee. What will people say? How old age comes to ruin men. What to do? Nevertheless there is the remedy of a wig, false teeth, etc but age can't be beat even with rods. Accursed years . . .

I was in Monterey some days past and saw your sister Dona Ramona and her daughter Dona Maria Ignacia. They are well and Dona Ramona says that as soon as Holy Week is over she is going to live in San Francisco and from there she will then go to make you a visit. I hope I can be present to have the pleasure of receiving her.

During the sixties the reversal by the United States Supreme Court of the Soscol Rancho confirmations increased the financial stringency in the Vallejo family. The General's wife wished to help. The grapes, apples and figs were bearing well; the Italian overseer, Giovanari, was able to dispose of $50 worth of fruit for Senora Vallejo. She, through the efforts of her daughter Jovita Haraszthy, then living in San Francisco, was able to sell some dried fruit, olives and chili peppers in the city. To further increase the Vallejo family income, Senora Vallejo made the suggestion to her husband that they establish a public bath at Lachryma Montis. As has been previously related, General Vallejo was at the Rancho San Cayetano in the Pajaro Valley, endeavoring to work out an agreement with his brothers and sisters, heirs to the rancho. He was impatient with the delays which, coming so soon after the Supreme Court's reversal, greatly increased his despondency, as can be seen from the following letter written to his wife on April 23rd, 1864:

Today, Saturday at six in the evening I received your letter of yesterday in which you mention the opening for public use of the little family baths because of the lack of things necessary for the family's use. Believe me, that for me, it was too grievous a blow which I received, a great pain and mortification. I am ashamed and I suffer excessively for I would never have believed that I would reach the point of having to give everyone access to the little private bath to hunt for a peso. Do what you want, do what seems best to you but I wouldn't do it. And in the event I did do it, first I would change the family to the Casa Grande in Sonoma and after arranging the baths in a manner capable of receiving the *public!* Then I would advertise it otherwise all the family will be the contempt of all honorable people, and of all those related to them. The first thing is that *one* small bathroom is not enough for the *public*, the second thing is that it is in the privacy of the family; the third is that those who bathe are very exacting, the fourth is that one should be warned of all that is needed, etc.

How I regret such a thing! I well know that you'll tell me that one must have *Money!* I know it too, and I know it because when I came to this place with the object of hunting for that accursed article (money) I left none in the house but I left all the rest that was necessary; I know it because I have suffered since I came the same need and the pain of not being with the family believing every day that I would arrange some business deal here and in spite of myself each day has been dragging on with hopes—false hopes. I haven't wanted to sacrifice this property as it is *one* of my last hopes and what they have offered me for it would not be enough to pay the debts in Sonoma and furthermore what good would it be to me to divest myself of a piece of property which could perhaps be the refuge of the family as it doesn't have any mortgage whatsoever on it.

You well know that there isn't any money anywhere, that I have looked for it anxiously in order to send it to you but I haven't been able to do it. Also I have been waiting for Frisbie to see if perhaps on that side one could get something but luck hasn't been propitious. How many families have I seen which have not even a house in which to live. They pay rent, buy what they need without any resource, without anything. The great evil of the day is that there is no money in circulation and one can't get it in any way . . . but when one has a big house, garden with as much as one could desire to eat, chickens, geese, etc, etc, one can't be reconciled to renting a little *bathroom* to the *public* in order to gain four pieces of silver. Por Dios, I want to die.

If all the property were not encumbered as you know with a mortgage, already I would have converted the brick warehouse and the stables into a bath house or lowered the Pavillion to a place where it could be converted to something; but waiting every day for fortune to blow from the good side I haven't done it; but I haven't wanted to do it until I could see the end of the Soscol business and others which depend on the action of the Government . . . If some other time you should ask me for advice for something, ask it of me *yourself!* and don't avail yourself of some other writer; there are things which no one ought to know and in which no one ought to be involved. I hope it will not be, but I think I shall know how to be decently poor when the time comes, just as I have known how to be rich and support a family; but I will not submit to any low thing.

I should like to write happy letters to you, full of comfort, perhaps of something which might make our lives less heavy, but we are poorly matched as far as that is concerned; we think differently.

If before my return, the house is converted into a public house, advise me through Ula, in order for me to make provision for the children and to hunt for a place to live.

The General's saving sense of humor caused him to add a postscript to his letter: "The first person to bathe should be Patrick." (Patrick Hayne was a laborer who worked on his ranch in Sonoma.)

Upon receiving her husband's letter, Senora Vallejo called Don Pepe (Jose de la Rosa) to whom she dictated an answer. But she later decided it was best to recopy the letter and let it go to her husband in her own hand:

I can't write quickly. I never thought that what I told you in the letter should be a secret from Don Pepe (since you, yourself, have discussed the baths in front of him) who is an old man who has known the family for many years and perhaps knows other secrets. . . . and I tell you again that in the letter which I sent you that there is nothing secretive . . . As you know I have a husband; I asked for his opinion to learn if you wanted my plan and if you liked it and at the same time to help you in some way on my own and this was my intention. I am so sorry, Guadalupe that in the least thing that I speak of or say to you—that you should put such a bad interpretation to it when not even in my imagination does there pass a desire to offend or mortify you . . . if I wanted, there would not be lacking to me a means of mortifying you.

Guadalupe, Guadalupe, what small consideration you give to me after so many years of living together. I well know the indifference with which you look upon me after so many years that I have served you as wife, as friend, as companion . . . If telling you of the needs that there are and of what the family lacks offends you, then I do it. Always the same problems, always the same difficulties. I think one way, you another. I think I do well and you say I do poorly—then which of the two is right? What I thought about the baths—since it doesn't please you nor has seemed good to you . . . it's finished business.

Also, I'll tell you about the orchard: I am delivering to the Hotel: vegetables; I'm delivering hens' eggs to the bakery . . . I am telling you now and if you don't like it, tell me so that I won't deliver any more.

You tell me in your letter that you would like to write me of happy things, of comfort, in order not to make life hard—but you are the one who makes it hard for yourself and for me—blaming me for whatever thing I may do, think or want. Guadalupe think differently about me . . . When you come home, don't come displeased—Come happy for that is what I want. I would rather die than to see you angry.

That the General deeply regretted having written his letter of April 23rd may be seen by the following written on April 26th, 1864:

It's been three days since I wrote to you and I suppose that you probably have received my letter which must have seemed to you not very loving and somewhat serious. At the time I answered you, I was enraged at the world, at all men, at the human race, at Fate, and at whatever exists under Heaven. In such a state I received the letter which you wrote to me, and without reflecting even an instant, I took my pen to answer you believing that you had actually posted the notices in Sonoma that the family baths were open to the public, which shattered my brain. But after re-reading your letter I see you are consulting me and you await my decision as to whether to do it or not; which has cooled me off and disposed me to write to you to the effect that if there is in that letter anything personal, don't look at it in that way or take it wrong for I am sorry about it. It is not the time to aggravate the present unfortunate circumstances in which we find ourselves, embittering them with useless complaints which would end in the total ruin of a family so dear to me and which must be so to you, too.

To remain poor because they have robbed me and not because of bad titles although they have tried to assert it, is a bad bit of luck which it has not been in my hands to remedy . . . To remain poor because the most powerful government in the world has *squatted* on my most valuable pieces of property is not my fault. The fact is that I haven't been able to defend them successfully because of the lack of material means to oppose the Government . . . I have had hopes for three years of getting out of my troubles with the accursed Soscol business which has embarrassed me on top of everything else making me in debt to those who have been serving me and the beginning of the mortgage on the property . . . I have suffered much physically and mentally, alone absolutely alone, making unheard efforts to sell and to get money to take home; but the DEVIL OF MONEY has disappeared from the country. Everyone barks, cries and whines for it. Some days past, I was in Monterey and believe me that place makes you ill. There are many families in such misery that were it not for the fishing they would die of hunger. Thank God, I said that in my home there are geese, ducks, chickens and all kinds of vegetables to eat. I made a point of comparison and was somewhat consoled and I even wish inwardly to share with them.

The greatest comfort to me in this secluded place has been the receiving frequently of correspondence from all the family, their letters lighten my heart, distract me and are a balsam which has cured me a little. Would that you, too had written . . . How much they would have cheered me.

I have been hunting with great care to learn if there can be found what is called *Happiness* among some people and I have not been able to find it in any one . . . Gossip, scandal, backbiting, calumny, lying, evil itself reign everywhere; in conclusion I haven't been able to do anything but be horrified by what I have learned here: but the great God, the good God, that God that sees everything, that knows everything and that, ought to take into account our actions, and of the use we have made of our tongues!!! that God—and our own conscience, I hope!!! will punish those that maliciously or innocently have done evil . . . This is not a sermon, it is a letter dictated from the heart, I want you to read it without bias. I need to unbosom my soul to one who (leaving to one side marital love) understands me.

The letters crossed, consequently Vallejo wrote again to his wife on May 6th from San Cayetano, upon receiving her letter:

At last you wrote to me in your own hand and a very long letter and I assure you it is very good except for the scolding. When you want to and also when you are inclined, you write well. You suffer from a lot of laziness and you try to write in the new style. There is no point in writing a pretty hand if the letter is not well written . . . You are doing right by sending the vegetables to the Hotel and the eggs to the Bakery Shop . . . Let's not talk of the baths again—but I wanted you to write in your own hand . . . Try to be happy when I come.

Francisca's last letter had given Vallejo many hours of reflection. She had written, "You think one way, I another." He was lonesome and he busied himself with a letter on May 10th to her from San Cayetano:

Lorenzo was here day before yesterday and with him I sent to the girls and Napoleon some rolls . . . Lorenzo promised me to take them to the house and to tell you he had seen me and how I am here alone in my mother's house. O how I wish I could have had a little money to send to you and that you could have come here to see me, not suffering so much on account of the absolute solitude in which I am, as I suffer in thinking of the bickering about my affairs and the failure to see my family.

You well know how I love the children and I can't stand being away from their side. I don't say anything to you because you won't believe me, but you ought to be convinced that being the father of such good sons and daughters, and you being the one who has given them to me, you can't be very far from my heart. What a pity that you haven't been able to understand me in so much time! Is it not true? It is certain that I am a very unusual man; but thus I am and only death will deprive me of the propensities with which Nature endowed me. It is a providential thing—that two persons of such different natures should have married without the rules of Physiology adopted as good by Society. They say in marriage it is necessary that the natures be different for the children to always to turn out well. As far as the children are concerned, the rule worked well.—but it doesn't please me to see you suffer on my account. You suffer and I am mortified . . . after making you happy by giving you such a fine family. God grant that they may always be good and not cause us any heartache. . . . Today I am awaiting Mr. Brooks to finish up here and then I'll come to see you. Would you like that? Tell me—and I'll come to see you at once. What do you say? Will you be happy? Will you give me—a kiss—with all your heart. I await your reply—but the reply of your head no less than your soul.

Vallejo was unable to return to Sonoma, finding it necessary to go to San Francisco where he hoped to form some contacts that might improve his finances. Still in a discouraged mood, he wrote to his wife on July 19th, 1864.

I am sending on the boat as you asked me to: sugar, coffee, tea, soap, ordinary candles and those of sperm . . . I am compelled to combat my difficulties in order to pay Mr. Madden, but at last I owe him the money which I need to pay him. I'm going to renew the mortgage on Lachryma Montis and Quiquiriqui for a year with the privilege of paying them off before that time since the interest that they charge us is 2 per cent a month compounded. I'll send the mortgage on Monday for you to sign. After this I need to work and sell other properties which I have still and pay off Madden as soon as possible before the interest surpasses the loan. We need to economize as much as possible.

The next day, July 20th, he wrote another letter home which also reflected his discouragement:

The more I work and the more I make myself hunt for the means to get money to pay the Madden mortgage and other unpaid bills of which you know, the less hope I see of suceeding. Seeing then, that it is necessary to take a prompt and resolute decision in order to save the house and lands at Lachryma Montis before Mr. Madden's mortgage absorbs it all with the interest which is accruing all the time, I have believed it is opportune and absolutely necessary to sell Quiquirqui with gardens and houses. I regret it, but it is necessary to pay the debts soon before things get into a worse state.

I see that a frightful crisis is coming close, and one must prepare oneself to see it come in time. If I could wait longer and see a better aspect to business I could wait a little longer, but nothing is clear; on the contrary all in the future is dark, threatening a monetary storm. I want, nevertheless, to put you and the family in safety, in order to be serene, fulfilling thus the duty of a man and a father. There is not one peso here, nor is one to be had. This letter is for you alone.

The General's financial worries blighted his usually happy disposition and, according to his wife caused him to mistreat her with words. He had been impatient with Andronico who finally gave up his work on the Lachryma Montis ranch. He was also impatient with his winemaker, Dr. Victor Faure. Senora Vallejo reported these tendencies to her daughter Fannie Frisbie: "Your Papa said that he was going to take the wine-cellar keys from Dr. Faure and give them to Andronico and Ula, and if Andronico doesn't come to receive them, he would put Ula there alone. He talked and said so many things against the Doctor . . . You all well know how he acts when he is furious with someone . . . For Dr. Faure they are building above the barracks. They are putting in divisions with two carpenters that earn four pesos a day, and are bringing from San Francisco the rest of the things. They have arrived already, three pieces of luggage and three carpet-bags and things which come in big boxes—and all these expenses, who pays for them?—your Papa . . . Tell the Captain [Frisbie] that he must not forget what we were talking about. In him I have every confidence, after God. Tell him that your Papa has kept here in the house three or four servants and has nothing with which to pay them. Tell him that if he can send me any money whatsoever to pay a very poor servant for whom I have to prepare food for those who before served me. Tell the Captain I don't ask for anything but your Papa's, for your Papa says that John holds all the property . . . Do all you can so that John will send me the money—400 pesos. Tell him that I am so mortified to have these people here in the house and have to feed them, when we don't have enough for ourselves and have to feed them at the table three times a day."

HOUSEKEEPING IN CITY OF VALLEJO

While the John B. Frisbie family were in the East in the fall of 1869, Senora Vallejo went to the City of Vallejo to care for her daughter Fannie Frisbie's home. Meanwhile Vallejo kept his wife informed as to the happenings in Sonoma. On Sunday, November 6th, he wrote her a lengthy letter about the recent visit of her brother Julio Carrillo to Lachryma Montis:

Francisca:

Today I sent for Vicente (old Indian retainer) and talked to him very slowly about what you charged me with, respecting the Indian Bernave, his son; and after he went to consult with Teresa, mother of B., he came to tell me that the mother didn't want to let the boy go.

Yesterday Julio was here. He came with two of his young daughters; he told me that one of them named Felicidad, he was going to send to Vallejo and that you were to take charge of her. He left her at Natalia's house so that he could send her perhaps on the stage. I offered to take her, but as it was a thing agreed upon beforehand, I suppose, I did not insist. She is a very pretty girl, and although I didn't know anything about your taking charge of her, it seems to me a good thing to help, although one be poor, the friends that need it. Poor Julio, I am so sorry for him because he has lost all his property, and he has a large family of little people to support.

Julio was seated in my room about an hour; he asked me many questions; among them was one that sounded like the following: "What are you working at?" At what I can; now as you see, I am reading, at other times writing my correspondence, other times making verses." "And to whom do you write letters and for whom do you make verses?" "The letters to the people with whom I have business affairs or friendship, to my men friends or *women* friends, (this with emphasis), to my relatives that are very numerous and to nice people; and the verses to the muses of poetry, to the sun, the moon and the auroa, to good weather, to rain, to Minerva and also to Midas, to beautiful women, to great men!" "Yes, but what do you work at?" "As you see," I answered him, "I need work for the mind and as for physical labor, in the first place I don't want to, nor need to." "Well, how do you live?" "Man works to seek a room or a house in which to sleep, in which to eat; I don't bother anyone, I don't get drunk, I don't frequent saloons. I work as I can and it has been a long time since I have been doing so." "Yes, but you have been a great spender." "Certainly, very certainly but always with benefit," I answered him, "and if not, cast your eye over my family and you will see I am right and proud, and it doesn't grieve me to say it. . ." "And Salvador, why doesn't he hunt for work? With a little two-wheeled cart and a horse, he could get work cleaning stables." "He can't," I answered him, "He is broken down and already old and besides he is in the house of his brother. He doesn't have any expenses, hardly eats anything"; that is the only thing I could answer him. "But before, I want you to know, before going to clean stables, he would lift off the top of his skull." "Well, how does it happen that I do it?" "Each one knows what he can do," I answered him. "I can do everything but there are those who can't conquer themselves and so goes the world." We ended the conversation and he went away perhaps very satisfied. We gave him a good lunch, wine, brandy, sardines, bread and cheese, stew with tomatoes and much red chile and very good salad of grapes with oil.

FAMILY LETTERS

During the Frisbie family's visit in Albany, New York, Fannie sent Senora Vallejo word of their doings:

Dear Mama:

I was seated on the sofa in my room when I heard the front door bell and it was a letter from you and one from Adela. You can't imagine how happy I was! I had been a little sad. John had gone to New York. It was six in the afternoon. I stopped being sad, and then the servant and I started to chat and the evening passed very pleasantly.

All the little ones are in good health now . . . They are going to have a show tonight and I have to take them their white clothes, that is for Benicia and Minnie who have to take part . . . Tell Miss Ana Frisbie that if she wants to buy the table, it cost me 25 pesos and the chairs, I don't know what they cost . . . but I think I'll need them when I return . . . John expects to return to California next month.

How is the daughter of my Aunt Luz? . . . I hope Zarela is better . . . How I regret that I'm not in Vallejo to help you, as Platon and his family are . . . How are you with your infirmities? Have you had to smoke the pipe with the fine powders? I hope you haven't found it necessary to do so again . . . My baby [David Farragut Frisbie] resembles Carlos [Jovita's baby] a great deal . . . I am glad Natalia is well. God has favored her with another little son. I hope the next one will be a girl. Tell her not to lose hope . . . How is Papa? Is his health good? Tell him to come and stay with me.

One of Fannie's servants remained with Senora Vallejo to help her to look after the house, thus giving her time to write to Fannie. A portion of her letter, dated March 25th, 1870 follows:

I am so glad when I receive your letters or those of the girls. When I or some one of the others receive your letters we pass the word around and give each other the good news that you and the children are well. Give them all many kisses. Tell them that their Grandma Vallejo always thinks of them all . . . Tell them that Grandma is always praying to the Most Holy Virgin of Light that she may light their way and keep them on the right path. Give many kisses to Josephine and David and to Platon and Bernardo, Sara, Pamila, Benicia, Fanny and you and John . . . I have been waiting for some news every day after they gave me the news that John had won over the Squatters. Everybody was excited. Four men came and lit a skyrocket in front of the house. I was very frightened of the Squatters but all is quiet.

After remembering all of Fannie's children Grandma Vallejo reported on the condition of her own children:

Ula came from Mexico, very ill. As soon as he got well, he wanted to return. Jovita was here for two months and on the 20th of this month, she went to San Francisco. Andronico working as much as possible but he is always very poor. Platon is here in the house, he and his wife Lili. Platon is always caring for the sick. Napoleon is in San Francisco earning his living. Natalia is well, also Attila and their children. Adela, Lili and the Doctor are as always in good health. Lulu and Maria are in the convent at St. Catherine's in Benicia. Your Papa is in Sonoma sometimes, other times in San Francisco and other times in Vallejo and he is well. I am well. I haven't had asthma again. God grant it doesn't return to me. Every Sunday I go to Mass . . . The rest of the relatives on both sides are well. Some of your old servants when they see me, remember you and send you greetings. They always enquire about you, John and the children.

Fannie received the letter and answered promptly—to her "Very Dear Mama:

I received your very much appreciated letter of the 25th of March in which you tell me all are in good health. . . You must have been happy when Ula arrived. How I would love to see him and give him a hug. You give it to him for me and tell him to send me his pictures before going to Mexico. I hope he finds work to do in California . . . John left Sunday night for California . . . I think that on Palm Sunday he will be in Sacramento.

I wish you could see these churches. They are much prettier than ours. The music is very good and the sermons very instructive; it is worthwhile going to Mass. I go to the Church of Santa Maria; it is very close to the house in which we live . . . The little ones miss the climate of our country. Little Minnie [Pamela] says she is very sad because you haven't written to her. Next week she will write to you . . . She says she can't write in Spanish. She received a letter from Papa and she couldn't read it and I had to translate it into English. She is very anxious to study Spanish in order to be able to write to her grandma.

Grandma Vallejo wrote on April first to her oldest granddaughter, Fanita Frisbie, saying:

The first time I have written to you—it isn't because I haven't wanted to but because I'm very busy. And I write so slowly that the desire to do so leaves me, and I write so poorly that I'm ashamed. Don't show this to any one.

Luisa and Maria are in the convent. I am very happy when you write to me in Spanish.

Now you must know how to write very well, and Benicia and Mimi. Tell them to write to me in Spanish even when I don't write to them. When I look at your letters I am very happy . . . All that your Grandma or *Abuela* wants, is for you to be good girls. Take good care of your Mama and your little brothers. Help them as much as you can. Do what your Mama tells you.

I can imagine how sad you all must be today your Papa will be away out here in California. Today, Palm Sunday, we are waiting for your Papa. Everybody is excited because he is coming. All are going to meet him at the station with soldiers and music.

The Frisbie girls' father was met by a delegation of Vallejo citizens when his train arrived in Sacramento. They continued their gala welcome in the City of Vallejo. The festivities terminated in a reception given by General Frisbie in his home to the welcoming committee. The excitement of the occasion was intensified for Senora Vallejo when General Frisbie told his mother-in-law he would like her to accompany him on his return to New York.

TRANSCONTINENTAL JOURNEY

Dona Benicia Vallejo made frequent trips to the City of Vallejo and to San Francisco to visit her married children, but it was in May, 1870, that she went on her longest and most interesting journey since the memorable one, early in 1833, as a bride, from San Diego to the Presidio of San Francisco. The May 1870 journey was transcontinental—across the whole United States just one year after the Golden Spike was driven at Promontory Point, Utah. She made it with General Frisbie; he, to join his wife; and she, to visit her daughter Fannie and her grandchildren in New York. Before leaving, she wrote to Natalia:

I am going from California for a little while to see another part of the world before I die, to see Fannie and the little ones. Don't be sad. If the girls, Luisa and Maria go to Sonoma to be with you, take care of them; advise them so they may know how to care for themselves and have them write to me and you too. Take good care of your Papa . . . If you go to the house, you and the girls, straighten it up for Papa so he wont have so much to do. When you pray with the children, tell them to pray for Grandma. Have Luisa and Maria pray a Rosary to the Virgin of Light so she will light my way and take me on a good journey.

Soon after getting settled with her daughter Fannie in the East, Senora Vallejo wrote to her husband. Her letter to the General was translated by the present author in June 1950, and the translation was mailed to Senora Vallejo's namesake and granddaughter, Francisca Vallejo McGettigan, who had just crossed the continent, herself, to visit her daughter Noel in Connecticut. Mrs. McGettigan's acknowledgment is of importance for its own sake: "Many, many thanks for the Benicia Carrillo Vallejo letter [on her way to New York]. It is certainly interesting to know her impressions and emotions as she rumbled and tumbled in the railroad train of 80 years ago. Her description is as apt as if it were written sitting beside me a couple of weeks ago." The English version of Senora Vallejo's letter of May 5, 1870 follows:

Guadalupe:

Since leaving home I have wished to write but had no opportunity. I put off making a letter. I wish I knew how to write well and promptly because I wish to mention all I have seen and heard since the day I left Sacramento. I felt a little sad but I gave a prayer and asked God and our Blessed Mother of Light to give me courage and to overcome all dangers which may happen.

To begin, the mountains of the Sierra made me remember you and the children. John came and told me that there was a Spanish lady in the car but I had not seen her; I was told it was my cousin. She was Rafaela Temple . . . She came to my room and we had some conversation for some time. I called her attention to the view of the mountains. Then the porter came to make the bed and my cousin went to her room to sleep. I had a small room myself. . . . I took off my clothes but there was so much noise it was not possible to sleep. I asked the Virgin that I might go to sleep as the cars made such a clatter and so much vibration. Finally I slept. In the morning, John came and told me to get up to see the view of the mountains of the Sierra Nevada, that it was a beautiful country. There were mountains, valleys and water like mirrors. The land was scarred by the railroad, by the numerous trails to take out the gold.

When we were approaching a place in the Sierra, John said it was the highest spot. When we went below the mountains and the cars climbed, climbed through the snow; cars, cars, cars and more cars . . . We had very good food, many ripe cherries and oranges, all that one could wish.

I think some good angel transported me, because the train speeded as though flying. I do not tire of giving thanks to God and to John for giving me the chance to see so much on this journey, so beautiful, so pleasant, so great for me . . . For four days and four nights we lived and traveled through a country so ugly and forlorn. There were many water stations . . . The land all colors, the water of many rivers ran slowly and very muddy. The water in abundance; the rivers are not like those of Sonoma, Napa and Sacramento . . . Some of the lakes are like the seas. Often I could not see the scenery well, as, I left my seat, the train shook so much.

The trains passed across the country of the Mormons, near a big mountain and beside the Salt Lake. It is a very pretty town. I saw the top of the mountain so majestic and full of snow. I do not tire of appreciating the greatness of God and the work of the Americans. I lack the ability to express the talent of the Americans, who built the Railroad and of God who made the scenery and who is good.

We went through the mountains all the day and night. Afterwards to sleep. The cars were speeding all night . . . then the plains so great that I could not see the end of the train. All the day we passed bridges, towns, and hilly land. We passed cars filled with wool, with coal, with lumber and with boxes. When we passed a city on the river we saw besides a boat a number of steamers and trains. We went over a bridge on a very large river, the Misisipi [sic] Oh! Oh! Oh! Oh! so beautiful Oh! what a great and beautiful river—so large.

When we arrived in Chicago, I saw the very pretty lake, the houses and railroads, the shops, the people and many things. On arriving at the city [Buffalo] we found we had a little time. Niagara is very beautiful. I had no occasion to go close to it but we were on the bridge joining the country of Queen Victoria. I did not like the houses, they are like barracks. Another day and night when we arrived at Albany at 7 in the morning, we were joined by Fannie and the children with much talking and kissing. All are well. I am also well. God be thanked. Greetings to all my children, the parientes and friends. God in his wisdom. BENICIA DE VALLEJO

Guadalupe take care of yourself and take good care of our children.

Upon receipt of Senora Vallejo's letter, her husband wrote her thus:

I congratulate you that you have arrived quickly, well and happy at Albany where you found your daughter and your grandchildren well, too. I envy you the pleasure you must have had—you and they—upon finding yourselves in a strange land so far from California from which you had never sallied forth. I am pleased you enjoy traveling through God's world, going up the beautiful and picturesque Sierra Nevada.

I imagine and see the impressions you must have felt since you left Sacramento, the climbing of the Sierra Nevada, the descent of it, the immense plains, Chicago, the new and big cities which you have seen, etc. All of this is marvelous and you always should keep it in mind and also think that the ways of Jhon [John] are fine and elegant, that he is always good to our daughter and to us. This makes up for what he has done to me sometimes. This reminds me that some times I have said to you that all men are not alike, either in face, feelings nor in manners. There are some that are men and they are only men, and others that by their manners, capture the good will of people and one ought to overlook some little faults in them. Jhon [sic] is good and we ought to be proud of him . . . God grant that the trip may result in your health improving so that when you return you'll be younger and with more understanding of the world.

The trip did a lot for the morale of Senora Vallejo. Letters written before making it show a capricious fretfulness and restlessness; little differences in the family were magnified into quarrels over petty matters. On her return her emotional fatigue had almost vanished with the widening of her horizon.

PLATON ADVISES HIS MOTHER

Dr. Platon Vallejo, who was very interested in all the members of his family, could not help giving them advice at times. His father accused him of writing "sermon letters." To his own mother he had the temerity to write such a letter on October 6, 1873:

I can't write to you satisfactorily about the mode or manner that Papa makes or disposes of his property in times past or in times when he did. He, perhaps confided in others more than he should have. The certainty of the case is now that he hasn't anything of which he can be robbed. Good or bad, everyone knows it and can not deny it. It is past! Experience is the mother of knowledge and that is true. Take care, then of what remains to us . . . Lay aside the past difficulties for which there is no remedy, for LAW, if it be according to the Law of God, will appraise it as Papa says, but especially for the one who has property, and, since he had so much of it, therefore they had to carve out and appraise more.

Dear Mama, I ask you with all my heart not to think so much of the past, for that which is yet to come may go unheeded by you now . . . Have patience with Papa, if you love me, for I love you so. God will assist you.

It was difficult for Dona Benicia to forget the past; the remembrance of the days of luxury contrasted sadly with the present days of denial. There was much to forgive—the conduct not only of the acquisitive Yankees but of some of the *parientes.* One evening Senora Vallejo wrote a letter expressing her resentment to a member of the family by marriage, but her husband would not allow her to send it, although what she had to say was true. She wrote Platon, "Your Papa would not permit me to send it . . . I have to obey your Papa. Were I an American, they would not deal with me in such a fashion, but I am Spanish and for that reason they do as they do."

RESTORATION OF THE MISSION

When Henry Cerruti was in Sonoma in 1874, gathering historic information for H. H. Bancroft, the little pueblo's mission church was once again being restored. The walls and roof had been completed, but $3,000 was needed to finish the work and for the purchase of benches, pictures and church ornaments. The local pastor appointed a subcommittee composed of Senora Vallejo and her daughters, Natalia, Luisa and Maria. In his *Ramblings in California,* Cerruti recalled that "A few days after the appointment of the sub-committee, a gentleman from San Francisco who happened to have business to transact with General Vallejo called at his house; the sub-committee engaged him in conversation . . . induced him to contribute twenty dollars toward the repair of the church . . . When the visitor had taken his departure, the General called his daughters to his presence, requested them to give him the keys of the church, expressed his displeasure at having been a witness to the begging scene. No sooner had General Vallejo got possession of the keys of the embryo chapel, than he sent for plasterers and carpenters, gave them instructions as to the manner in which he desired the work to be done and agreed to pay for it. The next thing he did was to send to San Francisco every worn-out Saint and picture with orders to have them truly renovated as he forwarded funds at the same time. The whole work was soon finished in good style. The General spent $2,700. The chapel was completed in genteel manner and the priests who a few months prior to this event were loud in denunciation of Mariano Guadalupe Vallejo as an heathen, were afterwards very loud in his praise."

More Family Letters

On January 22, 1875, Vallejo wrote to his wife from Monterey: "I am at last finishing the history of California. If you can, send me a little box with some sweet oranges. Some to eat and others to give to the young ladies who dont have anything to eat but acorns. And your husband will thank you."

There was no Mother's Day in 1876; however, on April 14th of that year, Vallejo wrote Senora Vallejo a letter which any wife would enjoy receiving from the father of her children:

I suppose you are surrounded by all the family big and small like the mother hen when she has many chicks and can't cover them all with her wings. This is one of the joys of life and the proof of having fulfilled the mission Nature destined for humanity and the Divine Commandant of the Supreme Creator—"Grow and multiply."

Fannie, a beautiful and good mother with her pretty brood; Adela, too, a beautiful woman, full of life but almost without family (having only one). She ougth to have a dozen in order to enjoy better health and to have something to keep her busy. Andronico is a good man who doesn't understand how to be other than upright; but, in this era that isn't good enough to live on and to have some rest and comfort in old age; one must "do as they do." 'Who with wolves run must learn to howl,' says the proverb. But poor Andronico has no aptitude for trickery.

Platon is a good youth, a doctor with fixed principles, a good Catholic, almost ascetic; his profession suffices I believe to support his family and he is happy, it seems to me with his position. So taking a good look at it, the family does us honor and I believe that you should be proud to be surrounded by them.

Natalia and the five younger children were not mentioned in this letter. In a teasing vein Vallejo closed his letter, "Make a good confession and repent all your wickedness. I authorize you to make my confession for me."

Although Senora Vallejo enjoyed receiving letters from her husband and children, she knew that if she was to receive letters, she must write. She was quite sensitive about her penmanship, no doubt comparing her own with her husband's beautiful script. Vallejo added a postscript to one of his wife's letters, "After Mama finished her letter, she brought it to my room so I could correct it saying to me, 'Don't laugh at me.' I corrected it and she wanted to do it again but I dissuaded her."

Whenever Senora Vallejo could persuade a member of the family or a close friend like "Don Pepe" [Jose de la Rosa] to write for her, she would do so. The following letter, dated March 5, 1877 was dictated to General Vallejo who wrote: "Dear Platon, your Mother asks me to sit down to write an answer to your last letter which you wrote to her. According to what she tells me (and I have seen it), it is in very good Spanish. She is seated at my right at the table in my room and this is what she dictates:"

Esteemed Son, Platon:

Your sermon-letter which you wrote to me some days ago is worthy of you and I value it completely not only because it is written in the language I understand but also for the thought that is expressed, for which I thank you. We all need counsel and advise so that we wont forget some of our obligations and duties toward God and our families. I know that my age is on the decline of earthly life and that old age brings us always frequent illnesses to remind us that we are nearing the tomb, in order to familiarize ourselves with death and passing to the life where as you say we shall be reunited through the grace of His Divine Majesty, the merits of our Lord Jesus Christ and our own good works. Is this not so? This is what I hope for and I shall try always with His Divine Grace to be prepared to receive what awaits us all—death—first to say with humility, 'God's will be done.'

All of us Christians ought to know that salvation is heavenly happiness, which should never have an ending, that being a belief that we can't follow except through Jesus Christ who came to earth to gain it for us through his precious blood after cruel pain, sacrifice and torment, all for the redemption of the human race.

Your Papa is in the midst of many, many difficulties about money, with the care of the family and thousands of other things, but even yet conserves a strength of will, rare for his age, a tremendous interest and furthermore a strong spirit full of life. His philosophy seems to increase with his labors. But sometimes I see him sad and thoughtful with some thought which preoccupies him. He needs company on his level, and some occupation that intrigues him. Your Papa suffers from his sight which he regrets exceedingly, since writing and his books divert him. He gets annoyed and in a bad humor many times ending in hopelessness.

The amanuensis for Platon's mother added his own postscript: "Why don't you come on the stage from Napa before the oranges are gone? You can take some sweet ones to your girls and some little trees. Bring Felipa."

1877

Most of the month of March, 1877, the husband of Senora Vallejo was in San Francisco trying to persuade their daughter Jovita Haraszthy to drop her divorce proceedings against her husband Arpad Haraszthy. The General called a family council and it was successful. On April 6th he wrote his wife:

Tomorrow I'll leave for Sonoma, not because I want to go, leaving the situation hanging as you know . . . I don't want to remain any longer in this hotel (Commercial Hotel) where I am, since the arrangements have been made by Jovita—the cancelling of the divorce proceedings . . . We who have been through so many good things, making castles in the air, but still I do not lose hope for it is also said in a proverb that "Patience conquers all." The worst of it is that I'm old and given to the rocking chair and while there is not much physical force left I shall have to live my own life and still live that of my family.

Jovita and Maria are well; everyday I see them at home, after a thousand labyrinthean ways and devilish deviations with land speculators. I am tired of driving in the streets; besides our Spanish speaking people are almost all of them uprooted from their own lands or impoverished and it is unbelievable that the majority of the time they have nothing to eat—so great is their poverty.

CHARLES E. PICKETT, A VISITOR

"Philosopher Pickett" was a frequent guest at Lachryma Montis. While visiting there on August 23rd, 1878, he handed Senora Vallejo this note:

To my old and ever faithful friend, Francisca Benicia Vallejo on her sixty-second birthday anniversary: My dear Madam:

Thirty years ago, the present month, you hospitably entertained me in your mansion. It was our first acquaintance. Often since I have passed many pleasant days under your roof. You have always made me welcome and placed me under deep obligation that I can never adequately repay you unless the ardent pulsations of a grateful heart shall be taken in return.

I am happy to greet you in person, this day at your lovely abode, so ornamented by your excellent taste, to find you in good health and enjoying the society of husband, children and grandchildren, all so worthy of your affection and of my esteem. That long years of health, peace and prosperity may be yours and theirs is the sincere desire of

Your always constant and devoted servant,
CHARLES E. PICKETT

The tall Italian cypress tree which overshadows the Lachryma Montis reservoir was bought for Senora Vallejo by Mr. Pickett in January 1864. He shipped it, with a sack of dahlia bulbs and an assortment of roots and cuttings of shrubbery on the steamer "The Princess" to the Sonoma Embarcadero.

On November 12th, 1878, Platon's mother wrote to him the following newsy letter:

In the first place you already know that I can't write fast and for that reason, I am availing myself of the hand of another to serve as amanuensis, in order to answer your letter of the 8th of this month which I have read with pleasure after there had passed many months, I should say years, without one of my male children having written me hardly any letters. Such indifference is painful for a mother who loves them so much. But what to do, my son? Times are like that; and it is much stranger in you, that forgetfulness, knowing I suffer physically and you being a doctor, that you haven't come to make a little visit, you being just two hours away.

Your Papa has been quite sick but he is better and he has had another relapse. He suffers his pains in silence and he suffers every day, physically and mentally. The death of Jovita has affected him deeply. Nevertheless the last two months he has written a great deal, helping a gentleman friend of his (Edward Vischer) to arrange a collection of pictures of all the Missions and Presidios of California which he could not have completed in twenty years but now, with the aid of your Papa, the very interesting work will be finished. Papa said to me "It is necessary for that man to complete that work and I shall help him because it is the same idea that Platon urged on me some years ago."

You tell me in your letter that the stamps from the P.O. are somewhat costly but it seems to me that 3 cents or more do not make one poorer than he already is. We surely are poor, that's true, but not as poor as that. Our very, very, very reduced circumstances do not prevent your Papa from writing letters. First he says he would fail to buy sugar and tea than to stop buying stamps for the mail. He says, too, when he complains of his children, "There are postal cards worth *one cent* and they are enough to write on."

We are well in health up to a certain point considering our age (Papa and I). Lulu is well. The embrace from you and Lily, Francisca, Felipa and Mary, we received with all our hearts and we return it to you with all the effusion of our souls. Moreover, we, Papa and Mama, add our blessing that "God, our Lord protect you and hold you in His Hand, Amen." You know, dear son, I love your wife and Felipa and Francisca, whom I haven't seen for a century. Why? Also I love Mary [Platon's maid] because she is good. I remember she was with me in Vallejo for a year, the two of us alone.

We receive regularly letters from Mexico. Fannie in every letter describes to us that city and its inhabitants in a very graphic style . . . Her letters are one continuous lament. She can't reconcile herself to anything . . . Nevertheless she wants to help John. It is probable that you have received letters from Mexico but as you have become so uncommunicative with the people of L. Montis we know nothing coming from Vallejo. I want to know if Andronico lives or dies and where he lives. If you know of him, give us news of his whereabouts.

A thousand thanks for the offer of the gentle mare of which you speak in your letter. If you want to send her we'll turn her loose in the pasture which has plenty of forage. We can't have more than one animal in the stable because it costs so much to maintain it. Here we have a small horse that doesn't eat much and it draws a little cart which Attila loans Lulu; with that we do our shopping. Papa sometimes raging but through necessity takes it to Sonoma. You can see this won't suit a big mare. Nevertheless, if you can send it, we will take care of it.

It is possible that Frisbie will make a trip here but I doubt it since he has not deigned to write nor send a telegram to your Papa who many times has said. "Times change and we change with it." Now there are no causes, gold, lands, herds, nothing! If you write to me again some time I'll surely answer your letter although it is with difficulty.

I haven't sent you fruit this year because it has been very difficult and at the same time it costs a lot to send it by express by way of San Francisco. My secretary can't see, his eyes pain him and he is begging me to make a period here. I do it. I greet you all with 1,000 kisses for Felipa and Francisca. Your mother who loves you with her whole heart.

SALE OF THE SAN FRANCISCO SOLANO MISSION

In 1880 it appeared that it was going to be necessary for Archbishop Alemany to sell the old San Francisco Solano mission and build a new church in Sonoma. It has been said that the mission was sold because the noise of the nearby railroad disturbed the services, and also because the communicants complained that the building was damp and cold. Senora Vallejo was deeply grieved. Her mother, Dona Maria Ignacia Lopez de Carrillo, who had passed away on February 9, 1849, had been buried near the baptismal font. At the time of the sale of the mission, Dona Benicia wrote her husband:

If my Mama and my brother [Juan] were not there [San Francisco Solano Mission] I would not feel so sad but having to move the dead is terrible. I trust God gives us strength and courage to do it. Poor little Mama, what a good Catholic she was. She herself prayed to Father Quijas to bury her near the Blessed Water. But now we have to take her away. I have faith that you will help me re-bury my dear Mama to where all our children, which are dead, are. When they are together I will be content.

Five of the six children who had died as infants, or as small children, were buried on the hillside near Lachryma Montis in the family burial ground, short distance beyond the Vallejo barn. A visitor to Lachryma Montis in 1861, after viewing the vineyards, orchards, and gardens, with the overseer, a Mr. Giovanari, spoke of visiting the Vallejo family cemetery:

There was one sacred spot to which we repaired, the family burial-ground, a quiet and beautiful place on the slope, enclosed by a neat pailing. Within were six graves; five children of General Vallejo and the ashes of Martin E. Cooke. The graves were covered with vases of flowers, statuettes and trailing plants, all neat, beautiful and appropriate. It was indeed a sacred spot and as such should always be the family sepulcher and in a garden of flowers too. We honor those who honor the dead and guard their resting-places.

In 1880 Senora Vallejo wrote to her sister Dona Josefa Fitch [widow of Captain Henry Delano Fitch] who was living in Healdsburg, asking for help to finance the removal of their mother's body to the Vallejo family cemetery. In her letter, Senora Vallejo mentioned that a bowling alley occupied the space west of the old mission.

DONA MARIA IGNACIA DE CARRILLO

The mother of Senora Vallejo had been a deeply religious woman. During her last illness she asked her pastor, Padre Quijas, for permission to be buried in the San Francisco Solano Mission near the Holy Water font, where drops of the Holy Water might fall on her resting-place.

Senora Maria Ignacia Lopez de Carrillo came to the pueblo of Sonoma in 1837 from San Diego, shortly after the death of her husband, Joaquin Carrillo. With Senora Carrillo came nine of her twelve children—four girls and five boys. The Carrillo family remained for a short time in Sonoma. Then on January 19, 1838, Vallejo's mother-in-law petitioned him for a grant of land in the pastoral valley of Santa Rosa. Four days later, the General gave her permission to occupy two leagues of land in the center of the valley. On September 30, 1841 ten thousand acres, called "Cabeza de Santa Rosa," were granted to her by acting-governor Don Manuel Jimeno. Senora Carrillo then selected a site on the Santa Rosa Creek where her sons, Joaquin, Jose Ramon, Julio, Juan, and Dolores assisted by Captain Salvador Vallejo and some Indians built the adobe home for the Carrillo family.

Senora Carrillo was active for a decade, riding her range and personally supervising the ranch. The hospitality Senora Carrillo felt for the Mexican colonists of the Hijar-Padres party in San Diego was not extended to the Norte Americanos, according to James C. Ward who was traveling in June, 1848 in the Sonoma District. In his diary he wrote that General Vallejo, who was said to be the most cultivated Californian, had kindly invited him to stay at his house which he said was comfortably furnished. Ward wrote, "I was tempted to pass through the valley of Santa Rosa but the road was longer and I should have been forced to trespass upon the hospitality of Senora Carrillo who, it is said, affections not our countrymen. One of her daughters is married to General Vallejo I know. Two beautiful ones are still at home with her."

Senora Carrillo fell ill in January 1849. Realizing that she was quite sick and might not recover, she called her sons to assist her in making her will, as she had not learned to write. She named all her children as her heirs, except her married daughters, Josefa, Francisca, Ramona and Maria de la Luz, who were married to men of wealth. Ramona was married August 4, 1826 at the San Diego mission by Fr. Vicente Pascual Oliva, to the dashing Don Romualdo Pacheco. Ramona became the mother of Romualdo Jr., who became the governor of California in 1875. Widowed Ramona married Captain John Wilson November 9, 1835. William Heath Davis wrote, "Dona Ramona was a handsome woman, queenly in her walk and bearing and among her country women who were noted for their beauty, she was one of the most attractive."

The next Carrillo girl to marry was Dona Josefa, who eloped with the thirty-one-year-old Captain Henry Delano Fitch in 1829. When Fitch died in San Diego in 1849, Dona Josefa came to Sonoma where she lived for a time before going to settle on the Rancho Sotoyome in Sonoma County, which had been given to her husband in 1841. In December 1875 Senora Fitch wrote to her brother-in-law General Vallejo regarding some land in lower California. On the 20th of the same month, Vallejo after clarifying the business matter wrote saying, "How happy you should feel! surrounded by your beautiful daughters and your grandsons who have no greater desire than to make a 'little money' and save it. It is known for many years you have been the wife of a Yankie and a very tight Yankie, whose virtues you inherited. But dear sister-in-law do not belabor the money: order fine carpets for your rooms, and better furniture, and live more comfortably; because in the end you shall die the same as I, and you cannot take money to the other life . . . you cannot fly with heavy cargo to the celestial regions."

The third Carrillo girl matrimonially inclined was Francisca Benicia whose marriage to Don Mariano Guadalupe Vallejo has been mentioned in detail. Maria de la Luz, older by two years than Francisca Benicia, did not marry until September 8, 1840, when she chose Don Salvador Vallejo.

After the death of Senora Maria Ignacia Carrillo, the "Cabeza de Santa Rosa" came under the management of 27-year-old Don Ramon Carrillo, who was described by Frank Marryat, the British visitor in 1850, as "a striking-looking fellow, well built and muscular with regular features, half concealed by his long black hair and beard . . . he was more picturesque in his mountain costume than the best Andalusian that ever got himself up in gold lace and silver buttons." Marryat, who had been seeking mules in Benicia for his proposed trip to the mines, was introduced by Captain John B. Frisbie to Frisbie's mother-in-law's brother, Don Ramon Carrillo. Carrillo invited Marryat to visit him at the Santa Rosa ranch. There he was welcomed in the long adobe house (built by the missionaries) by the Don and his wife, Dona Vicenta Sepulveda Yorba de Carrillo.

Marryat tells in his *Mountains and Molehills* of his enjoyment in riding with his host over the vast terrain and seeing Don Ramon's manada of horses. Tortillas and fresh milk were served for breakfast. In the evening, after an ample dinner of Mexican cookery, the wine of the South and cigarettes were passed. The vaqueros provided music from guitars; waltzing was enjoyed with the feminine members of the household—in fact, everything was enjoyed by Marryat except the Santa Rosa fleas, the so-called *Malditos*.

A NEW GRANDSON—DON TWEEDY

Maria, the youngest daughter of the Vallejos, was visiting at Lachryma Montis when her first baby, a son named Leo, was born in 1880. He was Maria's Sweet Baby, who in baby language became *Sweetie*, then *Tweedie*, and to be called by Grandfather Vallejo *Don Tweedie*. Upon Maria's return to San Francisco, Grandmother Vallejo decided to accompany her, so as to assist the young mother. While Senora Vallejo was there, her husband wrote to her:

> Just a few minutes after you left here, Adela went to Natalia's house, leaving me "alone with my soul." As you can imagine, raging with a toothache, half of my face swollen and in addition a sharp pain in the left eye. As I was alone and there wasn't anyone to make fun of me or to call me coward I began first to give plaintive cries and then to groan and to give bellows like a wounded bear. Oh! how I suffered for four hours . . . But at the end of that time I found means to bring the pain under control and I began to take great gulps of whiskey which burned me down to the soul producing abundant salivation and apparently it is easing the pain. God grant it may do so . . . I hope you had a good journey, without mal-de-mer and that you are happy.
>
> EL SOLTERO

Vallejo's relief from pain was temporary. He decided he would have to get Doctor Van Geldern to pull the molar that was causing his suffering. He went to the home of his daughter Natalia Haraszthy, where he met Adela Frisbie and the doctor, the latter carrying a box of instruments and some chloroform. The patient sat in a chair while Adela held his head against her breast and Natalia applied a handkerchief with the chloroform to his nose. Vallejo wrote his wife that the operation was worse than having half a dozen children! This must have amused her, who had given birth to sixteen! In his letter, he enclosed the offending molar.

Vallejo rented some of his land to the Caminata family whose seven-year-old Jacobino was a favorite with the General. Of Jacobino's visit on March 24, 1880, he wrote Senora Vallejo:

> No sooner had the locomotive given out its whistle announcing the departure of

the train which let out through the smokestack clouds of black smoke forming a serpent in the air, than Jacobino appeared with the little tin pitcher in which to carry milk, he greeted me and said: "Well, Patron, what can they be doing in San Francisco, the mistress of the house, Miss Lulu and Carmelita. Every day they go and go—and spend money—and the Patron alone, without money to buy anything, like a little meat and tobacco to smoke." But, I said to him "They are taking a trip, the Patrona is going to see Maria and the little baby. You see she wants to see her daughter. And he answered me, "Daughter doesn't matter, nor baby, nor anything, they aught to be here taking care of the Patron . . . Women have no business taking trips—and if the Patrona wants to take care of babies, let her have one of her own and she can take care of it.

But the Patrona can't have babies now that she is old! "Yes, she can," said Jacobino, "That's no job. Just look, Patron, my Mama is old and as fat as the devil and she makes babies. Well, I said to him, But the Patron can't. "No, How come? And how come my papa can? "Because your papa is Italian and Italians are full of Nick. "How are babies made, Patron? With a little machine like Adam and Eve's that you have heard of in the blue book. "Oh, boy! Listen Patron I want you to buy me a machine. I wonder if Mr. Shocken has one? "Yes, no doubt he has one but they say it is necessary for the Doctor to fix it . . . It's late, I am going to school and my mother is waiting for me . . . The poor boy went away and I remained alone, alone, alone.

A year later Senora Vallejo was again visiting Maria, and received the letter of July 19, 1881.

Francisca:

You have become very fond of San Francisco, surely you are very happy because Maria gets better when you are with her. Well, nothing is more natural, take care of her and stay with her as long as you like. Here we are all well, but I am very tired of the business of the water. I have to get up at five o'clock in the morning to go into Sonoma to distribute it, and at seven in the evening to turn on the machines and for what? Just to earn "our daily bread" with a great deal of trouble and weariness. If only I weren't so old, I could humble myself a little, then it would be a different thing since all the world works in order to live. Nevertheless I ought not to know such need at this age. It is God's will.

The sale of the church [Mission San Francisco Solano] was concluded and apparently they are going to build another new one in the plot that is near the entrance of the white gate where it leads out into the Alameda, with a convent and a house for the Father.

The water works from the springs of "Juan Viejo" for the new house of Attila are finished now and are very good; Attila as well as Natalia is crazy with delight. The house looks very good and now the time is approaching when it'll be finished.

A plague of little birds has come and they are eating the grapes and before they eat them up, I am sending a little box of them to Maria. Greetings to Maria, Harry and kiss Don Tweedy.

M. G. VALLEJO

The first Midnight Christmas Mass was held in the new San Francisco Solano Church which had been built on West Napa Street near West Third, the street which led to Lachryma Montis. Vallejo attended the Mass and wrote his wife who was again visiting Maria:

Lachryma Montis
Dece. 25, 1881

MERRY CHRISTMAS, FRANCISCA:

The Holy Night arrived at last and the first Mass was celebrated in the new church at 12 midnight. Luisa with her pupils sang quite well. In spite of much mud and such a dark night many people came and the church was full. Natalia and Lulu worked hard in arranging and preparing the altar, pictures and the rest.

The old church remains abandoned, in possession of Schocken to whom the Catholic Archbishop sold it after having been built and having served as a Temple for the Catholics for 45 years. Do you remember I built it for my soldiers? That in it Mass was said every Sunday and that the uniformed guard there convened and formed ranks and set out on marches. And at the time of raising the Chalice and the Host, it is done to honor the Divine Sacrament. And finally that there your mother and a brother are buried. It is better not to remember these things because it causes grief for one to see lost work and money.

It was a public insult that which happened to us with Jovita when the church repelled us when we wanted to give her burial [in S.F. Cathedral]. Do you remember? And it is the same person who sold a Catholic Church and the church serving as a Temple at the very moment! What a profanation! And they are called Christians, those who have in their care the true religion. The Protestants are justified in laughing at the abuses of the Catholics and in calling us fanatics. God wants only that He be worshiped "in spirit and truth."

It is 8 at night . . . Luisa in the dining room with Minnie, warming at the fire and I am writing this note to greet you and Maria and Harry. M. G. VALLEJO

SENORA VALLEJO—A SEMI-INVALID

During the early eighties, Senora Vallejo was a semi-invalid, with frequent bouts with pain. Her husband thus reported her condition to Platon: "Your Mama has been in bed for fifteen days without being able to take a step. She suffers terribly with some pains in her knees; from them, it passes to the sacral bone and then returns to the knees again. Thus I shall not be able to go on Saturday to visit you in Vallejo. And how is it possible to leave your mother alone, quite ill in bed. I am the one who personally does all the errands, going and coming to Sonoma, two or three times a day, and hunting for daily bread as God helps me." On another occasion, November 10, 1881 in language his professional son would understand, Vallejo wrote Platon: "It is 11 o'clock at night; a moment ago a violent pain attacked Mama, a very sharp one on the left side in the region of the spleen, or maybe in the left hypochondrium under the diaphragm between the floating ribs. It is a pain that has attacked her at other times when Dr. Wells was here, but he is not here and she ordered me to call you, and if it is possible for Padre Luis to come too. We have just called Dr. Lorenzo; who knows how he will work out?" Doctor Lorenzo arrived and told the Vallejo family not to be alarmed over Senora Vallejo's condition. The harassed husband went back to his letter writing, saying: "Everyone in the house awake. Mama was relieved a bit from the pain; the sick one sleeps, appears to be resting. If you can send some pills for Mama, or a medicine that will be an effective purgative for every day. You'll know what. Some pills of bread crumbs! The point is that you send them to her and tell her that they cure, and that they resuscitate the dead with them."

The Christmas Holidays found Senora Vallejo improved. It is not known whether credit must be given to Dr. Lorenzo's visits or to Dr. Vallejo's "bread-crumb pills."

SENORA VALLEJO'S LAST YEARS

In the years of affluence, it was General Vallejo's happiness to give his wife every luxury. Imported gowns from the exclusive J. Guerin and Company, located in the 1860s at 105 Montgomery Street, San Francisco, and at 43 Rue de Trevis in Paris; hoop skirts, tissue and silken gowns, mantilla, embroidered shawls, linens, silks, velvet and challis from A. A. Austens, also on Montgomery Street. From Joseph Brothers, jewelers in the Bay City, she bought silver dishes and napkin rings, gold thimbles and various pieces of jewelry, including a topaz set, comprising earrings, brooch and bracelet, which cost $110.00.

In later years, Vallejo's generosity was curtailed by growing financial reverses. It was then that Senora Vallejo assumed many tasks new to her. One day, evidently feeling tired and worn and a bit sorry for herself, and remembering her many Indian servants of bygone days, she wrote to one of her children:

> I am the cook. Now that I am, I suffer much. I have to clean the pots and pans, two or three times a day. I have no cook. I have to wash all the clothes and Lulu and Maria iron, sweep and clean the house. I have not even one servant to wait on me. I am the servant of all. When one is not accustomed to this kind of work, it makes it very hard and it is impossible for a lady of my age (59) to be glued to the floor, three or four days and so weary, too tired to go to the kitchen. My hands, they are all burned and cut; feet all swollen from standing and I don't mention everything that hurts me and what I suffer, for I never get through.

The situation of being without a servant must not have lasted any length of time, as Vallejo's account books show that he paid $20 a month for a "Chino-cocinero" over a period of years. Even though Senora Vallejo did not have to cook, her hands were never idle. When they were not making preserves from the figs, jelly from the tuna, the fruit of the cacti or marmalade from the oranges in the Lachryma Montis orchards and groves, they were embroidering or crocheting. Two of Senora Vallejo's most ambitious undertakings were the needle-point portrait of a lady whose arms are filled with flowers of many hues, and the linen crochet bedspread and matching pillow-shams—gifts to her youngest daughter Maria, and now, through the generosity of Maria's daughter, Alma, they ornament the historic Vallejo home.

Senora Vallejo's children's letters meant much to her, especially the letters from Fannie as they were always written in Spanish and as she was the child who was not near enough to visit. In April of 1889, Fannie had been in California. Before she left for her home in Mexico, she wrote to her mother from San Francisco on the 14th:

My dearest Mama:

How consoling it is to write and send remembrances and a word of affection. I know your heart must be full of sadness. We children are a source of tears for our parents . . . Mother, mine, I just can't tell you how I feel. No one but you can understand. We are going to be separated, I hope, for only a short time. . . I don't want either of you to be sick. I pray, dear Mother, that He will take good care of you and keep you in good health. If God only knew all we suffer, He would make life more agreeable to us.

Tell little Fannie, the girl you now have, that she must take good care of you. God bless her. How I would like to be in her place, to serve you and help you in everything. Her name being Fannie is enough to make me love her—but she is good to you too. A big kiss to all of Lulu's little ones and also to Natalia's. To Papa, loads and loads of love and kisses and good wishes and to you dear Mother all the love that a daughter can have for her mother.

FANNIE

After Fannie's return home to Mexico, she sent her mother another letter dated June 29, 1889 filled with expressions of filial affection:

Dearly Beloved Mother:

I received your letter two days ago and it gave me much pleasure, double pleasure; it being dictated by you and written by father. If I could really make an opening in my heart, I would tuck away in it all these letters, such precious heavenly messages from my dearly beloved father and mother. I wish you both might be near so I could lovingly embrace you.

Distance is cruel, my dear mother . . . I should like to enclose myself bodily in this letter but I am sending my soul instead. Bernardo is quite happy with his wife. Fanita and her children are all fine; her husband [Antonio Sequeira] is well and so are all the rest of the family.

FANNIE

GENERAL VALLEJO WRITES HIS WILL

That same month of June, 1889 on the 26th, General Mariano Guadalupe Vallejo prepared to give his last gift to his beloved wife of fifty-seven years. Alone in his study, he wrote in English the following holographic Will.

IN THE NAME OF GOD. AMEN:

I, Mariano G. Vallejo of the town of Sonoma, County of Sonoma and State of California of the age of eighty one years and being of sound and disposing mind and not under any restraint or under the influence of any person whatever, do make, publish and declare this my last Will and Testament in manner following, that is to say

1: I give and bequeath to my beloved wife, Benicia F. Vallejo, all my estate, real, personal or mixed and of every kind and description, that I may own at the time of my death, for her sole use and benefit.

2: I do not bequeath anything to my sons, Andronico, Platon, Uladislao, Napoleon or to either of them, nor to any of my daughters, Epifania, wife of General Frisbie, Adela, wife of Dr. Frisbie, Natalia widow of A. F. Haraszthy, Louisa, wife of R. de Emparan, Maria, wife of Mr. Cutter or to either of them, for the reason that I have already given to my said children and to each of them, what I consider their full share of inheritance.

I hereby appoint my said wife, Executrix of this my last Will and Testament, without bonds, hereby revoking all former wills by me made.

In witness whereof, I have hereunto set my hand and seal this 26th day of June A.D. 1889.

MARIANO G. VALLEJO
Manu mea propria

This will was made nine days before General Vallejo's 82nd birthday.

In the autumn of 1889, Senora Vallejo, in poor health herself, watched with foreboding the failing health of her husband. In December she telegraphed her son Platon, "Come and judge yourself. Not a well man." Platon came and also Andronico. When Senora Vallejo visited the sick room of her husband, which was in his former study, she usually came leaning on the arm of Andronico. Her oldest son seemed to have a special place in her heart, and he was a great comfort to her at the time of the final parting from her husband on January 18, 1890.

The Vallejo estate, "left for her sole use and benefit," had dwindled from approximately 175,000 acres of land to 228 acres surrounding the homestead; from thousands of cattle and horses to one cow and two ageing horses. But this mattered little to Senora Vallejo when her husband died. After almost fifty-eight years of marriage with her Guadalupe, she had little heart and courage to continue living without him. For some years she had been troubled with asthma and rheumatism. A Dr. John Rausch of Napa City, anxious to develop a sale for his remedy for rheumatism, wrote to Senora Vallejo:

> Some time ago I sent you some remedy for the rheumatism which I hope did you some good and cured you of all pain. I expected to hear from you if you got the remedy or not, but did not hear from you so I take the liberty of addressing these few lines to you to ask you if you would let me know if the remedy did you any good and if so pleas to write out a little statement about it for me . . . If you will pleas to alow me to use the statement in my cucrlars that I want to get printed.

If Senora Vallejo used Dr. Rausch's remedy, it did not benefit her. Her health did not improve. A few weeks after her husband's death she suffered a stroke which confined her to her bed. The *Sonoma Index-Tribune* ran an editorial entitled, "*General Vallejo's Widow.*" It called attention to the fact that the late Gen. Vallejo was adversed to accepting aid for services rendered his adopted country, but "had it not been for him, California might now be a dependency of Great Britain or France. His aged widow, however, survives him in the quiet retreat of Lachryma Montis . . . When all these things are taken into consideration and also the fact that Gen. Vallejo sacrificed his immense fortune for California, it would be no more than an act of gratitude on the part of the Government to provide liberally for the widow who has been left nothing out of a once princely fortune, if we except a mortgaged home and an honored name."

All of Senora Vallejo's daughters vied for the privilege of nursing their grieving mother. Natalia Haraszthy, who lived only a few blocks away, was on duty each day. Writing for the invalid, she sent the following letter to her brother Platon:

> Mama asked me if I would write to you to please come over; she wants to see you very much . . . Come over soon to see her now that she is bedridden. Sometimes it is heartrendering to see and hear her cry and moan . . . She has a good appetite, good pulse . . . We are going to buy Mama an invalid's chair with wheels so we can take her out under the trees and give her fresh air . . . We are going to pay for it on the installment plan. All her sons and daughters will contribute with pleasure. The chair will cost $50.

Natalia's little daughter Lolita also wrote to Platon saying:

> I know you must be anxious to hear how Grandma is, so I thought I would write you a few lines. Grandma is worse this morning, she can hardly move or bear to have us touch her. My Mama and all try to make her as comfortable as possible; she is so bad she does not get up any more only for us to fix her bed and then we have the hardest time in the world to get her back to bed again. Mama and I come over every day and stay all day and do all we can for her. Aunt Adela is here and she is quite handy . . . Uncle Nap and family have gone back home and we miss them so much; he was so handy in lifting Grandma and Aunt Mattie also.
>
> We need a man so much in lifting Grandma, we all together can hardly do it; we put a rag under her and by the rag, we lift her and turn her, she is so heavy, she can't be touched sometimes . . . just now she is asleep and very comfortable, she is always worse in the morning. Aunt Adela bought a new carpet for the room upstairs and they are going to move her there as soon as it is put down, they think she will be better up there . . . I think dear Uncle you aught to come over to see Grandma.

Senora Vallejo improved to the extent that she was able with assistance, to take a few steps. Her daughter Natalia said at the time: "Mama is doing very nicely. She can say a great many words and repeat what you ask her to say and is so much more intelligent than when you saw her last. Her appetite is splendid, her pulse sometimes a little too slow but otherwise good."

Dr. W. K. Vance, Senora Vallejo's physician whose office was in the Union Hotel, reported to Dr. Vallejo:

> I write with pleasure to say how our patient, your mother is doing. There is really no change to report; the case is stationary. Mrs. Emparan says the sick lady has made some attempt at articulation, some mono-syllables have come out. She seems mentally bright and content, appetite fair, oranges being much relished; bowels require castor oil occasionally, sleep tolerably sound . . . The ladies are quite busy at the old homestead, house cleaning, that awful domestic revolution.

On November 22nd, Senora Vallejo walked from her bed to the big armchair across her room and, after sitting in the chair for an hour, walked again to her bed; but that night about ten o'clock after her nurse Fannie Martin had retired, Senora Vallejo was struck with paralysis on the right side. Luisa Emparan was much concerned over her mother's physical and financial condition, so she decided to write to Alexander Montgomery, the president of the Society of the California Pioneers, for help. Her letter was dated December 18, 1891:

> I believe, Sir, that the time has come when the Pioneers, if not as a Society but as private individuals should come to the rescue of the aged, ill and destitute widow of the Pioneer of Pioneers, General M. G. Vallejo, my father. As you all well know my mother has been confined to her bed since my father's death and she is compelled to live from a very small income from the property my father left. My mother's condition becomes more critical, she having had a slight stroke of paralysis within the last 18 days and as I am living with her, it becomes my duty to nurse her and interest myself in her welfare. Among the Pioneers there are several wealthy ones who can without self-sacrifice assist in her days of misfortune, the widow of one who in his days of affluence gave warmest welcome to the newcomers with a generous and open hand.
>
> Captain Swasey, the bearer of this letter and an old friend of our family, can tell you I am not a beggar but the daughter of a noble and generous man who gave credit and honor to the people of the State in which I was born.

The president of the Society of California Pioneers read Mrs. Emparan's letter at a meeting of that organization and it was decided to post a request for help on the Bulletin Board. Before the month of December was over, help had come from many of its members, also from Mrs. General John Bidwell and a few friends, quietly given. Luisa Emparan and her sister Adela Frisbie wrote on black bordered stationery letters of thanks, December 29, 1890:

> To the Secretary of the California Pioneers:
>
> Allow me to thank you most sincerely and in my mother's name for the kind assistance you sent me from the Pioneer Gentlemen. It will indeed help to meet the many pressing demands of the moment for the invalid and aged widow of the generous Pioneer of Pioneers, General Vallejo. All our family likewise join in expressing their thanks.
>
> LULU V. DE EMPARAN

> Allow me to thank you in Mama's name for the kind assistance you have sent. I assure you that we feel grateful for all that Mama has received. Thanking you again, believe me to be
>
> Your sincere
>
> ADELA V. DE FRISBIE

The San Francisco Chronicle reported January 9th, 1891 that it was expected that "a bill to provide a suitable monument to the late General Vallejo and a pension or grant of some sort for his aged widow will be introduced at the present session of the Legislature by one of the representatives of Sonoma County."

In speaking of Senora Vallejo the newspaper article stated: "At the time of her husband's death a year ago, she was remarkably well preserved and was still a handsome woman. Her hair was raven black, her teeth sound, her memory clear and her movements agile, and she retained many traces of the beauty of the Spanish type which friends of her former years well remember. General Vallejo's death completely prostrated her and she has seldom left her bed since. A month ago she received a paralytic stroke, losing her speech, but the crisis passed and she is now expected to partly recover. Her portrait which appears in the January *Century*, was taken a few months ago and it is said is but little like her as she was a year before."

With the financial help from the Pioneer Gentlemen and friends, the Vallejo girls did not hesitate to authorize frequent visits from Dr. Vance who reported to Dr. Vallejo on January 27th:

> Our patient suffers from an attack of Bronchial Asthma and seems to get along comfortable enough. The wheezing has nearly ceased. This attack has of course reduced Mrs. Vallejo's strength. I do not anticipate any immediate collapse . . . Mrs. Vallejo is more amendable now than at former times, having submitted herself to any measure that we suggested.

The day after Dr. Vance sent his letter, Senora Vallejo became critically ill. Natalia telegraphed her brother Platon: "Come immediately, mother dying. Tell Andronico."

Reverend John J. Sullivan, who had administered the last rites of the Catholic Church to General Vallejo, was called and gave them to his widow. The end came at 6:15 on the morning of January 30, 1891.

Fannie Frisbie, when notified of her mother's death, telegraphed, "We mourn with you the death of our beloved mother. Funeral expenses provided as hereto. Advise." The Frisbies paid for Senora Vallejo's casket which was a duplicate of the one they had bought for General Vallejo.

The funeral took place on Sunday morning, February first, at ten-thirty. Escorted by the Sonoma Valley Band, the cortege, with the body of Senora Vallejo left Lachryma Montis and moved slowly down the tree-lined roadway to the St. Francis Solano Church. There it was carried up the aisle by her grandsons to the Altar for the Solemn Requiem Mass. The funeral sermon was given by the pastor, Reverend Sullivan.

Upon leaving the St. Francis Solano Church on Napa Street, the cortege passed around the Sonoma Plaza, which had been the scene of so many stirring events during her lifetime. The procession paused in front of the site of her old home, the Casa Grande, just as had been done for her husband the year before. Here the marchers respectfully removed their hats. Thence they proceeded to Mountain Cemetery overlooking the Valley of Sonoma, where the life companion of General Vallejo was laid to rest beside the body of her honored and beloved husband.

The little town of Sonoma grieved for the loss of their first citizens. So many expressions of sympathy were received that the Vallejo children saw that a card of appreciation was published in the Sonoma-Index Tribune thanking all "for the sincere marks of friendship held for our dear and justly beloved parents, Dona Francisca Benicia Carrillo de Vallejo and Don Mariano Guadalupe Vallejo."

Today a massive tomb of granite, quarried in California, covers the vaulted graves of those two Hispano-Californians. The tomb planned by Dr. Platon Vallejo was erected by the Vallejo children in loving memory of their parents.

Andronico Antonio Vallejo

Andronico Antonio Vallejo

The second son of Alferez Mariano Guadalupe Vallejo, Comandante of the Presidio of San Francisco and of his young wife Dona Francisca Benicia Carrillo, was born on April 28, 1834 at the lonely outpost, Castillo de San Joaquin, guarding the entrance to San Francisco Bay. This was one year before the founding of Yerba Buena, the site of the future metropolitan San Francisco.

The infant was given the classical name of "Andronico," the same name as had been bestowed on the Vallejos' first born, who had died a few months before. Andronico the second was baptized on May 2nd at the Mission Dolores. At the age of fourteen months, he was brought to Sonoma by his parents. No home awaited them, so the little family was forced to find a dwelling place in the abandoned San Francisco Solano Mission. There was ample room, as the principal house of this mission contained twenty-seven rooms.

The father of Andronico was away much of the time, building an empire and amassing his own personal fortune. Andronico's early years were therefore spent mostly in the company of his young mother: the educational details being left to tutors who lived in the Vallejos' new home, the adobe Casa Grande, west of the barracks and mission.

Spanish was spoken in the Vallejo household, but, during Andronico's growing years, his parents' home was the center of California hospitality for foreign visitors, especially those who spoke English; moreover two of his aunts, Tia Encarnacion and Tia Rosalia, were married to Americans. By the time Andronico was sixteen years of age, he was proficient in the use of English and thus could help his father in business affairs. As evidence of this is a letter dated March 25, 1850.

Esteemed Father:

Since the day you went away we have not had anything unusual here at home. The Captain [Frisbie] was here with my godfather on Monday and left the following day for Benicia. My mother and the girls and I are very anxious to see you. It seems that you've been away a thousand years from home. Father, Mr. Bruner spoke to me about wanting to put in an order to try to deliver four cattle, that I should see you about delivering them and at the same time tell me the price . . . Mr. William Boggs wants to take a little wood . . . He says he'll fix it up with you when you come. I think there are about 200 pieces or more. I don't remember well, just how many board feet there are. The other day a soldier died in a drunken bout and I assisted at his burial.

On April 2nd Vallejo replied from San Jose where he was attending the first Legislature telling Andronico that Mr. Bruner could receive four head of cattle, one each week, and that the price would be 25 pesos; that if Mr.

Bruner accepted the proposition, Jose could deliver the cattle to Sonoma from Petaluma. Vallejo added that it was good that William Boggs was cutting the lumber. In closing the letter, Vallejo told Andronico: "Always be a good man, today and always, and you will have the blessing of your father. Take care of the family, just as your mother wants you to."

ANDRONICO IN BENICIA

In the early spring of 1851, Andronico's 16-year-old sister Epifania married the American Captain John B. Frisbie from New York. When the young couple settled in Benicia, the seventeen-year-old Andronico became a frequent visitor. At this time, Dr. Robert Semple and Thomas O. Larkin had been given land by Andronico's father, for the development of the Benicia area. In turn, the two developers gave Andronico a lot on the swamp. Some years later, Vallejo was to mention this and call their gift "unheard liberality!!!

While in Benicia, Andronico told his father that he was speaking English all day with those who wished him to do so. He was glad of this opportunity to practice English because he knew that his father wished him to go to the U.S. Military Academy at West Point. A military man himself, it was natural that General Vallejo wished his eldest son to follow his profession.

Andronico had written Grandmother Vallejo in Monterey, telling her that he expected to be appointed to West Point; he referred to his grandmother's visit to Sonoma, saying, "We think often of the visit you made us some years ago [1842] and we wish very much for you to repeat it." Then Andronico enclosed ten pesos with instructions to buy chocolates.

With the idea of furthering General Vallejo's desire to send his boy to West Point, Thomas Jefferson Green (a colleague at the first session of the State Legislature in San Jose) wrote to Vallejo on September 13, 1850 from New York.

> The steamer Cherokee sails today and carries to your shores a number of our friends by one of whom Capt. Bale of Sacramento City, I send this, with some newspapers. You will see by the papers that California is admitted to the Union and our representatives are in their seats. I have done much and will do much more to bring our City of Vallejo into favorable notice . . . We are leaving on the 25th of November and reaching San Jose by the first of January so that I will be in my seat on the first day of the session, being the 6th of the month . . . I saw Thomas O. Larkin last night, he appears well pleased that our city joins his Benicia tract as he and Dr. Semple own that portion of the tract adjoining the survey.
>
> It is supposed at Washington City that the census now being taken will give California next year from three to four representatives and consequently many cadets at West Point will be entitled to admission the next June and September. Therefore should you still be desirous to enter your son you must early make interest with the Representatives for his nomination. The Hon. George W. Wright promised to nominate my son as a cadet before leaving California which he did February last but owing to our State not being admitted to the Union, the War Department would

not grant his warrant until I went to Washington and got an order from Pres. Fillmore for his examination on the 28th of last month so he was admitted and is now for the year, the only one from California, while she is entitled to two.

I also advise that you place your son at Kinsleys preparatory school which is within a half mile of the Academy at West Point. There his preparation would be perfect and it would give him a great advantage in his future course. I may be of some service which shall be cheerfully rendered. Mr. T. B. King can also do much in this matter. I will go in a few days to Washington and speak to him and Gwin upon the subject.

A little over three months after the first Congressmen, Edward Gilbert and George W. Wright from the new State of California were seated, a note was sent to Charles M. Conrad, the Secretary of War:

We the undersigned hereby nominate Andronico Vallejo as a cadet to the Military Academy at West Point from the State of California. Andronico Vallejo is a son of Don Mariano G. Vallejo, a native of California. He is about sixteen years of age and resides at Sonoma in that State.

This was signed by Edw. Gilbert and G. Wright. Gilbert had been a printer at Albany, New York, and had come to California in 1847 with Stevenson's New York Volunteer Regiment. He was one of the founders of the *Alta California*.

Two days after receiving the communication from the California Congressmen, Conrad, the Secretary of War, replied on December 23rd to Gilbert: "I have the honor to enclose to you a letter of appointment to Andronico Vallejo as a cadet to the Military Academy at West Point, made upon your nomination to this Department under the date of 21st inst." The Secretary knowing of George Wright's nomination of Thomas J. Green's son gave the privilege of naming Andronico Vallejo to Gilbert. The news did not reach California until February, 1851 when the *Sacramento City Transcript* carried the following item:

A CALIFORNIAN AT WEST POINT

By the last mail, says the *Alta*, Mr. Gilbert forwarded to Andronico, son of Mariano Guadalupe Vallejo his appointment as a cadet at West Point. Mr. Vallejo has the honor of being the first representative of California in the Military Academy.

It would appear from the letter of General Thomas Jefferson Green, quoted previously, that it was *his* son who held the honor of being the first appointee to West Point.

General Persifor Frazer Smith, Commander of the Pacific Division of the United States Army, a close friend of General Vallejo, had his headquarters in Sonoma. When he heard of Andronico's appointment, he was pleased to send the following letter to the Secretary of War, Charles M. Conrad, on March 3rd, 1851:

General Vallejo, a distinguished and well known citizen of California who resides here, has received notice that one of his sons, Andronico has been appointed a cadet in the Military Academy. He is highly pleased and flattered by this favor and extremely anxious to take advantage of it; but his son has had but few advantages in his education until very lately and is no means a proficient in the English language. You must be aware that until lately the persons who have settled themselves in this secluded place, coming from the United States were not of a class to aid by their intercourse, the education of a young lad.

General Vallejo would be very mortified if his son should not be able to pass his preparatory examination, or should, through want of previous instruction fail in his first year's endeavors; his return would seem like a great disgrace. At the same time the period remaining for the journey and taking the shortest route—via the Isthmus—for New York, he can only arrive a few days before that on which he is to present himself for examination in his preparatory studies.

Under these circumstances the General begs of me to solicit from you that the appointment of his son should be considered as commencing on the first of June 1852. In the meantime he proposes to send him to one of the schools in the neighborhood of the Military Academy where he will be fully prepared for his course.

I take the liberty of expressing my own desire that it could be made convenient to grant the General's wish. He estimates the honor done him even higher than it is generally considered among us. He is a very influential man among the California population and is heartily a good American citizen and more calculated than any other, among the former inhabitants to bring about unity of habits and feelings so desirable in a mixed population.

If it be thought proper to comply or indeed at any rate, may I ask that the answer be directed to him "Dn M. Guadalupe Vallejo, Sonoma, California." I will very probably not be here at the time of its arrival. I think I shall be required on the frontier; I understand that the first effort of the Indian Commissioners made to have a meeting with the hostile chiefs was unsuccessful.

Six weeks later (April 24, 1851), Secretary of War Charles M. Conrad wrote to Vallejo:

Major-General P. F. Smith has addressed the Department in behalf of your son, Andronico Vallejo who has been appointed a cadet this year, and requested that in view of his want of proficiency in an English education, his appointment might be made to take effect as June, 1852 and thus afford him time to prepare himself for the course of instruction at the Military Academy.

I regret to inform you that this cannot be done unless your son be renominated next year by the member who shall then represent the District in which you reside, in Congress. Should your son decline his present appointment the vacancy will remain open until the next Congress meets and then if renominated, it will afford me great pleasure to confer the appointment on him.

The Archives of the United States Military Academy record that in the summer of 1851 "Andronico Vallejo—Did not Report." Jackson W. Green from Sacramento, the son of General J. Green as mentioned before, was therefore the first cadet from California admitted to the Military Academy at West Point.

For some reason, Andronico gave up all thought of going to West Point; he chose, instead, a Catholic School, Mount St. Mary's at Emmittsburg, near

Baltimore, Maryland. He sailed for the East in 1852 with Robert McLane, a business associate of his father. Soon after their arrival in the East, McLane wrote to Vallejo:

I have this day placed Andronico safely and in good health as a student in St. Mary's College, Baltimore, Maryland. He spent ten days in New York as the guest of Mrs. Larkin and had for his companions his cousin (Rogerio Cooper) and young Larkin.

I send you by mail a prospectus of the college where I hope Andronico will pursue successfully his studies, he has a good disposition . . . though the visit in New York turned his head a little, so great was the whirl of pleasure and gayety constantly passing before his eyes that he seemed so happy at the end of the voyage that I could not deny him this recreation with his cousin and young Larkin.

I hope you will in your letters impress upon him to confine himself strictly to the habits and usages of the college which are simple but at the same time comfortable and good.

In his letter McLane wrote the General that he had returned from Washington where he had found an unfavorable state of things for California. The infamous conduct of the Indian Commissioners had been such that he abandoned the idea of bringing Vallejo's name to the President's attention. McLane said he had referred Vallejo's claim to the Senate Committee where it was in charge of Senator Bayard of Delaware, a gentleman of great energy and influence.

When the first collegiate year was over, Robert McLane wrote Andronico's brother-in-law, John B. Frisbie, that he was turning over to Andronico a memo of travel and college expenses which amounted to $1,275.98, out of the original sum of $1,300 placed in McLane's hands.

During his summer vacation, Andronico stayed with his sister Fannie Frisbie and her husband, and their infant son, Mariano Guadalupe (Lupe), at the Metropolitan Hotel in New York City. With Mrs. Frisbie at the time was the younger brother, Platon, twelve years old, whom Fannie had brought from California to attend school with Andronico. The two Vallejo boys accompanied the Frisbie family when they visited Niagara Falls, which, in the words of Captain Frisbie, were "the grandest, most imposing of Nature's wonders."

Andronico and Platon remained in school at Mount St. Mary's until November 1855. When they left, the President of the College, the Reverend John W. Caffrey, wrote to their father on November 30, 1855:

I can not let Andronico leave without expressing to you my high esteem for his character and the approbation of his teachers generally which he has merited by his good behaviour. I trust he will be a great help and comfort to you and I am sure he will if he pursues in the course he has thus far pursued. Platon has also been good and is doing well in his studies. He will I expect be a very successful student. He is a good and amiable child and we all like him and cherish the best hopes of his progress.

Reverend Caffrey also wrote a personal note for Andronico, viz., a letter of reference:

I hereby certify, that the bearer of this, Andronico Vallejo has been a student of Mount St. Mary's College from September 1852 until the present date; that his conduct has always been correct and honorable, that he has been a diligent student and a truly estimable and amiable gentleman and has merited the esteem and approbation of the Faculty of the College. Given at Mount St. Mary's College this 25th day of November, 1855.

JOHN W. CAFFREY

Another "personal note"—this time to General Vallejo from Robert McLane, (who, it will be remembered, had brought Andronico from California to Maryland and had watched over his finances)—was dated November 25, 1855, and was to be delivered to his father by the young man himself:

I cannot allow Andronico to take leave of me without a word of greeting to you, though I am so much engaged today at my office that I can only write a few lines . . . He is much improved in all respects, highly respected and beloved by all with whom he has had intercourse and will I am sure meet the expectations of yourself and his mother. I shall ever entertain for him sincere friendship and I hope he will not fail to keep me in his mind.

ANDRONICO STARTS FARMING

On the return of the two brothers to California, General Vallejo put Andronico to work on the Lachryma Montis ranch, working with Mortimer Ryan, the overseer, in the orchards and vineyards. The young farmer wrote his father on January 28, 1858: "Mr. Ryan begins to plough at Quiquiriqui first because the ground is very wet at Lachryma Montis . . . This letter is carried by Manuel Vallejo of Napa." Manuel was Salvador Vallejo's son.

During the summer of 1858, it was necessary for Vallejo to be away from home frequently; most of the time in Monterey where he was settling the estates of several of the Vallejos. While there he stayed with his sister Rosalia Leese in the Larkin House (which the Leeses had bought), and also at the Washington Hotel, which had been erected nine years before to house the delegates of the Constitutional Convention of which Vallejo had been a delegate.

The General's mind was at ease regarding his Lachryma Montis ranch, as it was doing well under the careful supervision of the overseer and Andronico. The ripening grain and fruit colored the fields and orchards; the vegetable garden was filled with fresh provisions for the family table; the second blooming of the roses, together with the flowering of the jasmine and the orange blossoms, spread a fragrance over the grounds—all of which was not lost on Andronico, an aesthete at heart, who was never meant to be a soldier nor was he geared to the mundane duties of a farmer.

Andronico did not live at Lachryma Montis but kept bachelor quarters in the adobe house built by John Ray in 1852. It was sold in 1853 to Andronico's mother, who gave it to her son, who in turn in 1860 sold it to Thomas P. Madden who held mortgages on much of General Vallejo's property.

From the space in front of the General's house, Andronico harvested 700 bushels of oats. These he put in bags and stored in the brick storehouse. After about six years of work on the ranch, Andronico tired of it, perhaps finding it difficult to please his father who was, at that time, under the strain of the Soscol litigation and the futility of his efforts to create harmony among the Vallejo heirs in the division of the property of the San Cayetano Rancho.

Andronico left Lachryma Montis without telling any one where he was going. It was presumed that he was in Napa with his Aunt Luz, his mother's sister. His twelve-year-old brother Napoleon wrote him a note in English on March 13, 1862, saying, "I write you a few lines telling you we are well. Mother says that what is the reason that you don't write to her. She don't know about you nor where you are." Andronico's mother also tried to reach him on April 6th of that year.

> Andronico, where are you? What are you doing? How are things with you? I don't know if you are alive or dead. Andronico, a young man educated as you are, by virtuous parents should also be virtuous; if by unhappy chance you find yourself in the world without worldly goods, without support and without being able to count on anything but yourself. Dear, dear Andronico, courage! Don't be afraid of work, don't be ashamed. Don't be lazy. Be an honorable man, be a worthwhile man and remember it is your Mama that is speaking to you.
>
> Every day I am waiting for a letter or news of you. You well know the girls never tell me anything, either good or bad. Andronico don't be indolent. Just take thought and remember that you have a mother, who doesn't forget you, not an instant. I ask everybody if they know if you are comfortable some place and they all say, they don't know. Oh! how many tears, how I suffer dear Andronico.

Andronico did go to Napa to visit his Tia Luz, wife of Vallejo's brother Don Salvador. Andronico was restless, not having found his niche in life. As his mother expressed it: "Andronico goes about like the wandering Jew. And all because of the bad temper of his father who hasn't known and doesn't know and never will know how to manage his children. I say it with a sad heart but it is the truth." After visiting in Napa, Andronico went to San Francisco where he boarded with a Mrs. Miller from whose residence he wrote his mother on May 18th, 1862:

> Right now, I'm in San Francisco but later on I don't know whether I'll go away. I am thinking if I can, of going to Mexico to see if in some other lands, I can seek something. The ideas I had for the mines, I have discarded because I think my luck won't be good and also the life is dangerous. My ideas about Mexico are in the event I can't do anything here.
>
> It is certain that I have been very poor and still am; this is not anything. I was in misery when my Papa was here and I wasn't capable of asking for a single coin in order to eat; but my Papa's secretary is always aided from my Papa's purse. I, his son, go about with a worn-out suit and Senor Estrada [secretary] with a new one;

my shoes aren't shined but those of Senor Estrada are; Papa's son walks without a cane; but Senor secretary has one that cost five pesos.

I smoke cigarettes and Estrada smokes cigars and expensive ones at that . . . I am banned from the side of my father and Estrada—he is the Jack of Diamonds of General Vallejo. I don't go to the theatre with my Papa but Estrada is the loyal companion of my father. If Papa subscribes to a paper, his secretary also takes one and has it delivered to the office. This man knows all the affairs of my father and family.

Estrada is given credit because my father pays, but when he pays for his son, it pains him greatly; To sum it up, I'll tell you that Estrada is at the right hand of my Papa; I am a blabbermouth, a rogue, a disobedient son but Senor Estrada is a saint . . . My father has not told the truth because I am not at fault. If Estrada tells you, he lies and I wish you would tell me if my Papa said that Estrada told him these tales so I could give him a beating. My Papa paid some bills of mine and some of Estrada's . . . I think that Estrada told him that I had expressed myself in an ugly manner against him. This is *false*, it is a lie and base calumny . . . Since my Papa is so liberal with Senor Estrada, he could pay me what this great man owes me . . . He tells me that he earns five pesos a day. With this he could pay me some $800 which Estrada owes me. He owes Mrs. Miller about $150 with interest . . . I am in good health, have been since I came. Mrs. Miller takes good care of me.

The evening of the day that Andronico's letter arrived, his mother sat down at her desk in her bedroom and started this letter to her son:

I have already read your letter so many times. I already know it by heart. It seemed to me there was nothing bad against your Papa. I thought it well to show him your letter for many reasons, and he would see that you had not spoken ill of him. I gave it to him to read and he was so enraged, I regretted having given it to him. But you know how your Papa is like; if one talks to him, he is annoyed and if one doesn't talk to him he is irked. It is enough to drive one crazy.

By express I sent you twenty pesos. Let me know if you have received them. My son always remember that the fear of God is the beginning of wisdom and without that quality one can not reach the second, nor have the moderation to be humble.

Leave the secretary, Senor Estrada, the Jack of Diamonds to the Blessed One . . . The great lord, the know-it-all, the one who knows the family secrets; let him alone. Don't put yourself in his company under any circumstances for any reason. At home all is well. It is eleven at night and the candle is going out. Goodbye, Andronico and remember your mother.

The foregoing letter was not mailed. Andronico's father evidently wanted his son to know that he was not angry with him, for he wrote the following letter in his own hand. His wife copied it and sent it to their son, under her own signature. It was dated June 4, 1862:

I received your letter in which you tell me what has happened between you and Estrada. I regret exceedingly that you have become involved in such a disagreeable dispute but when the natural duty to defend the honor of your father demands it, it seems to me that you have done right in not acquiescing. I'm not speaking just of that man but of anyone. You are beginning to be alone in the world and there will not be lacking occasions for realizing it, in that and a thousand disputes, but always try to evade them with dignity and also try to have right on your side, evading the occasions. Try to avoid dangerous company; be good and humble without servility and you'll see good results.

It doesn't seem to me prudent that you have gone to San Francisco without resources or employment which would help you with your needs. Come home where you will always be well received and you will have whatever we may have without need of embarrassments. Your Papa thinks your departure very strange and told me so. You know he loves you and if you have thought he is angry, he doesn't know why or wherefore.

They say a beating-up is paid with a fine of $25 and I am sending you enough for two! I asked your Papa without his knowing what for, for that reason a draft is on its way to the post office.

The vineyards are wonderful: they promise a rich harvest. This year there are 40,000 grape vines in fruit and your father needs anyone who will help him. You already know how the work is done and it will be a good thing if you offer your services as soon as you can. The family is well and send you expressions of affection. Hoping you will come soon.

BENICIA DE VALLEJO

The plea of Andronico's mother for him to return home was of no avail. The letter, it was true, contained an indirect apology from Andronico's father, but Andronico had grown tired of the duties on the ranch and of his father's impatience and querulousness.

Andronico received an offer to teach in Vacaville and accepted it for a short time. During a visit to his sister Fannie Frisbie, she persuaded him to settle in Vallejo, instead. This was in the year 1863. Fannie reported the fact to her mother as follows: "Andronico lives here in the house. He gives lessons in music and Spanish. They bring him in about forty pesos a month. That is enough to clothe him. He doesn't like to work hard. He is very fat and in good health." In reply, Andronico's mother wrote him: "I am glad you are employed and that you are happy for that is the one thing I desire. I pray to God and the Virgin that they will help you and light your way, so you can get along with all the people you are teaching. I have been ill but I am better. Dr. Von Geldern is curing me."

PROFESSOR A. A. VALLEJO—TEACHER OF MUSIC

On March 24, 1846 when Andronico Vallejo was twelve years old, his father signed an agreement which stated:

FIRST: Mr. Hoeppner obligates solemnly to teach Mr. Vallejo and his actual family to play the piano forte with all the science of the art, giving lessons of music, at least during five years or more if it should be necessary, until the complete instruction of the children to the male and female.

SECOND: Mr. Vallejo obligates himself to give to Mr. Hoeppner, a title to a tract of land of the Agua Caliente, bought from Don Lazaro Pina, to the extent of two leagues and a half long by ½ of a league wide.

The German musician, Andrew Hoeppner, had been in the employ of the Russians for some years at Sitka and had come to California with his attractive half-breed wife in 1845. After receiving the deed from General Vallejo to a portion of the Agua Caliente (warm water) property, Hoeppner developed it into a health resort and named it "Annenthal."

James C. Ward visited the Valley of Sonoma in 1847. He called on Hoeppner and found him to be a man of good taste who played delightfully on the piano. On Ward's second visit to the valley, he found that Hoeppner had gone to the mines, leaving his wife alone which made her wish that her husband would sell the place and take her back to Sitka. "Here are two of the most entertaining people in the world," Ward wrote in his diary, "burying themselves in an out-of-the-way place where all is contrary to their taste and living without associates and almost without acquaintances. He is one of the most agreeable performers on the piano I have ever met and they are both so entertaining and so amiable that no party in San Francisco is now complete without them."

Andrew Hoeppner furnished the music for the productions in Sonoma of the first Thespians, members of Colonel Jonathan Stevenson's Regiment. They played to crowded houses in the Colonnade Building owned by Salvador Vallejo. General Vallejo's secretary, Colonel Victor Prudon, appeared as Othello. When the news reached Sonoma of the Gold Strike, off went the stars and lesser lights, together with most of the audience.

About 1849, Hoeppner left his wife and adopted child and went to Chile and Honduras. As he did not fulfill his part of the contract, the land was sold by Vallejo to John B. Frisbie for $8,000. Part of that land is now Glen Ellen where Jack London once lived.

The piano used by Hoeppner in teaching the Vallejo children had been bought by Vallejo from Stephen Smith of Bodega. Regarding the sale, Smith wrote to Vallejo on January 31, 1844: "I answer your esteemed letter, dated the 28th of the present month in which you say of the household goods and pianoforte that they are high in price—in answer to which I tell you that if it were not for the fact that I have no house in which to put them I would not have suggested their sale because I bought them for my own use; but as you well know I have no place to put them so have wanted to sell them and I tell you as to the price that it is the very lowest for which I offer them and if it suits you to take them, you can deal with my brother-in-law [Manuel Torres]." In the letter which was written in Spanish, Smith also asked Vallejo to advise him how many heifers, bulls, lambs, calves and tame cows he could purchase from the Vallejo herds. In closing, Smith wrote: "I am always your friend and I wish you would call upon me to serve you."

Little did the Vallejo family realize that little Andronico's music lessons, started under Andrew Hoeppner, would lead to Andronico's life work.

After leaving Fannie's home, Andronico found bachelor quarters in Vallejo.

By 1870 he had built up his clientele of music students to such an extent that he could afford to rent studios in the Batcheller Building in Vallejo. Associated with him was Professor Washington V. Plise. Not to be outdone by his partner, Andronico decided to add the professional title to his own name. Advertisements, printed in the newspapers, announced that Professor Vallejo and Plise would give lessons in Spanish, French, piano, flute, guitar, harp, American lyre and also lessons in vocal music.

In 1879, Andronico maintained studios also in Oakland, on 12th Street between Broadway and Washington streets. According to an Oakland paper:

> Professor A. A. Vallejo was ready to give instructions on the piano by a short method, peculiar to himself, wherein a pupil could learn as much in three months as would be required in twelve months by any other method. He would give three lessons per week, full hour each time for $12.00 a month. Piano and music furnished without charge.

Another talent General Vallejo's oldest son possessed was for mathematics, particularly for mathematical puzzles. While teaching in Oakland he met another enthusiast, Jose Garcia de Cadiz, a bookkeeping instructor. The friendship resulted in their renting rooms at 1150 Market Street in San Francisco, where day and evening classes were given instructions in Spanish and bookkeeping as well as lessons on the piano, harp, flute and on some of the brass instruments. Andronico still kept his studio in Vallejo and had pupils in Sonoma for the piano. Among them his own sister Luisa and Celeste Granice, the daughter of the publisher of Sonoma's newspaper, the Sonoma Index-Tribune.

A press release in the Vallejo Evening Chronicle stated that:

> PROFESSOR A. A. VALLEJO
>
> All lovers of music will no doubt be proud to know this popular teacher is still forming classes on the piano, harp, American lyre and flute. His long experience and hitherto unprecedented success in his chosen profession is sufficient guarantee to all that they will reap the full benefit of money expended in studying music under his tutorage.
>
> Classes taught in any part of the county or State. Correspondence solicited. The Professor also gives lessons in the Spanish language. Prices for both music and language moderate. No argument is needed to show the many advantages accruing from a knowledge of music and the language he teaches. A mere appeal to the intelligence of our people is sufficient.

EL SOLTERO

Living in bachelor quarters and keeping house for himself, Andronico found pleasure in the Vallejo home of his sister Fannie Frisbie before she went to Mexico, and also his sister Adela Frisbie's home. He was also a frequent guest at the home of his brother, Dr. Platon Vallejo, whose wife Lily was an accomplished pianist. There were many enjoyable evenings, with Lily and

Andronico interpreting the four-handed arrangements of Mozart's Sonata in C and works by Schubert, with Platon forming the appreciative audience. At times Platon would join them by playing the violin. While at Platon's home, Andronico would usually find time to give Lily and her daughter, Felipa and Francisca, a lesson in Spanish.

Andronico, as indicated above, was the soltero, the bachelor of the Vallejo family. Once when visiting in Sonoma, he had taken a fancy to a Miss Mary Pickett. It is presumed she is the Miss Pickett that Henry Cerruti, one of Bancroft's literary agents, recalls having met at a dancing party at Lachryma Montis. Cerruti said she was a good dancer and was extraordinarily fond of fun, but, he regretted to say "she was a professional coquette, one of the silly girls desirous of being courted by every gentleman she came in contact with, giving encouragement to everyone who was neither old or ugly." The attraction of Andronico for Miss Pickett was only a temporary infatuation. The deep love of his life was for a young girl he met in Vallejo, an American girl who was his pupil and who possessed exceptional musical talent. But before the romance could mature she passed away, leaving a void that no one else could fill. To ease his heartache at the time (October 1873), Andronico's aunt "Tia Chiquita" (Mrs. John B. Cooper) gave him a trip to Los Angeles. Some years later, gossip has it that Professor Vallejo became infatuated with a married woman. Before the autumnal romance cooled, a little boy was born who grew to look so much like Andronico that the boy's schoolmates in Vallejo called the lad *Professor Vallejo.*

A FAVORITE OF HIS MOTHER

The eldest son of the Vallejos held a special place in the heart of his mother. As an infant, taking the place of her first born, he had kept her from being lonely during her husband's absence on military matters when they lived at the windy, sand-swept Presidio of San Francisco. As a mature man, Andronico gave his mother sympathetic understanding; to him she could express her moods of impatience and displeasure with his father, something she rarely did with her other children. It was Andronico who comforted her during his father's illness and during her own, in the year she survived her husband.

Although Senora Vallejo received care from all her children, Andronico was now the head of the family. He was at her side when she prepared her Will on February 23, 1890, shortly after her first stroke which was a slight one. She dictated to Mr. Clement, her attorney: "I desire my son, Andronico Antonio, to act as Executor of this my will without bond." She signed the document *Beicia F. Vallejo*, the slight misspelling of her first name. The witnesses were two of her children, A. A. Vallejo and Adela V. de Frisbie.

With all the Vallejo children except Ula at her bedside, Senora died on

January 30, 1891. Many letters of condolences came to Lachryma Montis. One dated January 31, 1891, postmarked Napa, addressed to Andronico, was especially appreciated. It was from their ever-faithful friend, William M. Boggs, son of the late Lilburn Boggs:

Andronico, I write to all the children of my dear departed friends, General and Mrs. Vallejo; your beloved mother whose death I learned took place yesterday. I have not words to express my sorrow. I mourn with you as I would at the loss of my own departed mother. Please convey my kindest sympathy to each of the members of your family, also the regrets of my wife and myself that we cannot be with you on this sad occasion of your dear mother's funeral.

Only a few days ago I wrote a long letter to Sacramento to one of the Senators urging him to use his influence in behalf of your mother and of the measure to pass a bill for her relief. Now it is too late but the memory of her and your honored father will ever remain. May Heaven's blessings rest upon you all is the prayer of your friend.

In her will Senora Vallejo left her estate to her two youngest daughters, Luisa and Maria. It was admitted for probate, without contest, on March 23, 1891. Both Andronico and his sister Adela were present in the Superior Court in Santa Rosa to acknowledge the signature was that of their mother, although in her illness she had misspelled her Christian name. Andronico had been named executor but declined to serve. Robert A. Poppe, a close family friend, an attorney of Sonoma, was appointed in his place.

It was only six years after his mother's death that Andronico became seriously ill with dropsy. His health had been such that for some time he had been unable to work. Edward McGettigan, the future father-in-law of Andronico's niece Francisca Vallejo, was president of the Solano County Board of Supervisors and saw to it that Professor Andronico Antonio Vallejo was given a pension. For fifteen months he was under the care of his brother, Dr. Platon Vallejo. In spite of excellent care, he passed away in the City of Vallejo on February 11, 1897, age 63, in his little apartment which was above a Mrs. White's millinery store. Two days after his death, on February 13th Dr. Vallejo and his twenty-two-year-old daughter Francisca brought the body of Andronico Antonio Vallejo to Sonoma for burial in Mountain Cemetery.

Epifania de Guadalupe Vallejo

Epifania de Guadalupe Vallejo

(Mrs. John B. Frisbie)

This child of the Vallejos—their first daughter—was born in one of the rooms of the deserted San Francisco Solano Mission on August 4th, 1835. This was about two months after the young officer, Mariano Guadalupe Vallejo, arrived with his wife and small son Andronico to found the pueblo of Sonoma. The baby's father had been commissioned by Governor Figueroa to act as Administrator of the mission during its secularization and to serve as Colonizer of the area north of San Francisco Bay.

Alferez Vallejo found that the pastor of the mission had departed for the San Rafael Mission, so Vallejo set about putting the chapel in order for services for the soldiers. It was not until the return of the Padre, the Reverend Jose Lorenzo Quijas, that the baby Vallejo girl was baptized on March 25, 1836 and was given the name of Epifania de Guadalupe. Her godfather was Captain John B. Cooper, the husband of Encarnacion Vallejo Cooper, the sister of Alferez Vallejo.

Epifania or Fannie, as she was more often called, was described by her brother Platon as having been during her girlhood "... a beautiful girl, with hair the color of a canary bird, large brown eyes and a complexion of pink and white and no freckles." On the subject of Fannie's girlhood beauty, we have also the opinion of James C. Ward, a pioneer traveler in California, who came to Sonoma as a guest of Captain J. E. Brackett, the first commander of the post, composed of men from Stevenson's Volunteer New York Regiment. Ward wrote in his diary in May, 1848: "On my return to town [Sonoma] I called on General Vallejo, whose eldest daughter came into the room while I was there; she is very handsome and will create a sensation in Washington, where her father intends to take his family before long." When Fannie was twelve years old, she and her sister Natalia became ill and were attended by Navy Surgeon Marias Duvall who said, "Natalia and Fanny (Fanita) were taken ill and fell into my hands; the most understanding patients I ever had. Fanny's softness and sweetness of character can never be forgotten." A year later Fannie was attended by Dr. Fourgeaud. The doctor wrote Vallejo on May 8, 1840, "I am much pleased to learn that the medicine I have sent your daughter Fanny has been of some service to her. I am entirely at your disposal, should you wish or need any further attention or advise in her case. I am much obliged to have her present: My wife admires it very much." In addition to her beauty and sweetness of temper, Fannie possessed a delightful sense of humor which prompted Gertrude Atherton to say, in her "Golden Gate Country,"—"She might have been an American girl with her quick wit, her sauciness, her frank gayety." Fannie played the piano with skill and was an amateur painter of ability. She completed a self-portrait which the family thought was a striking likeness.

Fannie's first music teacher was Andrew Hoeppner, with whom General Vallejo had contracted an agreement that for music lessons to be given to the entire Vallejo family for a period of five years Hoeppner, as previously stated, was to receive a certain tract of land. While Fannie was a pupil of Hoeppner, she wrote her grandmother in Monterey that she was playing the piano a little; her sister Adela, she said, played it well, and Andronico could play the March of Prague. "Papa called Natalia to play the Mexican March which she did and it pleased Don Luis a lot." Fannie added, "Nana Antonia, I know you speak English with the Americans."

The three Vallejo girls, Fannie, Adela and Natalia, and their brother Andronico all learned to play under Hoeppner's instruction, and often entertained visitors to the Casa Grande.

JOHN B. FRISBIE EMERGES INTO THE "VALLEJO TAPESTRY"

Next door to the Casa Grande was the cuartel or barracks which was built by Fannie's father during 1839–40–41 to house his Mexican soldiers. In 1846, it was the temporary home of some of the members of the Bear Flag Party; then it was occupied by the military outfit under the command of Lieutenant Joseph Warren Revere, and in 1847, after Revere's departure, the structure housed Company C of Stevenson's Volunteers under Captain J. E. Brackett.

Colonel Jonathan E. Stevenson's Regiment sailed from New York around the Horn on September 26, 1844 in three vessels, the *Susan Drew*, the *Loo Chew* and the *Thomas H. Perkins*. The flotilla arrived in San Francisco Bay with the wind blowing a gale, on March 5, 1847. On that day, General Vallejo was in Yerba Buena with his secretary, Victor Prudon and the two went out in a small boat to find out who the visitors might be. Little did Vallejo dream that on one of the vessels, the *Susan Drew*, was a young officer, Captain John B. Frisbie, who was destined to marry his daughter Fannie, and that the commander of that vessel, Lt.-Colonel Henry S. Burton, would become the husband of Senorita Ampara Ruiz, a cousin of his wife. Dona Ampara, a beautiful woman with a fine mind, had a book to her credit.

General Kearny reported their arrival in a letter dated March 15, 1847 to General R. Jones, adjutant United States Army, saying in part:

> On the 5th instant, Colonel Stevenson, with three companies of his regiment (the 7th New York Volunteers) arrived at the bay of San Francisco; . . . The heavy ordinance and stores brought out by that regiment will be landed at San Francisco, and be protected by the command to be stationed there; that brought out by the Lexington is still on board of her in this harbor, (Monterey) as at present there is no place on shore where I am willing to trust it.
>
> From the large amount of ordinance and stores sent to California by the department, I presume the territory will never be restored to Mexico; and it should not

be . . . The Californians are now quiet, and I shall endeavor to keep them so by mild and gentle treatment. Had they received such treatment from the time our flag was hoisted here, in July last, I believe there would have been little or no resistance on their part. They have been most cruelly and shamefully abused by our own people—by the volunteers (American emigrants) raised in this part of the country and on the Sacramento. Had they not resisted, they would have been unworthy the name of men. If the people remain quiet, and California continues under our flag, it will ere long be a bright star in our Union.

In this letter General Kearny said that the population of California was small, probably not exceeding 12,000 of which one-fifth were emigrants. Besides there were about 15,000 Indians, one third being called Christian Indians, the remainder the wild Indians who live in the mountains and subsist in a great measure upon the horses and cattle they steal. "The climate," the General wrote, "is pure and healthy—physicians meeting with no encouragement, as its inhabitants are never sick . . . The bays of San Francisco, Monterey and San Diego afford excellent harbors; they should be protected by permanent fortifications."

John B. Frisbie as Captain of Company H of Stevenson's Regiment was stationed at the Presidio of San Francisco under Major James A. Hardie. In later years Frisbie told Hubert H. Bancroft, "I made the first official expedition to the mines to arrest deserters and report on the mines." Frisbie made his report to Colonel Richard B. Mason, United States Military governor of California.

When Colonel Mason, himself, came up to the mines, he greeted Frisbie by saying, "I have come up to put you in a straight-jacket," referring to what he deemed exaggerations in Frisbie's report. Frisbie told the Colonel to hold the straight-jacket in abeyance until he had made some explorations himself.

Colonel Mason in his official reports, dated August 17, 1848, stated he could not bring himself to believe the reports that he had heard of the gold district until he had visited there himself but having made the visit with Lt. Sherman, he had no hesitation in saying that there was more gold there than will pay the cost of the war with Mexico a hundred times. With this report Colonel Mason sent specimens of gold donated by a number of persons which included John A. Sutter and John B. Frisbie as donors.

Upon Captain Frisbie's return to the Presidio of San Francisco from the mine district he received orders to transfer his Company H to Sonoma to relieve Captain Brackett. He arrived at Sonoma (which he said, was at that time esteemed the most desirable command on the bay) on August 5, 1848, just one day after Fannie Vallejo, the senorita who would one day become his wife, had celebrated her 13th birthday. Fannie, like many girls of Latin blood, had matured early into her feminine charms; so it is not to be wondered that young Captain Frisbie fell in love with the little California beauty living in the Casa Grande, next door to the Barracks. The Yankee Captain was welcomed into the Vallejo home; his courtship was impulsive, ardent and successful.

The Gold Rush which had begun in a big way the summer of 1848, had enticed men from all manner of occupations. Twenty-six soldiers had deserted from the post in Sonoma. Colonel Mason had been officially informed on August 6th of the end of the Mexican War and issued orders for the discharge of the Regiment of New York Volunteers. Consequently when Captain Frisbie received orders to disband the post at Sonoma, he was able to throw himself with all his Yankee energy, into the fast developing business and politics of the West. He interested the father of his fiancee in opening merchandizing stores in Sonoma, Napa and Benicia, to outfit the miners. The store in Sonoma was on the first floor of the Casa Grande; the one in Napa was at the junction of Napa Creek and Napa River. It was built of lumber which at Bodega mills had cost $300 per thousand feet.

Captain Frisbie also interested Fannie's father in the American brand of politics, and with his assistance, Vallejo was elected a delegate to the State Constitutional Convention held in Monterey in September 1849. While there, General Vallejo wrote home, "Tell Fannie that I hope that when I reach Sonoma she will already know English so that she can teach it to me."

Frisbie himself was not a member of the Constitutional Convention, but he was much in evidence. Frisbie ran on the ticket as candidate for Lt. Governor, with Capt. Sutter as Governor. They were defeated by Peter Burnett and John McDougall.

On April 25, 1850 in the old Mission San Francisco Solano, young Captain Frisbie with his lovely fiancee's mother and father acting as godparents, was baptized into the Catholic faith. It is recorded in the Second Book of Baptisms of the San Francisco Solano Mission that *Don Juan Frisbay*, No. 1739, had been baptized and that "Frisbay" had given up the sect called *Episcopal*. Captain Frisbie drew a line through "Episcopales" and wrote before it *Baptists*. Then, in his own hand, he wrote that he was 26 anos [years] and the "legitimate son of Eleazer Frisbie and Cynthia Cornell Frisbie; born at Albany, State of New York." The witnesses were Andronico Vallejo and Jose de la Rosa.

Some eight months later, Captain Frisbie was speaker of the day for the recently organized Society of California Pioneers at their first celebration, viz. on New Year's Day 1851. After a long parade of various organizations throughout sixteen blocks in San Francisco, the procession arranged itself before the old adobe building on Portsmouth Square where Captain Frisbie mounted the porch and gave his oration. "We are here to commemorate what we have done and to contemplate the fruit of our labors . . . When most of us arrived here, there were but some twenty houses in the pueblo; since then, only three summers have come and gone. Now look around you; we are in a mighty city . . . . That this mighty change has happened, Pioneers of California, is yours; and each member of this Society, looking at this wonderful achievement can say in soberness and truth—'This in part is my work!' "

That evening at six, the Pioneers gathered in the Armory hung with flags for dinner, Captain William D. Howard took his place at the head of the table. At eight, the champagne corks popped and as the glasses were filled, toasts were drunk to New Year's Day, to the President of the United States, to the Army and Navy, to the State of California, etc., etc.

General Vallejo was present and gave a toast in Spanish which was translated for the Pioneers by Mr. Teschmacher. Twenty-one toasts and many speeches later, Captain Howard formally ended the banquet which had cost $1,786.50.

FANNIE'S MARRIAGE

Fannie Vallejo, not quite sixteen and Captain Frisbie, not yet twenty-seven, were united in marriage on April 3rd, 1851 by Padre Anthony Delmas in the Mission San Francisco Solano. Colonel Joe Hooker and Felicidad Carrillo (the bride's cousin), were the attendants, with Fannie's former tutor, Senor Frederick Reeger, as witness.

The morning of the event, the bride's father wrote to his mother, living in Monterey:

> Yesterday was celebrated the matrimonial contract of Fanita, my oldest daughter with Don Juan Frisbie and today there will be the joining of their hands in my house and tomorrow there will be the eclesiastical ceremony.
>
> I believe it is my obligation to inform you and all my brothers and sisters that I believe Senor Frisbie is a fine chap. I have always thought this and in my opinion it will always be true. She has always taken my advice and her choice is her father's and all the family.
>
> I hope you will give her your blessing which will make her happy which is the wish of your obedient son who kisses your hand.
>
> M. G. VALLEJO

An idea of the festivities at the time of the wedding has been given by Jonathan Tibbett Jr., whose father and mother were among the invited guests: "A few days before the wedding, my parents arrived at the home of General Vallejo with anticipated interest and pleasure because of the brilliant festivities, they knew would follow. They were royally entertained and friendships were cemented that lasted during their life-time . . . My mother often related how the butter was molded into fanciful designs; a duck with her ducklings on a pond, a lamb curled up in sleep, a crouching lion with shaggy head and mane; a caballero mounted on a prancing steed and a centerpiece for the bride's table, representing a bride and groom."

The butter designs were molded by Mrs. Marie Brunner, whose talent in such creations had been commended by Napoleon Bonaparte and the Empress Josephine, during a stop they made at the tavern in Neuchatel, Switzerland, where Marie, then eighteen years old, was working as second cook. That her talent was still highly commendable at the time of Fannie's wedding may be judged from the praise she received for the design of the bride's centerpiece.

Mrs. Brunner allowed little Eliza Donner to accompany her when she delivered it to the Vallejo mansion. Eliza, together with her sister Georgia, were survivors of the Donner Party tragedy and had been given a home by the Brunners in Sonoma, where they continued to live until 1856.

Little Eliza recalled at the time of the visit to the Vallejo mansion, the Casa Grande that Senora Vallejo took her by the hand, saying in her own musical tongue, "Come little daughter and play while you wait." "She led me to a room that had pictures on the wall and left me surrounded by toys. But I could not play. My eyes wandered about until they became riveted on one corner of the room where stood a child's crib which looked like gold. Its head and foot boards were embellished with figures of angels; and a canopy of lace like a fleecy cloud hovered over. The bed was white but the pillows were covered with pink silk and encased in slips of linen lawn exquisite with rare needle work. I touched it before I left the room wondering what the little girl dreamed in that beautiful bed . . . The linen pillow slips were as fine as those Senorita Isabella Fitch showed me when she gave me the highly prized lessons in simple drawn work and her cousin Senorita Leese had taught me hemming. These young ladies were related to the Vallejos and also lived in a large house facing the plaza. In fact some of my sweetest memories of Sonoma are associated with these three Spanish homes. These people never asked unfeeling questions nor repeated harrowing tales and I did not learn until I was grown that they had been among the large contributors to the fund for the relief of our party."

FIRST HOME IN BENICIA

After their marriage the young couple went to Benicia to live. A prefabricated house—one with cut and numbered timbers, imported—was reassembled into a home for them in Benicia, the new city named for the bride's mother, which was being promoted by Robert Semple and Thomas O. Larkin. From Benicia, Fannie wrote her mother on May 19, 1851:

> This is a message of affection and love and Platon and the Captain join me. We are all well, thank God. Father's foot is nearly well. He gets about without a cane, up and down stairs. Platon has gotten over his case of boils. He hasn't gone to school because he was ill and also he spent the whole day with Papa on account of his lame foot.
>
> The village of Benicia is very gay, crowded. People come and go. Many soldiers and young ladies. They come from everywhere for the convention and the officials are building a platform for dancing.
>
> Sunday was very rainy and gloomy and I spent the whole day in my room reading.

Platon is very good company. We are frequently alone together in the house; every one goes his way, to his work and we stay here reading or playing the piano and when things get a bit lonely, suddenly the place is full of people, some visiting and others on business with the Captain. On Saturday 'Old Lady Shannon' was here. And she no sooner laid eyes on me than she began showering me with kisses. Then Papa began rapidly counting them up, "one for your Aunt, for Adela, for Natalia, for Benecita, Napoleon, Jovita and Ula" all of which he rattled off in a jiffy. He was right in front of me during all this kissing and making all manner of faces. He out did the old gal in foolishness. General Green sends greetings. Excuse my bad writing.

The letter was written in Spanish as are most of the Vallejo family letters.

The convention to which Fannie referred was the first Democratic State Convention in California. It was held in the Episcopal Church and nominated John Bigler for Governor on the sixth ballot. General John Bidwell was a delegate. Fannie's father and her husband were both members of the Democratic party. Frisbie, with his legal training and affable manners, had easily made friends with the California politicians.

After the Legislature moved the Capital the first time from Vallejo to Sacramento, Frisbie, a natural lobbyist, went to Sacramento to see what he could do to help his father-in-law. On March 31, 1852 he wrote Vallejo:

There is now a fair prospect of bringing the Vallejo business to a conclusion; the present indications are that the capital will go back and you released from your bond. A concurrent resolution passed the Assembly this morning, directing the Archives back to Vallejo after the close of the present session. Tomorrow we shall try the resolution cancelling the bond and I have no doubt that it will pass. Whatever is done, I think will be without delay.

The Legislature returned to Vallejo, only to move to Benicia for a session before returning to Sacramento permanently. Incidentally, among General Vallejo's first expenditures for establishing the capital at Vallejo was the sum of $98,450.00, one item being salary of John B. Frisbie, $1,200.00

FANNIE'S FIRST BABY

To the John B. Frisbies on July 29, 1852 was born a son who received the name of Mariano Guadalupe after Fannie's father. The infant was baptized in Sonoma, but not until January 30th, 1853, with Fannie's uncle, Juan Antonio Vallejo, serving as godfather, and her sister Adela del Refugio as godmother. The baby had been ill. His father wrote General Vallejo on January 11th:

Guadalupe is so very unwell as to render it impossible for me to visit Sonoma as there are many matters that I want to confer with you personally . . . Fany is well though much worn from the constant anxiety about our little boy; the Dr. however tells us that we have nothing to apprehend and that his sickness is nothing more than that always experienced by children in teething. We cannot however refrain from feeling the most anxious solicitude as the little fellow has never had a single sick hour.

Now that the Frisbies had started a family, he was more than anxious to provide financial security for it. His father-in-law's affairs needed prodding, such as the collection of some notes held by Vallejo. December 17, 1852 Frisbie had written Vallejo regarding one case:

"... they informed me that they will take them up. I will advise you of their payment soon as made which I have no doubt will be as promised in a few days as hay is now bringing 75 and 80 dollars a ton and they cannot have less than 800 or 1,000 tons on hand ... Upon the subject of the purchase of five thousand acres of land from Mrs. Mark West, let me suggest that Mr. Judah and myself join you in taking one half and you the other; the law business connected with it, to be transacted without charge. We also, advancing the five thousand dollars for the payment of her debts. Should you accept the proposition, please inform me of the same by return mail. The proposition I think highly favorable to yourself as you are not required to incurr any outlay of money or vexation, all this being assumed by us. We looking only to the property for our ultimate payment. I would like to know if the property was acquired by West [Mark West] after his marriage with Dona Guadalupe, if so, she is entitled to one half in her own right and we can get a good title without waiting for an administration of the estate by taking from her a deed for an undivided half or ten thousand acres.

In the spring of 1853, when Lupe (as the Frisbie baby was called) was not quite a year old, he and his parents sailed on the *Golden Age* for New York. With them was twelve-year-old Platon, who was on his way to join his brother Andronico at school at Emmettsburg, Maryland. Vallejo and his daughter Adela saw them off from San Francisco. While on board, Frisbie wrote to his father-in-law:

An opportunity offers in consequence of our touching at San Diego of dropping you a line. Fany and Platon are recovering from their seasickness; the baby has given us no trouble at all ... At Monterey we had an opportunity of seeing for a moment Juan Antonio ... Williamson who is a fellow passenger tells me he has left with his brother, the Doctor, three thousand dollars as a first payment on a thousand acres of land in Petaluma; the balance to be paid in six months with ten percent interest. Should they pay that amount, I think you would do well to sell.

In turn Fannie's father wrote to Frisbie on March 21, 1853:

It is eight o'clock in the morning and we are eating breakfast in the dining room and thinking of you, Fanita and Platon who are now at the port of Acapulco. After I said farewell to you in San Francisco, I returned with Adela to the city full of sadness, thinking of your journey ... the only thing to cheer me up was the hope of your arriving safely in N.Y. and meeting there Andronico and your lady mother and your Doctor brother ... to whom I beg you to give my affectionate regards, also from my family. My esteem is unlimited; I always feel a deep affection, especially for the persons I love with all my heart. Fanita is always my favorite daughter. She has exceptional qualities, if allowed to develop wisely. With training, she will be the joy and happiness to you and your family for which I advise you not to overlook this important subject ... When you introduce her into society, I am proud that she has a background and will know her position in the new society in which she will enter.

In closing his letter, Vallejo sent a thousand kisses to *M. G. Frisbie.*

THE FRISBIES IN NEW YORK

When Frisbie arrived in New York, he interviewed Mr. Aspinwall relative to the Vallejo property on the Soscol Rancho, which Frisbie believed he would have sold for $50,000 had not Bissell and Billings advised Aspinwall to delay buying it until such time as Vallejo would need money. Aspinwall offered $30,000 for the property; Frisbie refused. He was satisfied that if Vallejo would play their own game of assumed indifference, their appetite would become sharpened. "Great efforts," he wrote his father-in-law, "are being made here in behalf of the Benicia and Marysville Railroad and I am strongly inclined to the belief that they will succeed in raising the capital necessary for the construction of the road, this, and the generous progress and improvement of the country is daily enhancing the value of Soscol." On Sept. 5th, 1853 Frisbie wrote again to Vallejo:

I write you for the last time from this side of the Atlantic as it is our intention to return by the Steamer on the 20th and with an ordinary passage, we shall be in S.F. by the 12th Proximo. Since my last letter we have received yours containing the pleasing intelligence of the birth of our little sister Benicia and the marriage of Felicidad, for both events, which we tender our hearty congratulations. Andronico and Platon have been spending their vacation with us and returned but yesterday to their school. They are both in excellent health.

On the day the Frisbies were supposed to leave New York, Frisbie wrote again to his father-in-law:

I fully expected when I last wrote you that I would be the bearer of my own tidings by this steamer but important business connected with the settlement of my father's little estate rendered it indispensable that I remain until the next steamer. I have done nothing with the powers of attorney you gave me as I find no purchaser of the Vallejo or Petalumi property at anything like what I consider its value. Mr. Aspinwall will give $30,000 for the Vallejo property; this offer he keeps open until I have an opportunity of seeing you.

That Fannie made a favorable impression on her husband's relatives is apparent from the letter his sister, Cynthia, gave him to accompany a gift which she wished presented to General Vallejo:

"Will you accept the accompanying volume as a slight token of gratitude and affection I entertain towards you for your kindness to my beloved brother when a stranger in a strange land. I thank him for the dear sister he has given us and 'tis with a full heart we have this morning as she starts for her own native land. God guard and keep them and in due time restore them in health and safety to your arms. They bear with them the tenderest affection of our hearts. We hope ere long, dear General, to see you in New York.

We have a strong attraction here while we retain your boys [Andronico and Platon]. With much love to your good Lady and daughters."

A few months after the Frisbies returned to California they moved from Benicia to San Francisco where they boarded with Thomas Larkin's family on Stockton Street. At this time, the spring of 1854, one of Larkin's neighbors was James King of William who lived directly across the street. While there, Frisbie wrote his father-in-law:

I had hoped to have seen you in person, but upon the whole it was well you did not come down as the celebration of the Fourth was rather a tame affair or to use your favorite and forceful expression—a humbug. I have no doubt you enjoyed yourselves much more in your paradise of a home then you possible could have done in the noise, confusion, dust, fog, wind and smoke of San Francisco . . . You can not imagine my impatience to breathe once more even if it be but a few hours the pure atmosphere of Sonoma.

The Frisbies' next move was to the city of Vallejo which had recently been abandoned as the seat of California's government, and which General Vallejo and Frisbie had decided to develop into a commercial center. The General had given power-of-attorney to his son-in-law, trusting him with his business affairs and Frisbie had, in turn, great admiration for Vallejo. In a letter dated April 9, 1857, he expressed his regard:

I read with great pleasure the letter of O'Farrell [Jasper O'Farrell] which you had the kindness to enclose. Such proofs of friendship and esteem from those who have known you long and well, are peculiarly grateful at a time when many are prompted by mean and mercenary motives to blast the enviable fame which your life of distinguished public service has so well earned but General, you will outlive these vile calumnies, the record of your life will command the respect it so pre-eminently merits and your name will stand prominent among those distinguished as benefactors and patriotic servants of the state.

I regretted sincerely to hear of Mr. Cooke's [Martin E. Cooke] illness. I hope you will write me every day with regard to his health. Should he be no better by Sunday, Fany and myself will come over to assist in nursing him. I hope however a day or two will bring him out again but I beg you, you will not fail to let me know how he gets along.

Mr. Cooke failed to recover and was given burial in the Vallejo family cemetery.

LIFE'S PENDULUM — JOY AND SORROW

The Frisbies' second child, a daughter, so welcome, had been born on December 3rd, 1855. The infant was named *Fannie* for her mother and *Natalia* for her aunt. She became known as "little Fannie" or Fanita. The joy of possessing a baby girl was soon dimmed by the death of four-year-old Mariano Guadalupe [Lupe] on June 6, 1856 at the White Sulphur Springs developed by Frisbie in Napa Valley; only the day before Lupe seemed to be improving. Present at the little boy's bedside were his mother and father, his uncles, Dr. Levi Frisbie, Andronico and Platon Vallejo; his aunt Natalia, his paternal grandmother, Cynthia Cornell Frisbie from New York; his maternal grandmother, Senora Vallejo, with her four-month-old daughter Luisa in her arms. Present also was the heartbroken maternal grandfather, who wrote in his journal: "O Lupe, Lupe, Lupe, no one was appreciated more by your grandfather than you. You are in Heaven and we are left in this world of corruption and wickedness and your little sister is left in the valley of tears."

The Episcopalian Reverend John L. Ver Mehr, master of the Sonoma girls' school, St. Mary's Hall, read the funeral service as the regular Catholic priest was not in Sonoma. The little body was laid to rest in the Vallejo family vault in the gardens of the Casa Grande, before being taken to Vallejo for permanent burial.

On October 1, 1857 a little sister for Fanita Frisbie was born and was named *Cynthia Benicia* for her two grandmothers. Two years later another sister, Mary Pamelia, often called Minnie, arrived on the world scene, August 8, 1859. A year later Frisbie felt the need to go to New York. His wife insisted on going with the family, so Natalia was taken to help look after the little Frisbie girls. They sailed on the *Golden Age* in October 1860. During the voyage Frisbie wrote Vallejo:

> I can not but express my deep regret of being compelled to leave California with my family without your paternal benedictions. The circumstances have impressed me with a sadness which I find impossible to shake off, for if there be a person on earth for whom I entertain a sincere affection, it is yourself and it ever has been and ever will be a cherished object with me to merit yours in return.
>
> We are making good progress in our voyage but are all suffering from seasickness so much am I under the dreadful malady that I find it a very difficult task to write . . . Should I be successful in my mission to Washington I believe I shall be able to negotiate at Eastern rates of interest a sufficient amount of money to pay the debts. In the meantime if you will name a sum which you require monthly for yourself I think I can provide it for you so that you may receive it promptly for yourself during my absence by remittance from New York. The present revenue of our property will give over and above taxes and expenses about ten thousand dollars per annum. I hope you will find it convenient to drop me a line per Pony Express . . . so that I may receive it upon my arrival. Permit me in conclusion to bid you an affectionate farewell.

During this journey a heavy storm, which lasted twenty-four hours, not only confined all the members of the Frisbie party to their staterooms but gave Fannie a fever: Reporting her condition home she wrote, "I was awfully sick but that was nothing, say those who don't get seasick but I was sick, it was bad for me. We arrived in New York on the *Northern Light*." Soon after their arrival, Captain Frisbie got in touch with Platon and was happy to report to the family in California that Platon and Ula, who were attending school in New York, were in good health and doing well in their studies . . . On November 3, 1860, Frisbie wrote Vallejo:

We arrived here yesterday, after a rather rough but otherwise pleasant voyage: . . . Our wheat speculation promises exceedingly well. I was to have been introduced at the corn exchange today but it being a wet day (the rain absolutely pouring) I determined to defer it until Monday, as there would then probably be a much larger attendance. I am inclined to sell here as there are many English buyers in the market, they pay Liverpool rates, less charges. As soon as I sell I shall make you a remittance. The shipment of this cargo has given me a standing in financial circles here which I feel confident will enable me to negotiate funds upon highly adventageous terms.

My prospects at Washington I believe to be good and I look with confidence to a speedy realization of those hopes we have so long labored to obtain. Harkins writes me from Liverpool that he has no difficulty in buying iron for our road at greatly reduced rates, paying for it in the bonds of the country at eighty-five cents. The cars we can get here upon the same terms. The loan has not yet been effected but he apprehends no difficulty in this particular.

It is my honest conviction, General, that here is an immense fortune almost within our grasp; up to the present moment we have been going up stream but the tide is manifestly getting in our favor and when I meet you again I believe I shall be received with not merely a friendly but a warm paternal embrace as the reward of years of fidelity to our common interests . . . In my next, I hope to be able to inform you that the appeal in the Soscol Case has been dismissed. I shall write you again as soon as I shall have had an interview with the Atty General. The remittance to which I refer, you may look for in about a month . . . The only news I hear aside from what I have written which could be of interest to you is Political, the details of which you will get from the papers but it may be summed up in four words—LINCOLN WILL BE PRESIDENT.

With the election of Lincoln, the outgoing Buchanan Administration took no further action in the Soscol matter. On Washington's birthday, Frisbie wrote Vallejo: "I regret to inform you that the political complications upon this side are of a most embarrassing nature and have effectually prevented me from consummating the leading objects of my mission here. I leave here [New York] on the 25th for Washington to make one last effort with the outgoing Administration for Soscol . . . I shall have no difficulty in raising money as soon as I can obtain the order for a dismissal of the Appeal unless our State [California] should become inoculated with the Spirit of secession. Such an event would alarm Northern Capitalists who now regard us with great favor, in consequence of our remote position from the scene of Revolution."

The spring of 1861 was made memorable for the Frisbies and Natalia Vallejo by their attendance at the Inaugural Ball of President Lincoln. It was called the "Union Ball" and was held on March 4th. A few weeks later (April 19th), Fannie wrote to her mother from the Continental Hotel in Philadelphia:

I have not written you because we were hoping to leave on each ship but John can't leave due to his business in Washington. Within two or three weeks I expect to have another little one. I believe you weren't expecting the news so soon. Natalia is more apprehensive than I. She says it looks she is to be mid-wife . . . I can't write much because the noise of the soldiers and the drums in the hotel which is full of troops, men and women going to war. It seems that John is going to be a soldier again. I think that had it not been that I am ill he would have already have gone as an officer. The people are so excited that they don't know what they are doing.

Fannie's baby came on May 4th. There was some disappointment as it was another girl. She was given the name Sarah Monica, and was destined to be the most beautiful of the Frisbie daughters.

On June 18th, Frisbie wrote Vallejo: "I have just returned from Washington and have only time to say previous to the departure of the Pony that I sail with my family for California on Friday and shall probably reach California within a week from the receipt of this. It is doubtful whether I take any order for the dismissal of Soscol. I hope however to do so."

The Frisbie family accompanied by Natalia left New York on the *North Star* and were comfortably situated with four staterooms. The entire voyage was pleasant, the weather calm, fare sumptuous and the ship officers courteous and attentive.

GOVERNOR STANFORD APPOINTS FRISBIE A GENERAL

In the early 1860s, Fannie's husband began shipping wheat to Liverpool, England, on the ship *Oracle*. It was the first cargo of wheat to pass out of the Golden Gate and it was raised in Vallejo, California. Other shipments followed. One shipment got only as far as San Francisco where Frisbie sold the entire cargo, making a profit of $7,000. It was about this time that Leland Stanford, who had studied law in the same law office with Frisbie in New York State, became governor of California. On January 10, 1862, he appointed Captain John B. Frisbie adjutant-general of the State of California and Commander-in-Chief of the militia. Frisbie commented on the appointment to his brother-in-law, Platon Vallejo, "The only personal item is my appointment by the Governor to a Brigadier Generalship but as this relates only to the militia I do not feel much elated. I have been so long familiar with my old title, that I part with it with something like the reluctance I should experience leaving a companion of years."

Another trip East appeared to Frisbie to be advisable. There had been much Squatter trouble, even threats upon his life, and he was only too glad to leave California for awhile. This time he was leaving his wife at home and taking her father with him. It was now the "two Generals." They left San Francisco on the *Constitution* on January 4, 1865. Once again in New York, Frisbie took his father-in-law everywhere, trying to impress him with the wonders of his own native land. During this visit Vallejo wrote to his wife that he had heard that their daughter Fannie had given birth to a son (her third) on March 30, 1865. The second son, John Bernard, had been born on

April 17, 1863. The new baby was named Luis Platon, and the infant's godparents were Dr. Platon Vallejo and Fanita Frisbie, the baby's oldest sister who was not quite ten years old.

General John B. Frisbie had become the leading citizen of Vallejo. He was persuaded to become the nominee of the Union Party for the Assembly of the State Legislature. He was elected as the representative of Solano County and served one two-year term from December 2, 1867 to March 30, 1868. He did not seek re-election.

ADMIRAL FARRAGUT RETURNS TO MARE ISLAND

It was the month of August, 1869 that Admiral David Glasgow Farragut and his wife Virginia Loyall Farragut revisited the scene of the Admiral's first command at Mare Island which extended from September 16, 1854 to July 16, 1858. Briefly, the acquisition of the island which had received its name from General Vallejo's mare which had strayed from the herd and lived there among the elks, had come about as follows: In 1850, John B. Frisbie and his associates purchased Mare Island, offshore from the future city of Vallejo, from the original grantee, Victor Castro, for $7,000 and subsequently sold it for $17,500 to Aspinwall and Bissell of New York. The New Yorkers sold it in 1853 to the United States Government for $83,491 for a Navy Yard. Before the money was received from the government, William Stewart, the Washington, D.C., attorney for Thomas Larkin, advised him there was a possibility that Mare Island might be included in the Huichica Rancho adjoining Sonoma, a grant which Larkin had acquired from Jacob P. Leese. W. H. Aspinwall of the Pacific Mail wrote a letter of protest to Larkin saying, "I am informed that objection is being made to paying for Mare Island, recently sold to the Government in consequence of allegations by yourself and Col. Stewart that there is an older grant than Castros. I think there must be some mistake. I made the sale under the title derived from General Vallejo . . . Let me know if you doubt his right to give such a title?"

Shortly before, August of 1869, Fannie's sister Adela, who also lived in Vallejo, wrote to her mother: "Another piece of news I have not mentioned is that the *Generala* will soon have another baby in August; this I believe is why now she is so difficult to get along with." This would be Fannie's ninth child.

On Monday evening, August first, 1869, the City Fathers of the town of Vallejo met to make plans for welcoming the "brave old Tar." Admiral Farragut arrived the next day on the steamer *The New World* and a large cavalcade escorted him and his wife to the home of John and Fannie Frisbie where speeches of welcome were made. In response, the hero of Mobile Bay indicated that he felt his life was behind him and all that he wanted was a good rest.

The official visit to Mare Island was made on August 11th with Frisbie;

Farragut, the Navy's first Admiral, was given a 17-gun salute. Farragut also went to Sonoma to visit his old friend General Vallejo.

When the Frisbies' child, arriving on August 12, proved to be a boy, his parents decided to name him David Farragut after their recent distinguished guest. The two David Farraguts, both with Scotch and Spanish ancestors, died within a few years of each other; the Admiral in August, 1870 and the little David Farragut Frisbie in April 1874.

TRANSCONTINENTAL JOURNEY

In September 1869, shortly after the transcontinental railroad had been completed, the Frisbie family made the trip across the United States in company with General Vallejo. The General was a great help with the Frisbie family who then numbered eight; five girls, Fanita, 14 years old, Benicia, 12 years, Pamela or Minnie, 10 years, Sarah Monico, 8 years, Josefina, 2 years; and three boys, John Bernardo, 6 years, Luis Platon, 4 years, and the baby David Farragut, one month old.

Upon the family's arrival in the East, Fannie rented a house at 15 Elk Street in Albany, New York, opposite a park where her children often played. The older ones attended a Catholic school. Little David became ill with a mastoid infection which frightened Fannie, as she recalled that her mother had lost Plutarco, a three-month-old baby, with the same disease.

Fannie's husband spent the entire winter of 1869–70 lobbying in Washington. He urged upon the attention of members of Congress matters of vital importance to the town of Vallejo and Mare Island, particularly in making Vallejo a port of entry and Mare Island a first-class Navy Yard. Capitalists were also interviewed and financial aid secured for the Marysville Railroad which was to terminate at Vallejo.

General Frisbie returned to California in April 1870, leaving his family in Albany. As the train pulled into Sacramento he was met by a delegation from the city of Vallejo, and, upon reaching Vallejo itself, he received another welcome from members of the Society of the Vallejo Pioneers, an organization of which he was president. The Vallejo Rifles and the Frisbie Guards were also among the groups which escorted him to his home on Georgia Street. Genuinely pleased, Frisbie invited them all to come to his house that evening at eight o'clock. Champagne flowed profusely; toasts were drunk, and speeches made to honor Frisbie as Vallejo's first citizen and former legislator—the man most intimately identified with the progress of the town.

Senora Vallejo had been keeping house in the Frisbie mansion while the family was in the East, and she had written Fannie of the plans for the homecoming of her husband:

> Today, Palm Sunday, we are waiting for your husband. Everybody is excited because he is coming. All are coming to meet him at the station, soldiers, music, all the town . . . John arrived well and was well received by every one . . . I don't want

to return to Sonoma where there are no doctors to care for me and here in Vallejo are all my children. Yes, I can stay here while the girls are in school. They have a week's vacation; very soon they'll return to school, Luisa and Maria . . . Dear Fanny, your house and all you left here, I take care of it the best I can. If you want me to continue taking care of it, tell me and if you don't want me to; tell me.

Fannie replied on April 30, 1870, "I am glad you like to live in Vallejo. It is a happy little village, a little ugly but it surely pleases everybody, particularly us, its founders. How I would like to have been with you when John arrived. It is the first time they have received him with affection."

The latter part of April, 1870, Frisbie found it necessary to return to New York and Washington, D.C. He invited Fannie's mother to accompany him. As previously told, she accepted and had a most interesting and enjoyable time.

JOHN B. FRISBIE'S ENTERPRISES

In 1872 through the boldness and energy of General John B. Frisbie, the town of Vallejo boasted a modern hotel, the Bernard House. Previous to its opening to the public Frisbie gave a house warming. At nine o'clock on Wednesday, August 7th, General Frisbie and his lady received a host of friends and invited guests in the parlor. A San Francisco band played favorite airs while another under the leadership of W. H. Emmons entertained in the public parlor. At twelve o'clock supper, a profusion of delicacies, was served on tables with cut crystals and silverware dazzling in the gas light.

Mr. L. C. Fowler proposed a toast to their generous host and hostess. General Vallejo was called upon for a few words; he "commenced his remarks by alluding to his deficiency in the pronunciation of the English language, and intimated that his ideas would be given in Spanish, but warming with his subject, he seemed totally to forget his mother tongue, and gave the party a most excellent discourse in pure unadulterated Anglo-Saxon. His reminiscences of the early settlement of this section of the State were interesting in the extreme. Colonel McAllister responded to the usual toast to the Army and said he hoped to live to see the day when Benicia and Vallejo, now twin sisters in generous rivalry, would be one broad expansive city." To this General Vallejo concurred.

At this time the Frisbies were living in their second home in Vallejo—a handsome mansion of two floors with a large attic on the third. It took up almost a square at Virginia and Sutter streets, and was surrounded by gardens of flowers, luxuriant shrubbery and trees. It was no effort for Fannie to entertain, as the Frisbies had many servants, including personal maids, a cook, coachman, governess and gardener. The latter was Old Sam, who was often seen with his lame, shrunken, Indian-rubber leg, walking about "chewing on an old stump of a segar and squirting the juice upon the beautiful flowers."

It was the sudden dismissal of these servants in the early fall of 1876 which caused the fearful depositors of the *Vallejo Savings and Commercial Bank* to withdraw such large amounts that Frisbie, who was president, had to close its doors. This financial misfortune was partly caused by Frisbie's promotion of the railroad between Marysville and Vallejo and also his speculation in mining stocks.

Much of General Vallejo's holdings, which Frisbie was managing, were lost. Vallejo said, "Frisbie should not have risked or jeopardized what was not his, neither in his speculation nor in stocks." To Fannie he wrote:

Dona Carmelita Dominguez has just told me that you have suffered losses and that you haven't a cent, etc. If it is so, my house is at your entire disposal without reservation. I know nothing nor has John told me, not a small word, so I think there is some exaggeration. Neither can I believe (in case it is partly true that all my property that I have in the hands of Frisbie on trust and of which I receive $250 a month interest on $30,000 in money, besides the interest in the land and dwelling have been lost in the speculation in the bank failure. Above all, know that you have a refuge. I'm happy to receive you under my roof and we can be together again.

Your Papa,
MARIANO G. VALLEJO

The shock of losing his fortune caused Fannie's husband to become ill, but he soon rallied and was busy making plans to visit New York with money supplied by Patrick Lynch, the second husband of his sister Cynthia who had been the widow of Reverend Charles Van Loon. On November 30, 1876, Frisbie wrote to Vallejo, telling him of his plans:

Since I last wrote you I have been ill and still am quite ill; the pressure of necessity has however kept me upon my feet. I wrote to Mr. Lynch in regard to my Mexican project. As soon as he received my letter, he telegraphed to me not to engage in it but to come East as soon as possible . . . I was compelled to reply that I had not the means to make the trip. A few days since I received a draft from him to pay expenses and a letter urging me to come on with as little delay as possible. I shall therefore start on Saturday and shall probably be absent for a month. By a close squeeze I am able to send you $100. Would to God it were as many thousands. I know you must be in great need of money and it grieves me to the heart that it is not in my power to provide it for you.

Upon my return to California, I shall be prepared to determine some action in regard to my future . . . There are chances to make money here and in the East and I shall relax no effort until I am master of some one of them for I can have no peace of mind until I see you and my family in the possession of competence.

I almost feel that my late financial disaster in compelling me to abandon the hopeless task of building up Vallejo against the overwhelming influences which have combined to arrest its development, will accrue to my advantage, in-as-much as it leaves me free to employ my energies in any field of enterprise that is within my grasp and that my judgment inclines. The difficulty of re-establishing myself without capital, I fully realize, yet with health and the blessings of God, I am sure I can overcome it.

FRISBIE AND VALLEJO VISIT MEXICO

On Frisbie's return from his Eastern trip, he confided to Vallejo of his intention to visit Mexico in regard to an extensive railway scheme. As it had been a desire of long standing on the part of General Vallejo to visit Mexico, the native land of his father, he decided to accompany his son-in-law.

A rumor was started, by newspapers notorious for sensational fiction, that General Vallejo and General Frisbie were going to Mexico to work for the annexation of a part of that country to the United States. The San Francisco *Alta* commented on these reports: "Frisbie and Vallejo are men of too much intelligence to meddle with an annexation scheme as a private enterprise and they have no authority from the Administration with which they do not sympathize politically. Both are Democrats and neither have the least chance of being employed, even if the President favored annexation."

Frisbie and Vallejo arrived in Mexico in May, 1877. Soon after their arrival in Mexico City, Frisbie wrote to Senor Matias Romero, Minister of the Mexican Treasury, whom Frisbie and Vallejo had met some years before in Washington, D.C. Frisbie's letter ran as follows:

I would be pleased to have an interview with you at such a time as will be most convenient to yourself to discuss the practicability of certain business projects in connection with this country which I have in contemplation. There are also certain political matters of importance and interest in regard to which I should like to have your views.

Senor Romero replied that he would be happy to receive him. The prospects in Mexico immediately impressed Frisbie. He became increasingly anxious to return to his own country where contacts could be made with certain capitalists and where steps might be taken to promote the recognition of President Diaz by the United States. General Vallejo refused to leave with him because of the virulence of Yellow Fever at Vera Cruz, the port of departure. On September 26th, 1877, Vallejo wrote to Frisbie:

Dear John:

I am absolutely resolved through fear of nothing less than death itself, not to go to Vera Cruz for the ship. The same fear assails me in respect to you since you have a large family which also belongs to me. I should regret exceedingly for them to be deprived of two fathers. My conscience compels me to make these reflections to you. It is preferable to avoid this dismal result than want to remedy it when there is no remedy for it!!! How sad a fate to remain buried in a strange soil. What a sad and terrible affliction for our chilren and for all our mutual and beloved family.

I repeat to you, my conscience orders it of me and my duty demands it. If you persist in going by Vera Cruz and if (God forbid) misfortune assails you, I shall have done my duty by trying to avoid it.

I hope that the Supreme Being will keep you safe and sound and to give an account of your mission wherever it may be, regretting in my soul that I could not accompany you for the reasons given. I shall give an account to our families of our trip to this country which is so fabulously rich-poor.

From the Hotel Comonfort (named for a former Mexican president), Vallejo sent a copy of the above letter to his son Platon with the following comment: "I am sending you the attached copy of my objections so if some misfortune happens to Frisbie because of his insistence of going via Vera Cruz during the time the Yellow Fever is reeking such havoc, that the whole family will see that I tried to prevent it. Frisbie is very stubborn, almost obstinate; he says he has no fear and a thousand other foolish things." No misfortune happened to Frisbie and he returned safely to the United States.

In 1883, when Hubert H. Bancroft was visiting Frisbie in Mexico, Frisbie told him the following story: "I came down here [Mexico] with General Vallejo . . . I made the acquaintance of General Diaz and talked with him freely. There was no diplomatic relations between the two governments. Our Administration refused to recognize Diaz as the Executive of Mexico. I told Diaz that I was thoroughly in sympathy with him, that our Government was wrong and that I would go to Washington to see what I could do. I said that I did not want any commission from him but if he thought it prudent to give me a letter, I would tender my services if they could be made effective."

"On arriving in the United States I proceeded immediately to Washington . . . I called upon the Mexican agent [Mr. Mata] and found him busy packing his trunks to leave. He was discouraged and felt that war was eminent . . . He had been treated with marked discourtesy by the Administration and intended to leave. The first American I went to see was Gorham who was the Secretary of the Senate. . . . I explained to him the state of affairs. He said 'Frisbie, you can not stop any thing, there is going to be war . . .' "

I set to work with the Pacific Delegations from California, Oregon and Nevada and they with very little reluctance adopted my views of the question and made cause for Mexico."

"A prominent member of Congress from Onondaga County, New York was a personal friend of mine and exceedingly close to Senator Roscoe Conkling (N.Y.). He arranged an interview with the Senator and myself. It was to be at midnight, the Senator being so occupied that I could not see him any other time. I went to his hotel and we discussed the matter until the small hours of the morning . . . He introduced a Resolution in the Senate, asking for the appointment of a Commission to look into Mexican affairs . . . A similar committee was appointed in the House."

Frisbie appeared before Conkling's Committee and after a lengthy examination took the train for California for the holidays to be with his family. However he hastened back to the Capital to continue the battle. He received an intimation direct from the White House that the Diaz Government would be recognized. Frisbie, regarding it as authentic, went to New York and telegraphed the news to General Diaz.

While in Washington, Frisbie was interviewed at the Arlington Hotel. He gave a glowing account of the possibilities awaiting development in Mexico and he concluded his interview by saying that he planned to return to California to adjust his affairs. That accomplished he would return to Mexico with his family to engage in business.

Frisbie had confided some of his plans to his father-in-law while both were in Mexico whereupon Vallejo had written home: "Frisbie is planning to return to Mexico with all his family to recuperate what he has lost. Mexico has vast lands but to make money it is necessary to have capital or credit. I believe it is good for Frisbie but I do not believe it is for his family."

The Frisbie family had consisted of twelve children; of the seven daughters and five sons, all but three lived to maturity. The children lost during childhood were, as stated before: Mariano Guadalupe, the first born who died in 1856, and the two who died in the spring of 1874—Cecilia, a golden-haired three-year-old, and the five-year-old David Farragut.

The eldest daughter, Fanita Natalia, had been married in Vallejo, California, on September 23, 1875 to Antonio de Sequeira, scion of an ancient family of Portugal and an employee of the bank of which Frisbie was president. As a bride she had been gowned in white satin with a train, while a veil of tule with orange blossoms covered her head. The wedding occurred before Frisbie's financial crash; consequently an elaborate reception at the family mansion had followed the wedding ceremony at St. Vincent's Church.

Frisbie Leaves for Mexico

On January 22, 1878, Frisbie with the children left Vallejo, California, for Chicago en route to Mexico. The *Vallejo Rifles* and a delegation from the *Vallejo Pioneer Society* escorted him to the depot where he spoke a few words in parting; the scene was mutually affecting. Fannie and her eldest daughter left later with General Vallejo going to San Francisco to bid them farewell. The morning of March 21, 1878, he wrote Fannie's mother:

> Fannie the elder and Fannie the younger left this morning to be re-united with Frisbie (and the children) in Chicago and from there they will go to New Orleans on the way to Mexico. Last night until one A.M. we were together in some rooms wherein came many relatives on both sides to say goodbye . . . When the moment of parting came, Fannie could not control herself and threw herself in my arms sobbing . . . She charged me with tears to bid you goodbye, recommending you to God. In all it was a tender scene . . . This morning all of us accompanied them on the Ferry to Oakland where the train got ready to leave; the sorrowful scene was repeated.

Fannie sent her mother a postcard from Omaha, saying that they were all well and that they hadn't seen a green thing since leaving California.

Frisbie in Mexico

At the time the Frisbies moved to Mexico, the President of the country informed General Frisbie that his household property would be exempt from duty, but when the goods reached the Mexican border, the Custom officials put a tariff on them of nearly $4,000. President Diaz, who was fond of Frisbie, saw to it that the Mexican Congress passed an Act admitting Frisbie's household goods free of duty.

Through his friendship with President Porfirio Diaz and his own Yankee sagacity, Frisbie became a millionaire, as well as a figure of importance in the city of Mexico. He was a charter member of the American Club and was largely instrumental as we know in securing recognition of the Diaz regime by the United States Government.

December 1879, almost two years after going to Mexico, Frisbie was in New York to sell bonds in his mining company, one fourth of which had been subscribed. He wrote to Fannie's father from the Windsor Hotel, saying that she and the children were well and that there was another little Sequeira, a sister for "Agosto," "Juanita" who he said, was a beauty. Frisbie wrote further:

I have been here since the 7th ult. and I should have written you ere this but for pending negotiations and which I have been expecting from day to day to close and which if it is consummated will place me in a good financial position and enable me to lift the burden of poverty from your shoulders as well as my own. I deem my share in *El Oro* and *Real del Monte* Mines well worth a million dollars, as soon as I can command adequate machinery to utilize the immense ore bodies we have in sight.

I hope the balance (bonds) will be taken before the time for my departure. If so, my troubles will be over, the proceeds will give me the means of paying for the mine and an eighty stamp mill with which I can earn net, monthly $36,000. The mill will be in operation about the first of July.

I return home by way of Havana. Gen'l Grant and family will join the ship there and go to Vera Cruz. I think I shall be able to induce him to visit our mines some time during his stay in Mexico. We have a good house and will be able to make him quite comfortable.

Another visit to the United States and Frisbie writes to Vallejo in April of 1883:

It is about two months since I left Mexico. During the interval I have heard frequently from Fanny and the children . . . I came with President Diaz and have been with him most of the time during his visit to the United States. We sail this morning for Vera Cruz in the same steamer (City of Mexico) that took you and me six years ago . . . In about fifteen months railroad connections will be established between the cities of San Francisco and Mexico.

Bernardo [son] graduates in June, he is a fine scholar and a splendid boy. Although but twenty years old, he stands six feet in his stockings. After a short vacation he will enter upon his business career. I have secured him a position with a salary of $1,200 a year. Sarah will be married in October next, to Mr. Morgan from South Carolina. He is of good family, a thorough business man and has a capital of $25,000 . . . Mexico is making (for her) rapid progress. I am still in the employ of the Huntington-Stanford Railway.

A letter dated June 27, 1884, reports further, regarding the mines which Frisbie and James B. Haggan had been developing. "The mining properties in which I am interested are doing well but a heavy debt has been incurred for mill and machinery. This is being paid by the profits now made consequently I have no income from this quarter and can expect none for a year. My chief reliance is therefore upon my salary I am receiving from the Railroad Company. Working up hill at my time of life and that in a foreign country is not jolly and I must confess that at times I experience difficulty in restraining feelings of discouragement."

MARRIAGE OF SARAH MONICA FRISBIE

Sarah Monica Frisbie, considered to be the most attractive of the Frisbie girls, was married to Joseph La Motte Morgan of Georgetown, South Carolina, by the Archbishop of Mexico in his private chapel on June 28, 1883. The bridegroom was a son of P. H. Morgan, American Minister to Mexico. The twenty-two-year-old bride was gowned in white satin with train and a tule veil. In accordance with Mexican custom there was a Padrino and Madrina as attendants. President Porfirio Diaz and his wife Dona Carmen Romero Rubio de Diaz serving in the roles.

The bride's mother, Fannie Vallejo de Frisbie, was dressed in a brown satin gown trimmed with black Spanish lace. Her bonnet matched the dress. Carmen Diaz (herself a bride of the previous year) was a daughter of Don Manuel Romero Rubio, president of the Mexican Senate. As befitting her station in life, Senora Diaz wore a gray velvet dress embroidered in red roses; on her head was draped a black lace mantilla and her jewels were magnificent diamonds.

The feminine guests wore "simple walking costumes." After the ceremony, because of a recent death in the family, a wedding breakfast was served at the bride's parents home, at Calle Nueva No. 6, instead of a reception.

Dona Carmen Diaz gave the bride a handsome diamond marquise ring while President Diaz presented the young couple with a pair of rare Chinese vases for their new home on Calle de Empedrallo. It was in this house during the fall of 1883 that they entertained Kate Bancroft who was visiting with her father, Hubert Howe Bancroft.

The house was not occupied long, as Sarah Monica and her husband (who had been secretary to his father) moved to Pueblo. Explaining their change of residence to General Vallejo, Frisbie wrote: "It was a grievous trial to part with her and I fear I shall never be reconciled to the separation. The only consoling reflection in connection with it, is that Mr. Morgan is devoted to her and able to provide for her in a comfortable manner, aside from this, he is an admiral companion, intelligent, moral and an experienced business man."

In two years Sarah Monica Morgan was back in Mexico City. The marriage, which had held promise for a bright future on that June morning in 1883, was tragically terminated on December 13, 1885. Frisbie, the heartbroken father, wrote Vallejo:

On Sunday the 13th I telegraphed to you the sad news of the death of our sweet and dearly beloved child, Sarah. This great affiiction came upon us suddenly and unexpectedly. She, however had, for several weeks, although in usual health, a presentment that she would not survive the birth of her child and was thoroughly prepared for the better land to which her pure spirit has flown but we who loved her so devotedly can hardly endure the thought that we shall never look upon her sweet face again. She passed away gently and with but little pain, retaining her reason and conversing with us almost to the last. Two days prior to her death she gave birth to a dead male child weighing 9½ pounds. Her first-born, a girl died last summer and was but six months old. Her poor husband who is a noble man is left desolate without wife or child and his wild sorrow aggravates my own and excites serious apprehension for his health.

FANNIE'S NOSTALGIA

Though Fannie had tried to adjust herself to life in Mexico City of the 1880s, there were many things she did not like and of which she wrote in detail to her father: "I am doing everything possible not to take root in this place. If you could see the streets . . . You haven't any idea how bad they are, I mean the stench we smell day and night, like living over a sewer. It is really the devil's intestines! Excuse me, Papa, for telling you these things." To her favorite brother, Platon, she expressed her feelings thus:

John has been very busy with his mines. Four days ago he went to Pachuca where he has some silver mines which he hopes will soon be prosperous and if not, you will see me very soon again in California. It is true we have a very comfortable house. How I wish all of you were dropping in, like Lily and all the family did in Vallejo. The days here seem like years to me.

It is impossible to tell you how sad I am. I cry every day and I'm almost blind with my eyes all red. John doesn't like to see me sad but it is impossible for me to be happy in this country. Tell Felipa and Francisca to pray to the Virgin that their Aunt Fannie should come to see them.

The Frisbie town house was located in the center of Mexico City on the street now called "Calle Luis Moya," and was directly opposite the present-day *Prince Hotel.* Twenty-five servants looked after Fannie's household. The numerous servants, each doing a different task, were under the direction of Fannie's eldest daughter, Fanita Sequeira, whose natural ability as a supervisor of formal living was such as to have her father remark, "Fanita, why not give us more food and less formality?"

Among the servants was a Chinese boy brought from California who figured in a family anecdote told to the author. General Frisbie had forbidden his wife to go to a bull fight. The refusal of her husband's permission piqued Fannie; this, and her Spanish heritage increased her desire to go. As a lady could not attend, unescorted, Fannie insisted that the Chinese servant act in this capacity. He wore his regular dark blue suit with his queue hanging down his back while Fannie wore one of her silk dresses with a mantilla on her head.

During the three acts of the bull fight Fannie sat spellbound; first the "Picadores" or horsemen with lances; then the Banderillo, the men carrying the colored ribbon-decorated barbed stick, which was quickly placed in the muscles of the bull; then the "muleta" or crucial stage, when a small red cloth or cape was carried on the Matador's sharp sword for the final killing of the bull. When this phase was reached, Fannie, absorbing the excitement of the crowd with their shouts of "Ole, Ole, Ole" threw her purse into the ring.

Besides the Frisbie's city residence, they had a hacienda "Careaga" some fifty miles from town, both of which took a great deal of money to maintain. This fact caused Frisbie some concern when he had to refuse financial assistance to his father-in-law. General Vallejo had been told by the City of Sonoma that he must replace the wooden pipes carrying his spring water into town, with iron pipes. Much as he wished to assist Vallejo, Frisbie felt obliged to reply on August 31, 1885:

I have received your letter of August 19th and it occasions me more pain than I can express that you doubt my disposition to do all in my power in your behalf. Independent of the salary I am receiving, I am absolutely without resources. The mining interests to which you refer have thus far been a burden to me rather than a source of income and but for the aid of my brother-in-law [Mr. Lynch] I should not have been able to carry the stock.

No man ever struggled harder than I have to make a success in my life; thirty years were wasted in California in contending at the peril of my life and expensive litigation with Squatters and in efforts to build up Vallejo. I am now well advanced in years and have nothing but my labor to depend upon, for the maintenance of my wife and children. This is a sad prospect and still more embittered by the reflection that you require aid, which is not in my power to render. I will however strive to save something from earnings from time to time. Enclose herewith a draft for $50.

Fifty dollars were sent by Frisbie to Vallejo from time to time and the remittances were faithfully entered in the General's account book. Pressed by James Mervyn Donahue to pay the note of $1,500 borrowed from his father, Colonel Peter Donahue, Vallejo wrote again asking Frisbie for help who replied on January 15, 1886:

Your favor of the fifth inst. I received this A.M. I am pained to say in reply that it is utterly impossible for me to send the money you desire. I have no property at my command to sell or borrow upon, were it otherwise I should be only too happy to avail myself of it to come to your relief.

I have however in hand for negotiation which will yield me if I succeed a commission that will enable me to comply with your request; a few weeks will determine and if my hopes are realized the pleasure I shall derive therefrom will be greatly enhanced by having it in my power to come to your aid and which you may feel assured, I shall promptly do.

Herewith you will find a draft for $50 payable to your order.

Very affectionately yours,
JOHN B. FRISBIE

A few days later Fannie wrote to her father:

John just told me that he sent you the fifty pesos. You probably have them by now. I would like to have a million, Papa dearest. Sometimes I ask Providence to be generous with me and there are times when I pray with so much fervor that I find myself peering in all the corners to see if 'the little sack of pesos' is there.

It isn't too good for me to think too much of home because doing so engulfs me in sadness. How unpleasant it is to have to live here where one doesn't want to. How I would like to be home at this very moment. We are going to have lunch. The table is a very long one. We have a very large and beautiful dining room. I would give anything if you and Mama were here to have soup with me . . . The children are arriving from school and surely make a racket. I so wish we could see each other. We are so apart dear Papa. The tears blind me and are spotting my reading glasses . . . John noticed me crying and asked me to whom I was writing. He said 'I suppose you are writing home and sending your tears as well as your heart.' If it were possible, I would enclose myself in this letter.

When deep spells of homesickness would seize Fannie, she seemed to find comfort and emotional release in writing as above to her father and as in the letter which follows:

Today I received your very nice letter of June 20th. It is so good for the soul to see the handwriting of my adored father. I kiss the precious words again and again and cry over them. Knowing that it is you who sends them. I so deeply yearn to be with you. Every day I think of my beloved Sonoma where there are so many I love and who loves me. It is terrible to be so far away. You know what it means to be sad, I think of you constantly.

I am entrusting Leo (15 years old) to you all. I am content to know he is among those who love him. Adela has him under her wing. I hope he isn't a bother. As you know all boys can be mischievous. Leo has always been a good little fellow. Now that he is on his own I don't know how he is behaving . . . I am glad to have him in California. I do hope that Leo does well in school. I believe Luis Platon (20 years old) soon will start off on a trip to the United States and says he surely hopes he gets to California.

Oh that little flower in your letter is peering at me and saying 'Not long ago I saw your father and mother, I just came from there.' Now I kiss the jasmine that came in your letter. I hope you can send me two or three seeds of the spiney locust. Everyone has been interested in the thorns you sent me.

To assuage Fannie's nostalgia, her husband maintained a home in the city of Vallejo where he allowed her to spend some time each year, usually accompanied by one or more of her children, to enroll them in California schools. In 1887, Fannie took her oldest daughter, Senora Antonio Sequeira and her granddaughter Juanita Sequeira to California with her. During that visit she persuaded Senora Vallejo to go to San Francisco to have a group picture taken. This picture became the famous "Four Generations" picture; a copy hangs in the historic Vallejo Home in Sonoma.

General Frisbie in April 1889 was able to go with his wife and their two daughters, Minnie, age sixteen, and Magdalena, age 12. When the time came to end this visit Fannie wrote a goodbye letter saying in part: "Mother mine, I just can't tell you how I feel. No one but you can understand. We are going to be separated; I hope only for a short time. I don't want to cry because I will soon return. How I envy the good fortune of my brothers and sisters now that I have to go so very, very far away from my dearly loved father and mother."

On Fannie's way home she wrote to Platon from Chihuahua, Mexico:

Yesterday we left El Paso. We had a very good trip. Today we are in Mexican Territory. It's a pretty day and we are all well and happy and in good health. John is well and he hasn't had inflammation in his face. He appears much better. Minnie too seems to be thriving under the change. I hope God will help me the rest of the trip. As soon as we reach the city I'll write to you and tell you how the rest of the family is . . . I believe that Felipa would have enjoyed it very much. We are commencing to see the Indians at all the stations. They all speak Spanish.

I am sorry that Francisca didn't come with me. A trip like this is better than study for a young girl like her—so much to see. Every day we think of Francisca. Everything that Magdalena sees that is notable, she says she wishes *Frank* were here to see it. Greet Adela and Angelita; such pretty creatures. A kiss for all. Don't forget Aunt Fannie who loves them so much also greet the Chino and big Adela.

GENERAL VALLEJO'S 82ND BIRTHDAY

The Frisbies, having been to California in April of 1889, were unable to make the trip to Sonoma so soon again to join the family in celebrating General Vallejo's 82nd birthday on July 7th (his actual birthday was on July fourth, as his baptismal record plainly states). Nevertheless the Frisbies managed to celebrate it, in *absentia*, by entertaining Walt William Palmer, then a guest at the Hotel Iturbide, the luxurious hostelry where Vallejo had stayed in 1877. Fannie wrote on July 15th describing the evening to her father:

Mr. Palmer was here. We drank a glass of wine to your health. Poor dear Mr. Palmer's eyes filled with tears when your name was spoken. We drank in silence. The old dear is so handsome. He wanted to talk but he couldn't. He looked from one of us to the other—speechless. He sent us ten bunches of flowers to decorate the house. You would be amazed to see so many flowers. The whole place was filled with blossoms and I am sending you two pansies from one of the bunches. I want you to write your age and the date on one of them in your own handwriting and keep it for me when I return to California.

A few days later, July 20th, Fannie's husband also gave a description of the party:

Fannie has received letters from her sisters giving a most interesting account of the happy time all had upon your eighty-first [sic.: 82nd] birthday and I experienced a feeling of sadness that I, with my family was not permitted to be present at the eventful and joyful occasion, but although so remote from you, you were remembered by all.

Our parlor and dining room were beautifully decorated with flowers kindly sent by your good friend Mr. Palmer who was our guest at dinner. Children and grandchildren all joined in toasting you and Mr. Palmer cordially entered into the spirit of the festival. I fondly cherish the hope should we be spared another year to be present at your next anniversary. You will find enclosed a draft for $50.

This was followed by another note from Frisbie to Vallejo, enclosing a letter dated August 17, 1889 from Mr. Robert Underwood Johnson, associate editor of the *Century Magazine*:

We are now organizing for the Century Magazine a series of illustrated papers on subjects connected with the pioneer movement in California beginning with the explorations and the life in California before the Gold Discovery.

We have already approached General Vallejo, through a gentleman in San Francisco with a request that he should write a sketch of Spanish life at the time, but we fear that by reason of his advanced age, we shall not be successful. In this case we should like to know whether your experience would justify you in undertaking a paper on this subject, and if not, whether you could recommend any one to us qualified to prepare the paper of the interesting life of the old Californians.

We should also like to illustrate the papers thoroughly and to that end we request that you will be good enough to inform us where we may obtain portraits of General Vallejo, Alvarado, Pio Pico and Jose Castro. Is there not a daughter of Alvarado still living in Washington and if so, can you give us her address? We should prefer to make portraits from daguerreotypes or oil paintings, which could be photographed by any operator. It would be interesting to present portraits of some of the best known ladies of the time, in Spanish costume, if practicable.

Frisbie, in sending the above letter to his father-in-law, called his attention to the fact that the *Century Magazine* had a fine reputation and a large circulation. He said he had written to John S. Hittell suggesting that he prepare a paper. General Vallejo, himself, did not write anything for the magazine but he was instrumental, no doubt, in having his niece Guadalupe Vallejo, the daughter of his oldest brother, write, "Ranch and Mission Days in California" which was published in the December, 1890 number of the magazine.

Charles Howard Shinn visited Sonoma the latter part of June 1890, gathering data. He visited Lachryma Montis and his photographer, Warren, was permitted to take a picture of the invalid widow, Senora Vallejo. Her photograph, taken in a high-neck lace-trimmed night gown, with a woolen shawl, was published with Mr. Shinn's article, "Pioneer Spanish Families in California, With Special Reference to the Vallejos" in the January, 1891 number of the Century Magazine.

Fannie became somewhat negligent about writing home and her father called her attention to the fact in a letter dated October 21, 1889:

My very dear daughter Fannie:

The enclosed package contains, as you will note, the story of a letter belonging to your mother, written many months ago. It came from Mexico where you are residing and then landed in Washington, from whence it came to us, to Sonoma once again. The cause of its waywardness, I do not understand for it was well addressed, fortunately it contained nothing of importance.

I am sending you the letter so that you will know that your mother has written to you and thinks often of you and the entire family. She wonders exceedingly about your silence, but now that she knows that you did not receive the letters, things are somewhat straightened out. However, it does not satisfy me, for I believe in getting a letter or not getting one; a daughter (already a grandmother) should write to her loving old mother, in order to console her in her last days.

Your mother does not actually see, she cannot write and being seventy-three years of age, 'tis no plaything. As for myself, now I am merely kicking at the goad of old age and although I write and read without glasses still and there is no useless quivering of my pulse, nevertheless eighty-two years 'tis no plaything! So then don't put off writing to us; one letter is sufficient for father and mother together. Your letters make us live again, they entertain and bring you back to us since they are from our first little girl, our dear daughter.

Give our greetings to your entire family, the men and little women, grandsons and granddaughters. And don't forget the wives of Bernardo and Sequeira. Leo is well. He visited us some days ago. Andronico, Platon, Nap, Adela, Natalia, Lulu, and Maria are also well, each one in different places. Don't forget to write to us.

Your father who loves you,
M. G. VALLEJO

FANNIE'S LOSS

The visit of Fannie to Sonoma the spring of 1889 proved to be the last one in which she enjoyed the companionship of her father. Her next visit was in answer to an urgent telegram from her sister Luisa, sent January 4, 1890: "Papa gradually failing. Come as soon as possible." Luisa, watching by his bedside, was afraid that their dear Papa would not know Fannie, and she felt it would be a great disappointment to her sister if this should happen.

General Frisbie sent a telegram saying that Fannie and two of the children, Luis Platon and Josephine, would reach San Francisco on January 14th. Fannie arrived as scheduled in San Francisco and went immediately to Sonoma. After four days of anxious watching she sent a telegram to her husband announcing General Vallejo's death. Frisbie telegraphed in return, "Our tears mingle with yours. Do all possible for dear Grandmother. Pay all funeral expenses." Fannie ordered the casket and joined with her brothers and sisters in signing the letter sent to John B. Frisbie on January 22, 1890, written no doubt by Platon:

Papa sleeps in peace; having departed in the bosom of his numerous family. The memory of his saintly death shall forever remain sacred in the hearts of those who knew and loved him. He was resigned, gentle, affectionate. His faith in God was great, causing the love of his Maker to kindle in his breast the flame and trust in God, like a dove that has flown from a cage.

He received the last Sacrament of the Church with a holy love and joyous disposition. He died a truly saintly death, conscious to the last, repeating often the words "Into Thy Hands, Lord, I commend my Spirit." Though he attained the age of eighty-two, he retained in all freshness of youth his clear intellect and cheerful disposition. Papa's last days and every hour to the last moments of his precious life resembles a glorious sunset, the impression of which will ever remain a sacred consolation to us all.

He was buried from the church of St. Francis Solano with High Requiem Mass. A eulogy was pronounced by his pastor and confessor, dwelling upon his excellent traits of character and natural virtues, his generosity, his faith in God, his love of his family and home. The funeral services were conducted in a most satisfactory manner. Arriving at the Cemetery, he was temporarily deposited in a vault until a future time when the weather which has been unusually severe will allow us to bury him in his final resting place.

Mama desires us to express her most sincere and grateful thanks for the generous assistance you have rendered our beloved father, the echo of which sentiments resound in all our hearts. We have done all in our power to lighten the burden of the funeral expenses and we can truly say that Papa was buried in a most becoming manner. We trust in God's merciful goodness that his soul rests in peace.

A. A. VALLEJO — FANNIE FRISBIE — ADELA FRISBIE — NATALIA HARASZTHY — PLATON VALLEJO — NAPOLEON VALLEJO — LULU DE EMPARAN — MARIA CUTTER

On her way home to Mexico after the funeral of her father, Fannie wrote to Platon from El Paso, Texas, on March 13, 1890, saying:

It's been two months since I passed here with so heavy a heart and so frightened by what we thought could happen to us, which was the death of Papa, our beloved Papa. What I have been through these two months seems like a dream. What is to be done? With patience one earns Heaven. It is sad to live so far from one's relatives. I don't like it. Speaking of Papa's burial, it seems to me that the sisters didn't like the arrangement that we made for the vault. Write to Natalia and ask her if they at home liked the arrangement. According to what Maria told me, they had letters from many men that were going to make a statue for Papa.

The Native Sons of the Golden West considered erecting a statue of General Vallejo in Golden Gate Park in San Francisco, but nothing came of the suggestion.

In 1920, the *San Francisco Bulletin* conducted a contest to ascertain which among California's distinguished dead should be favored by having a statue in the National Hall of Statuary in the Capitol in Washington, D.C. General Vallejo received the largest number of votes, approximately 1,400 more than Father Serra. The third highest candidate was Thomas Starr King. The State Legislature was to make the final selection.

In 1921, California Concurrent Resolution No. 10 and Assembly Concurrent Resolution No. 8, identical measures, were introduced simultaneously, naming Serra and Vallejo as the two to represent California. The Senate Committee on Rules, however, in reporting back the Resolution, recommended its adoption with an amendment substituting the name of Thomas Starr King for that of General Vallejo. Senator Herbert L. Slater made a fight to have Vallejo's name retained, but on a vote of 20 to 19, King was chosen. It was not until 1927, after a great many other names had been suggested, that, with the backing of the Native Sons of the Golden West and also the Native Daughters and the California Federation of Womens' Clubs that Governor Young signed the Bill naming Padre Serra and Thomas Starr King as the two representatives of California in the National Statuary Hall.

Ettore Cadorin, a native of Venice, Italy, living in Santa Barbara, was awarded the honor of creating the statue of Padre Junipero Serra. Assisting him was a young girl, Marian Brackenridge, who has since become nationally famous as a sculptor. She now lives in Sonoma, the home of Vallejo, the California patriot who was eliminated because of religious prejudice.

In January 1891, Fannie and her husband took over the expenses of another Vallejo funeral, namely that of Senora Francisca Benicia Carrillo de Vallejo. Fannie's emotions are best expressed in her letters written at the time. On February 9th, she wrote to her niece Adela, a daughter of Platon:

Your Aunt is very sad. I should like to be with you and weep awhile and chat with your father. How many of the family were present at the hour of death of Mama? How sad when you think of all the things that have happened in one year. What does your Papa say about the sickness of grandma? Ask him if she suffered very much before dying. Tell me who dressed Mama, how they dressed her, and what kind of casket they put her in, what Father said the funeral Mass? I would like to know everything. Where they put Mama after her death, I suppose with grandpa.

Poor dears, how they suffered in life and in their last days. What illnesses the two of them had, but now they rest forever. We shall never hear them speak nor see our loved parents again. It is terrible not to have a Papa nor a Mama. You poor dear, God took away your precious mother at such a tender age. We must conform to the will of God. My dear, take good care of your Papa and love him. You don't find a Papa like yours every day.

On the same day, Fannie wrote to Platon, Adela's father:

I received a newspaper some days ago, telling of Mother's death. Just imagine what a strange thing it seems to be an orphan. Poor, poor Mama. How she suffered. One year she lived after the death of Papa. How sad the world seems to me now. Our children are the consolation that God has given us and we live for them.

I want you to tell me how Mama left things at L.M. I want what belongs to me. Most of all the pieces of furniture Mama had was mine and I want them back. Between you and Natalia, will you all collect everything. There are a number of broken chairs. Will you get them together so that they can be fixed because I want to live in California. The chair which I sent Mama and another one which Papa had in his room.

Tell the mistresses of L.M. that I am mistress of the furniture, the piano particularly. There are pieces of furniture that John gave me when he married me. Also the bed that Mama had in her room and bookstand . . . I want to come up at once to collect my things. I don't want anyone to deprive me of them. I shall be very selfish. Now that Papa and Mama are gone I have a right like all the others to what belongs to me. I should like a keepsake of Mama, like some pieces of clothing that she wore. I want a comb with the Mexican arms which Mama gave to me many years ago.

The "mistresses of L.M.," Luisa and Maria, sent the furniture and piano to Fannie's house in Vallejo which she occupied on her different visits to California. She was given her mother's brown taffeta gown, the ruffles of which were embroidered with black cut-velvet. While in Mexico the present author was given a ruffle from this gown by Magdalena Frisbie de Marron, the then last surviving child of Fannie Vallejo Frisbie.

THE GEN. JOHN B. FRISBIE STEAMER

Zepheniah Jefferson Hatch and his brother Charles Hatch entered the water transportation business with the steamer Monticello on August 10, 1895. As traffic increased they ordered the steamship General John B. Frisbie built. She was constructed in the State of Washington. She was 164 feet long and 29.3 feet in width. The 1,100-horsepower engines were installed in San Francisco.

The Hatch brothers incorporated as The Monticello Steamship Company. The maiden trip of the General John B. Frisbie was made in 1901. Among the prominent people on board for the maden trip from Vallejo to San Francisco were members of the Frisbie and Vallejo families. Mrs. John B. Frisbie had fitted out her nephews Carlos and Raoul Emparan, sons of her sister Luisa Vallejo Emparan of Sonoma, with new suits, hats and shoes.

The Gen. John B. Frisbie made the 30-mile run to San Francisco in an hour and forty-five minutes. The steamer was provided with the services of a restaurant, bar, shoe-shine stand and a barber shop. The bar was finally closed at the request of authorities at Mare Island Navy Yard.

THE FRISBIE'S GOLDEN WEDDING

In April 1901, Fannie and her husband celebrated their Golden Wedding at their San Nicholas Rancho, some miles beyond Chapultepec near Atzcapotzalco, where General Frisbie owned a sugar plantation; here he brought fifty guests in his private Pullman car from Mexico City to his ranch "Careaga." The high-ceiling rooms fronting on the broad stone verandahs of the U-shaped residence were filled with yellow blossoms.

Fannie wore a dark gown trimmed in Brussels lace, while over her hair, which only had a sprinkling of gray, was a white lace mantilla. She carried white lilies and gardenias. The groom wore a morning coat, gray pin-striped trousers, white vest, a bow-tie and a lily-of-the-valley boutonniere.

Mass was said in the Frisbie's private chapel by Padre Barajas. Afterwards the guests sat down to an elaborate banquet where toasts were drunk in champagne to the bride and groom of fifty years ago. The eldest son, John Bernardo, on behalf of his brothers and sisters, gave a speech filled with affectionate sentiments and presented his parents with a plaque of gold plate; in the center of which were likenesses of Fannie and John B. Frisbie, while surrounding them were medallions of the twelve Frisbie children, with engravings of their names and birth dates.

Fannie, somewhat heavier than when she was a bride in the pueblo of Sonoma and now looking very much like her late father, danced the La Jarabe with Padre Barajos. Vega's orchestra furnished the music. It was no effort financially for General Frisbie to engage the renowned Vega's Orchestra, because he had sold his El Oro Mine to an English Syndicate for $1,200,000 in gold retaining at the same time his interests in the Esmeralda Mine besides his interests in railroads, banking, stock raising, dairy farming and sugar mills.

DEATH OF FANNIE VALLEJO DE FRISBIE

Four years after the gala event of the Golden Wedding, Fannie became ill and was taken to Cuatla, a village saturated with tropical beauty of poinsetta, hibiscus and brilliant colored bougainvillea. There, in the warm climate south of Mexico City, it was hoped she would regain her strength. She enjoyed the warm baths but they failed to cure her and she passed away on February 14th, 1905, aged seventy years. Dr. Vallejo received on February 15th a telegram from her son Bernardo, which said, "Mother, from pneumonia, passed away. Please notify all relatives."

This daughter of California transplanted to Mexico had expressed a wish that after death she be taken to Sonoma for burial. Her body was embalmed, with the idea of carrying out her desire, but her children prevailed upon their father to inter her in Mexico, so that in future years they might be buried near her.

General Frisbie's death occurred four years later, within two weeks of his eighty-sixth birthday. He had been a convert and remained a devout Catholic. When he became seriously ill, he sent for Father J. A. Reis of the San Lorenzo Church, and with his children and grandchildren kneeling by his bedside, Frisbie was given the last Sacrament of the Catholic Church. He passed away at his home on Calle Ancha on May 10, 1909. His funeral was attended by the American Minister to Mexico and by many Mexican and American dignitaries as well as relatives and friends.

FRISBIE DESCENDANTS

Fannie and John B. Frisbie had twelve children, but by 1951, when the present author paid her first visit to Mexico, all had passed away with the exception of Magdalena, who was a child of two years when her parents arrived in Mexico. She in 1951 was an octogenarian, the widow of Senor Ramon Marron. Her residence in Mexico City was at 1343 Calle Insurgentes where she lived alone with the exception of a maid. Surrounding her were many of the beautiful art objects and paintings which once graced the palatial home of her parents.

In 1951, my traveling companion to Mexico was Cecilia Mendia Shegog, a great granddaughter of Maria Antonia Lugo de Vallejo, the mother of General Vallejo. Cecilia spoke very little Spanish but her large, sparkling brown eyes spoke for her. Our first mission on arriving was to present our gold seal, beribboned letters of introduction from California's Governor Earl Warren to the American Ambassador. We hailed a taxi in front of our hotel, the Del Prado, and were driven for some time along back streets, finally emerging into the Paseo de la Reforma where the Embassy of the United States was then located in a tall office building. We found to our chagrin that the Embassy was only a few walking blocks from our hotel. However, the needless taxi fare was soon forgotten by the warmth of the welcome of Ambassador William O'Dwyer who personally ushered us into his private office and cleared the way for my research work in the Mexican Military Archives.

While in Mexico I met many of Fannie's grandchildren as well as her daughter Magdalena. The Vallejo descendants in Mexico are prominent in many walks of life. An especially attractive granddaughter is petite Emma Frisbie, whose friendship and that of her pretty young daughter Martha I treasure. She addresses the author as "Mi muy querida hermana." It was Emma who said that she remembers, as a child, hearing her father, Luis Platon Frisbie, speak in such glowing terms of California that she felt it must be one of the rooms in Heaven.

I asked the grandchildren if they knew any anecdotes about their great grandfather Vallejo. They told me that their grandfather Frisbie had told them that every time the dignified General would pass a burro, heavily laden, he would take off his hat in a salute. When asked why he did this, he answered: "The little donkeys deserve it as they are the hardest working creatures I see in Mexico." I was also told that the first Christmas tree in Mexico was in Grandfather Frisbie's parlor.

During my first visit in Mexico I expressed a desire to Senora Marron to visit the grave of Fannie, her mother. She and her son Ramon Marron y Frisbie drove me out to the French Cemetery. Outside its high iron fence sat the flower vendors and from one of their baskets I selected a spray of crimson carnations. The three of us then walked through the ornate gate, near the Monument to the fallen French soldiers, to the main roadway, and, after a short distance, reached the Frisbie plot.

There on the white tomb of Fannie and her husband, I placed the carnations as a tribute to this daughter of the Don, she who had so loved California.

In December 1956, I was again in Mexico, my fourth visit. I again expressed a desire to visit Fannie's tomb with a floral offering. It was suggested that I take gladiolus as that flower was at its loveliest in December. I had a strong compulsion to take crimson carnations, and on the way to the cemetery my escort, Senor Luis Platon Samperi, visiting in Mexico City from Guadalajara, told me that the clavelas roja (red carnations) was actually the favorite flower of his grandmother Frisbie. Senor Samperi, as a child of four, had been placed in the care of Fannie Frisbie when his own mother, Cynthia Benicia Frisbie de Samperi, died in 1896.

Squatting that December day in the dusty road before the cemetery entrance were the flower vendors. In their baskets were gladiolus in hues of salmon pink, yellow and white; there were also violets, roses and orchids. One basket held a lone bouquet of carnations and they were crimson. These I bought and placed on the white marble of Fannie's tomb. Some of the flowers were laid on the nearby grave of Fannie's granddaughter Juana Sequeira de Carral who had given the Herz concert grand-piano, once the property of Fannie, to the historic Vallejo Home in Sonoma in 1950.

Before leaving the French Cemetery, Senor Samperi and I visited its chapel. Through the mullioned windows, variously colored light streamed through the stained glass as we knelt in prayer. In the sanctity and serenity of the chapel, my thoughts traveled to the village of Sonoma, where in the little adobe Mission of San Francisco Solano, Fannie was born, and where she was baptized and where she was married by the gray-habited and sandaled Franciscan padre; and then my thoughts came back again to the tree-shaded marble tomb where her body is at rest in the soil from whence had come her Castilian grandfather, Don Ignacio Vallejo.

Departing from Mexico, the author was quite ready to agree with Lieutenant Joseph Warren Revere who had served in Sonoma and wrote: "There is a nameless charm in Mexico which holds every one . . . which begets a longing to revisit it, which never fades."

Adelayda Vallejo

Adelayda Vallejo

(Mrs. Levi Cornell Frisbie)

The second daughter of the Vallejos, Adelayda or "Adela," was born on January 3, 1837, in the recently completed Casa Grande and was baptized by Padre Jose Lorenzo Quijas. The infant's godparents were her uncle Don Salvador Vallejo, intrepid Indian fighter, and her father's niece, Dona Maria Ignacia Soberanes, the wife of an Englishman, Dr. Edward T. Bale, who later acquired a ranch in the Napa Valley and established his mill there. About the time of Adelayda's birth, her father brought up from Monterey the Zamorano printing press to Sonoma where he set it up for his own use, printing proclamations and his individual bookmarks which read, "*Soy de la propiedad y uso de D. Mariano G. Vallejo.*"

Adela received her education from tutors, among whom were Colonel Victor Prudon, her father's secretary; Andreas Hoeppner, the musician; and the Belgian scholar Frederick Reeger. When she was twelve years old, her father signed a contract, dated August 8, 1849 in which "Senor Reeger obligated himself to instruct and teach the six oldest children of General Vallejo to read, write and figure; the languages, English, French, Castilian as well as Geography, and History, giving lessons in piano in the employment of which he will spend six hours a day. Senor Reeger being free the rest of the time. Senor Vallejo agrees in payment to give Senor Reeger a salary of 4,000 pesos a year beginning the first of January, 1850." For some unknown reason, the lessons did not start until May 16th.

Adela, the first of the Vallejo children to be born in the Casa Grande, was a decided brunette who had inherited the classical features of her mother, whose face when she was the teen-age Francisca Benicia Carrillo, the young Lieutenant Vallejo had called the most beautiful he had ever seen.

When Adela was just fourteen years old, she wrote to her Grandmother Vallejo in Monterey:

My dear Grandmother:

I take the greatest pleasure in sending you these lines. We are all well except Papa who is sick with a big boil on one cheek. All his face is swollen; he can't eat, he seems old. He went to Benicia sick. It rained on him, all wet and ill he reached home yesterday afternoon (March 27th) and he had to send to have the boil on him opened. Now he doesn't suffer so much and we hope that within a few days he will be well.

It's now been some time since Papa promised to take us to Monterey and we are waiting anxiously to take this trip, the idea which pleases a great deal. Meanwhile my respected and loved grandmother, receive the most affectionate greetings from your loving granddaughter.

Adela Vallejo

P.S. Here is a draft on the new government so that you can drink some little cups of chocolate to our early arrival.

Adela finished her schooling at the young ladies' academy, St. Mary's Hall, which was then located in her old home, the Casa Grande. When she was seventeen, she fell in love with Doctor Levi Cornell Frisbie, the elder brother by two years of Captain John B. Frisbie. Levi was born in Albany, New York, on May 1, 1821. He was of Puritan and Huguenot descent and, through his mother, was related to Ezra Cornell, the founder of the University of that name in Ithaca, New York. As a young man, Levi went to Williams College, later enrolling in the Albany Medical College from which he graduated in 1841. After graduation, he practiced medicine in Albany for eight years.

When his health broke down in 1849, Levi was persuaded by his brother, Captain Frisbie, to come to California, and to keep him out-of-doors, the Captain arranged to have Levi join the surveying party which was then laying out the proposed town of Vallejo. While the chains were being laid and the stakes driven for the boundary of the future town, the wild cattle became mixed with the wild elk and had to be driven out by the native vaqueros. Only eight miles from the proposed city was the Indian rancheria on the Napa Road.

ADELA'S ROMANCE

The romance between Adela and Levi was not popular with the Vallejo family, perhaps because of the differences in their ages, Doctor Frisbie being sixteen years older than Adela. On the other hand, it may have been because the family preferred William A. Cornwall, Secretary of the California Senate, who was in love with Adela. Cornwall wrote to Adela's father on February 20, 1855:

> I arrived in this city (Sacramento) this morning; I shall immediately resume my duties as Secretary. I shall await with the deepest anxiety your reply to the question which I proposed to you when I was at your house. If your reply is unfavorable, then I wish to die.
>
> For long years I have watched the growth of your sweet child, the development of her intellect. I have observed her amiable temper, her kinship to you, her father. Love and adoration for her was implanted in my heart and through those long years the hope which has sustained me has been that she might some day become my wife.

In spite of the fervor of this eligible suitor, Adela was constant in her affection for Doctor Frisbie.

During the summer of 1858, Adela's father was in Monterey, serving as administrator of the estate of his youngest brother, Don Juan Antonio Vallejo, and also assisting his sister Dona Prudenciana in handling the estate of her late husband, Don Jose Amesti. Impatient with her husband's continued absence, and feeling the need of his presence, Senora Vallejo wrote him on July 14, 1858:

> Guadalupe:
>
> Come, come, come, come, come, come. You say that you love me very much and also my family. If it be true, as you have told me so many times, now at present my

family needs your counsel. Remember there is not one, nor two but many of us. You speak of your duty and your obligations to your sisters. You can leave them and come and guide your family. I, myself cannot take care of everything. Andronico, Adela, Natalia, Jovita, Napoleon, Benicita, Luisita, Marilitta and big Benicia send you many embrazas, many little kisses. Much love,

BENICIA

Four days later Vallejo answered his wife's letter saying:

Francisca:

At last I received your letter dated the 14th of the present month, all in your own hand without your having made use of a stranger's hand, all of it full of your own thoughts which I know and want to know always. So you also use parentheses, eh? How much one can say with them! Can't you? And do you remember how much I said to you in my last letter? . . . I still haven't forgotten what you said to me the night before I came away. You were seated at the foot of my bed, taking off a stocking . . . and I was looking at you. What different sensations in that moment. I don't want to remember it almost but no, I do, too want to remember it. How many things you said to me. And as I was looking at you . . . How beautiful you seemed to me. Do you believe me and if you don't—I would die of grief. I believe that you will be happy with this letter and more over, more than happy as I am coming to see you soon. Keep in mind that as soon as I arrive I am going to plant a kiss on you, straight from the heart and will you return it? I am coming . . . I am coming . . . I am coming. A thousand kisses to everyone, everyone, everyone.

Yours forever,

M. G. VALLEJO

Adela herself, in her newly-acquired English, had likewise written to her father on June 20, 1858:

I feel so miserable to think that there is no person who is satisfied yet; Everybody has to say something about it. I know that very well but steel I do not listen to all complaints . . . Papa, we must love somebody on this earth. We cannot be without it. It is so natural, that you know very well. Well, dear Papa, what would you do if you were in my place. You have been married with Mama, in the same way.

Will you give your consent to me to marry the person I love? Papa, if you love your child, I do not think you refuse to give your consent that I have been waiting for four long years. I love the Doctor and no one else . . . But I trust in God, Papa, that you will give your consent upon this subject. Now Papa, do not be so cruel. Do let me know as soon as possible. I am very anxious about it. I hope you have answered the Doctor's letter. If you will, dear Papa, I will promise you and try to be a good child in the future.

Adela's plea was followed by one to Vallejo from Doctor Frisbie. Anxious to help Adela, Benjamin Brooks, the attorney, wrote Vallejo saying because of his refusal to approve Adela's marriage to the Doctor, the invitations which had been printed and some sent, had to be rescued from the post. In writing, Brooks said he wanted to remove the bone of contention and gain peace and happiness for all which he thought was necessary for the life and happiness of Adela.

Vallejo, in Monterey on June 30, 1858 wrote to his wife:

I've heard nothing of the wedding of Adela to whom I wrote answering her letter. If she is at home, tell her not to forget her promise and that I should like to hear her plead her case in her defense. She is very determined in her feelings and although even I am accused of the same thing; she really lacks an argument. I didn't marry against the wishes of the parents of my wife, although they resisted at first. I never before I married went against the domestic rules of the family. I never saw my wife more than two times and did not speak to her of marrying except indirectly and I asked for her by letter from a distance of 300 leagues. I have never violated that conduct and you know it yourself. You know me—I see things in a different way from the common run of people. I love my family very well from my wife down to the last one. I sacrifice myself for them, we rear them, we educate them and that is the proof. If they are grateful, they won't forget these services but how few children hold to their parents. Take care of yourself, take care of the little ones and dont forget Your affectionate M. G. VALLEJO

Some weeks later, Vallejo gave a reluctant consent to Adela's marriage. She lost no time in persuading her mother to take her to San Francisco to shop. They arrived in the city on July 12th and remained three days, chiefly in the dress shops along Montgomery Street, buying a $1,700 trousseau. Brooks, the attorney, wrote Vallejo, "When your wife was here, she asked me for 1300 pesos promising me to return them the moment you return and without question I gave them to her because I don't know how to refuse your wife—but you well know I have no money and it put me in a difficult spot and I beg of you to tell your wife not to ask me for such things."

Adela and her mother spent the nights at the Rassette House. Upon their departure they were presented with a bill, room and board $6 a day. $2 for the drawing room, with an additional charge of fifty cents for gas lights.

On July 13, 1858, Dr. Frisbie wrote to Senora Vallejo: "Adela is your child and I know you are deeply interested in her happiness and I pledge you to do all in my power to render her happy and hope to prove to you how much I prize your friendship and high regard. I want to see Adela and make final arrangements and decide when and where the matter shall be consummated."

The members of the Vallejo household, busy with the plans for Adela's wedding, had neglected to write to the General. Peevishly he wrote to his wife on June 30, 1858:

Three mails have been delivered since I've been anxiously waiting your letters and those from all the family. I suppose that they have been all absent or are busy about many things. . . . Now that I'm not bringing you to task particularly for you have asked me to excuse you at times but Andronico, Adela and Jovita, never would I pardon them such negligence with their Papa, for they promised to write me at least once a week, one letter each.

Final plans for the wedding were made for July 26th, and on July 23rd Adela wrote hopefully to her father:

Well, Papa, I must tell you all, all, as I promised you. We have been waiting for you for a long time to arrange all this matter about my marriage. You know that we set a date that was the 19th of June and you did not come. Of course the Dr. and I thought to have a letter from you to see what you would say.

We had an answer from you a week after the 19th. And now Papa, I have been waiting for you all this time. I saw the Dr. the other day in town. I told him that I must have an end to it one way or the other. And he told me he was going to come the 26th to be married. Now, Papa, the day is fixed. And how much happier I would be if you come to be present at that occasion. Will you, Papa dear, dear Papa, if you love your child, you must come. It is my only wish and I pray you will not be angry with me.

It was true that Vallejo had given his consent for Adela's marriage to Dr. Frisbie but not his approval and he failed to attend the wedding, purposely it seems. Instead he wrote a petulant letter to his wife from San Francisco in which he said, "Adela, poor crazy dear; God grant she will not be too remorseful."

ADELA'S WEDDING

The wedding of Adela Vallejo and Levi C. Frisbie was strictly a family affair occurring at four o'clock on the afternoon of July 26th, 1858 at Lachryma Montis, with Father Vilarrasa of Benicia performing the ceremony. The wedding certificate, in the script-hand of Captain Frisbie and signed by Francis Sadoc Vilarrasa, was witnessed by John B. Frisbie, Benicia de Vallejo, Natalia Vallejo, and Fannie G. Frisbie. Jovita was present but did not sign, perhaps because she was a minor.

The bride remained long enough at Lachryma Montis to write to her father: "It is five o'clock in the afternoon. I tell you that I and the Doctor married at four o'clock, Monday July 26th and we leave for Vallejo this afternoon. We were very sorry that you were not present. I hope you will find yourself in good health and that you may come soon."

The new Mrs. Levi C. Frisbie's sister Natalia also wrote to their father on the wedding day:

Well, Papa, at last Adela is married and gone; she was married at four o'clock this afternoon by Father Vilaraza of Benicia. Oh dear Papa how sad it is or it has been for us this day. How often I have thought of you and wished your presence. How bad it looked without you being here. Yes, Papa, your dear, dear presence but it can't be helped. She is gone forever. They just left for Vallejo together with the Captain and Fanny and we hope they will get home safely. Papa, how bad I feel, I must stop and kiss you goodbye.

July 30th, 1858, four days after the wedding, Benjamin S. Brooks, San Francisco attorney and esteemed friend of the Vallejo family, wrote to General Vallejo in the interest of Vallejo family harmony,

Mrs. Adela Frisbie with her husband came here Tuesday and are now at the Rassette House. I have visited your girl and she seems happy but she wants very much to have your approval. . . . Now that the thing is over and done with, to the world I say, it is a matter of indifference to you.

The Doctor who visited me yesterday made apologies for his letter which I had shown you. He put it in the fire with many expressions of regret for his foolishness. I visited him at his office and he appears happy but wishes you would receive him. Don't you wish to receive him? Do me the favor of permitting me to invite them to your reunion.

The tenth of August, Captain Frisbie and his wife are having a reception at their home in Vallejo and the cards of Adela and her husband are accompanying their cards. I absolutely insist that you should be there and should dance with your wife and Adela. Now we should bury the hatchet.

It is strange and hard to account for the aversion that General Vallejo had toward Levi Frisbie when he was so fond of the younger brother, John. "The hatchet" was still not buried six months later. At that time, Maria Benicia Ysabel, the little six-year-old child with the long dark curls, was seriously ill, and Doctor Frisbie was called by the family to Sonoma. His letter of January 7, 1859, explains the situation which developed:

Genl. M. G. Vallejo
Dear Sir:

Having been requested by the family to visit little Benicia (who was represented to me to be dangerously ill) I hastened to Sonoma and sought an opportunity to communicate with you before calling at the house but neither myself nor messenger was able to find you but in the interim I received from the house an urgent request to go up immediately which under the circumstances I could not consistently decline. I conferred therefore with Dr. Love who promised to meet me at the bedside of the patient which was accordingly done.

I have since learned that my motives have not been properly appreciated and the proffer of my sympathy and kindly feelings rejected indignantly. And while I regret, General, the course I have pursued, has proved so repugnant to your feelings, I must in all candour assure you, no gentleman, much more, no true physician could have done less, I, therefore withdraw entirely, from the case and leave the responsibility where it rightly belongs.

Very Respectfully Yours,
L. C. FRISBIE

A week later Benicia Ysabel Vallejo, *not* under the care of Dr. Frisbie, died (January 13, 1859).

Months later, regretting, it would seem, that he had not allowed Dr. Frisbie to handle little Benicia's case, Vallejo called him to attend his youngest son Napoleon, then nine years old, who had received a wound in his chest in an accident from an open knife. In September 1859, the doctor reported thus to General Vallejo on his son's condition: "Knowing full well the intense anxiety you feel in relation to Napoleon, it affords me great satisfaction to be able to inform you that he continues to improve rapidly and will in all probability be able to sit up in a day or two. I returned according to promise last evening and this morning made a thorough exploration of the chest. Respiration is more completely re-established in the left lung nor can I discover any indication of organic defect. His symptoms are all favorable." The letter was signed "Faithfully Yours"—in contrast to the "Respectfully Yours," signed a few months before. The increase of warmth in the relationship between the two men whom Adela loved so dearly made her happy. Another cause of happiness for Adela had been the birth of a daughter on May 19, 1859. She was given the name Francisca Adelayda but, for some unknown reason, was always called "Lily."

It was when Lily was quite young that Adela and her husband were members of a *Circle* interested in Spiritualism, a group which met in her father's house at Lachryma Montis. The Civil War had caused so many bereaved families throughout the United States, that Circles or seances were held in many homes. Dr. Charles Van Geldern, called to Sonoma in 1849 to attend Vallejo, seemed to be the leader of the Circle which met at Lachryma Montis. Other members were Natalia's friend, Mrs. Tracy, George Butler, Andronico and Uladislao Vallejo and General Vallejo. At these gatherings, Andronico's guitar floated about the room, striking the hanging crystals of the chandelier. At one seance a sheet of paper bearing vignette of General Vallejo's home and garden was taken from a portfolio and deposited at a center table, whereupon a message was written through the entranced George Butler.

These seances and others in California were reported in "Modern American Spiritualism" by Emma Hardinge who spent fifteen months in California lecturing and speaking in a campaign in favor of the re-election of President Lincoln. She said in her book that General Vallejo was one of the oldest and most respected persons in the State, "His wealth, position and noble character forbid the possibility of attaching a shadow of suspicion to his name and yet for years he pursued similar investigations under his own roof until his faith and that of his family became as fixed in the belief as the everlasting hills of his own California."

Years went by and there were no further additions to Adela's family. Her sister, Fannie Frisbie, then the mother of eight children, wrote: "Adela should have a baby boy; it is bad luck to be the wife of a doctor. I am going to see if John can study medicine and become a doctor to see if I don't have to have so many babies."

Adela's daughter Lily, though delicate from childhood, was a beautiful girl, and her uniform "Mascot of the Frisbie Guards" proved to be most becoming. The honor was bestowed upon her by her Uncle John, who had been appointed head of the California National Guard by Governor Leland Stanford.

Sometimes, through stress of duties as a mother and as the wife of a busy doctor, Adela had to neglect her correspondence. When her letters did not come to Lachryma Montis, Senora Vallejo was not timid about chiding her, as on April 15, 1867:

> It is some time since I've heard anything from you, either because you have forsaken your home or you are angry with me or something has happened to you. Perhaps the doctor has refused to let you come to see me, for now you have forgotten

you have a Mama. As for me, I haven't forgotten that I have a daughter Adela. I don't want to think ill of you. Tell me what is the matter. Why have you forgotten everybody? I have asked Natalia if you have written to her and she told me no.

Don Pepe [Jose de la Rosa] says he scarcely saw you and that with the husband you have, he doesn't let you go anywhere. It's been more than two years since I saw Dr. Frisbie. Never have I turned you away from home. On the contrary it pleases me greatly for all to come to see me here or wherever I may be.

It was in this letter that Senora Vallejo told of the tragic burning of the Casa Grande, two days before, mentioned in detail in the sketch of Senora Vallejo.

On April 24, 1867, impelled by one disappointment after another in connection with some of the business transactions which John B. Frisbie had been handling for him, Vallejo expressed his injured feelings to Doctor Levi C. Frisbie, the elder brother, as follows:

Dear Doctor:

I was ready to go to Vallejo with the family but I think it will not be good nor prudent to go now. My object was that Lulu might be getting ready to go with Fanny Frisbie (jr.) to the school in San Jose and Maria would remain in school in Vallejo. All this was arranged with Frisbie beforehand and not with Fannie. Therefore it is not necessary to send the carriage now.

I thank you for the offer of your home. Tell Adela not to bother now. If sometime I can build a little house in Vallejo, then I shall take what I call my family to my house and not to some one else's home . . . I saw in the paper that Frisbie and others have received patents but Frisbie has told me nothing which is very strange; but perhaps some day he will remember that I exist and that there is a "*General Vallejo*" *who remembers him at all times in all circumstances.* He knows what my family is suffering. He negotiates, receives money and forgets absolutely that the "bread of Prosperity ought to be divided among the poor who have produced that prosperity." But that's how the world is.

Vallejo will be a very important town; have no doubt about that. I have believed if for many years and as you say "founded in my imagination" more than a quarter of a century ago. Since 1830, when I made the first expedition to the Straits of Carquinez, I decided on that spot. Later Dr. Semple and Larkin thought that Benicia would be a better place for the convenience of the small boats that came and went from the mines. But in 1849 when the Capital was moved from Monterey I thought it was time to start my plan in Vallejo. The rest you know.

To my way of thinking, Benicia and Vallejo will be a single thing, when the state of California has the population of the state of New York. Nevertheless others want to take the credit for having started the project which is now being realized—but I assure you that no one thought of it ever, nor was it possible, since no one knew the place nor had the necessary things to come forward with such a big business, nor the credit, nor the reputation, nor the name except your father-in-law. I spent my capital and it is possible that I shall lose it, all except my honor and my name which I value more than everything. San Francisco has been the mortal enemy of Vallejo but those people ought to be content with what they are and leave the others in peace. San Francisco is very envious and greedy and wants everything for San Francisco. Time will be the one that shows up deceit.

Your servant who kisses your hand,
M. G. VALLEJO

RUNAWAYS

In January of 1869, a Mrs. Simonton, close friend of Adela and Fannie, passed away. The two sisters attended her funeral in Vallejo. Returning home, the team of General Frisbie's horses attached to the carriage became frightened and ran a long distance before the driver succeeded in stopping them. Fannie jumped out, and fortunately sustained no material injury. Three years later, another runaway and Fannie was not so fortunate. She and her husband were out riding on the Napa Road when the train came thundering down, just as the Frisbies were preparing to cross the tracks. The shrill whistle of the locomotive and the jarring noise increased the terror of the horses. Rearing and jumping, they backed toward the passing train, until, by a side movement, the buggy was upset and badly smashed. General Frisbie's ankle and wrist were sprained; and Fannie, severely bruised and frightened. When the engineer brought the train to a stop, first aid was given to both.

Returning to the year 1869—on February 10th, Adela wrote her mother a newsy letter:

Platon has received a letter from Papa, where he writes that he has been sick due to a fall he had coming down the stairs but it appears he is much better which makes me glad. We have to give thanks that he did not break any bones, as this on an old person is a much serious matter than on a young one . . . Please let me know in case Papa has a great deal of pain, so I can send him some liniment for rubbing it on the parts of the body where the pain is.

Today is Ash Wednesday and if my memory does not fail me, this day you were married thirty-five [sic. 37] years ago in San Diego. All the Catholic people went to Mass to receive the ash, as sooner or later some day we all have to die. Many people asked and took the ash and when I arrived, there was very little left on the plate . . .

Lillie Vallejo is much better but myself I have been sick with inflammations and have decided to not wait longer but to ask Levi and Platon for some medicine . . . In this town there are five doctors. Fanny's family is well. Napoleon is working for the Railroad as second clerk with a salary of 65 pesos per month . . . Arpad wrote to Fany that he has been three days out of the hospital and that he was feeling well although still with marks from the smallpox. Greetings to Natalia and the family, also to my uncle [Salvador], also Lulu, Maria, Papa and to Dona Carolina [Senora Moise Kahn] if she is staying with you.

When in her teens, Adela's daughter Lily went to visit her father's sister, Cynthia Frisbie Lynch, in Syracuse, New York, and, while there attended the Academy of the Sacred Heart. At eighteen years of age, she became engaged to Dennis McCarthy, treasurer of the City of Syracuse and youngest son of Senator Dennis McCarthy. Meanwhile, Lily's grandfather Vallejo was in Mexico City and her mother in California. To Adela, General Vallejo wrote in June, 1877:

How much pleasure it gave me to read your last letter of the 2nd of this month. I assure you, my daughter, that it is truly a joy; a *pater familas* feels happy when he receives in a far away land letters from his children. This is the one proof of love and affection towards those who have given us being; it is proof of gratitude and appreciation of open-heartedness and blessed joy towards our parents.

You, my dear daughter are a mother and through experience you must have felt the same happiness when you receive letters from your lovely daughter, the beautiful Adelita who is absent from you for the first time. So then I who have so much family, how do you imagine I feel when I receive the letters from all my children?

Now I shall tell you something about this city so famous in the annals of our history. The early Spaniards, our true ancestors founded it about 356 years ago and they continued the subsequent years up to 1821 to build it up with monumental edifices, secular in nature worthy of the grandeur and munificence of their creators. Since the last date (1821) nothing has been improved nor built except for some houses of adobe brick such as the mission ranch houses with tile roofs and others with roofs of shingles (without nails) held down, so that the wind wouldn't carry them off, with stones, rather rocks.

The city contains a population of 300,000 inhabitants, some forty thousand whites, all the rest of the population are Indians, untamed Indians, almost without clothes, all bare-footed, naked in other words. Everything here is Indian; Indians carry charcoal, forage, wood, barrels, reed mats, whips, whatever there is. Then there follows thousands upon thousands of burros with loads of everything from the neighboring country of sugar, coffee, cotton and alfalfa.

Grandfather was still in Mexico when Adelita's [Lily's] wedding to Dennis McCarthy took place on October 25, 1877, in St. John's Church, Syracuse. Mrs. Patrick Lynch, her paternal aunt, gave a reception to the bride and groom. A month later, traveling Grandfather Vallejo arrived in Syracuse and wrote home:

Yesterday (November 22, 1877) I arrived at this city in which I found Adela which gave me the greatest pleasure. Also Adelita, married to a young man named McCarthy who seems to be a splendid specimen and according to what every one says of very good character in addition to being handsome and with very beautiful manners, also from a very fine family. Since coming from Mexico I am feeling better. I am gaining back the forty pounds I lost in the Capital in six months' residence. On the contrary Frisbie grew fat because he led the easy life.

At the time the General was a guest in Lily's home he said he was given careful attention. Adela and her father returned to California together, their transcontinental trip seemingly being shortened by card games they enjoyed.

DEATH OF LILY FRISBIE MCCARTHY

The marriage which had begun with the promise of many years of happiness for two young people so much in love was terminated four years later by Lily's sudden death on Sunday, June 12th, 1881, as she was preparing to take her drive with her husband. She had been convalescing from a severe illness. Her husband had ordered the carriage and was waiting for his wife in the parlor of their home on East Fayette Street when Lily, in the bedroom above was seized with a spasm. Unable to breathe freely, she asked her maid to raise the window. But the fresh aid brought no relief, and when the maid returned to the side of her young mistress, Lily expired uttering no sound. The frightened maid called aloud for Lily's husband. He hastened upstairs, only to find his wife lifeless. The regular family doctor could not be located, so another physician was summoned, Dr. Dunlap, but found Lily Frisbie McCarthy beyond human aid.

The entire community was stunned by her death, as she was widely esteemed and regarded in Syracuse. A memorial brochure was published in which mention was made that "she was as pure as the prayer, childhood wafts above."

The funeral was held on June 15th, 1881 in Syracuse's St. Mary's Catholic Church where rich and rare velvet draperies mingled with the abundance of flowers. Candle lights from the altar and the gas jets cast a radiance over the congregation. Some ten priests participated in the service, and a choir of one hundred and twenty-five children from St. Vincent de Paul's Asylum, in which Lily had been especially interested, chanted the "De Profundis." Professor Fiske played Beethoven's Requiem on the organ.

Lily's young husband was too prostrated with grief to attend the funeral; nor were her parents present, as they were unable to leave California.

The Requiem Mass was celebrated by Father O'Brien. Reverend Dr. O'Hara, pastor of the church and a close friend of the McCarthy family, delivered the funeral sermon. He referred to Lily as the gifted granddaughter of General Mariano Guadalupe Vallejo, "noble and eminent patriarch of California" whom he eulogized by quoting from Bayard Taylor's *Eldorado.* "Truly," Reverend O'Hara continued, "our lifeless friend was of a grand Castilian race and eminent ancestry. In his advanced age of 77 [sic. 73] what grief shall fill the good old General's heart when he learns of his beloved granddaughter's death."

Upon being told of Lily's death, the "Patriarch" wrote to Adela on June 13, 1881, with his wife and daughter Luisa adding their names after his signature:

> Our souls and our whole being has been affected greatly by the sad and lamentable death of Lillie, your only daughter. We all accompany you and the Doctor in your great sorrow. God, only God can console on such occasions. His judgments supreme are incrutable although to us poor mortals, they seem to us unjust at times. Lillie, your dear daughter has obtained to the mansion of angels. There she will care for her dear ones and pray for those whom she left here disconsolate who some day will be reunited with her.

Dennis McCarthy, the bereaved husband and his mother left Syracuse

June 16th for California, bringing Lily's small son, Dennis Jr., to his maternal grandmother Frisbie. The boy spent a number of years with her, then he returned East and attended the Westminster School at Dobb's Ferry, New York.

Perhaps it was because of this deep personal sorrow that Adela was the compassionate member of the Vallejo family. It was Adela who tried to comfort Ula, the erring one, with her frequent letters, filled with news of the home he had so abruptly left. It was Adela who left her home duties in Vallejo to come to Sonoma, that she might aid her sisters in nursing their father during his last illness. Adela was at Lachryma Montis on January 3rd, 1890—her 53rd birthday. In recognition of the day, her ailing father went into the garden and picked a bouquet of its first blooming flower, the fragrant narcissus or Chinese Lily, to present to her. This was just two weeks before General Vallejo died. The flowers were pressed as treasured mementos.

DEATH OF DR. LEVI C. FRISBIE

Adela's husband was a successful physician, not only in the city of Vallejo but throughout northern California for forty years. He was a pioneer in his profession long before his wife's brother, Dr. Platon Vallejo, started practicing in Vallejo. Before coming to California, Dr. Frisbie was twice elected president of the Medical Society of his native county in New York state, and, after coming West, he was the first president of the Pacific Medical Society of the counties then comprising Solano, Sonoma, and Napa.

His interest in his work persisted to the last day of his life, which terminated at his residence, 169 York Street, on a September morning in 1892 from a heart attack. It was known that Dr. Frisbie had for many years a serious ailment, but he had not been obliged to neglect his patients.

Adela attempted to tell her far-away brother Ula about the death of her husband. She wrote on October 4, 1892: "Although we feel so keenly, how poor is language to express our deepest emotions, yet as words only can be employed by those separated by distance I shall now tell as clearly as I can about the last hour and death of my dear Levi." She recounted how she had seen her husband in his usual health at nine o'clock, Friday evening. The following morning Levi awoke and, finding himself in great pain, called the maid, Katie. Frightened at the Doctor's appearance, she called Mrs. Frisbie who tried to convince her husband that he was suffering from congestion of the lungs but he kept repeating, "I'm dying." Levi kissed Adela on the cheek, then walked to where his trousers were hanging. From them he took his keys and unlocked his secretary, from which he took two packages of papers. These he handed to Adela, saying, "Keep these, take care of them, they are for you."

Katie, who had gone for Dr. Platon Vallejo, stopped and told the next-door neighbors, the McKnights, who came immediately over to the Frisbies. Mrs.

McKnight asked Dr. Frisbie, "Are your lungs congested?" He replied, "No, it is my heart."

Adela wrote further in her letter to Ula that her husband continued to call for hot water:

I ran down to the kitchen to get some [water] . . . I put his feet in hot water. While I continued to chafe his feet and do all in my power to relieve him, his head dropped on one side. I supposed he was resting but in fact he was gone. So without a struggle other than he endured while walking about—'the silver cord' was loosened and I was alone with my dead. Mr. and Mrs. McKnight with Katie's assistance carried the dear form to my bed where with my own hands I had spread a blanket to receive him. I prayed in his ear for God to have mercy on him.

Andronico was the first to arrive and afterwards Platon, Mr. Topley and others . . . Mr. Callender took charge of the funeral. Levi was dressed in the coat which he wore at Lily's wedding . . . His appearance was that of one lying in a perfect sleep. After a prayer at the house the procession moved to the little Cornell Baptist church where Rev. Gaston (the pastor) assisted Rev. Mr. Chase (Presbyterian) Rev. Van Anda (Methodist), and Rev. Klink conducted the services. A solo "Flee as a Bird" was sung by Miss Winchell and a quartet choir sang other hymns . . . Reverend Chase said in part "Dr. Frisbie will be missed in many spheres. The little children of the Orphan's Home will miss him. He gave to them freely of his skill, his time, his sympathy. His companions among the Pioneers will miss him. The circle of those who come from the East to found a new commonwealth has been broken again and again. It will close again after this new loss but the time is not far distant when its last member will pass away."

After the funeral, Adela said that they rode through the streets with the church bell tolling, then took the train to Sonoma. With her were close relatives, including Edward Frisbie, Platon Vallejo and his 16-year-old daughter Francisca. The widow said that they left the casket in Mountain Cemetery in the new receiving vault surrounded by flowers.

Dr. H. H. Davis of Sonoma, the physician who had attended General Vallejo in his last illness, was never forgotten by Adela. She gave him her late husband's operating chair and in appreciation he wrote her on August 17, 1894:

Much to my surprise and gratification I find myself the possessor of a very handsome and complete Physician's Operating Chair and to your kind thoughtfulness and generosity am I indebted for it. How much I thank you I can not tell you. I shall ever prize it as a gift from the worthy daughter of a noble father, a man whom I was proud to call my friend and whose memory I fondly cherish. It will ever be a gratification to me to feel that I was permitted to be near and administer to his comfort in his last days and as I look upon my handsome chair I shall be reminded that his daughter kindly remembered my attention to him.

Some years later the practice of Dr. Davis with his office equipment including the Physician's Operating Chair was acquired by the young Doctor Allen M. Thomson who in 1902 married General Vallejo's granddaughter, pretty Anita Emparan.

After Doctor Frisbie's death, Adela tried valiantly to carry on. She was a frequent visitor to Lachryma Montis, to share the companionship of her favorite sister Luisa Emparan. There she spent many hours making over her late husband's clothes into short pants for her nephews, Carlos and Raoul. Perhaps to allow for growth, they were made roomy so the boys called them —"Rooms to Let."

Dr. Frisbie left Adela some valuable property situated in various parts of the City of Vallejo. She purchased the property known as "The Cornell" and conducted it as a private boarding house. This augmented her income and provided for certain companionship. As this time she was a member of the Native Daughters of the Golden West. The Vallejo parlor felt it had taken a forward step in having as a member "one so nearly and dearly connected with one of California's distinguished and historical characters."

Adela's added responsibilities, her increasing deafness and the loneliness of living without husband, child and parents proved too difficult. On Tuesday, April 2nd, 1895, as she was about to have her breakfast brought to her room by her maid, she suffered a fatal stroke. She was fifty-eight years old at the time of her death.

Adela was survived by four brothers, Andronico, Platon, Ula and Napoleon and by four sisters, Fannie, Natalia, Luisa and Maria. She was also survived by her aunt Encarnacion, Tia Chichita, the widow of Captain John B. Cooper. Being 87 and not too well, Mrs. Cooper did not attend the funeral but sent word that she was having Masses said for Adela.

Adela's body was taken to Sonoma, where it was buried near her husband and daughter in Mountain Cemetery. Lily had been buried in New York but her body was exhumed and brought to California by Adela soon after the death of her husband.

Dr. Platon was in charge of Adela's estate and he saw to it that Doyle Brothers of Vallejo, who had erected his parents' monument, build a handsome one for the three Frisbies, Levi, Adela and Lily. However, Adela's lasting monument was her life generously lived. As Luisa once said of her sister, "Adela has no equal. She has been a model daughter during her parents' illnesses working constantly night and day. She is truth and justice itself. I shall miss her like the flowers miss the dew and sunshine."

Natalia Veneranda Vallejo

Natalia Veneranda Vallejo

(Mrs. Attila Haraszthy)

The third daughter of the Vallejos, Natalia, was born in Sonoma on February 12th, 1838. She was named after her mother's sister, Maria Antonia Natalia Elijia Carrillo [Mrs. Henry Delano Fitch]; the name Josefa by which she was known, having been bestowed on her by her godmother, who had for the moment forgotten the Carrillo baby's name. The Vallejos' Natalia was baptized by Padre Jose Lorenzo Quijas in the San Francisco Solano Mission, with Don Salvador Vallejo and his wife, Dona Maria de la Luz Carrillo, as her godparents.

Natalia's first home was the Casa Grande on the north side of the Sonoma plaza. There she began her education with tutors. Then when she was sixteen, she became a student at St. Mary's Hall, the school established for young ladies by Dr. John L.Ver Mehr, the first pastor and founder of Grace Parish in San Francisco. The school occupied the large rooms of the Casa Grande after Natalia's parents had moved to their new home, one-half mile northwest of the plaza. Attending with Natalia were her two sisters, Adela and Jovita, and several cousins from the Fitch and Bale families. In June 1855, Natalia prepared the valedictory oration, extolling the beauties of nature, which was published in the *Alta California*.

Girlhood days for Natalia were filled with much "fon"—what with the meriendas (picnics) held in the meadows of the Valle de la Luna or on the grassy plains under the Oaks of Soscol, with band music; and what with the dances at home in the Vallejo parlor which were allowed to last until midnight. However, Senora Vallejo saw to it that her girls were useful. They were taught fine needlework, but they were also allowed to use the Howe sewing machine.

Attractive but not as beautiful as her sisters, Natalia possessed a sparkling personality which made her popular with the opposite sex. Among her admirers was Martin E. Cooke, a brilliant lawyer and active Democratic politician, who, with David Broderick, handled the bill in the State Senate establishing the Capital at Vallejo. When Natalia was about eighteen years old, Mr. Cooke gave her a handsome book, *The Republican Court, American Society in the Days of Washington*, which he inscribed "To Natalia from her dear friend, Martin E. Cooke." It was filled with engravings in color of portraits by Gainsborough, Stuart, Trunbull and Copley depicting the wives and daughters of Colonial statesmen.

Mr. Cooke was a business associate and intimate friend of General Vallejo. When Mr. Cooke became ill the spring of 1857, the General insisted that he stay at Lachryma Montis. In spite of the loving attention, Mr. Cooke's chronic illness resulted in his death on April 13, 1857. His mother wrote from the East that she wanted General Vallejo named as executor of her sons' estate but the local court would not allow him to serve, saying the association of the two men had been too close.

Martin E. Cooke was buried in the Vallejo family burial-grounds adjoining Lachryma Montis. General Vallejo's sorrow at Cooke's death he expressed on April 24, 1857 in a letter to his nephew, Pablo de la Guerra:

> Doubtless you have felt sad about the sudden death of our good friend, Mr. Cooke, and the sorrow that this unexpected event has caused me and which has condemned me to such sadness to overwhelm me. His friendliness, his advice, his right judgment in everything, in effect, his knack of knowing men always astonished me. I'll always remember him, or better said, we ought to regret his passing . . . As for me, not only have I lost an intimate friend but also a man who put my affairs in such good order that I could not have done as well myself. His conduct and good management made me think I was going to have good luck in my financial affairs, and just when we were beginning to realize a profit from such care, constancy and energy. The Easter Season has taken him from us by the stroke of Death. May the Mighty Hand of the Omnipotent God receive him among the Chosen. God grant that he has been ready.

Three days before Natalia's father wrote the foregoing letter, Pablo de la Guerra wrote on stationery of the Senate Chambers in Sacramento to Natalia, calling her "dear little cousin of mine" and telling her that he was in no mood for writing because of the death of Mr. Cooke. He said he learned through his Cousin Fanny that Adela had not received the flowering plant he had sent her. Through Salvador, he was sending a daguerreotype which Salvador, Andres Pico and he had taken together. He closed his letter by saying he might return through Sonoma, and added in English: ". . . will you both abuse me if I go there again? I should like to know before I make up my mind to visit you."

Another of Natalia's suitors was a man of some prominence in the Valley of Sonoma—a Kentuckian and a former member of the Bear Flag Party, who had amassed a fortune at the mines. General Vallejo was not adverse to having a rich son-in-law. He suggested to Natalia that she might take a fancy to him. Whereupon she let her father know, in no uncertain terms, her opinion of the Yankee backwoodsman:

> And now let me answer the question you ask in regard to Mr. Swift—Well, Papa, he may be good and I did not say he is not but there is something wanted in him. Oh! how bad it looks for a man like him, rich, very rich, young and we can say handsome, to be so awkward, to be so speechless as not to let a single word escape from his lips while he calls on the young ladies. He don't know how to speak, not even shake hands. Papa, he pumps instead of shakes. I am sorry to say, that is not the kind of a man that I would or could admire.
>
> The Bible says it is easier for a Camel to pass through the eye of a needle than a rich man to enter into the kingdom of Heaven so there is no chance for poor Mr. Swift. He is so rich that the very weight of them, will weigh him down. You must forgive me for saying so many things but that is just what I think. I am astonished

at you; the idea to think I could take a fancy to him. No, Papa, I am General Vallejo's daughter and I think I will have a better choice than that.

Natalia also had an admirer who was an elderly poet, Don Jose de la Rosa, a family friend of many years. He addressed a poem to "La Senorita Natalia Vallejo, the Darling of my Heart." It was of course in Spanish and composed by this one-time printer of the Zamorano Press. He had also been a clerk of the San Francisco Solano Mission under Padre Quijas, and was the courier selected to carry Vallejo's message to Captain Montgomery after Vallejo's arrest by the Bear Flaggers.

The mother of Natalia was away on a short visit and Natalia wrote her a note saying: "The party is tomorrow night. It could be we will not go so that Jovita and I will be home. Papa is very angry and ill-tempered. We have regretted coming home for the house seems like a prison. We hear no other sound but the voice of Papa like when he is reasoning with you and does not consider."

Senora Vallejo was not fond of writing letters. Whenever she could persuade some member of the family to write for her, she would do so. Often it was Natalia who would write to her father:

> Mama has been wanting me to write you these few lines and enclose a little list which she says not to forget to send. It is just what is needed at home for the present. Dear Papa, and if you have something to spare, do please get me an oil lamp for the parlor. I think it will not be as expensive as burning sperm candles and the Holy Days are near [1858] We will of course have some one or other in the house.

Not only during the Holidays but most of the year the Vallejos had guests and there were many social affairs in Sonoma. One long remembered was the reception that General Vallejo and his wife gave for Mayor John Cameron and his Lady. The invitations were printed on white satin.

In June 1858, Natalia attended a ball with the Haraszthys, the family of the man who was to court Natalia with serious attentions. Of this event she wrote her father:

> Well, I must tell you the good fun we had at the Ball, Thursday night. Oh! Papa it was one of the best Balls I ever was in before. It was splendid, the hall looked very handsome indeed. Papa, the Pikes were dressed with a great deal of taste, indeed the ladies as well as the gentlemen. The ladies looked charming. The music, it was the best from San Francisco. All of us went together with Mrs. Tracy and the family of Colonel Haraszthy. You ought to see the old lady and gentleman dance, they enjoyed themselves as well as the young ones. A great many came from San Francisco. Mr. Brooks was here and Mr. Harry Logan and Mr. Valentine. Papa, we did think of you and we wished you were present. Uncle Salvador's daughter went with us and enjoyed herself as well as the rest but I don't know if my Uncle will like her doing it.

The months of June and July of 1858 were busy ones with plans for the wedding of Adela to Doctor Levi Cornell Frisbie. During Adela's shopping visits to San Francisco with her mother, Natalia remained in Sonoma to watch over her two baby sisters, Luisa and Maria. On the day of Adela's marriage which occurred at Lachryma Montis, Natalia being twenty was allowed to sign as a witness to her sister's marriage. As previously noted General Vallejo remained in San Francisco and did not attend the ceremony.

NATALIA'S TRIP EAST

The Vallejos had Indian and Italian laborers in the fields and Chinese servants in the home. Natalia's mother enjoyed caring herself for her little ones. In this task Natalia was a great help, and she liked to let her father know of her home industry as she was aware of his teasing views on a young girl's indolence from a clipping he had placed in a scrapbook: "A girl will go to a dance and waltz seven straight hours without complaining; but just ask the same young lady to wrestle five minutes with a broom and she'll faint before she gets both hands fairly on the handle." With the idea of letting Papa Vallejo know of her sewing, she wrote July 15, 1858:

> Mrs. Tracy is coming to spend the day with me. We are to sew on the Sewing Machine and then we are going to Mrs. Tate's for a ride. We are invited to Mr. Swift's [Granville P. Swift] next Saturday. He is going to lay one of the cornerstones of the house and he is going to put in a bottle of Sonoma wine. He is to have many ladies and gentlemen as well as us.
>
> Papa, I have no more to tell you and Mrs. Tracy is coming. I can hear her gay laughter through the trees.

Because of Natalia's gentle way with children, her sister Fannie Frisbie persuaded General and Senora Vallejo to allow Natalia to accompany the Frisbie family to New York, to help care for little Fanita and Benicia on the long journey. The close companionship on this journey was the beginning of a life-long bond of affection. As Fannie said later: "Platon and Natalia are the relatives that are nearest my heart."

The Frisbies and Natalia sailed from San Francisco in October 1860 on *The Golden Age* for New York. The story of that journey was narrated in the following letter from Natalia to her mother:

> Since we left San Francisco Wharf, we had very good weather except two or three days were the only ones that made me seasick, the rest of the time I spent happily. Everything they tell you about the ocean wave, that the steamer is on one end and the other way down, there is no such thing. It is not as bad as they say. Of course one feels it very much if one is in a little boat that is being blown and buffeted but in a steamer like the Golden Age, it is a pleasure.
>
> When we arrived at Acapulco it was about two in the morning. Later John, Fanny and I and some four or five gentlemen got off together. The great city of Acapulco was about a mile from where the steamer was. We were delayed about an hour because they had to row; finally we got there. The men had to carry us in their arms because we could not get along any other way. Fanny and I fixed our petticoats. We removed our shoes and were ready to hold on to the arms of the men.
>
> We were ready to go into the City and had not walked three steps and upon

turning a corner, we were surrounded by natives; natives of all sizes; some dressed, other half dressed and many without clothing. There were there to sell to the passengers, to the Yankees their shells, snails, oranges, lemons, bananas and many foolish trifles. We bought some fruit, the men as well went looking for a hotel.

The houses were like Indian huts, made of simple tule and mud. About four-thirty we left Acapulco. In another seven days, we put in at Panama. We went ashore at seven in the morning, that is to say, John, Fanny, the babies, George Butler and I. We went to the Aspinwal House and had a good meal.

The first thing heard upon arriving, are the bells of the Church . . . The houses are all made of adobe mud bricks. On the roof of the house one sees growing all kinds of grasses, flowers, so that on the roof of the Cathedral the trees grow; that even bananas are seen; not only this but a thousand kinds of weeds among the statues of the Saints inside and out, mustard grows on them. Upon poor St. Peter radishes come out everywhere. Cutting is not thought of, for even cabbages I saw growing at the feet of I know not what Saint. But one thing pleased me in Panama—the country side. It is worthwhile to come from California to see the countryside. I can not tell all the kinds of trees, grass and flowers. We took the cars at twelve o'clock and by four we arrived at Aspinwall, another little Acapulco. At five in the evening, October 25th, we embarked on the steamer "*Northern Light*" for New York. Fanny became somewhat ill but I was carefree like the sailors.

On the second of November we arrived at the great city of New York. It pleased me immensely. We took a coach and went to the Hotel Metropolitan. Platon and Uladislao came as soon as they knew of our arrival and stayed with us Saturday and Sunday. We found them in good health.

After a short visit in New York City, the Frisbie family and Natalia went to Syracuse to visit Captain Frisbie's relatives. There Natalia continued writing her letter, saying:

Here we are in Syracuse for a few days I hope, for I want to spend the winter in New York and Washington, not in this old outlandish place, 250 miles from the City . . . Broadway Street there is one of the handsomest streets in the world but in mountains, hills, valleys, trees and flowers, none like our home. The country here is not to compare with our own California, what I have seen of it coming from New York, there are very pretty cities and that is all. You have no idea how cold it is outdoors. It is nothing but ice, snow, wind, mud and everything else that is disagreeable. Oh! it keels me and anybody else that comes from a decent climate like ours. California's climate, Papa, is Angel's climate . . . I will be home in three months but you can write regularly because there is the steamer, the Overland or the "*Pony Express.*"

Natalia's desire was realized and she went to Washington, D.C., with the Frisbies. The Federal City was crowded with visitors who had come for the inauguration of Abraham Lincoln as the sixteenth President of the United States. A ball was to be given in the *Muslin Palace*, a temporary building hung with blue and white muslin. Natalia, along with the Frisbies, had been invited. In great excitement she opened the official invitation and saw the American Eagle surrounded by 34 stars engraved on the invitation which read: "The honor of MISS VALLEJO's company is requested at the Union Ball on Monday evening March 4th at Washington, D.C."

Two hundred and thirty leading statesmen were present at the ball as *Managers;* among them were several appointees to Lincoln's Cabinet: Secretary of State W. H. Seward, Secretary of the Treasury J. A. Dix, Attorney-General E. M. Stanton, Postmaster General Horatio King. Andrew Johnson, the Vice-President, was also a manager, as was General Scott and the two United States Senators from California, M. S. Latham and William Bigler.

The grand march was led by President Lincoln and Mayor James E. Berret of Washington, followed by Mrs. Lincoln on the arm of Senator Stephen A. Douglas of Illinois. The First Lady was gowned in blue silk with a blue ostrich feather in her hair. The Marine Band furnished the music.

Natalia wore a handsome hoop-skirted gown of apple-green satin embroidered in flowers. It has been said that President Lincoln danced with one lady from each state; if that is true, Natalia may have represented California, as there is a tradition in the Vallejo family that Natalia danced with the Civil War President whose birthday was the same as her own.

Thirty-nine years later, Natalia lifted the historic gown from an ancient brass-studded camphorwood chest. Removing the blue tissue wrappings, she altered it to the prevailing fashion for her young daughter, Lolita, to wear to the turn of the Century Ball at Sonoma's Union Hall. There it again became "historic" as beautiful Lolita Haraszthy led the grand march with her partner Bob Pasch on New Year's Eve 1900.

NATALIA'S FIANCE

On Natalia's return to Sonoma from the East, she saw a great deal of the members of the Haraszthy family. With the impudence of the very young, she had called the Countess Eleanora Haraszthy "the old lady," and Colonel Agoston Haraszthy, "the old gentleman," in spite of the fact that both were only in their middle forties.

Colonel and Mrs. Haraszthy had two daughters and four sons. It was not long before Natalia knew that the second son, Attila Haraszthy, with his classical European education and his Continental manners, was her choice. Instead of "pumping" her hand, as the Yankee backwoodsman had done, Attila no doubt pressed a kiss upon it.

Attila had helped his father with the planting of the vineyards and gardens of Las Flores, a tract of land of about 211 acres near the Mission Dolores. In 1857 when the Colonel bought 560 acres in the foothills of the Mayacamas Mountains, northeast of the town of Sonoma, he sent Attila there to look after the vineyard which had been planted with cuttings from his Crystal Springs property. The Colonel called his new place "*Buena Vista.*" On one of the high spots he built a white Pompeiian-type villa with fountains and formal gardens; and it was at the Vintage Ball, given in the villa, that Attila showered Natalia with attentions.

While General Vallejo was at the San Cayetano Rancho in the Pajaro Valley during the spring of 1863, he received a letter from Natalia telling him of her promise to marry Attila Haraszthy. On April 15, 1863, the General wrote to his wife, discussing the engagement:

> Enclosed I send to you a letter for Natalia. It is my answer to one she wrote to me lately telling me that she was engaged to marry Attila Haraszthy but she doesn't say if she has consulted you or given you notice of such a thing. As you'll see in the aforementioned answer, I can't do more than assent to what she asks as she is old enough and has enough judgment to choose a man for a husband. I deem it my duty to send you the letter to read before giving it to her. It could be there is something which I don't know or that she may wish to surprise me; but if not, you should hand it to her.
>
> It is very strange that every time I come to Monterey the girls always want to get married and others always learn of it before I know about it. They have informed me that Jovita too is engaged to one of the other Haraszthy boys but I know it only by hearsay. We shall see where the rocket bursts. Mr. Haraszthy hasn't told me anything about the family business and it was natural that he should speak to me for the sake of courtesy unless he (H) doesn't know anything about the business.

Jovita was indeed engaged to Arpad Haraszthy. Natalia and Jovita were not as timid as their older sister Adela, who had pleaded for her father's consent. The two younger girls took things into their own hands, and made plans for a double wedding. Sonoma County clerk William L. Anderson, having duly issued the marriage licenses, Padre L. Deyaert of the San Francisco Solano Mission performed the double wedding ceremony on June 1, 1863. Countess Eleanora Haraszthy's gift to her son Attila was an inscribed Bible, which had been presented to her by David Broderick.

Natalia was ill during the first year of her marriage and lost her first baby, a son, born on August 2nd, 1864. The infant had been named Attila Agosto de Guadalupe, after its father and two grandfathers. The following Spring, Natalia was again expecting a child and again she was ill. Her father whose return to California from the East had been delayed because of the assassination of President Lincoln, was concerned over Natalia's illness.

On May 15, 1865, General Vallejo wrote to Natalia from New York City, on the stationery of the Fifth Avenue Hotel where he was staying. The hotel faced Madison Square at Broadway and 23rd Street, and was a gathering-place for notables. Three weeks before, the funeral of President Lincoln had passed his hotel. For several hours Vallejo watched the cortege composed of organized groups, Lodges, labor unions, commercial bodies interspersed with spectacular floats and military bands playing dirges. The hearse was drawn by sixteen white horses covered with black coverlets. The General felt that his daughter, who had been in Washington, D.C., in 1861 attending President Lincoln's first Inaugural, would be interested in the story of the late President's funeral procession in New York City. Consequently he went into considerable detail:

Dear Natalia:

Yesterday I received your letter of the 30th of March last, because it was addressed to Washington, it was held at the Willard Hotel but finally I received it and was very pleased, first, because you are living still, daughter of mine and I'll see you well and happy as before. Each time I think of your illness it frightens me.

We had decided to leave here on the 23rd of April but events have become so complicated that I have much unfinished business which I thought could be concluded. Since the evacuation of Charleston, the taking of Richmond and the surrender of General Lee with his Army; there have been celebrations everywhere in all cities as well as political discussions on the coming peace so long desired. Naturally business is at a standstill. About these public rejoicings, before they were over, the assassination of President Lincoln followed in their tragic wake as you already know from the public newspaper dispatches regarding the general consternation that followed.

The nation is covered with sorrow and the houses of business are closed for twenty days so we also lose time. I am afraid to look on this city of New York. Everything is in black; excitement at times, then consternation.

Finally the showing of the body of Mr. Lincoln in funeral honors as no one else in the world has received them. The line of march was twelve miles long, with some 80,000 men in the procession. From 900,000 to a million souls as spectators; a magnificent and stupendous spectacle. The singular thing about it was that in all that vast multitude, there was not one disturbance. When the catafalque passed, hats were all removed in respectful silence. Numberless bands of music played funeral marches, profound silence reigned, men and women in significant mourning with armbands; flags at half-mast with cannon shots every half minute, everything as solemn as could be.

The procession in front of the Fifth Avenue Hotel lasted six hours. Trees in the park were full of men and boys, they looked like crows. Two of the trees split and their dwellers toppled to the ground. When I get back I'll finish the story, it would take too long a letter.

I've visited many towns and am getting reconciled with the climate and with the greeness, nevertheless it rains nearly every day and I catch cold. Colonel Haraszthy arrived here, plenty sick after fourteen days of travel but the weather is good now. Today, the newspaper says that Jeff Davis has been taken prisoner. Poor man! Many say he will be hanged. I fear that many things can happen; it would have been better had he gotten away.

This letter is also for Mama. Tell her I cannot leave here until the 12th of June and if God wills and I don't drown en route I shall be in Sonoma at the end of June. Kiss Napoleon, Lulu, Maria and I hope she doesn't get sick. Regards to Mrs. Haraszthy, Jovita and Arpad. I received a letter from Attila and I am glad he is well. Tell Ula that I've not forgotten him and tell him to be good.

Your Papa who loves you from his heart,
M. G. VALLEJO

Colonel Haraszthy, Natalia's father-in-law, whom General Vallejo had seen in New York, had gone East to confer with a Congressional Committee in Washington, D.C., on the proposed wine and brandy taxes.

On September 6th, 1865, Natalia gave birth to another son, to whom she gave the name *Mariano* in honor of her father, who acted as godfather. Natalia's next son, her third, was named Agoston, for the baby's grandfather Haraszthy. This baby was a blond which appealed to Natalia, she wrote: "Mama, you should see how pretty Agoston (Gusti) is, with his fair skin and blue eyes, he looks like a little bird."

Natalia's next two children were daughters, christened Eleanora Benicia (familiarly known as Lolita), after the infant's two grandmothers; and Natalia, after herself, but called "Tala." The godfather of the last named baby girl was Ula Vallejo.

After her marriage, Natalia's first home was a house built in the center of one of Colonel Haraszthy's vineyards. She gave it the name "Champagne," and so designated it on her stationery. In April 1870, while she was living there, and her mother keeping house in Fannie's home in Vallejo, she wrote Senora Vallejo the following letter, in which she gave her a vivid description of the condition of the San Francisco Solano Mission church.

> I see by the papers that the Captain [Frisbie] arrived, how happy you must be. Since I came from Vallejo I have wanted to write to you but I have such a cold, I can hardly open my eyes and Mariano and Gusti too. I think I'm sorry I came, Mama since from the time I got here, Attila has been away almost all the time and now he is in San Francisco . . . Sunday we went to Mass and the church was so cold and damp that all of us suffered. But Mama, the strangest thing of all of this—instead of Father Deyaert giving each one a branch, as they do in all the other churches, he grasped a bunch of branches and threw them outside the railing and told the people that if they wanted branches they should come when they wanted to get them, that he didn't have time. It seemed to me that it was like giving a bunch of cows something to eat, the way he took the pile of green willows. I think he did not even bless them and the church was filled with people. Neither a sermon nor Holy Water at the door.
>
> A terrible smell inside of wet earth. In the big seat of ours, between the tablets and the wall, there is a hole big enough to put a cat in and through the hole there came a terrible draft . . . The Chinese that Attila hired when you were here, left the same day you left for Vallejo so there were 2 or 3 days without a Chinaman. Then we found another who is quite regular, makes very good bread, washes and irons . . . he cooks ala "pike."

Natalia was delighted when her father gave her 122 acres adjoining Lachryma Montis, facing 300 feet on Spain Street. On it Attila Haraszthy built a house from the borrowed blueprints of Vallejo's Victorian Gothic mansion. Natalia called it "Willows Wild" because of the willow trees growing near the creek. While they were living in this new home, little Agoston (Gusti) burned his face and eyes so badly with gun-powder during the Holiday season, that at first it was feared he might lose his sight.

On part of the 122 acres and with funds borrowed from the Sonoma Bank of which he was a director, Natalia's husband planted grapes. This was against the advice of friends, who had lost heavily because of the destruction of the vines by the insect Phylloxera. Attila did not heed their warning and lost everything. For a time he thought seriously of leaving Sonoma and opening a wine shop in San Francisco or in Vallejo, but financial worries brought on illness and he passed away at the age of fifty-one on February 2, 1886.

Henry Weyl was appointed administrator of Attila Haraszthy's estate, which was so heavily mortgaged that Weyl was able to save only the home for the widow and her children. Natalia's father was in straightened circumstances himself, and could only help by purchasing "leche" (milk) from her.

When Natalia's parents became ill, she spent some time each day in nursing them. Her mother's stroke after the General's death had made it necessary that some one be with Senora Vallejo all the time. During Natalia's visits, her mother discussed her will, which she had made in March 1890. Natalia thought that her mother had made a mistake in leaving her property to the two youngest daughters, Luisa and Maria, instead of sharing the estate with all the children. In a letter she wrote to her brother Platon on November 22, 1890, she quotes Senora Vallejo as saying: "Your Papa left everything to me so I could do what I think best . . . I want to leave my children equal parts . . . Your Papa left it all to me and it is mine alone . . . The lands that Papa gave them before, have nothing to do with what he left me. All this is mine alone and I will do what I want with it. Now my head is dizzy but in a few days I am going to do it." To this Natalia added a postscript: "All I have written is the truth and nothing but the truth."

On January 7th, 1891, she wrote again to her brother, saying: "I would like to talk to you about Mama's will. I think we ought to do something. I don't see why the girls must have everything. Mama doesn't want them to have it all. I wrote as much as I could remember of all Mama told me before she was struck by the paralysis."

It was natural for Natalia to feel that the estate should be shared. She had a real need for additional resources, as she had been widowed four years.

Senora Vallejo never changed her will. She must have felt it was only fair that the two younger children, who had been brought up without the advantages of travel or the gifts of land which had been given to the older Vallejo children, should receive the estate. She had often heard her husband say that that was his desire.

After Natalia's parents' death, she was anxious that their bodies which had been temporarily placed in the Duhring family vault, should rest in a vault of their own. She wrote Platon on February 12, 1891, her birthday, discussing the situation:

Inclosed you will find Fanny's last letter and by that you can see that we can begin the vault at once. How kind of John to do so much. I hope Fanny will come to California.

I have not seen a soul from L.M. Adela is still there. I am still under the weather but feeling a little better. If the girls have not done anything toward the vault, you and I ought to take it in hand and try to stop all this begging . . . Lulu said she had or she was going to write to Senator Ragsdale to help us or to build the vault. Have you seen anything in the papers? I hear there was an article in the Alta. Let *us*, Platon go to work and build Papa's vault and let those people see that we can do something without making so much fuss and newspaper talk. If Fanny comes to Cal. I guess she will straighten up matters.

Under the direction of Platon Vallejo, the vault was constructed in Sonoma's Mountain Cemetery. The sarcophagus, of California granite weighing 22 tons was executed by Doyle Brothers of the City of Vallejo.

NATALIA'S LAST YEARS

As the years went by, Natalia added weight to a figure which even as a child was chubby and as a young lady, plump. When her plumpness reached over two hundred pounds, she had a special carriage made for her outings, and, for her hours at home, a special rocking chair. Old-timers recall seeing this daughter of General Vallejo occupy the full front seat of a fringe-top surrey while her two beautiful daughters, Lolita and Tala, sat in the rear seat. She always drove and chaperoned them when they attended the dances at Glen Ellen.

Like many stout people, Natalia had a pleasant disposition. Her nephews and nieces all adored "Aunt Nat." The four little motherless daughters of Dr. Platon Vallejo loved coming to Sonoma during their vacation where they could be with their cousins, Lolita and Tala. Also visiting at Natalia's home, there might be two of her husband's young relatives, a niece Harriet Haraszthy [Bela Haraszthy's daughter] who had come from her school in Napa; and a nephew, "Georgie" Allan Hancock [son of Ida Haraszthy Hancock]. Young Allan Hancock came from the military school, Belmont College in San Mateo County, to visit at *Willows Wild*.

During these visits, Natalia's parlor would be filled with music, much as Colonel Haraszthy's villa had been at Buena Vista. "Georgie" would get out his harmonica or perhaps his cornet (he was the chief bugler for Belmont College) and play. Natalia or her daughter "Tala" would play the piano.

The years ahead would find Allan Hancock developing into a musician of consequence. His mother, in appreciation of her son's musical talent, gave him a rare Gagliano violon-cello, which enabled him to become an interpreter of the world's great composers, as a member of the Los Angeles Symphony Orchestra and the Philharmonic Orchestra.

OLD MISSION IN SONOMA SAVED

In 1905, the old San Francisco Solano Mission was saved from total ruin by means of a fund raised by the California Historic Landmarks' League, the Native Sons and Daughters of the Golden West, and other patriotic groups, under the auspices of the San Francisco Examiner. Natalia Vallejo Haraszthy expressed her feelings in a letter to the Examiner Editor:

Words are entirely inadequate to express my gratitude and my delight to you for the preservation of the landmarks of California, particularly for the saving of the

Sonoma Mission San Francisco Solano. The dear little church where I was baptized many, many, many years ago when my idolized father General Vallejo and my dear Angel mother, Francisca Benicia Carrillo Vallejo were young.

I remember our pastor Padre Quijas, a Franciscan priest with his long gray habit and sandaled feet with a capuchin over his head and rosary hanging at his side. Two of my ancestors rest within the Chapel walls. I was born in Sonoma, educated and married right here in old Sonoma City and I am here yet surrounded by my children, grandchildren and a host of dear friends.

A few years later it was with great sadness that Natalia left her residence in Sonoma because of ill health, relinquishing thus her nearness to her childhood home, the beloved Lachryma Montis where, as she said in a poem, "the waters caress the rocks and the air is a sacred concert of birds and leaves. Oh! Mountain Tear, home of those beings who gave us life, my father and mother."

Natalia moved to Oakland, to the home occupied by her daughters Tala and Lolita, where she was cared for lovingly. A fall forced Natalia into a wheel chair. One of Tala's daughters who became the movie star and dancer Natalie Kingston remembers her grandmother seated in that chair and when little Natalie temporarily provoked her mother, Grandmother Natalia would hide the small form in the folds of her garment.

In March of 1913, Natalia was saddened by the death in Los Angeles of her sister-in-law, Ida Haraszthy Hancock-Ross. Ida left $1,000 in her will for Natalia, but she was not to enjoy it long. Four months later, on July 30, 1913 a stroke of paralysis caused her death at the age of senventy-five at 119 Twelfth Street, Oakland.

Besides Natalia's children who were present at her passing, there was also Bess, the wife of Natalia's youngest son Agoston (Gusti). Bess was the little Irish beauty, Elizabeth Merry, who always said that her husband's mother was a fond and indulgent mother-in-law.

Among the letters of sympathy received by Natalia's children was one from their mother's brother Platon: "I see by the papers, the passing of your dear mother, my sister, Mrs. A. Haraszthy in Oakland yesterday. Perhaps at her advanced age it was to be expected that the Call would come sooner or later; nothing is more common to all than this universal change, the advance from one condition of existence to another, falling asleep here to awake in another greater life . . . Our Heavenly Father in his Mercy will receive her gentle beautiful soul. Believing this, there's a consolation, a mitigating balm left for us who mourn, not without hope, of a truer, better and eternal life with God."

Natalia's body was taken to Sonoma for the Requiem Mass at the St. Francis Solano Church. This fifth child of the Vallejos was buried in Mountain Cemetery next to the grave of her husband, Attila Haraszthy, the second son of Colonel Haraszthy, noted viticulturist, who is especially remembered each Autumn when the grapes color in the Valley of Sonoma.

Platon M. G. Vallejo

Platon M. G. Vallejo

The seventh child of the Vallejos was destined to be an understanding and devoted son. He was born on the fifth of February, 1841 in the large adobe house known as the Casa Grande, on the north side of the Sonoma plaza. The infant was given the classical name of *Platon* because, at the time of his birth, his father was absorbed in the Philosophy of Plato. To the first name was added that of his father, *Mariano Guadalupe.*

When Platon was only five years old, he unwittingly helped in the making of the Bear Flag. He was looking on while the square of cloth was being painted by a member of the Party. When a gust of wind ruffled the cloth, the amateur artist called the boy, "Hi, Sonny, put your foot on it." In later years Platon said it was the one thing in his life in which he took no pride.

Another incident of his childhood was when Platon, in a spirit of resentment against his mother's discipline, tied the tails of two of her pet kittens together and hung them on the clothes line. Their cries soon brought an Indian servant to the rescue.

At the age of eight, Platon was allowed to attend the burial services of his Grandmother Carrillo in the San Francisco Solano Mission and saw her body interred in the church near the Holy Water Font.

Platon was a great friend of his oldest sister Fannie, and when she began housekeeping in the new city of Benicia, Platon lived with her and went to school. One of his letters to his mother, written at that time (May 20, 1851), contains several items of interest:

Dear Mama:

Receive the greatest affectionate regards from me, Fannie and the Captain. Tell my Aunt Felicidad that I am very happy that she is ironing my shirts; tell Henry to take good care of my cinnamon colt, cleaning him with a brush . . . Fannie says she won the bet from Felicidad since I learned the Philadelphia polka in one day. On Sunday the 18th, it rained here quite a bit but in spite of this, many ships are always going up and down. I still haven't gone to school having been sick with boils but I will be going soon . . . Papa has been very sad because of his trouble and because he hasn't been able to send home the provisions that he wanted to send.

His father's "trouble" to which Platon referred was the General's concern over the permanent location of the State Capital.

In 1853, when Platon was twelve years old, he made his first trip East with his sister and her husband, Captain John B. Frisbie. Frisbie had gone East to promote his and General Vallejo's joint business enterprises, and Platon went with them in order to join his older brother Andronico who was at school near Baltimore. After two years in Maryland, where he did well in his studies, Platon returned to California and enrolled, along with his younger brother Uladislao ("Ula") at Mr. Crittenden's *San Francisco College,* which was on Bush Street between Mason and Taylor. The Vallejo boys occupied rooms situated in the back part of the school, and the following letter from Platon to his father indicated that things were going well with them:

We have had some two or three very foggy days since you went away. Last night it was so much so that we could hardly see twenty paces before or behind in the street . . . The best wizard in the world will be in San Francisco in a few days, also the Christy Ministrels, the best of the day . . . We are getting along well in our studies.

Ula has improved a great deal . . . Ula told me to tell you, to take this letter as from both of us. That he would write to you next mail. Ain't he a young villain? He wants to pay you back, he says it will be "capital fun," when you read the above. He does it in fun, you know.

A few days after July Fourth 1858, Platon wrote again:

My dear Father:

I received a letter from Adela yesterday and said they were all well at home. We bought a few fireworks on the Fourth and not wishing to have the fun all to ourselves, Ula and the son of Mr. Ross and myself went up near St. Mary's Hall and had the greatest fun you ever saw. The young ladies also in our exploits, also Mrs. Ver Mehr who was looking out the window . . . A young lady came up behind Ula and hit him on the back with a torpedo (this is a kind of firecracker that will crack as hard as a gun by striking against anything). After entertaining ourselves in this manner till about nine or ten o'clock, we bid Mrs. Ver Mehr and the ladies goodnight and retired to the Dormitory.

In spite of their many opportunities for "fun," the Vallejo boys did not neglect the serious practice of the arts while they were attending San Francisco College. In fact, Platon took violin lessons on an instrument his father had bought for $20.

That Platon was seriously inclined was evident from his ability when only eighteen to evaluate the *carta del consejo* (letter of advice) sent to him from his mother's cousin Ampara Ruiz de Burton, the wife of Colonel Henry Burton, former commander of the *Susan Drew;* one of the vessels which carried Col. Stevenson's New York Regiment to California. Her letter to Platon was written in 1859, before he went to school in New York City:

I am pleased that you accepted my humble and sincere advice. It was offered not only because I like you very much but because it is my ardent wish that all the Californians may cherish forever in their bruised hearts, that loyal attachment to their own race. But it should be cherished, my dear Platon, with liberality, that is without bitterness and aversion, which some seem to think, is the best proof of patriotism; without the narrowness of view which will not see virtues in others or faults in ourselves but with that judicious liberality, true magnamity which will grant their due to others fully and willingly.

We can keep sacred the holy feeling, the love of our own race. Unhappily many of our paisanos do not act out this principle, but act as if they thought that to draw into their shell of impotent disregard, is to be good patriots. How misled they are. They are so little conciliatory and the Americans so little generous . . . And now we have to beg for what we had the right to demand.

It cannot be denied that the Californians have reason to complain. The Americans must know it; their boasted liberty and equality of rights seem to stop when it meets a Californian. Witness the Land Commission! We are a child's handful in their mighty grasp; they can crush us with impunity. They know it and broke their faith as solemnly pledged at Guadalupe Hidalgo; broke it by stooping to a miserable stratagem. How shameful this, in this, in the conquering, the prosperous and mighty nation.

Her letter made quite an impression on Platon. He later shared it with his father who wrote: "A thousand times you have said to me, 'our race' and the 'Anglo-Saxon race' and I confess to you candidly that even now my attention has been aroused to such a degree that I take the liberty of asking you, 'What do you mean in those two distinct phrases?' I am surprised at what you assert in your letter in that respect. I do not believe that my race is condemned to an eternally inferior position with the only alternative of being mixed with the Yankee race . . . Do you believe that our blood is better than theirs? The Yankees have it over us in physique, in business acumen, crazy enterprises with no other God than money. We excel in enjoyment, pleasure, romanticism, etc. so that those two conflicting elements in the mixture of the blood in both races can do no less than produce a third, more beautiful, more energetic, stronger, sweeter in character, more temperate and I believe stronger. The climates in which they have developed naturally have produced opposite effects . . . in one, activity, in the other, softness."

MEDICAL STUDENT

In April 1860, when he was nineteen years old, Platon once again went East, this time to enter Columbia University as a medical student. With him was his brother Ula, who was to enroll at St. John's College, at Fordham, New York. Before Platon left California, Senora Vallejo took him shopping in San Francisco and bought him at Joseph's Jewelry Store on Montgomery Street a gold pen—a pen he kept over fifty years.

One Spring day in New York City, when the two Vallejo boys were strolling along Fifth Avenue, their eyes were attracted to a handsome turn-out, drawn by a pair of magnificent bay mares. Turning to Ula, Platon said, "Notice the brand!" Ula looked and saw the "inter-twined inverted spades," the brand of their father's stables; but with such fast-stepping horses, there was no time to ask the driver for the story of their shipment from California.

When summer arrived, Platon was quite conscious of New York's heat. As he sat in his room on July 19, 1860, writing to his father, he told him that the perspiration was running down his face and his shirt was soaking wet. Continuing, he said:

The vacation at St. John's commenced on Wednesday the 11th of this month. Ula was here in New York and spent the Sunday with me. He left on Monday and went back to the college to study. He says he is going to study this summer and make up one year. He likes the college and his professors. He is bent on study and determined he shall lose no time. I am glad to see the boy so earnest.

I left everything I had in Vallejo in care of Captain Frisbie except what was sold. The cattle you know I sold . . . they were very poor; the water in Vallejo did not agree with them, and they began to look miserable and I was afraid they would not go through the winter . . . The horses you know were sold at auction because I was going away . . . besides it did not pay to keep them, such a lot of scrubs while there is so much good stock in the country . . . I kept the best horses in the band and sold all those that were good-for-nothing. Those that I did not sell are now, Captain tells me, a part of Big John's family and are in good condition.

When Platon had finished his letter, he walked down to the Astor Hotel—a good three miles—and on his return he took a shower which he said was "co,co,co,cold."

On June 15, 1860 Vallejo wrote to Platon, telling him that he had received with pleasure his letters from Acapulco and Panama saying, "Last month I was elected MAYOR OF THE CITY OF SONOMA and although it pays no salary, it is an honor to be elected without opposition." He added, "I should like to know in what condition the little interests I gave you to manage in Vallejo were left, since I know nothing up to now. I would say nothing about this if you were twenty-one already." Platon replied to his father's question—"I left everything I had in Vallejo in the care of Captain Frisbie except what was sold."

Captain Frisbie reported to Platon in a letter dated October 11, 1860 on how he had managed the latter's holdings in California: "I have sold your farm at $50 an acre, $500 to be paid in cash, $2,000 in other property and the balance in one, two, three, four and five years with ten percent per annum but the interest will amount to much more than the rent this year. I have sold your place in Sonoma for $1,500, $300 cash and the balance in three years with interest. But these sales will I think enable me in the course of a year to take up your mortgage to Kelly and leave you an investment that will pay you from four to five hundred dollars a year, perhaps more. At all events that will go far toward paying your expenses at present and also assist you in starting your profession . . . I feel assured you are disposed to exercise a reasonable economy and fully appreciate the importance of acquiring prudent habits."

New Yorkers returning from the country to the city in the autumn of 1860 made it a lively place. For the Vallejo boys it was made particularly lively by the coming of Captain Frisbie, accompanied by his wife and their three little daughters (ages five, three and one). With them also was Natalia Vallejo who was to help care for the Frisbie children and to study music. Soon after their arrival, Captain Frisbie wrote Platon's father: "Platon has wonderfully improved in appearance and address and is regarded as one of the most distinguished medical students in the city. Indeed I was not prepared for so marked an improvement in so short a time. The only apprehension I have with reference to him is that the close application to study may impair his health." Shortly afterwards Platon himself wrote to his father: "I received your letter for Natalia and sent it on without delay. I suppose you have already heard from them by Pony Express. They [Frisbie family] spent two or three days here, then passed on to Syracuse. . . Yesterday I bought a small dissecting case which cost me $6 and tomorrow I begin to investigate the anatomy of the human body. The study is very difficult and dangerous and therefore it requires great attention and care in the pursuance of it. But I guess we can manage that. Tell Mother that I do not write to her at this time but this is for you and her and all the children to whom I send affection. Give my love and respects to Adela and the Doctor.

Affairs back in California had not been going so well for Platon's parents. His father had been under a severe strain due to the reversal of the Supreme Court on the Soscol grant. His mother shared her husband's worry over finances. She found some relief in writing to Platon:

The other day I wrote you a letter dictated by your Papa but this is by me alone and I'm telling you how I feel. God grant that you receive it. Dear, dear son, Platon, I want to tell you not to be like Uladislao who left his studies to come to Sonoma and lie around without learning anything . . . Platon, here this letter for you has been around here for some days and right now—about half an hour ago I received one from you in which you tell me that you are well and happy which is the important thing . . . Now we're going to speak of other things.

I and the family all are well. When I received your letter we were all together in the sewing room and all heard your letter read because Natalia read it to everyone. Each one took part and all said that they were going to write to you. It seems that Uladislao is annoyed with you because you haven't answered his letter; Henry as always well; Andronico isn't at home. He is in Napa with your Aunt Luz. He still doesn't find employment. He goes about like the Wandering Jew—poor boy. Yes, dear Platon—God grant that it isn't going to be the same with you . . . and all because of the bad temper of your papa who hasn't known, doesn't know and never will how to manage his children. I say it with a sad heart but it is the truth.

Platon, I am going to tell you why your Papa is so silent; why he is very poor. Captain Frisbie has given bad accounts to your father and the government of the United States has taken from him the Soscol properties and furthermore the little that remains to him is pledged to Mr. Madden and he also owes other people.

Platon, how many things I want to tell you but you see that I can scarcely write. In a few words, I'm going to tell you—your papa has lost everything in one way or another nor are there hopes of adjustment because he has such a bad disposition you can't stand him; at times he is so good that you can't believe it is your papa—in a little while he is so angry that no one can believe it is the same man. Sometimes I start to speak to him about something or ask him a question and he answers me so peevishly and with such bad words I am frightened. He changes from one moment to the next from one extreme to the other. Just think of me, Platon, dear, how sad I must be.

God is very great and I hope that He will give me strength to be able to bear up. Philosophy is very good, isn't it? Platon what are we going to do? I am happy when I see others poorer than we—and they live content.

Platon, the other day I was in Vallejo and learned that what you used to have in that town, you now have nothing. I didn't want to ask more as I don't know how you left things. They say they sold it all . . . So one loses on all sides. Your papa is very angry with Captain Frisbie but it doesn't do him any good—you know Americans. As they are intent upon appropriating the property of the Californians, all are the same, aren't they? You wouldn't think the Captain capable of treating your papa so badly, would you? But he is the worst of all. The others hardly knew us but this one is married to one of my daughters, is an ingrate and a shame but he is an American and we can't hope for anything but tricks.

Platon, it's been some days since I began to write this letter but I hadn't sent it to you because it seems so poorly written that I lost interest in sending it to you but I want to tell you not to go to war.

Platon did not heed his mother's advice but volunteered his services to his adopted country.

CIVIL WAR VOLUNTEER SURGEON

When the Civil War started, Platon interrupted his medical studies to join the New York Sanitary Commission Volunteer Surgeons. At the same time, a classmate and a close friend from Virginia cast his fortunes with the troops of the South. After the battle of Bull Run, at one of the improvised hospital tents, Platon encountered his rebel friend. They embraced, time and place forgotten in the joy of meeting again.

On January 26, 1863, his sister Fannie wrote:

It's been two years since we left New York and I haven't written you a letter. I am so lazy about writing. Knowing me, why haven't you written me? Your last letter was to John telling him that you were going to war. I suppose you must be back. John left San Francisco the first day of January for New York . . . Dear brother, do everything possible to help him and to console him . . . John will tell you all the trials he has suffered because of that Soscol. The only hope is in his going to Washington to see if he can do something with Congress. I have very little hope that he will succeed in what he wants.

After Platon's tour of duty, he returned to the College of Physicians and Surgeons, with transportation furnished from Washington City to New York by the United States Government. In the Spring of 1864 he passed all his examinations, and so informed his brother-in-law John B. Frisbie:

I am happy to state to you that I have passed all my examinations; I, here enclose a note from Doctor Parker to Sec. Stanton. If convenient please send me some money soon as you can; we (our class) have certain preliminaries to arrange before commencement and it is desirable that all should hand in their dues as early as possible in order to obtain music for the occasion . . . You have been a brother more than kind to me, aye, the adjective would not half express it, though you had been but half as good . . . The graduating fee alone is $30.

At the graduating exercises, Columbia Medical College, April 3rd, 1864, Platon took second prize, in a class of seventy-eight. A letter to his father at the time gave voice to his feeling:

After four long years of study I am happy to state that I have come to the successful termination of my studies and have possession of the diploma I have so eagerly coveted, so anxiously striven for and they tell me so creditably obtained . . . Our Alma Mater on the night of our commencement, that momentuous evening of our lives, dismissed us with fond and hopeful solicitude, into the world of struggle for ourselves. Well, if it must be done I would gladly continue my studies further but we must make a virtue of necessity and be heroes in the strife. Thank God for a little heart.

General Vallejo was prompt in replying:

Yes, I am happy, because brilliant is the triumph which you have had, upon ending your studies in the University of New York in which you have obtained a hood of Doctor of Medicine. The honorable character of your profession is the finest passport with which a young man of your age can present himself in all the societies of the world. I have always expected great success from your studies because I know of your application to them, your courage and resolution . . . But you should always keep in mind that Captain Frisbie had helped with his powerful influence in his native city and in every way to a favorable conclusion of your brilliant triumph in Columbia University. Gratitude is a virtue inspired by Heaven in noble and sensitive hearts.

Natalia and Jovita, you probably know already that they have achieved a brilliant success; they have married two of the youths of the distinguished family of Mr. Haraszthy. So that when you visit the domestic hearth again you will find it almost deserted, comparatively, with only Ula, Nap, Lulu and Maria.

PLATON RETURNS TO CALIFORNIA

When young Doctor Vallejo left New York City he carried with him a letter of recommendation (dated April 22, 1864) from Dr. Williard Parker, Dean of the College of Physicians and Surgeons:

Platon Vallejo M.D. is about to leave this city for his home in California. I beg to say he leaves me and my colleagues, the Professors of the College of Physicians and Surgeons of the State of New York with entire confidence in his success and our highest esteem and respect. He entered my office as a student on Medicine and Surgery more than three and one half years ago. He had been very industrious, pursuing the studies of his profession with uncommon zeal and devotion. The temptations of a large city had no influence in drawing him away from the one great object, his profession.

He had extensive opportunities for Surgical observation, being always ready to assist us and to take charge of my patients after operations. . . . His inaugural thesis was upon the Diseases of the Kidneys and he obtained one of the college prizes. I most heartily congratulate his parents and friends on his honorable and successful career and the promise which he gives of distinction and usefulness.

Through the influence of General Vallejo's friends in the United States Navy, Platon served for a short time as Assistant Surgeon on board the storeship "Farallones," stationed at Mare Island, California. Upon resigning in April, 1865, he accepted a position as Ship's Surgeon with the Pacific Mail Steamship Company.

On one of the Company's voyages that year, he met young and attractive Lily Wiley of Burlington, New York. She was on her way to California to visit her older sister, Anna Eugenia, the wife of Edward A. Poole, captain for many years on the Sacramento River boats.

Also a passenger was Emilia Melville. Although Dr. Vallejo took time out to coach the then young opera singer in the French version of *The Daughter of the Regiment*, he had eyes for no one but the fair-haired Miss Wiley. (Forgotten was "the little witch with black hair and blue eyes" of his New York college days.) Miss Melville, herself, playing in San Francisco in 1927 in "The Royal Family," recalled in an interview that voyage of 1865, and spoke of Lily Wiley as "a blonde-like angel."

Upon Lily's arrival in California, she lived with the Poole's at 1005 Stockton Street in San Francisco. Later she attended school at St. Catherine's Convent in Benicia, where several sisters of Dr. Vallejo were also enrolled.

A Broken and Mended Engagement

Lily Wiley was not lacking in beaux. Finally she was persuaded, by an influential relative [so Platon thought] to accept an engagement ring from a millionaire suitor. Heart-broken, Platon, on board the S.S. Constitution, wrote Lily as follows:

> You know Lilly, that you have yourself, with your own hand severed, be your reasons what they may be, every tie that can bind our hearts together except that limited and holy one of friendship. What ties did not your delicate hands snap the day you so tenderly avowed you had no love for me. Oh! I could not tell you how beautiful had been my dream. Oh! Lilly, have we parted as friends, mere strangers to grow?
>
> Another note followed, "Lily—I love you. Tomorrow I shall be here. Determine what you shall do, and let me know once for all. That ring, your engagement ring must be off your hand or speak no more of love, to me. If you love me and wish to be true, let me know when we meet again."

On Platon's return to the mainland, the same courage and resolution which he had put into his medical studies, he put into the contest to win back Lily's love, with the result that she broke her engagement and made plans for an early marriage to the young California doctor who, when in Port, stayed at the Occidental Hotel in San Francisco.

In August, 1867, on board the *S.S. Golden City*, Platon wrote to his fiance that he was on the deck of the finest ship of the Pacific; that he felt nearer Heaven than if he were on the highest mountain, and that he was watching their star. He added, "I keep San Francisco time and often as I look at my watch, I imagine what you are doing . . . Your pictures are a source of very great comfort to me. I never imagined a simple little picture could be the source of so much pleasure . . . It was your parting gift and it bears a sweet remembrance of the original." Platon also gave his sweetheart some ship news, "In the second class cabin is an old woman who swears I saved her life . . . and in the steerage is a whole company of soldiers that I served with, after the battle of Centerville."

One of the passengers remarked that Dr. Vallejo had endeared himself to the passengers and was particularly attentive to the sick. An old printer who fell desperately ill in the second cabin was visited by Dr. Vallejo, who took the man from his hot room and placed him in his [Platon's] room where he recovered, believing that he owed his life to Dr. Vallejo.

Among Platon's correspondents was Mary Parker, the wife of Dr. Williard Parker who had spoken so highly of Dr. Vallejo at the time of his graduation. She told Platon how concerned they were over the trouble between the Turks and the Greeks, and that her husband, who was, as already mentioned, Dean of Columbia University's College of Physicians and Surgeons, was sending instruments to a doctor in Athens. She also wrote that she was very much ashamed of Andrew Johnson.

THE WEDDING OF PLATON AND LILY

The wedding of golden-haired Lily and the raven-haired Platon occurred on the morning of November 14, 1867, in Trinity Episcopal Church, San Francisco. A Catholic ceremony followed shortly after in the City of Vallejo, with Father Louis Daniel officiating. At this time Lily was eighteen and Platon twenty-six.

A six-week honeymoon was spent at Platon's parents' home, Lachryma Montis, "amidst the olive, fig trees, pomegranates and orange groves." Platon in his newly-found happiness wrote a friend, "You know, Gerry, that I have always loved the fair sex, their beauty of form and sweetness of character. . . . I am willing to acknowledge that no microscope could enoble and magnify a man's heart as does the love of a woman."

After his marriage, Platon remained a few months with the Pacific Mail Steamship Company. His last voyage with the company was on the *S.S. Montana*, from which he wrote as follows to his bride:

> The day has been pleasant since we left and I should need nothing but your loving presence to make me happy during the whole voyage. I cannot go to bed, dearest without writing a letter to you by way of a devotional (and you know I believe in the communion of saints) to invoke your presence . . . I will return soon and then I will devote all my time to you and my whole life shall be an expression of love for you dearest Lily, my sweet little wife. I will close this short letter dearest Petty and write a letter to Mr. McLane tendering my resignation and excuse for so doing. I will send you a copy from Acapulco.

While still on board the *S.S. Montana*, on February 16, 1868 Platon "respectfully tendered" his resignation as Surgeon of the Pacific Mail Steamship Company, to its president Allan McLane, giving the reason that he was married and desired to establish himself on shore.

After the acceptance of Platon's resignation by McLane, a friend of Platon's father, the young couple settled in the City of Vallejo, for a time in the home of Fannie and John Frisbie. Platon's mother, visiting there, remarked, "Platon is here, he and his wife, Lili. Platon is always taking care of the sick. Some pay him and others don't have the wherewithall." The doctor's mother might have added that some paid him with a load of hay, a turkey, a pair of ducks, or a few chickens, or perhaps even a pig. If the patient was grateful and anxious to please, a game cock was given to the cock-fighting doctor.

This recalls the story told the author by Francisca McGettigan, daughter of Dr. Vallejo; one of the favorite game-cocks of the doctor lost a fight, and some of its feathers were given to his wife to decorate her bonnet. Because of many rough characters living in Vallejo in the early days, Mrs. Platon Vallejo was not allowed to remain away from home after dark. One winter evening, dusk having already fallen and Lily not at home, Platon's anxiety developed into a bit of Spanish temper. When at last she returned and removed her bonnet, Platon grabbed it and threw it into the fire. This little incident seen and remembered by Francisca, was in later years forgotten by her father—at least so he said.

During the early years of establishing himself in his profession, Dr. Vallejo's patients ranged from the town's leading citizens and the Navy Personnel of Mare Island to members of the Chinese colony. His resourcefulness in an emergency is well illustrated by another incident recalled by Francisca. As a little girl, she saw Ah Wah, their Chinese peddler, arrive on his weekly rounds, holding his swollen jaw and evidently in great pain. The Doctor helped him to take off the bamboo pole (from which his baskets of vegetables dangled) off his shoulders, and, telling him to stretch himself out on the porch, Platon disappeared into the barn where his favorite horse was stabled. He returned with an ominous pair of forceps used for equine disorders. Straddling the Chino's midriff, the Doctor's orders were, "Open your mouth, wide, wide, wider, wider." With a tug and a pull, out came the offending molar, which was held up for the relieved patient to examine.

When little Francisca was born on July 18, 1875, a Western Union Telegram was received from General Vallejo: "Congratulations again from the family. Our family name must be perpetuated, we want a boy. Go ahead." However, Platon was not to have a boy. His four daughters were Felipa, Francisca, Adela and Angela.

FAMILY LETTERS

Letters from General Vallejo to Dr. Vallejo's household were not always addressed to his son; sometimes he wrote to Lily, as he did on February 15, 1870:

My dear Fabiola:

Your pretty letter of the 9th of this month I received at the right time and I answer it saying that you should make an effort to write to me in Spanish. It doesn't matter that you make mistakes. I'll correct them and will be your teacher, if you don't disdain having your Papa as a teacher, your Papa who has so much affection and love for you.

It is much better for you to learn my language for you are young. I am old and don't want to set out *now* to write English which although I can do so slowly I can't do it correctly as my own language.

I am so glad that Mrs. Poole has already returned to California. I send back to her affectionate regards. Is she as beautiful as when she went away? When I go to the City I am going to ask her a thousand questions and pay her pretty compliments. I deeply regret that you are ill again. Have courage my daughter and don't give up. I think here in L.M. you will get better since the climate and the baths would help you a great deal. Believe me, dear Fabiola, as always your affectionate Papa who loves you with all his heart and wishes for you very good, good, good, good, good, good health and happiness.

About two months later (April 17, 1870), Fannie wrote from Albany, New York, to her brother Platon, chiding him about his penmanship:

You can't think what pleasure it gave me to receive your letter dated the 24th of March. I had quite a little trouble in reading it but finally we managed to understand it, each one guessing a word. Now we know it by heart. Fanita has received your letters and we had the same trouble. Minnie says that you love her more because her letter is better written.

We are very sad since John went away. It seems to me I am more sad being alone here than in California as I know no one in Albany. I am very glad that Lily's health is better. I hope she won't have rheumatism again. I believe from now on she will be strong and have better health. Tell Lily to write to me in English and I'll answer her in Spanish . . . You already know that John was in Washington all winter so I had to take care of all the family and the house, which is not a small thing. You well know how large the family is and all the little ones have been ill.

Don't let Ula leave until he is completely over the fever and the cold that he has. I take it for granted that he must be improved as he is thinking of going to Mexico again. When you see him tell him to send his picture since I can't see him . . . Tell John he isn't to sell the big piano. I put you in charge of all the pictures in the house. Tell John not to put them in his office . . . Don't let any one take them anywhere, particularly the picture of Lupe [the baby who had died 14 years before] which is behind the door in the parlor. Have them put in a chest all together. I'm glad that Mama is well as she says and that she hasn't asthma again. Give her a kiss and another one to Lily for me. Greet Tele [Salvador Vallejo's daughter]. Ask her how she likes the business of babies. She'll probably say 'Que Caramba'. Tell her I hope the next one will be a girl.

Rarely a letter was sent to Platon or to members of his family by Vallejo which did not contain an affectionate greeting for Father Luis. Father Luis Daniel, the beloved pastor of St. Vincent's Church, gave not only spiritual help but often material aid as well. He was always a welcome member of Dr. Vallejo's household. On one occasion, when he was hearing the Confession of little Francisca Vallejo, she was surprised to hear him whisper, "Tell Papa, I will be over for supper tonight."

Platon wrote his father about the visiting priest, Father Duggan, and Vallejo replied on March 7, 1874 rather proud, no doubt, that he could furnish his pious son with a bit of history of one of the saints:

Yesterday I received your long letter dated the 4th of this month in which you acclaim in mystical style, suggestive and sometimes powerful in which you sing the praises of the young Dominican preacher, Friar Duggan in his sermon alluding to the life of St. Tomas Aquinas, his exemplary virtues, also the life of his venerable parents which he imitated constantly. I regret greatly not having been present on the occasion to which you allude, since you know that I am an admirer of talent, especially when it starts to unfold in the mind of a young orator inspired by learning and under the aegis of the Saint whose panegryic the Rev. Duggan proposed to make.

Without question it is very beautiful to see a talented priest climb into the pulpit and to hear his sermon preached with eloquence before an illustrious and intelligent audience making shine the virtues of men who have been or were the lamps of Christianity among whom is counted St. Thomas Aquinas who after being canonized by the Pope John XXII in the year 1313, was given the title of Doctor of the Church by Pius V being at that time the most profound theologian, the wisest, the clearest in his arguments and conclusion because of which they called him or gave him the name of "Angels of the Schools"—(Dr. Angelico and Eagle of the Theologians.)

Actually, the story of St. Thomas Aquinas when he was young has some very interesting episodes and after professing in the order of St. Dominic he was always the one with a great deal of eloquence, fought heresy and defended with success and universal admiration the Christian religion; and as much for this as for the works which he published, principally his commentaries on the Psalms, on the Epistles of St. Paul to the Romans, to the Hebrews and of the First Corinthians and on his "Catena Aurea" on the Gospels, etc etc, there was attached to him the fame of a just and pious man and he was canonized.

Let us leave now our saint in Heaven and let us descend to this ungrateful world where one is accustomed to say "The one who slips away from a Saint doesn't stop at the Devil" . . . I couldn't continue because I had to go across and load a wagon with some wood to make a fence and while I was carrying the wood I got a splinter in my right hand which inconvenienced me greatly in writing. I reached the house, *I, myself* unloaded the wagon and your Mama who is and has been very ill with Asthma, took care of me and I can't write more.

Henry Cerruti, one of Bancroft's literary agents, said that General Vallejo was not a very staunch Catholic but he did contribute greatly to the support of the Sonoma Chapel for the sake of his wife and his favorite son, Dr. Platon Vallejo. Cerruti quoted Vallejo as saying, "That many bad priests had done more towards throwing discredit upon the Church of Rome than Calvin and Luther combined."

Dr. Vallejo, "a young man with sound religious principles," was pleased to receive from his father a letter dated January 3, 1872, which Platon always treasured.

Dear Platon:

Andronico gave me your letter last evening—the one that begins with the words

"AVE MARIA PURISIMA," "Conceived without sin" is the response to so worthy a salutation. How many memories it brings to my mind. My infancy, my adolescence and my young manhood comes back to me "face to face" from those days. Sweet is the remembrance of it and much more so when it is joined with the memory of persons so respectable and worthy of remembrance as Reverend Father Junipero Serra. I was born twenty or more years after his death but the missionaries who succeeded him were well known to me. Father Baltazer of the "Mission on the River Carmelo" baptized me. He was an intimate friend of my father and our family. Then, there was Fray Vicente Francisco de Sarria, Vicar Forans of the Alta California missions and consultor for the ecclesiastical province of New Spain, a very learned man, just and of truly hallowed candor.

A thousand times did I kiss his hand, a thousand times more was I his altar boy. An equal number of times did I hear him chat with my father about Father Serra. And about the same number of times did I receive candy from him after Mass for my progress in reciting the Litany of the Saints in company with other boys of my own age. He gave me my First Holy Communion in his convincing angelic ways. I remember him as if he were here today gazing upon me. How solemn is this remembrance to me! Even surpassing those days and times when things were done with much more pomp and ceremony than today, Father Sarria wanted to send me to Mexico City with Governor Sola during the year 1821 so that I could study for the priesthood; but I wasn't able to do it, and instead of professing celibacy, I accepted the "Matrimonial Order" of which you are a consequence, my son, rather than enter the Sacerdotal Order. It would take me a long time for me to tell you stories about the era contemporaneous with the persons to whom I refer.

"Ave Maria Purisima" was always said upon entering a house where our Catholic Christian people dwelt. The Indian catechumens and even the pagans were told to greet one another with the words "Amar a Dios" (Love God), and this charming phrase was known in all corners of the province in peace as well as in war. "Amar a Dios Amigos" (Mar a Yos Chene-ne) said the Indians on the road and in the fields. How many times to me, myself, on my military campaigns into the interior of the territory would the Indian chiefs present themselves with the words ("Mar a Yos Chene-ne") A harbinger of peace, a masonic like pass-word brought under the Propagation of the Faith—the "propagania fide." As I run out of this paper, I salute you the same with "Ave Maria Purisima" and "Amar a Dios." Tu Papa,

M. G. VALLEJO

When the John B. Frisbies returned from the East, Dr. Vallejo moved from their home into his own on Carolina Street. His father took a keen interest in helping him landscape the grounds and sent over from Lachryma Montis:

2 Rooted Olives
4 Rooted Pomegranates
4 Rooted Passion Flowers
2 Honey Locusts
4 Very Pretty Sentinal Poplars
4 Mixed or Venus Flowers
5 Rooted Grapes, White but very rare

Along with the plants, he sent the following note: "You, before being a

Doctor used to help me plant vines and trees and to work the earth and for that reason, I don't tell you how to transplant what I'm sending you." Vallejo also sent Platon a cane saying on October 18, 1874:

> Yesterday with the sailing of the steamer *Sonoma* to Vallejo I sent you as a gift my cane which since 1824, I should say for fifty years I have had it in my possession. I was then a cadet and I bought it from the son of the Vice-roy of Lima, Don Sebastian Arrieta whose initials are still legible on this cane. The son of the Vice-roy was a lieutenant of Cavalry. He died in San Juan Bautista near Monterey, squandered a fortune so that his father disowned him. As I was a cadet, I was made aid-de-camp of the Plaza by Governor Arguello and at the same time Captain of the Port and here I took the baston of command as indicated by the black tassels that are still on the cane hilt.

Referring to his own health, General Vallejo told his doctor-son: "I sleep from three to four hours, perhaps that is enough. My pulse is good (70–75). My tongue is a bit coated . . . I think the worst thing in being old, for after an attack of chills and fever the body doesn't respond so readily. I don't take any medicine and my food is simple and moderate. I drink no wine although I should but I don't like to give a bad example and I prefer always to have my conscience clear in order to preach against drunkards who do not know how to curb the accursed and unnatural vice. I am glad that you are now in your own home living independently, that means you are a family man now. Tell Lily she must watch out for the "old man" when he comes to your home. "Life begins so and it is better on the way up, than on the way down. I speak from experience. Nevertheless I have been very fortunate with my sons and daughters, honorable men and good girls. At least it seems so to me and I want to believe it always. I take great care as you tell me not to get my feet wet. Salvador sends you and Lily greetings and thanks for your thoughtfulness in regard to the frock coat. Your poor uncle, so rich in another time."

Platon was soon to be a real "family man." On March 11th, 1872 he and Lily became parents of a baby daughter—a fact, which he thus announced to his mother:

> My dear Mama;
>
> I merely wish to call attention to a little thing that has arrived here lately and it is very much in need of a name. Would you have any objection to spare it one of your beautiful names—Felipa? and allow her to be called after her grandmother. I hope you will not refuse our request but will lovingly grant it the name and honor of being called after you. Lily joins me in love for you all.
>
> PLATON

Three days later Platon's mother replied, "I doubly accept and concede your request, provided it proves the affection and endearments you have for your mother who wishes you and your wife, health and prosperity."

In early September, Lily, having taken Baby Felipa to visit her grandmother, wrote to her husband from Lachryma Montis: "I know you feel anxious to know how Felipa is doing. Felipa has been splendid all day, has slept well and seems to feel bright; she is talking to her Grandmother. Ula has just come home and all the girls are in great glee. Well, I guess I will take Felipa now. Take good care of yourself and accept much love from your loving wife."

On July 18, 1875, once again Grandmother Vallejo was asked to give another of her "beautiful names" to another granddaughter. The name *Francisca* was chosen and bestowed on the second daughter of Platon and Lily Vallejo. When she was four years old, Grandpa Vallejo sent her this note: "I send by Express a little box of figs, recently dried which Grandpa packed for you but on the condition that your Mama tells you when and how much to eat at a time. Induce your Papa to tell you his recollections of Lachryma Montis where he and all his brothers and sisters were children. Receive for Felipa and the baby (Adela) your Mama and your Papa, our affectionate greetings." When Francisca had reached the age of ten, Platon said she "is as sweet in disposition as a dove. She is very bright and looks a great deal like Lily."

The General was not the only one who liked to send gifts to Doctor Vallejo's family. On March 8, 1878, Platon's mother wrote him:

> After greeting you, Lily and your little ones, Andronico and Fannie, Adela and all my grandchildren, I'll tell you that I am sending you this little gift: a string of chiles, 2 dozen oranges, a bottle of jelly. There are for Lily 3 dozen oranges and the glass of sweets are for Fanny. One dozen oranges for Fanita. Moreover for Adela a string of chiles, 2 dozen oranges and a little blue glass of jelly for Adela. Andronico one dozen oranges, a little blue glass and a half dozen of fruit and a half string of chiles. Everything is coming in a box. 2 dozen oranges are coming for Father Luis . . . Don't laugh at my writing, Greet everyone.

A third daughter was born to the Platon Vallejos on October 12, 1879. She had a round dimpled face, dark curly hair and enormous brown eyes. The name chosen was Adela, after Platon's sister. A fourth daughter, Angela Josephine, was born on March 16, 1884, and she was described by her father in a letter to his parents (April 2, 1884) as ". . . a beauty and don't forget it; very much like her mother in certain respects but in many other respects (we know how to account for certain high-toned peculiarities) 'coses de Espana' that causes every one to remark at the first glance 'Oh isn't she like Grandpa . . . I think she also resembles Grandmother.' We have here a combination of the old folks, which is to me highly satisfactory. Lily and child doing well."

General Vallejo was disappointed that Platon had no boys; however, he enjoyed his little granddaughters and took pleasure in sending them gifts and writing to them. Little Felipa was a special favorite of his. He wrote this rather long but unusually interesting letter, dated March 29, 1876, which must have been in answer to one written for Felipa by her father as she was only four years old:

My dear Felipa:

Your last letter dated the 23rd of last month I received at the proper time. I haven't answered it because I have been very busy and also because my sight fails me at times, that is to say, my eyes hurt me so much that tears come. But I must write to you and I do it with much pleasure because my letter is for you.

I wanted to send you some things yesterday but I didn't as there wasn't a clean box in the house; now I've gotten one in Sonoma and I am sending you some oranges and some rolls—fresh—just out of the oven of the bakery.

Grandma says she can't write with her hurt wrist and for me to send you many, many, many greetings. But do you know the reason Grandma is disabled? Well, if you don't know, I'm going to tell you. Last year, Grandma went into the yard where the cows are milked, that is to say, where they take the milk out of their udders and put it into a jar or pail, to take it into the house and to drink with tea or coffee. When she finished milking the cow, Grandma went close to the creature and was caressing her, petting her on the back—when all of a sudden when she least expected it, the cow gave her a kick and knocked her about two yards away. Poor Grandma fell against some stones full length and upon falling, landed on her right arm and broke her wrist.

Grandma didn't know why the cow, a very gentle one had given her such a kick, but you know dear Felipa, that she has a little dog named 'Toni.' Well Toni went to the yard with Grandma and when she petted the cow, the dog went to the cow to smell her udder, the cow saw him out of the corner of her eye and aimed a kick at him but Grandma was the one who took the blow. That is the reason Grandma can't write to you and she tells me to tell you that if your Papa and Mama will let you come to L. Montis, she will take good care of you and you will get to know the cow that gave her the kick and her calves and you will drink fresh milk and will see how they are milked—and you will see very high hills covered with very large trees.

In those hills there are bears, deer, coyotes, rabbits and hares—and quails and robbins—and—larks—buzzards and big snakes and rattle-snakes which are very poisonous; when they bite, a person dies. Also there are other kinds of animals, worse than all the others called "*Squatters*"! These are really dangerous because they rob the trees, they steal the fences, taking them down at night—whole lengths of boards, unnailing them and then renailing them in their own fences—they steal the lambs and sell them in the markets and at night when no one is looking, they milk the cows, they carry off the milk and Grandma doesn't know how these things happen. Also they break down the fence and steal the horses—sometimes they take out the gentle horses and plow their land all night; it's worse when there is a moon—and then in the daytime the horses are very tired and then Grandpa curses and reviles them in Spanish because he doesn't know how to do it in English—and it is sure that if one complains to the authorities, he will lose the suit and moreover will pay for it.

But the hills, the trees, the birds are very fine, now especially there are many flowers. Some birds are flying about playfully, others are very busy building their nests into which to lay their eggs—and from the little eggs come the very tiny birds without feathers and after the feathers come out, they are very warm and the Mama bird brings them food to eat and puts flies in their mouths—and they open their mouths and beg—then the papa of the birds, comes and also brings them food—and the Mama leaves to hunt for more and meanwhile the papa takes care of them and when night comes the mama bird sits on them and covers them with her feathers and the papa is at her side watching over them and from time to time he is chatting with the mama, telling her a thousand pretty things, about their children and they sleep—and sometimes they awaken and start to chat with their parents and when dawn comes they start to sing.

On another occasion I'll tell you more stories about the frogs and the fish in the pond and how the latter swim and the former makes noises. My eyes are hurting, I can't continue the stories, so good night Felipa. When you say your prayers remember to ask God for his grace for your Grandpa and Grandma so that He can impart to them the portion of His Infinite Goodness that belongs to them so that they can gain from his boundless goodness the forgiveness of their sins and a great deal more mercy for Grandma because she gets angry at Grandpa. First kiss your Mama for me, then your Papa, then your little sister and if you see your Uncle Andronico, kiss him also and thousands and thousands of greetings to Father Luis and before the paper is used up, I give my blessing. GRANDPA VALLEJO

CALIFORNIA HISTORICAL RESEARCH WORK

There was much correspondence between father and son during the days that General Vallejo was busy dictating the history of California to Henry Cerruti for Hubert Howe Bancroft and gathering historical documents as well; and it did not take long for Cerruti and Bancroft to realize that their success depended on winning the good favor of Dr. Vallejo. This was done, and on January 26, 1875 Bancroft wrote him:

My dear Doctor:

I thank you many, many times for your kindness in permitting your father to give me the documents. I can assure you most emphatically that you and your family and your friends shall always have access to all my library contains, and more than that, I want you to write something for me. I saw the perusal of your letter which your father kindly let me read. I see that you have marked ability as a writer. It is these finer shades of thought, Doctor Vallejo, which you so beautifully throw into your letter that I want in my study of character.

I wish you would write out and send me as soon as you can—be it little or much—your conception of early character. Give me the eyes your father looked through, their thoughts and inner life as well as their habits and customs . . . Tell me what you think of Mission life, of the conversion of the natives, of a thousand things you have heard your father and his friends talk about. I will use it as I shall use your father's most valuable history, that is, as a manuscript by yourself, quoting it always in your name and preserving it permanently in my library. You can give me something splendid if you will and I believe it will pay you to do it.

With sincere regard, I am

Very Truly Yours,

H. H. BANCROFT

Cerruti, wishing to aid Bancroft, added his request that Dr. Vallejo prepare a manuscript: "Mr. Bancroft has returned to San Francisco. I spoke to him about your work [Literary] and he felt highly pleased to perceive that you had not forgotten him. Please write all you can remember about ancient customs and manners of the native Californians, that is the material Bancroft needs the most, because history can be written with the perusal and research of official documents but the manners and customs of a noble race cannot be described without the assistance of an eye-witness. I also beg to assure you that Mr. Bancroft in his great history will do you full justice besides giving you credit for every line he may quote from your manuscript."

Soon after writing the letter, Cerruti went to the city of Vallejo and gave Platon several chapters of the *History of California*. After Cerruti's visit, Platon wrote to his father on July 17, 1875:

Mr. Cerruti was here a few days ago and left for my perusal several chapters of the sketches of Early Life in California. Archbishop Alemany was visiting Vallejo at the same time and I showed him the proofs. He took a rapid glance at them.

How glad I would be if you were to submit them before printing to his correction and regard, any little item that may catch his ever vigilant and paternal eye. Let your work be complete, adhering strictly to the historical facts and be cautious not to mix unnecessary with the dogmatic teachings of the church . . . Can it be that Cerruti has been tampering with the history? But it is yet in my possession and I will try to hear from you before Cerruti comes to claim his writings.

I asked Archbishop Alemany if he would not write a little letter to you. I think, my dear Papa, that he would and could give you much assistance and if you are guided by his good counsel, I am certain that your work would become one worthy of the perusal of schools. I think you should submit your whole work before it is translated or printed or extracts can be taken from it to some good Catholic man of letters and sound judgement as Governor Burnett or to our beloved friend and Father, Archbishop Alemany. It is most proper and just. And listen attentively to the advice and rest assured that conscience will be better at ease and our work will have the weight of his counsel or influence of the shadow at least of the highest clerical authority in California. Without it, the work will be interesting to some; with it to innumerable people. So I would most urgently request you as I said before to submit it nobly to the critical revisal of Archbishop Alemany with power to correct.

General Vallejo knew that his historical research had been thorough; his recording, factual and truthful, and there was no need for Archbishop Alemany to review the work. To explain his viewpoint, the General wrote his son:

I have read your letters in which you deal with the manuscripts which Cerruti loaned you for *your personal* inspection. In answer I'll say to you that in the compilation of the history of California, I have confined myself strictly to the truth and even where it has been possible for me I have strengthened my statements with official documents. It may be unintentionally I haven't done complete justice to the merits of all the illustrious men who have contributed to the glory of our country but in such case I am not to blame but others.

I tried to get all the documents there were of the olden days. Some of the people had them in their possession were generous in lending them but others either refused my request or consented under such conditions that it was impossible for me to make use of their offerings. Numbered among the first there stands out the Reverend Father of Santa Clara and the priests of the ex-missions of San Jose and Monterey,

Casada and Casanova; the latter was so agreeable that with his own hand he copied several notes that I have included intact in the history.

Among the second figure; the fathers of the Mission Santa Barbara who refused to lend their documents to my friends, not-with-standing the fact they offered them a bond of 10,000 pesos as guarantee that they would be returned intact and also your so-admired friend, the Archbishop Alemany refused to loan to my secretary some books which contain letters written by the old missionaries of whom I have made many and favorable mention. To the little help of those people can be attributed the lacks, errors and omissions which I have made but as the history which I have written is not yet finished there is still time to remedy that which is not well done. You can rest easy that I shall do what is in my power to please you where I can do it without clashing with right and justice. As for the revision of the history of California I'll tell you I have no objection to submitting my writings for judgment but I do object to the revision of Alemany.

Platon continued to be deeply concerned over the manner in which he thought Bancroft planned to chronicle the history of "the Holy and venerable men," the early California missionaries. His attitude displeased Bancroft who wrote him, "You do me a great injustice if you think I sneer at sacred things. Whether I can go as far as you in faith (which could I not, I should consider it my misfortune), whether I satisfy you in my delineation of your people or not, of one thing you may rest assured, I shall speak in every instance with respect and affection and without prejudice. If you will allow me plainly and truthfully to include their few faults, with their many good qualities, I am sure you will be satisfied and of the faults and wrong doings of the Anglo-Americans I shall speak unreservedly. What I want you to do is to write out as many pages of manuscript as you can on the character, customs, habits and proclivity of the early Californians. Give me a picture of them and their daily life. I believe I have expressed the belief a hundred times that the missionaries who planted the line of Alta California missions did a work unique and individual in the history of the Church. It is without a parallel. Help me to picture it properly."

On February 7, 1875, Bancroft wrote Platon again:

I think you will be satisfied with my treatment of the Spaniards before I get through with them. They certainly were in some instances cruel to the natives, not more so than the Yankees in Cal. And the Spaniards were not half so much to blame as the Anglo-Americans for the former work was done in an age of cruelty, the latter when the world is supposed to be more refined and gentle. Of course in this work I could only speak of Europeans in connection with the Indians. The facts are there and it surely would be wrong to disguise them. I think the way the gold-hunters treated the Indians of Cal. was most dastardly. I can excuse the Spaniards but for these cut-throats and murders of three centuries later, there is no excuse.

Anxious for a report from Platon, Cerruti wrote him: "How are you progressing in your writings? The History of California written by Gen. M. G. Vallejo is drawing to a close. I consider it a splendid work, sufficient by itself to give the General a great literary reputation. I am certain that no living man can write a better one, more reliable and so free from prejudice."

Most of Cerruti's work for Bancroft was finished, but he kept in touch with the Vallejos for whom he had formed a deep attachment. About this time he started borrowing money which he invested in mining stocks. The bonanza for the *few* enticed the *many* into speculation, this engendered a whirlwind and Henry Cerruti was caught in its destroying blast. The only solution seemed to him to be suicide. A few months before he took his life in Sonoma at the Union Hotel, Cerruti sent this friendly letter to Platon Vallejo:

Dear Sir and Friend:

Though the weather is very cool I cannot abstain from acknowledging receipt of your welcome favors. I assure you that it pleases me very much. General M. G. Vallejo's history is a thousand times better written and a million times more interesting than your Uncle's letter (Jose de Jesus Vallejo); your cousin Alvarado's four volumes, also pretty well done with much material. I am sure Mr. Bancroft will be able to write a correct history of the native land of your forefathers.

While at Lachryma Montis General Vallejo ordered you in case of his death, (which I hope will be long delayed) to take charge of his correspondence and keep it for ever; the Right Reverend Father Lewis [Luis] and I were present when Gen. M.G.V. made the request; but as I know that there are living in Vallejo parties who plundered the General most shamefully I would suggest that General M.G.V. should give you written authority to that effect because the want of a legal document may cause interested parties to suppress correspondence which will go far toward branding them as thieves. I make the suggestion so that you may act as your clear judgment may dictate.

Wishing yourself and lady, happiness and prosperity, I remain

Very Sincerely, Your Well Wisher,
HENRY CERRUTI

General Vallejo's insight into the causes underlying the tragedy he expressed in a letter dated October 16, 1876 to Platon: "I am very sorry about General Cerruti. He was a good man and very honest. He fell into the hands of men without honor or conscience. They rushed him, he was ruined and he ruined others and had no alternative than to commit suicide when he saw that he had been deceived. Poor man!"

The Native Races of the Pacific States, the first of Bancroft's works to be published, was well received and at Christmas time 1875, Bancroft presented General Vallejo with a full set. Telling his son Platon of his gift, Vallejo wrote on January 1, 1876:

On the 24th of last month I received a gift from Mr. Bancroft as a Christmas present and bound as for the library of a prince, which gift is the work entitled "Native Races of the Pacific States." I commenced to read it—and the first pages gave me the idea to write a sonnet and send it to him which I did on the 25th, the day following the arrival of the gift. I enclose a copy of the sonnet.

You well know that it is very easy for a poet to make a *long* poem and to include in it a whole epoch but a Sonnet is very difficult because in 14 verses, no more, one has to encompass a whole epoch, one single thought sufficiently developed, having to end in the last verse with a notable flourish. Such are the special rules set up by the most distinguished teachers. Return to me the poem which is very satisfactory for a Poet, ordinary as I am, who makes no pretensions in being a half-way good one.

General Vallejo in turn gave the five volumes of *The Native Races*, simply bound in linen, to his nephew, Don Juan B. Alvarado.

GENERAL VALLEJO ENTERTAINS MEXICAN OFFICIALS

After Vallejo had played host to some visiting Mexican officials, he wrote to Platon about it: "The other day I saw the president of the Mexican schools. He is a handsome subject, a very wise man, recognized as such by everyone, also his ministers. We talked a great deal on all subjects. I took them to the Cliff House, the Park and to a great part of the city with which they were pleased. If I can and have the wherewithall, I will take them to Vallejo one of these days. I want, in effect, to tire them out and to amaze them, as the saying goes, for ulterior motives. They are all literate men with very profound learning and are fine gentlemen. The man of the world would say: 'It is a good thing to light two candles, one to the Virgin and another to the Devil.' "

The General was in the habit of quoting proverbs. He had a well-thumbed and well-marked book of classical sayings from Latin, Greek, French, Spanish and English authors. This book was given to the author by his youngest grandson, Raoul Ricardo Emparan. In reading Vallejo's letters, one is sometimes confused to know if a particular saying is his own or a bit of borrowed wisdom.

THE PAINTINGS OF ORIANA DAY

Among the close friends of the Platon Vallejos were John A. Day, a store clerk on Mare Island, and his wife Oriana Day, who was a talented artist. Dr. Vallejo suggested to her that she undertake the painting of the California Missions under the personal supervision of General Vallejo. Mrs. Day took up the idea with a great deal of enthusiasm; she visited the ruins of the Missions, read historical documents, and acquainted herself with Edward Vischer's drawings, which proved to be very helpful. Speaking of Vischer's drawings, Vallejo said:

As for the collection of the old Missions of California compiled by the deceased Dr. Edward Vischer in 20 years of work, I tell you that it is a work as rare as it is interesting. That gentleman deserves the eternal gratitude of the sons of the country, that know how to appreciate it since as you say in your letter, they are the relics that remain to remind us of the men who commenced to sow the seeds of Christianity with self-denial and selflessness with good example, their stainless conduct and their old time Christian virtues without hypocricy, without ostentation and full of Faith. Would to God that they had many imitators. Would some miracle would raise up another Sarria, another Amores or another Payeras. They would see in what a state the missions are or they would die again because of not seeing anything of the past, yet there is in the whole world, everything is perishable, everything changes, everything is upset and regenerated under the supervision of the Intelligence of the Supreme Creator.

In everything is seen the finger of God, directing the Universe without one single atom escaping, one atom that moves invisible to us in space. He guides us and protects us and with his Infinite Mercy he aids us and gives us hope (putting ourselves under the obedience of His divine mandates) of reaching Eternal Bliss.

General Vallejo spent many hours in Oriana Day's studio, helping her with his pencil sketches, tracing the lost outlines of the mission buildings and indicating the pastoral scenery. He recalled historic personages, costumes and ancient ceremonies. As a result, Mrs. Day was able to place in her paintings Spanish soldiery, Catalian guards, the Cuerra or leathercoated ones, riding in processions; priests, drawn by oxen or mules in carretas; padres standing by open doors; and fiery vaqueros, with their lariats, chasing wild horses, while Indians stood with their bows near huts of grass.

Oriana Day not only painted the Missions of California but also the Presidios. In addition she painted General Vallejo's Casa Grande (with the adjoining buildings) on the north side of Sonoma Plaza, and a portrait of General Vallejo himself. Mrs. Day planned that the paintings would illustrate a book, the text of which she wished Vallejo to write:

We hope the opportunity and leisure will be afforded you with the Doctor's aid to complete the contemplated work. We are sure that the material and knowledge you have on the subject when put into concise form and expression, will in connection with the illustrations, be a gem of a book which will be a credit and honor to yourself and a valuable contribution to the history of California and which will always be of paramount interest in the future.

About this time, Vallejo wrote to his son Platon: "I believe that you should be my secretary and no one can write on that subject [the Missions] in English better than you. It is just the matter of earning for ourselves some thousands of dollars. Mr. and Mrs. Day have already written to Boston for a bookman to take charge of the publication."

Platon hoped to have the portrait of General Vallejo painted by Oriana Day placed in Sacramento. He wrote to his cousin, Congressman Romualdo Pacheco, who replied: "I am extremely pleased to know that the work on the pictures is progressing and agree with you that your father's portrait merits a place in the Capitol. It is gratifying to know that the artist has been so successful. To secure a place in the Capitol for the portrait of your father would be beyond my control as it would require an act of the Legislature. Upon my return to the West I will see what can be done in the matter."

A newspaper reporter visited Mrs. Day's studio in the Phelan Building in San Francisco, and wrote up her restoration of the California Missions on canvas. He wondered how a daughter of the East, a young woman still on the sunny side of mid-life could envisage ruined buildings she had never seen, and so reproduce them that they were recognized at once by old settlers. The answer to this question, he felt, would signify a vast amount of study on her part, of the history of the Missions, and also securing the assistance of General Vallejo who, the reporter said, was "one of the noblest men who represent the old order of things and who is, today a bright ornament to the present California . . . Vallejo who held out against the blandishments of both Russia and England . . . A nobler specimen of the genus homo walks not the streets of San Francisco, nor one more worthy to be the representative of the past and present and if the Legislature of California at its next session, does not procure his life-sized portrait, which we saw in Mrs. Day's parlor and place it in their State House, they will lose an opportunity of honoring themselves as well as one of the historic characters of the State, which may never present itself again."

"This universally honored gentleman though of Castilian lineage, is more proud of being called a *Californian* and dislikes very much to be regarded as being, or having been, any other than what he was the day when at the head of the Mexican troops in California, he bowed and did obeisance to the Stars and Stripes—An American Citizen."

Unfortunately the stories of the California Missions were never written by Vallejo or by his son Platon—perhaps because of the illness of Platon's wife or because of Vallejo's financial worries. To explain his own situation, Vallejo wrote on August 4, 1880 to his son:

> It isn't for lack of desire that I do not leave here to make a visit to the inhabitants of Vallejo. No, it is because in these times, one cannot travel without the purse being well provided with that which in Latin is called "ready money" and in Sonoma or rather Lachryma Montis, the lack of money is in full force . . . Entire months go by without one single peso being seen in the house; it is for that reason that I haven't fulfilled my promise to visit you and it pains me more the circumstances of not being able to help the beautiful artist, Mrs. Day, in her monumental work of the past of our historic California.

Many have thought that Dr. Vallejo was the favorite son of General Vallejo, though he was known to be devoted to all his children. A letter dated April 18, 1876, from Rosalia Vallejo Leese to her brother would give some credence to the idea: "I have received two letters from you including one from Platon. I haven't answered because I have been sick in bed with a bilious attack. I see you are very proud of your favorite son, Platon. You have reason to be . . . God preserve that son of yours until you give your last sigh. . . . Would that all mothers could have a son like him." More evidence is revealed in a postscript to a letter, dated February 5, 1877, which the General wrote to Platon: "I think that you and Lulu are my two children who care for me the most. It is possible for a man of my age to be mistaken. . . No, I do not wish to be hasty. All my children appreciate me but I do believe that they do not love me as much as you all do." Be this as it may, it was to

Platon that Vallejo seemed able to show many facets of his character withheld from others. There must have been a light-hearted comradeship between father and son for the following comment to be appreciated by the younger man: "I received the paper that has the picture of the Prince of Asturias, Don Carlos. Everyone in one voice, 'How much he looks like Platon.' Well, my son, I have never been in Oviedo."

On March 4, 1881, Vallejo wrote that he had been worried over Platon's silence and he thanked God when he received his letter dated February 26th. The General went on to say:

Today is the inauguration of the president of the United States. Heaven grant that he will be good for all the people and that the nation may prosper in peace during the period of his administration. Pacheco is a very intimate friend of Mr. Garfield and it is very probable that he will send him to Mexico as the Minister Plenipotenciary which is the best mission to which your cousin can aspire. It would be a political move and doubtless beneficial to both countries; and it would be fitting for Pacheco in every way as much for his health as for the fact that it is a "fat office" to which is added the honor and the representation of the native Californians after the sale in "Guadalupe Hidalgo" by the Mexicans.

Mexico is going to enter into a new era; the railroads have already reached her borders along the Rio Grande: Mexico is a country extraordinarily rich in uncultivated lands ripe for agriculture; proverbial are her mineral riches, she possess mountains of iron, immense strata of coal, an excellent climate, etc. . . In 25 years from this date, it will be a land stupendously rich and the wonder of the world. "Manifest Destiny" say the Americans, and I say: the finger of God points to it and His decrees are immutable. What I regret is that I am so old that I shall not see the great metamorphosis.

Platon Vallejo's Wife

Lily Wiley Vallejo was a gentle, quiet individual. According to Platon, "she was not given to worldly mindness nor to the usual frivolities that consumes so much of women's time." Her family, her music and her church service filled her life. After her marriage Lily was baptized into the Catholic Faith on St. John's Day, 1868 and given the name Juanita. She embraced her husband's faith with so much ardor that she was asked to join the Third Order of St. Dominic.

For some years Lily had suffered with rheumatic fever, which prompted her father-in-law to express his deep concern over the state of her health to Platon:

In your last letter, I see that my dear Juanita is better but Platon, it seems to me that it is necessary to bring her to Lachryma Montis. The climate, the water, the house, her Mama and yours, who love her so much and want to help her and give her comfort. Her little sisters, Lulu and Maria who always every day, plead and supplicate me for they want Lily here, to take care of her so she may get well quickly and finally myself who love her so much—as much as you perhaps because she needs paternal affection which she has lacked since childhood. Mama also requests it and if Lilly can get out I'll bring her at once. Lulu and Maria say to me every once and awhile 'Platon ought to do what you tell him, shouldn't he?' 'Yes, daughters, that is the duty of children but sometimes——.' 'No, Papa, if the thing is good that Papa commands, one ought to obey anyhow.' They love Lily so much. I can't reason with them. Therefore my son, as much because that here she will improve, so that all beg for it, I hope you'll be able to arrange for her to come.

Platon wrote to his father that although Lily was feeling better and was able to take walks, after two or three blocks she would get very tired. By centering her activities in her home and church she was able to conserve her strength, but by the spring of 1885 her rheumatic heart condition became serious. On a Saturday in June in accordance with her usual duty as president of the Altar Society she went to St. Vincent's Catholic Church to dress the altar with candles, roses, and her favorite flower, the St. Joseph Lily. Returning home, she was tired, very tired. The next day, returning from Holy Communion, she sat down at the breakfast table and told her husband of a curious dream.

Lily was devoted to Saint Brigid, the Saint who had promised her devotees to warn them at least three days before they were to die. It seems that in her dream Lily saw a catafalque whereupon stood a black object, resembling a coffin, and also long lighted candles like those on the church's altar. Lily said she could not tell who was in the casket—she, herself, or her little fifteen-month-old baby, Angela; but Lily had come to the conclusion that it was to be herself. The story of the dream depressed Platon, so he turned the conversation at the breakfast table to something more congenial, and the dream was never mentioned again.

It was not long before Lily was forced to take to her bed, saying "not an inch of my body is free from pain." She tried, because of her loved ones, to fight the disease, but with her constant suffering she became resigned and willing to submit to what seemed to be the will of God. Although weak, she retained her mental faculties until the last. On June 5, 1885, at two in the morning, Lily Vallejo passed away peacefully at the age of 36 years. The morning after her death Platon held his five-year-old daughter Adela in his arms and told her what had happened; to which she is said to have responded: "Well, Papa, is not Mama better off in Heaven than suffering here?"

The Dominican Sisters cut off Lily's long golden hair and dressed her in one of their habits for burial. The Requiem Mass was at St. Vincent's Church where the Reverend Father Louis Daniel delivered the eulogy before her many friends and relatives, General Vallejo being one. After the final ceremony in St. Vincent's Cemetery, Platon wrote to a friend: "Do not pity me dear friend, but rejoice with me that I have such a treasure in the Heavenly Paradise. While she lived she was the world to me. Now she is linked with my hopes for a Happy Immortality. I doubt not but she is better able to help us in her present state than ever before. She was our comfort and our idol. I worshipped her and loved her as a child of God and my children drew from her not only their bodily sustenance but she instilled into their souls the food that gave them everlasting life by loving and constantly instructing them by word and example in the paths that lead to Heaven and God."

As Platon looked at his four motherless children—Felipa, Francisca, Adela and Angela—he murmured, "What can I offer in return for the loss of a dear mother? The answer can come only from above." A solution appeared to offer itself: on July 7th, 1885, a month after Lily died, General Vallejo wrote to Platon:

> Since I reached home after my last visit with your family, I haven't been able to lift my hand. I have been sick, profoundly affected by the death of Lily. I have been thinking of her a great deal and the little family that she left and who miss her so much. It was certainly at a time when they will miss her the most but so Heaven ordained it and one must bow to the decree of the Creator.
>
> What cares and what a great responsibility you have in your charge, my son. How I wish I could help you in some way to endure it but I haven't been able to find the way yet. Apropos to that thought, I am enclosing for you a letter which I have just received from Mrs. Poole, the older sister of Lily who reared her and now with very good will offers to take charge of the little family that her sister left. The letter speaks for itself; I suggest that you read it and tell me (returning it to me) what you think. Mrs. Poole is a good woman and I believe would fulfill her duties toward her nieces, with the same blood as hers and her sister's daughters . . . She is a fine intelligent woman and I believe sincerely that her letter is written with her hands on her heart. Think well about it and do the best says a Spanish axiom.
>
> As I understand in Mrs. Poole's letter, she would come to your house to care for the family under your protection and it should be that as much as an example as for affection toward her little nieces she would take a step from Episcopalianism to Catholism and thus we would accomplish two important objects. Don't you think so? . . . Mama is always ill a bit; she can't now do anything; she thinks about Death a great deal and wishes to die in peace with every one.

Platon decided not to accept Auntie Poole's offer, but to employ a housekeeper. Nevertheless in a letter to Mrs. Poole he assured her, "We try to carry on everything as if dear Mama were here yet . . . I think that her spirit though invisible and enwrapped in the vision of God, cannot be far from us nor can be indifferent towards us in what we do and what we are."

Among the many letters of sympathy Platon received, he saved a few from his closest friends and relatives. In thanking his niece Benicia Frisbie, he wrote: "I don't know what to say to you, my dear Bennie except that your Aunt's soul has passed to a blissful immortality. A return to nothing is absurd and an impossibility. A virtuous life seeks its just reward."

Benicia's sister wrote her Uncle that her Mama "wanted to know if you buried Lily near the little ones in our plot. Her beautiful hair did you cut any off? . . . When next you visit her grave put some flowers there in the name of 'Little Fannie'."

The letter from his niece's father, General John B. Frisbie, was dated June 15, 1885 from Mexico City:

Would that words of consolation could fly from my pen that would lift from your heart the great sorrow that I know too well which weighs heavily upon it but I can only remind you that it is the good God who has taken from you your beloved wife, that she may be with Him in a better land where pain, disappointment and grief are unknown. This home was too poor a home for her pure spirit, her exalted Christian character better fitted for companionship with angels . . . For you my brother and your sweet little children I feel the deepest sympathy and earnestly pray our Heavenly Father to sustain and comfort you in your affliction.

Another brother-in-law, Arpad Haraszthy, wrote Platon on June 27th:

It is but a few moments ago that I learned from Henry Blackman of the death of your dear wife Lily. I cannot tell you how shocked I am not to have known of it before and to have offered you the assurance of my sympathy in this irreparable loss. The General had told me a short time ago that she was quite ill but I had not the slightest thought the result would prove so serious. Be assured my heart goes out to you and your dear little ones in your bereavement.

The next day Platon answered Arpad's letter: "My dear Brother Arpad: I have just received your beautiful letter and I thank you for your kind sympathy for myself and the little children. We are indeed very lonely and no human sympathy or consolation can satisfy the void which is left in our hearts and home by the loss of a beloved wife and companion . . . God knows best what to ask of his creatures and we do not withhold from His Sacred Heart the sacrifice which he requires from myself and the little babes and we are resigned to His Holy Will."

To Platon his motherless daughters were part of his dear wife and he found solace in performing duties now facing him. His sister Fannie had observed his devotion to his children on her different visits to California and so apprised her father on July 15, 1889:

I received your nice letter with one from Platon in which he tells me that his little ones went to Sonoma to visit grandma and grandpa. Precious children. I think Platon raises them very well, not having a wife to help him. It is a tremendous load, the responsibility of a family of girls. I saw nothing finer in California than Platon's family and how he manages them. Poor soul. They are splendid children . . . May the good Lord always keep them well and a consolation to their father who so much loves them. The love of parents for their children is so great as to be beyond measurement or comparison.

The four girls—Felipa, Francisca, Adela and Angela—usually went to Sonoma during the summer vacation and spent the time with their grandparents and with their Aunt Natalia Haraszthy. Francisca remembered in later years: "Grandpa used to love to hear my sister and me play piano duets. There was one selection that ended with a long run. Grandpa thought that was marvelous and he would come up and kiss our fingers, then ask each of us to dance with him . . . Grandpa would wake up at 6 when the church bells played the angelus and order his chocolate. Then we grandchildren would all run in to see him. The first to answer 'Who loves Grandpa the best?' would get the first teaspoon of chocolate."

Platon wrote to his girls frequently. On one occasion he wrote, "The little white doll with the blue bonnet, says I ought to write to you tonight and tell you the secret we have. Well, Papa is going to send you by Express, Taffy Candy." Felipa, to whom the letter was sent, replied, "The box arrived yesterday afternoon and I thank you very much for being so kind. I would have probably have received the box sooner but you addressed it to Grandpa instead of Aunt Nat . . . Papa you must write to Grandpa, he thinks so much of you."

This was Grandpa Vallejo's last summer at Lachryma Montis and Platon's daughters were to remember it for years. That winter Dr. Vallejo had left his practice in Vallejo with another physician to come and help nurse his father through the night hours. Platon was amazed when his father was told by the Sonoma doctor to take exercise, to see the General jump out of bed and began to imitate the Indian war dance; on being told that it was a bit too strenuous he changed to a favorite waltz.

The loss of his father in January 1890 and of his mother in January 1891 were crosses almost as hard to bear as the one in June 1885 when he lost his wife, the mother of his four daughters.

On February 5, 1891, Platon wrote a card of thanks to the Editor of the Sonoma Index-Tribune saying:

The undersigned desires through your paper to thank on behalf of the members of the family of the late General M. G. Vallejo and Mrs. Vallejo; the Sonoma Band and the choir of St. Francis Church together with the people of Sonoma and other localities for their kind attention, sympathy and many other proofs of kindness and respect shown toward the venerable and beloved dead. The members of the family of the late Gen. and Mrs. Vallejo truly appreciate and will ever cherish in the memories the warm and sincere marks of friendship and esteem and respect, in which they always held our dear and justly beloved parents. It is a consolation for us which in our present loss help to sustain our broken spirits and give us courage to try and bear in future this last affliction.

DR. PLATON VALLEJO

WILLIAM HEATH DAVIS' WORK

Eight months after the death of Platon's father, the history-loving Doctor received the following letter dated September 20, 1890 from William Heath Davis, written from his office in Room 23, No. 66 Montgomery Street, San Francisco, saying in part:

Some time since, Mr. Napoleon P. Vallejo, your brother called at my office and bought one of my volumes, "Sixty Years in California" in which your deceased father is mentioned throughout the book, as one of the distinguished and representative men which this genial land produced. I am preparing a second book to be published soon, which will be longer and wider in scope than the present one, with not less than 1,000 pages of interesting reading matter. I will have in the book from fifty to seventy illustrations of the early scenes of California prepared in the best possible manner to make it more attractive.

Between the scenes there will be portraits of some of our historic native Californians and of Argonauts of the time anterior to and of 1849 whose names I have procured beyond the figure ten, and I will continue canvassing for more until I have obtained twenty in all. These likenesses will be made from steel plates and the work will be the first class in every respect with a biographical sketch of each individual appended thereto for $250.00 for each one. It would give me infinite joy to have your father's fac-simile and biography in my coming volume, surrounded with his own near relatives and other distinguished people of his time and only of that class will I place in my history.

Platon could not at that time afford the $250 necessary to have his father's portrait and biography included in Davis' projected book. Three years later (1893), Davis was still gathering material to add to a revised, enlarged edition of his *Sixty Years in California* and he decided to call on Dr. Vallejo, whereupon the Doctor wrote him, "I sit down with pleasure to write you, I will expect you soon and perhaps I ought to say correct (to help to correct) some erroneous ideas respecting California's early historical events. I look upon all and every work and item upon the history of California with jealousy, understanding with solicitude lest a word or thought improperly written by a wandering historian gives a wrong interpretation to the best acts and intentions of those who came before us . . . The pages of history are black with falsehoods and the worst of it, is that there is a demand for it, just as there is a demand for adulerated liquor. To my taste, pure running water."

Davis' visit was delayed, so Platon wrote him the following letter June 28, 1893 after Davis had sent him some of his manuscript for the Doctor's perusal.

Your favor of the 14th of the present month was duly received, together with the enclosed fragment of history relating to early times in California and as the history of California must be written for the people too, pleasant, truthful and understandingly such a history would please a native Californian like myself, if you please. I had both of my eyes levelled upon the pages which you were kind enough to send. You see Mr. Davis such scripture as had kept the attention of the world disgusted with the Californians of Spanish descent is not worth mentioning to my mode of thinking. Let me whisper it in your ears for I know you will jump up and thank me for concurring with you that the history, the true history of the character of the discovers, conquistadors and early possessors of this blessed land has never been written nor understood by Bancroft nor anyone else; they could not write what they did not know . . . California was suspected of being a rich and beautiful country long before the so-called American conquest. The Russians pressed their claim disagreeably close, the French sent that coyote De Mofras to tempt the unsophisticated Californian with bull frogs and champagne. The English came darn near getting ahead of Uncle Sam for the fair fairer, fairest of all the provinces of the known world.

You don't know how my father loved California. He loved his country as he would love his sweetheart. I knew it and I am a chip of the old block . . . I was born here . . .

We discovered America and invited you here, still I envy you the ten years that you came to California before I did. I was born in Sonoma Valley in 1841 . . . My father was the man that gave the country, the biggest boost the baby California ever got when he threw her into dear Uncle Sam's long reaching arms.

As has been mentioned, William Heath Davis had come to California in 1831 and married into the prominent Estudillo Spanish family.

When he got his manuscript ready for publication, he had lived in California seventy-five years. He had received much help from a reporter of the San Francisco Examiner, named Ike Parsons. During the Earthquake and Fire of April 1906, his manuscript was in his office in the Montgomery Block. Parsons, thinking to save the manuscript, removed it to his own office only to have the fire change its course and the flames destroyed the precious manuscript. From Davis' notes his enlarged work *Seventy-Five Years in California* was published in 1928 in a handsome edition by the John Howell Book Company of San Francisco. It is now being printed in a new edition by Lawton Kennedy who has been called "The Prince of California Printers."

PLATON'S AVOCATIONS

When all of Dr. Vallejo's daughters were married and settled in their own homes he found time to devote to some of his personal interests such as raising blooded horses and fine game cocks. His favorite horse Billy had been trained to kneel down, roll over and stand up and bow his head at the crack of a whip like a circus horse. He taught his roosters to fight by the viewing of their reflections in a mirror. Platon also had a pet goat. One day it strayed into the neighborhood of the Protestant church. Before Platon had missed the goat, he received a telephone call from the minister of the church. "Doctor, your goat has entered my church." Agitated, Dr. Vallejo exclaimed: "Por Dios, my Catholic goat in a Protestant church!"

Platon also turned to his favorite avocations: California history and sculptoring. As a confidant to his father for many years, he was in a particularly favored position to become a repository of information on the early days of California, and he was generous in sharing it with those who sincerely wished to learn the truth. His "Memoirs of the Vallejos," dictated to James H. Wilkins, has become an important source-material for those doing research work in the archives of California. Platon had little patience with some of the Californian historians, such as Theodore H. Hittell. On the fly pages of Volume 2 of his set of Hittell's History of California, he wrote the following criticisms with apparent relish:

This "History" of the American "Conquest of California" reminds one (who knows better) of the story of the "Wolf and the Lamb." What an atrocious lie! What a malicious cruel use of an opportunity to malign and cast odium upon those that deserve better of the world.

The trouble with the Californians was that they were only a handfull of people standing against a great and powerful nation; and the Bear Flag marauders if they did not succeed with their villainy would be nothing but they were a band of robbers who wanted to oust the Pioneers of Spain from their possessions *before* they came into the Union led by General Vallejo to settle their land titles and confirm them in their possessions according to law as the General assured and promised them would be done if they followed his advice and directions.

The Bear Flaggers were treacherous malcontents who did not deserve well either of Mexico or the United States. The Californians, certainly suffered from their presence and their treachery. And now they and their descendants have Mr. Hittell writing a history that reminds us of the story of the wolf and the lamb.

The intention of General M. G. Vallejo from his earliest career, from the beginning of his public life was to educate the Californians to freedom in religion, liberty in form of government and industry and improvement of the race by education and proper intermingling of society. To bring from Europe the industrious and well deserving and give them all means to induce them to remain here and make them happy in this beautiful land of sunshine and otherwise untold wealth. And so it would have been without war of "Conquest" by the United States or the Bear Flag Party.

Upon questioning the General one time what he [Vallejo] thought of these things, Vallejo paternally replied: "My son . . . Everything has turned out for the best. Let be, as it is. We are here. Writers write according to their views many times with the wrong ideas to inspire them. But facts speak louder than a waste of words and we are in the United States, soon to be the foremost nation on earth, Love everybody. Be good. Obey just laws. Que mas? Harbor no rancor in your heart. Speak well of everybody. Remember De Mortuis nil nisi bono. We live."

When Platon insisted that he wished to give the world certain facts, his father said, "No, let it go. What good to keep open an old sore? Let the wound heal. I brought this upon myself. I did what I thought was best. It was best for the country and so far as I am concerned, I can stand it."

PLATON'S LAST YEARS

The years slipped by. Platon's daughters finished their prescribed education. Francisca, the second daughter, who had been named for Grandmother Vallejo, graduated from Dominican College at San Rafael where she had majored in music, playing both the piano and guitar and doing some composing.

The spring of 1901 ushered in a typical situation of which Francisca wrote to her father:

My dear Papa:

You will not be surprised I think at what I am going to tell you and I hope Papa dear you will be pleased and make me quite happy by your approval. Night before last, Charles asked me to marry him and I said 'Yes.' He is very dear to me indeed. I did not realize how fond I was of him until lately and I know he loves me—so what else must I say. He is to write you by this mail so I will let him speak for himself . . . I feel we shall be very happy and I know Charles is as good as gold.

You have always been the best father in the world to me and though I do not say so often, you know Papa dear, accept my love and write to me soon.

The night Charles McGettigan proposed to Francisca Vallejo, she was visiting at the home of her Aunt Mattie Vallejo, who lived with her father, "Judge" Harvey Brown, on Myrtle Street in Oakland. This was eleven years after Mattie had divorced her husband Napoleon Vallejo. The divorce had not lessened the affection Platon and his family felt for Mattie (who was the innocent party) and for her remaining son Harvey (Bun) Vallejo.

Doctor Vallejo's consent was given. The engagement of Francisca Carrillo Vallejo and Dr. Charles McGettigan was announced in the newspapers on April 16, 1901. Little did the city of Vallejo's most popular obstetrician realize that when he brought into the world thirteen of the children of Mary O'Grady and Edward McGettigan, one of the babies was to become his son-in-law. The son-in-law to be was a graduate of St. Mary's College and of the Medical College of the University of California.

Father Joseph P. McQuaide on January 22, 1902 united in marriage Charles McGettigan, age 28 years, and Francisca Vallejo, age 25, with Ed McGettigan and Angela Vallejo as witnesses.

Among Dr. Vallejo's correspondents was the author Eva Emery Dye of Oregon City, Oregon, whose story of Dr. McLoughlin, Fort Vancouver, agent of the Hudson's Bay Company, was published by Harper Brothers. On June 9, 1894, Mrs. Dye had written Dr. Vallejo: "I do not see how I can come down again at present but if I ever do write a book 'In the Days of Alvarado' I shall hope to look to you for the most charming part of a historical romance. Even the very names of your brothers and sisters (written on the back of the picture you sent) have kindled my imagination and my fancy. A gem of art could certainly be produced, setting forth the Arcadian time of the Spanish Californians. How in the world Bret Harte and Joaquin Miller and others have overlooked that poetic field, I can not understand."

GRANDFATHER PLATON VALLEJO

Like many surgeons, Dr. Vallejo's skillful fingers found relaxation and pleasure during idle moments modeling clay and carving in stone, animals, birds and human figures. He executed an intaglio of his father which is considered an excellent likeness of General Vallejo.

In the early 1920s, Dr. Vallejo lived with his daughter Adela Peters at 420 Carolina Street where many of his carvings might be found on the larger rocks under the trees. He also spent much time in San Francisco at the home of his second daughter Francisca McGettigan and her husband Dr. Charles McGettigan. At this time the McGettigans had one daughter and six sons. In spite of her large family, Francisca found time to write poetry, compose music, prepare radio programs on California history, and winning many awards and not sacrificing her youthful beauty. It might be added that Alec and Mary de la Cruz, who have served the McGettigan family for over forty years, must take some credit for having relieved their mistress of most of the household responsibilities.

Francisca set aside a room for her father on the top floor of her home where he had an expansive view of the Bay and the Marin hills. Before him lay Temelpa, the sleeping Indian maiden whose reclining form was outlined against the sky north of the Golden Gate or "Yulupa," as Dr. Vallejo preferred to call the entrance to San Francisco Bay. Yulupa was the name used by the Suisun Indian tribe.

Dr. Vallejo's enjoyment of his visits with Francisca and his grandchildren he described in a letter to his sister Luisa in Sonoma:

> Sometime in the summer if we live, we will talk things over when I go up to visit you but now I can't promise you. I do not feel strong enough to be away from my old quarters . . . I have been here at Francisca's at 2644 Filbert Street in San Francisco spending the winter with my daughter who loves to have me here. I love to be with her and the children and the great Grandfather Vallejo gets the credit, alright. They are a beautiful family—six boys and one girl. The oldest Noel has married lately and two of the boys, men now have gone to sea to learn their trade.
>
> Indeed Time flies, changes and we change. But would it not be monotonous if we remained in one spot always and never saw new things. And I, myself begin to look more like Mount Shasta on top and less like Mount Diablo . . . The Indians averred that Piu dwelt there, when he moved it shook the earth, hence they accounted for earthquakes, slides and tital waves.

Platon was an authority on Indian lore and legend, and was able to speak several Indian dialects. One of his greatest pleasures had been to sit with Carroll, his eldest grandson, and tell him the Indian tales told to him by Old Tomo and Chief Solano upon whose mighty shoulders he used to be carried. Chief Solano spoke Spanish well, and Platon remembered that his father had said of Solano: "To the bravery and in particular to the diplomacy of that great chieftain of the Suisun Indians, civilization is indebted to the conquest of the territory which today composes the counties of Solano, Napa, Sonoma and Lake."

There were times when Carroll's brothers, Paul, Kevin, Daniel, Bernard, Edward and their sister Noel had listened in the past to Grandfather's tales about El Diablo, about Piu and old Cocasui, the sly fox who listens and spies for his master, the Piu of the Contra Costa Mountain.

Francisca Vallejo McGettigan has preserved many of these legends for posterity in her book of poems, *Along the Highway of the King*. In the foreword of the book, Gertrude Atherton, the eminent novelist, wrote: "Of the distinguished men of California, the most outstanding was Don Mariano Guadalupe Vallejo, Lord of the North, a great soldier, a far-seeing statesman, a man of rock-bound strength and stern integrity . . . He was a poet, too, and the woman he married, Francisca Benicia Carrillo, was a cultivated musician as well as a model wife and devoted mother. How could their granddaughter

Francisca Carrillo Vallejo be other than gifted? . . . She is the Voice of California, an authentic poet and composer."

It was in the home of this gifted daughter that Dr. Platon Vallejo died on June 1, 1925. Although he was eighty-four years old, he had been busy working on a dictionary of the Suisun Indian language, including the tribe's nomenclature.

It was on Wednesday, June 3rd, that it seemed the entire town of Vallejo constituted itself a guard of honor while the body of Dr. Vallejo was being taken from the boat to St. Vincent's Catholic Church where he had been a communicant for sixty-two years, the same church where the cherished family friend, Father Louis Daniels, had served for so many years.

The church was thronged with old friends from all over Solano County where he had been known for years for his charities where he ministered to many for miles driving in his one-horse buggy.

After the Requiem Mass conducted by Reverend Christopher Lanz, Dr. Vallejo's body was carried to St. Vincent's Cemetery, situated between Vallejo and Benicia, the cities named for his father and mother.

The body of the first native-born physician, Platon M. G. Vallejo, was laid to rest next to that of his wife who had passed away forty years before. Now as he once said, he was "Close-knit with her in Blessed and Happy Immortality."

Jovita Francisca Vallejo

Jovita Francisca Vallejo

(Mrs. Arpad Haraszthy)

On February 23rd, 1844, in the family home, the Casa Grande, Jovita Francisca, the ninth child of the Vallejos was born. A few weeks before Santa Ana had appointed General Manuel Micheltorena governor of California, succeeding Don Juan B. Alvarado, General Vallejo's nephew. The infant's godparents at her baptism were her ten-year-old sister Epifania and her aunt Encarnacion Vallejo Cooper.

In her early teens Jovita attended Dr. Ver Mehr's St. Mary's Hall in Sonoma, where her two older sisters, Adela and Natalia, were students. John Ver Mehr, an Episcopalian minister had been persuaded by General Vallejo to come to Sonoma and establish a school for young ladies, but upon arriving in Sonoma in 1853, Ver Mehr found that it was not convenient for the General to turn over the Casa Grande for the school as he had promised, so Ver Mehr had to locate it in the home of Senora Fitch on the west side of the plaza. The Senora's house had been erected by Jacob P. Leese in 1843; subsequently he sold it to General Vallejo and Captain Frisbie, who leased it for a time to General Persifor F. Smith and then later they sold it to Senora Fitch.

By 1854 General Vallejo was able to redeem his promise to Dr. Ver Mehr and the latter moved St. Mary's school into the Casa Grande. It succeeded so well that in 1855 the number of pupils nearly filled Vallejo's spacious mansion, and Dr. Ver Mehr found it necessary to obtain more space by converting the adobe building in the rear into additional class rooms. The building, still standing, had housed Vallejo Indian servants as well as the kitchen for the household.

Many of the students at St. Mary's Hall were from early California families; and were as Dr. Ver Mehr remarked ". . . docile and faithful." Among them were Jovita's cousins, the daughters of Senora Fitch and the Bale girls from Napa.

During the summer and fall of 1856, an epidemic of diphtheria struck the Valley of Sonoma. Four of Dr. Ver Mehr's daughters—Bella, Amy, Ida and Fanny, age three to eleven years—died from the virulent disease. Dr. Ver Mehr in his autobiography "Checkered Life" told that "the daughters of General Vallejo, and many other friends came and laid Bella out," crowning her with laurel and olive leaves. The bodies of the Ver Mehr girls were given temporary burial in the private vault in General Vallejo's garden, at the rear of the Casa Grande, where General Vallejo's grandson "Lupito," his daughter Fannie's first born was placed in June 1856. In December, Dr. Ver Mehr put four little coffins on wagons going to Lakeville. There they were transferred to a steamer bound for San Francisco, where they were taken to Lone Mountain Cemetery for burial. Dr. Ver Mehr, his wife Fany, and their remaining daughter Gertrude followed on the stage. As Dr. Ver Mehr was leaving Sonoma, a letter arrived by Express from San Francisco and was handed to him. He opened it to find that the handwriting was unfamiliar and there was no signature, only these words, "I was sick and thou visitedst me." With it was a check for one hundred dollars. The gift and letter did much to soften the sadness of the Ver Mehr's return to San Francisco. A collection of $900 was taken up in five of the San Francisco churches, and with the addition of other funds, Dr. Ver Mehr was able to re-open St. Mary's Hall in a good-sized house on the corner of Geary and Powell.

Jovita transferred to the new St. Mary's Hall; homesick she wrote to her mother:

> Gertrude Ver Mehr was playing the waltz that Natalia plays and I felt so sad. I remembered all my dear sisters and brothers. Nothing can be as sad to here of things that have been played in there dere sweet home . . . It seems to me like an enchanted place when I think of all the beautiful up there. Well Mamasita, you must excuse me for writing in english but I had to do it to improve my english. I think one of the girls will be so kind to translate it to you.

In June, 1858, Dr. Ver Mehr moved St. Mary's Hall to a three-story building on Bush Street in San Francisco. It had large parlors, class rooms and a dormitory. There, too, Jovita was a student and there she received merit awards and gift-books for excellent scholarship. On stationery bearing a print of the new St. Mary's Hall, Jovita wrote to her father in her newly acquired English:

> Dear Papa:
>
> We have just come home from a long walk in which we most appeare like a flok of geese; I suppose some people must laugh to see a long string of young ladies going about town but we always try to go where we would not be seen so much . . . To staye in the house the whole blessed day is pretty bad, to hear other people talk of going to such and such a place or having been to such and such a place although I don't mind it much myself. I like to staye in the house sometime. Fannie came down to the Ball that was given at Tucker Academy. I here it was a very fine thing. I was sorry you could not attend it . . . I am getting along nicely in all my studies but I think the trip to Europe would do me more good than anything else, if we could only go soon; how happy I would be, let us go in April. I wish your business were all arenged so that we could go soon.
>
> I would like to go and spend next Suterday and Sunday at Caroline Larkin. She was hear yesterday and she made me promise that I would go, so can't I go? Just as you saye, I will do everything that (you) tell me to do you know. I regret very much not being with you at that little pic-nich that you had, I am sure I would have enjoyed myself very much. I must now bring this to a close by sending my love to my dear friends, and the rest for yourself.
>
> From your little girl,
>
> JOVITA

Caroline Larkin had been a friend of the Vallejo girls for some years. In May of 1854 she was visiting them in Sonoma and wrote to her parents, "Uncle Cooper is going away tomorrow. All the Vallejo family are very handsome. I think the youngest girl who is a year old [Benicia Ysabel] has curles all over her head and large black eyes with very long eyelashes. Mrs. Vallejo is handsome." Five years later the Vallejos were to lose this beautiful child when she was not quite seven years old.

While Jovita was attending school in San Francisco, General Vallejo rented a pew at old St. Mary's Cathedral, in order that his little girl (she was only fourteen) could go to Mass as well as his boys, Platon and Ula, who were enrolled at Mr. Crittenden's College in San Francisco.

After Jovita's return home, she liked to correspond with her father when he was away. It gave her an opportunity to practice her "english" and, at the same time it kept her father posted as to the happenings at Lachryma Montis; for example:

Dear Papa:

On the 17th, Wednesday morning the Ryan house at Quiquiriqui burnt down; nothing could be safe but a few clothes that belonged to Ryan. Fire broke out from the stove. When Ryan saw it, the house was all on fire, as he was working in the orchard.

Mother looks over my shoulder and tells me for you to send some tea, sugar rice for we are out of them. We are all well, Lulu and Mary send their love with min[e] also thanking you for the candies. My love to all my friends. It is raining just now.

From your little JOVITA

Jovita's studies when she was at school in San Francisco had included painting, but she gave it up to concentrate on music. An old family friend, Senor de la Rosa, recalled in after years how beautifully she sang *Ave Maria* in the San Francisco Solano Church. She played both the piano and guitar and in 1862 her father playfully drew up a formal contract whereby Jovita was to teach two of her brothers to play the guitar. She was required to give them three lessons a week, and as compensation was to receive from the boys one cow, red in color, and one colt named "Barragan," provided the boys were able to play a Baca (a lively tune) on the guitar.

The General always corresponded in Spanish with his children; yet one time when he was in San Francisco, he wrote a bi-lingual letter to Jovita. It appears that Senora Vallejo had requested her husband to buy some earrings. On January 17, 1861, he wrote that the earrings had been made to his liking and he was enclosing them in the letter:

Jovita: Mama me encargo unos arillos y los mando inclusod en esta carta estan hechos a mi gusto and I do not know if she likes them. I hope she will do. I think they are very pretty indeed. How you like my engles? You understand it? If not tell me the truth.

JOVITA MARRIES ARPAD HARASZTHY

The fourth daughter of the Vallejos, with her large brown eyes and classical features, was considered by members of the family to be the most beautiful of the Vallejo girls. When she was nineteen, she fell in love with Arpad Haraszthy, four years her senior. He had just returned from Europe. His education and experiences there made him a suitor no girl could reject. The wedding—a double one, as Natalia was marrying Jovita's fiance's brother Attila—occurred on June 1, 1863. This was the year that the Haraszthy brothers' twenty-year-old sister, Ida, married Major Henry Hancock, engineer and lawyer at an elaborate wedding in San Francisco. Ida had first met Major Hancock when she was nine years old.

Attila and Arpad Haraszthy were the sons of Colonel Agoston Haraszthy, a nobleman of Hungary, where he had owned a large estate planted in wine grapes. In 1840, as a political exile he had come to America, returning two years later to bring his wife and his three sons, Gaza, Attila and Arpad, together with his parents, to the United States. They settled in Wisconsin, but his mother did not long survive in the new world. In 1849, because of the Colonel's asthmatic condition, the Haraszthys left Wisconsin; his physician advising him to go either to Florida or to California. The discovery of gold on the west coast had created such excitement that California was chosen for their new home, and, in the fall of 1849, one could have seen a family party of dignified appearance crossing the plains—Colonel Haraszthy's father with his second wife (Matilda Richardson of Massachusetts) and Colonel Haraszthy with *his* wife (Countess Eleanor) and five of their six children; a third son, Bela and two daughters, Ida and Otelia, having been added to the family. Ida in later years recalled the long journey with hostile Indians lurking along the trail and how a Comanche chief offered to exchange four squaws and two ponies for herself—the beautiful six-year-old Ida.

Upon their arrival in California, the Haraszthy family settled in San Diego from which district the Colonel was elected a member of the State Legislature that met temporarily in Vallejo in 1852–53. Colonel Haraszthy's future son-in-law, Captain Henry Hancock, was also a member of that Legislature.

In January 1857, Colonel Haraszthy bought 560 acres of land northeast of the town of Sonoma—a purchase which post-dated his ownership of "Las Flores" and the land at Crystal Springs, where in both places, he had found the climate unfavorable for the raising of grapes.

Arpad Haraszthy, Jovita's husband, was born in Futtak, southern Hungary, on June 28th, 1840. After coming to San Diego, his mother, finding so few educational institutions in California, took him and several of other children around the Horn to New York to place them in school. Arpad remained there at school until 1857. During the vacation period, he traveled throughout the southern and eastern states and Canada with funds supplied by his father. Soon after his return to California, he left for Paris for the purpose of completing his education as a civil engineer. To please his father, Arpad left Paris and went to Epernay, in the Champagne district, to receive instructions in the art of making champagne.

In July, 1861 Arpad's parents and his sister Ida had gone to Paris. Colonel Haraszthy kept a journal and in it said: "My son, Arpad had been four years in Paris and latterly in the Champagne District where he is now learning the manufacture of champagne and other wines. He proved a great assistance to us during our stay in Europe; he acted as my secretary; my correspondence with scientific societies increasing daily as well as with prominent officers of different governments."

Colonel Haraszthy and Arpad visited France, Germany, Switzerland Italy and Spain where the Colonel collected and shipped to California about 200,000 vines embracing 300 varieties, which were due to reach San Francisco by steamer in January 1862 in care of Wells-Fargo & Company. When the shipment arrived, Colonel Haraszthy took charge of the planting of the vines, and the rooting of cuttings which were then distributed throughout the State. In spite of initial difficulty with the pest Phylloxera the high quality of California's wines today is, in large part, due to Colonel Agoston Haraszthy's foresight.

FIRST HOME OF JOVITA AND ARPAD

After the marriage of Arpad and Jovita which had occurred as mentioned before, on Monday, June 1st, 1863 with Father Deyaert officiating at the double Haraszthy-Vallejo wedding, Colonel Haraszthy bought the Butler place near Sonoma and gave it to Arpad. There in the nearby foothills, Jovita said that her husband "built a little shanty, up in the ravine, a beautiful spot." The Colonel also placed Arpad in charge of the cellars of his Buena Vista Winery. The Colonel wishing to expand the development of his property, incorporated it into the Buena Vista Vinicultural Society with a number of members; William C. Ralston and other capitalists being in the background. Agoston Haraszthy was made the superintendent with Arpad as champagne master.

Arpad's father-in-law had been receiving prizes for his wines and champagne, but, in 1863, in deference to his new son-in-law, General Vallejo did not enter his champagne in the fairs. On the other hand, Arpad exhibited his product under the name of the Buena Vista Vinicultural Society and took first prize. The only ingredient that entered Arpad's champagne besides the juice of the grape was a small amount of rock-candy, dissolved in white wine of a certain age. In France not only flavoring but brandy or alcohol were often added.

After several years with the Buena Vista Vinicultural Society attended by success and some failures in the making of sparkling wines, Arpad left their employ and entered into partnership with P. D. Giovanari, who had worked in the vineyards of General Vallejo. The firm Haraszthy and Giovanari carried on a wine business, selling wines and brandies wholesale, and bottling the same for shipment, up to 1866 when Arpad moved to San Francisco. There in the Haraszthy parlor, Arpad and Jovita, with benches filled with apparatus, developed the "*Eclipse*," named after a popular brand of cigars. This champagne was to win international awards. At the opening of the Palace Hotel in San Francisco on October 5th, 1875, the toasts were drunk in Eclipse Champagne.

A few months earlier, some of the sparkling wine had been brought out to the home of Jovita and Arpad to toast Arpad's sister Ida Haraszthy when she gave birth in her brother's home in San Francisco to twin boys, George Allan and Harry, on July 26, 1875. Harry was short-lived but George Allan lived to be 89 years old.

Captain Allan Hancock was a man who played many roles in life with success as an oil operator, farmer, banker, real estate developer, navigator, aviator, scientist, patriot, water witcher, musician, philanthropist for colleges and causes. Sharing his interests during his sunset years was his wife Marian Muller who gave him a happiness which often seems reserved for the young.

Arpad Haraszthy's wife, Jovita, was essentially a home-loving woman, finding pleasure in her domestic duties and in caring for her daughter, born on April 11, 1864 and named *Agostine* after Arpad's father. Jovita found time to write to her mother, who in turn liked to relieve her pent-up feelings to this understanding daughter as she did in January, 1867:

> It's been some days since I received your letter in which you tell me that you are well, you and Arpad and Agostina and that you are happy with your sewing machine which pleases me very much . . . Your Papa and Andronico are always quarreling. You, well know your Papa, he is so ill-tempered and how stubborn and proud. What a task it is to live with ill-tempered people, he has no patience and we have no one to help us do things. I am always a bit ill.
>
> Jovita write to me when you can. Don't do as your brothers and sisters do, who never are able to write even a little letter to their mother. The only one who used to write to me was Adela and now even she scarcely remembers me. Perhaps it is because I am poor. They may be afraid that I'm going to ask them for something. Only from you and Natalia have I received some little things. One knows that is affection. Not Andronico, nor Platon nor Fani, nor Adela. I say nothing about Ula as he is not here [He was in Mexico]. I don't want anything of worth, just any thing of love.
>
> Your Papa came from Napa and brought me some printed calico for a dress. It has rained here a lot, so much that one can't go out in the streets. They are very muddy, the carts can't move. They drive the wagons with three pair of horses and then the men can go out with difficulty. Sonoma is a very sad place, especially Lachryma Montis and Buena Vista. Give Agostina many kisses and Arpad an embrace. Take care of yourself.

A month later, on the 13th, Jovita tells her mother:

I received your nice long letter. I was just busy cooking dinner when Arpad brought it to me. I was so glad that I let my dinner burn but we did not mind it. I am real sorry how things are going on there for your sake and my two little sisters but things will change; misfortune can not always last.

Let me tell you a piece of news about myself, better to hear it from me first than from others. Agostine [three years old] is to have a playmate in about twelve weeks, that is next May. I know you will be surprised but don't feel worried about me for I have not had a day's sickness in all six months and I feel happy to think I will have another little one to love me. Adela has been here and stayed all day with me and she has promised me to come and stay with me at that time so I feel very glad to have some of the family with me. She is going to embroider my flannels for me. Fannie has been down, she spent a whole day with all her little girls with me . . . She too is going to present John with a pledge of her affection next August. It is a general increase all around—a sure sign the world won't come to an end. My love to all and tell Maria that Snookie [Agostine] has her letter and sleeps with it all night . . . Arpad wrote for Otelia [his sister] to come and stay with me whilst I don't feel well. I am expecting him to send me a bed and things so when Otelia goes back, I expect you to let one of the girls come and stay with me.

When Jovita's mother learned of her daughter's expected child, she wanted to go to San Francisco to be with Jovita during her confinement, but Jovita thought otherwise: "I don't think it necessary for you to do so for two reasons first Adela has promised to be with me and she will take care of me, secondly Doctor Precht in whom I have all confidence will attend to me and see me safely through . . . Arpad has promised me a servant to do all the work after I have recovered."

Jovita's second child was a son. She thought the infant resembled her brother Uladislao: The baby was baptized *Carlos Juan Uladislao* with Captain John B. Frisbie and Adela Vallejo Frisbie as godparents. Soon after the birth of the Haraszthy heir, Arpad wrote his mother-in-law: "You have of course been already told that Jovita and baby are doing well and that all danger is now over. Jovita sits up every day a few hours. And in a few days will be able to move about again. Now if it would please you, we would like you to come down and spend at least a couple of weeks with us. I hope we are not asking too much. Our house is No. 1007 Mason Street."

When Carlos was old enough to travel, Jovita took her two children and her twelve-year-old sister Luisa to the city of Vallejo, where they were the guests of the John B. Frisbie family. From Vallejo she wrote to her mother on March 28, 1868:

It is a long time since I have written to you and I know you are worrying about Lulu; you must not let it give you any trouble. I take good care of her. We have been detained in Vallejo longer than we intended. Agostine brought the black measles with us and all the children took them. It is three weeks today but thank God they are all up today and doing nicely. Agostine and little Fannie had the worse time. Adela's little girl did not take them as soon as the others but has taken them three days ago and is very sick now. Was I not unfortunate to bring trouble to this household of children?

How are you getting along? All alone, no cook, no Salamaia [Indian servant] no Lulu: well I hope it will not always be so. How is Maria? Carlos misses her yet, he thinks Lulu is her. I must close now, he is crying. Kiss Papa, Uncle and Maria for me. Agostine and Carlos press their dear Grandma to their little hearts over and over again. Good night.

From your affectionate daughter,
JOVITA

To facilitate the task of making garments for her two little children as well as for herself, Jovita bought a sewing machine. She sold some personal jewelry in order to purchase material. In a letter to her mother she tells of these transactions, along with news.

How does Natalia like her corset that I sent her? Tell her that I have bought a beautiful sewing machine for $25 from a lady that wanted to get rid of it. I am very fortunate in getting it so chip. I sold those two old bracelets of mine which were not much account and I got six dollars for them, with which I bought beautiful cotton for under clothing. I am glad to hear through Napoleon, who is stopping with Fannie at the Occidental Hotel and that you liked the goods I sent you. I suppose you will make them up as soon as you can and the girls will go to school, as things have taken a different turn now.

On the last steamer from Mexico, Don Victor Castro arrived. Have you any news of Ula? Tell Lulu and Mary I will soon answer their nice little letters. Oh! how much they have improved. I was real proud of them. I read them to Fannie's children. They cannot write as well as our pets. Tell Mary that Agostine has a great big doll, one of those large babies; it shuts and opens its eyes by itself.

On May 7, 1874 Jovita sent a sewing machine to her mother which delighted Luisa and Maria. When it arrived the two girls went to their sister Natalia's house for lessons. That afternoon they began sewing on the Calico material for which their father had paid $10.

Jovita welcomed the visits of her two younger sisters, Luisa and Maria, to her home, especially Luisa who shared Jovita's love for music and could sing duets with her. One such occasion was when Luisa was seventeen; in regard to it Jovita wrote her mother on February 10, 1873: "You must be put out because I have used my influence to have Lulu here because this is her only chance to cultivate her voice and you can rest assured that I will make her practice for I am determined she won't be like other young ladys, they think only of their pretties and that is all. I shall take good care of her, in fact I don't think she will have much enjoyment unless it is in her music but as she is a good little girl, I will not have much trouble . . . So make up your mind to not see her until we all go to Sonoma in the month of May and then *hurra* boys for a good time."

Senor Mancusi was selected as the maestro for Luisa. Jovita was very proud when he reported that her little sister had an excellent voice. Jovita also took lessons in singing, and on Sunday she sang in the French Catholic Church.

Realizing that the upkeep of her father's ranch and the education of the two youngest girls kept him "hunting for money," Jovita was anxious to help her family increase their income. She wrote her mother: "It is a long time since I heard from you but I must write to you on business about your dried fruit. I have found a person who buys all those kind of things, also your olives. I want you to write to me or make Nap or Luisa write for you. Now is the time to sell all those things. Mr. Jordan's brother-in-law had business from here to Portland and says he will do the best he can; the market price is from 12, 15, and 20 cents a pound for dried fruit. You are to send the things direct to him and he is to deliver to me whatever he makes from it and I will manage it as nice as I can . . . You had better pack up all the best you have and have it ready so that when I let you know when and where to direct them. Pack them up in what you have, boxes or barrels, it matters not."

JOVITA'S UNHAPPINESS

As the years went by, with Arpad giving more and more time to the commercial end of the wine business (his partner was now Isidor Landsberger) and to civic affairs, an irritability on his part developed and Jovita found the sea of matrimony a bit rough. As early as the summer of 1876, General Vallejo was disturbed over the domestic atmosphere he found in Jovita's home. Finally in 1877, after fourteen years of marriage, Jovita threatened to get a legal separation which increased her father's distress. Because of Jovita's children and the prominence of the Vallejo and Haraszthy families, such a termination was to be avoided and the General felt it was his duty to try to prevent it. He went to San Francisco and spent days, in fact weeks, with Jovita but found her unyielding. Meanwhile he kept his wife informed, his first letter after his arrival being dated March 13, 1877, from 1126 Pine Street Francisca:

From the moment that I reached the wharf I have been with Arpad and in his office; he laid bare to me the "hows and whys" (in his way) of the business of the divorce between him and Jovita. Then I came to see Jovita and she, too, gave me her reasons. The fact is that Arpad wrote her a letter telling her he would ask for a divorce, etc. and she who wanted it at once went to see Mr. Brooks and took the business in her hands. Then I went to see Brooks with whom I talked a long time. This Mr. Brooks doesn't like divorce in any way; but he has to do what Jovita asks of him if the scandal can't be avoided. He would like Jovita to go to live with us for one year as a test; but Jovita doesn't want to, as she says that she would lose the right to the house furnishings in a law suit, etc. and that surely after the year was up, she would be in the same position that she is in now, to give Arpad half of the property that they have accumulated together and moreover to have to support the children—so that I don't know what to think or what to do.

Arpad wants me to manage the case because I will look after the interest and honor of Jovita, of her children and also the interests of the Haraszthy family. I could wish with all my heart to avoid a scandal and to placate Jovita a little but she is determined in everything. Tomorrow I shall see what I can do and tonight I shall talk a little more.

Another letter to Francisca, dated March 22nd, reported no progress:

After thousands and thousands of words and long conversation with Jovita, now as a friend, now as a counselor and also a father, I haven't been able to make my advise prevail under any point of view in the question of the divorce. In spite of my liberality (so far) in such things, I am very surprised to find in Jovita such obstinancy. She told me that she had no alternative than divorce, the insane asylum or suicide that she did not consult me at the beginning because she knew that I would tell her that she should join her husband. "Papa" she says to me "only the one who carries the coffin knows how much the dead one weighs."

Arpad has written several letters to her asking her pardon. I have seen that reconciliation is impossible, divorce inevitable and that a cursed scandal will result. To prove cause for divorce in the courts, you need a great scandal and many dollars especially if one of the party persists and fights the case. Moreover it is dragged out so. Adela has probably told you how stubborn Jovita is.

It is certain that the men (many of them) are usually to blame for out of ten ones there are nine bad ones and among the women, I believe that out of ten there are nine good ones. You see how I look at the thing; but the family is the only thing which keeps up society. I truly find no way out. Civilization pushes up toward the Abyss. How I wish that the exalted Hand of the All Powerful or the Spirit of His Infinite Divinity should interfere in the well being of his creatures.

Although living in the same house with Arpad, Jovita was not speaking to her husband; so he communicated with her by a conciliatory letter:

With feelings of kindness, I address you this time and ask you once again to forget the past and return to me as my wife. I am not only willing but even anxious to acknowledge to you, all those errors that I have committed as I have already acknowledged them to your father, to General Frisbie and to Mrs. Hancock. And I hope, Jovita, you will pardon them. I must own that my nature is hasty and impetuous, that I get angry easy.

We have misunderstood each other for years and the incidents which have lately transpired have proven a painful lesson, which I shall never forget . . . Why not, then, since we know the cause, come together once again and with the example of the past before us, endeavor to lead a new life and wring from the future many happy days—more than we ever had in the past. If you will consent, I assure you that I will do everything in my power to secure our mutual happiness. There is always plenty of time to appeal to the Courts; but when the case gets so far, there is no receding. It must go on to the bitter end.

Arpad's conciliatory letter reached Jovita on March 26th, 1877, and she granted him an interview. Her father was able to report progress on the same day to his wife:

It is nine o'clock at night and I set out to write to you to tell you something of the sad and unfortunate affair between Jovita and Arpad. After many talks, advice to one and then to the other; listening to the complaints and serious accusations, some of them grave and others apparent; consultations with some members of the two families such as Adela Frisbie and also Ida Haraszthy de Hancock, who have all, now with one means and now with another tried to persuade Jovita to a reconciliation. Still nothing have they been able to effect in spite of repeated letters from Arpad begging her pardon, repentant a thousand times, like the Magdalene of having sinned in provoking the divorce.

Right now Arpad asked for a verbal explanation with Jovita since they had not talked with each other—and they are in the parlor talking and I am in Jovita's room waiting for the result which will not be final but which will have a tendency towards a good understanding and will spare us the killing sorrow of the last two weeks which have been truly cruel. 11 at Night

The conference ended.—Jovita gives in (not because she wants to) only for the sake of the children. This week I expect to finish the *cure* and will go home to rest from so much turmoil and then I'll tell you everything . . . Arpad has promised us so much that now we are afraid.

General Vallejo remained ten days longer in San Francisco after the reconciliation. On April 4, 1877, he wrote a reassuring note to his wife, saying, "It seems that after the furious storm that had been let loose in the matter of Jovita, a calm has followed. The sea that had been so stirred up has subsided; it is serene and peaceful. Please Heaven, that it continues so that we shall not again have to hear and see such things among our own people that are so disagreeable; this time without anything on our side to be ashamed of."

Now that the marital difficulties of Jovita were solved, her father turned to his own troubles, the hunt for "dinero." His hunt was successful; some money was advanced to him and he was soon in the midst of plans for his trip to Mexico with John B. Frisbie. While in Mexico, Vallejo was pleased to receive letters from Jovita. He thought she deserved happiness but from her letters he thought she suffered. Vallejo wrote his wife, "My heart is very sad when I remember Jovita, poor girl, I dream of her all the time and the dreams are sad." Arpad himself wrote his father-in-law "a very flattering letter," but Vallejo said "I haven't answered him yet."

On Vallejo's return home, he noticed that Jovita wanted some member of her own family to remain with her in her home; usually it was Adela, Luisa or Maria; then again it was Ula, the brother so like her handsome little son Carlos. Vallejo told his wife, "Jovita wants it that way and this proves she is fearful about something . . . Jovita is the same, seemingly, but she is dejected in spirit and seems very sad because the birth of the child is near . . . Jovita awaits your visit. I am sorry and have great compassion for her. Poor woman!"

THE DEATH OF JOVITA

The year 1877 passed, and with the arrival of spring 1878, there were many important happenings in the Vallejo family; the General himself was busy with land litigation, seeking witnesses and translating documents with the help of Ula and Maria; Fannie Frisbie, the eldest daughter, was leaving California with her family to make her home in Mexico; Maria engaged to young Harry Cutter, was busy planning her wedding for May 8th, the 21st anniversary of her birth; and Jovita expecting her third child.

The Civil Courts in the spring of 1877 had not separated Jovita and Arpad, but in the spring of 1878, death did. It happened on May 5th, 1878. On that day, Jovita was convalescing from the birth of her third child, a daughter named Jovita, who had not survived. Jovita was in bed, her luncheon tray on her lap as she sat up to eat. Suddenly she was seized with a fatal heart attack. Her terror-stricken husband put a mirror in front of her lips to see if there was evidence of the breath of life. But her heart was stilled; the heart which had been heavily burdened with domestic troubles could no longer bear the added sorrow—the recent death of her infant daughter. Arpad sent telegrams to the members of the family, and Jovita's father went immediately to San Francisco.

For an unknown reason, there was some delay in receiving permission to bury Jovita from the San Francisco Cathedral.

The distressed father wrote to Platon May 8, 1878:

> I received your telegram and as the Archbishop is not here, I haven't seen him nor do I have the heart to talk about anything, particularly of ecclesiastical matters, which cost your father so much work and grief.
>
> The business of the burial of Jovita has been very, very disagreeable to me; the Vicar has deceived me in spite of my good faith and best intention. I have gone from top to bottom and at last, every one has seen the deceit, the rebuff, indeed the implied insult to all my family, etc, etc. Scandal results and who knows where we are to stop.
>
> It is the plan of Arpad himself and mine so that when the time comes the proper rites should be celebrated in the Cathedral and as soon as they are over, the body should be taken to Sonoma. If the Vicar refuses to perform the ceremonies in the Cathedral, we'll see what happens. Neither I, nor my family, relatives and friends deserve such rude and tactless treatment. God is Everywhere—in church and out of it. In any case I am greatly aggrieved. Tomorrow, we all leave for Sonoma.

Returning to Sonoma, Vallejo again wrote to Platon: "Today I came from San Francisco with my heart crushed with sadness, with shame and mortification because of the action of the Catholic fathers in the honors, rather the half-honors for my daughter, Jovita. I and the family have resented it very much . . . I know I do not merit such rude and cruel treatment. The Archbishop was in this 'Vale of Tears' to bless the house of the *Rich* proprietor, Colonel Hooper: he passed here the *Poor* house of General Vallejo and he didn't deign to come to even to 'console the sad' as the works of mercy demand; and this knowing your mother was very, very ill."

Two days later (May 11, 1878), General Vallejo wrote to Archbishop Alemany:

> His Excellency, the Most Reverend Archbishop of San Francisco
>
> In order to avoid more difficulties and murmurs regarding the funeral from the

Cathedral of my daughter Dona Jovita de Haraszthy, deceased, whose body lies in the Mausoleum of Calvary Cemetery. In the name of her husband, Senor Haraszthy whom I represent, I do write to ask that funeral honors be given my daughter with all the pomp due her position as a Catholic . . . With all due respect, I sign myself,

Your obedient servant
M. G. VALLEJO

Platon felt that he knew the cause of the withholding of permission for Jovita's funeral from the Cathedral, and took it upon himself to secure the records of the marriage of Jovita and Arpad by a Catholic priest. When the records were received, Archbishop Alemany concerned himself with the case and wrote this reassuring letter to Dr. Vallejo:

Dear Doctor:

I was sorry that all things concerning your sister's burial were not as agreeable as I might have wished. Just at the moment we did not know whether the marriage had been made right and not having the certificate from the Pastor, all that could be done at the time was to place the body in the receiving vault. I am most happy to receive your favor on the subject and to learn that not only her marriage had been made right but that a certificate had been issued.

I received also a letter from the General just when about leaving for Los Angeles to attend the funeral of Bishop Amat and I seized a moment before leaving to state to him that I had left instructions with my Vicar-General to the effect that he should facilitate the funeral in the Cathedral or other place for his daughter. I hope the good General will understand that under the circumstances all was done that the Church regulations allow. With kind remembrances to Mrs. Vallejo, I remain

Siempre Suyo,
J. S. ALEMANY

Platon notified the relatives about Jovita's death. From Mexico he received this message from his sister Fannie Frisbie, dated June 15, 1878:

I received your sad letter dated May 6th in which you tell me of the death of Jovita. What a terrible blow for all of the family and particularly for the two children who will be without their mother who loved them so much. When you write to me again, tell me everything about how it was and from what Jovita died. It seems strange for a woman recently delivered. Is her husband very sad? How sad it was that Maria wasn't married on the 8th of May, instead, there was a burial . . . When I stop to think that I shall never see dear Jovita again, I am filled with much sadness.

The entire Vallejo family were deeply affected by Jovita's death. When the General last looked upon her face, he cut from her hair a raven black ringlet which he carried in his wallet the rest of his life.

Judging by a letter written to Archbishop Alemany, the prelate made some overtures to Vallejo but the latter had not forgotten. He addessed the Archbishop: "I have your very worthy letter dated October 26th past. I appreciate very much your honorable mention which you made of my respected mother . . . Regarding yourself, it appears the conduct was unjustifiable on the sad occasion of the burying of the remains of my dear daughter, Jovita. I do not know what thing was represented to you of such gravity that you were obliged to submit us to shame with an insult that only misconduct would merit. The marriage of my daughter Jovita was performed by a Catholic Priest . . . If you had the kindness to ask, I could have told you the truth. You should not have pronounced the sentence without hearing the defense, for the reason that Death had closed the lips of the innocent accused, whose right to be defended was most sacred. As to whether she had completed her Easter duty, also your informer was able to slander. Who was that person who knew the life of Jovita so intimately and why do they believe an accusation without permitting us a chance to defend her?"

ARPAD'S LAST YEARS

The immediate months after Jovita's death were busy ones for Arpad, what with the care of his fourteen-year-old daughter and his eleven-year-old son, but the responsibility gave him a certain comfort. Much time was also given to expanding his business and to participation in civic affairs. Arpad had been a friend of Mark Twain and Bret Harte. He was a charter member of the Bohemian Club in 1872, and through the years had enjoyed the companionship of many of its members who possessed special talents. One of these was the artist, William Keith. Keith, whose studio was above the California Market in San Francisco had painted the hills about the Buena Vista Vineyards and, in appreciation Arpad had often sent him barrels of wine, which Keith shared with his fellow Bohemians.

Like his father, Colonel Haraszthy, Arpad wrote articles and books on the cultivation of the grape and on wine making. In March 1880, the State Board of Viticulture was created, consisting of nine commissioners. Arpad Haraszthy, the Commissioner from the San Francisco District, was named president, and held the position many years. Later he became Commissioner for the State at large. As president of the Viticultural Commission, he prepared in 1888 a comprehensive report for Governor R. W. Waterman. In closing his report, he spoke of the protective tariff: ". . . a high tariff on foreign wines has been the means of introducing our wines among our own citizens, extending the area of our vineyards and giving employment to more than 30,000 souls."

In 1880, one of the members of the State Viticultural Board, the vintner Charles A. Wetmore, who had been a staff writer on the old *Alta California* and whose vineyards were in the Livermore Valley, selected the name *Ojo del Vintage* for his wine, but, finding the name difficult for many to pronounce, he chose *Lacryma Montis* or "Tear of the Mountain." Hearing of this, Arpad told Wetmore, "My father-in-law, the General, is going to give you a piece of his mind when he sees you. You have stolen the name of his vineyard and his wine." Wetmore thought it impossible that he could have invented a name previously in use but Arpad produced an old bottle bearing not only the name "Lachryma Montis" on the label, but also a picture of the residence and the brick storehouse. Arpad said the name was the translation into Latin of the Indian name Chiucuyem (Weeping Mountain). Thereupon Wetmore mailed a letter of apology to General Vallejo, assuring him that the mistake would be corrected. This he did by calling the vintage "Cresta Blanca" after the mountain with the white magnesium scar in the Livermore Valley.

Arpad always held his father-in-law in affectionate regard. He had never forgotten the General's delicate handling of Jovita's threatened divorce; and during Vallejo's last illness Arpad had allowed Napoleon (who was in his employ) to take time off in order to nurse his father. He had hoped to visit the General, himself, but business affairs prevented it as he explained in a letter dated December 28, 1889:

Dear General:

I am in receipt of your letter of the 26th and shall strain a point to enable you to have Nap to assist and comfort you in your illness for awhile longer. Be assured in the meantime that I feel deeply for you to whom I bear the most sincere respect and affection and deplore my inability to visit you in this great illness. I am not absent from your bedside from choice but because it has been absolutely impossible to leave Town even for a day.

The work I have to attend to on Sundays is quite as great if not greater than the ordinary days of the week. For the last three weeks, changes and complications have risen for me that bind me down like a slave. I have to often return to the office after dinner and work to midnight. Besides this Agostine has gone to join her husband at Vallejo and Carlos has gone to New York and I have chosen to move into another dwelling and have to do what I can to fix my things in some kind of shape to bring them out of chaos. This is of itself a herculean task, great enough to drive one crazy. Though my effects were moved 15 days ago, the carpets are not yet down, the pictures not hung, the boxes only half opened and about 1,500 hundred volumes of books strewn over the floor of several rooms.

And all this is simply because I am unable to devote a couple of hours a day to arrange them. Mrs. Hancock has however come from Los Angeles and will now assist in getting things into order for me.

But now comes the annual taking of stock at the Store and Cellars, when every bottle and gallon of wine have to be counted, valued and reckonned up. If everything goes smoothly, even in the operation, it never is completed under ten days, comprising the numerous hours of work done at night. Besides this my correspondence seldom fails under 14 letters a day. In fact I am so pushed that I am compelled to refuse seeing people who call on me with various proposals.

I tell you all this, not as an excuse but to show you how I am situated and how utterly impossible it has been for me to leave the City. I cannot hold out on this scale much longer and shall take the first possible moment to leave and visit you. Trusting that you are now just convalescing and will soon be yourself again,

I remain, Affectionately yours,
ARPAD HARASZTHY

General Vallejo, as we know, did not recover and Arpad Haraszthy served as one of the pallbearers.

CHICAGO WORLD COLUMBIAN EXPOSITION

When the California State Legislature appropriated $300,000 for its State Building at the World's Columbian Exposition in Chicago, Arpad decided to exhibit his wines in the State Building and also in the Horticulture Building, where the display was arranged in a mammoth Redwood tree. His awards were for Muscat, Claret, Chateau, D'Orleans, Cabernello and Sauterne wines.

Arpad Haraszthy never married again; his business and his civic and social affairs filled his life; for relaxation he enjoyed good music and was a regular patron of the opera. His children grew to maturity and lived with him from time to time. Agostine married George B. Strickland, a Naval officer. Her hobby was photography which she developed into a commercial enterprise in New York City. Carlos Arpad's son died before he did.

Jovita's husband survived her twenty-two years. In November 1900, while returning home along Hyde Street from a pleasant evening spent with a friend, he suffered a fatal heart attack. After his death Agostine looked after his affairs, with advice in certain matters from her father's sister, Ida Hancock, who came from Los Angeles to assist her niece.

On December 3, 1900, Agostine wrote to her Uncle Platon Vallejo: "It was kind of you to write me such a beautiful letter. It comforted me and sustained me and I thank you with all my heart. Aunty Ida has returned to her home in L.A. and so I'm alone, attending to my dear father's affairs."

The years passed, and Jovita and Arpad's children, Agostine and Carlos, grandchildren of two noted vintners of Sonoma Valley, died without leaving any heirs.

Uladislao Vallejo

Uladislao Vallejo

Uladislao, the tenth child of the Vallejos, was born on November 6, 1845, and baptized the same day in the Mission San Francisco Solano. He was given the unusual name of *Uladislao*. The infant's father was a reader of the classics and was evidently impressed by the story of Uladislao, the King of Hungary in 1077 who fostered Christianity. The baby's godfather was Don Andres Castillero and the godmother Maria Ignacia Lopez de Carrillo, his maternal grandmother. When the baby was seven months old (the youngest of the eight then living Vallejo children), his father was temporarily made a political prisoner by members of the Bear Flag Party.

Uladislao's first home was the Casa Grande, where his family had been living for almost ten years. It was both his home and his schoolhouse, because the tutors for the Vallejos lived there also. When Uladislao, or "Ula" as he was usually called by the family, was nine years old, he left Sonoma to attend the *Family Boarding School for Boys* in Benicia. It was an institution founded in the *Athens of California*, by the Reverend Charles M. Blake, and said to give thorough instruction in English and the Classics. The school was built on a lot donated by General Vallejo, Robert Semple and Thomas O. Larkin, the three developers of Benicia.

The school at Benicia was the third such undertaking in California by the Bowdoin College graduate, his previous attempts being at Stockton and at Grass Valley. Horace Greeley, Col. J. C. Fremont, Gov. John Bigler, C. M. Weber, and S. C. Hastings, all gave him permission to use their names as references for the Benicia School, but enrollment was slow. The necessity for cash impelled him to write as follows to General Vallejo: "Little Uladislao is doing very well and we are pleased with him. He needs drilling to acquire habits of study. I am much in need of funds just now and I should be greatly obliged if you could send me some money this week. Mr. Barrows probably informed you that I offered to take $300 (half price) for the year, paid in advance."

Dr. Blake's need of funds was caused by California's first *Depression*—the financial disturbances and business failures in San Francisco in 1854 and 1855, plus the effects of moving the State Capital from Benicia to Sacramento.

In 1858, Ula was a student with his brother Platon at the San Francisco College run by a Mr. Crittenden. Ula, under the influence of his studious brother, grew ambitious. He wrote home: "I have begun to study French and I think I will get along very well. I am also reading several histories: the Roman, the English and the United States. I am going to study Latin very quick and maybe Philosophy and a few other things."

Ula's reports at the San Francisco College for attendance, studies and conduct were satisfactory but he tired of school in the city and wished it were in Sonoma, away from brick walls pasted with signs informing the public of the plays at the McGuire Opera House, the lectures at the Lyceum, and the coming of the Christy Ministrels, diverting entertainments, which the Vallejo boys' studies did not permit them to attend.

ULA GOES EAST TO SCHOOL

In April 1860, Ula started on the first journey of the many he was to take. He went East to New York with Platon; he, to enter St. John's College (now Fordham University), and Platon to enter Columbia University. Ula enrolled on June 4, 1860, in a class called Third Academic, a sort of upper grade high school. He was then fifteen years old. Soon after his entrance to the Jesuit Institution General Vallejo wrote his son:

> I have great hopes that when you enter the school you will devote yourself to your studies with constancy in order thus to achieve the hopes of your parents. Be obedient to your teachers so thus you will succeed in learning to know the sciences which course is indeed somewhat laborious at first. Time and devotion make them light and even pleasant.

To reassure their father Platon wrote home on July 20, 1860:

> Ula will not spend any time out of college except on Sundays when he may come to see me here in New York. He is in for study and has made up his mind to go to work hard this vacation and gain one year of study. It is surprising how much good these last few weeks have done him while he has been at St. John's. The place he thought he would dislike so much and peeved to go because it was a Jesuit Institution and it looked so much like a prison. But now he thinks precisely the other way; he likes it first rate; he likes his professors; the rules are not severe, he likes to study and his studies seem easy and pleasant under such good teachers.
>
> He begins to like his religion more than he ever did. Ula says he is getting corns on his knees instead of his toes. I am sure he will get along better than you expected when he left home. He has grown a great deal and he looks gay and lively. I have no doubt the fancy dinners he gets at the college have a great deal to do with it.

Ula wanted his father to write to him in English. The General sent a message to Platon on January 21, 1861: "Greet Ula and tell him that in order to write to him in English it costs me a lot of work and a short letter will have to do—that many long ones rob me of time and patience."

Ula added his own bit of encouragement to his father:

> I am getting along very well in this college. If you will let me stay here six years more, I will be all right; by that time I will graduate. I want to study for a Doctor in New York. Three years more and then I will have three diplomas. The first will be for my A.B. and the next one will be for my A.M. and then for my M.D. and after those three, I will be all right.

These scholastic ambitions were nothing more than day-dreams. Ula lost interest in his studies even before he had finished his first selected course. He left St. John's College on October 4th, 1861, and on November 11th, 1861 Ula's father notified Platon of Ula's arrival in California:

I send you word by telegraph of the arrival of Uladislao on the sixth of this month. He gave me your letter in which you explain to me the reason for his coming and the motives behind his leaving school which has seemed to me very sensible as well as disagreeable; but it has happened and can't be helped. What bothers me and alarms me the most is that if in such a reputable school at such a great distance he has not been able to remain, I have very few hopes for that youth who shows his repugnance for studies as well as a headstrong, fickle and disobedient nature. It is very regrettable that after so many expenses occasioned for his benefit, his education secured, he should be capable of not seeing nor appreciating the earnest desires I have had for him; all of which seems to me a bad sign. God grant that I am mistaken; grant that Ula's faults do not lead him to a precipice.

Ula would meet a precipice in future life—one which would hurt his loved ones as well as himself—but that was twenty-six years ahead. At the moment he did not want to return to a classroom (California's first "drop-out"); he wanted to seek work in A. Austin's Department Store on Montgomery Street in San Francisco. Austin's dealt in dress goods and all the fineries which the feminine sex, which included his mother, delighted in buying. His brother-in-law John B. Frisbie wrote on November 19, 1861 that there was a vacancy at Austin's, as young Timens, who had worked there, had gone to Mazatlan, Mexico. "I deeply regret his [Ula] having left his school," Frisbie wrote, "but as the step has been taken, I sincerely pray it may prove for the best." When Ula returned the Vallejo family were living in the Casa Grande as improvements were being made on the house at Lachryma Montis.

ULA'S FIRST TRIP TO MEXICO

In 1864, Ula decided to go to Mazatlan himself. There he fought in one of the skirmishes. Vallejo reported news of 19-year-old Ula to his mother:

The news that I have of Ula is that in the last movement made in Mazatlan against the government, he gave a good account of himself, taking the side of the government. After the battle he was taken prisoner at the side of Governor Garcia Morales and it fell to his lot to be exiled to Lower California. As soon as I learned of it, I came from the Parajo on the run in order to pay his return passage to Sonoma and I have arranged it all so that wherever the boat is, they will bring him. I fear that Ula with his restless and rash nature may have gone to join Senor Juarez but I hope not.

The prodigal son returned home! His father, September 14, 1864 wrote Ula's mother from San Francisco:

The day before yesterday, I wrote to tell you of the arrival of Uladislao . . . I've kept him here for two days because he wants to know what's been going on in this part of the world. Poor boy! is so sick and so, languishing. I've sent him home by way of the City of Vallejo first so that Platon might give him some medicine and that he might visit his brothers [Andronico & Platon] and his sister [Adela] . . . The misfortune that he suffered for the cause of Mexico and his ancestors, the calamities and the ill-luck that he has supported during a period of five months . . . He left here strong, full of life and full of illusions and with patriotic ardor . . . Uladislao has acted like an honorable man. He has placed himself on the side of justice, of honor, of duty and of patriotism, giving an example of bravery and good sense . . . His sacrifice and renunciation is known and spread abroad after being taken prisoner in battle, deported and he returns almost dead to his paternal hearth. Poor Ula. Now I love him more than ever and I know you will soon think the same.

The family were glad to have "Ula" back, especially his sisters who enjoyed his teasing; however, nothing in the way of work developed for him. The following year, 1865, General Vallejo was in the East. Probably he spoke to General Halleck about Ula, as that autumn although busy with affairs in Washington, D.C., Halleck took the time to write a letter in Ula's behalf to the Secretary of the Navy. Still nothing developed for Ula. Halleck had been a friend of General Vallejo since the days of the Constitutional Convention in Monterey; Vallejo was then a delegate from the Sonoma District, and the young Brevet-Captain Henry Wager Halleck was Secretary of State under the military rule in California, as well as a delegate from Monterey to the Convention.

Ula's Second Trip to Mexico

His second sojourn in the country south of the Rio Grande came about in the following manner. Ula's father had been in San Francisco in May, 1864 and had met General Placido Vega, former governor of Sinaloa, who was in California as an emissary of Benito Juarez. Vega was seeking financial aid with which to buy military supplies for the uprising against Austrian Archduke Ferdinand Maximilian, who was serving as Emperor of Mexico. Vallejo returned to the Pajaro Valley where he wrote his wife on May 6th telling of the meeting:

At the present time in San Francisco is the Mexican General Vega of good reputation, a gentleman and well-to-do. I have made some arrangements with him for our wayward son so that he may go under his protection to Mexico and he has promised me if the fortunes of the war against the French for the independence of Mexico are favorable, Ula will be made a General.

I have written him that he will find Ula a well-educated young man in the American way, but very juvenile and with a heart as big as the world, brave and anxious to fight in defense of the country of his ancestors . . . I am expecting a letter from Senor Vega and we shall see what is to be done. Poor Ula! It seems I already see him in General's finery.

War is dangerous, yet it is the profession of very brave men. The enemy fires the shots but you dodge them; when one fights for a just cause, it is necessary not to think of risks . . . "Nothing ventured, nothing gained."

It was not until July 1866 that Vega had collected enough money for his project. Victor Castro, Augustin Alviso and M. G. Vallejo advanced approximately $9,000. The barque *Josephine* was chartered and loaded with 7,000 rifles, powder, percussion caps, revolvers, 3,000 uniforms, etc., etc. With General Vega on the *Josephine* went the recently commissioned Captain Uladislao Vallejo, a soldier-of-fortune of twenty years, eager for adventure and full of sympathy for the thirty Mexican officers who were returning to their native land, after having been exiled by the French authorities then in control.

Also on board were about forty American volunteers. After landing at a small fishing village in the State of Sinaloa, they conveyed the military supplies 600 miles into the interior to Chihuahua, where Benito Juarez used them to equip his troops for immediate attack, and thus was able to win victories which were highly beneficial to the cause of Mexican independence.

President Juarez had been the first head of State to congratulate President Lincoln on his assumption to the Presidency of the United States, a courtesy of State which Lincoln never forgot, telling Congress on one occasion of "the simple virtues of the heroic Mexican people and above all, its inextinguishable love of liberty." Lincoln's coming to power alleviated Mexico's fear of intervention from the United States.

From Chihuahua, in November 1866, Ula wrote home, telling his father that he had been admitted to President Juarez's Guard and was a permanent soldier in the Mexican Army. Four months later (March 18, 1867) he wrote from San Luis Potosi that he was sending his father 'Power of Attorney' which was certified by an English official as there was no American Consul there. In closing his letter, Ula wrote, "Maximilian is at Queretaro, almost starved to death. We will seize him with his twenty thousand men. I think we will catch him alive. What do our Imperial friends think of it? The President [Juarez] is at present in this city."

Ula's figures were somewhat exaggerated as historians have estimated that Maximilian left Mexico with 2,000 men February 13, 1867. After three months siege, the Republican forces captured Queretaro and sentenced Maximilian and his two Mexican aides, Miramon and Mojia, to death which was carried out at dawn on June 19, 1867.

While in Mexico, Ula wrote his mother: "I am always thinking of you although I don't always have an opportunity to write to you. It is true I am half crazy or at least a dare-devil but nevertheless I never forget you. Mother, I am well. I lack for nothing. There is only one thing that bothers me. I am in love with a Mexican girl. Certainly, I won't marry her because she is poor, not as poor as we might say but I need a richer one . . . Tell Don Pepe [Jose de la Rosa] that all of his family there no longer exists one because the other day I was in Puebla; I enquired and got no result so I suppose that all have died."

In time, Ula's restlessness or the ruggedness of the Mexican campaign dulled his enthusiasm for army life and he wished to return to the peace of the Valley of Sonoma. He wrote his father that he would like to return home.

His father reported to Ula's mother: "I have been hunting for some money to send Uladislao who asks for him to receive it in time; $150, so that he can come by way of Guadalajara where a gentleman will take him as far as San Blas, then General Vega will take care of the rest."

On February 6, 1870, Placido Vega wrote Ula's father: "Finally Don Ula has made up his mind to go away and he will do it tomorrow, on the *Juanito*, that goes to Mazatlan and take the Continental . . . I send 450 cigars for you."

Ula arrived safely in California but was rather weak from the fever he had contracted in Mexico, and it was some time before he was rid of the chills. He remained with his father at Lachryma Montis while his mother was in the town of Vallejo looking after Fannie's house while the Frisbies were in the East. During his mother's visit to New York he wrote her on June 15th:

> Yesterday I saw a letter from New York where it says that you left for Syracuse with General Frisbie to visit the relatives of that gentleman. I suppose that he has quite a few but we have more. Tell me how you like to travel on the Railroad. What do you think of those huge mountains and plains? As Papa says the sun rises ahead of you and one travels all the day going tototàn, tototàn, tototàn and the following day the same, tototàn, tototàn, tototàn . . . Which do you like better Albany or Syracuse? The two places are very beautiful. Yesterday I came from Natalia's house and right now I am writing to you in the Delirio. Papa went to San Francisco this morning and left the keys to the house so I am fine.

On November 6th, 1870, Ula celebrated his twenty-fifth birthday. To quote his father: "We celebrated it with a duck stew and a bottle of wine, but none but myself was with him but he [Ula] says that is enough. No one in the family had remembered him."

Uladislao Vallejo—Viniculturist

When Napoleon returned from Santa Clara College, the General decided to turn over to him and Uladislao the Quiquiriqui Vineyard which lay directly in rear of the adobe buildings on the north side of the Sonoma Plaza. Their father said that his principal reason for doing this was to give his sons, still at home, a way of earning their living honestly, payment for actual work. He would rent the Quartel or Barracks for $40 a month, in order that they might live separate from the family. Vallejo said that the house was very large; it had rooms in which to live and space for making and storing wine; there was a very good well and there was a pump. There was also a place to keep tools and field implements. Their father helped to get them started by giving them 3,000 gallons of wine. The Vallejo boys might have made a success of viniculture, had not the vines become infested with the scourge Phylloxera.

The following letter, written some time later to Ula's mother, is interesting and a portion concerns Ula.

Jan. 19, 1875
Monterey

Francisca:

On the 24th of last month I reached this place and as it was Christmas Eve I was invited to the home of Mr. Abrego where after a good dinner there was a dance "in the style of the country" and a thousand cascarones [eggs] were broken which gave me a great deal of pleasure. I thought of you a great deal, and much more did I think of Lulu and Maria who have never seen that kind of game which is so much fun for the young people. The cascarones were full of little things of tinsel and little colored papers. They also broke some on me; but I got even except with a girl who was passing me on the street said to me, "How are your chickens? Cluck, cluck, cluck!" As the eggs are broken up to the eve of Ash Wednesday I hope to get my revenge although I don't know where she lives. Since I arrived I have been very busy with the history and General Cerruti. He sends greetings to you and all the girls.

Confidential!! Ula wrote me and wants me to give him the rental of the Barracks and I answered him no, that the rental was for you and the family. Also he wants the little vineyard and I answered him that I was going to work that for the family and to pay taxes and that I would pay Nap to cultivate it. He also wrote me about his business with stones or making a quarry and I answered him that if he could make the deal he could finish it at 2 reales a ton, reserving the mineral rights and that he should make out the papers. It is very strange that Ula after receiving 1,000 pesos in silver can't start a business that will keep him busy and maintain him in decency. I'm not at all pleased with his conduct.

I expect to finish soon and then I shall come to Sonoma. Greetings to Lulu and Maria, Napoleon and Dona Carmelita. Don't get sick, don't worry, don't lose sight of the work of Demetrio.

Yours,
M. G. VALLEJO

Ula was next given the opportunity of collecting water-rents for his father's Sonoma Water Company. The Lachryma Montis Spring not only supplied water for the ranch but also for Sonoma residents who did not have wells. After a few weeks of collecting, Ula gave up the work, and his patient but disappointed father remarked, "Ula needs what a little tree needs—a great big post for support." Meanwhile Ula still indulged in his own day-dreams. He told his father that he was going to be richer than "the Bonanza men of San Francisco." Vallejo added, "May God help him to be a good and honorable man and if some day Fortune is kind to him, may he remember the needy poor with whom the world abounds."

ULA VISITS SAN LUIS OBISPO

The members of the Vallejo family thought Ula was the handsomest of the good-looking Vallejo boys. He was tall, well built, with regular features, fair complexion, and chestnut-brown hair. He was popular with the Fair Sex and he in turn was appreciative of their charms though somewhat of a tease. At forty years of age, he was still a soltero (bachelor) and was trying out a position with the railroad near San Luis Obispo, the birthplace of his paternal grandmother, Dona Maria Antonia Lugo. While there, he wrote to his sister Lulu on July 10, 1881:

I am down here surveying a Railroad which is called S.L.O.&S.M.V.R.R. (guess what all those letters mean). I have come among a lot of relatives which are the Mallaghs and Tia Ramona's family. All of which have been very glad to see me and when two or three days pass without my going to see them, they send for me. Tia Juanita has a large family—five girls and as many boys; of the girls there is only one married, her name is Helena; then there is Jennie, Felicidad, Maria and Anita who is about twelve years of age.

Jennie is very pretty, the best looking of the family and resembles Carolina Kahn, a great deal, so much so, that the first time I saw her, before I knew who she was, I stopped to speak to her, thinking it was Carolina. Tia Ramona is quite old and infirm. She was also glad to see me but I do not go there often because she is very religious and wants me to go to confession and questions me in Christian Docterine and I, of course, knowing that, always take one of the Mallagh girls with me and do not give my Aunt a chance to start on religion.

The surveying work at San Luis Obispo was terminated and Ula went to Darwin, Inyo County, with $100 given to him by his father in April 1882, to try his luck at mining. There Ula found a family poorer than himself, so he interested himself in their plight and asked Platon to send them medicine. In a short time, Ula was back in Sonoma, where he tried to help his father by serving as his secretary and by translating documents to be used in some of the General's lawsuits still pending.

In 1885, Ula asked his brother-in-law, John B. Frisbie, who was an agent in Mexico for the Pacific Steamship Company, to use his influence in getting him a position in Lower California. The following letter from Frisbie to President Porfirio Diaz stated the case:

My very esteemed Sir and Friend:

Conquering the natural sentiments of delicacy that I feel and with your proverbial deference, please excuse and permit me to recommend very particularly the young Don Ula Vallejo, whom you know is the brother of my wife. He served with the Republican Army of Mexico during the epoch of the French intervention, assisting Sir President Juarez.

Senor Vallejo was curator of the Maritime Custom House of the fleet of all lower California and is now solicitating the employment of the Custom House at Cape Celadores. He is a useful official. If you would be so kind as to consider my recommendation, it would be a favor very much appreciated and for which I await your acknowledgment,

Your friend,

JOHN B. FRISBIE

To let Ula's father know what he had done in Ula's behalf, Frisbie wrote to the General on June 30, 1885:

Not knowing the address of Ula, I enclose for him herewith a copy of a letter I addressed to the President in his behalf and his Excellency's reply hereto. Mr.

Ryerson of Lower California informed me that Ula desired the position I have applied for, hence I took the liberty of interesting myself in the matter, hoping my efforts might prove of service.

Mr. Morgan, Sarah's husband mailed to you the day before yesterday an obituary announcing the death of their little child; she was a beautiful baby and we all sadly miss her . . . The poor mother is almost heart broken and in wretched health. Yet her doctor speaks encouragingly of her recovery. All the members of the family join me in much love to you, Grandma, and such of the dear friends we have left in precious California.

For the last eighteen months, business affairs have not thrived with me. Railroad enterprises in this country have not proved renumerative, on the contrary, all are losing money . . . Throughout the Republic, consequently foreign capital is being retired and none coming in. I am hopeful however that the administration of President Diaz will be able to restore confidence and reanimate the present torpid industries of this God-favored but man-cursed land.

The copy of President Diaz's letter which was enclosed was dated June 23rd and stated:

My Esteemed Friend:

Obliged by your favor of the 19th instant and with the desire of seconding the recommendation which you have made in favor of Senor Vallejo, I declare that this very day I gave the name of such a worthy young man to the Minister of Agriculture in order that he make use of his talents in the employment to which reference is made, at the first opportunity which presents itself.

Your friend and devoted servant who is pleased to serve you

PORFIRIO DIAZ

Nothing permanent came of President Diaz's interest in Ula. In December 1885, Luisa's husband, Ricardo de Emparan, who was the Mexican Consul in San Diego, found work for Ula, and in appreciation Vallejo wrote: "I thank you for the favors that you did for Ula and Senora Vallejo does too. God grant that he behaves well and carries out well the post you have given him. The post of Todos Santos will take in considerable revenue. Ula with the experience that he had in Upper California ought to be able to choose a good location and ought to identify himself from now on with the place. He ought to open a Book of Registry of all the places that are being settled so that in after years he would have an office called *Searcher of Records*, a very important office and of value everywhere since lawsuits are never lacking and also abstracts elegantly drawn always bring good money."

THE PRECIPICE

Ula did not stay in Lower California for any length of time. Back in Sonoma and through his father's influence with the Town Trustees, he found work as Town Marshal and Tax Collector. After eight months, the said Marshal and Tax Collector sailed on Wednesday, November 30, 1887, on the steamer *Costa Rica* for Mexico with $1,152.50—the entire proceeds of the Sonoma tax levy for the year 1887—in his pockets.

The *Sonoma Index-Tribune* printed in its weekly edition:

The friends of the departing Tax Collector are at a loss to account for the insane freak that seized him to forsake home and friends in so unceremonious a manner. On Thursday the excitement in town was somewhat allayed when it became known that the full amount of money collected by Marshal Vallejo in exact figures, $1,152.50 had been paid over to the City Treasurer at the time required by law, to wit, the first day of December.

U. P. Vallejo was appointed Marshal and Tax Collector some months ago by the City Trustees and in so far as a Peace Officer was concerned, was the most efficient Marshal the City ever had.

With a heavy heart General Vallejo, Sonoma's justly-loved citizen, called on two of his friends for a loan, John F. Clewe, the merchant who, years before, had wished to marry his daughter Luisa, and C. Aguillon, manufacturer of brandies and wines, who sent him Christmas gifts of wine each year. They gladly loaned him the full amount, which was thereupon paid to John Tivnen, Treasurer of the City of Sonoma.

The *Petaluma Courier* reported on the incident thus:

We understand that the General has made good every cent of the amount to the City and now has the Treasurer's receipt for the amount. General Vallejo who for his manly walk through a long life should have the title "Right Honorable" prefixed to his name and his venerable and estimable wife, while under a shadow of affliction doubtless more unbearable to them than death, have the sympathy of the entire community.

Months later, there was still discussion of Ula's malfeasance and his father wrote a letter to the Editor of the Santa Rosa Democrat assuring the public "without any fear of contradiction that U. P. Vallejo does not owe a cent to the City of Sonoma."

ULA IN GUATEMALA

Ula did not long remain in Mexico. He found work in Guatemala on the Ferro-Carril Central de Guatemala, the railroad which ran from the port to the Capital. Riding on the trains gave Ula an opportunity to appreciate the grandeur of the natural beauties, both scenic and feminine. On December 8, 1890 he wrote about both of these aspects to his sister Adela, who was always sympathetic to those in trouble.

We stop at a great many stations and it is one of the most beautiful roads you ever saw. This country is always green and fresh looking. From the time we leave the Port, it is a continual climb and up grade until we reach the Capital at the elevation of 5,000 feet above the level of the sea. You can not form an idea of the varied scenery we have, winding in among the volcanoes and then running many miles along the shore of some of the most beautiful lakes you ever saw or read of; the Lake of Amatitlan is surrounded by volcanoes, two are about 18,000 feet and another 14,000 feet.

The beautiful Guatemallicans! There are some very handsome girls here, just as pretty as you can find them in the United States and some more so, on account of the peculiar Central American type. I tell you, they are stunning and very beautiful.

It was not long before Maria, one of the beautiful "Guatemallicans," captured the interest and heart of the long-time *soltero* and run-away Californian. He wrote home for a copy of his baptismal record at the Mission San Francisco Solano, and, also a statement that he had never married. These formalities, duly attended to, he and Maria were married and became the parents of a son, born on December 9, 1891. Ula named his first-born *Mariano* after his father and *Prudencio* after himself.

Ula could not forget what he had done in Sonoma. That it weighed on his mind is apparent from the letter he wrote Platon on October 5, 1890 from Escuintla, Guatemala:

It is now nearly three years since I misteriously disappeared from Sonoma and under the circumstances, I suppose there is not one of the family over anxious to know my whereabouts and I do not blame them, for I have most shamefully disgraced the name Vallejo, of which we were all so proud and I do not doubt but what that action of mine hurried father to his grave. I shall never forgive myself and I assure you that since I read the notice of his death in the San Francisco papers, I have worried so much that my hair has turned nearly all white.

Poor Father, I hope that he has forgiven me for all the bitter days I have caused him. God bless him. I hope he made all the necessary reconciliations with the Almighty before he was taken away but then he is now happy and we are suffering, particularly myself as I have made up my mind never to return to California and much less to Sonoma. I have separated myself from the rest of the family as long as I live. I want you to write to me and give me all the home news. I dare not ask it from any other member of the family. I know you are indulgent and will to a certain extent overlook my faults . . . I should like you to get me a collection of pictures from all the family particularly father's and mother's, as that will be my only consolation while I live. . . . Send me when ever you can the Sonoma paper "Index-Tribune" and any other S.F. paper you can get hold off.

About this time Ula wrote to his sister Adela:

I received your letter of the 11th, also a lock of father's hair which I assure you I shall preserve as long as I live. It is very thoughtful of you to send me the lock of hair as it is the only relic, you might say, that I posses of father.

The first account I saw of Father's death was in the San Francisco Bulletin. I was standing on the street of the house I lived in at the City of Guatemala and an acquaintance of mine happened to pass by and asked me if I had seen the San Francisco papers. I told him I had not, he then told me about the announcement of father's death. In the evening I went to his rooms and got the papers and through those means I was informed or rather got acquainted with the details of the death and funeral of that good, honest, honorable man. He was too great a soul for this world. As much as I grieve his loss, still I am satisfied knowing that he died a saintly death. He is now enjoying and associating with God and the angels. He has simply gone to see the rest of the family. You know we have quite a number of brothers and sisters in heaven.

As if to comfort Adela who had lost her only child, Lillie Frisbie McCarthy, nine years before, Ula continued: "Lillie is with him now Adela, they are all happy where they shall never be molested again. God bless them."

Adela, in sympathy for her wayward brother, sent him a package, which he acknowledged on December 1, 1890:

I received the package containing your two pictures, two silk handkerchiefs, Papa's smoking cap and a lot of different articles clipped from newspapers. I am ever so much obliged to you, Adela, for sending me all those things, particularly Papa's cap. I prize that more than anything else. I did not have a single thing of Father's and that is all I want. I will treasure it as something precious all my life.

I am very sorry to hear that Mother is so sick and helpless. Poor Mother, it must be trying to her not to be able to move around as she was always a busybody, always doing something . . . Not to be able to walk, it must be awful. Be good to her as she is one of the best mothers in the world . . . I should like very much to see mother, poor good old mother but how can I under the circumstances; I am too ashamed of myself. I could never endure to be in her presence. No, it is utterly impossible. I can not face that good and best of mothers and I assure you I would willingly return to Sonoma but again I repeat I cannot go back. When you see her kiss her many times for me and assure Mother that she has not a child who loves her more than I do.

At present I am not employed but just as soon as I can, I will send Mother what few dollars I can. You see, money in this country is only good here; in other countries it is not worth a single cent; it is not like United States money that it passes all over the world . . . At any rate I will do what I can to help poor mother. She is certainly very deserving that we all should help her . . . I want you particularly to go to see Nat, hug and kiss her for me lots of times. Attila also, tambien the children. Lolita must be a fine looking girl by this time. Of course Tala, as my godchild is my favorite of the whole family. I hope she has gotten over her partial paralysis—good little girl she is. I only wish I was rich to give her a fortune.

Senora Vallejo was showered with love and care from her children who had remained close to nurse her back to health; but in January 1891, in spite of their care, the tired seventy-five-year-old mother of sixteen children passed to her reward. Her truant son wrote again to Adela on February 25, 1891:

It is just three years and five months since I left San Francisco and just think what a terrible change there has been in our family. No father and no mother to tease as I used to do. I cannot for a moment realize that they are dead and gone. I never think of home unless I see the old folks at their usual places; father on the front porch or writing in his room and mother either mending or making some kind of preserves in that old shed near the wash house and old Martin helping her but it is only too true they are gone forever.

Well, Adela, I am at present employed by the Railroad Company, just simply making a living and patiently waiting for something to turn up . . . Adela, I am sorry to see the children quarreling about who shall get the largest piece of Lachryma Montis . . . I am referring to those who have had already the lion's share of Father's property in the good old days, such as Fannie Frisbie, Andronico and in fact all the family, everyone has received something except Lulu, Maria and myself but as far as I am concerned, I am willing and ready to give my share to Lulu and Maria providing the rest of the heirs do the same. Lachryma Montis has always been acknowledged by all the family that when father and mother should die, Lulu and Maria should be the owners of the property. I have written to Natalia telling her the same thing. Natalia cannot claim a single inch for Mariano, simply because father was Mariano's godfather . . . Platon has in his possession that old case of silverware belonging to father. You must remember it; father always kept it in the closet in his room, that case of silver must figure in the personal property . . . Nap has in his possession father's gold headed cane.

The case of silver mentioned was a general's field chest composed of an entire dinner place set for three with large silver pieces; writing and shaving and toilet articles. It had been given to General Vallejo by the Russian government in 1834 after his visit to Fort Ross; given it is said in appreciation of the protection afforded the wife of Count Rotchef, the Princess Helena Gagarin, niece of the Czar of the Russians when Chief Solano became enamored with the "blonde squaw." The General is quoted as saying, "The beauty of this lady excited so ardent a passion in the breast of Prince Solano, Chief of all the Indians about Sonoma that he formed a plan to capture by force or stratagem the object of his love and he might have succeeded had I not heard of his intention in time to prevent its execution."

Another letter from Ula was written in September 1892 to Adela and informed her that his wife Maria and he were expecting their second child:

Next month I will commence to prepare for the next baby. I have to take these things in time and buy a little every month so that when the time comes I will have all that is required; we poor folks have to do that as I have not the money to buy everything at once—poco a poco se anda lejos [little by little you go far]. I am now without employment but I am in hopes soon I will find something to do in connection with the Government, then I will be more easy . . . I am ever so much obliged to you for sending me the photographs of mothers and father's tomb. Well, at last father and mother are placed and resting forever in their own vault. Yes, the Duhring family deserve the thanks of all of us and not only that but we are under everlasting obligations to them for allowing the bodies of our dear dead parents to be deposited in their family vault for such a long time. When you see them, thank them for me and tell them I shall never forget it and I shall never tire of thanking them to the last day of my life.

ULA'S DISAPPOINTMENT

Ula wrote home that he was looking forward to the arrival of their cousin, the Honorable Romualdo Pacheco, as United States Minister to Guatemala, to replace Mr. Mizner of Benicia, California. Pacheco, son of Ula's religious Aunt "Tia Ramona," had been Lieutenant-Governor of California, then Governor for a short time. He was a Republican and an intimate friend of President Garfield. Now he was in the United States foreign service assigned to Guatemala. Ula planned to welcome him at the port of San Jose. He was confident that Pacheco would help him to secure employment, connected in some way with the Government. Were they not first cousins? their mothers sisters?

Mr. Nanne, the superintendent of the Guatemala Railroad, said that he would speak in Ula's behalf if Pacheco would come with him for the interview with the officials. Pacheco refused. In anger Ula said that he had heard that the Honorable Romualdo Pacheco, the former Governor of California, was known to never help a native Californian; that he believed that Pacheco was a consumate ignoramus and as far as he, Ula, was concerned, Pacheco could go to Hell.

Without work, Ula's wanderlust took hold of him and he wrote his brother Platon that he was considering going to Argentina. The baby his wife was expecting when he wrote to his sister Adela in September 1892 proved to be another boy who was named Ula Francisco. There was a third child who was given the name Maria Jesus. By a strange twist of fate, Maria Jesus, a grown woman in 1933, met her father's sister, Luisa Vallejo Emparan when Mrs. Emparan was the official hostess of the S.S. Santa Rosa of the Grace Line on its maiden voyage. Among the Caribbean countries, the ship stopped at Guatemala. This niece, Maria Jesus Vallejo, was overjoyed to meet her father's sister. Afterwards, Maria Jesus wrote her Aunt:

"After so long a time of hoping to meet you, you can not imagine how I felt . . . To me it is only a dream to have had the pleasure of holding you in my arms. I still feel your kisses. Your coming was like a light rain, showering my soul, for since my dear father died, I missed that love and finally God gave me yours. You have a place in my heart today next to my mother . . . Your presence reminded me of the living image of my father. There are moments in which it all seems like a dream from which I do not wish to awaken, except to see you again.

Some time later Maria Jesus Vallejo married Leonidas Galindo Rangel and they had a daughter named Guerda Judith.

Meeting Ula's daughter was a source of pleasure and comfort to Luisa Vallejo Emparan, knowing that the "rash and restless one" of the Vallejos had had the love and care of a wife, two sons and a daughter through the years.

Napoleon Primo Vallejo

Napoleon Primo Vallejo

The youngest son of the Vallejos was born in the Casa Grande on December 8th, 1850. At that time, his father was purchasing the last parcels of land to complete his Lachryma Montis estate and was making final plans for the erection of his new home. A great many loads of course and fine gravel were hauled before the builders began operations.

General Vallejo gave this child the name *Napoleon* after one of his military heroes, the Little Corporal. He selected *Primo* as the infant's second name to differentiate it from Napoleon the Third, the grandson of Empress Josephine. Padre Anthony Delmas baptized Napoleon Primo at the Mission San Francisco Solano, April 3, 1851, the wedding day of the infant's fifteen-year-old sister, Epifania Guadalupe and Captain John B. Frisbie. The young bride and groom acted as godparents of the four-month-old Vallejo baby.

Napoleon spent much of his earlier years with his father. He was his little "Companero." Napoleon once said, "I knew my father better than any of the brothers and sisters of our family because I ate with him, I slept with him every night, I played games with him." The General took Napoleon with him on many of his journeys to San Francisco on the stage and steamer. On one of these occasions when Napoleon was almost four years old, his mother wrote her husband:

Guadalupe:

I was seated in the sewing room waiting for you for some moments; thinking that perhaps you weren't coming since it had been some time since the stage had arrived and you didn't arrive at the house when Billy entered with a letter from you in which you tell me of the misfortune that almost befell us with Napoleon. I realize and think how you must have been in these moments when you were looking for him and didn't find him. Dear God! What would I have done if Napoleon had been lost. Guadalupe—watch over Napoleon. Since the moment I left him on the ship I haven't had a moment's pleasure. The days are longer for me than before in thinking about the boy because I know he is michievous and if he doesn't see you he is capable of wandering where he wills in search of you and perhaps you'll lose him again . . . It is true that I had thought of going to San Francisco on Tuesday of next week . . . I have the girls (Adela, Natalia, Jovita and Benicia) here so that they could make their clothes. Tell Fanny that the girls are sending her two bonnets so she can send them out to be covered with green on the outside and on the inside with whatever seems best to her but don't put flowers on them either inside or out.

In closing her letter Napoleon's mother sent greetings to Fanny, Fanny's husband and to "Lupe," the first Vallejo grandchild who was then two years old. When Napoleon was seven years old he was given a pony. At that time Stephen William Shaw was in Sonoma, painting portraits of the older members of the Vallejo family; and Napoleon was proud when the artist put him on his pony and his father on a favorite horse, together, in the painting of

Lachryma Montis with the residence and the brick warehouse and gardens.

At this time Napoleon had not learned to write, so his sister Adela took the dictation of a letter of the seven-year-old for his father:

Dear Papa:

I am taking care of your room and I don't let anyone enter except my Mama. And I am taking care of the house too. The baths are clean. Adela cleaned them this morning and I helped her to shake the rugs. And when I go to bed I think of you a great deal. I haven't dreamed of you but I have thought of you. I always think of you. I wish you would give me permission to go to the Circus tomorrow. There is going to be one here and I should like very much to go. I am well.

Your son,
NAPOLEON

A year later, when Napoleon was eight years old, he attended the District School in Sonoma where a Mr. Tallarand was principal. One morning in early autumn, Napoleon left for school accompanied by a neighboring schoolmate. In order to reach the school, they had to walk along a very rough lane, Napoleon looked at his fingernails and decided they needed attention. He pulled out his jack-knife and, with the open knife in his left hand and not watching his steps, and also busy conversing about school problems, he stumbled against a boulder. As he fell, the open knife entered his left side. Napoleon's schoolmate screamed when he saw Napoleon pull the blade of the jack-knife out of his breast and the blood spurt out over his clothes. The little boy ran and gave the alarm at the school. He soon returned with the principal and a number of older boys who found Napoleon on the ground unconscious. They placed him on a door they had brought with them and took him to Doctor Victor Faure's office, where Napoleon's mother soon arrived to comfort him while the doctor stopped the flow of blood.

Napoleon was away from school for some time. During his convalescence he asked to have his Indian boy friends come to see him. Napoleon appeared to be on the road to recovery, later he had a relapse and his father sent for Doctor Levi C. Frisbie under whose care Napoleon was placed.

In later days, Napoleon, recalling his illness wrote in his personal notes, "I said to Mother, 'Raise me up in bed and put one or two pillows under my head . . . I heard the chant and I heard you pray for me because you thought I was going to die; Mother kneel down if you can; Father do the same; each of you take hold of my right and left hands and in silence pray to God, thanking him for sparing my life; I am not going to die; I feel better.' " Napoleon remembered that he had felt a prickling sensation dart through his veins; his hands, which were held by his father and mother, were warm and his pulse began to beat strongly. From that moment, he said, he began to improve. His body was renewed in vigor and he enjoyed good health most of his life.

A Pow-wow was given in Sonoma to honor Napoleon upon his recovery from his severe illness. It was a gathering together of about seventy-five Suisun Indian Chiefs from the Seven Tribes who were scattered in the counties of Mendocino, Lake, Sonoma, Solano and Marin. Their leader was a son of Chief Solano. Napoleon's uncle, Salvador Vallejo, was put in charge of the provisions. It took six weeks to complete the arrangements. The Sonoma Indians were appointed to send out the invitations and to prepare sleeping wigwams and shacks.

Food was to be provided for fifteen days. General Vallejo ordered five bulls slaughtered every day. Hogs and sheep and chickens were also supplied as well as beans, Chili sauce, onions, bread, tortillas and pinole. Contributions of cake, coffee and milk were contributed by Sonoma's townspeople; many of the ladies volunteered to serve.

Indian games and dances were enjoyed each day. At the request of General Vallejo, the Indians donned their war gear and danced the war dances; afterwards they smoked the Calumet or Peace-Pipe.

Every night of the Pow-wow, Napoleon was wrapped up by his mother and taken to see the mystic dances. By his side as he sat on a table, stood two Indian boys. During the celebration Napoleon was presented with a wampum belt which was valued by the Indians at $50 in American money. Among the entertainers was the Indian boy Comola, the dancer. Comola was dressed in a shirt, white and soft of doe-skin and ermine; ornamented with beads and wampum; his moccasins were of buck-skin. On his head were eagle feathers and on his heels, tails of foxes. In one hand Comola carried a bunch of quills, an Indian pipe in the other. His first movement was slow in step and gesture, stepping gently like a panther in the flame-light and in the shadows; then he began a swifter dance, singing and spinning round in circles, leaping through the flames of fire, till he became exhausted and in the darkness disappeared. After a short time he returned and sat down among the assembled guests and fanned himself with his bunch of eagle feathers.

The little Indian boys taught Napoleon how to make bows and arrows. The bows were usually made from a young ash branch, or a sprout of the yellow willows or from a young shoot of pecan; these woods were more pliable and could more easily be bent. The Indians called Napoleon *Napus*, and his father *Huckawin*.

When Napoleon was ten, he sent the following letter, dated January 1, 1861 to his brother Platon, who was in New York at the Medical College of Columbia University:

Dear old Boy:

I have just finished Nat's [Natalia Vallejo who was in the East] letter and I think I must write to you. I am having very good fun since I came home with all the little Indian "chaps" playing marbles from morning to night; good fun you bet but with all that Papa makes us clean the place after we get through. Your horse *Nap* is just as fat as he can be—well taken care of. Goodbye Doctor Plato.

The little Indian chaps were Napoleon's playmates. One was Joaquin, a grandson of Chief Solano, who was a sweet singer who fashioned flutes from the hollow reeds of the elder. Napoleon's parents liked to hear him sing Indian songs in the Suisun dialect. Another was Comola the dancer, and there was Hace, the champion swimmer, also Yoela. Napoleon hunted and fished with them and learned to eat roots and grasses, wild fruit and berries.

When Napoleon was about fifteen years old, his father had a cottage, called the *Hermitage*, built for him above the Reservoir, behind the cacti patch. In describing his occupancy of it, Napoleon said: "In it I had five shotguns, three rifles and half-a-dozen pistols, split bamboo fishing rods and fish nets. I had fourteen dogs (pointers, setters and hounds) two monkeys, three cats and a parrot." At that time he said he mastered the art of converting the skins of bears, panthers, deer, foxes and skunks into leather by means of chemicals and proper sun exposure. Instead of papering the walls of the Hermitage, he used the skins to cover them and to carpet the floor. There the adolescent lived in seclusion, feeding and playing with his animals and parrot.

Napoleon considered himself a great hunter; he wrote, "I was always considered a crack shot, both with rifle and shot gun. I did my shooting from right eye and right arm as well as with left eye and left arm. In other words I could shoot as well from left side as from right side." He tells of saying to his mother, "Don't buy any meats of any kind at the butcher shops; I want to see how long I can keep the house in game." She replied, "Very well, Polle, only take care and don't get hurt on your trips." His first day of hunting saw him bring home four dozen valley-quail, three doves, and six cotton-tail rabbits. A later trip resulted in a fine buck—a five-pointer which weighed 136 pounds dressed.

COLLEGE STUDENT

Before Napoleon was ready for college, his quick temper had caused him to be reprimanded by the principal for fighting and using profanity. The General decided to send his son to the College of Santa Clara. Before his departure, Napoleon spent some time in the spring of 1867 with his sister Fannie Frisbie in Vallejo. In a letter home he wrote: "I went to church this morning and prayed for you all with the greatest devotion. I am teaching the first two classes in catechism in the Vallejo Sunday School . . . I am going to Santa Clara tomorrow or the day after. Captain Frisbie is going to take me down. Andronico, I hear, is teaching at Vacaville near Sacramento City."

Napoleon enrolled at the Santa Clara College in April 1867. Aside from his regular courses, he became interested in dramatics and was assigned a role, aptly described in a letter to his mother:

> Your kind letter reached me last week bearing the melancholy news of your illness. Believe me I am still uneasy for I know how much you suffer from the terrible 'Asthma.' It is an abominable disease.

Last Thursday, the 11th of December we had a grand display of our abilities on the stage of our theatre, here in the college which proved to be very successful. As I had the most ravenous, savage, violent, angry, furious role (and by many words it may be styled) I was not liked very much by the audience for such is generally the case whenever a drama is played, especially if it be a tragedy; there is always one that is not liked very much; that part I had the honor to take, for my first attempt on the stage.

It was strange that Napoleon should have been selected to play the part of the villain. In appearance he was like the hero. He was an extraordinarily handsome young man, of fine physique and with brilliant dark eyes and wavy black hair. It has been said that many a fair-haired miss and dark-haired senorita lost their hearts to this debonair scion of the Vallejos.

Other college plays in which Napoleon took part were *Henry the Fourth* and *Robert McCaire*. How serious was his theatrical interest was apparent in the textbooks which he kept in his library, for example Sol Smith's "Theatrical Management in the West and South." Napoleon also had a good singing voice, and he played the guitar with skill. Both talents he had used many summer evenings when the Vallejo boys and girls climbed the steps to the tree house (the nest) which Napoleon had built by himself in one of the large trees at Lachryma Montis.

While at college, Napoleon's mother sent him a bit of advice, "I am very pleased when I see your letters and in them, I see your advances. Study, study as much as you can. Don't waste time." Among Napoleon's fellow students at Santa Clara College were several who made names for themselves, such as Clay M. Greene, D. M. Delmas, and Father McQuaide.

When Napoleon left college, he secured his first position in the town of Vallejo with the Pacific Railroad as second clerk—or, as Napoleon referred to it, as "second agent"—at $65 a month. Captain Frisbie, who was promoting the railroad, had given the position to his wife's youngest brother. Frisbie said he thought Napoleon was well employed in the railroad business and was happy. As for Napoleon's father, he hoped that his son would not get discouraged and would "continue energetically doing what was entrusted to him." This was in 1869. Napoleon's own version was as follows:

The Railroad is getting along very rapidly. It is now within a few miles from Sacramento, that is at Davis' ranch on the Putah Creek. The road is a beautiful one. I saw today two locomotives, one called 'Vallejo' and the other 'Solano,' both of equal size and almost the same value. There are besides two others up near Suisun, carrying rails for the continuation of the road. People are constantly asking for places on the Railroad; young men from good and distinguished families come to see the Captain for positions.

When Napoleon's brother Uladislao returned from one of his several visits to Mexico and needed employment, General Vallejo decided to form a partnership between the two younger boys and himself, for the growing of wine grapes at the Quiquiriqui Vineyard. Their business failed because of the plant louse, Phylloxera, which attacks the roots and leaves of the wine grape and which had been introduced into the Sonoma Valley on infested grape-cuttings from Europe. Napoleon and Uladislao next became associated with their father's Sonoma Water Works. This, too, proved to be of short duration. Vallejo disappointed in Napoleon, wrote to Platon that, "Napoleon is coming to see you. He needs a good sermon and I hope he will get it because he is very independent and it would be a good thing for him to get settled in something."

Once again Captain Frisbie came to the rescue and in December 1871 appointed Napoleon to act as agent and telegraph operator in Marysville. There he made friends with men who were hunting enthusiasts. They formed the Marysville-Buttes Shooting Club in which every member was a first class shot, superior in every way in the field with a gun and a dog.

One of the rules of the Club's Constitution was that all birds should be shot on the wing, and the person violating this rule had to forfeit one hundred dollars which was applied towards defraying the cost of a champagne dinner. When not shooting quails and ducks, the members had sport in steeple chase runs.

One wonders if Napoleon's horse carried the $1,500 silver-mounted saddle which he said his father bought for him at the time Vallejo purchased his own, costing $2,000. The president of the club was Oscar Stone (manager of the best and largest Dry Goods Store in the City of Marysville); Napoleon was vice-president.

A year before Napoleon went to Marysville, his mother crossed the continent to visit her daughter, Mrs. John B. Frisbie, in Albany, New York. On her return several months later, Senora Vallejo went to the studio of J. G. Smith in Vallejo and had a photograph made which became General Vallejo's favorite portrait of his wife. He wanted to give a copy to Senora Teresa de la Guerra Hartnell who had requested one; and Napoleon, being asked to take up the subject with Platon wrote him, "At Father's request I write you for the purpose of asking you to do him a favor of going to Smith's to have some pictures of Mother struck off. The kind he wishes is that in which Mother has a veil over her head. I think Fannie has one in her bedroom. The picture was taken shortly after Mother came from the East. Father thinks it a good picture and wishes to have one dozen of them." The General's wife was fifty-five years old when this particular photograph was made; it is the one most often published of her.

NAPOLEON'S MARRIAGE

In the year 1875, a blond Yankee miss, Martha Brown, the daughter of Harvey S. Brown, attorney for the Southern Pacific Company for many years, won Napoleon's questing heart. Martha, a graduate of Mills College, was a

Protestant, and some concern was felt in the family that there was to be another mixed marriage; but Napoleon was too deply in love to allow his family's views to influence him.

The wedding occurred on Wednesday, October 20, 1875, at the residence of the bride in Oakland, with Reverend Mr. Ackerly officiating. The bride was twenty-one and the groom twenty-five. Regarding the marriage, the General commented in a letter dated October 26th, 1875:

> I always thought nobody would come from Vallejo to the wedding of Nap in view of the rumors I heard before I left, but now he is married and well married. Regardless how much they feel, from the first to the last, the Archbishop, the priests and others will give the Church's interdiction against him and all the ones that attended the ceremony but 'what is done is done.' I will have to deal with them and to fight them until their anger is gone.

In spite of adverse feelings among members of the Vallejo family, the bridal pair were welcomed to Lachryma Montis where they spent part of their honeymoon before going to Cloverdale.

Martha and Napoleon Vallejo settled in Oakland and became in time the parents of two sons. The first was named for his paternal grandfather and thus became Mariano Guadalupe Vallejo, the second. He was called "Lupe" by the General. The second son was named Harvey Brown Vallejo after his maternal grandfather. When Harvey was born, Napoleon wrote his brother Platon: "On Tuesday, the 26th of November [1878] at half-past four in the afternoon, Mattie became the mother of another little boy. Funny that you should have all girls and I boys." The second little boy's godmother was Mildred Pacheco Tevis, the daughter of Romualdo Pacheco, former short-term Governor of California.

Napoleon and his wife and their little sons were frequent visitors at Lachryma Montis. The Christmas Holidays of 1882 were memorable for Harvey and Lupe, aged five and six. Although Grandmother Vallejo was absent, there were enough "Parientes" in Sonoma to have much Christmas cheer and fun. Senora Vallejo had gone to San Francisco to help nurse her daughter Maria Cutter's boy "Don Tweedy" (Leo) who was ill. The General wrote his wife the day after Christmas, describing the Yuletide festivities:

> You well know that Mothers are always the comfort for their daughters, especially when their children or they, themselves, suffer some illness. Mamas are the ones who provide sympathy; it has been said they provide the cloth for tears.
>
> You tell me that Leo is still ill which I regret. Pet him for that often does more good than medicine. We spent the Holy Night here well enough. There was in the parlor a "Christmas Tree" for Lupe and Harvey. Carmelita found in one of her wardrobes a mask and appropriate clothes. Napoleon accumulated a big and immense stomach and without the children smelling a rat, he appeared with a big white beard. Laden with toys, he went to the tree; the children half trembling watched

Santa Claus amazed. Little by little, they got friendly with him, greeted him and kissed him. After awhile Santa Claus said goodbye. After he left, Napoleon returned in a little while; Lupe and Harvey telling him what had happened, causing much laughter.

Afterwards there were some performance with the Deaf One, Mr. Estrella acting out with signs. Then they danced a bit and exactly at 12 we had punch (egg nog) and each one retired. . . I forgot to tell you that we ate a very fine stuffed turkey. I sent Mr. Aguillon as always, a basket of oranges and he sent me a case of wine, a demi-john of brandy and another of Angelica.

The Mr. Estrella mentioned as having attended the Christmas party, taught at the Berkeley School for the Deaf and was a frequent visitor at Lachryma Montis, occupying the Hermitage, then the guest-house on the hillside in the rear of the Reservoir.

In the early 1880s' Napoleon spent some time at Lachryma Montis raising chickens and teaching Spanish to some of the Sonoma ladies. One was Mrs. Horatio Appleton, the wife of the vineyardist who discovered that the phylloxera, which was destroying the vineyards in Sonoma Valley, was a plant louse. Mrs. Appleton brought with her for the lessons her little daughter Carrie, who in later years became the much loved Carrie Burlingame of Sonoma.

In the late 1880s, Napoleon traveled in the Northwest Territory as salesman for Arpad Haraszthy's company established in 1864 and famous for the internationally known champagne, "The Eclipse." Martha or Mattie, as his wife was usually called, wrote soon after he left on one of his trips:

Dear Nap:

We have just finished dinner and such a good dinner; a lovely steak, mashed potatoes, hot with Chili, the Chili pickles you made for a relish. I know you would have enjoyed eating, had you been here . . . Well, now I will go back to last night. After you left I got dinner and after washing the dishes we came to the dining room and the boys studied their lessons. Fred came and stayed until eight and helped "Bun" [Harvey] with his examples. At nine, we were all in bed. We slept fine, just as warm and nice, in fact, slept too well; did not wake until eight this morning. I tell you, we had to fly around to get breakfast . . . I think we have either lost or left a small valise in Sonoma as I can not find it anywhere.

Lupe also wrote to his father:

I made the hot-house and planted my seeds; the lettuce and the cabbage have just come up. About the time you get back, they will be quite large. Think I will subscribe for the 'Youth's Companion'; they have some fine presents. I am going to get a little air-rifle for $3.00. It is something like the one I have; a boy had one down here . . . The birds have a large nest; the old female was on the nest from three o'clock till morning. They must have eggs. We have not gone rabbit hunting yet. I hope you will bring me home a pair of moccasins.

Lupe wrote a letter to his Grandfather Vallejo, asking for stamps and received this letter in reply:

My very dearest Lupe:

Many months have passed since you wrote me a very nice letter asking for some postage stamps of different nations and I answered immediately and included some stamps but as I did not know the address of your father's house, the letter was returned to me as it had my return address. My first and second name is your family name too.

So now that I know your address I'll answer again and include the stamps, promising to send more. Grandma and Grandpa send you herein all their love and also to your little brother, with their blessing, asking you to be a good boy.

THE ORIGIN OF THE VALLEJO DEGREE

Napoleon Vallejo became a member of the Oakland Parlor of the Native Sons of the Golden West. He attended one of the celebrations of Admission Day of the Native Sons and Daughters of the Golden West. Among the honored guests were Governor and Mrs. Stoneman; also General Vallejo, a member of the Sonoma Parlor. It was at this celebration that General Vallejo originated the Vallejo Degree. A Native Daughter approached the General to ask for an exchange of cards and a handshake. He raised her hand in courtly fashion and pressed a kiss upon it whereupon she smiled and said, "You should have reserved the kiss for my lips." The General was not slow in following the fair one's suggestion. There were requests from other Native Daughters and thus the rite became an initiation to "*The Vallejo Degree.*"

With the General was his youngest son, Napoleon, who said, "Pop, aren't you getting tired? Can I help you?" His father answered, "I am willing my son, but you are not General Vallejo."

Through the years this rite was observed on occasions. One occasion which Napoleon remembered was when a National Convention of School Teachers met in San Francisco. Arrangements were made for a tour. Napoleon, who was at that time in charge of excursions for the railroad between San Francisco and Ukiah, arranged for the teachers to come to Sonoma. Four cars and an engine took them to the Red Gate of the Vallejo estate where they found the master of Lachryma Montis sitting on the porch. Napoleon introduced his father who not only delighted his feminine visitors with stories and served them choice wine and luscious fruit of Sonoma Valley but as an added pleasure for the young ladies as well as himself, bestowed the *Vallejo Degree.*

NAPOLEON NURSES HIS FATHER

When Napoleon's father became ill in the winter of 1889, Napoleon spent as much time as he could from his travels and from his own family to assist his sisters in nursing him. After one of his visits to Lachryma Montis in December he wrote the invalid:

My dear Father:

I arrived home last night at 6:30 safely. Andronico left us at Vallejo at about 4:30. I thought of you all the time on my way home and last night I looked to see the hour that you ate supper; you all in your respective places and I wished I was with you to do my share. I am going away today to Portland and shall be away probably to the 23rd or 24th of the month. Mattie will be with you in a day or two and she will take with her our two boys.

I shall write to her every day and she will do the same for me whilst I am away. I will give her the dates of my arrivals at different towns. Don't let the sweet oil rubbing of your liver by John Tomley be forgotten. Have the rubbing done once a day without fail. I am going to the market now. Will write again later on. Goodbye Papa. Be patient with your trial. You will be all right in a little while. Love to all.

Your loving son,
Nap

When Napoleon was not at Lachryma Montis, faithful John Tomley took over the task of rubbing the patient. At night he slept on a blanket, spread on the floor near General Vallejo's bed and thus was ready to answer any call.

It was a comfort to the General to have his youngest son perform the tasks that were beyond the strength of the girls. Vallejo wrote to Arpad Haraszthy (Napoleon's employer) to see if Napoleon could be excused from his work for a while. Arpad was willing and Napoleon returned to Sonoma to assist in the care of his father who was suffering from a jaundice condition.

Back on filial duty, Napoleon reported the condition of his father to his brother Platon:

Father had a very severe attack of vomiting, feeling very faint, weak, with no appetite. I was notified on my arrival from the North of father's condition and I came up right away. Yesterday he was quite bright but towards noon he became very sick. He had some soup, squash (boiled) and a little boiled beef. After he had his lunch he commenced to complain of nausea and sour stomach. He vomited several times and was threatened with a chill.

I rubbed him with hot towels; I was at him for nearly an hour, rubbing. This morning he feels very much fagged out; expresses a desire to stay in bed and continually says he is very weak and tired. I think you had better come up right away and see him again. I am here since the 24th and Mattie came up on the 9th of the month. Adela is here also, Natalia comes every day. Andronico is here to. Yes, come up tomorrow, if you can. I am neglecting my home, business and everything else to be here but I cannot leave under the circumstances.

Platon, brother and physician replied:

So you see my dear boy, here you have Papa a sensitive person to a superlative degree, concerning eatables, always so by nature and time itself has been unable to remove. Now he has been suffering from the consequences of a disease which of itself though not always dangerous, still more or less disagreeable and producing and exaggerating the nausea and vomiting. Be careful not to allow Papa to go out on the wet ground, even if it clears up above.

Though the December days were dark and filled with rain, his father did not forget that the 39th anniversary of Napoleon's birth would occur in that month. He wrote him a "royal quatrain" in which his name is emphasized:

Tienes muy bien corazon
Napoleon
Por eso tanto te estimo
Primo
Eres de mi alma reflejo
Vallejo
Si te miras al espejo
Veras mi retrato vido
A lo cual yo me suscribo
Napoleon Primo Vallejo

Before the bleak month of January, 1890 was over, Napoleon's father had passed away, in spite of the loving care of the Vallejo children and the professional care of Dr. H. H. Davis and Dr. Platon Vallejo. The task of sending out announcements of the General's death to the Press, and dispatching telegrams to relatives and close friends, was assumed by Napoleon.

Napoleon, Andronico, Platon, and the sons-in-laws were the pall-bearers. Napoleon's sons were honorary pall-bearers. Among the floral pieces, one of the most noticeable was the one with the satin ribbon bearing the name of Napoleon's fourteen-year-old son, Mariano Guadalupe Vallejo, the second.

Eight days after the funeral, Napoleon wrote to his mother:

I have not written you before because I have been expecting to go up to Sonoma every day. As it is you may expect to see me at any moment. I have written Platon to name the day that may be convenient for him and Andronico, then we can go up and look over Papa's papers. I am anxious to do this work before I start on one of my long trips. Some times I stay away for two months and I think an examination should be made soon.

I am commencing to feel better now that I have been at home and had some sleep. I lost fourteen pounds during my stay in Sonoma whilst father was sick. I shall remain here for some days yet owing to the bad conditions of the railroads all over the country. It is impossible to travel and very much more it is impossible to ship merchandise and goods. The roads are all washed away, the telegraph wires are down and the devil is to pay in general.

This had to be a very severe winter for all kinds of business for all the people; for the sheep and the cattle; for the steamers and the railroads; and to think that poor Papa should have gotten sick this very cruel rainy season. The days were cold, raw, damp and cloudy. Not a chance to take advantage of a good spell of sunshine to get him out. All was against us. We did all we could to save him. There was no one ever had better care, more loving attention than he did.

I dream of him every night. I think of him all the day long. His picture is in my parlor with a bouquet of flowers, fresh every day, put by it. It is hard to think that we shall never see him again. To think that we shall never hear him say his original sayings, his proverbs, etc. He is now in the other world awaiting for us, where we shall all soon find him.

To emphasize his desire to be on hand when his father's papers were examined by his two brothers, Napoleon wrote to Platon: "I would like to be present when the search is made of Papa's papers. It is impossible to stay away longer from duty. I am a man of family and must earn my bread and butter. Arpad is alright but the partners will kick if I remain away longer . . . I would like very much to have you wait till I return before anything is done."

NAPOLEON VALLEJO DIVORCED

Domestic inharmony, combined with the temptations inherent in the protracted absences from home that are a part of a salesman's profession, caused a breaking of home ties and resulted in a divorce obtained by Napoleon's wife Martha, shortly before the close of 1890. Napoleon chose to announce it to the family in a brief note from Portland, Oregon, to his sister Adela Frisbie: "Prepare to hear of a surprise. On December 2nd 1890, I was divorced in Oakland, California and it was on January 12, 1891 I was married again in Tacoma, Washington. I was single 21 days." Napoleon had married a Miss Kate Leigh Stokes, daughter of a tavern keeper. Reverend E. Copeland of the Unitarian Church officiated. By the second marriage, Napoleon had a daughter whom he named Jovita after the favorite sister who had died fourteen years before.

All the members of the Vallejo family were unhappy over Napoleon's action. They were devoted to his first wife. Fannie Frisbie expressed the sentiments held by the Vallejos in a letter she wrote to Platon from Mexico:

> What do you think of the barbarities that our little brother has done? Neither his wife nor his children have meant anything to him. I think Nap is crazy. What low things he has done and will be doing. He must not have any shame. What is he thinking of? How sad must his abandoned family be. Death is nothing in comparison to what this man has done. I know nothing of what happened but they have written me that it is all Nap's fault.

After the divorce, the Vallejo boys, *Lupe* and *Bun*, missed their father, especially the fishing and hunting trips with him, but they found it easy to transfer their love to their maternal grandfather, "Judge Brown," who undertook the care and financial support of Martha and her boys. Harvey Brown had crossed the plains in the pioneer days and, soon after arriving in San Francisco, he was practicing law in a tent on Market Street. Later he had a suite of offices which took up an entire floor of the Flood Building.

Frequent visitors to Judge Brown's home in Oakland were the daughters of Dr. Platon Vallejo. Felipa was there in 1895 and wrote to her father: "Poor Aunt Mattie has been having a trying time. Her Papa has been very sick with pneumonia. Grandpa Brown (as I always call him) is a dear old man and a very good father to Aunty and Bun. Outside of our own family, they are the truest people and friends I know and as good as I ever want. Good people are so scarce."

Harvey, the younger of Napoleon's sons, had been given the nickname of "Bun" by an Irish nurse, because he reminded her of a little Bunny as he scampered about. "Bunny" was shortened to *Bun*, and the name "*Bun*" *Vallejo* remained as an appellation through the years. Some time later Bun recalled the visits he and his brother made to Lachryma Montis when their Grandfather Vallejo was living. The General usually took them to town in the old carriage. They sat in front with him and the Chinese servant in the little rear seat, with his queue flapping in the wind. At dinner, the General sat at the end of the long walnut table with his back to the west window. When the large bowl of frijoles topped with cheese, was brought into the dining room by the *Chino Cocinero*, it was placed in front of Grandpa Vallejo, who said in English to the hungry, eager grandchildren, "Who loves Grandpa the best?" The child answering first received the first serving of beans, the melted cheese streaming from the spoon to the bowl.

Harvey Vallejo said his brother was a brilliant student. He was a high school senior with a smooth face when many of the male students had moustaches; College was denied Lupe as he developed tuberculosis. In spite of his devoted mother's care at a mountain ranch, Mariano Guadalupe Vallejo, the second, passed away when he was seventeen years old.

NAPOLEON VALLEJO—ARTIST

In the late 1890s, Napoleon was living in San Francisco at 704 Dolores Street, the old Spamar home. He opened a studio there and spent much time painting California landscapes; for a period, this was the chief source of his income. A little neighborhood boy, Billy Carr, sold him milk and eggs and ran errands. Billy loved the thrill of watching a real artist paint a picture. One day, Billy's sincere appreciation of Napoleon's art was rewarded by a gift from the artist of two paintings: one, a painting of the old Mission Dolores (this was for Billy himself), the other, a painting of snow-covered Mount Shasta, was for Billy's brother. Fifty-five years later, Billy, a successful railroad official, presented the two paintings to the state-owned home of Napoleon's parents in Sonoma. Perhaps Billy and his brother reminded Napoleon of his own sons' boyhood which he had missed.

Some time later, the second Mrs. Napoleon Vallejo passed away, and Napoleon, then sixty-one years old, turned his thoughts to his first love, Martha Brown. They were remarried in June 1911. The newspaper account said, "Vallejo gave his age as 61 years and his bride for the second time blushed when she said she was 57 years of age."

NAPOLEON VALLEJO—STUDENT OF CALIFORNIA HISTORY

As the years accumulated, Napoleon became interested in the annals of the Vallejo family, and in the contributions the Carrillos and the Vallejos had made to the history of California. He said his purpose in writing a biography of his father was to refute the maligners and traducers of General Vallejo and to present a true and sincere story. He found stimulating pleasure in corresponding with his brother Platon, who was considered an authority. One of Napoleon's letters, dated October 26, 1911, read:

Dear "Doc":

With all due respect to your grey hairs and the eight or nine years that makes you my senior, I take upon myself the responsibility of addressing you in the familiar way that I begin this letter. My calling you "Doc" does not convey the idea that I wish to be disrespectful or too familiar in any way, on the contrary I wish to say right here that I feel very proud of you as a brother and as an instructor and one skilled in a profession and branch of the highest knowledge that requires a savant and master. I am younger than you are and probably not as well educated as you are but in experience and sin, I am a 'dod-gasted' good second to you.

Napoleon's enthusiasm for the historic work increased. On February's added leap-year day in 1912 he wrote Platon:

I am enthusing more and more every day with the idea of you and I writing a history of one volume of California. I have a plan upon which I am constantly trying to find a beginning. It is a favorite and ever recurring theme and discourse, thought and effort and I must say occupies a lot of my attention night and day.

I visited Mr. Robertson, the book publisher yesterday and he asked me if I had my manuscript written and I told him I had the material consisting of data and brains and that the manuscript would be forthcoming with but little effort and time. I asked him some questions regarding the cost of one volume book and the cost of a two volume to be illustrated on good paper, revised and put on the market for a sale. He then told me to come again and 'talk it over' with him.

I have a hunch (do you know what a hunch is?) that if we were to put our forces together, we would suceed even though we are beginners. Our book would not be the first history of California but I think that we are particularly the proper persons to compose and write a book. We would not be translators nor compilers as much as we would be "The Distinguished and Efficient Sons of the late General M. G. Vallejo!" Many things that have never been written about that the public knows nothing of, we can create and enlarge upon. The history that Father wrote for Bancroft was alright (I helped him to write it) until it was turned *upside down* instead of the truths as written by Father.

I am slowly getting data of everything I can think of, beginning with the name of California the Explorers, the Indians, Portola, Cabrillo, Drake, etc, etc. The coming of the stranger (American) Bear Flag People (Los Osos). The Discovery of Gold in the San Fernando Valley, first and then by Marshall. The lively times between 1840 and 1860. The Vigilantes. How well I remember parading on Montgomery Street in 1856. I had one hand in Father's and the other in Andronico's.

What we would write would come nearer being the genuine history and our documents we can call genuine when we can trace back our authorities many years to the author or authors from whom the true facts are supposed to emanate. Isn't it a shame we are so short of funds? G-Whizz if I had a little money, I would say 'Doctor, you and I can do it, let's. And we can do it in a manner that Father would surely approve and be proud of. So many things, I have in store to write about. Each I would treat so as to be friendly with the people generally. As soon as I can, I will begin with my hobby. I think that our cousin Jacob R. Leese would help us materially. He is full of genuine information. He belongs to this Society [Pioneers].

It was well that Napoleon had this interest as his beverage sales had dropped. He wrote Platon on April 23, 1912, "The Liquor business is going to pieces more and more especially so since the women vote."

About this time, an unscrupulous real estate operator of Oakland had been able to convince Napoleon that he could recover some of the San Francisco Presidio property and have it returned to the Vallejo heirs. Napoleon's father had fought the case unsuccessfully for a number of years. Napoleon gave the slick operator, who had married a Castro, power-of-attorney besides money. It was thought by Harvey Vallejo that he had been given Vallejo family relics, including the gold-headed cane which was presented to General Vallejo on his Golden Wedding day. The real estate man was found guilty of a felony charge of swindling another man out of $1,000 and was sentenced to three years in San Quentin. Commenting on this sentence, Napoleon said, "If I had appeared with Mattie during the suit in court and put in our complaints, he would have been sent up for probably ten years, but we thought of his wife and three little daughters. He is getting what he deserves and when he comes out in three years from now, he will know better. The original power-of-attorney which we all signed, he told me he had sent to Washington, D.C. but I do not put any credence on anything he says."

While gathering material for his history, Napoleon came across a book, "California, Its History and Romance." The author was John Steven McGroarty. After reading a review of it in a local newspaper, Napoleon wrote Platon:

I am sending you under separate cover a copy of the San Francisco Examiner, dated March 21, 1912 which contains some very anger producing lies about Father in the early days of California when he was in power. I have read the article two or three times since yesterday and I have been completely upset by it. I have been roused. The injury which the infamous lie has excited or produced towards us is not a supposed or temporary one but with the full and lasting intent to injure us in the public's eye and mind, those that are gone as well, as those that still live; descendants of the Spanish Californians. I can hardly control my wrath, rage, fury and indignation and I think that we all ought to make known our great displeasure and resent that man's awful lies—in some way or other.

He surely has been misinformed as to historical facts or else he or some one very near him is an enemy to our dear father and the other Spanish Californians. In his writings he seems to show wrath and ire and expresses the feelings of one who had been bitterly provoked . . . For that reason I will drop my enthusiasm for the book I have been trying to get up and devote some energy and power forcibly exerted toward the man from Los Angeles.

A few weeks later, Napoleon, in a better frame of mind, wrote to his brother again: "This is the day, April 18th. The day of all days to be remembered by San Francisco and California for a great, many years to come. Six years ago today, *all day*, I didn't know whether I was afoot or horse-back. The people were all dazed and dodging earthquakes. And whenever I met anyone I knew, I would extend my hand and say 'shake.' I experienced by actual count 68 different shakes." The first fires he said began at seven and eight o'clock. Napoleon was then living at 1748 Market Street. He packed a suit-case with clothes and sleeping material, and, with $300 in gold, left his quarters.

Napoleon wrote to his brother asking him to suggest some appropriate books of history for him to read and to give his opinion of some of the authors of historical works on California. Platon replied promptly April 6, 1915 saying: "Yesterday I received your letter asking me to give you my opinion on several historical works. H. H. Bancroft's I have not seen and Hittell's and McGroarty's lies are awful . . . Bancroft's histories, books or works, I have not so much as seen the outside [covers] of them yet! McGroarty's is so outrageous, it leaps beyond the boundaries of credibility, and destroys itself. I consider his atrocious calumnies so far beneath the notice of my family, that I would not waste time in refutation (I refer to the newspaper clippings). It seems to me that these writers did not write for the sake of telling the truth and the most desirable of the beautiful historical events and romantic incidents consequent upon the discovery and acquisition of our incomparable California, of which there is abundant material,—but that they were rather led by the spirit of commercialism and making money; and for the pleasure of throwing mud, to create attraction and incite the curiosity of the public to purchase their misleading tales at so much a volume. They would sacrifice the truth and destroy the good name and personal character of men of distinction and representative individuality, to please the invidious, and provoke the malignant hatred of their own class to which they belong by natural propensity and affiliation. How many lies have been told which would require volumes to refute?"

When Napoleon began the actual writing of the biography of his father and the History of California, he became totally blind in his right eye. He applied to Doctors Barkan, Rosenthal and Buckland for treatment. The first named physicians pronounced his condition *incurable*, but Doctor Buckland prescribed for him. He advised against an operation because of the exorbitant cost and of the uncertainty of a successful outcome, saying that when an operation was a failure, generally both eyes became totally blind, caused by the sympathy of the one good eye with the other. In this condition Napoleon found himself on the first day of January in 1915; he was out of employment and could get no work of any kind because he had passed the age limit. He said he was "old, blind, out of employment and flat broke." He began to lose his appetite. He lost forty pounds and was on the verge of a nervous breakdown. He said that he felt that he had three alternatives: to starve, steal or commit suicide. He pondered and meditated, then prayer came to his rescue. He fervently asked God to spare his sight in one eye till he completed his book. Soon after, he was offered a position, then he began his work on the biography of General Vallejo. He spent hours in research work in the rooms of the Society of California Pioneers at No. 5 Pioneer Place in San Francisco. Much of the manuscript was written on the stationery of the Society which he joined in 1903.

It was a source of encouragement to Napoleon to read some of the letters which he received from people who had known his father. Robert E. Cowan, the well known book collector, wrote Napoleon on October 12th, 1915.

I am greatly interested in the fact that you are engaged in preparing the biography of your famous father, General Vallejo. The position he occupied was of so great importance and his career so distinguished in the history of California, that with so brilliant an inspiration it cannot be but that you will render the subject full and ample justice. Indeed it would appear that above all others you should be eminently qualified for this work.

To have lived in his presence and to have known him intimately, has been a privilege that has been denied all later historians. To have heard history as he recited it from the wealth of his mighty experience, should also be a supreme advantage, and these advantages have been yours.

It is opportune and timely too that a work such as yours, should now appear. The character of General Vallejo has been brought into disrepute by certain recent writers, self-styled historians. The impoverished historical knowledge of these writers has been greatly supplemented by an exotic imagination, and a wide departure from the truth has been the result.

It is well that falsity of these, and all historical fictions be corrected before too great a time has elapsed, and such malignant seed, has had time to become deeply rooted.

A month later, on November 15th, H. H. Bancroft wrote to Napoleon:

I take pleasure in availing myself of the opportunity of saying a few words in relation to my long and familiar intercourse with General Vallejo during the latter part of his important career in shaping the destinies of this country.

I never met a man of purer patriotism or kinder heart. I never heard him speak ill of an enemy, while cruelity of any kind was far removed from his nature. I have seen tears in his eyes, in speaking of the fatal effects upon the Indians of the smallpox, brought upon them by the incoming white people. The trickeries played upon him by Fremont and the Bear Flag filibusters, he treated as something as a joke which were nearer akin to villainies in the minds of those familiar with the circumstances at the time, and the subsequent career of that greatest fraud of the day, Jessie Benton's husband . . . General Vallejo, in heart and conduct was ever for California for American occupation, as well as for his own people, who were rather scurvily treated, as we all know by Polk and Taylor politicians, and the Southern lawyers, who controlled the courts of that day.

Our great work, the greatest perhaps of his illustrous life, it gives me infinite pleasure to record the years he spent with me and my secretaries in gathering material for my historical work and writing a history of California from his own personal and actual experiences which stand now forever preserved in the archives of the University of California, in the form of fifty large quarto volumes, containing tens of thousands of original documents nowhere else existing and five folio manuscript volumes of "Historia de California" by Mariano G. Vallejo.

Let those who have done more, using while abusing his work, cavil and criticise, if they can derive any pleasure or profit from it.

Another letter Napoleon received was from Herbert Vischer, son of the noted artist Edward Vischer, and was dated March 27, 1916:

It will be a great pleasure to show you the collection of diagrams and drawings made by and under the direction of your much esteemed father, General Vallejo, of the Presidios of California while still a part of Mexico. They comprise a very valuable addition to the collection of sketches of the Missions of California during that period, made by my father, Edward Vischer. As I have already told you, my father visited all the Missions in 1842, while they were still centers of all the life of the community, visiting them in an official capacity, and seeing them very thoroughly. He came back to make California his home in 1849, and began in 1861 to visit what remained then, and make sketches, finishing the collection in 1879, just before he died.

He had met your father in 1842, and was acquainted with him afterwards, but in the course of the last named years they became intimate friends, owing to the lively interest which General Vallejo took in the sketches, which was so keen, that your father offered to make a contribution covering the Presidio, which he did in the accurate and painstaking manner which was his characteristic trait. Your father went to considerable expense and gave much time, without any idea of recompense of any sort except to preserve a record of institutions of a former period, which both our parents looked back to with enthusiasm and veneration.

And the two men became very intimate, and spent much time together, discussing former days and past experiences, sometimes at Lachryma Montis. I can recall perfectly seeing your father for the first time, about the year 1861 or 1862, on the Napa boat, a fine soldiery man of imposing presence, and about my father telling me who the General was, and about the part he took when the State became American.

In the final years, I met him very often, but I learned to know him better through anecdotes which my father repeated to me. Therefore, I can assure you my dear Sir, knowing your father as well as I have known him, that it was a great surprise to have you tell me that there are writers at this time who are making charges that your father was a brutal slaughterer of helpless men, and had found it amusing sport to make them suffer; whereas, I know him to have been a polished, kindly, courteous friend and gentleman, at the same time a man of military training and conceptions.

The garrisons in those days had the duty to keep order in a sparsely peopled country, among settlers and among Indians; some of them subdued and attached to the Missions, but surrounded by Indians which were tribal, and wealth consisted entirely in stock and cattle. Border conditions prevailed on the out-skirts.

I can recall my father telling me narratives, recounted to him by General Vallejo, of expeditions which were no pleasure jaunts, but arduous undertakings. And I know that my father was not the man to extend intimate friendship if such accusations were believed about your father at that time . . . You can rest assured that your father was quite prominent enough for anything very bad to have been brought out long before now, if there was any foundation, and the opinion of his contemporaries, and authentic records, will be the basis of his reputation. And fortunately, there are plenty of records in the collections—the Bancroft Library and others.

Particularly in your father's case, because he stood out prominently, was a man of color through and through, an acknowledged leader with his own people, and was deservedly liked by Americans, because nobody more than he accepted the new conditions more gracefully, or showed greater ability to adjust himself . . . He mixed with the new people. Loyal to the old order, he was loyal to the new and a loyal Californian till he died . . . He was a man of capacity, well educated and a sterling exponent of the splendid qualities of the race which produced him—a race which may claim to have done as much as any of the races to pioneer civilization and spread knowledge. This was how my father regarded him and esteemed him and loved the General accordingly. A true Caballero, through and through.

Also among the letters which Napoleon added to his collection of research material was one from John F. Naughton, former Recorder of Sonoma County, who had written on April 9, 1915:

I will say that I was well acquainted with your father Gen. M. G. Vallejo of Sonoma, Cal. for thirty years back. He was a man modest in demeanor, of stirling cardinal habits and had the respect of the best people in California. When I was recorder of Sonoma County in his lifetime, he appeared as witness in Spanish land suits before Justice Jackson, Temple and Pressley and I as County Recorder had to produce the original records and be present guarding them during the trial and the profound respect and friendly treatment accorded your father by these Justices would never be extended any but a worthy man. He was not only generous and kind but also one of the best dressed men in America.

Still another letter was one dated February 22, 1916, from T. H. Chandler of San Francisco, who wrote in part:

One of the pleasantest recollections of my life was the knowing of General M. G. Vallejo. He was plain, unassuming and possessed the finest characteristics of any man I ever knew and a more charitable and conscientious man never lived. Gen. M. G. Vallejo did more for California than any other man that ever lived and it is a burning shame and a base ingratitude that no monument or statue is in evidence to commemorate his name, the greatest man that California has ever produced . . . His face was his most attractive feature, for it was the face of a good man who had lived a noble life . . . He was five feet, eleven inches in height, a most distinguished and attractive looking man and when standing still, his every pose was graceful, suggestive of intelligence and power . . . He died as he had lived, a loyal and faithful son, a most model husband and the best of fathers leaving a memory fragrant with the sweetness of a great life, possessed of ardor, courage, humility and resignation.

Under the heading PERSONAL NOTES, Napoleon wrote:

General Vallejo was very orderly, very neat and clean. He was a very particular man about keeping everything in order, in its proper place. The moment a person disarranged anything, the General, himself, would at once replace it, and yet, do so with a military politeness, without offense. In this respect, I flatter myself in saying that I am the only one in the family that is exactly like him.

He had a most wonderful memory which he retained until his death. I have seen him read eight and ten pages of ancient history out loud to us, at home and then close the book or give it to one of us to look at while he repeated, word for word the ten pages he had just read.

At the age of seventy-five, he began to dictate the five volumes of the History of California from 1815 to 1846, and he finished his great work in three years. He could read and write without the aid of glasses . . . His wonderful eyes were like deep pools when his intellect and spirit stirred him. He had the temper and disposition which delighted in contributing to the happiness of others. He was tenderness itself; mildness and goodness were in all his acts overflowing with benignity, compassion and clemency.

Napoleon was disappointed in not having his manuscript published; however, his literary talents found an outlet in the early 1920s in the San Francisco Chronicle's *Safety Valve*. He and a number of regular contributors, who wrote on the various topics being locally discussed, were often cartooned in sketches in the Sunday editions.

ILLNESS AND DEATH OF NAPOLEON VALLEJO

The last years of Napoleon Vallejo's life were spent in San Francisco at 400 Cole Street where he had been living alone after the death of his wife Martha on November 12, 1917, his hope that his daughter Jovita by his second marriage would come from the State of Washington and keep house for him did not materialize.

In February of 1923 Napoleon wrote Governor Friend W. Richardson asking for an appointment as Notary Public. His sponsors included five leading San Francisco bankers, James Rolph Jr., Mayor of San Francisco, U. S. Webb, Attorney General, Ex-Congressman Joseph R. Knowland, Julius Kahn and the Judges William W. Morrow, William C. Van Fleet, Charles A. Shurtleff and Curtis D. Wilbur. However, in October of that year he became ill and was taken to St. Mary's Hospital. When it was evident he would not recover, his son Harvey saw to it that his father was given the last rites of the Catholic Church, although Harvey, himself, had accepted the Episcopal faith of his mother.

Napoleon Primo Vallejo died on Friday, October 5, 1912, at the age of seventy-three. Funeral services were conducted by Father Gleason from a private chapel. The body was taken to Sonoma by Harvey and his wife Grace, where services were conducted October 8th by Father Costa, acting-pastor of the St. Francis Solano Catholic Church. At Napoleon's request, he was buried in the Vallejo family plot at the foot of the granite monument which shelters the graves of his parents in Sonoma's Mountain Cemetery.

Napoleon's son, Harvey Brown Vallejo, who inherited physical resemblances and many of the noble qualities of character that distinguished his grandfathers, was, like his father, a prize-winning marksman. He shared many duck-shoots with "Pop" Warner of Stanford football fame and with Duck-a-Minute Bill Banta. Harvey had a record, too, of years of devoted care of his invalid wife Grace, whom he said it was a privilege to serve. After her death in 1958, he continued to live in their apartment at 1706 Grove Street, San Francisco, with his dog "Boots."

Early on the morning of December 3rd, 1959, aged 81 years, Harvey Brown Vallejo, passed away from a heart attack. His ashes were brought to Sonoma by his devoted daughter, Jovita Vallejo, his only child. They were placed with the petals of some late-blooming roses of Castile from the gardens of Lachryma Montis, in the earth near the graves of his father and grandparents, by the Reverend Doctor Livingston, pastor of St. Stephens Church in Sebastopol. Thus passed the last in California of General Vallejo's grandchildren bearing the name VALLEJO.

Luisa Eugenia Vallejo

Luisa Eugenia Vallejo

(Mrs. Ricardo de Emparan)

The meadow larks, the song birds of the Valley of Sonoma, were just beginning to return to Lachryma Montis that 27th day of January in 1856 when another child, the fifteenth, was born to the Vallejos. This baby was baptized Maria Luisa Eugenia at St. Vincent's Church in the City of Vallejo on April 20th with her sister Adela and her brother-in-law John B. Frisbie as Godparents.

General Vallejo wrote the names of his children and the day of their births in the large Vallejo Family Bible, the gift of Padre Deyaert. He added on March 9, 1887 the names of the three grandchildren who had been born at Lachryma Montis, in the following manner:

> ANITA ADELA FRANCISCA DE EMPARAN
> Nacio el dia 7 de Junio de 1883
> en la casa abolengo Lachryma Montis, Sonoma Valley
> CARLOS HIDALGO
> Nacio el dia 14 de Setiembre de 1884 en el mismo cuarto que Anita.
> RAOUL RICARDO ROLANDO
> Nacio el dia 30 de Octubre de 1885 en la misena casa que sus dos hermanitos arriba mencionados.

On the nearby margin, the fond grandfather had written in Spanish the coincidence that Luisa, the mother of the three children, had also been born in the paternal home of Lachryma Montis.

Little Luisa was destined to be the song-bird of the Vallejo family; she started singing almost before she could lisp the Castilian words of her nurse's lullabies. Her babyhood passed into childhood, a childhood believing in Santa Claus at the age of nine, as her letter written in December of 1865 indicates:

Dear St. Clause:

I espect you will bring me something at Christmas night and I will hang up my stocking by the fireplace with a chair, if you will bring me something nice and pretty. Next day when I wake up, the first thing I do is to go to the fireplace and see what you have brought me. I will try to learn as much as I can. I will be good and love you. Goodbye, my St. Clause, in the night of 1865.

LULU VALLEJO

The note was written in English which she had been taught at the Sonoma Public School. Luisa or Lulu as she was called when her euphonious Spanish name was anglicized. In 1869 she went to St. Catherine's Convent in Benicia with her younger sister Maria (b. 1857). The daughters of Luisa's sister, Fannie, the wife of Luisa's Godparent, John B. Frisbie, were students there as well as her future sister-in-law Lily Wiley. Once a week, on Thursdays, the pupils were allowed to write letters as mentioned by Luisa, on September 28, 1869, in a particularly revealing letter to her "Dear Mama."

It is just eleven o'clock when all the girls are writing . . . I thought I would write you a few lines. I wrote Papa yesterday and told him if he or you wanted me to take guitar lessons from Mr. Ferris from the City. He comes once a week for twelve dollars a month. Do you think that is too much? Mr. Ferris was very glad when I told him that I might take lessons. I also told Papa if he was willing to send me the guitar that we have at home and when I go home I can play with Uncle Salvador. Give my best love and many kisses to my dear Uncle and tell him to excuse me for not having written to him in Spanish, I can't even to you, Mama. I have to write in English. I am getting along very well in my classes.

Dear Mama, next time you go home be sure to bring me my music books. Every time I go to my music lessons, my teacher scolds me for not having my own books. I would also like you to bring me my worsted box and Mary's and our worsted shawls we begun and my crochet needles and thread. They are all in the first bureau drawer in the sitting room.

When you come, bring us a box of fruit and a bottle of the syrup of pears you made last year, a big bottle. Such things seem splendid at school . . . What I would like to have now are my music book, nail brushes, little square glasses (mirrors) for combing the hair in the morning, writing paper, mattresses, blankets and spreads.

After making these requests, Luisa added a postscript: "I wanted to tell you that you need not buy the mattresses, the straw ones will do, just bring two blankets. I can just as leave sleep on straw."

Two months later, eleven girls at the Convent came down with chicken-pox and the younger sister Maria wrote to her mother about it, with surprising diagnostic skill: "We are not at all well, some kind of pimples—they are full of water and each [itch] like everything . . . Poor Lulu, she has them very bad, she has it on her head very bad . . . We can not even comb our hare or wash our face, for water is very bad for it . . . Now Mama please see about this and come over immediately." As usual, recovery from the attack was not too difficult.

Once during a vacation, Luisa and Maria were at Lachryma Montis when Charles E. Pickett was a guest. He had lost his teeth and they had not yet been replaced. At dinner, the girls giggled audibly at his difficulty in eating and were straight way sent from the table by their father. Afterwards the General reprimanded—and embarrassed them by saying, "I am alive today because of Mr. Pickett's kindness when I was a prisoner at Sutter's Fort."

While Luisa and Maria were at St. Catherine's Convent, Maria made her First Communion; Luisa had made hers in the summer of 1869 with her nieces, Fanita and Benicia Frisbie at the new St. Vincent's Church in Vallejo. In 1871 Maria and Luisa went to the Vallejo Seminary and by 1872 they were ready to enroll at the Convent of Notre Dame in San Jose. Their father thought well of the Convent. In recommending it to Dr. Levi Frisbie for his daughter Lily, General Vallejo wrote: "It is based on a curriculum of teaching of the first class. There, one can learn as in any foundation of learning. Those who direct it are persons of respectability. A lay-out of the buildings is the best and most comfortable in the whole state. The same goes for its cleanliness and discipline."

The Mother Superior, Sister Maria Teresa at Notre Dame, was Luisa's cousin, the daughter of her uncle Don Jose de Jesus Vallejo, elder brother of General Vallejo and Administrator of the San Jose Mission at the time it was secularized. His wife was Soledad Sanchez, a granddaughter of Don Gaspar Portola.

In 1868, when Luisa was twelve years old, she had been the favored companion of her uncle, Don Salvador, who was then living with his brother in Sonoma. On long summer evenings, Don Salvador would softly accompany her on his guitar as she sang the twilight hours away, while Senor Papa read and translated the classics in his study. During one of Luisa's visits to the home of her sister Fannie Frisbie in Vallejo, she wrote her father: "Tell Tio Salvador that every time I sing, I think of him, what nice times we used to have. Ask him if he still looks at two little stars near the moon."

Besides her voice lessons, Luisa studied piano with her brother Andronico who had his studio in Vallejo, and went once a week to Sonoma to give her lessons. The piano on which Luisa later preferred to play was a rosewood concert-grand imported from Paris. Its maker, Henry Herz, Vienna-born French pianist came West during the Gold Rush; his first concert in California being on April 1, 1850 at the National Theatre in San Francisco. At his second concert Herz offered his "fashionable" audience a special thrill by introducing the national airs of the different countries. Stephen C. Massett, who was later to dedicate one of his songs to Luisa, was on the program with Herz, singing and giving comic recitations.

LUISA'S GIRLHOOD DAYS

Photographs of Luisa, taken when she was in her "teens," show her as a beautiful girl with long dark hair and large brown eyes. Those who knew her as a girl say that her eyes could sparkle with humor, or, at times, with coquetry. She was popular with both women and men. With the latter, Luisa was credited with a number of serious conquests, not only among the "*caballeros*" but among the *Yankee Gallants*. As her sister Maria remarked, "Lulu is now 17 years old and she wants to marry, yet she doesn't know how to mend nor cook."

On January 27, 1874, Luisa's father wrote her a poem in Spanish beginning: "Today you complete eighteen years, daughter of mine, Under a good star" and ending, "Would that the Lord Almighty grant you a happy future.' Several months later, Hubert Howe Bancroft's agent, Henry Cerruti, came to Sonoma to procure historical data from General Vallejo; he was quite impressed with the eighteen-year-old Luisa. In his "Ramblings in California," he described her as "a highly accomplished young lady of bright intellect and refined manners, who besides being well versed in the English language is also a good Spanish scholar."

When Luisa was twenty, she became engaged to one of the most eligible young men in Sonoma, the merchant John Frederick Clewe who had come from Germany to join his sister Mrs. Duhring, a teacher at Dr. Ver Mehr's St. Mary's Hall for young ladies in Sonoma.

General Vallejo recorded in his journal that on July 14, 1876 he called Luisa to him and asked her if she had already consented to the young merchant's proposal. She responded, "Yes." The journal continues: "I revealed the difference in religion, the consequences with the Catholic Archbishop and the excommunication of the Church and that my family was all Catholic and that it would be good to see the Archbishop. I invited the one who had asked for my daughter's hand in marriage and after a long sermon, gave my consent." In spite of parental approval, Luisa changed her mind; the engagement was short and the ring returned. How this happened, Luisa's father explained to his son, Platon, in a letter dated August 9, 1876.

> It is said often with reason "that from the cup to the lips is a great distance." The proverb has been borne out in the engagement of Lulu. It's a month more or less since Mr. Clewe of Sonoma asked for her hand and she accepted. I called her into my presence, and also Mama. I made to her as many observations as the situation suggested and which might be required in such cases; she verified the promise of marriage in our presence and that of her fiance, without pressure, willingly and spontaneously, seemingly with delight. The day for the ceremonies was planned, anticipating dispensation from the Archbishop since the fiance is a Protestant; the engagement ring was given.
>
> I hunted for some money to get Lulu ready with a thousand things longed for. She went to San Francisco to buy them and a couple of days ago to my surprise, she said to me that she, Lulu, had reconsidered very carefully the business of marriage and that she regretted it . . . I wrote a letter to Mr. Clewe, Lulu also wrote one; the ring and other things were returned to him by Express . . . After all and in spite of the good qualities of Mr. Clewe, I believe that Lulu has done the right thing . . . The boy said upon leaving that he would go to Europe soon.

Mr. Clewe did go to Europe to visit his parents and there found consolation two years later in his marriage to a beautiful German girl, Marie Riensch. After a European honeymoon, he brought his bride to Sonoma where she was accepted with affection. Mr. and Mrs. John Frederick Clewe were close friends of the Vallejo family through the years. In after years, the Clewe residence was the only home where Luisa's two sons, Carlos and Raoul, were allowed to visit when they were in their teens.

DEATH OF TIO SALVADOR VALLEJO

Lachryma Montis had been saddened during February 1876 by the serious illness and death of General Vallejo's brother, Don Salvador, on the seventeenth. For some time he had been ailing, and Luisa was among those who nursed him in the room which Henry Cerruti described as containing weapons, modern and ancient, carpenter's implements, watchmaker's tools, blacksmith's hammers, a sleeping couch and half-a-dozen demi-johns filled with good Sonoma wine. Also in the room was a tin cup treasured by Captain Vallejo as the means of saving his soldiers from dying of thirst, when his entire supplies were destroyed in a battle with the Indians.

General Vallejo wrote a short poem describing Don Salvador's last Sacrament, administered to him by Padre Luis of Saint Vincent's Church in Vallejo. Luisa mailed the verses to her brother Platon in her letter of March 3, 1876:

> Enclosed you will find a little piece of poetry which I stole from Papa's table, dedicated to Uncle Salvador's last beautiful action while on earth. We think Father Luis could more truly appreciate the few lines than most any other person and it would please Papa to see it in his possession. We all, Papa in particular, think of dear Uncle every day and of his many laughable anecdotes.
>
> I suppose you heard of Tonita's death at the San Jose Mission. Aunt Luz is still with us and we have enjoyed her visit very much. Uncle Salvador's room has been cleaned out and the doors left open for airing. Every time any of us look in that direction, we imagine and almost believe he is there. All his little trinkets have been distributed among us all, which we truly appreciate. Aunt Luz takes with her the blue coat which you gave him and many "recuerdos."
>
> Poor Uncle, we have missed him beyond expression but then what a consolation to know he acted his part nobly towards the last. He has left this world of trials and disappointments to one of uninterrupted and ineffable happiness. Your last letter giving an account of the funeral was translated by Papa and enclosed a copy to each of his sisters.

On the 10th of March, 1876, Luisa again wrote to her brother Platon:

> Poor Uncle, he little thought he would be the sole subject in our letters, all this time and I think we can hardly do him justice. How we miss him, how we think and speak of him all day long. Sunday if the day is pleasant we will take to his grave some flowers. Pobrecito (poor dear). Today we received the news of another death in the family; Jovita Castro, our first cousin and a very sweet young lady died on the 8th inst., and will be buried in the City. We can not possibly attend the funeral. Mama feels very badly as she, Jovita was Aunt Felicidad's only child and quite a favorite of mother's. We may well mourn for the loss of our uncle and two first cousins. . . . I didn't know you could write poetry. Allow me to congratulate you upon your great success. Your poetry has pleased Papa exceedingly and he is exerting himself to study them and digest every line. He is proud of his son, the poet. Ahem! Says your poem is very graphic and touching. You are a regular chip of the old block. What a shame we haven't the advantage of you in Vallejo in having the church and everything so near at hand and so very convenient whilst we have to wait for our turn twice a month to hear Mass and then if it rains we cannot venture in the mud.

When General Vallejo was in the midst of his California historical work he took Luisa and Maria on one of his visits to Senora Hartnell's ranch near Salinas City. A letter to his wife on one occasion says: "Yesterday afternoon, we came from San Francisco and at once we went to a little ranch to visit Teresa who was happy to see the girls. On arriving at her house, I hid but let them enter and the first thing she said 'these are Vallejos, daughters of Guadalupe or Luz.' Then there was no longer any use to hide and I came out. There was much talking, 1 ½ hours. She wanted us to spend the night with her."

It was during this trip in 1874 that Vallejo took his two youngest daughters to Monterey where Luisa said her father while walking on the beach bent down and filled one of his hands with the white sand and reverently kissed the soil of his beloved California. After their visit to the Monterey peninsula, they went to San Francisco where Vallejo said they "visited the mother of Frank Curtis (Frank a beau of Luisa) she as well as her children have treated us very well. The lady is very amiable and kind."

The following year, 1877, Luisa's father made his trip to Mexico. Returning to the United States, he wrote Luisa from Syracuse, New York:

Today I received your two letters, one dated the 6th of October and the other the 7th of the same month. Benicia [Benicia Frisbie] sent them to me from Washington as soon as she learned of my arrival at this city [Syracuse]. As I am to leave here 'homeward' very soon (I believe on the first day of December next) I am omitting the answering of all the points that you mention in them; I will only tell you that I was anxious while in Mexico to receive news from home but the blame for my involuntary detention in the country was truly for fear of passing through Vera Cruz, a truly terrible place for Yellow Fever, a devilish sickness and because of the terrifying and frightful hurricanes that are prevalent in that accursed locality in the months of August, September, October and November, especially.

Not being able to remain longer in Mexico I resolved to leave there after the plague had calmed down a bit on the 14th of this month. I left on the train at 12 at night, taking leave of the great Tenoxtitlan, monumental city, historic in Mexican annals. The train left there and passing through the highest mountains in the world, reached Vera Cruz on the 15th at 7 in the evening. The American Consul received me at the train (thanks to the Minister Foster of the Consul General Skelton who telegraphed to him at Vera Cruz from Mexico City) and I embarked at once in a boat of the American Steamship "*City of Merida*," truly a magnificent ship. In the night it put out to sea and I began to feel a very noticeable sense of well being, so much so, that I ate with appetite; I breathed the pure air of the sea and from then on I was much better in every way, physically and mentally.

At each instant, the hurricane from the north was expected but it didn't appear while we were crossing the gulf of Mexico. It occurred to me to say to the passengers in my conversation on board with them that fortunately Jupiter was having a big ball on Olympus where he had called all the gods. The zephers, with very good will carried us to N. Orleans in the ship without any untoward event in three days of good weather. I arrived here (Syracuse) in the train from N.O. and in another three days I shall leave for Sonoma.

John B. Frisbie's business detained him in Washington, D.C., and prevented Luisa's father from leaving Syracuse the first of December as he had expected, so he wrote again to Luisa:

Much time has elapsed since I received a letter from you although neither you nor I am to blame. Circumstances, many times make things appear in a different light from what they are in reality and so it has happened now. Nevertheless I have always written to Mama so that you all could hear from me and at the same time, letters to her, serve all the family without causing any one to be jealous. Moreover when one is traveling on the road so much and whose eyes cause him to suffer it is not easy to write to all the members of a family as large as ours.

I am living in the home of young Denis McCarthy, the son-in-law of Adela, waiting for Frisbie to return from Washington to continue our trip to California. Adela is still here overseeing her daughter on the duties of a household while she is waiting to return to California and awaiting a letter which the Doctor is to send her as she has been advised by wire. It is possible that he will tell her that she can stay with Adelita all winter or that she should leave immediately and in the last event it is possible we will go together. [Which they did.]

It is snowing without being cold. The houses, streets, trees and everything that exists under the sky is covered with snow, white as the dress of a virgin who in her betrothal covers herself with the mysterious veil of innocence. It is very pretty to see it rain snow but very inconvenient for those like myself who can not endure such a rigorous temperature . . . Syracuse is a pretty city of more than sixty thousand inhabitants. There passes through it day and night, every twenty minutes, immense trains of passenger cars and freights; canals with thousands and thousands of vessels that go from the lakes to N. York and return and go up by means of locks; wide streets, well lined with trees. I saw the town 11 years ago [sic. 12 years ago] and it contained ten thousand inhabitants.

LUISA'S CHUM

A little over one year separated the birthdays of Luisa and Maria and the two sisters were very close. After Maria's marriage on May 12, 1878, Luisa would have been very lonely had it not been for her special girl friend, Elizabeth ("Lizzie") Chipman, daughter of Mrs. W. W. Chipman, who was also the mother of two other daughters, Alice and Fannie, and two sons, "Willie" and "Sherry." Later, Mrs. Chipman was widowed and married the noted attorney John W. Dwinelle. The Chipman girls were frequent visitors at Lachryma Montis, and Luisa was often a guest at the Chipman home at 438 Second Street in San Francisco. After one of these visits, Luisa wrote Lizzie (February 24, 1880): "I arrived home safely and was so lovingly welcomed home by all my folks. *WELCOME HOME* was put above the dining room door; two large bouquets, a lovely wreath and a dear little bunch of violets in the parlor. Papa went down on the train to meet me at the steamer and we were so glad to see each other."

Confidences were shared with Lizzie about topics of great interest to young girls, BOYS! In November 1879, Luisa attended a house-party in Sonoma

Valley about five miles from her home and on the 10th she wrote Lizzie that she had a jolly time, but, she confessed: "I only regretted one thing, namely, the male department didn't suit me. One was 16 years of age, another 49, another 45 and the very homely Manuel whom I see as a brother." Another letter on the aforesaid topic was written on May 10, 1882.

It pleased me to see your splendidly spoken Spanish. I can tell you, you have been to the *S.S. Mexico* and have been 'playing the mischief' with the officers. Yes, I have met the 'Comandante' and isn't he lovely for an engaged gentleman? Mr. Montalbo, their 'jefe' is also engaged to be married. But you wouldn't think so to see how he cuts up. They are all great flirts and they notice everything about you. Be sure to have your feet just so, for they are the next things they look after your 'lindos ojos'! [pretty eyes]

Lizzie's mother, Caroline Chipman Dwinelle, was also a frequent visitor to Lachryma Montis and in her later years recalled "seeing the dear General with portly form, radiant face, reaching high for a choice cluster (orange blossoms) and then his droll search for a pin to fasten the boutonniere which was presented in grandiose style . . . the old gallant that he was! To hear him say with so much pride, 'Senora Caroline, the reason they are so much better, we give them water, water, water!' And showing me what they, the oranges, liked, he dug a deep valley around a favorite tree and then turned on the water, which disappeared as if by magic. 'You see, Senora, how thirsty they are. Of water they never get enough and that is why the oranges of General Vallejo are so much better.' "

During the 1870s Luisa was a frequent guest at the homes of her married sisters: Fannie and Adela in Vallejo and Jovita in San Francisco. While at Jovita's home she took singing lessons in Italian. Her father was proud to report "the singing teacher says that Lulu has an excellent voice." As for Luisa herself, she was very pleased with the maestro, Senor Mancusi who had "such beautiful eyes." At this time the *Gazette* announced that Stephen Massett (Jeems of Pipesville) had composed a piece of music and dedicated it to Miss Luisa Vallejo who was not quite 18 years old.

GENERAL GRANT VISITS CALIFORNIA

During General U.S. Grant's tour of the world, he stopped over in September 1879 in the San Francisco Bay area to visit the cities of Oakland and San Francisco. Luisa and her mother attended the welcoming ceremonies which Luisa described in a letter to her father who had remained at home. On September 27th, 1879, he acknowledged it as follows:

I just received your letter. Tell Mama that it pleases me that you all have had such a good time. The picture that the newspapers have printed about the ovation given to General Grant; that of Oakland must have been more impressive to the American Chief. There, of course was not the luxury of the Babylonian city of San Francisco. The innocence of little children, 1,500 appearing with flowers and their families formed the background. How friendly and sublime.

Perhaps with the idea that it might hasten the return of Senora Vallejo and Luisa, the General reported what he had been doing at Lachryma Montis (a great deal for a man of 72 years): "I have been gathering up the fruit before the ants get it, gathering baskets for the winter. I have picked apples and pears. But it causes me much trouble to get down from the trees. I've fallen twice out of the apple trees. When I go to bed, I dream of falling; but what to do. I haven't bought anything since Mama went away except a bread tort from the new bakery; two dollars for meat, forty cents for fish, beans and tea . . . I haven't touched the dirty clothes; it is better for another person to do my washing."

When Senora Vallejo and Luisa returned to Lachryma Montis, they found the house packed with fruit, from one end to the other. Luisa commented: "You can imagine the state of things."

HELP FOR THE NEW CHURCH

Luisa was a member of the choir of the St. Francis Solano Church, located in the old mission building where her mother was president of the Altar Society. The mission was sold by Archbishop Alemany in 1881, and Luisa with a desire to help in the building of the proposed new church, directed a fair and was able to collect $450. In April 1881, after the new church had been completed on West Napa Street, Luisa wrote to Lily Vallejo, her sister-in-law: "We have our new church right near us and we feel proud of it. You have no idea how Nat [Natalia Haraszthy] and I worked to make our fair a success and now we see our reward. I am training a lot of girls for the choir while Nat attends to dressing the altar every Saturday . . . I have to watch the old folks for although they know 'heaps' more than I, they forget their ages and venture out in the cold without necessary wraps."

LUISA'S COURTSHIP AND MARRIAGE

During one of Luisa's visits to Mr. and Mrs. Joseph Schleiding in San Francisco, she met at a dinner party a handsome young man whom her father admired, Don Ricardo de Emparan, son of Jose de Emparan and Countess Anna de Arriola, members of old Spanish families of distinction in Vera Cruz, Mexico. Streets in Vera Cruz and Mexico City to this day bear the name Calle Emparan. Ricardo's father, Jose de Emparan, was *El Ministro de Fermento Colonizacion e Industria* under President Benito Juarez, and Ricardo de Emparan was appointed a Consul by President Porfirio Diaz and was assigned to San Diego.

Courting General Vallejo's attractive daughter, the young consul sent a box of sea-shells to Lachryma Montis; among them were the spiraling white *Fusus Colus*, the crimson *Thorny Oyster*, the *Rose Mure*, also the porcelain enameled *Auger Shell*, and the bowl-like *Sea Urchin* decorated with exquisite bas-relief—just the ornaments for the shelves of the "What-Nots" in the

Lachryma Montis parlor. The General told of their arrival in a letter written to the donor on January 31, 1882:

The shipment arrived by Express and I gave it to Natalia and Lulu who had agreed to share it between themselves. Of course, there were many exclamations such as 'How wonderful.' 'This shell is so beautiful,' 'these are divine,' 'Nothing so exquisite as these mother-of-pearls shells,' And after so many phrases of praise to the beautiful gift, they turned to the donor 'How nice and thoughtful is Senor Emparan, how much we appreciate his thoughtfulness.'

The romance between Luisa, aged 26 years, the last daughter remaining at home, and the young Mexican Consul, aged 29 years, progressed rapidly. Due to the necessity of Luisa's fiance having to be at his San Diego post, the wedding plans were hurried and a dispensation was received from the necessity of publishing the banns.

Luisa chose her mother's birthday for her wedding day. The day of Luisa's marriage, August 23, 1882, the parlor at Lachryma Montis was filled with flowers from the garden, including a floral bell whose clapper was a fresh, waxen-white bud from the one large Magnolia Grandiflora tree on the estate. This variety starts blooming in June and bears blossoms through the month of August.

Luisa followed the Spanish custom of having for her attendants her mother and the groom's eldest sister, in place of his mother who had recently died. Father Esser of the St. Francis Solano Church performed the ceremony. The guests gathered at Lachryma Montis for the reception and the serving of refreshments from the tables set up in the orange grove west of the house. Following the festivities, the bride and groom left for San Francisco, staying at the Palace Hotel for a few days before boarding a steamer for San Diego, where the young Emparans were to make their temporary home.

Three days after the wedding, and after the family had retired to their rooms for the night, Luisa's father wrote her the following letter dated August 26, 1882. It is indicative of the banter that he and Luisa's mother often engaged in, relative as to the superiority of their respective birthplaces, Monterey *vs.* San Diego:

Dear Lulu:

As is our custom when the moon came up over the horizon we were sitting on the porch to see it come up. Mama, Adela, Mattie, Nap and I thinking of you. Some were saying that perhaps you might be traveling admiring the grandeur of the sea. Others said, you might be seasick, others that perhaps the quiet sea was making the moon shine on the calm waves while you were chatting on deck with Emparan and some passengers and acquaintances, perhaps thinking of us at the hour and I who know the coast and the time the ships make going down it, said 'right now the ship which is carrying Lulu and her husband is sailing in the Santa Barbara Channel; it will touch this point and will arrive at San Pedro in the morning. They leave very early in the train for Los Angeles where they lunch; they take a walk tomorrow in the afternoon. Sunday they go on shipboard again. They'll greet Monday in RE-

NOWNED San Diego. As I said these last three words, intentionally looking at Mama. She then took over the conversation and started with Monterey. After the arguments pro and con, we came to a halt in what you know—nothing!

Under the table there were four watermelons which I bought this morning and we began to divide it into slices. It was half-past nine: all went to bed and I, dear daughter set myself writing to you.

As General Vallejo started for bed, he laid the letter to Luisa on his desk in the study. Next morning, Luisa's sister Adela added her message to it: "I have just returned from church; we missed your sweet voice in the choir . . . We all had a good day's work in packing your things. I know full well you will say within your heart 'Do they miss me at home?' Yes, dear darling sister, you will be missed more than all of us, for you filled Papa's and Mamas hearts, as you know we all loved you dearly. Goodbye, Sweetheart."

Another postscript was added by Lizzie Chipman, the girlhood chum, the sister of Alice and Fanny. The three Chipman girls were called by Luisa's father "The Three Graces." He said that Alice, who resembled her mother, was so pretty that he never tired looking at her. Lizzie wrote on the margin of the General's letter to Luisa: "I suppose by this time you feel quite at home in San Diego but do not fall in love with it for San Francisco and Sonoma can not get along without you. I feel quite favored to have been at your wedding."

Napoleon, who had come for the wedding, added a few lines: "The bird has flown and the nest is empty. Your room is forsaken, dark and empty. I miss you oh! so much, so much. I shall always think of how pretty, amiable and kind you looked your last two or three days at L.M. Tell Dick to take good care of you."

Napoleon's wife also wrote a few lines: "How do you like traveling by sea? . . . Lizzie returned home today and when Adela goes I shall feel alone. As yet I cannot realize you are gone for good. Hope soon you will live in San Francisco and then you can come home often. Love to Ricardo and yourself. Lovingly your sister Mattie."

Although the wedding guests had been few in actual number, many engraved announcements had been mailed and General Vallejo was particularly appreciative of the congratulatory message from Benjamin S. Brooks, his attorney during the 1850s and 1860s when there was a super-abundance of litigation. Mr. Brooks' letter, written in Spanish, was dated September 9, 1882:

Shall we congratulate you? We are very happy to learn of anything which adds to your happiness or Mrs. Vallejo's and I suppose you are pleased that your last daughter is united with the man of her choice and of whom you approve. We, the parents must feel an anxious desire to see our children, especially daughters settled in life before we are compelled to leave them and therefore we desire sincerely and warmly to congratulate you on this happy event. Yet you must feel a pang in parting with your daughter—your only daughter, we might say—to go so far away from you. I am afraid you will be lonesome with all your children gone.

But every day makes the distance shorter. Railroads are growing fast in all directions. San Diego will soon be in railroad connection by the Southern Pacific, perhaps, it is already and link by link they are building, a road along the coast from Mission to Mission so that we shall be able soon to retrace by steam the route traveled by the old Padres on mules. A Century and Nine Years! What is a hundred years in the life of the World? But does it not seem to you as if more than its share of important events have crowded into the last fifty years? The Steamer, the Railroad, the Magnetic Telegraph, the Ocean Steamship, the Sub-Marine, Telegraph, the Printing Press, the Street Railroad, the Cable Road (which my son Ben invented).

And what changes you have seen . . . For a time in 1836, you and Alvarado declared California independent of Mexico. In 1846 she became practically a part of the United States of the North. And then came the discovery of Gold and the Treaty of Peace in 1848 and since then everything has changed.

I do not see you often but I do not cease to think of you always and wish we could see each other often. I wish you would come to see us. We have a new house at Broadway and Gough; from the windows of my library I can see the old Presidio where you so long held sway. I look out to the Golden Gate, I can see Punta del Castillo, Punta Bonita, Carallo, Sausalito, Isla de los Angeles, Alcatraz and Tamalpais. All the vessels that go and come pass my chamber window. I can see all the Bay, almost to Sonoma.

LUISA'S SAN DIEGO DAYS

Those who had said that Luisa might be seasick on the journey were right. After arriving in San Diego, the bride wrote to Lizzie Chipman on September 15, 1882:

I had a miserable time on the steamer. I had all the attention that could be expected by my dear husband and the kind stewardess and the good Captain . . . I am rather pleased with San Diego and have met a circle of friends whom I used to hear Dick speak of repeatedly. I have had trouble in finding a house furnished and have moved from the hotel to the rooms Dick had formerly, where I am cozily fixed; I am married and I cannot realize the step I have taken. It seems as though I am still 'Lulu Vallejo' and full of mischief as ever . . . We are in hopes every day of receiving orders to go to the City [San Francisco] and live there for awhile. I would so much like it if we could be there by December so as to enjoy our Christmas together at home.

But coming home for Christmas was not "in the cards" for Mr. and Mrs. Ricardo Emparan, and they spent their first Christmas together in San Diego. Instead of sending a conventional gift to Luisa's parents, the young couple decided to send money for the taxes on the home place. Luisa told her mother that if her father had succeeded in paying them, then she, Mama, was to take half of the money and give the other half to Luisa's father.

Ricardo was accepted by Vallejo as another son which was evident by Vallejo's note written on September 4, 1882.

Esteemed Ricardo, these lines are for you: You call me by the name of father, not by reason of being so by nature but by virtue of your joining with my daughter Luisa. Well. I accept with pride and pleasure such a substitution with all my heart and my wife accepts at the same time the title of mother . . . How I wish we could serve you as guides in the few years that remain to us of life and would that we could be representatives worthy of those that from Heaven approve the joining of our families.

Be good, Ricardo, take care of Luisa and receive the blessing of your new parents.

M. G. VALLEJO BENICIA DE VALLEJO

On December 6, 1882 Vallejo shared his thoughts, political and otherwise, with the esteemed Ricardo:

I owe you so many answers to your letters that I don't know where to start and you must not think that it has been because of negligence nor lack of will to do it nor lack of affection . . . You know that I keep up my correspondence in spite of my years and if in the future I fail in doing so, you must not blame me because I am now alone, alone in every meaning of the word. Before, the last four months Lulu served me as secretary but now she is not under the paternal roof. It has really been *first* sickness of the eyes (not the sight) and rheumatism in the right hand and *second* personal business at Lachryma Montis and away from it, such as in Santa Rosa and other places and the *third*, the daily meeting of visitors whom I alone can entertain and I am obliged to answer all the questions that they ask of me as if I were the public information officer. Add to all of that what I have mentioned, the Elections of the 7th, last month: the result of which has been sad for the Black Republican Party and the triumph for the Democrats . . . This county has always been known for carrying the banner of the Democratic Party and this year or better said, in the recent elections it has come out better than ever.

The triumph of the Democratic Party in California and in the other States of the Union is the prelude of what will happen in the year 1884 in the presidential election, if I am not deceived. The triumph is a national necessity; the opposition party has abused scandalously the power of the Treasury and the public funds to the detriment of the masses who are those who have supported and do support with patience the excesses and wastes of the Administration for twenty years. Believe me, Ricardo, American Democracy is the Best Democracy in the world, that is to say, under the principles enuciated by the celebrated and very famous Jefferson.

General Vallejo's prophecy was not self-deception. The Democratic Party's nominee, Grover Cleveland, carried the vote of the country in 1884, the first Democratic victory since before the Civil War.

THE YOUNG MOTHER

Shortly before Luisa expected her first child, she returned to Lachryma Montis in order that the baby could be born in her parents' home. A letter to Lizzie Chipman on May 2, 1882, transmitted the latest news on the subject:

I am busy preparing my little trousseau and have gotten ready for the new arrival. Maria sent me a lovely basket with all the necessaries and my other sisters have given me several little presents. It is so sweet to look at the dear little things and I can hardly realize they are for me. My sisters will all be here to welcome him or her to Lachryma Montis and strange it was, here, where I first saw day-light. Now I know this is too much baby-talk and I have tired you.

The baby was born on June 7, 1883 and was named Anita Adela Francisca. When she was six months old, Anita was taken by her parents to Mexico City where the Emparan family were guests of Luisa's sister Fannie Frisbie.

On December 31, 1883, Fannie's husband, General John B. Frisbie, wrote to Luisa's father: "Lulu and her husband are living with us but expect soon to go to housekeeping. They are a pleasant addition to our family circle and we shall greatly miss them when they leave us. Anita is a little cherub and naturally a favorite with all."

Another year passed and Luisa found that Little Anita was to have a play-mate. Accordingly Luisa persuaded her husband to let her return to Sonoma so that her second child could be born at Lachryma Montis. On June 27, 1884 as she was about to leave Mexico City, General Frisbie wrote to her father:

Lulu leaves us this morning: her departure will make us all feel intimately our exile from beloved California. All of us long to see the grand old state again. I had hoped that we might be able to do so before the close of the present year but from the present indications I fear that it will be impossible to absent myself from business long enough to realize this cherished desire, combined with this obstacle is the expense attending such a trip. My family is so large that to provide for it is about all the money I can earn.

The mining properties in which I am interested are doing well but a heavy debt has been incurred for mill and machinery. This is being paid by the profits now made consequently I have no income from this quarter and can expect none for at least a year. My chief reliance is therefore upon my salary I am receiving from the Railroad Company . . . Yes, I succede [sic] and work on determined to force my way to fortune. When General Diaz returns to power. I have good reason to believe that my progress will be certain and rapid as I am promised his aid in carrying out an enterprise I have in hand in connection with some capitalists that will be of great Public advantage and highly renumerative to the Promoter. As Lulu will tell you all about our social and domestic life and Emparan everything of general interest and so much better than I can, I will not attempt to forestall their narrative.

The pleasure of the homefolks at the prospect of Luisa's return to Lachryma Montis was expressed to her by Natalia in a letter dated May 20, 1884:

I received your sweet long letter only today and I have read it over and over again. Oh! Lulu, I am so happy you are coming back to California. Dear, sweet Ricardo, to bring you back. Kiss him for me, once, twice, three times. Oh! I am so glad. When I think of your coming back, it makes me feel better, it seems as if I can stand what ails me better, to have near me one I love so dearly . . . Dearest Lulu, just think of *you* with another baby. I feel so sorry but what can you do. This is the way with us married people. Never mind Lulu, you will get over it this time nicer and easier . . . Just think of all I went through with no doctor, just Mama and Attila. You will not have such a hard time.

Dear little Anita, I can just see her dear little face with all her beautiful long hair.

How fond Emparan must be of her and I suppose you don't love her a bit, do you Lulu? Sonoma's month of May, as beautiful as ever with flowers, green fields and the air so mild, soft and pleasant. Oh! Lulu, I am very happy and contented with my home and its location . . . Attila's business is all here, Mari [Mariano] is busy with the cultivation of the vineyard; Gusti [Agoston] at school and my two little girls are growing so nicely. I am proud of them; they go to school every day to the darling Sisters, so near and convenient.

I saw Mama yesterday, she is pretty well . . . Papa is in the City, he is also well. Poor old folks, they begin to look so old and gray, more so, Papa.

Luisa returned home as planned. Her second baby, born on September 14, 1884, was a boy and was given the name of Carlos Hidalgo. Another year (1885) and Luisa was once again expecting a baby. Meanwhile business interests called Ricardo back to Mexico, but he decided to leave his wife at Lachryma Montis so that their third child could be born at the family home. From Mexico he wrote to his wife on October 29th, 1885:

My Adored Lulu:

Soon I will have the pleasure of embracing you again. How long it seems, centuries for days, away from you. How many times I have desired to see my babies. So alone, except for the Vera Cruz packages. I wonder when I am going to see our new little child. How pretty you are with your baby. If it is a boy, we will call it Raoul or Ricardo and if a girl Gabriela. Do you like the names? I'd like also, if it is a girl to give it your name. But it doesn't matter to you but never-the-less to me it seems LUISA is pretty . . . I have just received your letter and one from Papa on the 20th. Kiss my children for the love of your

RICARDO

The birth of the "new child" was announced to Ricardo in a letter written by General Vallejo on October 30, 1885, the day of the infant's arrival:

Dear Ricardo:

Last night at this same hour (6 P.M.) we had tea with Luisa, nothing transpiring, no signs of the impending birth but at ten P.M. pains were coming on. Doctor Davis was sent for and came right over. After some hours the new arrival came into the world, healthy and bright as a patena, chubby and well developed. Luisa was very happy as all of us are too. There was no suffering by the patient, no use of chloroform nor other medicants. I assure you, it was a happy, blessed event. Senora Vallejo and the Doctor attended to everything with admirable care and discretion. I can sum it all up with mentioning good, good, good. The day dawned bright and clear . . . Anita and Hidalgo are in very good health. Hidalgo is ready to learn to walk.

A postscript was added by the young mother: "Don't worry or concern yourself about anything. All is well. I am in the care of Anita, Hidalgo and the baby, as if you were here." The third Emparan baby was baptized by Father J. C. Esser on November 25, 1886 at the new Catholic church, St. Francis Solano. He was given the name of Raoul Ricardo Rolando and his godparents were General Vallejo and his wife.

BUSY DAYS AT LACHRYMA MONTIS

Motherhood provided Luisa with an outlet for her desire to serve others. Even at twelve years of age, she had been a veritable little mother to her nieces and nephews, Fannie Frisbie's children in Vallejo, who were near her own age. Once when visiting her sister Fannie, Luisa wrote home: "I have been busy helping Fannie and Jovita with all the children; they have been so sick with the measles, from little Fannie down to the babie; Lillie, Snookie and Carlos all had them. But, thank God they are better." Now in 1887 her own babies required the usual amount of personal attention as she wrote Lizzie Chipman: "My little cherubs are all well and making the greatest noise imaginable. The day being a cloudy one and cold I have kept them indoors. I declare a Saint would not be able to stand their noise." The "three cherubs" were Anita, four years, Carlos, three years, and Raoul, two years.

Luisa's father, who was in Monterey at this time with the father of the "three cherubs," wrote to Senora Vallejo:

> Lulu wrote to me and told me in her letter everything about home and that every one "so far" is well for which I'm glad. I've gone out walking showing Ricardo the environs of Monterey and I believe he likes the landscapes, the Bay, Pacific Grove, the Big Meadow, Cypress Point, the Fisherman's Wharf, the Pines, Mount Parnassus, Hotel Del Monte, etc, etc. He will tell you about our trip when he returns.

With careful planning Luisa found time to assume more and more of the household duties at Lachryma Montis, thus relieving her mother who suffered from rheumatism and asthma. In addition Luisa acted as secretary for her father.

Fortunately, the Vallejos were able to afford the services of a Chinese cook and to employ the old farmhand Martin and his daughter Fannie, as rarely a week went by without visits from one or more of the *Parientes*. No longer could bowls of gold coins be placed in the bedrooms of guests; instead, the golden fruit from the orange trees (horticultural descendants of the seeds from Acapulco) filled the bowls, along with magnolia blossoms if the visits were in the summer. These offerings were visual evidence that, in spite of the change in fortune, General Vallejo was still the gracious host.

It was noticeable since Ula's trouble that Vallejo's health had begun to fail. Luisa longed to remove the financial worries from her father. She felt that if he could be assured of a regular income, his health would be restored. On January 23, 1889, she wrote to Louis Litzuis, a friend in Sacramento:

> I avail myself of this opportunity to write and suggest to you, the following noblest action. As you are Papa's friend and know fully his circumstances, advanced age and many other considerations which entitle him to what I believe to be a debt of gratitude from the State. It is this: that the State give Papa a pension, as given Sutter. Papa more than deserves this, for if California today belongs to the United States and not to England or France as the State history asserts. He also assisted the immigrants with money and hospitality . . . Papa can well be called the Father of

this country and if others have received compensation, he surely deserves this distinction now at his advanced years and for which the Treasury will not be troubled many times as he has reached his 82nd birthday. Papa as you know is a Democrat and it is certain the Republicans as well as the Democrats will vote for this reward as I am certain the Governor will sign the bill.
P.S. This idea is unknown to Papa as I would not like at his age to have a disappointment.

Luisa followed up her letter to Mr. Litzuis by writing to all the members of the Legislature.

In December of 1889 when General Vallejo's illness became critical, a number of his sons and daughters returned to Lachryma Montis to help nurse him; and though the burden of the enlarged household fell on Luisa's shoulders, she never allowed her father to see that she was tired. She was never too weary to smile or to sing him a favorite song as she sat on the edge of his bed. In spite of the loving care of his family and that of Doctor Davis, as we know, General Vallejo died on January 18, 1890.

Luisa spent the following twelve months caring for her invalid mother who, after several strokes, passed away on January 30, 1891. Among the many letters of sympathy which were kept was one from her cousin Anita Fitch Grant, who, like Luisa, had a beautiful voice (it was said that Adeline Patti wanted to adopt Anita as a protégé).

My dearest Lulu:

To you and the loving daughters I saw at your dear mother's bedside and of course to all the family I extend my heartfelt sympathy. Often have I thought of the beautiful picture and I rejoiced that her last days could be so comfortable and sweet. The pain of bereavement cannot be assuaged except by Time's kind soothing hands. Words seem meanless and I cannot tell you how I would comfort you if possible.

I promised my Aunt to take mother (Josefa Carrillo de Fitch) to see her. I found when I told Mother of her sister's condition, it would not do for she was quite overcome and I felt that a visit to the old home where she would the more vividly realize your father's absence and your mother's hopeless condition would be more than she could bear . . . Please accept our tender love and remembrance and believe me,

Your sincere friend and cousin,
ANITA F. GRANT

From Encinal Park, Alameda, Lizzie Chipman's mother, Caroline E. Dwinelle, wrote that upon hearing the news of Senora Vallejo's death that she was quite depressed; "if it had not been for the hope of the glorious future where we shall all meet in a happier circle again never to part, what could we do?"

Another dear friend, the wife of General John Bidwell, wrote on February 1, 1891 from Rancho Chico:

I can not express to you my emotions on learning at eleven o'clock last night of the departure of your dear mother for her everlasting home. For some reason your letter to me of January 14th was received on the 24th and I think it was postmarked as having been mailed on the 23rd though so dim is the mark that I could not be sure of it. In the letter you mentioned that your mother was 'doing as well as could be expected.' Also said that she had had a slight stroke of paralysis which pained me much to learn.

I have been quite ill myself since December 15th so went to the City to see Dr. Hirschfelder where he kept me a few days whence I returned not long since and am almost myself again. But he forbade excitement of every kind and complete rest. So I have not read the papers so did not know anything save as communicated by you . . . the past week was our tree planting time at our Indian village which I had to superintend and as there are many trees and plants to set out that occupied the rest of my time. We have laid off the Rancheria anew, which involved much planting.

Could I have telegraphed you, I would have done so (last night). Today would have been too late as the office is only open in the evening. I cannot tell you how sadly I feel that no word of sympathy was received by you from me before the last rites were performed or how deeply disappointed I am not to have seen your noble mother. My husband has promised and promised to take me to Sonoma, first to see your father, then your mother but it seems impossible to get there—so many demands upon his time. But we will see those who have gone to the Father when we reach His "house" also.

I was so glad to see the picture of your dear mother in the late Century (magazine). Hers is a grand face. Now I must close with expressions of loving sympathy with every member of your dear father's and mother's family; bereft indeed, in the loss of such noble and beloved parents and so nearly together. God grant you His Peace, which the world can neither give nor take away is the prayer of

Affectionately yours,
ANNIE K. BIDWELL

Fannie Frisbie and her husband assisted with the funeral expenses for Senora Vallejo just as they had done for General Vallejo. The permanent vault was yet to be built. In connection with this, Luisa wrote to her sister Adela, "Many thanks for your dear little note . . . I am sure the sale of the paintings [Oriana Day's paintings] as you will see by a copy of a letter of Mrs. Gamage [Mrs. Day's daughter] and which we have sent to Mrs. Stanford. I only hope she will be induced to help us with the vault for Papa and Mama. Isn't it very kind of the Gamages to donate $500 toward our purpose. God bless them; they love his [Vallejo] memory and are of the few who see or realize the ingratitude done Papa by the Americans. You ought to hear them talk. How good if the rich will buy the pictures. We can then start on the vault, resting place of our dear Papa and Mama."

WIDOWED LUISA EMPARAN

Luisa and her sister Maria were the heirs to Lachryma Montis where Luisa continued to live while Maria's home was in San Francisco. The responsibilities of maintaining the estate was on Luisa's young shoulders as her husband, Ricardo, a brilliant intellectual was busy with Consular affairs. Luisa had Chinese help in the kitchen while the care of the grounds was left to some of the young Italians. Ascanio Catalani, the major-domo was a man of education but willing to do all the chores. He taught the youngest Emparan boy, Raoul, to speak beautiful Italian which was used through the years more often than the Spanish.

The operation of the Water Works was turned over to the Robin brothers but Luisa's three children, as they were growing up, were taught to be useful. Anita's task was to fill the kerosene lamps, trim the wicks and clean the chimneys. Carlos and Raoul kept watered the Roses of Castile which bordered the entrance roadway. Carlos brought in the wood for the cooking stove and numerous fireplaces while his younger brother Raoul closed the windows and outside green shutters in each room every night and opened them each morning.

The three Emparan children started their education at the Presentation Convent on Napa Street about six blocks from their home. They were taken there on foot by Fanny Martin, the daughter of one of the old servants who had worked for General Vallejo. Whenever a visitor of importance visited the Convent, the Emparan children were called from class to meet the visitor who was told that they were the grandchildren of the late General Vallejo, the founder of Sonoma.

Luisa with a well ordered household had time to sing at home and at church. When the third St. Francis Solano Catholic Church was dedicated on January 10, 1897, she and her niece Natalia Haraszthy sang together. That same year, 1897, Luisa sang at Sonoma Valley's original Vintage Festival held at Rhine Farm.

Senor Ricardo de Emparan found it necessary to make frequent trips to Mexico and it was there, in Ensenada, in his native land, that Luisa's husband passed away on June 4, 1902 at the early age of forty-nine. His death prevented Carlos and Raoul from going to college and they entered the business world to help their mother.

ROMANCE OF ANITA EMPARAN

Luisa's only daughter, Anita, when grown, was one of the prettiest girls in Sonoma, resembling in a dainty way her father. She graduated from the Sonoma Valley Union High School in June 1902 and about a week later, she and Sonoma's popular young physician, Dr. Allen Milo Thomson, drove in his buggy to Santa Rosa, where they were married in the civil ceremony in the parlors of the Occidental Hotel by Major John Brown, an old family friend who had known Anita since infancy. The *Sonoma Index-Tribune* reported the event as follows:

> A romance that startled all Sonoma came to light Tuesday last when the marriage of pretty little Miss Anita Emparan and Dr. A. M. Thomson, was announced. Cupid was sly, for while love was a-kindling no one even suspected that the doctor was wooing the charming dark-eyed granddaughter of the late Gen. Vallejo.

The secret of their engagement was well kept until last Tuesday when they drove to Santa Rosa and were quietly wed. In the old days we could have called it an elopment but in the Twentieth Century it was just a quiet wedding for Cupid often fools people that way. The doctor and his bride-to-be drove a spanking team up to the county seat and there applied for a marriage license, the ceremony was gone through and Judge John Brown pronounced them man and wife. The bride was attired in the white organdy dress she wore at her graduation from the High School just a week previous and with her black hair down her back, looked as girlish as the night she received her diploma.

After the ceremony the young couple drove home to herald the surprise to their friends and to tell the bride's mother Mrs. Emparan, who ever kind and forgiving gave them her blessing but insisted that the Catholic rites be performed in addition to the civil ceremony.

On Sunday, June 22nd, in the parlor of the Vallejo home, Anita and the Doctor were married according to the rites of the Roman Catholic Church. The bride again wore her graduation organdy dress, and on her curly black hair was a tule veil kept in place by orange blossoms from the trees planted by her grandfather Vallejo. Sweet peas and maiden-hair ferns formed the bride's bouquet; the time was one o'clock; the wedding march was from Lohengrin; and the exact site of the ceremony was under a floral bell in the window-alcove of the parlor. Father Leahy, pastor of the St. Francis Solano Church, officiated. The bridesmaid was Miss Bertha McGimsey, dearest friend and classmate of the bride; the best man was Milton McGimsey.

The bridegroom, Allen Milo Thomson, had been born in Missouri and was graduated from the Medical School in Columbia, Missouri. Through correspondence with an enthusiastic friend living in California, Dr. Thomson decided to move West—but the move landed him further West than he anticipated, for, soon the Spanish-American War broke out, and Dr. Thomson was appointed physician-surgeon on the Army transports plying between San Francisco and the Philippine Islands. At the termination of the war, he was offered a position at the Sonoma State Hospital which he accepted. However, he tired of institutional work and moved to Sonoma, where he took over the practice of the retiring Dr. H.H.Davis, the Vallejo family physician.

MADAM PRESIDENT

At the time of Anita's marriage, the Emparan boys, Carlos, 18, and Raoul, 17, were finishing their education and were about to start their business careers. The mother, with more free time on her hands, became interested in civic and club affairs, in addition to her regular church work which had been her avocation since girlhood. In 1919 she was prevailed upon to accept the presidency of the Sonoma Valley Woman's Club, of which she had been a charter member in 1901. Repeatedly she had been asked to serve as president but had always declined. For the benefit of the Sonoma Valley Woman's Club she opened the gardens of Lachryma Montis where in the midst of the palm and orange trees, musical moonlight fetes were held; the grounds lit up with myriads of small Chinese lanterns. As president Luisa Emparan brought in fifty new members and inspired new life in the organization. Her recording secretary was Carrie Burlingame, daughter of Horatio Appleton, pioneer vineyardist who sold much of his grape output to Mrs. Emparan's brother-in-law, Attila Haraszthy.

Luisa was active in the preservation and beautification of the Sonoma Plaza. She gave in 1892 an oak tree in memory of her father. Major Edwin A. Sherman conducted the planting there with Luisa turning the first shovel of earth and "Rendering" a solo. Luisa's voice aided many causes. Although a Catholic she had put many a shingle on the Protestant churches.

Madam President Emparan found that there was a debt on the Sonoma Valley Woman's Clubhouse; to help liquidate the debt, Luisa suggested that each member bring in five dollars by the next meeting; the money to be earned through some talent of the individual members—by the sale of needlework, art work, handpainted china or examples of culinary art, such as homemade pies, cakes or bread. If a member was completely devoid of talent, Madam-president Emparan suggested that such a member might rob her husband's trouser pockets.

Madam-president Emparan, after giving some thought to what she could do to raise her five dollars, gathered up some of the most prized Vallejo heirlooms and placed them on General Vallejo's desk in the library; the exhibit to be viewed for a small fee. Her son Carlos nailed a diminutive sign on the gate of Lachryma Montis which stated that the historic Vallejo articles could be seen for twenty-five cents, the proceeds to be given to the Sonoma Valley Woman's Club. The venture was a success. After the showing, a request was made to Mrs. Emparan, that the exhibit be continued, in order that others might have the privilege of seeing the historic articles. The number of heirlooms taken from the Vallejo family chests was increased, thus by 1923, a small museum was started.

It was in 1923 that Sonoma held the Sonoma Centennial Celebration which featured the founding of the Mission San Francisco Solano. Garnet Holme wrote and directed the play in which Luisa Emparan sang so beautifully "La Golandrina" and her young son Richard Raoul Emparan, raising natural sideburns, played the role of his grandfather, General Mariano G. Vallejo, looking strikingly like the young Comandante Vallejo, the founder of Sonoma.

MARRIAGES OF THE EMPARAN BOYS

The two Emparan boys, although of Spanish blood on both sides, chose American wives. Carlos married Agnes Moss of Geyserville on April 24, 1919. They had one son, Robert, who in June 1951 married Phyllis Reed in the

Monterey Presidio Chapel where 144 years before the groom's great grandfather, Don Mariano Guadalupe Vallejo, had been baptized as a one-day infant.

Ricardo Raoul, the younger boy, left Sonoma and became one of the younger executives of the Crane Company in San Francisco. He returned to Sonoma as Richard R. Emparan in 1914 to manage the Sonoma Water Company for his mother and to clear the Vallejo estate of all indebtedness. When he had accomplished this fourteen years later, he felt free to marry. He was married in Oakland on November 7, 1928 to Julia Sheehan, a business girl of San Francisco. Although married 36 years, they had no children.

When Richard Raoul Emparan became a widower, he selected for his wife, Mrs. Edmund N. Brown (familiarly known as Madie Brown), whom he had known since she was a State Park Commissioner and who with Mr. Will Chipman was largely responsible for the State of California acquiring Lachryma Montis as part of the State Park System.

On the third day of Christmas, St. John's Day, December 27th, 1965, the marriage of Richard Raoul Emparan and Madeleine Luisa (Madie Brown) was solemnized at a high noon Nuptial Mass in the St. Francis Solano Catholic Church in Sonoma. The Reverend John S. Roberts read the rites; Communion was received by the bridal pair after they had exchanged golden wedding rings, under the symbols of both wine and bread; a privilege extended by the Vatican Council.

The bride's son, Robert Minge Brown, a former Rhodes Scholar and a descendant of Benjamin Harrison, a Signer of the Declaration of Independence, gave away the bride who wore a pastel blue gown with a full length mantilla of soft silk lace, an heirloom which had belonged to the groom's grandmother, Dona Francisca Benicia Carrillo de Vallejo. The bride carried a bouquet of Lilies-of-the-Valley.

Serving as Matron of Honor was Alice Gallagher; Henry Masonnave was Best Man. Don Sebastiani and Mike Cahill were altar boys. Reverend John O'Hare [later Monsignor O'Hare] who had instructed and baptized the bride into the Catholic Faith as Madeleine Luisa, was at the side of the Altar with Patrick Scheblich, lately returned from Spain.

Among the relatives who attended the wedding were the groom's brother, Carlos Emparan, and his wife. The bride's two grown daughters, Colleen Simmon and Natalie Williams and their husbands and Gloria, her son's wife and seven grandchildren. Among the friends who filled the church were twelve children from Claudia Drive, age two years to ten, all present to wish Mr. and Mrs. Richard Raoul Emparan many years of happiness.

Raoul's wedding gift to his bride was a necklace of pearls which she wore. Beautiful though it was, the gift the happy bride valued the most were his words to her: "You are my reward for being good to my mother, Luisa Vallejo Emparan. She always wanted me to be happy."

PLATON VALLEJO WRITES OF HISTORIC DAYS

Luisa enjoyed receiving letters from her brother Platon as he wrote well, and they were often filled with historic bits gleaned from their father's reminiscences. One such letter was written to Luisa in 1910. Platon thanking her for her remembrance of him during the Holiday Season, said although there might be long periods of silence between them, he knew there existed a deep affection in the family with such a father and mother that they were fortunate in having. Platon spoke of the California of 150 years before, when it was a beautiful wilderness, not a desert. He wrote of the Big Trees and the wild oats, of the mighty grizzley and the foxy coyote; then he spoke of Don Gaspar de Portola, Padre Junipera Serra, and of Don Ignacio Vicente Ferrerr Vallejo—"three persons in whom we as Californians and descendents of Castile, my dear sister, are most particularly interested." Platon's long letter continued:

> The year 1835 when the decree for the secularization of the Missions came and the work of many years ceased and the foundations of the original mission churches were left to crumble and come to naught under the influence of the wind, and rain and general neglect attending the change of government. When this change came and the old order began to pass away, our father, then Director of Colonization for the District of Sonoma and the north side of the Bay began to promote the building of a house of worship for the families of the colony of Sonoma and the aboriginal inhabitants who remained and resided in the Valley. This was the little chapel, the ruins of which still stand there on the corner of the Plaza, where Fannie was born and where we were all baptized and received our Christian names. Only the foundations of the original mission were erected, never completed. . . . The adobes that were used for the construction of the venerable little chapel were the very ones that were intended for the construction of the projected original Mission Church which was never completed. Thus the Mission Church did not appear, only a few feet from the ground and the material went for the construction of the soldiers' chapel as it was called, for the soldiers and their families and the Christianized Indians. This hasty scrawl is not intended for a sermon as dear Papa used to affectionately and jocularly call my "Carta sermonies" when I enjoyed the privilege and happiness to address him a few lines.

OFFICIAL HOSTESS

A red letter day in the annals of the Grace Line and of Luisa Vallejo Emparan was November 26, 1932, when the $5,000,000 Grace liner, the *Santa Rosa*, left New York for San Francisco on its maiden voyage, with Mrs. Emparan as official hostess. On board, mounted on a slab of redwood burl, was the threshold of Lachryma Montis, over which the great and humble had trod to see Luisa's father, General Mariano Guadalupe Vallejo. On the train trip to New York, Mrs. Emparan had as her companion Mrs. Agnes Parramore. They stayed at the Waldorf-Astoria Hotel where Mrs. Emparan's suite on the thirty-first floor was decorated with red roses, the gift of the former governor of New York, the Honorable Alfred E. Smith. During the voyage to California, the *S.S. Santa Rosa* cast anchor at Cuba, Panama, Costa Rica, El Salvador, Guatemala and Mexico, where Luisa's knowledge of her parents' native tongue and her own gracious personality and charm made her thrice welcome.

At the port in Guatemala, as mentioned in Uladislao Vallejo's story, she met her brother's daughter, her lovely niece Maria Jesus Vallejo.

MEMORIAL TO GENERAL VALLEJO

The memory of Luisa's father was very precious to her. She kept in her heart and mind the dream that eventually California would recognize his greatness and acknowledge him in some appropriate way. Soon after General Vallejo's death in 1890, the Native Sons of the Golden West, inspired by one of its members, William Farragut Chipman of Alameda, considered erecting a stature of General Vallejo in San Francisco's Golden Gate Park. Mr. Chipman, the "Willie" of earlier days and the brother of Lulu's chum, Lizzie Chipman, wrote to Luisa Emparan on May 30, 1890:

Dear Lulu:

I have just returned from Chico. I called on Mrs. Bidwell, a charming lady and had a very pleasant conversation with her; the subject so dear to us all, your noble father.

I gave her a copy of some resolutions that I intend to present to the Grand Parlor. Although the sentiment was that something should be done, it was not thought adviseable that a Committee from the Native Sons should go to the Legislature. It was argued that it would be a political measure and hence not in accord with the fundamental principles of the order. I sincerely hope that something will be done by the State at the next meeting of the Legislature. Depend upon it, Lulu, that something must be done as I am anxious to further the matter.

Years later Luisa still cherished her dream for public recognition of her father. She decided to write to James Rolph Jr., the Mayor for almost 19 years of San Francisco, who had just announced his candicday for Governor of California; she wrote:

I am a daughter of the late Genl. M. G. Vallejo, whom you undoubtedly know as one of California's noblest sons and benefactors. I am by forceful circumstances prompted to approach you and hope through your influence persuade the state of California to purchase this the last home of my father. The State should own this historical home. It is the home of my sister and myself, we have no income save the monthly rent of $60 and are obliged to seek relief, taxes are exorbitant and life is a struggle with us. Our near and dear ones are in no position to help us.

You no doubt are the coming Governor of California and I assure you my support and all connected with me . . . Hope you will favor me with a line and if you send me a button, shall be proud to wear it and say "Hurrah for James Rolph Jr. Governor of California."

"Willie" Chipman's project did not develop; however, after forty-three years this devoted friend had not forgotten. He conceived the idea of honoring General Vallejo and, at the same time, helping the last surviving daughters, Luisa and Maria, by having the State of California acquire Vallejo's old home, Lachryma Montis, as a state-owned historical monument. On July 2, 1931, when the present author was a member of the California State Park Commission, Mr. Chipman sent her a letter which follows in part:

> I personally knew General Vallejo when but a small lad. My father attended to some law matters for him and his family and ours have been most intimate for many years . . . Mrs. Emparan and Mrs. Maria Vallejo Cutter, daughters of General Vallejo are living at the old place, consisting about 200 acres, which is all that remains of the vast estate of the late General. These daughters are dependent upon the small income from $300 to $400 a year, paid them in fees to visit the museum which is in the old house . . . California may rejoice in being a Star in our galaxy of States, primarily by reason of the patriotism and deeds of General Vallejo, to our State. Recognition of his services, generosity and loyalty, in the judgment of many should be tangibly acknowledged.
>
> Mr. Colby, the Chairman of the State Park Commission tells me that he bespeaks of your keen interest and that you are primarily instrumental in the preservation of California landmarks, noting particularly your good works at present in regard to the San Juan Plaza and historic buildings and the Mount Davidson Park and other places of import.

The present author was happy to offer her suggestions and to work with Mr. Chipman in his plans to place Lachryma Montis within the State Park System as a fitting tribute to a great native Californian. Mr. Chipman, with the assistance of members of the General Vallejo Memorial Association, which he organized and of which he was president, raised the necessary money to match the State's contribution to the fund for acquisition of the Vallejo residence, the brick-timbered storehouse, and twenty acres of surrounding grounds.

As early as October 1917 mention was made in the San Francisco Examiner that "The residents of Sonoma are discussing the matter of the purchase of the old home of the late General Vallejo at Sonoma as a memorial park and landmark." The suggestion was also made in 1924 in the *California History Nugget:*

> It would be fitting for some person or group of persons, loving California as Vallejo loved it, to purchase the Vallejo homestead for the State. In that way it might be preserved as a little treasure-house of California relics; and as a memorial to a man whose career of public service and whose honor, love of country and generosity have made his name merit remembrance.

THE DEDICATION OF THE VALLEJO HOME

Lachryma Montis was dedicated as a State Historical Monument on July 7, 1933. On the day of dedication, Luisa Vallejo Emparan, dressed in white, seemed really young although the Vallejo family Bible would show that she was seventy-seven years old. Her long cherished dream was being realized. It was with deep emotion that she handed the deed of Lachryma Montis, on behalf of herself and of Leo and Alma (the grown children of her late sister Maria) to the Honorable Joseph R. Knowland, a member of the State Park Commission. Luisa's father was being recognized and appreciated by his native state. A song was in her heart as well as on her lips as I and the others heard Luisa sing the Spanish songs her parents loved. Francisca Vallejo McGettigan, Luisa's talented niece, was at the piano where she played a number of her own compositions.

In congratulating Mr. Chipman, this author wrote to him: "While I am sure your work has been a labor of love yet that fact did not lessen the amount of time which was necessary for you to give nor lighten the economic conditions under which you worked. All true Californians are grateful to you and your associates of the General Vallejo Memorial Association. I hope the State Park Commission will be able to work out a plan whereby Mrs. Emparan will be appointed the Custodian of Lachryma Montis. She would to all practical purposes be the *Castellana* of her home as of old, but with the added advantage of a monthly salary and with no taxes to pay. This would indeed be a small tribute for California to pay in return for the services her noble father, General Vallejo gave to California." This viewpoint was shared by the other members of the State Park Commission. Thus, Luisa Vallejo Emparan was appointed the *First* Curator of the historic Vallejo Home and wore with pride the star-shaped badge of office.

The land adjoining the acreage acquired by the State was sold by Mrs. Emparan to a former Italian emigrant boy William Montini who had rented it for a number of years for pasturage for his dairy cows. Mrs. Emparan was fond of him and saw to it that the Vallejo barn was reserved for him with his purchase of her land.

Mrs. Emparan appointed in 1933 as Custodian (Curator) was still serving in 1941 at the age of eighty-five was able to sing La Paloma, Estrellita, La Golondrina and other Spanish melodies for the entertainment of the visitors to the historic Vallejo Home. Her gracious welcome was given to all, regardless of social position. Her friends during the depression of the 1930s ranged from the vagabonds camping along the ties of the nearby abandoned railroad, tramps whom she helped to feed and clothe to the Chief Executive of the nation, Franklin Delano Roosevelt, who sent her the following letter dated December 20, 1939:

> I am grateful to you for the cordial greetings which you sent me through Congressman Lea and want you to know that I appreciate deeply your kind thought of me. May I, in reciprocating all your wishes, add the hope that your days will be full of peace and happiness and quietness of soul.

LUISA'S LAST DAYS

It was in the midst of her family and close friends that Luisa Vallejo Emparan observed her eighty-seventh birthday on January 27, 1943. Although she was confined to her bed, she insisted on draping her head and shoulders with a black lace mantilla and placing a crimson rose near her cheek. That memorable day, her last birthday, the California Legislature passed a resolution, introduced by State Senator Herbert W. Slater of Sonoma County, extending felicitations to the daughter of one of California's first State Senators. The resolution was thereupon engrossed on parchment and bound in red leather for formal delivery to the "daughter" thus honored. That day a telegram was received from a relative, the famous movie star Leo Carrillo who wired, "Many happy returns of the day to you darling. I am thinking of you today. God bless and keep you for many, many years. You are the most beautiful flower in California."

The months of illness which followed were borne without complaint. Luisa's nurses often spoke of her bright spirit and their enjoyment in listening to her stories and Spanish songs. It is recalled that on July 22nd about dusk, several of her loved ones were gathered about her bed; her daughter Anita, her son-in-law Dr. A. M. Thomson, her youngest son Raoul and James Baines, a life-long friend. To the group's amazement they heard the strains of *Estrellita* being softly sung by Luisa. It proved to be her *swan song*, as early next morning, July 23rd, death stilled the song in a heart that had beat so bravely for eighty-seven years.

The flag at the gate of Lachryma Montis was lowered by her son Raoul to half-mast. They carried her body from her home to the St. Francis Solano Catholic Church where she had conducted the choir for many years. The church was crowded with life-long friends, State officials, Army and Navy officers. The Superior Court of Sonoma had adjourned so the Judges could attend the funeral. After the Requiem Mass, the cortege passed around the Sonoma Plaza and paused in front of the site of her parents' first Sonoma home, the Casa Grande. This mark of respect had been observed at the funeral of General Vallejo and also that of his wife. Many of the flags in Sonoma were at half-mast, evidence that the passing of her presence was mourned by the Sonoma residents.

Luisa was buried in Sonoma Mountain Cemetery where many of her dearest ones had been laid to rest. Her grave on each birthday and on each Memorial Day is adorned with roses from the garden planted in her memory at the historic Vallejo Home, in 1951, on the 95th anniversary of the birth of Luisa. At the time of the dedication of the garden, Luisa's recordings of Estrellita and La Golondrina were played as poignant reminders that although the "Songbird of the Vallejos" had gone, the memory of Luisa Vallejo Emparan would as the melody of a song linger and inspire others to cherish dreams no matter how delayed their fulfillment.

Maria Ignacia Vallejo

Maria Ignacia Vallejo

(Mrs. James Harry Cutter)

On May 8, 1857, the fragrance of the Roses of Castile, honey-suckle and jasmine filled the upper master-bedroom at Lachryma Montis, where, close to her mother, lay a tiny baby girl with dark ringlets and darker eyes. At her baptism in the Mission San Francisco Solano, she was named "Maria Ignacia" after the Holy Mother of Christ and her own grandmother, Dona Maria Ignacia Lopez de Carrillo, who, eight years before, had been laid to rest in the old Mission near the blessed-water font. Baby Maria's elder brother, Platon, was present as godfather, at the christening.

Dona Benicia said of her baby "... muy vivita y todos ojos" (very vivacious and all eyes). General Vallejo called this final child of his sixteen "... the last spark of my soul."

When Maria (or Marillita, as her mother often called her) was at the toddling age, she sometimes got into mischief. On one such occasion, she ran from her mother into the orange grove. There she saw her father, and, he sensing the situation, quickly hid her in the folds of his long Spanish cloak. When Maria was seven she received a joint letter with Luisa from her father who was at the Rancho San Cayetano. He wrote:

> Now I'm going to tell you how I'm getting along here. I am alone with Estrada in a house above, on an elevation from which you can see the sea, the village of Watsonville, . . . a river in front. Also you can see the town of Santa Cruz, the pine forest of Monterey and you can always hear the heavy roar of the waves of the big sea as they break on the beach. I am in this house, then, and very early I get up, dress with just my socks, white shirt and on top the red smoking jacket I had when I was ill in San Francisco, then I put on my head that cap with the teensy-tiny beads and Ula's green tie that he loaned me for the trip and I begin to take a stroll round about and I look very much like Robert Mackies, he of the big book of monkeys. Do you remember? Well I look like him.

Maria, in recalling her childhood birthday to her sister Luisa, who had sent her birthday greetings, told how "Mama always used to make wreaths for me, wreaths of the choicest flowers. She made these wreaths, these '*coronitas*' before breakfast so that when I came down-stairs she could place them on my head." Continuing Maria said:

> On the eighth of May, I thought of Mama and the pretty wreaths she made for me and with her own dear hands, placed on my head, so gently, so lovingly. I can see 'Lachryma Montis' as it was then; two happy little girls playing or strolling about. One with long braids, the other dressed in white, with long curls with a wreath on her head. Oh! sweet beautiful memories. I am so glad I was born at Lachryma Montis. I once asked Mama if I was a pretty baby, she said, "Eras todos ojos" and of course I drew my own conclusion. I was her *baby* and I remained her baby.

To her father, Maria was always *the baby*. When introducing his children to visitors, General Vallejo would mention each by name, until he came to Maria; then it was just "here is my baby." Nevertheless he kept track of the recurring additions to her years. For instance when she was a young matron living in San Francisco, he wrote: "To congratulate you on your birthday, we had intended to send you a box of flowers but it rained so hard today, rather yesterday, that circumstances have deprived us of that pleasure. We must be content to wish you many years of happiness and may you enjoy this day, happy at the side of your husband."

On another birthday, Maria's father sent these verses:

Tu natal es este dia
MARIA
Que Dios to conserve en gracia
YGNACIA
De mi alma ultimo reflejo
Procina ser el espejo
De tu nombre y nada mas
MARIA YGNACIA VALLEJO

School Days

Maria first attended the public school with her sister Luisa, there being only fifteen months' difference in their ages. Later, the two girls went to St. Catherine's Convent in Benicia where Maria made her first Communion at the age of twelve.

All the Vallejo girls were given piano lessons. Maria's love for music was sincere, but she felt that her real talent lay elsewhere, as her letter to her mother of September 9, 1870 shows:

> I only intended to write you these few lines and ask you if I may leave off taking music lessons. I do not know why it is that I can not get music into my head. You need not think that I am lazy for you know I love it and I do wish I had a good ear for it. Lulu always learnt piano lessons much faster than I have and has a better ear. I have been drawing every week and intend to go on but the piano lessons I can not get. If you think it would be better for me to leave it off I shall do so and then I would have more time to study my other lessons but if not, I shall try and do my best and if I can learn anything it shall be all for your own sake.

The years ahead were to prove how right little Maria was, to wish to give most of her time to drawing.

While the two youngest Vallejo girls were students in Benicia, their mother for a number of months was living in nearby Vallejo, where she could see them more often. General Vallejo remained in Sonoma; he was trying to keep house with his brother Salvador. Nevertheless he found time to write to the two girls, with a special letter dated March 5, 1870 to Maria:

> Yesterday I wrote Lulu a nice long letter and after writing it, I couldn't rest because I got to thinking you might feel sad because I didn't write to you too, even

though you haven't written your Papa. So I take pen in hand to send you good wishes and to remind you to be diligent in your studies so you can give a good account of yourself when your class has its examinations—and also you can send your Papa letters beautifully written.

The weather is fine now. Spring is benignly smiling upon us; and the wild flowers are beginning to send forth the aroma and fragrance which so many times has delighted us here at Lachryma Montis where you first saw the light of day. The whole place is profuse with growing things.

Every night little owls come and make their entrance into your Uncle's room; they are easily caught and I believe they are the ones you tamed two years ago. We let them go each morning and they return at night. The larks sing in great choruses nicely balanced on the garden fence; the sparrows with their little mates are also happy as larks and busily engaged in making their nests in the orange and olive trees. The Delirio is covered with honey-suckle blossoms of many colors and the roses in front are already in bud.

Every time I go to sweep the dust from the hall and clean the ballastrade, I think of you and Lulu. I have been a long time alone with your uncle; however we make very good stew, with corn and really fine beans with tortillas of tapioca flour. Whenever I sit down at the table I think of both of you.

I haven't anyone to rub my aches and pains, nor to have tea with me in bed in the morning and it makes me feel sad; but I say to myself 'Never mind, if you keep on living, Lulu and Maria will be here again.' Give my best wishes to the Sisters. Be a good girl and remember your Papa who send his love and blessing.

M. G. VALLEJO

The *El Delirio*, mentioned in Vallejo's letter, was a small cottage on the grounds built in 1854—a kind of retreat for members of the family or for their guests. It has been said that much of the history of California, composed by General Vallejo for H. H. Bancroft, was written there.

GIRLHOOD DAYS

When Luisa and Maria left St. Catherine's Convent in Benicia, they became students at the Convent of Notre Dame in San Jose, where Anderson's *Common History of the United States* was one of Maria's textbooks. Her reaction to the chapter on President Polk's administration and the Mexican War, can only be surmised from a certain independence of thought that characterized her later in life.

The winter of 1873, Maria, not yet sixteen, took a severe cold. Her sister Adela insisted that she stay with her, so that Dr. Frisbie could look after her. Meanwhile Adela kept her mother informed on the condition of Maria's health:

Of course the first thing you would like to know is how Maria is getting along with her throat trouble. It is better. The Doctor gave her his latest medicine remedy for her chest, Tincture of Iodine, every other day and night. Maria's sickness is too little patience; little by little, is the way to get along and not to worry, to be careful, not to go outside when the weather is cold, to keep the feet warm, to wear wool and to eat well and to go out walking as the best exercise. Levi tells her every day to go out walking and one thing more he recommended is the kitchen, not too much, but enough to get her mind off herself and to think of something better.

When Henry Cerruti was in Sonoma during 1874 gathering historical material for H. H. Bancroft, he was much attracted to the seventeen-year-old Maria, to whom he gave his inscribed photograph. It was at about this time that Maria afterwards recalled having been alone with her father at Lachryma Montis when some subject was being discussed and a difference of opinion arose. Sharp words were exchanged between them. With a haughty expression on his face General Vallejo said, "Aqui, yo estoy rey" (Here, I am king). With equal hauteur Maria replied, "Y yo hija del rey, yo soy princesa" (And I am the daughter of a king, I am a princess). Vallejo, disregarding the apparent defiance of his daughter, and no doubt secretly amused, softened, kissed her, and, petting her on her shoulder, said, "Ponge tu sombrero y nos vamos a pasear." (Put on your hat and we will go for a walk.)

VALLEJO'S LETTER FROM MEXICO

When General Vallejo was at the Iturbide Hotel in Mexico City, he called in a professional letter-writer and dictated a letter to twenty-year-old Maria:

> Maria, your letters are picturesque and gracious and they leave me with a beautiful impression. They mitigate somewhat the ennui of separation which I am anxious to terminate. At my age, when love of family is so strong and when one is proud to have children and a good loving wife, it is not possible to remain a long time so far from the family hearth without feeling a bit homesick for Mama . . . So it is when I read your letter, my soul revivifies and fills with gladness as I seem to see you for a moment, framed as an image stamped upon the paper.
>
> I ask Heaven to preserve you always with the character of a pure heart, never worried by the adversities of life . . . You asked me for a memento from Mexico and I offer it to you as you deserve. I have bought something for every one. Goodby until the day when I can give you an embrace. Now I send my blessing.

ROMANCE OF MARIA

There was a time when it appeared that the two youngest girls would be the third set of the Vallejo sisters to marry brothers. Maria met Will Curtis at a ball given at Hubert H. Bancroft's mansion in San Francisco—the same ball at which Luisa met Will's brother Frank. The two girls became engaged to the Curtis brothers, but the youthful infatuation did not last for either girl.

Later while visiting her sister Jovita Haraszthy, Maria met the handsome native son, James Harry Cutter, born of California pioneer parents from New England. The meeting occurred at a party at the home of Jovita's neighbor, Lily Coit, who was the mascot of the Volunteer Firemen. Among her guests was young J. H. Cutter, Jr., son of James H. Cutter who, in the fall of 1850 had organized the Knickerbocker Engine Company No. 5 and was elected its foreman. The company had no superiors in fighting the conflagrations that swept over San Francisco in the early 1850s. In 1860, J. H. Cutter Sr. was named Harbor Master of San Francisco.

Young Mr. Cutter was most attentive in his courtship. Maria, on her part, enjoyed his companionship so much that in order to see him more frequently she offered to stay with her father in San Francisco and help him translate Spanish documents into English for use in his court cases.

At Christmas 1877, Harry Cutter's courtship was rewarded by having Maria hang about her neck his gift, namely a golden locket which enclosed a hand-painted miniature of himself. He told his friends that he was going to marry the most beautiful girl in California and have her preside at the *head* of his table.

Maria's father liked the young man, but he was not for giving up his youngest child without a bit of discreet investigation. From San Francisco, Vallejo wrote to Maria's mother: "Since I came from Sonoma, I have been busy in different things. As soon as I came I began to enquire about the young man who wants to marry Maria and up to now everything seems favorable. Tomorrow if it doesn't rain I'll go to Oakland to get information from Mr. Brown [Napoleon Vallejo's father-in-law] who is supposed to know the Cutter family." After a trip to the East Bay, Vallejo wrote: "I've been in Oakland and all my enquiries with respect to the family of Harry and himself have been satisfactory . . . Tell Maria that she should not forget me. She may want much money before leaving home." Vallejo added that Adela had given Maria "a dress of silk, very elegant, which she wasn't using."

There was some discussion in the family regarding Maria marrying a Protestant. Platon wrote his youngest sister a letter filled with brotherly admonitions. Maria replied on March 30, 1878, as follows:

> Your kind and well meant letter reached its destination this noon and I hasten to answer to set your mind at rest. You must not think I have consented to the serious step I am about to take without thinking hard and trying to have matters arranged that we could be married by a priest.
>
> I find in Mr. Cutter so many qualities that are desirable in a good husband. He and Mama talked it over. He says, of course I shall follow my own faith, that he shall always go with me to the Catholic Church and about the eventualities of the future, it shall be left to me, in other words, if there are any children, they shall be baptized and brought up Catholics. His family are all strict Episcopalians and I should not be blind to the sacrifice he makes. God knows I am not leaving my church. I shall no doubt be a better Catholic in the future.
>
> Now that I have found the right one I feel I must get married. If you think that Jesus will not listen to my prayers for marrying the man I love, if you think that He will turn away from me *I do not*. I shall be married here from my home with Papa's and Mama's blessings.

On April 4, 1878 Maria's father told the concerned members of the Vallejo family that "paternal authority has very sacred limits and when children are old enough to contract marriage they should be advised and nothing more." As was the General's custom in the case of a prospective mixed marriage, he had the young folks consult the Archbishop, with the result on April 30th, The Reverend Joseph S. Alemany wrote to Maria's father as follows:

> I am very pleased with the agreeable and intelligent young man, Mr. J. H. Cutter who has happily consented to that I asked of him so I include the necessary dispensation. Unfortunately they have made the engagement for me on the 8th of next month at the home of Mr. Hooper. Very probably I shall not be able to solemnize the marriage vows of your daughter and so I have sent word to Father Luis Daniel so that he may be ready in the event he is given notice. But perhaps the time of your daughter's wedding will be at an hour in which I shall be free from ceremonies at Mr. Hooper's house and in this event I would have no objection but rather satisfaction in uniting them in Holy Bonds. I appreciate Mr. Cutter for having complied so well what I imposed of the Laws of the Church.

Mr. Hooper, one of the wealthy men of San Francisco, had built a new home in Sonoma Valley and the Archbishop Alemany had promised to bless it, on May 8th. Maria had planned her wedding on that day as it was her 21st birthday but it was postponed until May 12th because of the sudden death of her sister Jovita Haraszthy on May 5th. Naturally Maria's wedding at Lachryma Montis was a quiet one.

SAN FRANCISCO, MARIA'S NEW HOME

Mr. and Mrs. James Harry Cutter set up housekeeping in San Francisco. From Sonoma, Maria took her girlhood bedroom set made of walnut, and many other usefull as well as ornamental things, which Senora Vallejo gladly shared with her daughter. As a wedding present, the Senora gave Maria a beautiful needlepoint portrait of a lady carrying a basket of flowers, which she, herself, had made.

The Cutter's first child, Leo, was born in February 1879 at Lachryma Montis, with Dr. Wells and Maria's mother in attendance. General Vallejo sent word of the event to Mrs. W. W. Chipman, a close friend of the family: "More news: Maria, my baby also has a baby, a son born on the night of the 10th of February . . . Lulu is the only one left me. You have such pretty and lovely daughters, so interesting, so good. How have you escaped becoming a mother-in-law and all the rest that follows?"

Leo was called "Tweedy"—baby-talk for "Sweetie"—by his mother,which was dignified into "Don Tweedy" by his grandfather.

When Maria was first married, her mother was a frequent visitor at the Cutter's home in San Francisco, especially after the arrival of Leo. On July 19, 1881 Senora Vallejo's husband did his best to bring her up-to-date on the hydrographical, physiological, clerical and ornithological doings in Sonoma.

Francisca:

> You have become fond of San Francisco. Surely you are happy because Maria is

better when you are with her. Well nothing is more natural, care for and stay with her as long as you wish.

Here all are well but I am very tired with the business of the water. I have to get up at five A.M. to go to Sonoma to distribute it and at seven in the evening I have to return to change the machinery. And for what? For only to gain daily bread with much labor and fatigue. . . Every one works to live, nevertheless I do not have the necessities at this age. Be it God's will and let more work come.

They have consummated the sale of the church. I think they will construct another new one on the lot which is near the entrance of the White Gate . . . There has come a plague of birds which are eating the grapes. I have ordered a small box for Maria. Greetings to Maria, Harry and kiss Don Tweedy.

On one of Senora Vallejo's trips to the Cutters', she took the steamer, being accompanied by Luisa, who was going to visit her chum Lizzie Chipman. On board, Senora Vallejo took one look at the weather; then she went directly to her stateroom, and took a nap. She awakened to find a "fierce storm" brewing and immediately became seasick. In recounting her experience in a letter to the family, Senora said:

When the boat arrived at the wharf, I was completely gone. Lulu accompanied me to Maria's house then she left. I remained all alone as Maria wasn't home. There was an old lady, the one who was minding the baby and a Chinese boy in the kitchen . . . Finally the old lady came in and asked if I wanted something to eat. She offered me a cup of tea and put it on the table but it wasn't possible to drink it.

What would you like? she asked me in English. Then I asked her if she had a little whiskey. 'No' she said, 'but down below there is a place where they sell it.' 'Can you go and buy a little?' 'Yes' she told me and went and bought a little bottle. I made a punch and took it and my stomach commenced to get better. After awhile I made another punch and my stomach was cured. I was in the house about two hours when Maria arrived; in a little while Jari [Harry] came and he received me with much affection.

While at Maria's home, Senora Vallejo expressed a desire to go to Mass on the coming Sunday, which would be Easter. Maria took great pleasure in preparing her mother's Easter toilet, and the Senora took equal pleasure in writing to Sonoma about Maria's efforts:

Maria said 'I want you to look pretty,' I said to her—'What am I going to do if I don't look pretty?' then she said 'Did you bring your dress of black satin?' 'No' I said to her. 'Then we must send for it.' 'But how?' I asked her. 'Sending a telegram to Papa for him to send it.' 'Here I have the key to the wardrobe, we will send it to him.' Maria said, 'Give it to me. I'm going to write a note to Harry so that he will go himself and give the key to the Captain of the Sonoma boat so that he can give it to Papa.'

Maria dressed and went out into the street and came back very happy with some ribbons and said to me 'Mama, give me your bonnet. I'm going to put some ribbons on it. They are using them a lot now.' I gave it to her and she fixed it up pretty.

It seemed that the satin dress had strayed. It was thought that if it did not come by the Sonoma boat, it might come by the one from Napa or from Petaluma. After much waiting, a boy delivered two boxes to Maria's home. In one were two skirts, and in the other the bodice of the dress. Maria put the gown on her mother, catching up the train as she said "they are not wearing long dresses this season." The gown was re-adjusted, and Maria's mother was ready to go to the Easter Mass in the new church of San Ignacio; however, Maria thought her mother was not quite ready to go—she needed a bit of "glamorizing." Senora Vallejo described it in this way:

Maria said to me 'Stand in front of the mirror.' And when I stood where she told me, she began to throw white powder on me and said 'Just wait, Mama and see how pretty you are going to look.' 'Por Dios! you have messed up my face.' I said, 'No, Mama, you look prettier! Don't put too much on me, take off some; so so much won't show. What will people say?'

Maria didn't stop fixing me and said 'Now look at yourself in the mirror. You'll see you look much prettier, a thousand times prettier.' All this she was saying as I was being dressed. We went to the coach, from there to the home of Harry's mother. The lady came out, very well dressed, got into the carriage and we went to church.

As soon as I took the Holy Water, I crossed myself. It seemed I was being flooded with something Holy; my head, my body, my soul, my spirit; it all seemed I was filled with Glory. I couldn't pray, I couldn't say any more than 'Holy God, Holy Fortress, Everlasting God, free us from all evil. Blessed be the Most Holy Sacrament of the Altar. We reached the railing, knelt and crossed ourselves. All the church was full of lights and very pretty. How beautiful everything appeared, all the church filling with people. The music started, they opened all the stops of the organ and then they disminished until there only remained two or three soft voices. How beautiful, how sublime, I said and closed my eyes. What a beautiful Mass! the priests stood and began to do a thousand acts that belonged to the Mass. I was enraptured.

MARIA'S SECOND BABY

Maria's mother and her sister Luisa went to San Francisco the last of February in 1881 to be with Maria. They had gone at the request of Maria who was ill and needed as the General said "Affection and the 'cluckings' of her mother. Her illness, he said, was that she was "under restraint or pregnant again." Again in September of the same year Senora Vallejo was visiting Maria in San Francisco. It was fortunate for Maria that her mother was there when the second child of the Cutters was born. It was a little girl and was named Alma and dedicated to the Virgin.

At the time of the approaching event, the physician, Dr. McNutt, said that the birth would probably take place on the evening of October the second. Instead it took place on the evening of October the first. No doctor was present, so Maria's mother brought little Alma into the world as a birthday present to Maria's husband, who celebrated his own birthday on October first. The happy father insisted on giving the amount of the physician's fee to Senora Vallejo. At first she refused, but, upon her son-in-law's urging she accepted the money as a token of gratitude and love—a love she was proud to have earned as a mother-in-law.

The new baby was called "Alma Linda" (pretty Alma) by her grandfather Vallejo. When she was very small, a Charity Bazaar and Baby Show was held at the Palace Hotel in San Francisco. The Press reported the affair, and for the first time in newsprint appeared an appraisal of Alma's charms, which was not only true then but also prophetic:

The event of the afternoon was the remarkable beauty of a little girl, Alma Cutter, three years of age, who fairly took by storm the hearts of all the ladies by her loveliness and the winning sweetness of her manners. The large crowd present and several of the ladies of the committee, unanimously declared that had this child put in an appearance at an earlier hour she would have been awarded the highest prize by acclamation. As it was, she did not arrive until the voting was over and was not a competitor, there being an impression among the many that only children in arms were to compete.

As it was, the future International Party giver, Elsa Maxwell, received first prize. It was about this time that Maria celebrated her 27th birthday anniversary. Her father brought flowers from Sonoma and Maria wrote to her mother thanking her in Spanish:

Millions of thanks for the bright flowers that you sent with Papa when he came last night; but we were not at home, we had left, Harry and I, and we did not return until about 10 P.M. Papa had already gone to bed but we made so much noise seeing the flowers which you sent that I thought he could not sleep.

How pretty the orange blossoms were and how large the roses with so many buds. Among the roses I kissed were the roses that since I was a little girl I named 'Las Mias' [Mine]. These bunches of roses grew next to the window which is now the room of Napoleon. When I was a little girl and until I was a "young lady," each birthday you made me a crown of these roses and buds with orange blossoms and myrtle branches. I shall ever remember dear Mama those times and you every time you go by my bed of roses which bloom so bright on May 8th, you remember me.

The prettiness of Alma's babyhood developed into a maturity of beauty for which the Carrillo women of California were noted. Those who have known Alma Cutter (Mrs. Robert McLennan) well, and this was the author's rare privilege, believe that her beauty was a sort of outer reflection of a spiritual beauty within. She had a radiant personality, a tender compassionate nature.

When Alma was eighteen years old she was given a debut-party by her parents. She wore a pink satin and chiffon gown, trimmed with looped strings of pearls and tiny pink roses. Her cousin Juan B. Alvarado Jr. sent her a bouquet of American Beauty roses, whose stems were so long that the rose petals brushed her cheeks. These unusually beautiful crimson roses were the creation of George Bancroft, noted historian who was Secretary of the Navy during California's critical days of 1845–46. It was Secretary Bancroft who sent secret and confidential letters to Admiral John D. Sloat advising him to pursue a policy of peace but at the same time to remember that should Mexico commit acts of hostility he should with the forces under his command possess the ports of Monterey and San Francisco.

At the celebration of the Fiftieth anniversary of the organization of the Legislature and State government at San Jose, Alma was selected to represent *California.* The beauty of her gown was enhanced by the jewel medallion portrait of her grandfather Vallejo which she wore.

As a rule Alma celebrated her birthday with her father which strengthened the natural bond of affection between Alma and her father. She was proud that her Papa had been a gold-medal recipient at the old Lincoln Grammar School in San Francisco; his report cards, with a straight "A" in every subject, were treasured by his wife and later by herself. Mr. Cutter was one of California's earlier conservationists. Many a Sunday was spent climbing Mount Tamalpais with his friend, Congressman Kent, and other members of the Sierra Club. In fact there was a point on the trail which his fellow-climbers called "Cutter's Peak." Another close friend of Mr. Cutter was James Rolph Sr., the father of "Sunny Jim" Rolph Jr. At the beginning of young Rolph's career, Harry Cutter Junior wrote a congratulatory letter to Rolph's father:

> It gives me the greatest pleasure to felicitate you upon the triumphant victory won by your son, James Rolph Jr., for I feel the people of our city are to be congratulated upon the successful outcome of the very remarkable campaign he has conducted to a splendid finish. The office having sought and found a man who is truly a representative chief executive; the new era with its glorious possibilities opens before us as citizens of the great Metropolitan City of the Pacific Coast and with James Rolph in the Mayor's chair San Francisco will come into its own.

Under James Rolph Jr., the Builder, San Francisco arose from the debris of the Earthquake and Fire of 1906 to become one of the great modern cities of the United States. After serving San Francisco as mayor for 19 years, Rolph was elected Governor of California. It was the author's privilege as a member of the California State Park Commission (to which Governor Rolph had appointed her) to select one of California's beautiful redwood groves to bear his name.

MARIA, THE ARTIST

Like her youngest brother Napoleon, Maria Vallejo Cutter was interested in the theatre and had considerable dramatic talent. Many of the Vallejo family gatherings were made enjoyable by Maria's recitations. Naturally there could be no thought of a daughter of the Vallejos going on the stage, but Maria was allowed to give a formal recital in the Crocker home and also at Hubert H. Bancroft's San Francisco mansion.

Maria's granddaughter, Paloma, has inherited not only the features and large dark eyes of her grandmother but also her dramatic gifts. In addition, Paloma has a beautiful voice. She was selected by the grand opera prima donna, Mme. Pasquali, as San Francisco's best child singer and as such was starred in many of Mrs. John Cuddy's children plays.

A natural corollary to Maria's enthusiasm for the stage was her creative ability with canvas and paint. She was not content with still-life sketches but studied figure-painting with Mme. Tojetti, the wife of the celebrated California artist. Maria's copy of Adolphe W. Bouguereau's *Charity* is an excellent replica and hangs in the Vallejo parlor. It was fortunate for Maria that she had Katie Shea to look after her children, and Charlie the faithful *Chino-cocinero* to preside in her kitchen. These helpers gave her time to perfect her art.

The family home at Lachryma Montis always held a charm for Maria. Her visits and regular correspondence kept filial ties close. Most of her letters were to her father: "Tell mother," she wrote him once, "that I do not write to her in Spanish as my heart would dictate as I have become such a gringa." On March 30th, 1889 she wrote: "Letters from home do me as much good as everyday meals. Sometimes more, for I always enjoy them. La Demajaunito [demijohn] de "Agua vitani" also reached me yesterday afternoon shortly after your letter. I had to smile and I thought Dear Papa how he didn't forget. Immediately I got a glass and saying, "Here's to our health," I took a good long drink. It went to the spot . . . Thank you dear Papa for gratifying my 'autojo.' When I was so sick I used to think if I could only drink some water from home, how I would enjoy it."

On General Vallejo's 77th birthday, Maria and her husband sent him a congratulatory letter dated July 7, 1884 which was copied in a Sonoma newspaper:

Today you have passed another milestone in your journey through life. A journey so marked with rich and varied experiences, so full of promise, so full of realization. The destiny of modern invention and genius, all were subjects of your prediction. All have passed before your vision. We, your children are proud of such a father and are very happy today to be able to congratulate you on your continued strength and vigor of mind and body. We pray for many, many returns of this day, many mile-stones yet to pass. With much love,

Your children,
MARIA AND HARRY

Five years later (1889), Maria's visits to Lachryma Montis became more frequent because of her father's illness. Harry could not always accompany her, and, instead, sent a letter of explanation, such as the following:

I would have been so glad to have arranged to have accompanied Maria on her visit to you on Sunday last but had some outside office work to attend to. It seems such a long time since I have had your friendly greeting. I think of you so often and am pained to learn of your continued illness but I know you will bear it with the patient fortitude of a soldier: and the loving sympathy and kindly wishes of your many friends will go out towards you and such good medicine will help you more than physic towards a speedy recovery of your customary vigorous health. I often brag of your mental and physical vigor so well preserved.

Today I met a young man from Chico, one of the Native Sons of the Golden West who recited to me with much gusto the particulars of the reception tendered to the Son whom they most delight to honor, your respected self. He was enthusiastic over the affair and especially over the felicitous remarks you made at the time. You may be sure I left much interested and coincided with him in approval of the proceedings. With my kindest wishes for your rapid restoration to health, I remain

Yours affectionately, Your Son
HARRY

After one of Maria's visits in December 1889, she wrote her father:

I arrived home safely. Harry went to the wharf to meet me. Had quite a pleasant trip home. The weather was milder when we arrived in the city than I expected; this morning however it is very cold, a very heavy frost fell last night and the whole country around is white this morning. There is a heavy fog and all together it looks cold and uninviting.

I promise you, dear father, I shall call and see Tia Chiquita [Encarnacion V. Cooper] in your name. I presume you know that the Leese family and their father [Jacob P. Leese] have been re-united. I thought of you all the way home. Mr. Clement and I spoke of you so often. Tell Mama please, that the fig preserves she so kindly gave me to bring home, tasted fine after I arrived at the Pigeon House. I had no trouble in bringing it. Pobrecita Mama! She is real brave for she does not feel well either. Goodbye, I hope I will find a still greater improvement in your condition the next time I see you.

Another visit to Sonoma, and, on her return to San Francisco, another letter:

Precious Papa:

Did you think I was a naughty girl to run away without saying "goodbye"! You know dear Papa, partings are never very pleasant so when you were nearly fast asleep I stole up to your bedside and gently kissed my lips to your forehead. Papa, I did not want to leave you, but with Mama's sickness the day before, the extreme cold weather and malaria in my system, which will manifest itself in spite of me, altogether I felt it would be better for me to come home, since Adela had arrived and not be sick up there.

I may not have proved myself a competent nurse but I was so willing and I loved to wait on you. I need not assure you that I think of you constantly for you must feel my spirit is ever near you. I am always wondering whether you are awake or asleep, how you are feeling, which way you are turned, who is in the room with you, who is giving you your beef tea, medicine or a glass of water. I do not forget you dear, darling Papa. I love you so and am so proud of my dear grand noble Papa.

It has been piercing cold here in the City . . . I wish we could have all the bad weather here in '*Frisco*' and let Sonoma have all the good weather . . . Just wait Papa some day when you are well again and we can take another lunch together and then go on a little visit to the Presidio; you will look back to these days of long tedious sickness and the world will seem fairer and the sun shine brighter.

The hope of finding her father better was not to be realized. His strength in December, like the days of the year, grew less and less. January came and the Vallejo children were called home. Maria was at Lachryma Montis when the General died; but, because of the serious illness of their son Leo, it was necessary for the Cutters to return to San Francisco. Once home, Maria eased the tension of her grief by writing to Luisa at Lachryma Montis:

Mi pobrecito Leo esta muy enfermo . . . I can think of nothing else but of him whom I shall never see again in this world. I feel too full, Lulu. I can't write. Oh! what a terrible experience I went through Saturday night when we landed at the wharf. I was walking along close to Harry when I heard first one newsboy, then it seemed hundreds yelling '*All about the Death of General Vallejo.*' Oh! I clung to Harry's arm and involuntarily I cried out. I sat in the car and no sooner were we seated when one little newsboy, then another would jump on the car and pass through, calling what was like a sharp dagger thrust through my heart. I kept my hands over my ears whenever I saw one jump on till Harry had to go and request the conductor not to allow any more to get on the car. They were like flies for they would go around the other door to get near where we sat and Harry had to keep his cane against the door to keep them from coming in. Oh! it sounded awful. It made me feel terrible. It was the worst nightmare I ever experienced or want to experience again. How my little boy cried when I got home. Poor child, he always said Grandpa was his ideal of a man. He put his arms around my neck and Oh! how he cried. How everyone mourns our precious Papa.

Maria found Leo sufficiently improved in health to allow her to return to Sonoma for the funeral. Harry was one of the pall-bearers.

THE UN-OPENED LETTER

After General Vallejo's funeral, Maria returned to San Francisco where she found a letter awaiting her. The envelope was addressed in the handwriting of her brother, Napoleon, and bore the cancellation mark "Sonoma, January 17, 1890." On the reverse side was "San Francisco, January 18, 1890." It was early on January 18th while it was yet dark, that General Vallejo had passed away. The outer envelope enclosed another envelope, neatly addressed to Mrs. Maria Vallejo de Cutter by General Vallejo. Maria in her grief laid the letter aside. One month later she picked it up, only to leave it unopened and write on the cover, "Papa died one month ago last night. Oh! how I miss him. How I want him back again. This letter has never been opened. This was the last letter written to me before he died. Darling Papa, his soul is with God. A better, nobler man never lived. My heart is breaking. My eyes are blinded with tears for him. I shall never again see him on earth."

The years passed into the next century, but Maria never opened the letter. In 1953, during some of the present author's research work, it was found still unopened. Finally Maria's daughter Alma was persuaded to open the envelope. Inside was not a farewell note but a letter, written early in July 1889 which her father had neglected to mail. It had been found, stamped and ready for mailing on General Vallejo's desk by Napoleon. He put it in another envelope and addressed it to Maria.

Maria lived in San Francisco for fifty-three years. Handsomely gowned and wearing a black lace mantilla during the Portola Festival of 1913, she rode along the city's streets in her father's old carriage, which had been called "*The Waterloo*." With her was her daughter Alma and the baby granddaughter Paloma. The sight of three generations of the well-known Vallejo family riding in the flower-decorated carriage was enough to arouse enthusiastic applause from the crowds watching the parade.

STATE OF CALIFORNIA ACQUIRES LACHRYMA MONTIS

Upon the death of Senora Vallejo, Lachryma Montis was jointly inherited by Maria and Luisa. To Maria it was a kind of earthly paradise; when lucrative offers were made, she steadfastly refused to sell. Her consent was withheld until she knew that the State of California wished to acquire the home of her parents as a mark of respect to her father. She wrote her sister: "Lulu, you say in your letter, 'Maria, lets make up our minds to dispose of the entire property to the State. The State will restore it and give it the prestige it deserves . . . But Oh! Oh! Oh! how difficult it is to make up my mind to part with our dear beautiful Lachryma Montis . . . Dear, grand, noble Papa, have we your consent? . . . But circumstances being such as they are, I have been thinking and thinking it all over and with an aching heart, tears in my eyes and with a reluctant hand, I wrote the word 'YES'." After its purchase, Lachryma Montis was made a part of the State Park System, while James Rolph Jr. was California's governor as mentioned previously.

For many years Maria was in delicate health, but she was blessed in having a devoted husband to look after her; and when Harry Cutter died in 1925, his son and daughter continued the watchful care over Maria. Some seven years later Maria became seriously ill. She was taken to St. Joseph's Hospital where Dr. Philip King Brown attended her. Leo wrote his Aunt Luisa: "Some people when sick desire that their relatives and friends visit them. Some on the other hand do not. Mama is that kind. That she has her Leo near her to take care of her is entirely sufficient and she desired and enjoys Alma's visits." Hope for Maria's recovery being abandoned, she was given the last rites of the Catholic Church, and on March 10, 1932 she died at the age of seventy-five years.

Her two children brought their mother's body to Mountain Cemetery in Sonoma where it was placed beside that of her husband in the Vallejo family plot, next to Maria's parents. Each year on May 8th, Maria's birthday anniversary, flowers from Lachryma Montis are placed on her grave—an annual tribute to the "baby" of THE VALLEJOS OF CALIFORNIA.

Acknowledgment

During the writing of a book, an author is the recipient of many courtesies, personal and literary. I wish to express my gratitude to the following persons whose encouragement and assistance was appreciated. First in importance were

THE TRANSLATORS

Mary Bean
E. P. Bly
Ralph W. Dix
Peter Narvaez
Brother Veronius Henry
Jose de la Mora
Charles B. Trevino

and

Emma Alexander, Lorraine Andrews, Eleanor Arnold, William Bauder, Florence Becker, Sonoma Belis, Paloma Vallejo Boyden, Dr. J. N. Bowman, Marian Brackenridge, Helen Bretnor, Dr. Adelaide Brown, Hon. Edmund G. Brown, Gloria Brown, Robert Minge Brown, Carrie Burlingame, Marian Crabtree, Monsignor James Culleton, Betty Diggett, Ray Duer, Alma Easton, Dr. Elliot Evans, Armand Franquelin, Emma Frisbie, Alice Gallagher, William Getchey, Helen Giffin, E. Edwin Gledhill, Laura Gregory, Margaret and Palmer Griffith, Ann Guillaumin, Honore Guiney, Dr. George Hammond, Marian Hancock, Carol Heche, I. Warren Hellman, Renie Hess, Janet Holmes, Lottie Huenergardt, Mary Hussong, Virginia Jordon, Lawton Kennedy, Dr. Clark Kerr, Ivy Loeber, Mabel Middlebrook, Dr. Robert Mollenhauer, Ruth Murgatroyd, Brian McGinty, Rev. John McGloin, Gladys McPhun, Nan Norgren, Monsignor John O'Hare, Charles Oliva, Allan Ottley, Robert Parmelee, A. L. Paulson, Edward Planer, Rev. John S. Roberts, Fred B. Rogers, Rodney Rulfoson, David Ryder, Margaret Sanborn, Cecilia Mendia Shegog, Colleen and Starling Simmon, Sister Incarnata, Archie Stevenot, Dr. Albert Shumate, Dr. John Barr Tompkins, Jovita Vallejo, Harriett Weaver, Natalie and Robert Williams, Gladys Wickson, Dr. Richard Coke Wood, Marie M. Manly.

Copyright Releases and Literary Courtesies

AUTOMOBILE CLUB OF SOUTHERN CALIFORNIA Touring Topics 1931 (Westways).
Lydia Lothrop's *The Noblest Roman.*

BANCROFT LIBRARY Dr. George Hammond; Dr. John Barr Tompkins.
Permission to quote from Vallejo documents and letters.

CALIFORNIA STATE LIBRARY Dr. Allan R. Ottley, Librarian, California Section.
Use of Vallejo material in files.

CALIFORNIA HISTORICAL SOCIETY
Permission to quote letter of condolence from General Vallejo to Mrs. Jacob Snyder May 2, 1878.

CALIFORNIA STATE PARK COMMISSION
Permission to use copy of Peter Van Vallanburgh's sketch of General Vallejo and to use copies of Senora Vallejo and Andronico Vallejo portraits painted by Stephen W. Shaw.

DEPARTMENT OF THE ARMY Col. J. S. Hardin, Acting Chief of Staff, West Point, N.Y.
H.Q.U.S. Military Academy. Information relative to Andronico Vallejo, June 1851.

DODD, MEAD & CO.
Permission to quote from "The Wife of the General" by Ishbel Ross.

GENERAL SERVICES ADMINISTRATION; NATIONAL ARCHIVES AND RECORDS SERVICE
Photostats from War Department—1851.

HANCOCK, CAPTAIN ALLAN AND MARIAN
Permission to quote from "Pioneer Heritage" by Samuel T. Clover.

HARDING, GEORGE
Permission to quote from "Don Agustin Zamorano" by George Harding.

HECHE, CAROL
Permission to use Lulu Vallejo's letters to Lizzie Chipman.

HISTORICAL SOCIETY OF SOUTHERN CALIFORNIA Lorrin Morrison, Publisher
Permission to quote from June–September Quarterly, 1945—"California Reminiscences of Jonathan Tibbett Jr."

HOWELL, WARREN R.
Permission to quote from *Montgomery and the Portsmouth* by Col. Fred B. Rogers. *Journal of Marius Duvall,* A Navy Surgeon in California. Edited by Col. Fred. B. Rogers. *Seventy-five Years in California* by Wm. Heath Davis. Letter of Wm. Heath Davis. Sept. 20, 1890 to Dr. Platon Vallejo.

HUNTINGTON, HENRY E. LIBRARY
Permission to quote from *Life and Adventures in California of Don Agustin*

Janssens. Pub. by Huntington Library. Letters: Wm. A. Cornwell to Gen. Vallejo Feb. 20, 1855 (Va. 179) Secretary Buchanan to Consul Larkin (Va.-150 B.) List of clothing and supplies issued to Nathan Coombs by Lt. Joseph Warren Revere. Stephen Smith's letter (Bodega. Jan. 31, 1844) to General Vallejo.

JONES, IDWAL
Permission to quote from *Vines in the Sun* by Idwal Jones.

MEXICAN MILITARY ARCHIVES—MEXICO CITY
Legajo No. 2 Book D. Vol. 23. December 11, 1841.

MONTEREY COUNTY COURT HOUSE—SALINAS
Vallejo Family Records.

MONTEREY—FRESNO CATHOLIC DIOCESE Monsignor James Culleton.
Courtesy of researching early Church records.

PACIFIC CENTER FOR STUDIES IN WESTERN HISTORY, UNIVERSITY OF THE PACIFIC
Permission to quote from original documents of St. Gertrudis Ranch, Baja, California. Signed by President Benito Juarez and Don Jose de Emparan, Minister of Colonization and Industry.

POWER, ROBERT H.
Permission to quote General Vallejo's letter to his wife. Feb. 19, 1850.

ROBERTS, REV., JOHN S.—ST. FRANCIS SOLANO CATHOLIC CHURCH
Courtesy of researching Baptismal and Marriage Records of the Mission of San Francisco Solano.

SANTA ROSA PRESS-DEMOCRAT PUBLISHING COMPANY Ruth W. Finley, President and Publisher.
Permission to quote from "Santa Rosans I Have Known" by Ernest Finley. Use of Santa Rosa Press-Democrat Library.

SONOMA COUNTY COURT HOUSE—SANTA ROSA
Research of old records of Sonoma County.

SONOMA PUBLIC LIBRARY AND SONOMA CITY HALL Librarian Marie Barr; Mayor Talbert W. Bean.
Use of books. Use of records.

SHUMATE, DR. ALBERT
Permission to quote from General Vallejo's letter of Dec. 20, 1875 to Senora Josefa Carrillo de Fitch.

SOCIETY OF CALIFORNIA PIONEERS Dr. Elliot Evans; Helen Giffen.
Permission to quote from *This Sudden Empire* (Published by Society). Use of Napoleon Vallejo letters and the Will Chipman collection.

STANFORD UNIVERSITY PRESS
Permission to quote from *Mountains and Molehills* by Frank Marryat.

UNITED STATES NAVAL INSTITUTE Commander R. N. Adrian, Secretary.
Permission to quote from *A Long Line of Ships* by Lt. Commander Arnold S. Lott.

UNIVERSITY OF CALIFORNIA PRESS
Permission to quote from *Philosopher Pickett* by Lawrence Clark Powell.

WHELAN, REV. J. S., Our Lady of Sorrows Church Record photographed by W. Edwin Gledhill, Santa Barbara.

Permission to use Marriage record of Don Ignacio Vallejo and Dona Maria Antonia Lugo.

WINE INSTITUTE

Permission to quote from *The Authentic Haraszthy Story* by Paul Fredericksen.

Bibliography

ANNUAL REPORTS STATE BOARD OF HORTICULTURE: 1885–86, 1888, 1889.
AMERICAN GUIDE SERIES: *California.*
ATHERTON, GERTRUDE: *Golden Gate Country.*
BANCROFT, HUBERT HOWE: *Literary Industries,* Volume XXXIX.
BASHFORD, H., & WAGNER, WM.: *A Man Unafraid.*
BEAR FLAG PAPERS: MS (Bancroft Library).
BELL, HORACE: *On the West Coast.*
BIDWELL, JOHN: *California in 1841 to 1848.*
BIGELOW, JOHN: *Life of John Chas. Fremont.*
BOGGS, WILLIAM M.: *Reminiscences of 1846.* MS
BOLTON, HERBERT EUGENE: *Guide to Material for History of California in Mexican Archives.*
BOYES, MARCIA EDWARDS: *The Legend of Yerba Buena Island.*
BROWNE, JOHN ROSS: *Reports of Debates of Constitutional Convention.*
——— *Muleback to the Convention.*
BRYANT, EDWIN: *What I Saw in California.*
CALIFORNIA STATE PRINTER J. WINCHESTER—1850: *Journal of the Senate of the State of California,* 2 Volumes: First Session–Second Session.
CERRUTI, HENRY: *Ramblings in California.* Edited by Margaret Collins and Virginia E. Thickens.
CLOVER, SAM T.: *Pioneer Heritage.*
COLTON, WALTER: *Three Years in California.*
CULLETON, MONSIGNOR JAMES: *Indians and Pioneers of Old California.*
DAKIN, SUSANNA BRYANT: *The Lives of Wm. Hartnell.*
DANA, JULIAN: *Sutter of California.*
DANA, RICHARD H.: *Two Years Before the Mast.*
DAVIS, WILLIAM HEATH: *Seventy-five Years in California.*
DELKIN, JAMES LADD: *Monterey Peninsula.*
DEVOTO, BERNARD: *The Year of Decision.*
DOBIE, CHARLES CALDWELL: *San Francisco, A Pageant.*
DOWNEY, JOSEPH T.: *Filings From an Old Saw.*
DUVALL, MARIUS: *A Navy Surgeon in California.* Edited by Fred B. Rogers.
DYE, EVA EMERY: *McLoughlin and Old Oregon.*
ELDREDGE, ZOETH SKINNER: *The Beginnings of San Francisco.*
EMPARAN, LUISA VALLEJO, and HONORIA TUOMEY: *Mission, Presidio and Pueblo of Sonoma.*
FORBES, ALEXANDER: *A History of California, Upper and Lower.*
FORD, TIREY L.: *Dawn and the Dons.*
FREDERICKSON, PAUL: *The Authentic Haraszthy Story.*
FREMONT, JOHN CHARLES: *Memoirs of My Life.*

FRISBIE, JOHN B.: *Reminiscences.* MS (Bancroft Library)
FRISBEE, EDWARD D. D.: *The Frisbee-Frisbie Genealogy.*
GRAY, A. A.: *History of California.*
HANNA, PHIL TOWNSEND: *California Through Four Centuries.*
HARDINGE, EMMA: *Modern American Spiritualism.*
HARDING, GEORGE L.: *Don Agustin V. Zamorano.*
HAWTHORNE, HILDEGARDE: *California Missions.*
HITTELL, THEODORE H.: *History of California,* 4 Volumes.
HOUGHTON, ELIZA DONNER: *Expedition of the Donner Party.*
HOUSE OF REPRESENTATIVES: *Document No. 17–31st Congress.*
HOOVER AND RENSCH: *Historic Spots in California.*
HUBBARD, HARRY D.: *Vallejo.*
HUGGINS, DOROTHY: *Continuation Annals of San Francisco.* Files of Contemporary Newspapers and Magazines.
HUNT, ROCKWELL D.: *California's Stately Hall of Fame.*
——— *John Bidwell, Prince of California Pioneers and Californians.*
IDE, WILLIAM BROWN: *The Conquest of California.*
IRVING, WASHINGTON: *History of Columbus.*
JANSSENS, AGUSTIN: *Life and Adventures in California.*
JONES, IDWAL: *Vines in the Sun.*
——— *Ark of Empire.*
LARKIN, THOMAS OLIVER: *Larkin Documents.* MS (Bancroft Library)
LEESE, JACOB P.: *Bear Flag Papers. Letters of 1836.* MS (Bancroft Library)
LOTHROP, LYDIA: *The Noblest Roman* (Touring Topics).
LOTT, ARNOLD S.: *A Long Line of Ships.* U.S. Naval Institute.
LYMAN, GEORGE D.: *John Marsh, Pioneer.*
MARRYAT, FRANK: *Mountains and Molehills.*
MENEFEE, C. A.: *Historical and Descriptive Sketch Book, Napa, Sonoma, Lake and Mendocino Counties.*
MOFRAS, EUGENE DUFLOT DE: *Travels on the West Coast.* Translated by M. E. Wilbur.
MAC MINN, GEORGE R.: *The Theatre of the Golden Era in California.*
MCKITTRICK, MYRTLE: *Vallejo, Son of California.*
MC GLOIN, REV. JOHN B.: *California's First Archbishop.*
——— *Eloquent Indian.*
MURPHY, CELESTE G.: *The People of the Pueblo.*
OLDER, MRS. FREMONT: *Missions and Their Romances.*
PHILLIPS, CATHERINE COFFIN: *Jessie Benton Fremont. The Woman Who Made History.*
——— *Portsmouth Plaza.*
POWELL, LAWRENCE CLARK: *Philosopher Pickett.*
POWERS, LAURA BRIDE: *Old Monterey.*
PRIETO, GUILLERMIO: *San Francisco in the Seventies.*
REVERE, JOSEPH WARREN: *Tour of Duty in California.*
——— *Keel and Saddles.*

ROBINSON, ALFRED: *Life in California.*
ROGERS, FRED B.: *Montgomery and the Portsmouth.*
ROYCE, JOSIAH: *California.*
ROWLAND, LEON: *Los Fundadores.*
RUSH, PHILIP S.: *A History of the Californians.*
SANCHEZ, NELLIE VAN DE GRIT: *Spanish Arcadia.*
SCHERER, JAMES A. B.: *Thirty-first Star.*
SHERMAN, EDWIN A.: *The Life of Rear-Admiral John Drake Sloat.*
SHERMAN, WILLIAM T.: *Memoirs of General Sherman.*
SHUCK, OSCAR T.: *Representative and Leading Men of the Pacific.*
SIMPSON, LESLEY BYRD (Translator): *The Laws of Burgos 1512–1513.*
SIMPSON, SIR GEORGE: *Journey Around the World.*
SOULE, FRANK ET AL: *Annals of San Francisco.*
SUTTER, JOHN A.: *New Helvetia Diary.* Letters. MS
SWASEY, W. F.: *The Early Days and Men in California.*
TAYLOR, BAYARD: *El Dorado.*
TEISER, RUTH: *This Sudden Empire.*
TIBBETT, JONATHAN JR.: *Reminiscences.* (Historical Society Southern California).
TUOMEY, HONORIA: *Sonoma County.*
TORCHIANA, H., A. VAN COENEN: *Mission de Santa Cruz.*
UNDERHILL, REUBEN L.: *From Cowhides to Golden Fleece.*
VALLEJO, MARIANO GUADALUPE: *Historia de California,* 5 Volumes (Bancroft Library).
VANCOUVER, CAPTAIN GEORGE: *Voyage of Discovery.*
VER MEHR, REV. JOHN L.: *Checkered Life.*
WALKER, FRANKLIN: *San Francisco's Literary Frontier.*
WAUGH, LORENZO: *Autobiography.*
WILLEY, REV. S. H.: *History of the Colleges of California.*
WILKES, CHARLES: *Narrative of the United States Exploring Expedition.*
WISE, HARRY: *Los Gringos.*

INDEX

BY ANNA MARIE AND EVERETT G. HAGER